Public Relations
A Values-Driven Approach

FOURTH EDITION

David W. Guth
The University of Kansas

Charles Marsh
The University of Kansas

PEARSON

Boston   New York   San Francisco
Mexico City   Montreal   Toronto   London   Madrid   Munich   Paris
Hong Kong   Singapore   Tokyo   Cape Town   Sydney

Acquisitions Editor: Jeanne Zalesky
Project Manager: Lisa Sussman
Marketing Manager: Suzan Czajkowski
Editorial Production Service: Omegatype Typography, Inc.
Composition Buyer: Linda Cox
Manufacturing Buyer: JoAnne Sweeney
Electronic Composition: Omegatype Typography, Inc.
Interior Design: Carol Somberg
Cover Administrator: Kristina Mose-Libon

For related titles and support materials, visit our online catalog at www.ablongman.com.

Between the time website information is gathered and then published, it is not unusual for some sites to have closed. Also, the transcription of URLs can result in typographical errors. The publisher would appreciate notification where these errors occur so that they may be corrected in subsequent editions.

ISBN-13: 978-0-205-56945-8
ISBN-10:   0-205-56945-5

Library of Congress Cataloging-in-Publication Data

Guth, David.
    Public relations : a values-driven approach / David W. Guth, Charles Marsh. — 4th ed.
        p.   cm.
    Includes bibliographical references and index.
    ISBN-13: 978-0-205-56945-8 (pbk.)
    ISBN-10: 0-205-56945-5 (pbk.)
    1. Public relations. 2. Public relations—Moral and ethical aspects.   3. Public relations—Case studies. I. Marsh, Charles. II. Title.
    HM1221.G87 2009
    659.2—dc22
                                                                            2007039695

Printed in the United States of America

10 9 8 7 6 5 4 3 2 1   RRD-VA   11   10   09   08

Credits appear on page 580, which constitutes an extension of this copyright page.

NEW to This Edition

We share a belief in the value of providing students with the most up-to-date statistics, the latest research, and the most current examples of public relations practice. The dynamics of public relations practice and academic study change rapidly. The fourth edition of *Public Relations: A Values-Driven Approach* reflects our belief that if today's students are to be prepared for a future in public relations, they need the most current coverage of these exciting and important changes. We remain committed to this book's focus on the role of values in our personal and professional lives. Additionally, every effort has been made to present relevant information in the conversational style of writing that our readers say they prefer. We have tried to practice what we preach by making editorial judgments based on what we believe to be the needs of our audience. It all comes down to values. We value our student readers and their investment in their education.

The fourth edition of this book is our best effort to reflect the public relations profession as it is today. The world has evolved with increasing complexity since this book first appeared in 2000. We believe the substantial revisions in every chapter of the fourth edition will help students place the profession within a more appropriate context. Pages xxiii–xxiv of the preface provide a detailed listing of just some of the revisions in each chapter. In addition to a sentence-by-sentence and image-by-image revision, this new edition:

- Introduces new information on social exchange theory, priming theory, fully functioning society theory, Image Restoration Discourse, postmodernism, message "stickiness," partner relationship management, and Hofstede's cultural dimensions in an effort to strengthen the book's strong theoretical underpinnings.
- Reflects the rapid technological changes reshaping our world, with a significant amount of new material addressing the growth of social media (blogs, podcasts, and more) as well as a new section on writing for the web and a completely restructured and renamed Chapter 11, "Cyber-Relations in the Digital Age."
- Details the latest reports on the status and future of the profession, including the 2005 Public Relations Society of America Membership Survey, the 2006 report of Commission on Public Relations Education, new diversity statistics on the public relations workforce, and new data from the U.S. Bureau of Labor Statistics.
- Analyzes the public relations implications of recent events, including Hurricane Katrina, the Virginia Tech shootings, the war in Iraq, global warming, Dove's Campaign for Real Beauty, and corporate/industry scandals.
- Includes 15 new case studies as well as several that have been updated from earlier editions.
- Features nine new QuickBreak sidebars, four new Memos from the Field, and three new Values Statements.

BRIEF Contents

Contents

CHAPTER **2**

Jobs in Public Relations   33

CHAPTER **3**

A Brief History of Public Relations   57

CHAPTER 4
The Publics in Public Relations   90

CHAPTER **5**

Communication Theory and Public Opinion   133

CHAPTER 6
Ethics and Social Responsibility in Public Relations   165

SECTION **TWO**

The Public Relations Process

Now that the foundations for the practice of public relations have been established, this section of the book focuses on the discipline's four-step process: research, planning, communication, and evaluation. Although this process is both strategic and tactical, an emphasis on values remains at its core. Successful practitioners rely on critical thinking skills introduced in these five chapters.

CHAPTER **7**

Research and Evaluation

CHAPTER 8
Planning: The Strategies of Public Relations
233

CHAPTER 9

Communication: The Tactics of Public Relations 261

CHAPTER **10**

Writing and Presentation Skills

CHAPTER **11**

Cyber-Relations in the Digital Age   336

SECTION **THREE**

Public Relations Today and Tomorrow

Public relations practitioners operate in a dynamic and intense environment. We live in a time of great changes that test our values. The final section of this book examines the profession's critical issues. Emerging professionals will confront many, if not most, of these challenges in the coming years. These five chapters bring those challenges into focus.

CHAPTER **12**

CHAPTER 13
Public Relations and Marketing 407

CHAPTER **14**

Cross-Cultural Communication   435

CHAPTER **15**

Public Relations and the Law   464

CHAPTER **16**

Your Future in Public Relations   506

APPENDIX

Public Relations Society of America Member Code of Ethics 2000   539

Preface

IN THE THREE YEARS SINCE the publication of the third edition of this book, the world has been a tumultuous place. There have been armed conflicts around the globe, including Iraq, Afghanistan, the Darfur region of Sudan, Lebanon, and Somalia. When human beings haven't been trying to kill one another, many have struggled against the forces of nature. More than 230,000 people were killed in just one event, the Indian Ocean tsunami of December 26, 2004. And, of course, there was New Orleans. Many countries, including the United States, have struggled with weighty issues such as immigration, nuclear proliferation, health care, sexism, racism, violence, and the delicate balance between national security and personal freedoms. Even the sports and entertainment pages of our newspapers often read like a police blotter.

It is in this environment that young women and men prepare for what the U.S. government says is one of the fastest growing careers: public relations. And it is why the authors of this book remain committed to what we call values-driven public relations.

The late and highly respected public relations historian Scott Cutlip wrote about the practitioner's potential for helping what he called "our segmented, scattered society" to replace "misinformation with information, discord with concord." Although the profession has fallen short of that goal, we join Professor Cutlip in that hope. It all comes down to who you are, what you believe, and how you want to be seen by others. It all comes down to whether your actions will match your words.

It all comes down to values.

It has been more than 100 years since the first public relations agency opened in the United States. During the 20th century, the practice of public relations grew from a vague notion to a powerful force in democratic societies. Today, while the profession has made impressive gains in respect and access to power, public relations has a public relations problem. Although its roots date back to the beginning of recorded history, the fact remains that public relations—both as a profession and as a discipline—remains largely misunderstood.

Public relations is an honorable profession with a glorious past and a brilliant future. Like any other human pursuit, it also has its share of flaws. However, at a time when much of the world is embracing democratic institutions for the first time, public relations is an important catalyst for bringing change and promoting consensus. Through the practice of public relations, organizations and individuals communicate their ideas and advance their goals in the marketplace of ideas. This concept is increasingly understood within the nations of Eastern Europe, where, since the fall of communism, the demand for public relations education has skyrocketed.

Public Relations: A Values-Driven Approach introduces this dynamic profession to the practitioners of the 21st century. Through a realistic blend of theory and practical examples, this book seeks to remove the veil of mystery that has shrouded the profession from its very beginnings. Using the conversational style of writing favored by today's college students, this book takes the reader on a journey of discovery, often through the eyes of leading practitioners and scholars.

Values-Driven Public Relations

As the title suggests, however, these pages contain more than just a recitation of facts and concepts. This book champions what we call *values-driven public relations*: an approach that challenges practitioners to align their efforts with the values of their organization, their profession, their targeted publics, and society itself.

Values-driven public relations is a logical response to a dynamic and diverse society in which complex issues and competing values bring different groups of people into conflict. This approach links communication with an organization's values, mission, and goals. Today, public and private organizations are increasingly held accountable for their actions by a variety of stakeholders. No longer is an organization's behavior measured solely by traditional indicators of success, such as profits, stock dividends, and jobs created. Additional measures of social worth now include an organization's relationships with its employees, its communities, its customers, and its physical environment. Stakeholders expect decisions to be made within an ethical framework. *Public Relations: A Values-Driven Approach* prepares future practitioners and the organizations they represent for a world of increased responsibility, scrutiny, and accountability.

Public Relations in the Social Context

Another notable feature of this book is its discussion of relevant issues within a broader social context. Public relations did not develop, nor is it practiced, in a vacuum. Throughout history, the practice of public relations has been shaped by great social forces. Its emergence in the United States was linked to the Industrial Revolution and the related Populist Era reforms. The 20th century's military and social conflicts served as catalysts for the profession's growth. Public relations was also transformed by the economic globalization and technological advances of the 1980s and 1990s. *Public Relations: A Values-Driven Approach* provides this broad social context so that future practitioners can have a clearer understanding of the so-called real world they are about to enter. The book includes full chapters on history, ethics, law, cross-cultural communication, and the role of the profession in the Digital Age. Throughout the book, students are directed to online sources of further information.

Features

A major goal of this book is to strengthen students' problem-solving skills. Every chapter opens with a hypothetical but realistic **scenario.** Each scenario places students in the shoes of a practitioner and challenges them to create an ethical, values-driven, effective solution. Each chapter also includes relevant case studies that expose students to successful as well as unsuccessful public relations approaches. Following each scenario and case study are questions designed to engage students in a meaningful analysis of the issues raised. The book further promotes problem-solving skills by introducing a variety of processes that guide students through the stages of research, planning, communication, evaluation, and ethical decision making.

Public Relations: A Values-Driven Approach also contains pedagogical elements that engage students in the subject matter. Each chapter begins with a list of learning **objectives** that set the stage for the topics that lie ahead. **QuickChecks,** a series of questions focusing on the book's content, are interspersed throughout each chapter. **QuickBreaks,** lively and relevant sidebars, bring depth and texture to each chapter. In keeping with the values focus of this text, **Values Statements** from a broad range of organizations are scattered throughout the book. A list of **key terms** appears on each chapter opener, and a full **glossary** is provided at the end of the book. Each chapter also includes a **Memo from the Field,** a message to students from one of today's leading public relations professionals. These professionals represent a broad range of public and private interests and reflect the diversity of the society upon which they wield so much influence.

Chapter-by-Chapter Revisions

Substantial changes have been made in every chapter of the fourth edition of *Public Relations: A Values-Driven Approach.* New current events include the aftermath of Hurricane Katrina, the shootings at Virginia Tech University, the Dove Campaign for Real Beauty, the firing of radio shock jock Don Imus, the philanthropic work of rock star Bono, the spying scandal at Hewlett-Packard, and much more. In addition to a sentence-by-sentence and image-by-image review, the chapters contain the following revisions and additions:

Chapter 1: New survey results on attitudes toward public relations; updated statistics on public relations employment and income; a new organizational values statement (Hallmark); and a new case study ("The Lessons of Katrina").

Chapter 2: Introduction of social media; new information on U.S. Code restrictions of federal publicity efforts; new Bureau of Labor Statistics job data; introduction of postmodern public relations theory; new salary data; and a new case study ("Stormy Weather").

Chapter 3: A new opening scenario; a new QuickBreak ("Thank You for Smoking"); a new organizational values statement (Ivy Lee's Declaration of Principles); and a new case study ("The March of Dimes").

Chapter 4: New data on employee publics, news media publics, government publics, investor publics, multicultural community publics, constituent publics, and business publics; and a new QuickBreak introducing social exchange theory.

Chapter 5: A new chapter introduction; introduction of priming theory; a new organizational values statement (APCO Worldwide); a discussion of U.S. media relations in Iraq; and a new Memo from the Field.

Chapter 6: Introduction of fully functioning society theory; new data on the relationship of ethics and profits, and a new case study ("Canada's Family Channel Battles Bullies").

Chapter 7: A new opening scenario; a new QuickBreak on the cost effectiveness of research; a new Memo from the Field; and a new case study ("Big Bang PR").

Chapter 8: The addition of "strategies" to a public relations plan that includes "goals," "objectives," and "tactics"; a revision of the planning grid to reflect resource dependency theory; new data on practitioners' access to top management; and a new case study ("Grape Expectations: Planning to Save California Wines").

Chapter 9: The introduction of social media tactics; revision of the communication model to reflect social media; the expansion of pitch letters to include e-mail and telephone pitches; updated information on political action committees; a new QuickBreak on creating memorable messages; a new Memo from the Field; and two new case studies ("Fleishman-Hillard Prompts Young Singles to Shout Yahoo!" and "No News at Senatorial News Conference").

Chapter 10: New data on the importance of writing and presentations; a new section on "Writing for the Web"; inclusion of social media; and a new case study ("Ghost Story").

Chapter 11: A thorough overhaul, including a new title: "Cyber-Relations in the Digital Age"; inclusion of social media, Web 2.0, and RSS; a new QuickBreak on web site design; a new QuickBreak on Wal-Mart's use of blogs; a new Memo from the Field; and a new case study ("Corporate Podcasting").

Chapter 12: Up-to-date examples of crisis responses; an updated IABC study on crisis planning; a new QuickBreak on apologia theory and Image Restoration Discourse; and a new case study ("False Hope").

Chapter 13: Inclusion of social media; introduction of partner relationship management; new data on the prevalence of integrated marketing communications; and a new case study ("Dove Soars with Real Beauty").

Chapter 14: New data on the diversity of the public relations workforce; new QuickBreak on Hofstede's cultural dimensions; and a new case study ("Pro Bono").

Chapter 15: New statistics on public opinion regarding freedom of expression; updated examples of public relations practitioners facing legal troubles; introduction of the National Do Not Call Registry; and updated statistics on the prevalence of litigation.

Chapter 16: Updated U.S. and world population figures; updated Hispanic economic figures; updated statistics on women in the workplace, sexual harassment, and salary equity; discussion of the Commission on Public Relations Education 2006 report; a new QuickBreak on global warming; a new Memo from the Field; and a new case study ("Guns and Greens").

Supplemental Resources for Instructors and Students

Instructor's Manual and Test Bank: By David W. Guth and Charles Marsh, The University of Kansas. This detailed Instructor's Manual and Test Bank contains sample syllabi, discussions of chapter-opening scenarios, and answers to chapter discussion and case study questions. In addition, the Test Bank portion of the manual contains numerous multiple choice, true/false, fill-in-the-blank, and essay questions. Available in print and online on our Instructor's Resource Center at www.ablongman.com/irc. Please contact your Pearson representative for an access code.

Computerized Test Bank: By David W. Guth and Charles Marsh, The University of Kansas. This user-friendly interface enables instructors to view, edit, and add questions, transfer questions into tests, and print tests in a variety of fonts. Search-and-sort features allow instructors to locate questions quickly and arrange them in preferred order. Available only online on our Instructor's Resource Center at www.ablongman.com/irc. Please contact your Pearson representative for an access code.

PowerPoint Presentation Package: By David W. Guth and Charles Marsh, The University of Kansas. A PowerPoint presentation provides lecture slides based on key concepts in the text. Available only online on our Instructor's Resource Center at www.ablongman.com/irc. Please contact your Pearson representative for an access code.

MyCommunicationLab for Public Relations: This state-of-the-art interactive and instructive solution for introductory public relations courses is designed to be used as a supplement to a traditional lecture course or to completely administer an online course. The site gives instructors and students access to a wealth of resources all geared to meet the individual teaching and learning needs of every instructor and every student. Combining an e-book, a portfolio builder, multimedia, video clips, activities, research support, practice tests, and exams, MyCommunicationLab for Public Relations engages students and prepares them to enter the world of public relations. Access code required. Visit www.mycommunicationlab.com or contact your Pearson representative for additional information.

Public Relations Study Site: By Holly Pieper, Mansfield University. This web site features public relations study materials for students, including flashcards and a complete set of practice tests for all major topics. Students will also find web links to valuable sites for further exploration of major topics. The site can be accessed at www.pearsonpublicrel.com.

Acknowledgments

The authors want to thank the dozens of people, many unknown to us before the writing of this book, who contributed greatly to this effort. The authors want to thank Dean Ann Brill and the faculty, staff, students, and alumni of the William Allen White School of Journalism and Mass Communications at the University of Kansas for their advice, support, and patience during this project. The authors also extend their gratitude to the dozens of companies, agencies, and individuals who gave their permission for the use of photographs, publications, and other artwork used in the text.

Sixteen men and women gave their valuable time to write memos to students who will read this book. The authors gratefully acknowledge the contributions of Judith T. Phair of PhairAdvantage Communications; John Echeveste of Valencia, Pérez & Echeveste Public Relations; Edward M. Block, formerly of AT&T; David A. Narsavage of The Aker Partners, Inc.; Jane Hazel of Health Canada; Carol Cone of Cone, Inc.; David Rockland of Ketchum; Timothy S. Brown of Delmarva Power/Atlantic City Electric; Deborah Charnes Vallejo of Bromley Communications; Regina Lynch-Hudson of The Write Publicist; Craig Settles of Successful.com; Wayne Shelor of the Clearwater (Florida) Police Department; Vin Cipolla of National Park Foundation; Bill Imada of IW Group; James F. Haggerty of The PR Consulting Group, Inc.; and Kevin Saghy, 2006–2007 national president of PRSSA.

A group of dedicated educators provided many suggestions for this fourth edition and, in doing so, helped the authors maintain a focus on the needs of students who read this book: Daniel D. Fultz, Bluffton University; Majorie Keeshan Nadler, Miami University; Brent Northup, Carroll College; Astrid Sheil, Northern Arizona University; and Amy Thurlow, Mount Saint Vincent University.

Once the text was written and the necessary artwork and permissions secured, the burden of this project shifted to the talented editors, designers, and technicians of Allyn and Bacon, including Lisa Sussman, Jeanne Zalesky, and Karon Bowers, as well as the team at Omegatype Typography, Inc.

Public Relations: A Values-Driven Approach would not have become a reality without the unwavering love and support of our families. They are our inspiration and motivation. Our wives, in particular, are our best friends and best editors. We lost a valued member of our team in March 2007. For that reason, we dedicate this book in loving memory of Jan Marie Guth.

David W. Guth, APR
Charles Marsh, Ph.D.

ABOUT the Authors

The authors of this book come from very different backgrounds but share a passion for public relations education. Both are associate professors at the William Allen White School of Journalism and Mass Communications at the University of Kansas. In addition to this textbook, they have collaborated on two textbooks: *Adventures in Public Relations: Case Studies and Critical Thinking* and, with colleague Bonnie Poovey Short, *Strategic Writing: Multimedia Writing for Public Relations, Advertising, Sales and Marketing, and Business Communication*.

Before becoming an educator, David W. Guth served as a broadcast journalist in six states and won numerous local, state, regional, and national reporting honors, including the prestigious George Foster Peabody Award. He has also served as a public relations practitioner in the public and private sectors, including holding several positions in North Carolina state government. As an educator, Guth coauthored *Media Guide for Attorneys*, a publication that received regional and national awards. In addition to his teaching and research responsibilities, Guth has served as crisis communications consultant to several government agencies and public utilities. Guth is an accredited member of the Public Relations Society of America. His international experience includes public relations work in Japan, Italy, Russia, and Turkmenistan.

Charles Marsh has a Ph.D. in English literature and 20 years of business communications experience. He is the former editor of *American Way,* the in-flight magazine of American Airlines, and the former senior editor of corporate publications for J.C. Penney. He is the author of *A Quick and (Not) Dirty Guide to Business Writing* (Prentice Hall, 1997) and has won national and regional awards for writing and editing. In addition to teaching, Marsh has been a communications consultant to J.C. Penney, Ralston Purina, the USA Film Festival, the United States Information Agency, the American Management Association, and other organizations. His international experience includes public relations work in France, Italy, Spain, Kyrgyzstan, and Costa Rica.

What Is Public Relations?

OBJECTIVES

After studying this chapter, you will be able to

■ explain the definition of public relations

■ understand the different roles public relations practitioners play

■ describe the four-step public relations process

■ appreciate the role of personal, organizational, and societal values in the practice of public relations

Bad News on the Doorstep

The first thing you see as you pick up the morning newspaper is a front-page story about your employer. A recent decision to move some of its operations to another location has generated criticism from community leaders, employees, union officials, and area business owners. The article also voices the concerns of several nonprofit organizations that your employer may be backing away from its commitment to local charities.

All of this comes at a time when your employer plans to approach government and business leaders about a new business venture, one that could generate new jobs and help spark the local economy. However, there's a catch: Your employer cannot do it alone. This new venture will require the government's commitment to an expensive upgrade of the city's infrastructure and the chamber of commerce's willingness to assist in the training of new workers.

You also know that your company has no intention of backing away from its support of the local community. The company's values statement says one of its goals is "to bring health and prosperity to the communities where our employees live and work." And until this morning's news story, no one had ever questioned your organization's commitment to its values.

Finishing that first cup of coffee, you know that you have to act. The decisions you make and the advice you give will affect the company's relationships with a wide range of publics. It is a tough job—but you are up to the challenge.

You work in public relations.

Public Relations: Everywhere You Look

If you want to get a sense of the mixed feelings people have about public relations, just ask them.

That's exactly what the world's largest organization of public relations practitioners did during 2005 in a nationwide survey about attitudes toward media, marketing, and the public relations profession. Nearly three out of four people surveyed said public relations practitioners help raise awareness about important issues and help get the news media to address issues they might otherwise ignore. However, by similar margins, they also said practitioners sometimes take advantage of the media to present misleading information and are only interested in disseminating information that helps their clients make money. That's not exactly a ringing endorsement.[1]

The term *public relations* and its abbreviation, *PR*, are often used (and abused) by those who have little or no understanding of its meaning. Some treat *public relations* as a synonym for words such as *publicity*, *propaganda*, *spin*, and *hype*. Some use the term as a pejorative, something inherently sinister. Others think of it as fluff, lacking in substance. The news media often contribute to the confusion. According to a study of 100 news stories that used the term *public relations,* fewer than 5 percent of them used it correctly. Researcher Julie K. Henderson wrote that 37 percent of the stories used *public relations* in a negative manner, and only 17 percent contained a positive reference.[2]

There are times when it is easy to see public relations at work. In the first decade of the 21st century, a variety of critical issues—questions of war and peace, disputes between science and religion, and the balance between public safety and personal freedoms—have dominated the news. Public relations practitioners often play a highly visible role in these debates by articulating their clients' values and orchestrating events that grab the public's attention. Other practitioners contribute by communicating vital information to help people important to the success of their organization cope with what are, by any measure, difficult times.

However, it may be more often that people do not recognize the connection between public relations actions and their outcomes. Faced with a serious shortage of blood supplies in 2005, American Red Cross officials in Puerto Rico turned to a public relations agency for help. GCI Group organized "Descubre el Regalo que llevamos dentro," the "Discover the Gift Inside" tour. A truck trailer converted into an interactive mobile museum toured the island and educated residents about the importance of giving blood. Donations increased by 20 percent over a four-month period.[3] In New York, Boost Mobile, a cellular telephone service provider popular among youth, teamed with RockCorps, an organization that harnesses the power of music to inspire volunteerism, to strengthen its brand image. Five thousand young people received free tickets to an exclusive hip-hop and alternative rock concert at New York's Radio City Music Hall in exchange for four hours of community service.[4]

Many try to define public relations strictly in terms of these kinds of high-profile images. However, *publicity* and *public relations* are not synonymous. As you will learn in Chapter 9, publicity is just one of many tactics used by public relations practitioners. Perhaps it is best to think of public relations as a tapestry, with many parts intricately woven into one whole cloth.

Public relations fosters mutually beneficial relationships. During the 1980s, the Adolph Coors Company was under fire from civil rights and feminist groups over its hiring practices. The brewer also was transitioning from a family-owned private company to a stockholder-owned public company. Through a variety of tactics that included the creation of eight employee diversity councils, Coors reached out to publics it once had viewed as its sharpest critics. These initiatives brought both financial and social rewards. Coors is the third-largest brewer in the United States with net sales of $5.84 billion in 2006.[5] The company has received recognition for its diversity efforts from several national magazines, including *Business Ethics, Black Enterprise,* and *Hispanic.*[6]

Public relations also builds corporate and product identities, a process known as **branding.** In their 2002 book *The Fall of Advertising and the Rise of PR,* authors Al and Laura Ries shook up Madison Avenue with the argument that it was public relations—not advertising—that successfully launched brands such as Starbucks, Palm, The Body Shop, Wal-Mart, and Red Bull. They said the key to this success was the credibility associated with effective public relations.[7]

RockCorps Promotional Materials Cellular telephone provider Boost Mobile strengthened its brand image and inspired volunteerism by teaming with RockCorps to create a series of highly targeted messages. Thousands of young people engaged in community service in exchange for concert tickets and promotional items. (Courtesy of Boost Mobile and RockCorps)

Some of the best public relations activity occurs when it appears as if nothing at all has happened. Few think to attribute high employee morale, increased productivity, or good corporate citizenship to public relations. But they should. When an orchestra sells out a concert or when a growing number of people decide against drinking and driving, it is easy to forget that these successes may well be benefits of sound public relations strategies. Even knowing where to vote, go to school, and shop is often the result of good public relations.

Public relations casts a broad net.

The Search for a Definition

So what is public relations? To update a phrase from a popular 1950s television game show, that is the million-dollar question. Unfortunately, there is no definitive answer. The modern practice of public relations first came under serious study in the early 1900s, and educators and practitioners have struggled ever since with its definition. At the beginning of the 21st century, defining public relations remains an issue.

This confusion was illustrated in a survey of accountants, attorneys, and public relations practitioners. The three groups were selected because they had something in common—a counselor relationship with their clients. Each group was asked about its profession and its place within organizational structures. Although the accountants and attorneys clearly understood their roles, the public relations practitioners did not. This caused the study's authors to raise a pertinent question: If public relations practitioners are unclear about who they are and what they do, why should they expect anyone else to understand?[8]

There isn't even any consensus on what to call the profession. Because of the supposedly negative connotations carried by the term *public relations,* many organizations opt to use euphemisms such as "public affairs," "public information," "corporate communications," or "community outreach" to describe the function. Burson-Marsteller, one of the world's largest public relations agencies, describes itself in its web site as a "communications counseling firm."[9]

Other organizations, especially government agencies, try to hide their public relations practitioners from the eyes of jealous rivals and zealous budget-cutters by giving them seemingly innocuous titles, such as "special assistant" or "information manager." One state agency had its listing removed from the North Carolina state government telephone directory in an effort to avoid detection. Instead of answering the telephone by saying "public information office," the staff was instructed to answer by repeating the office's extension number.[10]

Public Relations Defined

In 1976, in an effort to eliminate some of the confusion, public relations pioneer and scholar Rex Harlow compiled 472 different definitions of public relations. From those, Harlow came up with his own 87-word definition, which stressed public relations' role as a management function that "helps establish and maintain mutual lines of communication, understanding, acceptance, and cooperation between an organization and its publics."[11]

QUICKBREAK 1.1

The Definition Debate

The struggle to define the profession of public relations continues well into its second century. While many may see this as an intellectual exercise, others say the failure to reach a consensus on what, exactly, public relations is may undermine its future.

The **Public Relations Society of America (PRSA)** has tried to lay the matter to rest on several occasions. The PRSA Assembly adopted an Official Statement on Public Relations in 1982: "Public relations helps our complex, pluralistic society to reach decisions and function more effectively by contributing to mutual understanding among groups and institutions. It serves to bring the public and public policies into harmony."

The statement went on to describe public relations as a management function that encompasses monitoring and interpreting public opinion, counseling management on communication and social responsibility issues, and researching and managing organizational communication.[12]

Recognizing that its own attempt at defining the profession ran more than 400 words, PRSA settled on a more concise and somewhat vague alternative in 1988: "Public relations helps an organization and its publics adapt mutually to each other."[13]

PRSA's efforts to define public relations appear only to have invigorated the debate. The argument over what public relations is and how it should be defined raged throughout the1990s and into the new century. Practitioners, scholars, and textbook writers (including the authors of this book) continue to add fuel to this fire.

The challenge is deceptively simple: Find concise terminology that captures the values, purpose, and spirit of a complex and dynamic profession. The solution, however, remains elusive.

"If the field of public relations wishes to master its own destiny, it must settle on a definition," wrote James G. Hutton of Fairleigh Dickinson University. To that end, he proposed a three-word definition: "managing strategic relationships." While acknowledging his definition's potential drawbacks, Hutton believed that it captured the essential elements of the profession.[14]

Predictably, this attempt to settle the debate was met with skepticism. Writing in *Public Relations Review* in 2001, four European public relations professors found Hutton's approach "commendable, yet a bit flawed." Their major complaint was that Hutton's definition—and most U.S.-based definitions—focused only on U.S. theories and practices. "It is only after we are able to take into consideration the full richness of the present state of thinking and practicing public relations around the globe that we will be able to draw conclusions towards what the public relations profession is in the world at the beginning of the 21st century," the European scholars wrote.[15]

Even with dramatic advances in public relations research and technology during the last century, we are no closer to defining the profession than when Edward L. Bernays first coined the phrase "public relations counsel" in 1923. As one author wrote more than 40 years ago, public relations remains a discipline "of some 100,000 whose common bond is the profession and whose common woe is that no two of them can ever agree on what that profession is."[16]

In recent years, some have referred to public relations as *reputation management*, *perception management*, or *image management*. However, others express misgivings. They say these are superficial titles that do not reflect the depth of the profession.[17]

One area of agreement among public relations practitioners is the definition of the term **public:** any group of people who share common interests or values in a particular situation—especially interests or values they might be willing to act upon. When a public has a relationship with your organization, the public is called a **stakeholder,** meaning that it has a stake in your organization or in an issue potentially involving your organization.

The fact is that as long as people are people, they will continue to view the world with differing perspectives. That's why it may be best to avoid the debate over the exact wording of a public relations definition and, instead, to concentrate on the various elements of the profession itself. Here is where one finds consensus. Common to any comprehensive definition of public relations are the following elements:

- *Public relations is a management function.* The relationship between an organization and the publics important to its success must be a top concern of the organization's leadership. The public relations practitioner provides counsel on the timing, manner, and form important relationship-building actions should take. In other words, practitioners aren't just soldiers who follow orders; they're also generals who help shape policy. And like all managers, they must be able to measure the degree of their success in their various projects.

- *Public relations involves two-way communication.* Communication is not just telling people about an organization's needs. It also involves listening to those same people speak of their concerns. This willingness to listen is an essential part of the relationship-building process.

- *Public relations is a planned activity.* Actions taken on behalf of an organization must be carefully planned and consistent with the organization's values and goals. And since the relationship between an organization and the publics important to its success is a top concern, these actions must also be consistent with the publics' values and goals.

- *Public relations is a research-based social science.* Formal and informal research is conducted to allow an organization to communicate effectively, possessing a full understanding of the environment in which it operates and the issues it confronts. Public relations practitioners and educators also share their knowledge with others in the industry through various professional and academic publications.

- *Public relations is socially responsible.* A practitioner's responsibilities extend beyond organizational goals. Practitioners and the people they represent are expected to play a constructive role in society.

You may have noticed a common theme running throughout this list: the concept of **relationship management.** Farsighted, well-managed organizations know they must have good relationships with publics important to their success. A landmark study that sought to define excellence in public relations noted that having good relationships with these publics can save an organization money by reducing the likelihood of threats such as litigation, regulation, boycotts, or lost revenue that result from falling out of favor with these groups. At the same time, the study said that an organization makes more money by cultivating good relationships with consumers, donors, share-holders, and legislators.[18] Therefore, nurturing these relationships is one of the most important roles public relations practitioners can play.

However one chooses to frame its definition, there is one other important aspect to public relations: It plays a critical role in the free flow of information in democratic societies. When American colonists declared their independence from Great Britain in 1776, they said, "Governments are instituted among men, deriving their just powers from the consent of the governed."[19] The meaning of this phrase is clear: For democratic societies to function in a healthy manner, the government and the people must reach a consensus on matters of importance. Consent cannot occur without the exchange of information and ideas. That, in turn, requires communication. Those who cannot communicate effectively in democratic societies are left at a distinct and sometimes dangerous disadvantage.

Public relations plays a critical role in effective communications. Through public relations, individuals and organizations enter the great marketplace of ideas. And, through the proper application of public relations, practitioners participate in the search for consensus.

A Profession Gaining in Respect

It wasn't that long ago that the attitudes of corporate executives toward public relations were ambivalent at best. Former Mobil Corporation executive Herb Schmertz expressed the sentiments of many when he wrote in the mid-1980s that "public affairs is far too important to be left to public affairs professionals."[20] About the same time, survey research identified divergent opinions about the role public relations plays in organizations. While most practitioners surveyed said they saw their jobs as developing "mutual understanding" between management and the public, their bosses said the role of public relations was "persuasion, information dissemination, or propaganda."[21]

But that was then, and this is now. Recent surveys suggest that corporate executives are beginning to see the value of good public relations. A USC Annenberg Strategic Public Relations Center (SPRC) study reported that among companies included in *Fortune* magazine's Most Admired list there is greater support for the public relations function than among those of similar size not on the list. The report also said, "There is a demonstrable connection between a company's use of public relations and its own reputation and stature."[22] Another study reported that while many CEOs "still keep their PR executives at arm's length," an increasing number of practitioners are gaining access to upper-level managers.[23] These findings have been confirmed by similar studies in Japan and the United Kingdom.[24]

"There are two very contradictory and simultaneously held views of public relations," said SPRC Director Ian Mitroff. "In short, the profession is doing commendable work but suffers from low-self-esteem. Perception needs to catch up with reality."[25]

Whatever the perception and reality, there is one undeniable fact: Public relations is big business. *The Economist* reported that spending on public relations in the

United States reached $3.7 billion in 2005 and will grow by almost 9 percent a year through the end of the decade.[26]

The Hunt-Grunig Models of Public Relations

A major reason that recognition of the value of public relations has come so slowly is the many diverse roles practitioners play within different organizational structures. In short, one size does not fit all. Researchers Todd Hunt and James Grunig have identified four models that they say public relations practitioners generally follow:

1. In the **press agentry/publicity model,** the focus of public relations efforts is on getting favorable coverage, or publicity, from the media. In this model accuracy and truth, Hunt and Grunig contend, are not seen as essential.[27] In a recent survey of award-winning professionals worldwide, none said they preferred to emphasize this model.[28]

2. In the **public information model,** the focus is on the dissemination of objective and accurate information. Hunt and Grunig say that people following this model serve as "journalists in residence," acting in much the same manner as news re-porters.[29] In that same study of award-winning professionals, only 6.3 percent said they preferred to emphasize this model.[30]

3. The **two-way asymmetrical model** is a more sophisticated approach in which re-search is used in an effort to influence important publics toward a particular point of view. Hunt and Grunig describe this as a "selfish" model, one that does not lend itself to conflict resolution.[31] In the previously mentioned survey, 18.6 percent of the award-winning professionals said they preferred to emphasize this model.[32]

4. The **two-way symmetrical model** is the model Hunt and Grunig prefer. It focuses on two-way communication as a means of conflict resolution and for the promotion of mutual understanding between an organization and its important publics.[33] Among those award-winning professionals we have mentioned, 56.3 percent said they preferred to emphasize this model.[34]

Which public relations model—or combination of models—an organization chooses to follow depends on several factors. In smaller organizations, which often deal with fewer people and have less-complex issues to address, the practitioner tends to be more a communications technician than a counselor. Organizations that rely on public relations practitioners with relatively little experience usually limit the practitoners' role to technical tasks, such as news release writing and brochure design.

An organization's internal environment also can dictate the degree of influence public relations has. Sometimes corporate culture can inhibit good public relations practices. One study of organizations identified four barriers that practitioners often face in the corporate culture: a lack of access to top management, an unwillingness of management to pay for or grant authority to gather information, a resistance to timely and accurate disclosure, and differences over how managers and practitioners view the role of public relations.[35]

You may be wondering what, if anything, this means to you. If you are planning a career in public relations, it can mean a lot. The Hunt-Grunig models are not abstract concepts. They can help you predict the future. As the previously mentioned research suggests, organizations that embrace public relations tend to be more successful than those that don't. And it doesn't take a rocket scientist to understand that the closer one is to management—the more influence one has—the greater the opportunities for career advancement. Knowing how a potential employer sees the public relations role can make quite a difference in your future.

Public Relations and Marketing

Another definitional issue is whether public relations should be considered a separate discipline at all. Some very learned people argue that public relations is a component of a different field encompassing many persuasive communications: **integrated marketing communications (IMC)**. (This topic is discussed in significant detail in Chapter 13.) However, other, equally learned individuals bristle at the thought of public relations being covered by an all-encompassing IMC umbrella.

The authors of this book support the latter view. We see IMC as a customer-focused marriage of three distinct disciplines: advertising, marketing, and some functions of public relations. As you may have noticed, some people think of public relations as "free advertising" and of advertising as marketing. However, each term represents a distinct discipline:

- **Advertising** is the use of controlled media (media in which one pays for the privilege of dictating message content, placement, and frequency) in an attempt to influence the actions of targeted publics.
- **Marketing** is the process of researching, creating, refining, and promoting a product or service and distributing that product or service to targeted consumers.
- **Public relations** is the management of relationships between an organization and its publics.

Not every marketing situation requires the use of all three disciplines. Marketing, the central concept in IMC, focuses on customers. We respectfully suggest that public relations practitioners engage in relationships that go far beyond customer communications. Although this is a debate that may best be conducted in an atmosphere that includes beverages and peanuts, the debate is indicative of the broader struggle public relations practitioners have faced since the dawn of the 20th century—to have public relations accepted as a separate and significant profession.

The confusion over what public relations is demonstrates why any attempt to define the profession is best done in broad strokes. In truth, public relations is part art and part science. It is a dash of inspiration and a lot of perspiration. It is also very hard work that is often at its best when it goes unnoticed. This, in part, explains why public relations was ranked 12th in a list of the 250 most stressful jobs in the United States—ranked as less stressful than being a police officer or an air traffic controller, but more stressful than being a college basketball coach or a member of Congress.[36]

1. What are the five essential elements in the definition of public relations?
2. How is public relations related to the concept of relationship management?
3. What are the Hunt-Grunig models of public relations, and why are they significant?
4. How do public relations and marketing differ?

Why a Public Relations Career?

You may already be asking, "Why would anyone want a career in a field as misunderstood and demanding as public relations?" Good question. Now, a better answer: because there is no other job quite like it. Public relations skills are transferable across a broad range of career opportunities. Regardless of a person's career interests—such as health care, sports marketing, environmental management, government and politics, business and finance, or public service—there is no organization that cannot benefit from wise public relations counsel. Every organization has a need to maintain healthy relationships with its important publics. That is where the public relations practitioner exerts influence. Public relations is a profession that demands and rewards creativity and integrity. It's a profession in which you can see the results of a job well done. It is a career in which you can make a difference.

A Profile of Practitioners

In its most recent report, the U.S. Bureau of Labor Statistics (BLS) estimated that 188,000 people were employed as "public relations specialists" and another 58,000 as "public relations managers." The BLS predicts employment in public relations "will grow faster than average for all occupations through 2014" and that there will be "keen competition for entry-level jobs." The BLS said this growth was because "the value of a company is measured not just by its balance sheet, but also on the strength of the relationships with those on whom it depends for its success."[37]

In a broad sense, public relations can be practiced within five organizational structures:

1. *Public relations agencies:* companies that contract to provide or supplement public relations services for others. These agencies are often affiliated with advertising agencies to provide integrated marketing communications (IMC) services for their clients (see Chapter 13).
2. *Corporations:* public relations units within companies. Corporate practitioners are company employees.
3. *Government:* public, taxpayer-supported units within government agencies. These units offer counsel on governmental policies and disseminate information vital to the healthy functioning of a democracy. These practitioners are government employees.

A Profession or a Trade?

Adding to the confusion about what public relations is and where it fits into an organization's structure is an ongoing debate: Is public relations a profession or is it a trade? This is a debate over more than mere semantics and prestige. The salaries practitioners earn, their influence on decision making, and the degree to which they are regulated hang in the balance.

Generally recognized qualities that distinguish professions from other career pursuits are

- the need for a certain level of education as a prerequisite to entering the profession;
- support of the profession by ongoing research published in scholarly journals or in professional association publications;
- the establishment of ethical standards, usually in the form of a code of ethics; and
- some form of licensing or government control.

Doctors and lawyers are professionals who clearly meet these criteria. Both have to receive an advanced academic degree and are expected to remain informed on the latest developments in their fields. Both professions are supported by significant bodies of research and have established codes of ethics. And one cannot be a doctor or lawyer until a state licensing board gives its stamp of approval.

When it comes to public relations, the dividing line between profession and trade is not as well defined. In one nationwide survey, there was little consensus on what constitutes a standard of professional performance. Answers varied significantly, depending on the respondent's age, level of education, race, level of experience, and geographic location.[38]

Licensing proponents, including the late Edward L. Bernays, an acknowledged "father" of modern public relations, see licensing as a way of weeding out unqualified practitioners and raising the stature and salaries of those who are licensed. Others see government-sanctioned licensing as burdensome and as an infringement on First Amendment rights to freedom of expression.

Organizations such as PRSA and the **International Association of Business Communicators (IABC)** have sought to promote public relations as a profession through the establishment of voluntary accreditation programs. Practitioners must gain a certain level of experience and demonstrate a certain degree of knowledge before receiving accreditation: **APR,** for **Accredited in Public Relations,** by PRSA and/or **ABC,** for **Accredited Business Communicator,** by IABC. With the creation of the **Universal Accreditation Program** in 1998, PRSA opened its accreditation process to members of eight additional public relations organizations, including the National School Public Relations Association and the Religion Communicators Council.[39] Both IABC and PRSA also promote professionalism with support of scholarly research and through the enforcement of codes of ethics.

4. *Nonprofit organizations or trade associations:* public relations units that serve not-for-profit organizations or specific business/interest groups. These practitioners usually are employees of the organizations they serve.
5. *Independent public relations consultants:* self-employed public relations practitioners. These practitioners may contract with clients on a per-job basis or may be placed on a retainer, much like a public relations agency.

With public relations unlicensed, it is nearly impossible to provide an accurate picture of the entire profession. A 2005 PRSA membership survey provides a glimpse into the state of the profession. Almost 7 out of 10 respondents were female. The largest number of respondents, 25 percent, worked in corporations, followed by those working in nonprofit organizations/associations (19 percent), and public relations agencies/consulting firms (17 percent).[40] While percentages differ, a 2005 analysis of IABC membership yielded similar rankings.[41] According to the PRSA study, nearly all the respondents had at least a bachelor's degree, with nearly a third having a master's degree, as well. More than one-third were managers, with males more likely to be in management positions and females more likely to be in staff positions. Ninety-three percent were white.[42] (These data raise equity issues discussed in Chapter 16.)

Not only is public relations practiced in a wide range of settings, but its practitioners use a broad spectrum of communications skills. Some of the more traditional public relations tasks include news release writing, brochure design, creation of annual reports, and development of marketing materials. In recent years, however, there has been a revolution in communications technologies, and public relations practitioners have been at the cutting edge of change. Practitioners now engage in web site development, blogs, and podcasts. They produce interactive CDs and DVDs. In the post-9/11 world, there is increased emphasis on government information programs, multicultural communications, and crisis communications.

QUICK ✓ CHECK

1. Is public relations a profession? Why or why not?
2. What are the five organizational structures in which public relations is commonly practiced?
3. Is the number of jobs in public relations growing?

The Public Relations Process

Although the technology used in the practice of public relations is constantly changing, the process that guides public relations is one that stands the test of time. Most public relations experts agree that public relations is conducted within the framework of a four-step process. But would this really be public relations if there were agreement on what to label each of the steps? Remember: This is public relations, the profession of a thousand definitions.

The Traditional Four-Step Model of the Public Relations Process

A variety of names have been used to describe the four steps of the public relations process. Some instructors, in an effort to help students memorize the various steps for the inevitable midterm exam, have favored the use of acronyms such as ROPE (research, objective, planning, and evaluation) and RACE (research, action, communication, and evaluation). In adding our two cents' worth to the debate over what to call each of the four steps, we opt for a more straightforward, if less glamorous, approach: research, planning, communication, and evaluation.

1. **Research** is the discovery phase of a problem-solving process: practitioners' use of formal and informal methods of information gathering to learn about an organization, the challenges and opportunities it faces, and the publics important to its success.

2. **Planning** is the strategy phase of the problem-solving process, in which practitioners use the information gathered during research. From that information, they develop effective and efficient strategies to meet the needs of their clients or organizations.

3. **Communication** is the execution phase of the public relations process. This is where practitioners direct messages to specific publics in support of specified goals. But good plans are flexible: Because changes can occur suddenly in the social or business environment, sometimes it's necessary to adjust, overhaul, or abandon the planned strategies. It's worth repeating here that effective communication is two-way, involving listening to publics as well as sending them messages.

4. **Evaluation** is the measurement of how efficiently and effectively a public relations effort met the organization's goals.

Although there is a simple elegance in defining the public relations process using this traditional model, it does not reflect the real world. It depicts a linear process: Step two follows step one, step three follows step two, and so forth (see Figure 1.1). How often does your own life move in such an orderly fashion? If you are like most people, life is constantly changing and full of surprises. Public relations is no different.

The Dynamic Model of the Public Relations Process

In the real world, public relations involves a dynamic process (see Figure 1.2). While practitioners move along a general path of research, planning, communication, and evaluation, it is often necessary to switch directions. They do this because the world is an ever-changing place. To put it another way, what was true yesterday may not be true tomorrow.

For example, the implication of the traditional four-step model is that evaluation is the last thing done. However, in this era of downsizing and increased accountability, evaluation should occur during *every* phase of the public relations process. Research should identify ways to measure the effects of a public relations program. Those measurements should then be built into any plan that is developed. As the plan moves into the communication phase, practitioners should be sensitive to the need to adjust their efforts to any miscalculations or changes in the environment.

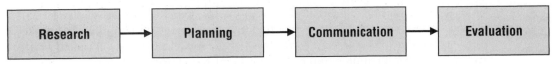

FIGURE 1.1 The Traditional Four-Step Model of the Public Relations Process

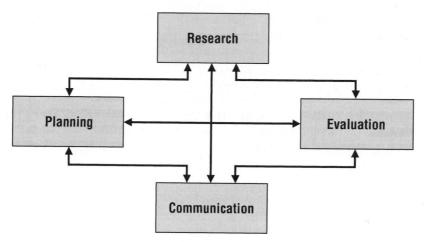

FIGURE 1.2 The Dynamic Model of the Public Relations Process

That, in turn, may require additional research. Finally, the evaluation phase provides critical information on whether the goals of the plan were met. But it also sets the stage for future actions.

The public relations process is not a step-by-step process followed much like a cook follows a recipe. It is a critical-thinking process involving a constant analysis and reevaluation of information.

The Role of Values in Public Relations

Although the dynamic model of public relations more closely resembles the real world, it is still missing a key component: **values.** For the purposes of this discussion, values are defined as the fundamental beliefs and standards that drive behavior and decision making. To put it another way, values are the filters through which we see the world and the world sees us. Everyone has values. Organizations have values. Actions communicate values. Even thoughtless actions taken with little regard for one's beliefs and standards communicate a value.

Think about the process you and your friends follow when planning a spring break trip. As you begin to research where to go, you first identify your values: fun, companionship, safety, price, and so forth. Those core values establish the framework within which you'll gather research, plan your trip, go on your trip, and, finally, evaluate its success.

Let's use a second hypothetical example to illustrate what we mean. If an organization says it values the opinions of its employees, it would not make any sense for that organization to conduct research that doesn't take into account the employees' opinions. And it would make even less sense to launch a plan that, in the pursuit of some other short-term gain, winds up showing that the organization is insensitive to employee concerns. That is why it is necessary to understand an organization's values before engaging in the public relations process. And because good relationships with important publics are critical to any organization's success, it is equally important to understand the values of those publics. Some may argue that this approach limits information gathering and creativity. However, that is exactly what values are supposed to do: establish the boundaries within which we are willing to operate.

This lack of focus on values is perhaps the biggest flaw in the traditional four-step model of public relations. At a time when organizations are being held accountable far beyond the balance sheet, their values-inspired mission and goals must be at the forefront of all their research, planning, communication, and evaluation.

A common complaint against public relations practitioners is that they occasionally act as if the ends justify the means. Some choose to flirt with or even to ignore the boundaries of ethics. Others, failing to pause and consider their organization's core values, sometimes find themselves in the uncomfortable position of trying to place their actions in an ethical framework after the fact. Isn't it much better to snuff out a fire before it causes irreparable damage? Issues of values, ethics, and social responsibility must be addressed throughout the public relations process: The continued growth of public relations as a profession depends on it.

1. What are the four steps of the traditional public relations process?
2. Why is public relations considered a dynamic process?
3. What are values, and what role should they play in the public relations process?

Actions Speak Louder Than Words—Part I

Too often, unintended actions speak louder than the lofty words found in an organization's mission statement:

■ The local, state, and federal government response to Hurricane Katrina in 2005 could be likened to a comedy of errors—except no one was laughing. Images of human misery in the face of bureaucratic blunders played out on live television before a worldwide audience. Some of the harshest criticisms were leveled at President George Bush, who early in the crisis commended Federal Emergency Management Agency Director Michael Brown for doing "a heck of a job." That praise came before both the scope of the disaster and the government's inadequate response were known. In the aftermath of the debacle, Brown resigned and Bush's approval ratings plummeted to the lowest levels of his presidency. (See Case Study 1.2.)

■ An internal investigation into news leaks at Hewlett-Packard evolved into a major scandal in 2006. HP Chairwoman Patricia Dunn and Chief Ethics Officer Kevin Hunsaker were fired and later indicted for spying on journalists and members of the company's board of directors. Through a controversial tactic known as pretexting, company investigators allegedly obtained Social Security numbers to gain access to a wide range of personal information, including telephone records.[43]

■ At first, it appeared as if Wal-Mart had grassroots support in its battle against critics who question the retail giant's hiring and marketing practices. Two Internet blogs, Working Families for Wal-Mart and Paid Critics, vigorously defended the company. However, the disclosure that Edelman, a public relations firm, orchestrated the blogs undermined Wal-Mart's credibility.[44] (See QuickBreak 11.4.)

Why did these organizations get black eyes? Because their actions—real or perceived—didn't live up to their stated values. Such incidents always leave a stronger impression than the inspirational words of a mission statement.

Values-Driven Public Relations

How can organizations try to ensure that their actions match their words? We advocate an approach we call **values-driven public relations.** Values-driven public relations incorporates a dynamic version of the four-phase process of research, planning, communication, and evaluation into the framework defined by an organization's core values (see Figure 1.3). We offer an alternate definition of public relations: *Public relations is the values-driven management of relationships between an organization and the publics that can affect its success.*

Values-driven public relations is the process of uncovering not just where an organization wishes to go but also the principles the organization will observe in getting there. The process begins with the consideration of values during the research phase—those of the organization and the various publics important to its success. Those values, in turn, are incorporated into planning and communications. Values-driven public relations also means being accountable for adherence to those values when we evaluate our actions.

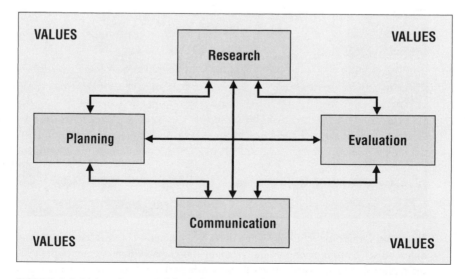

FIGURE 1.3 Values-Driven Public Relations

If that sounds easy, it isn't. We live in an increasingly diverse and complex world. New technology and the forces of globalization bring different interests into greater contact—and often into conflict. One need only look at recent history. Violent protests accompany practically every meeting of the World Trade Organization. Much of Seattle's downtown was shut down by pitched battles during WTO meetings in 1999. Four years later, trade talks in Cancun, Mexico, were marred when a South Korean farm leader killed himself to protest the WTO's agricultural trade policies.[45] Meanwhile, a frustrated WTO director-general told arguing delegates to expect "less Mr. Nice Guy" from him."[46] If anything, these events were the antithesis of values-driven public relations: A lot of heat was generated, but very little light.

Actions Speak Louder Than Words—Part II

At the same time, a variety of publics are holding public and private organizations more socially accountable. No longer is the bottom line seen as the only thing that matters. Although social responsibility may seem idealistic to some, its applications are very real-world:

■ Confronted with research showing that two of every three women believe that the media have created an unrealistic standard of beauty, a major player in the beauty

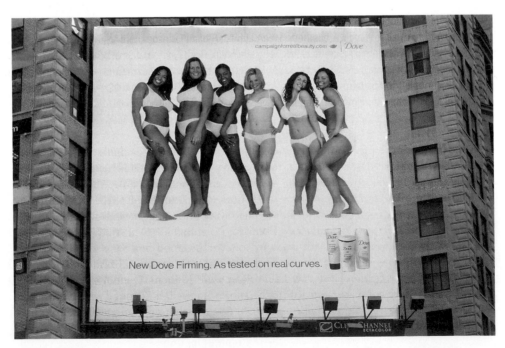

The Dove Campaign for Real Beauty used real women—not supermodels—in an effort to enhance self-esteem among young women. This award-winning campaign includes positive examples of values-driven public relations, where the values of an organization and a targeted public coincide. (Copyright 2005 The New York Times Company. Reprinted with permission.)

industry set out in 2004 to change those stereotypes. Unilever, maker of the Dove line of personal care products, launched the Dove Campaign for Real Beauty. The company used real women—not supermodels—in its integrated marketing campaign. The effort included Real Beauty Workshops that were designed to enhance self-esteem among young girls. Unilever's efforts prompted Canadian marketer Shirley Lichti to write, "In a world where media depictions of beauty are based on physical attractiveness and airbrushed images, the Dove Campaign for Real Beauty is a breath of fresh air."[47] (See Case Study 13.1.)

■ Southwest Airlines company officials wondered how their employees could find a meaningful way to contribute to their local communities. From this desire, the airline's award-winning Adopt-A-Pilot program took flight. The program pairs Southwest pilots with fifth-grade students across the country in an educational mentoring program. Its goal is to show students how important education is to achieving one's goals. Greg Crum, Southwest's vice president of flight operations, said, "We hear from teachers that many students have gained increased self-esteem and determination for future careers as a result of the Adopt-A-Pilot program."[48]

■ Based in Kansas City, Missouri, Hallmark Cards acted on its values (see Values Statement 1.1) in February 2006 when it donated the complete Hallmark Photographic Collection to a local museum. With 6,500 images by 900 artists, it is

VALUES STATEMENT 1.1

Hallmark Cards

Hallmark Cards, founded In 1910, is the leader in the personal expression industry. The Kansas City, Missouri, company reported consolidated net revenues of $4.1 billion in 2006. Hallmark products are distributed in more than 30 languages to more than 100 countries.

THIS IS HALLMARK

We Believe:

That our products and services must enrich people's lives.

That creativity and quality—in our products, services and all that we do—are essential to our success.

That innovation in all areas of our business is essential to attaining and sustaining leadership.

That the people of Hallmark are our company's most valuable resource.

That distinguished financial performance is imperative to accomplish our broader purpose.

That our private ownership must be preserved.

We Value and Are Committed To:

Excellence in all we do.

High standards of ethics and integrity.

Caring and responsible corporate citizenship for Kansas City and for each community in which we operate.

These beliefs and values guide our business strategies, our corporate behavior, and our relationships with business partners, suppliers, customers, communities and each other.

—Hallmark Beliefs & Values Statement

QuickBreak 1.3

How Organizations Establish Their Values

J.C. Penney has *The Penney Idea,* a group of seven governing values written in 1913. One of the values is "To test our every policy, method, and act in this wise: Does it square with what is right and just?"

Hallmark Cards has *This Is Hallmark,* a statement of "Beliefs and Values." One of the statement's five beliefs declares "distinguished financial performance is imperative to accomplish our broader purpose." One of the statement's four values is "ethical and moral conduct at all times and in all our relationships."

Johnson & Johnson is governed by the one-page *Johnson & Johnson Credo,* which begins, "We believe our first responsibility is to the doctors, nurses, and patients, to the mothers and fathers, and all others who use our products and services."

How did these respected, successful organizations—and others like them—develop their written statements of values? Each organization has its own system, but two ingredients seem common to the values identification process. First, it's a job for a dedicated committee, not an individual. Debating with others helps us clarify what we truly believe. Second, a statement of values must be written, must be well known, and must play an active part in an organization's everyday operations. Only in that way can it be tested and improved.

If an organization lacks a written statement of values, its public relations program is a ship without a rudder. An organization can begin to develop a **values statement** by forming a committee or committees to answer these questions:

1. Why are we in business?
2. What does our organization want to be known for—both today and a generation from now?
3. What should our publics expect from us?
4. What are our highest priorities?

considered among the most significant private collections of American photography. Many of the images, such as the late Joe Rosenthal's "Flag Raising at Iwo Jima," are instantly recognizable. Hallmark created the collection in 1979 out of a belief that photography is an important art form. When asked why the Nelson-Atkins Museum of Art was selected as the home for this important collection, Hallmark Chairman Donald J. Hall said, "We selected them because we like them." As the *New York Times* reported, "A Hallmark card couldn't have said it better."[49]

Whose Values Should You Follow?

In the research phase of the public relations process, an organization must, of course, identify and consider its own values—but it must also do more: It must identify the values of involved publics and, perhaps, the values of society itself. Sometimes it can be difficult to decide which values to follow. If there is conflict between organizational and societal values, organizations must make a difficult choice.

This does not imply that one must always adhere to society's values. For example, there was a time in the United States when society condoned slavery, denied

5. Where do we want to go, and whom do we want along for the ride?

6. What should our role be in our community and in our industry?

7. Whose organization is this?

8. To whom do we have obligations?

9. Why should someone want to work for this organization?

The answers to these questions should be used to create a short statement of the organization's core values. Stating each value as a principle can help you move from a values statement to a **mission statement;** in other words, stating each value as a principle can help you move from an idea to a proposed action. For example, J.C. Penney values justice in all its actions. In *The Penney Idea,* that value is stated as a principle: "To test our every policy, method, and act in this wise: Does it square with what is right and just?"

Let's look for a moment at the first question: "Why are we in business?" The obvious answer for

many organizations might seem to be "to make money." But it's not money that people crave as much as it is what money can provide: a nice home, food, education, the ability to help others. Hallmark's statement of beliefs and values notes that money is not an end; rather, it's a means toward accomplishing Hallmark's broader purpose.

The *Johnson & Johnson Credo* has served that company particularly well. The company won praise from customers, politicians, journalists, and other key publics for its immediate willingness to put the safety of its customers ahead of company profits during two product-tampering incidents in the 1980s. By adhering to its *Credo,* Johnson & Johnson emerged as one of the most respected companies in the world.

Like many strong, values-driven organizations, Johnson & Johnson periodically evaluates its *Credo* in the context of current business situations. In a values-driven organization, a statement of values or a mission statement should be as much a part of the everyday environment as coffee, meetings, and lunch plans.

women the right to vote, and allowed children to work long hours in unhealthy conditions. An organization may choose to swim against the tide of public opinion. If it chooses to do so, however, it should do so by choice, not chance. Values-driven public relations can be a catalyst for making this crucial decision.

Values-driven public relations is similar to the traditional four-step approach to public relations but it has significant differences. In values-driven public relations the role of organizational, public, and societal values is explicit, rather than implicit. Values-driven public relations also employs a decidedly nonlinear process, in which there are constant checkbacks on values, research, strategies, and execution. Most important, the practice of values-driven public relations answers the most ardent critics of public relations by placing ethical decision making first.

Let's close by returning to that opening scenario in which your company's actions are under close scrutiny. Faced with several public relations challenges and opportunities, the CEO has just asked, "What do you think we should do?"

Part of your answer should be "research." And to that one word, you'll add a key request: "Let's be sure that our actions reflect our company's values."

Welcome to values-driven public relations.

QUICK ✓ CHECK

1. How do you define *values-driven public relations,* and how does it differ from the traditional definition of public relations?
2. In values-driven public relations, whose values should we follow?
3. What are some examples of public relations decisions in which values played a key role?

Summary

Public relations is a very important but often misunderstood profession. Even those who practice it have difficulty in developing a definition for public relations with which everyone can agree. Despite differences in wording, proper definitions of public relations contain five basic elements: Public relations is a management function, involves two-way communication, is a planned activity, is a social science based on research, and is socially responsible. There is also broad agreement that relationship building is at the heart of good public relations. That requires knowledge of values, the beliefs and standards that govern one's actions. And not just our own values but also those of the various publics important to our success.

The manner in which public relations is practiced depends largely on the structure of the organization it serves. Although public relations should be a major concern of management, some organizations relegate its practitioners to the role of technicians. Some view public relations as an element of integrated marketing communications. However, others—including the authors of this book—view it as a separate and distinct profession.

The traditional view of public relations is that it is performed through a four-step process: research, planning, communication, and evaluation. The problem with that view is that public relations is a dynamic process in which any of these four phases can occur at any time. When practitioners conduct this process while closely adhering to values—those of the practitioner, the organization, and the society—the process evolves into what is known as values-driven public relations: the values-driven management of relationships between an organization and the publics that can affect its success.

DISCUSSION QUESTIONS

1. Before you read this chapter, how would you have defined *public relations*?
2. Why, in your opinion, is there so much disagreement over a standard definition of public relations?
3. In your opinion, should some form of licensing be mandatory for public relations practitioners?
4. What role does relationship management play in public relations?
5. How would you describe values-driven public relations to a friend who was curious but knew very little about public relations?

Memo from the Field

Judith T. Phair, APR; Fellow PRSA; PRSA President 2005; Vice President, Graduate Management Admission Council, McLean, Virginia

Judith "Judy" T. Phair, APR, Fellow PRSA, is vice president of communications for the Graduate Management Admission Council, a nonprofit education association of 154 top graduate business schools from around the world and the provider of the Graduate Management Admission Test (GMAT). She leads the council's worldwide strategic communications planning and oversees all marketing, advertising, media relations, and print and electronic communications. Phair is a seasoned public relations executive with extensive experience in marketing, media relations, fund-raising, legislative relations, and communications. Her résumé includes service as vice president for public affairs on the Council on Competitiveness, vice president for institutional advancement at the University of Maryland Biotechnology Institute, assistant dean of external relations at Johns Hopkins University, and vice president for public relations at Goucher College. Phair is a former president of PRSA. She has written and spoken extensively on public relations and marketing issues in the United States and abroad, including China, Italy, the United Kingdom, and Croatia.

I'll admit to being a bit envious of a new generation of public relations professionals. The reason: This just may be the best time ever to begin a career in our dynamic and demanding business. True, the profession is facing the greatest challenges in its history. But the opportunities are also practically limitless.

The evolution of public relations over just a few short decades is remarkable. We've come a long way from being seen as simply publicity agents whose main job is to get our client's name in the press. Today's public relations professional needs to understand financial spreadsheets and communications theory . . . corporate governance and behavioral science . . . the global marketplace and the 24/7 news cycle.

First, let's take a look at some of the challenges. Americans place a premium on trust and values—in government, in corporations, in nonprofits. Yet trust and confidence in all three of these areas is at its lowest ebb in years. The culprits include corporate and nonprofit scandals, the horrors of 9/11 and the rising tide of terrorism, and a worsening American image abroad. The fact is, all too often as public relations professionals, we have been behind the curve, not ahead of it.

At the same time, we're facing some dramatic changes in our own profession, spurred on by new technology and a shrinking world. In an increasingly specialized society, we are now expected to have highly specialized knowledge in specific market segments, rather than to simply be "generalists." Our clients and employers want us to be accountable and measurable. And the public wants us to be ethical and credible communicators—not "spin doctors" switching our messages every time a new poll shows a shift in opinion.

The stakes are high, but public relations—perhaps more than any other profession—is uniquely poised to make a difference. We can take our profession to a new and higher level—and, in the process, we can play a major role in restoring trust and confidence, at home and abroad.

You can be part of the best generation of public relations professionals ever—ethical, credible, knowledgeable, and ready to show the true power of public relations as an agent of positive change for our nation and our world. Are you ready? Here are a few guidelines, based on observation and hard-won experience, for advancing your career as a professional, as well as our profession.

- **Think globally.** You are entering a profession that has become global in scope, no matter where you work. Just about every corporation and every organization now has some international connection. Consider the West Virginia utility that was acquired by a Dutch firm—or the tech support for your computer that is based in India. Read international as well as national and local news, travel whenever you can, master another language, or two, or three. Learn—and respect—cultural differences.

- **Be accountable.** Our profession has become both more specialized and more comprehensive. You will need to know your organization's business from top to bottom if you want to be a truly effective and respected counselor. You'll also be expected to measure and evaluate results—to show how you contribute to the bottom line.

- **Stay flexible.** Adopt and adapt new technologies, new theories, new approaches to problems and issues. The definition of public relations continues to broaden, and that heightens our value. When I began my career, most of my colleagues shunned marketing tools and techniques. Now we realize that these are important additions to our public relations portfolio. Be willing to take on new assignments that may not "match" your job description or skill set—but can open the door to expanded opportunities.

- **Listen actively.** Two-way communication is an active process. All too often, we are our own greatest barriers to communication. If we really listened—not just heard—our bosses, our clients, our target audiences, we could engage in real dialogue and set the stage for successful exchange. It's so easy to let our own thoughts and theories crowd out the message we are receiving. The result is that we shortchange ourselves and our clients.

- **Think strategically.** Ask "why" before "how." Think before doing. When a client presents a problem, it is tempting to focus immediately on specific tasks—or tactics—to turn it around. Without a broader plan—a strategy—individual tactics may end up being temporary patches to make the edifice look good while the foundation is crumbling. Strategic thinking takes care of the long term, so that you can deal with the short term.

- **Keep on learning.** It's impossible to know "enough." There is always more to learn—both about our profession and about other areas that impact our lives and our careers, our world. Lifelong learning isn't an option; it's a requirement.

- **Embrace leadership.** In today's world, a solid background in public relations can take you as high as you want to go. Top public relations executives are now becoming presidents and CEOs—an almost unheard-of leap just a few years ago. It makes sense—we possess the skills and sensitivities that can make us great leaders. Take every opportunity—in your community, in your profession, on the job, to learn leadership skills and take on leadership roles. Indeed, PRSSA and PRSA leadership offer excellent opportunities to develop leadership, teamwork, and negotiating skills, along with the chance to get to know other current and potential leaders. Building relationships, after all, is still one of our most important contributions as public relations professionals.

CASE STUDY **1.1**

Closing the Gap on Sweatshops

When Paul Pressler became president and CEO of Gap, Inc., in 2002, his teenage daughter confronted him with what could have been an uncomfortable question: "Doesn't Gap use sweatshops?"[50]

However, the question didn't surprise him. The company was just one of many clothing retailers under fire for selling products manufactured in garment factories where workers labor under poor conditions with low wages. Many U.S. corporations have moved their operations overseas to take advantage of lower labor and production costs. This economic globalization has given rise to a growing chorus of labor and human rights advocates voicing concerns about worker safety, child labor, employee harassment and abuse, and less-than-living wages.

So how did Pressler respond to his daughter? He said, "I was able to tell her how the company was working to fight sweatshop practices and improve garment factory conditions around the world."[51]

Gap, Inc., based in San Francisco, owns three of the world's most popular clothing chains: The Gap, Old Navy, and Banana Republic. At the start of 2007, the corporation operated more than 3,100 stores and had more than $15.9 billion in annual net sales.[52] The company's 153,000 full- and part-time employees—as well as its board of directors—are required to follow a corporate code of business conduct. "Gap Inc. was founded in 1969 on the principle of conducting business in a responsible, honest and ethical manner," the code states. "Today, Gap Inc. remains committed to meeting the highest standards of business conduct. Nothing less will do."[53]

The company had set a high standard for itself. The question among many of The Gap's critics was whether the company was willing to keep its word.

An answer came in May 2004, when Gap, Inc., issued its first *Social Responsibility Report*. In it, the clothing retailer acknowledged that workers at many of its overseas suppliers were being mistreated. The company said it uncovered thousands of violations at more than 3,000 factories in 50 countries. "Few factories, if any, are in full compliance all of the time," the report said.[54]

"We believe that garment and other manufacturing workers around the world deserve better than the reality that many unfortunately face," Pressler said. "We recognize and embrace our duty to take a leadership role."[55]

The report detailed the company's ongoing global monitoring program launched in 1996. The 90-person compliance team made 8,500 factory visits in 2003. As a result of these visits, the team cut ties with more than 100 new garment facilities seeking The Gap's business and revoked prior approvals for 136 other factories because of violations of its vendor code of conduct.[56]

Many of The Gap's critics praised the company for its candor. But they also noted that other apparel companies, such as Reebok International, Ltd., had been more forthcoming on the issue. "It's positive that they're coming out with a report that moves this issue of social responsibility forward," said human rights activist Medea Benjamin, who had organized protests and boycotts of Gap products in the 1990s. "But the reality is that the Gap produces in countries where workers don't have basic rights and they leave countries where workers do have basic rights.

"They're coming late to it definitely, and they came kicking and screaming," Benjamin said.[57]

Public relations experts tended to render a kinder judgment. "There was full disclosure with good, key messages embedded, including the news that the company terminated contracts with factories found in violation of its code of vendor conduct," said Katie Delahaye Paine, CEO of KDPaine & Partners. "The resulting PR makes Gap appear ethical, concerned and morally superior to its competitors."[58]

The release of the *Social Responsibility Report* was the latest in a series of moves designed to help Gap, Inc., live up to its code of business conduct. Just a few weeks earlier, company officials and leaders of the nation's largest apparel and textile workers' union had announced that they would work together in support of displaced garment workers in El Salvador. Together, they would help open that country's first independent and unionized apparel export factory. Its owners had closed the factory because of labor disputes.

"We've had our differences with Gap in the past, and we may in the future," said union president Bruce Raynor. "But when we started talking with them about this situation and others like it, we realized that we could work together and create positive changes for workers in El Salvador and elsewhere."[59]

However, even this kind of cooperation comes with a price. Raynor said, "My daughter asked me if it was OK to shop at Gap now, and when I said 'yes,' it instantly cost me $80."[60]

DISCUSSION QUESTIONS

1. In your opinion, why did The Gap release its *Social Responsibility Report*?
2. How important are a company's foreign workforce conditions to your personal buying habits?
3. Is social responsibility compatible with making profits?
4. Who do you believe were the most influential stakeholders in The Gap's decision to address working conditions in foreign garment factories?

CASE STUDY **1.2**

The Lessons of Katrina

As a child, you may have heard the fable of the Dutch boy who averted a flood and saved his community by sticking his finger in a leaky dike. But as we learned in the wake of Hurricane Katrina, pointing fingers, alone, is not enough.

According to the National Hurricane Center (NHC), "Katrina was one of the most devastating natural disasters in United States history."[61] The storm packed 125 mile-per-hour winds when it made landfall south of New Orleans on August 29, 2005. Four months after the catastrophe, the death toll stood at more than 1,300 with hundreds still missing. The NHC also estimated property damage at $75 billion, making Katrina the most costly natural disaster in U.S. history.[62]

Although the disaster area was equal in size to the United Kingdom, much of the world's attention focused on New Orleans. At first, it looked as if the Crescent City had weathered the storm. However, the levee system protecting New Orleans—a Gulf Coast city that mainly lies below sea level—failed. Nearly 80 percent of the city flooded under as much as 20 feet of water. An estimated 1.5 million people were displaced.[63]

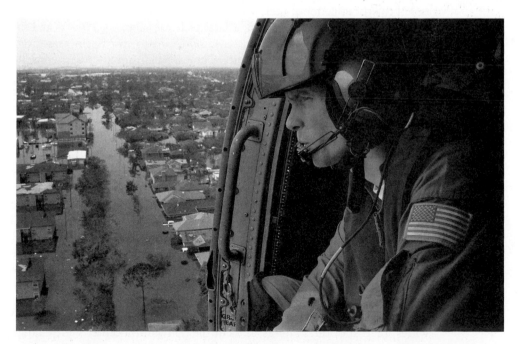

A U.S. Coast Guard helicopter searches for survivors on New Orleans rooftops in the aftermath of Hurricane Katrina. The Coast Guard was one of only a few government agencies that did not come under intense criticism for an inadequate response to the disaster. (U.S. Department of Defense)

Compounding this misery was an inadequate response and poor crisis communications at the local, state, and federal government levels. Risk assessment and preparing for the worst are the essence of crisis planning. Communicating those plans to key stakeholders—most notably the victims—is critical. However, a week would pass before many received relief. There were dead bodies abandoned on city streets. This human drama played out on live television to a worldwide audience. And the same question was asked time and time again: How could this happen in America?

Katrina was much more than a public relations failure. It was a system failure. "This country's emergency operations, awesome in their potential, are also frighteningly interdependent," *Time* reported in a post-storm analysis. "At every level of government, there was uncertainty about who was in charge at crucial moments."[64]

Following the terrorist attack on the World Trade Center four years earlier, lives were lost and rescue efforts hampered because police, fire, and ambulance workers were unable to talk with one another. *The 9/11 Commission Report* called for "improved connectivity in public safety communications."[65] This was not done. The resulting confusion delayed getting help to Katrina's victims.

It was also painfully obvious that there had been inadequate emergency planning. New Orleans officials had used the Louisiana Superdome as a shelter during Hurricane Georges in 1998. At that time, they were criticized for not making adequate preparations. Seven years later, conditions at the stadium were no better. The city had failed to stockpile food, fuel, and other supplies necessary to do the job.[66]

Perhaps most damning was a lack of leadership. As *Time* noted in its analysis, "Leaders were afraid to actually lead, reluctant to cost businesses money, break jurisdictional rules or spawn lawsuits. They were afraid, in other words, of ending up in an article just like this one."[67]

Regarding failed leadership, there's plenty of blame to spread around. New Orleans Mayor Ray Nagin was slow to order an evacuation but quick to blame others. E-mails from the office of Louisiana Governor Kathleen Blanco painted the picture of an administration that appeared to be more concerned with boosting its image than providing disaster relief. President George W. Bush appeared to be out of touch when he praised FEMA Director Michael Brown for doing "a heck of a job" in responding to Katrina despite mounting evidence to the contrary.

"There was no one who was able to balance compassion for the victims with a sense of hope, direction and confidence," said Ed Nicholson, director of media and community relations for Tyson Foods.[68]

Katrina became a perceptual crisis fed, in part, by competitive, around-the-clock news coverage that sometimes distorted reality. The situation at the New Orleans Convention Center is a prime example. Public safety officials were unaware of thousands of refugees stranded there without adequate food and water—until they finally saw it live on television. However, it since has been documented that TV reports of widespread shootings and assaults at the convention center were exaggerated.

Even with the best planning and response, Hurricane Katrina would have been a tragic event. However, the pain was unnecessarily compounded by the government's inability to adequately communicate with the people it is supposed to serve.

Joe Trahan, a noted New Orleans media trainer and educator, put it best when he observed, "If you can't or don't communicate, the frustration and anger will get out of control."[69]

DISCUSSION QUESTIONS

1. What were some of the specific failures of government officials in their response to Hurricane Katrina?
2. The case study criticizes some officials for "pointing fingers" at one another. However, isn't assigning blame part of the evaluation process?
3. Do you agree that there was a failure of leadership when it came to the government's response to Hurricane Katrina? Why or why not?
4. What role do public relations practitioners play before, during, and after a natural disaster such as Hurricane Katrina?

NOTES

1. "Executive, Congressional and Consumer Attitudes Toward Media, Marketing and the Public Relations Profession," Harris Interactive Public Relations Research, prepared for the Public Relations Society of America, June 2005, online, www.prsa.org.
2. Julie K. Henderson, "Negative Connotations in the Use of the Term 'Public Relations' in the Print Media," *Public Relations Review* (spring 1998): 45–54.
3. "Descubre el Regalo que llevamos dentro," 2006 Silver Anvil Award Winner Profile 6BE-060 1D02, Public Relations Society of America, online, www.prsa.org.
4. Nathan Burchfiel, "Rewarding volunteerism; concert tickets lure youth to community service," *Washington Times,* 23 August 2005, A2.
5. Molson Coors Brewing Company Form 10-K 2006, online, www.sec.gov.
6. "Doing Our Part—Awards and Honors," Coors Brewing Company, online, www .coors.com.
7. Al Ries and Laura Ries, *The Fall of Advertising and the Rise of PR* (New York: HarperCollins, 2002).
8. Eric Denig, ed., *A Geography of Public Relations Trends: Selected Proceedings of the 10th Public Relations World Congress* (Dordrecht, the Netherlands: Martinus Nijhoff, 1985), 244–249.
9. "Vision & Mission," Burson-Marsteller, online, www. burson-marsteller. com/ pages/ about/ vision.
10. David W. Guth, "Crises and the Practitioner: Organizational Crisis Experience as It Relates to the Placement of the Public Relations Function" (master's thesis, University of North Carolina–Chapel Hill, 1990).
11. Rex F. Harlow, "Building a Public Relations Definition," *Public Relations Review* (winter 1976): 36.
12. "Official Statement on Public Relations," *Public Relations Tactics: The Blue Book. The Green Book 2003* (New York: PRSA, 2003), B3.
13. "About Public Relations," Public Relations Society of America, online, www.prsa.org.

14. James G. Hutton, "The Definitions, Dimensions, and Domain of Public Relations," *Public Relations Review* 25, no. 1 (summer 1999): 199–214.

15. Dejan Verçiç, Betteke van Ruler, Gerhard Bütschi, and Bertil Flodin, "On the Definition of Public Relations: A European View," *Public Relations Review* 27, no. 4 (winter 2001): 373–387.

16. John E. Marston, *The Nature of Public Relations* (New York: McGraw-Hill, 1963), 4.

17. J. G. Hutton et al., "Reputation Management: The New Face of Corporate Public Relations?" *Public Relations Review* 27, no. 3 (fall 2001), 247–261.

18. James E. Grunig, ed., *Excellence in Public Relations and Communication Management* (Hillsdale, N.J.: Lawrence Erlbaum, 1992), 1–30.

19. *Declaration of Independence* (Washington, D.C.: Commission on the Bicentennial of the United States Constitution).

20. Herb Schmertz with William Novak, *Good-Bye to the Low Profile: The Art of Creative Confrontation* (Boston: Little, Brown, 1986), 5.

21. "Survey Confirms Practitioner/Management Goal Conflicts," *Public Relations Journal,* February 1989, 9.

22. "Public Relations Pays Off for Corporate America, Report Shows," USC Annenberg School for Communication/Council of Public Relations Firms, distributed via Business-Wire, 20 November 2002.

23. "Survey: CEOs Becoming More Confident in Their PR Executives," *PR News* 59, no. 16 (April 2003): 21, online, LexisNexis.

24. Yoshikuni Sugiyama, "Top Executive Must Recognize PR role," *Daily Yomiuri* (Tokyo), 20 May 2003, 9, online, LexisNexis; and Graham Sidwell and Michael Murphy, "Marketing & PR: New Role for Public Relations Industry," *Birmingham Post* (UK), 17 November 2003, online, via LexisNexis.

25. "Public Relations Pays Off for Corporate America, Report Shows."

26. "Do We Have a Story for You!" *The Economist,* 19 January 2006, online, www .economist.com.

27. Todd Hunt and James E. Grunig, *Public Relations Techniques* (Fort Worth, Tex.: Harcourt Brace College, 1994), 8–9.

28. Ayemir Okay and Alya Okay, "The Place of Theory in Public Relations Practice," in *Public Relations: From Theory to Practice,* ed. Tricia L. Hansen-Horn and Bonita Dostal Neff (Boston: Allyn & Bacon, 2008), 314.

29. Hunt and Grunig.

30. Okay and Okay.

31. Hunt and Grunig.

32. Okay and Okay.

33. Hunt and Grunig.

34. Okay and Okay.

35. Michael Ryan, "Organizational Constraints on Corporate Public Relations Practitioners," *Journalism Quarterly* (summer–autumn 1987): 473–482.

36. Les Krantz, *1995 Jobs Rated Almanac,* as cited by *USA Weekend,* 2–4 February 1996, 5.

37. *Occupational Outlook Handbook, 2006–07 Edition,* U.S. Bureau of Labor Statistics, U.S. Department of Labor, online, http://stats.bls.gov/oco/home/ htm.

38. Glen T. Cameron, Lynne M. Sallot, and Ruth Ann Weaver Lariscy, "Developing Standards of Professional Performance in Public Relations," *Public Relations Review* (spring 1996): 43–61.

39. "Universal Accreditation Board," Public Relations Society of America, online, www .prsa.org.

40. *Public Relations Society of America 2005 Membership Study,* Executive Summary, conducted by the Southeastern Institute of Research, online, www.prsa.org.

41. "About IABC," International Association of Business Communicators, online, www .iabc.com/about.

42. *Public Relations Society of America 2005 Membership Study,* Executive Summary.

43. Verne Kopytoff, "Hewlett-Packard Says It Spied on Reporters," *San Francisco Chronicle,* 8 September 2006, A1.

44. "PR Firm Admits It's Behind Wal-Mart Blogs," CNN, 20 October 2006, online, www.cnn.com.

45. "Suicide Mars WTO talks," CNN, 11 September 2003, online, www.cnn.com.

46. Guy De Jonquieres, "Trade Chief to Get Tough," *Financial Times,* 26 January 2004, online, LexisNexis Academic.

47. Shirley Lichti, "Dove Campaign Reflects a Beautiful Strategy," *The Record,* 21 June 2006, F1.

48. "Southwest Airlines Adopt-A-Pilot Educational Program Encourages School-To-Career Path," Southwest Airlines news release, distributed 1 February 2005, via PR Newswire.

49. Kathryn Shattuck, "For a Dear Museum: Love, Hallmark," *New York Times,* 18 February 2006, online, www.nytimes.com.

50. *Gap Inc. 2003 Social Responsibility Report,* online, www.gapinc.com, 2.

51. *Gap Inc. 2003 Social Responsibility Report,* 2.

52. Gap Inc. Securities and Exchange Commission 10-K Report for the Fiscal Year Ending January 31, 2007, Commission File No. 001-07562.

53. *Code of Business Conduct: Doing the Right Thing,* Gap, Inc., 3 (distributed as exhibit 1.4, Gap, Inc. Securities and Exchange Commission 10-K Report).

54. "Gap Seeks Better Conditions at Global Garment Factories."

55. *Gap Inc. 2003 Social Responsibility Report,* 2.

56. "Gap Inc. Provides Comprehensive Look at Its Efforts to Improve Factories."

57. "Gap Seeks Better Conditions at Global Garment Factories."

58. Katie Delahaye Paine, "Gaps PR Fall Into Place While Wal-Mart's Is a Mess," *PR News,* 24 May 2004, online, LexisNexis.

59. "UNITE and Gap Inc. Set Aside Differences to Work Together on Garment Factory Conditions; Unionized Garment Factory Opening in El Salvador, Result of Cooperative Relationship," news release distributed via PR Newswire, 19 April 2004, online, Lexis-Nexis.

60. "UNITE and Gap Inc. Set Aside Differences to Work Together on Garment Factory Conditions."

61. Richard D. Knabb, Jamie R. Rhome, and Daniel P. Brown, *Tropical Cyclone Report— Hurricane Katrina 23–30 August 2005,* Miami, FL: National Hurricane Center, 20 December 2005, 1.

62. Knabb, Rhome and Brown, 11–12.

63. Knabb, Rhome and Brown, 9.

64. James Carney, "Four Places Where the System Broke Down," *Time,* 19 September 2005, 34–41.

65. *The 9/11 Commission Report—Final Report of the National Commission on Terrorist Attacks on the United States,* Executive Summary, 2004, 20.

66. Knabb, Rhome and Brown, 37.

67. Carney, 36.

68. Ed Cafasso, "Going Back to Basics: Hurricane Katrina Illustrates the Importance of Aligning Action and Communications," *Public Relations Tactics,* October 2005, 25.

69. Cafasso.

2

Jobs in Public Relations

OBJECTIVES

After studying this chapter, you will be able to

■ name the basic areas of employment in public relations

■ discuss specific jobs and related duties within public relations

■ explain the differences between public relations managers and public relations technicians

■ describe salaries and levels of job satisfaction within public relations

KEY TERMS

An Inquisitive Friend

You've just found a quiet corner in the library, and you feel like putting a sign on the table: "Do not disturb. Serious studying in progress." Just as you open your public relations textbook, a good friend slumps down into the chair across from you.

"Public relations, huh?" he says, tipping back his chair. "Hey, I'm a people person. I love going to lunch. Tell me about public relations."

Stifling the urge to ease a leg forward and push him over, you realize that this could be a good opportunity to review what you know about public relations. You could define the profession for him: Public relations is the values-driven management of relationships between an organization and the publics that can affect its success.

You could tell him that public relations ideally is a function of management and that it's a socially responsible activity based on research, planning, two-way communication, and evaluation.

But what if he looks you in the eye and asks, "So what are the jobs in public relations? What would my duties be? How much money would I make?"

Good questions, you think. And you know that if you could just read Chapter 2, you'd have some answers.

Where the Jobs Are

In the above scenario, as you explained the profession of public relations to your friend, you might also remember to tell him something else you learned in Chapter 1: Broadly speaking, jobs in public relations exist in five different employment settings:

1. corporations;
2. nonprofit organizations and trade associations;
3. governments;
4. public relations agencies; and
5. independent public relations consultancies.

Each of these five areas contains a variety of sometimes startlingly different public relations jobs. Ideally, however, each job helps an organization fulfill its values-driven mission and goals by building important relationships. To help you answer the question about jobs and job duties, let's start by examining the different jobs within these five categories.

Corporations

You could tell your friend that not only do corporations offer most of the jobs in public relations, but they also offer the greatest variety of jobs. Corporations are organizations that produce goods or services for a profit. They include manufacturers such as The North Face, for-profit health-care providers such as Humana, retailers

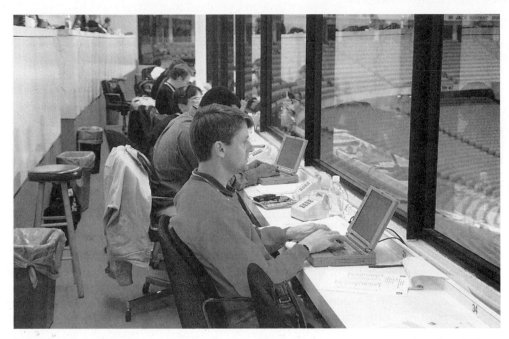

Press Box An important tactic in sports public relations is operating a press box for visiting media, such as those attending this Major League Soccer match. (Photo by David Guth)

such as The Gap, sports organizations such as NASCAR, and a host of other for-profit organizations.

In most corporations, public relations jobs focus on specific publics. Corporate public relations practitioners often specialize in one of the following: employee relations, media relations, government relations, community relations, business-to-business relations, or consumer relations (or marketing communications). If the corporation is publicly owned—that is, if it sells stock—some practitioners specialize in investor relations. In each of these areas, ideally, practitioners conduct research; advise the organization's top management; and plan, execute, and evaluate relationship-management programs.

Ideally, public relations practitioners should understand and appreciate all sides of a relationship between their organization and a particular public. Practitioners call this function **boundary spanning** because they span the boundaries that separate their organization from important publics. As boundary spanners, practitioners act for the good of relationships, knowing that healthy relationships are vital to their organization's success. And as boundary spanners, practitioners must sometimes ask their own organizations to change to benefit an important relationship.

One difficulty with the concept of boundary spanning is that it suggests a simple relationship between only two parties. In actuality, public relations practitioners often are intersection managers, operating at points where several publics come together simultaneously. Experienced practitioners know that their relationship-building efforts with one public can affect relationships with other publics. For example, a corporation's cost-cutting measures may please stockholders but discourage employees. In such cases, an organization's public relations team must be keenly aware of the values of the organization and the affected publics.

Although we certainly don't want to downplay the importance of research and counseling, the reality is that most young practitioners begin their careers by creating communications such as newsletter stories and web sites. Therefore, let's look at some of the traditional entry-level tasks.

- **Employee relations:** Communication tasks in employee relations can include production of newsletters and magazines, video programs, web sites, and special events.

- **Media relations:** Communication tasks can include production of news releases and e-mail pitches (see Chapter 9) and assistance with news conferences. More advanced communication tasks can include speechwriting and preparing scripts for video news releases. Media-related counseling duties can include preparing executives for interviews.

- **Government relations** (sometimes known as *public affairs*): Communication tasks can include producing brochures, reports, and videos for lobbies and political action committees (see Chapter 9). Advanced duties can include testifying before government fact-finding commissions, monitoring the activities of government units at all levels, and preparing reports.

- **Community relations:** Communication tasks can include maintaining contact with local special-interest groups such as environmental organizations. New practitioners also often help coordinate special events such as tours of their organization's facilities. Upper-level duties can include overseeing a corporation's charitable contributions, organizing employee volunteer efforts, and lending support to special events such as blood drives and United Way fund-raising campaigns.

- **Business-to-business relations,** also known as *B2B:* Communication tasks focus on building strong relationships with related businesses such as suppliers and distributors. Entry-level duties can include writing for newsletters and web sites and helping to plan special events. Management duties can include orientation meetings to discuss shared values and goals.

- **Consumer relations,** also known as *marketing communications:* Communication tasks usually focus on product publicity. Such duties can include preparing news releases and e-mail pitches, implementing direct-mail campaigns, organizing special promotional events, enlisting and training celebrity spokespeople, writing blogs, and coordinating communication efforts with advertising campaigns.

- **Investor relations:** Communication activities that target investors and investment analysts can include producing newsletters and other forms of correspondence directed at stockholders, producing an annual financial report to stockholders, planning and conducting an annual meeting for stockholders, maintaining a flow of information to investment analysts, and other activities designed to inform investors

NEWS

Federal Communications Commission
445 12ᵗʰ Street, S.W.
Washington, D. C. 20554

News Media Information 202 / 418-0500
Internet: http://www.fcc.gov
TTY: 1-888-835-5322

This is an unofficial announcement of Commission action. Release of the full text of a Commission order constitutes official action.
See MCI v. FCC. 515 F 2d 385 (D.C. Circ 1974).

FOR IMMEDIATE RELEASE
November 14, 2006

NEWS MEDIA CONTACT:
Rudy Brioché: (202) 418-2300
e-mail: rudy.brioché@fcc.gov

COMMISSIONER ADELSTEIN COMMENDS THE CENTER FOR MEDIA DEMOCRACY AND FREE PRESS FOR ITS CONTINUED STUDY REGARDING VIDEO NEWS RELEASES

Washington, DC. – In connection to the Center for Media Democracy and Free Press' second video news release study, " Still Not the News: Stations Overwhelmingly Fail to Disclose VNRs," Commissioner Jonathan S. Adelstein issues the following statement:

> Many broadcasters are apparently ignoring the FCC and their own ethics guidelines in running VNRs without disclosure. All the warnings in the world don't help if nobody's listening. When the flock ignores the shepherd, it's time to build a fence. Since the industry is patently incapable of self-regulation, it's up to the FCC to enforce our disclosure rules.

> Some stations have developed such an ingrained pattern of running VNRs that even a direct investigation by the FCC isn't enough to snap them out of it. Maybe some have run so many red lights it seems like the normal way to drive. It's time to start handing out citations.

> This is not a First Amendment issue. Newsrooms are not allowed under the law to run commercials disguised as news without an honest and adequate disclosure. Clearly, the embarrassment of informing viewers they are merely transmitting corporate propaganda in lieu of real news is leading many to actually eliminate disclosure supplied by the VNR producer. The issue is not free speech -- it is identifying who is actually speaking.

News Release An enduring part of public relations involves delivering stories to news media through news releases. This news release, part of the media relations program at the U.S. Federal Communications Commission, addresses another media relations action: the sometimes controversial use of video news releases by television stations and networks. (Courtesy of the U.S. Federal Communications Commission) about a corporation's financial health and business goals. Investor relations practitioners often oversee the legally required disclosure of financial information to stockholders and to the government.

Nonprofit Organizations and Trade Associations

Let's now tell your friend about public relations jobs in nonprofit organizations and trade associations. And, once again, let's focus primarily on entry-level communication tasks rather than on research and counseling. Nonprofit organizations can include universities, hospitals, churches, foundations, and other groups that provide a service without the expectation of earning a profit. Some nonprofit organizations, of course, are local. Others, such as the United Way, are nationally known. Still others, such as the Red Cross and Amnesty International, have international duties and reputations.

Public relations duties within a nonprofit organization often are similar to public relations duties within a corporation. Well-run nonprofit organizations have practitioners in employee relations, media relations, government relations, community relations, and sometimes marketing communications. However, because nonprofit organizations have no stockholders, they don't engage in investor relations activities. Instead, they have donor relations; fund-raising; and, if appropriate, member relations.

Communication tasks in donor relations, fund-raising, and member relations can include producing newsletters, videos, and web sites; writing direct-mail solicitations; and organizing special events.

Trade associations are often grouped with nonprofit organizations because, like those organizations, they offer services without the primary motive of earning a profit. Trade associations include such groups as the American Library Association and the International Guild of Professional Butlers. Trade associations offer their members benefits that can include insurance programs, continuing education, networking, and a unified voice in efforts to influence legislative processes. Public relations jobs in trade associations include member relations, media relations, government relations, and marketing communications. Communication tasks in member relations are often designed to educate and update members through newsletters and other publications, web sites, videos, and special events such as annual conventions. The American Medical Association, for example, offers its members the prestigious *Journal of the American Medical Association*. Another task in member relations involves recruiting new members through such actions as direct-mail campaigns.

Governments

Maybe your friend would be more interested in conducting public relations for the government. Tell him not to limit his search to the federal or central government of a nation: Jobs in public relations can also be found within state and local governments. Political parties and independent agencies created by the government, such as the U.S. Postal Service, also employ public relations practitioners.

VALUES STATEMENT 2.1

Public Relations Society of America

PRSA is the world's largest organization for public relations professionals. Its 28,000-plus members, organized worldwide in more than 100 chapters, represent business and industry, technology, counseling firms, government, associations, hospitals, schools, professional services firms, and nonprofit organizations.

PRSA MEMBER STATEMENT OF PROFESSIONAL VALUES

This statement presents the core values of PRSA members and, more broadly, of the public relations profession. These values provide the foundation for the Member Code of Ethics and set the industry standard for the professional practice of public relations. These values are the fundamental beliefs that guide our behaviors and decision-making process. We believe our professional values are vital to the integrity of the profession as a whole.

Advocacy

- We serve the public interest by acting as responsible advocates for those we represent.
- We provide a voice in the marketplace of ideas, facts, and viewpoints to aid informed public debate.

Honesty

- We adhere to the highest standards of accuracy and truth in advancing the interests of those we represent and in communicating with the public.

Expertise

- We acquire and responsibly use specialized knowledge and experience.
- We advance the profession through continued professional development, research, and education.
- We build mutual understanding, credibility, and relationships among a wide array of institutions and audiences.

Independence

- We provide objective counsel to those we represent.
- We are accountable for our actions.

Loyalty

- We are faithful to those we represent, while honoring our obligation to serve the public interest.

Fairness

- We deal fairly with clients, employers, competitors, peers, vendors, the media, and the general public.
- We respect all opinions and support the right of free expression.

—From "PRSA Member Code of Ethics 2000," PRSA web site

Public relations jobs within government units generally focus on four key publics: voters, the news media, employees, and special-interest groups.

Government public relations practitioners operate under a variety of job titles, including **press secretary, public information officer, public affairs officer,** and **communications specialist.** Entry-level communication duties can include writing news releases, responding to constituent concerns, and writing position papers that help politicians articulate their beliefs. Upper-level duties can include speaking with reporters, writing speeches for politicians, and briefing officials on public opinion.

The Values of Successful Employers

What do enduring, successful companies have in common? In the book *Built to Last: Successful Habits of Visionary Companies,* authors James Collins and Jerry Porras examine the workings of companies that have thrived despite occasional adversity and changing environments.[1] One foundation of such companies, the authors say, is a set of clear, strongly held, companywide core values:

> Core values [are] the organization's essential and enduring tenets—a small set of general guiding principles; not to be confused with specific cultural or operating practices; not to be compromised for financial gain or short-term expediency. . . .
> The crucial variable is not the content of a company's ideology, but how deeply it believes its ideology and how consistently it lives, breathes and expresses it in all that it does. Visionary companies do not ask, "What should we value?" They ask, "What do we actually value deep down to our toes?"

Built to Last examines the long-term success of 20 companies, including IBM, Johnson & Johnson, Motorola, Procter & Gamble, and Walt Disney. "Yes, they seek profits," say the authors, "but they're equally guided by a core ideology—core values and a sense of purpose beyond just making money."

As you consider a career in public relations and as you evaluate the different kinds of employers and job duties, be sure to study the values of those employers. Many organizations now list their values statements on their web sites. What, if anything, do those organizations say they value? Do their actions match their beliefs? Are their values so clear that they can guide public relations policies and actions? In the words of James Collins and Jerry Porras, will you select an employer that's built to last?

At the federal level in the United States, the term *public relations,* with its connotation of persuasive communication, is rarely used. Public relations practitioners within the federal government prefer euphemisms such as *public information.* One reason for their skittishness is the United States Code (a compilation of the permanent governing laws of the United States). Title 5, Section 3107 of the code flatly declares, "Appropriated funds may not be used to pay a publicity expert unless specifically appropriated for that purpose." Similar restrictions can exist at state and local levels.

Because many people incorrectly equate public relations with publicity, government units tend to avoid that term. Voters in most countries clearly don't want their tax dollars used for campaigns to persuade them of the wisdom of governmental actions and policies. However, voters also insist that government officials communicate with citizens and respond to their needs and concerns. So public relations *does* exist at all levels of government—but rarely, if ever, is it called by that name.

Public Relations Agencies

Maybe a **public relations agency** is the place for your friend. Public relations agencies assist with the public relations activities of other organizations. Corporations, nonprofit organizations, trade associations, governments, and even individuals hire public relations agencies to help manage and execute various public relations functions. A corporation, for example, may have its own in-house public relations staff—but for its annual report to stockholders or for a complicated overseas venture, it may hire a public relations agency for research, planning, communication, and evaluation. As we'll discuss in Chapter 13, many public relations agencies have merged with advertising agencies to provide a wide range of integrated, consumer-focused communications.

Practitioners in public relations agencies often are assigned to accounts. An account includes all the public relations activities planned and executed for one particular client. Individual accounts are managed by an **account supervisor** and, often, one or more **account executives.** Also working on each account are writers, who often are called communications specialists; designers; production supervisors;

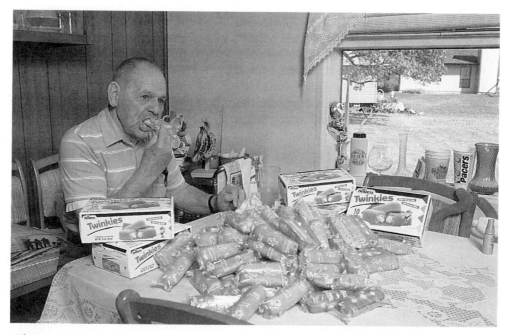

When Interstate Brands Corporation—the baker of Hostess Twinkies snack cakes—learned that Lewis Browning had eaten a Twinkie a day since 1941 (20,000-plus Twinkies), it turned his story into a news release that gained national attention and won a top award in a regional public relations competition. (Courtesy of Interstate Brands Corporation/Hostess Twinkies)

researchers; and, increasingly, online specialists for web site design and mainte-nance. Workers within an account sometimes wear more than one hat; for example, a writer may also be a researcher. Additionally, practitioners often are assigned to more than one account.

Public relations agencies can range from small shops with only a handful of em-ployees to divisions within advertising agencies to huge international operations such as Hill & Knowlton, Burson-Marsteller, Fleishman-Hillard, and Edelman.

Independent Public Relations Consultancies

Maybe your friend would prefer to work for himself. An **independent public relations consultant** is, essentially, a one-person public relations agency. Organizations or in-dividuals hire the consultant to assist with particular public relations functions. Gen-erally, however, a public relations consultant offers a smaller range of services than an agency. Many consultants, in fact, specialize in a particular area of public rela-tions, such as crisis communications, speechwriting, web site design, or training oth-ers in the basics of good public relations.

Some independent consultants, however, thrive as generalists. In the book *Real People Working in Communications,* author Jan Goldberg writes:

> Those who work as generalists in the field must be able to perform a wide array of duties at the same time. On any given week they may write press releases for one client, design a brochure for another, approach an editor for a third, meet with a talk show host for a fourth, implement a promotion for a fifth, set up a press conference for a sixth, put to-gether a press kit for a seventh, work out the beginnings of a client contract for an eighth, and field media questions for a ninth![2]

Note that eighth duty well. Like public relations agencies, independent consul-tants often must seek new clients even as they conduct business for current clients. The major appeal of independent consulting is also its biggest burden: The consul-tant alone bears the responsibility for success or failure.

Public Relations outside the Workplace

As you educate your friend about the broad categories of jobs in public relations, you might want to impress him with a touch of postmodern theory. Postmodernism is a philosophical perspective that almost defies definition—not even postmodernists agree on what it is and isn't. But broadly speaking, postmodernism resists conven-tional wisdom and seeks out voices and opinions that the mainstream tends to ignore. Postmodern critics point out that discussions of public relations (like this one, so far) generally focus only on jobs with paychecks.[3] Those critics correctly add that public relations skills can transcend the ordinary workplace. For example, volunteers for ac-tivist organizations often work to build relationships with reporters and government officials. Is that a salaried job? Not really—but it remains public relations. The the-ory and the practice of public relations are not limited to the workplace.

QuickBreak 2.2

Getting That First Job or Internship

You may be reading this chapter and thinking, "Great. I'm beginning to understand where and what the jobs are. But how do I get one?" Although the *Occupational Outlook Handbook* from the U.S. Bureau of Labor Statistics reports that "employment of public relations specialists is expected to grow faster than average for all occupations through 2014," it adds this caution: "Keen competition likely will continue for entry-level public relations jobs."[4]

We'll examine your future in public relations more thoroughly in Chapter 16. But let's preview a few dos and don'ts about communicating with potential employers.

Do This:

- Do thoroughly research a potential employer before applying.
- Do send an error-free application letter and a flawless résumé, whether online or on paper.
- Do realize that, according to one national survey, almost one-third of employers will check you out on web sites such as Facebook and MySpace.[5]
- Do prepare for a job interview by reviewing your research on the potential employer and developing knowledgeable questions to ask.
- Do create a portfolio of real work done for real clients, including work done as an intern or volunteer.

Don't Do This:

- Don't send a form letter asking for a job. Instead, include specific, organization-related information that shows why you want this particular job.
- Don't ask about salary. Let the potential employer introduce that subject.
- Don't forget to send a brief, typed thank-you letter after each interview.

Comprehensive studies over the past decade confirm that good writing is the top quality that public relations employers seek in new employees.[6] One study of almost 1,000 public relations professionals identified the top-three desired qualities for entry-level employees:

1. Strong written/oral communication skills;
2. willingness to learn/enthusiasm; and
3. personality/culture fit.[7]

One more thing, *étudiants.* Experts say "the ability to communicate in a foreign language may open up employment opportunities."[8]
Bonne chance.

QUICK / CHECK

1. What are the five broad areas of employment within public relations?
2. What criticism do postmodern theorists sometimes level against descriptions of public relations jobs?
3. How does the United States Code affect public relations within the U.S. federal government?

Public Relations Activities and Duties

You've conveyed all this information to your friend, and you've done a great job. But your success generates even more questions: Now he wants to know specifically what kinds of tasks he'll be performing at least five days a week for at least eight hours a day. You *could* excuse yourself for a moment and sneak out of the library—but instead, let's humor him. As a public relations practitioner, how *would* he spend his days?

Public relations researchers devote a great deal of time to answering that question. Professor David Dozier, who has extensively studied the daily duties and tasks of public relations practitioners, groups public relations practitioners into two broad categories:

1. **Public relations managers:** They solve problems, advise other managers, make policy decisions, and take responsibility for the success or failure of public relations programs. Public relations managers are most often found in organizations that operate in rapidly changing environments and in organizations that encourage employee input.

2. **Public relations technicians:** They rarely make key strategic decisions, and they rarely advise others within the organization. Instead, their primary role is to prepare

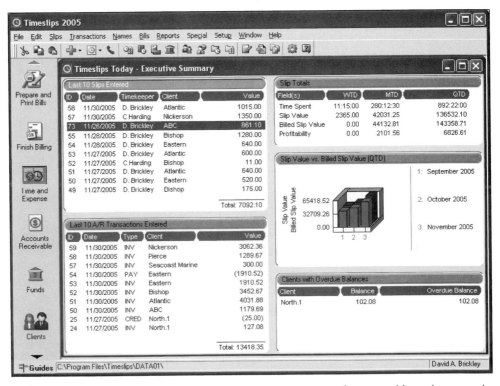

Time Sheet For billing purposes, public relations practitioners often record how they spend each working day. (© Best Software SB, Inc. All rights reserved. Timeslips Today is a registered trademark of Best Software SB, Inc.)

TABLE 2.1	How Public Relations Practitioners Spend Their Time[9]			

TASK	RANK FOR FEMALE TECHNICIANS	RANK FOR MALE TECHNICIANS	RANK FOR FEMALE MANAGERS	RANK FOR MALE MANAGERS
Disseminating messages	1	1	13	13
Writing, editing, producing messages	2	2	15	15
Implementing decisions made by others	3	6	17	17
Making media contacts	4	3	6	11
Implementing new programs	5	7	3	5
Correspondence/telephone calls	6	4	12	14
Implementing event planning/logistics	7	5	9	7
Managing public relations programs	8	8	2	2
Meeting with peers	9	11	16	16
Planning public relations programs	10	10	1	1
Making communication policy decisions	11	12	4	3
Evaluating program results	12	13	8	8
Conducting or analyzing research	13	15	14	12
Meeting with clients/executives	14	14	7	10
Planning and managing budgets	15	9	5	6
Counseling management	16	17	10	4
Supervising the work of others	17	16	11	9

communications that help execute the public relations policies created by others. They are more likely to be found in organizations in which the environment is stable and predictable.[10] Many organizations employ both public relations managers and public relations technicians.

Based on a national survey of PRSA members, Table 2.1 shows that public relations managers and public relations technicians do indeed spend their working hours in different ways. The most time-consuming task for managers is planning public relations programs, which ranks 10th for public relations technicians. The most time-consuming task for public relations technicians is disseminating (or sending) messages, which ranks 13th for public relations managers.

Table 2.1 also suggests that gender may affect how public relations practitioners spend their days. Public relations scholars express some concern that such studies may standardize gender-role differences. In other words, descriptions of job duties become prescriptions—the way things should be—and thus limit women's access to top managerial roles.[11] For more information on gender equity issues in public relations, see Chapter 16.

As you might expect, oftentimes it's not a matter of being always a manager and never a technician, or vice versa. Several studies show that public relations practitioners can have jobs that combine both managerial and technical duties.[12]

QUICKBREAK 2.3

Student Misperceptions of Public Relations

As a college student, you probably have realized that professors will study just about anything. Professor Shannon Bowen of the University of Maryland studies you: students in introductory courses in public relations.[13] Bowen's research has identified four qualities of the public relations profession that often surprise students in introductory courses.

1. *Diversity of duties.* "You can do more things throughout the field," said one student. "I never realized you can take on so many roles." Bowen's research found that many students had believed that public relations was simply publicity.

2. *Management responsibilities.* "I never realized there was so much management in PR," said another student. Bowen discovered that students in introductory courses had expected simply to learn about news releases and other tactics. The profession's focus on research-based planning surprised many.

3. *Research.* "I didn't know that research and statistics were a part of it or I might not have taken this course," confessed a candid third student. Despite the occasional difficulty of research, Bowen found that research pleased many students by increasing the legitimacy and credibility of public relations.

4. *Relationship maintenance.* "Now I understand that PR has to manage good relationships by using research, research, research, and getting background knowledge," concluded a fourth student. Bowen found that most new students had viewed public relations simply as a one-way communication process.

Bowen reports that although the unforeseen challenges of public relations discourage some students, they inspire others. "It certainly feels like it is a more difficult and challenging field than I thought," said one student, "but it offers advancement and more responsibility."

Let's mention a final public relations task that's rarely mentioned in surveys of working professionals: recording how you spend your time. Public relations agencies generally bill clients by the hour, and in an agency your supervisors will want to know how you spend each 15-minute block of time. Many corporations, odd as it may seem, also chart time in this manner. For example, a corporation's public relations department may bill the corporation's college recruiting department for the preparation of brochures and web sites. An important part of ensuring the financial success of your organization or your department may well be your scrupulously detailed record of how you've spent your working days.

QUICK CHECK

1. What specific job duties consume the most time in public relations?
2. How do the job duties of a public relations manager differ from those of a public relations technician?
3. Why do public relations practitioners record how they spend their working hours?

Working Conditions and Salaries

Now that you can exhaustively tell your friend about how public relations professionals get hired and spend their days, you may want to anticipate his next questions: "So what are working conditions like? And how much money will I earn?"

The U.S. Bureau of Labor Statistics reports that public relations technicians work 35 to 40 hours a week—"but unpaid overtime is common." Approximately two-thirds of public relations managers work more than 40 hours a week, according to the BLS, and "long hours, including evenings and weekends are common." The BLS offers this description of working conditions:

> Occasionally, [public relations practitioners] must be at the job or on call around the clock, especially if there is an emergency or crisis. Public relations offices are busy places; work schedules can be irregular and frequently interrupted. Schedules often have to be rearranged so that workers can meet deadlines, deliver speeches, attend meetings and community activities, or travel.[14]

According to a University of Georgia study, the median starting public relations salary for 2005 graduates of U.S. journalism and mass communication programs was $30,000. Among all graduates of those programs, new employees in the Northeast and West commanded the highest salaries; new employees in the Midwest commanded the lowest. Slightly more than 70 percent of those new hires received some form of medical insurance as part of their salary and benefits package.[15]

QuickBreak 2.4

The People in Public Relations

A 2005 survey of Public Relations Society of America membership offered this snapshot of PRSA members:[16]

- Sixty-nine percent are female. Older members are more likely to be male; younger members are more likely to be female.

- Ninety-three percent are white; 3 percent are black; 1 percent are Asian; and 3 percent are of Hispanic, Spanish, or Latino origin.

- Thirty-three percent have a master's degree; 3 percent have a Ph.D.

- Fifty-eight percent have been PRSA members for five or fewer years.

- Sixty-three percent are members of more than one professional association. Members who belong to four or more associations tend to have higher salaries.

- Thirty-one percent work in organizations with more than 1,000 employees; 21 percent work in organizations with 10 or fewer employees.

- Members' most time-consuming job duties involve media relations and marketing communications.

- Fifty percent have a salary in the $50,000–$99,999 range; 20 percent are in the $35,000–$49,999 range; and 13 percent are in the $100,000–$149,999 range.

Each year, Spring Associates, a New York–based executive recruiting agency, surveys thousands of public relations professionals to determine average annual salaries. Its 2006 report included these findings:[17]

- At public relations agencies, account executives (with two to four years of experience) averaged $49,950, including an annual bonus. Senior account executives averaged $59,960, including an annual bonus, and account supervisors averaged $78,805, including an annual bonus. Vice presidents averaged $114,398, including an annual bonus.

- At corporations, communications specialists (with two to four years of experience) averaged $71,000 (additional annual bonus: $5,767). Managers averaged $93,000 (additional annual bonus: $13,487), and directors averaged $118,000 (additional annual bonus: $7,805). Vice presidents averaged $136,000 (additional annual bonus: $39,334).

- At nonprofit organizations, public relations directors (primarily involved in media relations) averaged $55,000. Marketing directors earned $62,917, and directors of conventions/meetings/exhibitions averaged $61,800. Directors of member/constituent/chapter/affiliate relations and services averaged $64,170.

- Federal public information officers had a 2006 starting salary range of $24,677 to $32,084.[18] Local government PIOs earned approximately $45,000.[19]

- Annual salaries differ by gender, with women, in one comprehensive survey, earning 77 percent as much as men for comparable work.[20] Practitioners' length of service and other variables may affect this disparity, but gender discrimination remains a reality in many professions.[21]

National surveys can provide significant insights into practitioner salaries, but their findings, at best, are only approximations of what you might expect to earn. However, as we'll see in the next section, public relations practitioners enjoy their jobs so much that salary is not their top consideration in job satisfaction.

What's Important in a Job?

Finally, you may want to turn the tables and ask your friend a question: What does he want in a job? His answer may surprise you.

According to a survey by PRSA's Counselors Academy, 73 percent of senior public relations executives said that they retain their best employees through "personal satisfaction." Only 12 percent believed that salary was the key to loyalty and motivation.[22]

In the 2000 PRSA/IABC survey, salary was at best seventh on the list of important job-satisfaction attributes.[23] Some 95.5 percent of respondents said that salary was important to job satisfaction—but that high percentage was exceeded by the 99.4 percent who said creative opportunity was important, the 99.2 percent who said access to technology was important, the 97.7 percent who said professional development opportunities were important, and the 96.2 percent who said recognition by colleagues was important.[24]

Some evidence suggests that job satisfaction may not be as high for practitioners who are members of minority groups. In a 2005 survey of 132 non-white practitioners, 45.8 percent of respondents were satisfied with their jobs; 30.1 percent were dissatisfied; and 24.1 percent were neutral regarding job satisfaction. "Part of the industry is doing your own PR," one respondent suggested. "You have to know this before you even set foot in the workplace. You're going to have to pull yourself up. And you can't count on a person of color being there to help you."[25]

In surveys of practitioners regardless of race and ethnicity, job-satisfaction figures are higher. A workinpr.com survey found that 73 percent of practitioners are "somewhat satisfied" or "extremely satisfied" with their jobs. Only 16 percent said they were "not satisfied."[26] Even as experienced professionals, they seem to share the enthusiasm of the student in an introductory public relations course who declared, "I feel a lot better about the major now. . . . If you do your job well and do it honestly, you can move up in the PR field. There are a wide variety of employment opportunities . . . and you can move up as far as you will work to go."[27]

That might be a good answer for your friend as you pack up your books and leave the library. Before parting company, you can look your inquisitive friend in the eye and state with confidence that public relations professionals find their careers satisfying and rewarding.

QUICK CHECK

1. What is the average annual starting salary for entry-level jobs in public relations?
2. Do women practitioners earn as much as men practitioners?
3. How many hours per week do public relations managers work?
4. Is salary the most important aspect of a job in public relations?

Summary

For all their differences, public relations jobs have one thing in common: Ideally, each public relations job has the mission of helping an organization build productive relationships with the publics necessary to its success. Most of the jobs in public relations can be found in five broad settings: corporations, nonprofit organizations and trade associations, government, public relations agencies, and independent public relations consultancies.

Within those five broad areas, jobs and job duties vary widely. Public relations practitioners function as managers who counsel other managers and design public relations programs or as technicians who prepare communications. Oftentimes, a practitioner fulfills both roles, depending on the task at hand.

Salaries vary within the profession, but studies of practitioners show that salary is not the most important factor in job satisfaction. Such qualities as creative opportunity rank higher than salary in many surveys. Studies of public relations practitioners show that most enjoy their work and believe that they are meeting their personal career goals.

DISCUSSION QUESTIONS

1. Why do corporations have so many different areas of employment for public relations practitioners?
2. What evidence, if any, indicates that discrimination may exist in public relations salaries and job duties?
3. What are the attractive elements of a public relations manager's job? What are the attractive elements of a public relations technician's job?
4. What do you consider to be the most important element of job satisfaction? How does your answer compare with the findings of national studies?
5. Now that you've read this chapter, what is your opinion of the public relations profession? Does it seem to be an attractive career? Why or why not?

Memo from the Field

John Echeveste; Partner; Valencia, Pérez & Echeveste Public Relations; Pasadena, California

John Echeveste is a partner with Valencia, Pérez & Echeveste Public Relations based in Pasadena, California. Established in 1988, VPE is one of the country's largest Hispanic-owned agencies, handling a diverse roster of consumer, social-marketing, and public affairs accounts. Echeveste has helped develop public relations programs for major national brands such as McDonald's, AT&T, Disneyland, Target Stores, DirecTV, and General Mills. He is a founding member of the Hispanic Public Relations Association and recipient of its Premio Award. He also received the Public Relations Society of America Pioneer Award in 1994. He served as president of the Public Relations Global Network, an association of 30 worldwide PR agencies, in 2003–2004. He is a graduate of California State University Fullerton with a bachelor's degree in communications. He can be reached at john@vpepr.com.

I spent two years in high school and four in college studying for a career in journalism, only to discover after nine months as a reporter that it wasn't the job for me.

What happened? After my short stint as a news and feature reporter at one of the largest dailies in Los Angeles County, I realized that I was too far removed from the center of the action. Nothing wrong at all with being a journalist, but what I discovered all too soon was that reporting was a hands-off job and I was a hands-on person. So I put my journalistic skills to work and bounced around, working for a big corporation (stifling), managing a few political campaigns (exciting, but no future), and writing a documentary film (great fun, little money). In all of these positions, I was developing strategies, testing ideas, making things happen, and seeing results. That, for me, was a lot more satisfying and a lot more challenging than reporting on the things other people were doing. When I combined all these experiences, they pointed in one clear direction: public relations.

I mention this because the road to a PR career isn't always a straight one, and many of us don't end up in the professions we thought we would. But after 30-some years in the profession, the one thing I can tell you is this: Public relations puts you right in the center of the action.

So 16 years after starting an agency, I never regret that early career correction. Every day has brought new challenges, new discoveries, and new opportunities. And what keeps me most energized is working with bright new faces eager to make their own mark in the field.

So what does it take to succeed in this ever-changing profession? Here are the top qualities I look for when interviewing candidates:

■ *Learn to write like a reporter.* I can't overemphasize the importance of good writing skills. *I can't overemphasize the importance of good writing skills.* It's essential to everything else in the profession and the foundation of a successful career. The best way to learn good writing is by taking journalism writing classes—learn to write like a reporter and how to write under deadline. Even better, take an internship with a news organization where you can see the inner workings of a news operation and get some solid writing experience.

■ *Be inquisitive.* In public relations, you need to know a little about a lot of things. What I mean by that is that you need to be aware of what's happening in the world and how it impacts your clients or your organization. That means reading a daily newspaper thoroughly, monitoring news and trade magazines, and watching news/public affairs programs. The most effective PR practitioner is the one who arrives in the office every morning knowing what the day's top news stories are. Stay up with trends and with what's happening outside of the office.

■ *Show common sense.* This is one they don't teach you in college. I'm convinced that the most effective public relations programs are those that are the most straightforward. Too often, we develop convoluted, confusing initiatives that fall flat on their face. Keep it simple.

■ *Be committed.* Anyone expecting PR to be a 9-to-5 job should seek employment elsewhere. Deadlines (and clients) don't wait. You need to be willing to put in the long hours that can make the difference. And on top of that, you need to find the time to be involved in a worthwhile community or charitable cause that exposes you to a whole new universe of contacts and issues.

■ *Be an expert.* People who come in with a level of expertise in another field—sports, fashion, health care, a foreign language, music, etc.—are a step ahead of the rest. Your passions and hobbies can be an important personal marketing tool that adds extra value to your credentials.

Public relations is an evolving profession. I've seen it grow to become more inclusive and responsive to our multicultural society; to be used as a powerful marketing tool in launching new products and services and building brand equity; and to become a more valued management function. It is also a profession that thrives on those who are the brightest, most creative, and self-starters. So if you're willing to work long hours, answer to multiple bosses, and make less money than many of your college colleagues in exchange for being where the action is, then welcome to the wild, wonderful, sometimes wacky world of public relations. Enjoy the ride!

CASE STUDY 2.1

Stormy Weather: Eight Months in a Professional's Life

College students who monitor weather reports in anticipation of Spring Break know that March often enters like a lion and exits like a lamb. But for Carrie Martin, senior officer of strategic planning and communication for the American Red Cross, March 2006 began like a lamb and roared out like a dragon.

On March 2, Martin won one of the most coveted prizes in U.S. public relations: Public Relations Professional of the Year, as named by *PR Week* magazine. The profession's elite gathered at New York's Tavern on the Green restaurant to honor Martin and approximately 32 other award-winning public relations campaigns, tactics, teams, and individuals. In naming Martin the best of the best, the editors of *PR Week* declared:

> Martin showed adaptability and eagerness to expand her role at the Red Cross, and became a valued thinker and contributor to the communication and marketing department's senior management team. Over the past year, she was tapped to serve as the lead of the Red Cross media team made up of individuals representing each line of service in the organization. Hosting biweekly meetings, Martin increased communication and coordination among media team members and was able to provide management with a clearer picture of the organization's proactive media outreach activities.[28]

At almost the same moment Martin was accepting her award, national news media were directing their attention to a federal report titled *A Failure of Initiative: Final Report of the Select Bipartisan Committee to Investigate the Preparation for and Response to Hurricane Katrina*. The report included these devastating conclusions: "Katrina, however, was too much for the Red Cross. . . . The Red Cross was challenged by the sometimes-disorganized manner in which shelters were established. Some shelters were unknown to the Red Cross until after they were already opened by local officials."[29] Other reports accused the Red Cross of waste and fraud in its Katrina efforts.[30]

U.S. Senator Charles Grassley, then-chairman of the Senate Finance Committee, declared, "After hurricanes devastated the Gulf Coast in 2005, Americans again responded with tremendous generosity by donating hundreds of millions of dollars. It's a shame the Red Cross leadership did not rise to the occasion. Unlike the heroic efforts put forth by Red Cross volunteers in the aftermath of the disaster, the top dogs at the Red Cross failed their mission."[31]

Only days before the awards ceremony in New York, Martin helped craft an official response to the congressional report: The Red Cross announced that it already had begun its own investigation. In response to Senator Grassley's allegations, Martin served as the media contact person for a Red Cross news release that announced, "We are fully cooperating with the Senate Finance Committee and Chairman Grassley in response to their questions regarding the operations of the American Red Cross. The American Red Cross is committed to learning from our prior challenges and making the necessary changes to improve the delivery of services to the American people."[32]

On March 24, Martin announced through a national news release that the Red Cross was investigating allegations of financial misdeeds involving Hurricane Katrina volunteers.[33] Days later, another Red Cross news release revealed that the organization was turning its findings over to the FBI.[34] Exactly 28 days had passed since Martin had received her Professional of the Year award.

On April 4, the Red Cross announced the formation of the Independent Governance Advisory Panel to recommend any necessary changes to improve the organization's disaster relief efforts. During the next seven months, as the panel met and pondered changes, the Red Cross went about its business, assisting victims of storms in Tennessee, earthquakes in Indonesia and Pakistan, floods in New England, war in Lebanon, measles in Kenya, and much more.

In November, Red Cross leadership met with Grassley to discuss the changes proposed by the advisory group and accepted by the organization. Grassley was impressed. "I'm pleased with the vote by the board of the Red Cross to make real changes to the governance at the American Red Cross," he said. "The board has followed the recommendations of the Independent Governance Advisory Panel to make the changes necessary that will help ensure that the Red Cross has the necessary leadership and governance to succeed."[35]

After that statement—seven months and 28 days after the magical evening at Tavern on the Green—public relations' Professional of the Year Carrie Martin may have had time to breathe a sigh of relief and enjoy her award.

DISCUSSION QUESTIONS

1. Red Cross news releases may have helped publicize the organization's problems. Should the organization have kept silent about its responses to government charges? Why or why not?
2. How might Martin have conducted boundary spanning during the response of the Red Cross to government charges?
3. Organizations that rely on volunteers may have difficulty operating on shared values. How might such organizations avoid values clashes with volunteers?
4. What were your impressions of disaster relief during Hurricane Katrina? In your opinion, how did the Red Cross and other agencies perform?

CASE STUDY **2.2**

A List to Avoid

One of the highlights (or lowlights, if it shines on you) of the year for public relations practitioners is the release of an irreverent list of the worst public relations disasters of the past 12 months. Compiled since 1995 by Fineman Public Relations of San Francisco, the list balances an utter lack of mercy with a wicked sense of humor. It offers a wealth of case studies on how *not* to conduct successful public relations.

Among the recent winners of this dubious distinction:[36]

■ *Grand Theft Auto:* "As if best selling video game 'Grand Theft Auto, San Andreas' didn't have enough violence and debauchery already, its maker, Rockstar Games, added hidden animated sex scenes. The soft-core porn ignited a political firestorm, forcing a new 'adults-only' rating, reported the *Wall Street Journal.* Other coverage said Best Buy and Circuit City pulled the game from their stores."

■ *WPYX-FM, Latham, New York:* "As a promotion, the radio station holds what it calls 'Ugliest Bride' contests. From newspaper wedding announcements, the radio hosts pick the bride they deem the ugliest. Callers win by guessing which photograph was chosen. [Once], in a departure from usual practices, the station aired the bride's full name and place of employment. Hello, $300,000 lawsuit, an AP story, and a mean-spirited image."

■ *Tom Cruise:* "Tom Cruise's *War of the Worlds* press tour blew up on the *Today* show after he got on his Scientology soapbox and lit into host Matt Lauer. Cruise's diatribe against psychiatry included criticizing Brooke Shields for the medication she received during her post-pregnancy depression. . . . Cruise's other bizarre antics in 2005, including Oprah Winfrey's sofa jumping escapade to show his love for actress Katie Holmes, also earned him public ridicule."

■ *Target Stores:* "Those Salvation Army bell ringers with collection kettles outside department stores have been around for a century and are as meaningful to many consumers as any store-hired Santa Claus. So when Minneapolis-based Target announced it would ban Salvation Army collectors at all its stores, outraged consumers called for a national boycott."

■ *America West Airlines:* "After two America West pilots were fired for allegedly being drunk in the cockpit, the airline was supersensitive about the ensuing barrage of bad publicity. . . . When a woman boarded an America West jet in San Francisco and jokingly asked, 'Have you checked your crew for sobriety?'—the crew overreacted by kicking her off the plane."

■ *Harvard University:* "Publicly expressing sentiments that women are not good at math and science is not the kind of stereotyping you might expect from Harvard. So when Harvard's [former] president, Larry Summers, said gender differences are why fewer women than men excel in those areas, the school's outraged faculty and alumni called for his ouster."

There you have it: how not to conduct successful public relations. If you decide to pursue a career in this wonderful, challenging profession, we hope you'll set many lofty goals for yourself. One of them should be never to appear on the annual Fineman list.

DISCUSSION QUESTIONS

1. Which of the above public relations blunders is, in your opinion, the worst? Why?
2. Many of the above gaffes were committed by people not in public relations. How could public relations practitioners within the organizations have prevented those errors?

3. Should the organizations cited respond to their presence on the annual Fineman list? Or should they ignore it?
4. Suppose that you're head of public relations for each of the above organizations or individuals. The terrible event has just happened. Now the reporters are at your door. What do you tell them?

NOTES

1. James Collins and Jerry Porras, *Built to Last: Successful Habits of Visionary Companies* (New York: HarperBusiness, 1994), 8, 73, 88.
2. Jan Goldberg, *Real People Working in Public Relations* (Lincolnwood, Ill.: VGM Career Horizons, 1997), 88.
3. Patricia A. Curtin and T. Kenn Gaither, "Privileging Identity, Difference, and Power: The Circuit of Culture as a Basis for Public Relations Theory," *Journal of Public Relations Research* 17 (2005): 94.
4. *Occupational Outlook Handbook, 2006–2007*, U.S. Bureau of Labor Statistics, online, www.bls.gov.
5. "More Than One Quarter of Organizations Have Googled Job Candidate Profiles," news release issued by the National Association of Colleges and Employers, 11 July 2006, online, www.naceweb.org.
6. Don Stacks, Carl Botan, and Judy Van Slyke Turk, "Perceptions of Public Relations Education," *Public Relations Review* 25 (1999): 9–29; "Workinpr.com State of the Industry Survey 2002," online, www.workinpr.com; "Qualities/Skills Employers Look for in New Hires," National Association of Colleges and Employers, online, www.jobweb.com/joboutlook/2004outlook; "Council of Public Relations Firms Survey Shows Continued Industry Growth so Far in 2006," news release issued by the Council of Public Relations Firms, 7 June 2006, online, www.prfirms.org.
7. "Workinpr.com State of the Industry Survey 2002."
8. *Occupational Outlook Handbook, 2006–2007*.
9. Elizabeth Toth, Shirley Serini, Donald Wright, and Arthur Emig, "Trends in Public Relations Roles: 1990–1995," *Public Relations Review* (summer 1998): 145–163.
10. David Dozier, "The Organizational Roles of Communications and Public Relations Practitioners," in *Excellence in Public Relations and Communication Management,* ed. James E. Grunig (Hillsdale, N.J.: Lawrence Erlbaum, 1992), 341–352.
11. Larissa A. Grunig, "Feminist Phase Analysis in Public Relations," *Journal of Public Relations Research* 18, 116.
12. Greg Leichty and Jeff Springston, "Elaborating Public Relations Roles," *Journalism and Mass Communications Quarterly* (summer 1996): 467–468; Toth, Serini, Wright, and Emig; *Occupational Outlook Handbook, 2006–2007*.
13. Shannon A. Bowen, "'I Thought It Would Be More Glamorous': Preconceptions and Misconceptions among Students in the Public Relations Principles Course," *Public Relations Review* 29 (2003): 199–214.
14. *Occupational Outlook Handbook, 2006–2007*.
15. Lee B. Becker, Tudor Vlad, Maria Tucker, and Renée Pelton, "2005 Annual Survey of Journalism & Mass Communication Graduates," online, www.uga.edu/AnnualSurveys.

16. "PRSA 2005 Membership Study Findings Highlights."
17. "Salary Tables by Industry," CareerJournal.com, online, www.careerjournal.com/salaryhiring/industries/index.html; "Who's Making Money in Public Relations? PR News Releases Annual Industry Salary Report," news release issued by Springer Associates, 26 July 2006, online, www.emailwire.com.
18. "Public Relations Specialist," Michigan Career Portal, online, www.michigan.gov; United States Code, Title 5, Section 5332, online, www.law.cornell.edu/uscode.
19. *Occupational Outlook Handbook, 2006–2007.*
20. "Profile 2000: A Survey of the Profession, Part I," *Communication World,* June/July 2000, A1-A32; "PRSA/IABC Salary Survey 2000," online, www.prsa.org/ppc.
21. James G. Hutton, "The Myth of Salary Discrimination in Public Relations, *Public Relations Review 31* (2005).
22. "The Satisfaction Factor," *PR News,* 13 January 2003, online, LexisNexis.
23. "Profile 2000: A Survey of the Profession, Part I," *Communication World,* June/July 2000, A1–A32; "PRSA/IABC Salary Survey 2000," online, www.prsa.org/ppc.
24. "Profile 2000: A Survey of the Profession, Part I"; "PRSA/IABC Salary Survey 2000."
25. "Multicultural Survey of PR Practitioners," report issued by City College of New York and Howard University, 9 June 2005, online, www.ccny.cuny.edu/prsurvey.
26. "Workinpr.com State of the Industry Survey 2002."
27. Bowen, 211.
28. "PR Professional of the Year," *PR Week Online,* March 2006, online, www.prweek.com/us/events/ awards.
29. "A Failure of Initiative: Final Report of the Select Bipartisan Committee to Investigate the Preparation for and Response to Hurricane Katrina," report issued by the U.S. House of Representatives, 15 February 2006, online, www.gpoacess.gov/congress/index.html.
30. Tom Vanden Brook, "Red Cross to Release Results of Fraud Inquiry," *USA Today,* 27 March 2006, 3A.
31. "Raising a Red Flag: Wake Up Call for the Red Cross," news release issued by U.S. Senator Charles Grassley, 15 March 2006, online, www.senate.gov/~grassley.
32. "American Red Cross Response to Senator Grassley Letter of February 27, 2006," news release issued by American Red Cross, 27 February 2006, online, www.redcross.org.
33. "Statement: American Red Cross Currently Investigating Allegations," news release issued by American Red Cross, 24 March 2006, online, www.redcross.org.
34. "Red Cross Refers New Orleans Investigation to Federal Bureau of Investigation," news release issued by American Red Cross, 30 March 2006, online, www.redcross.org.
35. "Grassley Comments on Red Cross Governance Reforms," news release issued by U.S. Senator Charles Grassley, 30 October 2006, online, www.senate.gov/~grassley.
36. Fineman Public Relations' annual list is released through PR Newswire and can be accessed online via LexisNexis.

CHAPTER

3

A Brief History of
Public Relations

OBJECTIVES

After studying this chapter, you will be able to

- discuss how public relations evolved before it was formally recognized and given a name

- identify the forces that have shaped the modern profession's development

- recognize the major figures and events that influenced the growth of public relations

- explain the issues and trends that are shaping the future of public relations

KEY TERMS

Bernays, Edward L., p. 70
Committee for Public Information (CPI), p. 69
Crystallizing Public Opinion, p. 72
"Declaration of Principles," p. 67
downsizing, p. 77
Federalist Papers, p. 62
First Amendment, p. 62
Four-Minute Men, p. 70
Industrial Revolution, p. 59
Lee, Ivy Ledbetter, p. 66
Office of War Information (OWI), p. 74
Progressive Era, p. 60
propaganda, p. 69
Publicity Bureau, p. 64
rhetoric, p. 59
Seedbed Years, p. 64
vox populi, p. 59

Risky Business

Countries, much like corporations and individuals, often engage in public relations practices to attain their goals. That's why you were excited when officials of the Democratic Republic of Tranquility, a small South Seas island nation known for its tropical beauty, asked your agency to submit a bid for a tourism promotional campaign. They promised generous compensation in exchange for your expertise.

This seemed like just the break your struggling firm needed—until you did your research. You learned that the Democratic Republic of Tranquility is neither democratic nor tranquil. It is run by a brutal military regime that has been widely condemned for its human rights abuses. You also learned that the government wants to boost tourism revenues to support a military expansion that threatens neighboring countries.

On what basis should you decide whether to bid for this contract? Is everyone entitled to public relations counsel? Does history provide any examples from which you can learn?

Why History Is Important to You

At first glance, public relations appears to be a 20th-century invention. It is logical to link the emergence of the profession to the dramatic growth in mass communication technology during the past 100 years.

However, a closer examination reveals a remarkable history—a discipline practiced in many forms long before the nephew of a famous doctor gave it a name. History also tells about a profession that, at its very best, has been a positive force for change and, at its worst, has created challenges we continue to face.

History and the public relations profession are both values-driven. Both are filled with examples of where people acted—or failed to act—on their beliefs and standards. Both are also open to each observer's interpretation—also shaped by values. You faced this challenge in the opening scenario of this chapter: What values will govern your decision on whether to bid for the Tranquility contract? Can public relations help to change a client's bad behavior? Does the client's reputation matter?

The scenario also posed the question "Does history provide any examples from which you can learn?" For this particular scenario, history provides a dramatic—some might say tragic—example involving two public relations pioneers. Two men, confronted by similar choices, chose different paths—one to acclaim, the other to ignominy.

History is full of examples in which people have learned—or failed to learn—from the actions of others. William Shakespeare wrote in *The Tempest*, "What is past is prologue." To put it another way: Pay attention to history. You may be watching coming attractions.

Premodern Public Relations

Although the phrase "public relations" did not attain its current meaning until the 20th century, the practice of public relations has been evident since the dawn of recorded history. One example of public relations, in which primitive agricultural extension agents gave advice on how to grow better crops, dates back to 1800 B.C. in what is now Iraq.

Some historians believe that the development of public relations is a direct result of Western civilization's first true democracy: the city-state of Athens led by Pericles from 461 to 429 B.C. The dictatorships of the past had been overthrown, and suddenly the male citizens of Athens were free to debate, create, and implement public policy. In that environment, citizens began to study public opinion and the methods of influencing it. That study, known as **rhetoric,** is often seen as the beginning of public relations as a social science based on research, planning, and two-way communication. The practice of rhetoric fell into disuse with the demise of democratic Athens but flourished again in the freedoms of the final century of the Roman republic (100 B.C.), when a philosophy of *vox populi,* the voice of the people, was embraced.

The spread of Christianity during the Middle Ages could, in a modern context, be linked to the application of public relations techniques. Before the development of mass communication technologies, the faith was passed along by missionaries using word of mouth. Among the most notable of these missionaries was Francis of Assisi, who spread his teachings of self-imposed poverty and service to the poor across Europe and the Middle East. He died in 1226, but his religious order, the Franciscans, survives to this day. Johannes Gutenberg's Bible, printed in 1456 by means of a revolutionary movable type process, heralded the use of mass communication technologies. The Catholic Church's outreach efforts became more formalized in the 1600s when it established the *Congregatio de Propaganda Fide,* or Congregation for the Propagation of the Faith, to spread church doctrine.

Trends Leading to the Development of Modern Public Relations

The growth of modern public relations was not limited to just one nation. Aspects of what we now know as public relations emerged independently in several societies. For example, organized government public relations efforts in the United Kingdom preceded those in the United States by more than a decade. The National Association of Local Government Officers began in 1905, in part to educate the public about the role of local government in British society.[1] However, the earliest development of the profession appears to have emerged in the United States, where privately owned business and industry embraced public relations in the 1880s. In comparison, private sector public relations was not prominent in Britain until after the Second World War.[2]

The march toward modern public relations began in earnest in the United States after the Civil War. To a large degree, this development paralleled the country's transition from an agricultural to an industrial society. The **Industrial Revolution** brought with it growing pains, which, in turn, redefined the relationships among government, business, and the people. Historians often refer to this period of reforms as the **Progressive Era,** which ran from the 1890s to the United States' entrance into World War I in 1917. It was a period in which democracy as well as social and governmental institutions matured. Public opinion grew more important; the nation reexamined and, to a certain extent, redefined itself.

Let's look more closely at how the development of modern public relations is linked to five social trends that had their beginnings in the Progressive Era.

The Growth of Institutions. The Industrial Revolution spawned the growth of big companies. The resulting concentration of wealth among early 20th-century industrialists, such as J. P. Morgan, Andrew Carnegie, and John D. Rockefeller, ran against the traditional American inclination toward decentralized power—as evidenced in the checks and balances established in the Constitution. This, in turn, led to increased regulation of these businesses and consequent growth in the size of government. Led by the University of Michigan in 1897, U.S. colleges and universities began to promote themselves by creating publicity offices.[3] By the 1930s, labor unions began to have clout. As business, government, and labor organizations grew larger, the need for effective communication increased. All three sectors experienced a second growth spurt in the economic boom that followed the end of World War II.

The Expansion of Democracy. Progressive Era reforms such as giving women the right to vote and the direct election of U.S. senators brought more people into the political process and increased the need for public discussion of policy issues. That expansion continued into the mid- to late 20th century. As a result of the civil rights movement, black citizens and other minority groups gained greater access to the political process. During the Vietnam War, 18-year-olds were also given the right to vote. With the fall of communist governments in Europe and Asia near the end of the 20th century came a growing need for effective communication in emerging democratic societies. Because of the increasing importance of persuasion and consensus, public relations has become an integral part of the democratic process.

Technological Improvements in Communications. Each new communication medium presents both challenges and opportunities for reaching audiences both large and small. In the early 1900s the growth of national news services such as the Associated Press and the birth of national magazines such as the *Ladies' Home Journal* gave muckraking reporters a wider audience. The introduction of commercial radio in 1920 and commercial television in 1947 launched the era of instantaneous electronic communication. Developments in satellite and computer technology in the second half of the 20th century further revolutionized communications. With the dramatic expansion of the Internet in the 1990s, the power to communicate with mass publics began shifting away from media companies and toward individuals.

The Growth of Advocacy. In the late 1800s, a wave of immigrants who brought Old World political ideas to the New World—and, to some extent, the reaction of native-born citizens to this human wave from abroad—gave birth to increased

A great wave of immigrants (shown here receiving health inspections on arrival at Ellis Island) changed U.S. society and helped set the stage for the development of the new profession of public relations. (Courtesy of The Statue of Liberty–Ellis Island Foundation, Inc.)

political activism. Newspapers evolved from the organs of partisan "yellow journalism" of the 19th century into instruments of social advocacy in the early 20th century. The period after World War II also witnessed the growth of significant social advocacy, including movements for civil rights, women's rights, environmentalism, consumerism, antiwar ideals, children's rights, multinationalism, rights for persons with disabilities, and gay rights. Both those who advocated change and the institutions forced to deal with it found an increasing need for public relations.

The Search for Consensus. U.S. society is built upon consensus. The nation at one time believed itself to be a melting pot in which various cultures and philosophies would combine into something distinctly American. In recent decades, however, that concept has been largely discredited. It is now accepted that people can *both* be American and retain other cultural identities. Beyond the United States, the world population is growing at a rapid rate. The emergence of a global economy has highlighted the increasing competition for Earth's dwindling resources. With the threat of thermonuclear war on one hand and global environmental disaster on the other, the need to span cultural and philosophical differences is greater than ever. Organizations and individuals are learning that the positive application of public relations can help bridge those gaps.

As you will read in the coming pages, the development of public relations closely mirrors the growth of the United States. Although the profession evolved in other societies as well, it was in the United States—the great experiment in democracy—that public relations flourished.

Pre-20th-Century America

Although it would be more than a century before the discipline had a name, the use of public relations tactics was evident in pre-Revolutionary America. Perhaps the most famous example is the Boston Tea Party, a publicity event designed to focus attention on British taxation without representation. After the Revolution, public relations tactics were used to change the course of history. In what some have described as history's finest public relations effort, the **Federalist Papers** appeared in newspapers between October 1787 and April 1788. Written by Alexander Hamilton, James Madison, and John Jay under the single nom de plume Publius, these essays helped lead the reluctant former colonies to ratify the Constitution of the United States.

The ratification of the Constitution and the Bill of Rights in 1789 remains the most important event in the development of public relations in the United States. The 45 words of the **First Amendment** define the liberties that allow the free practice of this vital profession:

> Congress shall make no law respecting an establishment of religion, or prohibiting the free exercise thereof; or abridging the freedom of speech, or of the press; or the right of the people peaceably to assemble, and to petition the Government for a redress of grievances.

This guarantee of free expression, however, is not absolute. It is constantly being interpreted and refined by the U.S. Supreme Court. There have been times, during war or civil unrest for example, when freedom of expression has been severely tested. But more than two centuries after ratification, the First Amendment still stands as the singular liberty that distinguishes U.S. democracy and, as a consequence, the practice of public relations in the United States.

In the 1800s democracy in the United States continued to mature. Public education was introduced, which resulted in a more literate and well-informed society. As the right to vote was extended to men who did not own property, vigorous public debate emerged. The influence of that debate on the government was clear when President Andrew Jackson appointed Amos Kendall to his so-called kitchen cabinet. Kendall was the first presidential press secretary, serving as Jackson's pollster, counselor, speechwriter, and publicist.

Two other figures in the premodern period of public relations are worth noting. During the Civil War, Jay Cooke headed the United States' first fund-raising drive: Through an appeal to patriotism, Cooke sold government bonds to finance the Union's war effort. Better known, but less fondly remembered by practitioners, is Phineas T. Barnum, who created his circus in 1871 and later proclaimed it to be "The Greatest Show on Earth." Barnum was the father of press agentry in this country. A master showman, Barnum generated extensive newspaper coverage of his often bizarre enterprises through exaggeration, distortion, and outright lies. To the shame of the profession, some wanna-be publicists still practice Barnum's "publicity for publicity's sake" approach today.

QuickBreak 3.1

The American Revolution

It is not a stretch to say that the United States owes its existence—at least to some degree—to the successful practice of public relations. The American Revolution was a triumph of ideas and sacrifice, but it could not have happened without public support. While revolutionary leaders may not have called this relationship-building process *public relations,* that is exactly what they were doing.

One example is Thomas Paine, who came to America in 1774 with a passion for liberty and a flair for self-expression. In January 1776, he wrote a 79-page pamphlet, *Common Sense.* In it, Paine laid out the rationale for a permanent separation from the crown.[4] More than 100,000 copies of *Common Sense* were sold within three months of its publication. George Washington credited its "sound doctrine and unanswerable reasoning" with convincing reluctant colonists of the need to break from England.[5]

In its own way, the Declaration of Independence served as a news release, announcing the birth of a new nation and the principles on which it had been founded. When one looks at the drafting of the document and the framing of its messages, it is easy to see its resemblance to modern practice.

Thomas Jefferson was the lead writer, assisted by a committee of editors, fellow delegates to the Continental Congress. As one does when writing a modern news release, Jefferson wrote a lead de-signed to capture and hold the reader's attention. He wrote, "We hold these Truths to be self-evident, that all Men are created equal, that they are endowed by their Creator with certain unalienable rights, that among these are Life, Liberty, and the Pursuit of Happiness."[6] After the declaration's adoption on July 4, 1776, the Continental Congress ordered copies printed and distributed throughout the new nation. Newspapers reported its contents and, in many cases, published its text in full.[7]

Declaring independence was one thing. Winning it was another. Maintaining popular support was critical. To help in this cause, Paine published a series of 13 pamphlets, *The American Crisis,* in which he urged colonists to continue their struggle for independence. "These are the times that try men's souls," Paine wrote. "The summer soldier and the sunshine patriot will, in this crisis, shrink from the service of their country; but he that stands *now,* deserves the love and thanks of man and woman."[8]

"Methods to move mass audiences that are precious in modern America were vital in early America as well," wrote practitioner and historian Jason Karpf. "The Founding Fathers counted many PR masters among their ranks."

"As a nation, we are most fortunate for their PR triumphs."[9]

QUICK CHECK

1. What are some of the earliest examples of public relations—even before the profession was known as public relations?
2. What are the major social trends that have influenced the development of public relations?
3. What remains the most important event in the development of public relations in the United States?

The Seedbed Years

U.S. society underwent profound changes in the period following the Civil War. The Industrial Revolution transformed the nation's economy and helped fuel a flood of immigration. As already noted, reaction to the growth of mammoth corporations spawned a progressive movement and calls for reform. In this environment, publicity was first embraced as a means for shining a public light on government and corporate wrongdoing. New York banker Henry Clews proclaimed in 1906 that publicity was "our great remedy." However, by the 1920s, it was considered a corporate tool. One journalism professor condemned publicity as a weapon used to control public opinion.[15]

This evolution of publicity signaled the birth of a new industry, public relations. Public relations historian Scott Cutlip called this period the **"Seedbed Years,"** a time in which the new profession began to take root.[16] It was during this period of growth in U.S. society that organizations first felt the need for formalizing their communications. For example, in 1888 the Mutual Life Insurance Company created a "literary bureau" to publicize its services. One year later George Westinghouse hired a newspaper reporter to help him earn public favor in his battle with Thomas Edison over competing electricity distribution systems. Presidential candidate William Jennings Bryan inaugurated the practice of whistle-stop campaigning during 1896, in large part out of the need for publicity to counter William McKinley's well-financed campaign.

The nation's first public relations agency, the **Publicity Bureau** in Boston, was created in 1900 in recognition of the fact that corporations needed to voice their concerns amid a rising tide of critics. The Publicity Bureau came to epitomize the practice—and the challenges—of modern public relations in its infancy. The Publicity Bureau's clients, which included American Telephone & Telegraph and the nation's railroads, hoped that this new craft known as publicity might stem the increasing demand for government regulation.[17]

Other pioneering practitioners would soon follow. William Wolf Smith opened the national capital's first "publicity business" in 1902. The Parker and Lee agency, the nation's third, opened in New York City in 1904. However, it folded after only four years. That was a common fate of these early agencies.

Credibility was their problem. Publicity agents zealous to put forward a favorable view of their clients often provided inaccurate information. Sources were often hidden, creating a public increasingly suspicious of anything carrying a "publicity" label. There were also ethically challenged reporters—moonlighters—who wrote bylined stories for their newspapers in the morning and anonymous publicity releases in the afternoon.

Early public relations practitioners also faced stiff resistance from newspaper publishers. Some of this hostility stemmed from the tactics of early practitioners, which included bribes, gifts, and outrageous publicity stunts. Journalists also resented the growing number of people at their doorsteps seeking news coverage. Many journalists were contemptuous of former colleagues who switched to public relations careers. This was ironic, because many of the same critics complained bitterly about their own poor wages, negative reputations, and difficult working conditions.[18]

Thank You for Smoking

Thank You for Smoking, a 2006 film based on Christopher Buckley's novel, follows the exploits of lobbyist Nick Naylor, who, as one reviewer noted, championed the cause of the tobacco industry "ruthlessly and with a commendable lack of shame."[10] It is a funny movie—one that hits too close for comfort for many public relations practitioners.

Public relations has a long—and controversial—association with the tobacco industry. In the eyes of many, this collaboration has stained the profession's reputation. The most memorable moment in this relationship came on Easter Sunday 1929. Public relations pioneer Edward L. Bernays recruited 10 debutantes to walk down New York's Fifth Avenue carrying lighted cigarettes aloft in protest of restrictions against women's smoking in public places. The so-called Torches of Freedom march generated nationwide publicity and made it more socially acceptable for women to smoke. Bernays wrote decades later that "a beginning had been made, one I regret today."[11]

A 1952 *Reader's Digest* article, "Cancer by the Carton," dramatically brought home the danger of smoking to Americans. The tobacco industry responded by creating the Tobacco Institute Research Committee, which it said would sponsor research into health issues raised by smoking. It evolved into the Tobacco Institute, which at its height employed more than 120 public relations practitioners and spent more than $20 million annually promoting tobacco.[12]

A major shift in public policy came in the 1990s, fueled by the publication of internal industry documents suggesting that tobacco executives had ignored research showing smoking was harmful. Those documents also raised doubts about industry claims that it doesn't encourage smoking among minors.

Under the threat of a mountain of personal injury lawsuits, the tobacco industry finally admitted in 1997 that cigarettes are addictive and harmful to health. It also agreed to submit to nicotine regulation by the Food and Drug Administration, restrict its marketing tactics, and earmark more than $200 billion for health and antismoking education programs.[13]

In an ironic twist, public relations practitioners—once scorned for doing Big Tobacco's bidding—are now being praised for their role in reducing the rate of cigarette smoking. A 2003 report in the *Journal of the National Cancer Institute* credited a federal antismoking campaign with a decline in tobacco use. And it said the reason this effort succeeded where others had failed was because of the effective use of public relations.[14]

Theodore Roosevelt (1858–1919)

Early publicity efforts—especially those targeted at halting the increasing influence of government regulation—achieved only limited success for yet another reason: Theodore Roosevelt. The youngest person to date to serve as president, Roosevelt dramatically transformed the relationships among the White House, big business, and the electorate. Before Roosevelt's succession to the presidency upon the assassination of

Theodore Roosevelt, the nation's youngest president, is best remembered for using the White House as a "bully pulpit," from which he could rally public opinion in favor of his reform policies. (Courtesy of the Library of Congress)

William McKinley in 1901, the attitude widely held by Washington officials was, in essence, "What is good for big business is good for America." But Roosevelt saw big business' increasing concentration of power—an estimated 10 percent of the population at that time owned 90 percent of the wealth—as a threat to democracy. Roosevelt's administration proceeded to sue 44 major corporations in an attempt to break up monopolies and increase business competition.

Roosevelt also understood—probably better than any other person of his time—the power of harnessing public opinion. He transformed the presidency into what he called his "bully pulpit." Traditional power brokers were opposed to the reforms of Roosevelt's Square Deal, but the president understood the mood of the people and courted their favor through the muckraking press. As researcher Blaire Atherton French has written,

> Theodore Roosevelt was the first to initiate close and continuous ties with reporters, and may be accurately called the founder of presidential press conferences. He brought the press into the White House literally as well as figuratively. The tale goes that he looked out his window one rainy day and saw a group of reporters manning their usual post by the White House gate. Their purpose was to question those coming and going from the White House and in that way to gather news or leads. When T. R. saw them miserable, wet, and cold, he ordered that there be a room in the White House set aside just for them. In doing so, T. R. granted them a status they had never previously enjoyed and would subsequently never lose.[19]

Although many of his proposed reforms were thwarted by a stubborn Congress, much of Theodore Roosevelt's success and widespread popularity was a result of his skillful application of public relations. As another researcher has written, Roosevelt "figured out how a president can use the news media to guide public opinion. He did not just hand out information and leave matters in the hands of reporters. He created news."[20]

Ivy Ledbetter Lee (1877–1934)

A man who deserves more credit for the growth of public relations than he has received is **Ivy Ledbetter Lee.** His was a career that began in triumph and ended in a controversy that outlived him.

VALUES STATEMENT 3.1

Declaration of Principles

Ivy Ledbetter Lee and George Parker, veterans of Democratic Party politics, joined forces in 1905 to form the public relations firm of Parker and Lee. The agency drew public criticism for its representation of anthracite coal operators during a 1906 miner's strike. In an effort to stem the tide of hostile muck-raking reporters who doubted the veracity of the agency's public statements, Lee issued his "Declaration of Principles."

This is not a secret press bureau. All our work is done in the open. We aim to supply news. This is not an advertising agency; if you think any of our matter ought properly to go to your business office, do not use it. Our matter is accurate. Further details on any subject treated will be supplied promptly, and any editor will be assisted most cheerfully in verifying directly any statement of fact. Upon inquiry, full information will be given to any editor concerning those on whose behalf an article is sent out. In brief, our plan is, frankly and openly, on behalf of business concerns and public institutions, to supply to the press and public of the United States prompt and accurate information concerning subjects which it is of value and interest to the public to know about. Corporations and public institutions give out much information in which the news point is lost to view. Nevertheless, it is quite as important to the public to have this news as it is to the establishments themselves to give it currency. I send out only matter every detail of which I am willing to assist any editor in verifying for himself. I am always at your service for the purpose of enabling you to obtain more complete information concerning any of the subjects brought forward in my copy.

—Published in *American Magazine,* September 1906[21]

The son of a Methodist minister in Georgia, Lee studied at Princeton and worked as a newspaper reporter and stringer. After a brief foray into politics, Lee joined George E. Parker, once President Grover Cleveland's publicity manager, to form a publicity bureau in 1904. The new agency boasted of "Accuracy, Authenticity, and Interest."[22]

This philosophy evolved in 1906 into Lee's **"Declaration of Principles,"** the first articulation of the concept that public relations practitioners (although the term *public relations* had not yet been coined) have a public responsibility that extends beyond obligations to a client. "This is not a secret press bureau," Lee wrote. "All of our work is done in the open." (See Values Statement 3.1.)

Lee's "Declaration of Principles" also declared, "In brief, our plan is, frankly and openly, on behalf of business concerns and public institutions, to supply the press and public of the United States prompt and accurate information concerning subjects which it is of value and interest to the public to know about."[23]

Lee's statement, issued at a time when he was representing management's side in a coal strike, changed the direction of the evolving field of public relations. He established ethical standards by which others could judge his work. In doing so, he also brought credibility and professionalism to the field.

Although credited with bringing an ethical foundation to the fledgling profession of public relations, Ivy Lee is most remembered for unfortunate choices that damaged his reputation long after his death. (Courtesy of the Mudd Manuscript Library, Princeton University Library)

Of course, actions speak louder than words, and Lee did not always live up to his own words. Perhaps a kinder interpretation is that he often defined accuracy in very narrow terms. For Lee, accuracy meant correctly reflecting the views of the client—but it did not mean checking to see whether the client's statements were truthful. Because of that questionable logic, during his controversial career Lee often supplied misleading or false information to reporters. The resulting mistrust of Lee and his motives would eventually be his undoing.

Lee had an impressive list of clients. It was Lee who, along with pioneer practitioner Harry Bruno, helped to promote public acceptance of the new field of aviation. Lee was crucial in gaining the needed financial support for a nationwide publicity tour by aviator Charles A. Lindbergh. Lee is also credited for his work with what would eventually become General Mills and the creation of three of its most enduring symbols: Betty Crocker; Gold Medal Flour; and Wheaties, the Breakfast of Champions.[24]

You are judged by the company you keep. The appropriateness of representing controversial clients is an age-old problem for public relations practitioners—for example, will you decide to represent the Democratic Republic of Tranquility described in this chapter's opening scenario? Many of Lee's clients were controversial at the time they retained his services. They included the Anthracite Coal Operators, the Pennsylvania Railroad, and John D. Rockefeller.

However, it would be Lee's worldview and extensive travels that would cause the most damage to his reputation. In many ways Lee was a man ahead of his times. He supported recognition of Soviet Russia at a time when most of his compatriots were fearful of the recent communist revolution in that country. Lee was scorned for his desire for cooperation between the two nations. In less than a decade, however, cooperation between the United States and the Soviet Union would lead to an Allied victory in World War II.

The sharpest criticism was leveled at Lee's work in 1934 on behalf of I.G. Farben, the German Dye Trust. This episode occurred at a time shortly after Adolf Hitler assumed power in Germany. Lee's services were retained by industrialists to help counter a growing anti-German sentiment in the United States. Lee accepted a $25,000 fee with the stipulation that he only provide counsel and not disseminate information for the Germans within the United States. Lee, often referred to by his detractors as "Poison Ivy," was accused of being a Nazi sympathizer. Making matters worse, Lee ignored the advice he had often given others and refused to answer reporters' questions about his German business interests. In what now appears to be a very naive notion, Lee thought he could positively influence the behavior of the government of the Third Reich. In fairness, Lee was not the only person to underestimate the evil embodied in Adolf Hitler. However, this association would stain his name long after his death in 1934.

War and Propaganda

America's entrance into World War I in 1917 had a profound effect on both society and the growth of public relations. The war thrust the United States onto the world stage—a place where many U.S. citizens were reluctant to be. Isolationism grew out of a desire to separate the New World from the problems of Europe. In an earlier time, that had been quite possible. However, with the Industrial Revolution came the growth of U.S. economic power and ties to other nations that were an unavoidable consequence of a growing global economy.

World War I also focused public attention on the use of the mass media as tools of persuasion. People were becoming more familiar with the concept of **propaganda,** which is the attempt to have a viewpoint accepted at the exclusion of all others. The word's etymology stems from the Roman Catholic Church's efforts to propagate the faith during the 17th century. *Propaganda,* as a term, did not carry the negative connotations at the beginning of World War I that it does today. However, its abuse by its most evil practitioner, Nazi Propaganda Minister Joseph Goebbels, discredited propaganda both as a word and as a practice.

To rally the nation behind the war, President Woodrow Wilson established the **Committee for Public Information (CPI).** It became better known as the Creel Committee, after its chairman, former journalist George Creel. Creel was a longtime Wilson friend who had tried to persuade him to run for president as early as 1905, while Wilson was still president of Princeton University. Wilson had been reelected to the White House in 1916 on a promise that he would keep the United States out of the bloody conflict that had been raging across Europe since 1914. With involvement in the war now on the horizon, Wilson leaned toward the advice of his military experts that the press should be strictly censored. Creel, however, as military historian Thomas Flemming has noted, "convinced Wilson that the country needed not suppression but the expression of a coherent pro-war policy."[25]

During the two years that the United States was at war, the CPI churned out more than 75 million pamphlets and books with titles ranging from "Why We Are Fighting" to "What Our Enemy Really Is." Through what may have been the largest speakers' bureau ever created, the **Four-Minute Men,** 75,000 speakers gave 755,190 talks to drum up home front morale.[26] (The name "Four-Minute Men" came from the length of time volunteers spoke between reel changes at cinemas, which were the most important form of mass entertainment at the time.) CPI filmmakers also produced features such as *Pershing's Crusaders* and *Under Four Flags*. These films not only fanned patriotic fires but also raised $852,744.30—not bad for the days when the price of a movie ticket was only a nickel.[27]

1. Why did most of the early publicity agencies fail?
2. What contributions did Ivy Ledbetter Lee make to the development of public relations?
3. In what ways did the outbreak of World War I influence the growth of public relations?

Edward L. Bernays (1891–1995)

World War I and the propaganda surrounding it sparked interest in the study and manipulation of public opinion. There was a growing demand for publicity agents to represent the interests of private companies and public agencies. The Creel Committee proved to be a training ground for many of these practitioners. Notable among them was **Edward L. Bernays,** an acknowledged "father" of public relations. Although Bernays had served as a press agent in several capacities before joining the Creel Committee in 1917, it was after the war that he made his indelible mark.

The Austrian-born Bernays was a nephew of Sigmund Freud, and he played a major role in having Freud's theories on psychoanalysis introduced to America. Before joining the CPI, Bernays served as a newspaper reporter and a theatrical press agent. For the most part, Bernays received high marks for his work with the Creel Committee. However, Bernays' lifelong propensity for self-promotion eventually led to the dismantling of the CPI. At the war's end, Bernays traveled with President Wilson to Paris for the Versailles Peace Conference to provide the president with technical assistance in dealing with reporters. Bernays issued a news release upon his departure announcing that he and 15 other employees of CPI were traveling to France as the "United States Official Press Mission to the Peace Conference." In the release Bernays wrote that "the announced object of the expedition is 'to interpret

The Scopes Monkey Trial

It was one of the great trials of the 20th century. It involved a historic clash between science and religion. The opposing attorneys were giants of their age. Almost 80 years later, it remains a subject of intense debate.

And, oh yes—it was also a publicity stunt.

The State of Tennessee v. John Scopes—better known as the Scopes Monkey Trial—was the flash point of a theological and political struggle over Charles Darwin's theory of evolution. When Darwin published *The Origin of Species* in 1859, he wrote that human beings evolved from apes through a process of natural selection and adaptation. In a backlash against Darwin, the Tennessee legislature made teaching evolution in public schools a criminal offense in March 1925. The American Civil Liberties Union, eager to test the constitutionality of the law, offered to defend any teacher willing to challenge it.[28]

When Dayton, Tennessee, businessman George Rappleyea read about the ACLU's offer, he immediately recognized an opportunity. Dayton, a small agricultural community located in the southeastern part of the state, had hit hard times.[29] Rappleyea realized that a court battle over evolution would attract national attention that would revive Dayton's economy.[30]

But if his scheme to attract publicity was going to work, Rappleyea had to identify a defendant—a local teacher willing to be arrested and placed on trial for violating Tennessee's antievolution law. He recruited John Scopes, a popular 24-year-old math and physics teacher who coached football. After some reluctance, Scopes agreed. Rappleyea—a staunch evolutionist—swore out a warrant for Scopes' arrest and then called the ACLU. When the

civil libertarians agreed to defend the coach-turned-defendant, the game was on.[31]

Dayton embraced the controversial trial with a gusto rarely seen before or since. A Scopes Trial Entertainment Committee was established to arrange visitor accommodations. As the trial neared, the town was adorned with pictures of apes and monkeys. Robinson's Drugstore served "simian soda," and the town constable's motorcycle proudly displayed a "Monkeyville Police" sign.[32]

The trial's two lead attorneys dominated the stage, Clarence Darrow for the defense and William Jennings Bryan for the prosecution. The trial began with jury selection on July 10, 1925.

The nation closely followed proceedings in the Rhea County Courthouse over the next 12 days—it was the first trial ever broadcast over the relatively new medium of radio. Newspaper reporters from around the world descended on Dayton. They included H. L. Mencken of the *Baltimore Sun,* known for his sharp—often cutting—humor.

"Here was an unexampled, almost miraculous chance to get Dayton upon the front pages, to make it talked about, to put it on the map," Mencken wrote. "Two months ago the town was obscure and happy. Today it is a universal joke."[33]

For the record, Scopes was convicted and fined $100. Five days after the trial, Bryan died and became a martyr for the antievolution cause. Because of technical errors in the proceedings, the case never reached the U.S. Supreme Court. In Dayton, tourists travel to the Rhea County Courthouse every summer to commemorate the trial. Eight decades later, the town remains a focal point of the evolution debate.[34]

Edward L. Bernays, an acknowledged "father" of public relations, was the nephew of famed psychoanalyst Sigmund Freud and the first person to coin the phrase "public relations counsel." (Courtesy of the Museum of Public Relations, www.prmuseum.com)

the work of the Peace Conference by keeping up a worldwide propaganda to disseminate American accomplishments and ideals.'"[35] Creel was angry that Bernays had overstated the CPI's role. Wilson's detractors in Congress began to look upon the CPI as the president's personal publicity machine and pulled its plug.

The inevitable finger-pointing ensued. Creel blamed Bernays for undercutting the mission of the CPI in a search for personal glory. For his part, Bernays cast blame on Creel for helping to lose the peace. "Lack of effective public relations between President Wilson and the people of the United States, historians confirm, was one of the reasons for the rejection of the League of Nations by the United States," Bernays wrote. "The final breakdown of the League in the early Thirties was due in large part to the same lack of good public relations."[36]

It was Bernays who, in his 1923 book, *Crystallizing Public Opinion,* popularized the phrase "public relations counsel." He said he used the phrase because of the negative connotations attached to terms such as *propagandist, publicist,* and *press agent:*

> I wanted something broader than publicity or press-agentry. I called what I did "publicity direction," by which I meant directing the actions of a client to result in the desired publicity. A year later Doris [Bernays' wife] and I coined the phrase "counsel on public relations," which we thought described our activity better—giving professional advice to our clients on their public relationships, regardless of whether such an activity resulted in publicity.[37]

Bernays was not the first to use the term *public relations.* President Thomas Jefferson used it in an address to Congress in 1807. Attorney Dorman Eaton also used the term in an 1882 talk before the Yale Law School graduating class.[38] However, Bernays was the first to use it to describe the discipline that bears its name.

In his book, Bernays was also the first to articulate the two-way communication concept of public relations. In the same year that *Crystallizing Public Opinion* was published, Bernays taught the first public relations course, at New York University.

Through the years Bernays promoted the interests of a wide variety of clients, including the American Tobacco Company, Lithuanians seeking independence from the Soviet Union, and Procter & Gamble. Bernays took credit for pushing CBS Radio to develop news programming to build up its image. He also acknowledged his role in encouraging women to smoke cigarettes—something he said he regretted much later in life.

QuickBreak 3.4

The Mother of Public Relations

If Edward L. Bernays is most often credited with being the father of public relations, it is both logical and just that his wife, Doris E. Fleischman, be recognized as the profession's mother. Fleischman was more than Bernays' life partner. She was an equal—yet often invisible—business partner in one of history's most important and successful public relations agencies.

The original power couple of public relations met as children at a beach resort on Long Island, where their families had summer cottages.[39] Fleischman, whose father was a prominent attorney, became a women's page writer for the *New York Tribune* in 1914 and a freelance writer in 1916. She went to work for Bernays in the summer of 1919 at $50 a week as a staff writer. (He paid his male staff writers $75 a week.) At that time Bernays was engaged in what he called "publicity direction" for clients such as opera legend Enrico Caruso and the Russian Ballet.[40]

Bernays and Fleischman married on September 16, 1922. In an act that would come to symbolize this partnership, Fleischman—with her new husband's encouragement—registered at the Waldorf-Astoria for their wedding night using her maiden name. "I had an inner fear that marriage (though I wanted it fiercely with Doris) would take away some of my liberties as an individual if there were always a Mrs. added to my name," Bernays wrote in his memoirs. "I wanted both the ties and the freedom."[41] During their 58 years of marriage, Fleischman and Bernays were truly a team. "My relationship with Doris was at two levels," Bernays wrote. "At the office we were fairly businesslike and professional, but after working hours our relationship became highly personal."[42] Bernays gives credit to his wife for helping him coin the phrase "public relations counsel." Bernays told one interviewer that his wife "played an equally important role with mine, except that her insight and judgment are better than mine."[43]

Although they may have been equal partners, they certainly haven't received equal recognition: Fleischman remains a shadow lingering in the background of Bernays' career. That is largely because of the way this unique partnership operated. Although the couple closely collaborated on all projects, Bernays made all the client contacts and speeches—and not just because of his propensity for self-promotion. It was a time when women were a rarity in the business world. Many companies were uncomfortable and unwilling to embrace women's ideas. Though this reality was a bitter pill to swallow, the couple played the game by the rules of the day and, by all measures, won.

Even though Doris Fleischman has not received the acclaim achieved by her husband, Bernays was his wife's greatest champion. "These are difficult times, being alone after 58 years of happy twenty-four-hour-a-day companionship," Bernays wrote after Fleischman's death in 1980. "She was a rare woman."[44]

Public relations historian Scott Cutlip wrote that Bernays believed in self-promotion to the point that he lost the respect of many of his contemporaries. In one instance, Bernays was fired from an account he had with General Motors because he had gotten more credit for GM's Depression-era relief efforts than had the company.[45] Nevertheless, in recognition of his role in the advancement of public relations, *Life* magazine named Bernays to its list of the 100 most influential Americans of the 20th century.

Bernays remained a leading advocate for professional public relations until his death at the age of 103 in 1995. Late in his life, Bernays favored the licensing of public relations professionals. "Any dumbbell, nitwit or crook can call himself a public relations practitioner," Bernays told an interviewer. "The only way to protect yourself from dumbbells and crooks is to install intellectual and social values that are meaningful and keep out people who only hand out circulars in Harvard Square."[46]

Why Bernays and Not Lee?

Why isn't Ivy Ledbetter Lee, whose "Declaration of Principles" preceded Edward L. Bernays' *Crystallizing Public Opinion* by 17 years, considered the real founder of modern public relations? It appears that timing and circumstances favored Bernays.

That both men deserve recognition is without question. At a time when what was to become known as public relations was in its infancy, Lee gave the profession credibility and ethical standards. Later, Bernays gave the emerging profession a name and direction.

However, it is also true that both men were not saints. Lee proclaimed the value of truth and accuracy, but he didn't always apply those standards to his own work. As for Bernays, his penchant for self-promotion cost him numerous contracts, caused him to be despised by many of his competitors, and may even have helped to dash hopes for a lasting world peace after World War I.

Both men faced a similar fork in the road during their careers. Their choices helped to seal their reputations. With what may have been good intentions, Lee worked for the Nazis. Bernays declined the same opportunity.

Lee's death in 1934 stilled his voice and ended any chance he might have had to salvage his tarnished reputation. Bernays, however, outlived his contemporary critics. In his writings and in his promotional literature, Bernays actively portrayed himself as the "father of public relations," and he was embraced by an industry that had itself sought recognition and acceptance for so long. Now that they are gone, perhaps history will treat both men as the flawed but notable figures they really were.

The Postwar Boom

Government public relations efforts expanded at the start of U.S. involvement in World War II, when a 1942 presidential order created the **Office of War Information (OWI)**. Headed by veteran newspaper and radio commentator Elmer Davis, OWI had a twofold mission: to coordinate and control the flow of information from the battlefield to the home front, and to engage in experiments in psychological warfare against the enemy. The OWI was the forerunner of the United States Information Agency, which had more than 7,300 employees and an annual budget of approximately $1 billion prior to being absorbed by the U.S. State Department in 1999.

Like its predecessor, the Committee for Public Information, OWI became a breeding ground for a new generation of public relations practitioners. During World War II approximately 100,000 people were trained as public information officers.[47] Once the war was over, many of these "battle-hardened" practitioners turned their wartime activities into careers.

The postwar period witnessed a rapid growth in public relations education. It was during this period, in 1948, that the Public Relations Society of America was formed by the merger of the National Association of Public Relations Counsel and the American Council on Public Relations. The International Association of Business Communicators began in 1970 following the merger of the American Association of Industrial Editors and the International Council of Industrial Editors.

Postwar Social Activism

The period following World War II in many ways resembled the period of the Industrial Revolution: It was a time of significant growth in the size of government, businesses, industries, organizations, and population. The United States was the only economic power to emerge from World War II with its industrial base virtually untouched by the destruction of war. A consumer economy that had been slowed by the Great Depression and put on hold by the war was finally unleashed. Great advances were made in telecommunications, including the introduction of the most important mass communication medium of the 20th century—television.

The postwar decades also saw great social reform and upheaval, including the civil rights movement, consumerism, environmentalism, the antiwar movement, women's rights, gay rights, and multinationalism. Looming over all of this was the Cold War and the constant threat of thermonuclear war. Never had there been a time when the need for effective communication among nations, organizations, and individuals was greater.

In the highly competitive environment of the postwar period, public relations was seen by corporations as well as consumer advocates as a means for achieving strategic goals. This often led to a clash of values. One of the most significant conflicts came in what *Fortune* magazine called "the Railroad-Truckers Brawl." Because of the competitive pressures that came with the growth of the consumer economy, a group of railroad executives hired the public relations firm of Carl Byoir & Associates to orchestrate a campaign to increase government regulation of the trucking industry. This included weight restrictions the railroad executives said were designed to minimize the wear and tear on public highways. It also had the effect of making long-haul trucking less cost effective. When these efforts succeeded, the trucking industry fought back. It filed an antitrust suit in 1956 that, in essence, accused railroad executives of using public relations tactics to create an illegal monopoly in the long-distance freight industry. The case was decided five years later by the U.S. Supreme Court, which unanimously ruled for the railroad executives. As researchers Karla K. Gower and Margot Opdycke Lamme noted, "It was the first time that the Supreme Court directly addressed public relations, establishing it as a legitimate activity when used in furtherance of a political agenda."[48]

Consumer advocate Ralph Nader also used public relations tactics to change the way big businesses operate. Nader burst on the scene in 1965 with his landmark book *Unsafe at Any Speed,* in which he documented safety problems associated with automobiles, especially General Motors' Corvair. Unhappy with the negative publicity, GM sought to discredit Nader, prompting the consumer advocate to sue the company for investigating his private life. General Motors settled out of court and paid Nader $425,000—which he used to create a watchdog group, the Project on Corporate Responsibility (PCR). Nader then became a GM shareholder, which gave him access to the company's annual meetings. Although GM management defeated several PCR resolutions placed before shareholders, Nader was successful in coaxing GM to change its operations in several areas, including concessions on minority representation on the board of directors, environmental awareness, and consumer safety.[49]

Ironically, during the Industrial Revolution, many advocates of social change saw public relations as an attempt by big business to maintain the status quo. During the social upheavals of the second half of the 20th century, that view changed. Grassroots organizations adopted public relations tactics to influence the actions of business and government. In many ways, the flow of public relations had reversed.

In the spirit of "if you can't beat 'em, join 'em," well-managed companies came to realize the importance of cultivating important publics through public relations.

QuickBreak 3.5

Other Notable Figures from Public Relations' Past

Leone Baxter—with her husband and partner, *Clem Whitaker,* formed the first agency specializing in political campaigns in 1933.

Carl Byoir—a Creel Committee veteran; formed one of the earliest public relations firms, Carl Byoir & Associates.

Harwood Childs—a Princeton University political scientist who expanded upon Bernays' theories and stressed that practitioners should be students of "social effects and corporate conduct."

Pendleton Dudley—an influential figure in early public relations whose firm evolved through the years to DAY, which was acquired by Ogilvy & Mather.

Rex Harlow—a practitioner and educator; founded the American Council on Public Relations, which evolved into the Public Relations Society of America in 1948.

E. H. Heinrichs—a former Pittsburgh newspaper reporter hired by Westinghouse in 1889 to run the nation's first corporate public relations department.

John W. Hill—with partner *Don Knowlton* created Hill & Knowlton, one of the world's largest public relations firms, in Cleveland in 1927.

George V. S. Michaelis—a leading force behind the creation of the Publicity Bureau, the nation's first public relations agency.

Arthur W. Page—a vice president with American Telephone & Telegraph in 1927 who set the standard for corporate public relations, particularly employee relations.

Theodore Vail—organized the first public relations program for AT&T, based on the then-revolutionary concept that public utilities had to please their customers through good service and fair rates.

Hamilton Wright—a vigorous promoter of the growing state of Florida and a pioneer in the promotion of land development and in representing foreign nations in the United States.

As Edward Grefe and Martin Linsky note in their book *The New Corporate Activism,*

> A new breed of public affairs professionals began emerging who recognized that to build grassroots constituent support, it was necessary to present potential coalition allies with a positive program they could support. Following the example of grassroots organizers, these professionals fostered strategies that would not be simply against something but equally *for* something.[50]

Late-20th-century public relations practitioners became increasingly important in a wide variety of areas, including crisis communications, community relations, employee relations, and investor relations. Practitioners also played a part in strategic planning, although the scope of their role varied widely throughout the industry. "Within the public relations profession, the ability to influence strategic planning varies widely," wrote Robert W. Kinkead and Dena Winokur in *Public Relations Journal.* "Some practitioners get involved in developing game plans at the highest corporate level, while others simply implement communications moves once a strategy is set by others."[51]

QUICK ✓ CHECK

1. Why is Edward L. Bernays most often credited as being the "father" of modern public relations?
2. How did the end of World War II influence the growth of public relations?
3. In what ways have social movements such as civil rights, women's rights, and consumerism affected the development of public relations?

The Downsizing of the United States

Changes in the world's economic climate brought dramatic consequences starting in the 1970s. The United States had an aging industrial infrastructure that made it difficult for U.S. businesses to compete with more modern facilities in other nations. Former adversaries Germany and Japan, having risen from the ashes of war, began to compete successfully against U.S. companies both in this country and abroad. Those nations had also adopted many management practices that had been pioneered in the United States but seemingly forgotten here. As a result, business and industry began a sometimes painful process of modernizing and **downsizing.** They trimmed layers of middle management, sold unprofitable divisions, and focused on core enterprises. Jobs that had once seemed certain to last forever suddenly disappeared.

This process was hastened in the 1980s when President Ronald Reagan's New Federalism initiative began the process of downsizing the federal government and shifting many of its responsibilities to the states and to the private sector. In part because of tax cuts, deregulation, and reduced payrolls, the 1980s were a period of sustained economic growth. But they were also a time in which the gap between rich and poor widened in the United States.

The downsizing trend had a major impact on public relations. Many in-house public relations departments were either reduced or eliminated entirely. This, in turn, created opportunities for agencies and private consultants to fill the gaps. The irony, of course, is that this downsizing occurred at a time when organizations needed public relations practitioners more than ever—especially when it came to explaining why people were being laid off while their employers reported record revenues and rising executive salaries. A positive development has been a greater awareness of the need for corporate responsibility and volunteerism—areas in which public relations play a major role.

The Baby Boomers Come of Age

At the same time these economic changes were occurring, a technological revolution was taking place. With the invention of silicon microprocessing chips, computers became more powerful, smaller, and more affordable. Desktop publishing came into existence, along with fax machines, e-mail, and teleconferencing. Information became the nation's top commodity. Workers, especially public relations practitioners, became more productive, and record number of new jobs were created. Unfortunately, these new information-based jobs often paid lower salaries than the old ones they replaced.

Another important change came in the demographic makeup of the workforce. Women entered the job market in record numbers. Civil rights legislation also created opportunities for African Americans and other minority workers. The face of immigration also changed. A century earlier, the majority of immigrants coming to the United States had been from Europe. The nearly 20 million foreign-born residents counted by the U.S. Census in 1990 presented a different picture. Of that number, 44 percent had been added in the 1980s; and of the new arrivals, almost half came from Latin America and nearly one-third from Asia.

Public relations practitioners began to take on a much higher and sometimes negative profile during the 1970s and 1980s, especially in the area of government and politics. This trend actually had begun in the 1960s, when a large percentage of citizens felt that the Johnson administration was not telling the truth about its conduct of the Vietnam War—creating what commentators often referred to as a "credibility gap." In the 1970s, public relations also was criticized for its role during the Watergate scandal. In reality, many of that scandal's principal figures had advertising, not public relations, backgrounds. Had Richard Nixon followed good public relations principles, he might have been able to avoid the ignominy of becoming the first person to resign the presidency.

Following Bill Clinton's use of rapid-response public relations tactics to defeat incumbent George Bush in the 1992 presidential election, public awareness of political counselors—so-called spin doctors—increased dramatically. Some of these counselors, such as James Carville and George Stephanopoulos, later became network political pundits, a role once exclusively held by reporters. Political public relations took center stage in the presidential election stalemate of 2000. Both George W. Bush and Al Gore, trying to appear presidential and above the fray, relied heavily on surrogate spokespersons during the 36-day deadlock.

The New Millennium

The world is very different from what it was in the days of Teddy Roosevelt, Ivy Lee, and Edward Bernays. And so is the practice of public relations.

The terror attacks of September 11, 2001, have shaped public attitudes toward the profession in many ways. In the days and weeks following 9/11, practitioners won high praise for their efforts to inform a frightened nation, rally public support for victims, and help restore a sense of normalcy. If but for a brief time, the profession appeared to be fulfilling its potential as a catalyst for social consensus.

However, as the months and years passed, there was the inevitable reassessment. The head of the American Red Cross was forced to resign because her agency made misleading statements about how it used money raised in the name of the 9/11 victims. The newly created Department of Homeland Security became the object of public ridicule for a color-coded terror alert system that few seemed to understand. The Bush administration's public information campaign prior to the 2003 Iraq war led many to believe that they were misled—especially after the invasion failed to uncover a promised cache of weapons of mass destruction.

The reputation of public relations was further damaged by a series of scandals. They included three Fleishman-Hillard executives who resigned amid allegations they billed the City of Los Angeles for work that was never done. Two were eventually convicted of fraud and conspiracy. The incident became a focal point of that city's 2005 mayoral election and contributed to the defeat of the incumbent.[52] Later that same year in Canada, the government of Prime Minister Paul Martin fell after a parliamentary vote of no confidence. It was triggered by an investigative commission's report that the government had funneled millions of dollars to advertising and public relations agencies for work that was not done.[53]

At a time when the public relations industry should be celebrating a century of achievement, it finds itself answering the very same questions about integrity and values confronted by Ivy Lee and Edward Bernays. It raises a question all practitioners should ponder: Does history have to repeat itself?

QUICK ✓ CHECK

1. How has corporate downsizing affected public relations practitioners?
2. In addition to downsizing, what other social forces influenced the development of public relations near the end of the 20th century?
3. After more than a century of evolution, why does the profession of public relations still face questions about its values and integrity?

Summary

Although public relations did not acquire its name until the 20th century, it has been practiced in some form since the beginnings of recorded time. At the time the United States was formed, public relations tactics were used to rally colonists to the cause of independence and later to support the adoption of the new nation's Constitution.

Modern public relations was born during the Industrial Revolution and began to take root during the period known as the Progressive Era. Its development throughout the past century has been nurtured by great social trends—the growth of institutions, the expansion of democracy, technological improvements in communications, the growth of advocacy, and the search for consensus. The profession's development has also been advanced by historical figures such as Theodore Roosevelt, Ivy Ledbetter Lee, Edward L. Bernays, and Doris Fleischman.

By the end of the 20th century, public relations had begun to take a more central role in social discourse in the United States. Practitioners began to acquire more public visibility—even on some occasions when they would have preferred otherwise. As organizations downsized in an effort to become more efficient and effective in a global economy, public relations practitioners played a pivotal role. And in a post-9/11 world, the profession is challenged on two fronts: building its own credibility while helping to build global consensus.

DISCUSSION QUESTIONS

1. Whom do you consider the "father of public relations," Ivy Ledbetter Lee or Edward L. Bernays? Why did you choose one man over the other?
2. In addition to Lee and Bernays, who are some of the other major figures who contributed to the development of modern public relations?
3. What major forces have shaped the development of public relations in the 20th century?
4. What is propaganda, and why has its use been largely discredited?
5. What do you consider the most significant lesson to be learned from the history of public relations?
6. Would you accept the Democratic Republic of Tranquility as a client? Why or why not?

Memo from the Field

**Edward M. Block,
retired public relations
executive**

Edward M. Block was senior vice president for public relations, advertising, and employee information at AT&T Corporation for 12 years. He was also assistant to the chairman of the board and a member of the Office of the Chairman. He has received numerous awards for achievements in public relations, including the Public Relations Society of America's Gold Anvil. Most recently, he was cited by *PR Week* magazine as among the 100 most influential public relations people of the 20th century.

On page 76 you will find the names of Theodore N. Vail and Arthur W. Page, two executives whose pioneering ideas remain as enduring principles of corporate relationship building.

Vail is the chief executive whose utterly unique business model built the Bell Telephone System, a quasi-monopoly that created a new industry and dominated telephone service in the United States for nearly a century, becoming, at its zenith, the biggest company in the world. He welcomed government regulation, believed that profits need only be sufficient to sustain good service, and established a company-paid pension trust based on identical payout formulas for all employees, management as well as nonmanagement. He invested heavily in research to ensure continuous innovation. He also employed national magazine advertising to explain the policies and plans of the company to the public, no doubt the first demonstration of what would be called "transparency" today. These were remarkable innovations in an era best remembered for its robber barons.

Page elaborated and institutionalized Vail's concepts throughout that giant enterprise. A former magazine editor, he was hired by the parent company, AT&T, in 1926. He thus became the first individual elected to a senior executive position in charge of what we now call public relations. Subsequently, he was elected to the board of directors. He established modern public relations organizations in the Bell companies, delegating to them a cluster of responsibilities still found in most communications departments in U.S. corporations: employee information. Media relations. Community relations. Financial information. Institutional advertising and communications policy. Philanthropy.

Page was above all a counselor, and he made counseling a top priority in the far-flung PR organizations he created. He persistently argued—and demonstrated throughout his career—that when you get your corporate policies and business practices right your public relations programs will succeed. Conversely, he argued, that when your corporate policies are out of sync with the expectations of your publics you cannot sustain effective constituency relationships—so don't bother. Moreover, he warned, communications efforts intended to support wrongheaded policies will only make matters worse.

As an important extension of this focus, Page conceived of public relations as an institutional mind-set, not a functional department, and therefore a priority consideration in every decision, not only by top management, but also by supervisors in the field or on the shop floor. His conception is perhaps best summed up in the modern understanding of the term *corporate culture*. He ardently believed that public relations is everyone's job, a bias, an attitude that strives to fashion policies, actions, and business practices that project integrity and build trust over time.

People employed in the PR departments that Page established were expected to be experts in the communications arts and were hired and incessantly trained in these skills. But more important, they were widely deployed throughout the Bell companies' operating divisions to provide on-the-spot counsel in matters large or small. Their peers in the functional departments routinely took account of their judgments and acted on them.

The Page emphasis on counseling may seem a quaint idea in an era that seems to prize so many of the currently fashionable communications functions such as marketing support and investor relations. But his disciples abound and continue to insist that counseling will sooner or later reassert its importance. Why? Because counseling is by definition a value-added function, providing, as it does, a unique and critical perspective in managing the affairs of businesses whose constituencies are many and varied. Moreover, timely counseling is not overhead. It comes free as part of a total communications package.

Today, a 300-plus member Arthur W. Page Society exists expressly to promote his concepts in a context of contemporary business issues and to serve the needs of senior corporate executives as well as public relations counseling firms.

The Page concepts are captured, albeit cryptically, in the following "principles" espoused by the society's members: Tell the truth. Prove it with action. Listen to the customer. Conduct public relations as if the whole company depends upon it. Remain calm, patient, and good humored, especially in the face of criticism.

When you think about them, these admonitions are nothing more complicated than plain, old-fashioned horse sense. Makes you wonder why so many businesses today seem not to have any.

CASE STUDY **3.1**

The March of Dimes

One of the greatest ironies of the 20th century was that a man who successfully hid his physical disabilities from most Americans was also the most visible spokesperson in the fight against the disease that had crippled him.

Franklin Delano Roosevelt was the only person elected president of the United States four times. From his inauguration in March 1933 until his death in April 1945, FDR held a commanding presence in the minds of U.S. citizens. Historians consider him among the greatest of presidents for having led the United States through the Great Depression and to the brink of victory in the Second World War.

He is also remembered for his courage in overcoming polio (poliomyelitis), a viral disease that attacks the central nervous system and can lead to paralysis and death. Children were most often the victims of the disease, which is transmitted through contaminated food and water. When FDR contracted polio at the age of 39 in 1921, he lost the use of his legs. But with careful event planning, the assistance of the Secret Service, and the acquiescence of the news media, the extent of Roosevelt's physical disability was unknown to most people.[54]

While FDR may have hidden his own physical limitations, he was not shy in showing his support for others who had suffered the same fate. Initially, his efforts centered on Warm Springs, Georgia, where he had first gone in 1924 to bathe in the area's therapeutic warm spring waters. Roosevelt purchased the property in 1926. A year later, with the help of former law partner Basil O'Connor, FDR established the nonprofit Warm Springs Foundation as a center for polio therapy and research.[55]

With the onset of the Great Depression, the Warm Springs Foundation faced severe financial difficulties. A nationwide series of Birthday Balls was organized on January 30, 1934, coinciding with President Roosevelt's 52nd birthday. The Birthday Balls ranged from a lavish gala at New York's Waldorf-Astoria to a wheelchair dance for patients at Warm Springs.[56] The event was promoted with the slogan

Franklin D. Roosevelt (center), shown here in Warm Springs, Georgia, in 1932, managed to hide from the U.S. public his inability to walk. Note that in this carefully staged photograph, FDR steadies himself by holding the arm of an unidentified man. (Courtesy of the Franklin D. Roosevelt Presidential Library and Museum)

"Dance so that others may walk." It was so successful that it was repeated for several years.[57]

"Birthday Balls exploited the prestige of the presidency to collect monies for the Warm Springs Foundation," according to media historian Douglas Gomery. "It was often difficult to tell the difference between these polio balls and similar fund-raisers staged by the Democratic Party."[58]

Though the close connection between charity and politics may have been coincidental, it is undeniable. While Roosevelt had genuine sympathy for polio victims, being seen as their champion also helped his public image. Gomery notes that several interest groups, especially the entertainment industry, embraced the Birthday Balls as a means to gain favor from the Roosevelt administration.[59]

The relationship between FDR and the entertainment industry spawned the signature fund-raising campaign for which Roosevelt is best remembered, the March of Dimes. Roosevelt established the National Foundation for Infantile Paralysis on January 3, 1938. It marked the creation of the first permanent self-sustaining source of medical research funding based on small individual contributions rather than on money given by a few wealthy patrons. Eddie Cantor, a 1930s film and radio star, called this grassroots fund-raising effort the "March of Dimes," a play on the title of a popular newsreel series of the day, *The March of Time.* Cantor asked the public to send dimes to the White House to support polio research.

Two days after Cantor's initial radio appeal, the White House received 30,000 pieces of mail, virtually all of which had coins taped to the letters. The next day, the White House received 150,000 letters.[60] This is especially impressive when you consider that a dime in the 1930s was the equivalent of $1.27 in today's money. "The March of Dimes had become the most beloved (and richest) charity in the USA with coffers brimming over with totals measured in the millions of dollars," Gomery wrote.[61]

The story did not end with FDR's death on April 12, 1945. On the 10th anniversary of Roosevelt's passing, March of Dimes officials announced that a polio vaccine developed by Dr. Jonas Salk with their support was both safe and effective. As a result, the threat of polio has been virtually eradicated in most of the world.

This grassroots fund-raising effort, which tapped into the generosity of a nation at the height of its worst economic crisis, has had one other lasting imprint. To commemorate Roosevelt's crusade against polio, the U.S Mint began issuing dimes with FDR's image on January 30, 1946, the 64th anniversary of his birth.

DISCUSSION QUESTIONS

1. In your opinion, why was the March of Dimes so successful—especially in the midst of the Great Depression?
2. In hindsight, does Roosevelt's decision to hide his personal disability undermine his credibility as a champion of polio victims?
3. The case mentions the relationship between the charity and partisan politics. What were the benefits and risks of this relationship?
4. At the time of its creation, what made the March of Dimes unique among medical research charities?

CASE STUDY **3.2**

Too Much Blood and Money

Within minutes of the September 11, 2001, terrorist attacks, the American Red Cross was doing what it had done throughout its 120-year history: helping people in need. Who would have imagined that within a few weeks, the nation's largest charity would be rocked by a scandal—all because it may have been *too* successful?

One problem was that the Red Cross had collected too much blood from tens of thousands of donors eager to help the victims. Blood is perishable and has a shelf life of only six weeks. Within the first 48 hours, the nation's blood supply had tripled.[62]

However, it also had become painfully obvious that although approximately 3,000 people had died, very few people were injured and in need of blood.

Jim MacPherson, executive director of America's Blood Center, said, "Even on September 12, the day after the attacks, we called the Red Cross and we said, 'Would you join with us with a message to people that the blood supply is adequate and let's stop the collections right now so we can minimize the wastage.'"[63]

To the dismay of MacPherson and other critics, the Red Cross continued publicizing the need for blood donations. Red Cross official Jerry Squires said the solicitations continued because the future was unpredictable.

"We were hearing that September 11 might not be the end," Squires said. "We really felt that sort of calling a halt to blood donations was probably not the wisest or safest thing to do."[64]

News reports said that directors at several Red Cross blood centers were discarding 20 percent of their donations.[65] Red Cross officials acknowledged that some blood donations could no longer be used for transfusions because the red blood cells had died. But because they were able to use other blood by-products, such as plasma, no donation was wasted.[66]

As difficult as the blood situation was, an even bigger controversy erupted over Red Cross fund-raising. The agency had established a special fund to aid 9/11 victims' families, the Liberty Fund. Within seven weeks of the attacks, it had received an astonishing $547 million in pledges.[67]

By creating the special fund, Red Cross President Bernadine Healy unwittingly sparked a firestorm of criticism. Under normal circumstances, the Red Cross places donations in the National Disaster Fund, a pool of money available to all its chapters. Because the Liberty Fund was separate from the National Disaster Fund, the money was off-limits to local officials.

"My phone has been ringing off the hook with chapters angry about the Liberty Fund," wrote one Red Cross board member. "Creating a separate fund is unacceptable."[68]

Healy also came under fire from victims' families. Less than half of Liberty Fund money collected had gone to the families. Approximately $43.8 million had been dispersed in direct financial aid, with another $66.9 million going to "other immediate disaster relief needs."[69] The families were angered when they learned that the Red Cross planned to set aside more than $300 million for other needs, including a reserve fund for dealing with future terrorist attacks.[70]

"You can't raise the money for purpose A and spend it on purpose B," then-New York State Attorney General Eliot L. Spitzer told Congress. "My patience has run out."[71]

Healy was forced to resign in late October 2001. Red Cross officials ended active solicitation for the Liberty Fund. From that point on, all contributions were directed into the National Disaster Fund unless specifically earmarked for 9/11 victims.[72]

"We are going to try and be good stewards of the money," said interim Red Cross President Harold Decker. "That is what donors expect."[73]

Red Cross officials took other steps to restore public confidence. By mid-November, the organization reversed course and said that all Liberty Fund money would go to victims' families.[74] A month later, they named former U.S. Senator George Mitchell to oversee the payments.[75] After conducting a series of meetings with family members, Mitchell announced a three-part plan to distribute almost all of the remaining funds before the first anniversary of the attacks.

"The Red Cross deserves credit both for acknowledging its mistakes and changing its policies as necessary," Mitchell said. He also praised the agency "for meeting its historic and traditional role to provide emergency relief to thousands of people at a time of real pain, grief, and need."[76]

The Red Cross changed its advertising and public solicitation policies in June 2002. In doing so, the organization acknowledged that it had not clearly explained to donors that money collected for a local disaster could be used anywhere in the country.[77] The new program was called Donor DIRECT, or Donor Intent REcognition, Confirmation and Trust. Under it, the Red Cross asks donors to confirm the purpose of their donations.[78]

The Charities Review Council, an industry watchdog, concluded that although the Red Cross was well prepared to address the consequences of the September 11 attack, "by deviating from its traditional policies, it entered uncharted seas." The CRC concluded, "The Red Cross did the right thing by reversing course and openly admitting mistakes."[79]

DISCUSSION QUESTIONS

1. With concerns about the danger of future terrorist attacks, were Red Cross officials wrong to withhold some donations for future use?
2. Were local Red Cross chapter officials justified in their concerns about the creation of the Liberty Fund?
3. What could the Red Cross have done differently to avoid these controversies?
4. What steps did the Red Cross take to restore its credibility? Were they enough to do the job?

NOTES

1. Jacquie L'Etang, "State Propaganda and Bureaucratic Intelligence: The Creation of Public Relations in 20th Century Britain," *Public Relations Review* (winter 1998): 413.
2. L'Etang.
3. Gary A. Warner, "The Development of Public Relations Offices at American Colleges and Universities," *Public Relations Quarterly* (summer 1996): 36.
4. Sherman Morse, "An Awakening in Wall Street: How Trusts, after Years of Silence, Now Speak through Authorized and Acknowledged Press Agents," *The American Magazine* 63 (September 1906), as cited by "Teaching PR," Grady College of Journalism, University of Georgia, online, http://teachingpr.blogspot.com/2006/09/100th-anniversary-of-declaration-of.html.

5. Norman Foerster, Norman S. Grabo, Russel B. Nye, E. Fred Carlisle, and Robert Falk, eds., *American Poetry and Prose, Fifth Edition/Part One* (New York: Houghton Mifflin, 1970), 139.

6. Foerster et al., 139.

7. *The Constitution of the United States and the Declaration of Independence* (Washington, D.C.: Commission on the Bicentennial of the United States Constitution, 1992), 35.

8. Jason Karpf, "Adams, Paine and Jefferson: A PR Firm," *Public Relations Tactics,* January 2004, 12–13.

9. Foerster et al., 146 (emphasis in original).

10. Andy Dougan, "Smokey and the Bandit," *Evening Times* (Glasgow), 15 June 2006, 4, via LexisNexis.

11. Edward L. Bernays, *Biography of an Idea: Memoirs of Public Relations Counsel Edward L. Bernays* (New York: Simon & Schuster, 1965), 387.

12. John Stauber and Sheldon Rampton, "How the American Tobacco Industry Employs PR Scum to Continue Its Murderous Assault on Human Lives," *Tucson Weekly,* 22 November 1995.

13. "States' Attorneys Are Weighing Whether to Sign Deal," The Associated Press, as reported in *The Kansas City Star,* 18 November 1998, A4.

14. Frances A. Stillman et al., "Evaluation of the American Stop Smoking Intervention Study (ASSIST): A Report of Outcomes," *Journal of the National Cancer Institute* 95, no. 22 (19 November 2003) 1681–1691.

15. Karpf, 13.

16. Kevin Stoker and Brad L. Rawlins, "The 'Light' of Publicity in the Progressive Era— From Searchlight to Flashlight," *Journalism History* 30, no. 4 (winter 2005): 117.

17. Scott M. Cutlip, *The Unseen Power: Public Relations: A History* (Hillsdale, N.J.: Lawrence Erlbaum, 1994), 1.

18. Cutlip, 10–25.

19. Fred Fedler and Denise DeLorme, "Journalists' Hostility Toward Public Relations: A Historical Analysis," paper presented at the Association for Education in Journalism and Mass Communication annual conference, Miami, Fla., August 2002.

20. Blaire Atherton French, *The Presidential Press Conference: Its History and Role in the American Political System* (Lanham, Md.: University Press of America, 1982), 3.

21. Carolyn Smith, *Presidential Press Conferences: A Critical Approach* (New York: Praeger, 1990), 22.

22. Cutlip, 37–45.

23. Cutlip, 45.

24. Cutlip, 139.

25. Thomas Flemming, "When the United States Entered World War I, Propagandist George Creel Set Out to Stifle Anti-War Sentiment," *Military History,* The History Net, online, www.thehistorynet.com.

26. Charles A. Lubbers, "George Creel and the Four-Minute Men: A Milestone in Public Relations History," *Business Research Yearbook: Global Business Perspectives,* vol. III (New York: International Academy of Business Disciplines, 1996), 719.

27. Flemming.

28. "The Scopes Monkey Trial," Court TV Online, www.courttv.com/archive/greatesttrials/ scopes.

29. "People & Events: The Site of the Trial: Dayton, Tennessee," *American Experience: Monkey Trial,* online, www.pbs.org/wgbh/amex/monkeytrial/index.html.

30. "The Scopes Monkey Trial."

31. Edward Caudill, *The Scopes Trial: A Photographic History* (Knoxville: University of Tennessee Press, 2000), 5–6.

32. Caudill, 6.

33. H. L. Mencken, "The Monkey Trial: A Reporter's Account," *Baltimore Sun,* 9 July 1925, online at "Famous Trials in American History: *Tennessee v. John Scopes,*" University of Missouri–Kansas City Law School, www.law.umkc.edu/faculty/projects/ ftrials/scopes/scopes.htm.

34. Caudill, 18–19.

35. Bernays, 161.

36. Bernays, 177–178.

37. Bernays, 288.

38. Kathleen O'Neill, "U.S. Public Relations Evolves to Meet Society's Needs," *Public Relations Journal,* November 1991, 28.

39. Bernays, 218.

40. Susan Henry, "Anonymous in Her Own Name: Public Relations Pioneer Doris Fleischman," *Journalism History* 23, no. 2 (summer 1997): 52.

41. Bernays, 217.

42. Bernays, 216.

43. Cutlip, 169–170.

44. Cutlip, 170.

45. Cutlip, 159–225.

46. Alvin M. Hattal, "The Father of Public Relations: Edward L. Bernays," *Communication World,* January 1992, 15.

47. Cutlip, 528.

48. Karla K. Gower and Margot Opdycke Lamme, "Public Relations on Trial—'The Railroad-Truckers Brawl,'" *Journalism History* 29, no. 1 (spring 2003): 12–20.

49. Patrick Jackson and Allen H. Center, *Public Relations Practices: Managerial Case Studies and Problems,* 5th ed. (Englewood Cliffs, N.J.: Prentice Hall, 1995), 167–178.

50. Edward A. Grefe and Martin Linsky, *The New Corporate Activism* (New York: McGraw-Hill, 1995), 3 (emphasis in original).

51. Robert W. Kinkead and Dena Winokur, "How Public Relations Professionals Help CEOs Make the Right Moves," *Public Relations Journal,* October 1992, 18–23.

52. John Spano, "Douglas Dowie's Lawyers Seek to Get His Ex-Employer to Pay His Legal Bill," *Los Angeles Times,* 3 October 2006, B3.

53. Gail Chiasson, "Advertising Scandal Fells Canadian government," *Advertising Age,* 5 December 2005, 81.

54. "Franklin Roosevelt Founds March of Dimes—January 3: This Date in History," the History Channel, online, www.historychannel.com/tdih.

55. "The March of Dimes Story," March of Dimes, online, www.marchofdimes.com.

56. Douglas Gomery, "Health Politics and Movie Power," *Historical Journal of Film, Radio and Television* 15, no. 1 (1995): 127–128.

57. William H. Helfand, Jan Lazarus, and Paul Theerman, " '. . . So That Others May Walk': The March of Dimes," *American Journal of Public Health,* 1 February 2002: 158.

58. Gomery, 128.

59. Gomery, 131.

60. Gomery, 131.

61. Gomery, 132.

62. Transcript, *NewsHour with Jim Lehrer,* 19 December 2001, online, www.pbs.org. newshour.

63. Transcript, *NewsHour with Jim Lehrer.*

64. Transcript, *NewsHour with Jim Lehrer.*

65. Transcript, *NewsHour with Jim Lehrer.*

66. "Red Cross Head Steps Down," CBS News, 26 October 2001, online, www.cbsnews.com.

67. "Liberty Fund Closes Up Shop," CBS News, 30 October 2001, online, www.cbsnews .com.

68. Sharyl Attkisson, "Financial Irregularities at the Red Cross," *CBS Evening News,* 31 July 2002, online, LexisNexis.

69. "Red Cross Closes Liberty Fund, Names Interim Head," CNN, 30 October 2001, online, www.cnn.com.

70. "Defending the Liberty Fund," CBS News, 6 November 2001, online, www.cbsnews.com.

71. Ian Wilhelm, "NY Attorney General Weighs Legal Action Against American Red Cross," *The Chronicle of Philanthropy,* 8 November 2001, online update, http:// philanthropy.com.

72. "Liberty Fund Closes Up Shop."

73. "Liberty Fund Closes Up Shop."

74. "Red Cross: Victims Will Get All Liberty Fund Monies," CNN, 14 November 2001, online, www.cnn.com.

75. "Former Senate Leader to Oversee Red Cross Fund," CNN, 27 December 2001, online, www.cnn.com.

76. "Red Cross Unveils Plan for September 11 Funds," CNN, 31 January 2002, online, www.cnn.com.

77. Lena H. Sun, "At 'Turning Point,' Red Cross Picks Chief; New President Says the Organization Needs to Build Trust," *Washington Post,* 28 June 2002, A02, online, LexisNexis.

78. Paul Barbagallo, *Target Marketing* 25, no. 8 (August 2002): 15–16, online, LexisNexis.

79. "September 11: The Philanthropic Response," Charities Review Council, online, www.crcmn.org/donorinfo/disaster.htm.

CHAPTER

4

The Publics
in Public Relations

OBJECTIVES

After studying this chapter, you will be able to

- define the term *public* as it is used in public relations

- name and describe the different kinds of publics

- list the kinds of information that practitioners should gather about each public

- identify and describe the traditional publics in public relations

Pop Goes Your Wednesday

Wednesday starts peacefully at the Kablooie Microwave Popcorn Company, where you are director of public relations. You are planning to spend the morning getting ready for next week's annual meeting of stockholders. Kablooie is a new company, and you are eager to tell stockholders about its recently completed Statement of Values, which begins with these words: "Kablooie Microwave Popcorn Company exists to provide value at a fair price to its customers; to provide a competitive return on investment to its stockholders; and to provide a humane workplace and fair salaries and benefits to its employees."

Then:

- *Your assistant tells you his 13-year-old daughter just telephoned. A new online video shows Kablooie Microwave Popcorn blowing the doors off microwave ovens and injuring teens. One comment posted with the video says that a popular rock star has been hospitalized in critical condition after being injured by a Kablooie explosion. In other comments, kids are telling one another to boycott your product.*

- *Your assistant is still talking when a reporter from your local newspaper calls to ask about the rumor that Kablooie Microwave Popcorn is exploding in microwave ovens and injuring people. You emphatically deny the rumor and promise to call back in 15 minutes.*

- *A beep from your computer tells you that a new e-mail message has arrived. It's from a nationally known investment analyst, asking whether there are any new issues you're expecting to deal with at next week's annual meeting for stockholders. Evidently, she hasn't yet heard about the online video.*

- *Your secretary brings you a letter from a local Boy Scout troop. In two days the troop will begin selling your product door to door as a fund-raising project. The letter is thanking you for the early delivery of 10,000 packages of Kablooie Microwave Popcorn.*

You immediately decide to implement your company's crisis communications plan (see Chapter 12). Like all good public relations plans, it asks you to identify the most important publics with whom you must communicate.

In this scenario, who are your publics? Which are the most important? Can the new Statement of Values help?

What Is a Public?

Public relations. That's what we call this challenging, rewarding business.

Take a good look at that first word: **public.** That's where we start. Publics are literally the first word in our profession.

So what is a public? As you may recall from Chapter 1, a public is any group whose members have a common interest or common values in a particular situation. A political party can be a public. Upper-level managers in a corporation can be a public. Fans of a popular music group can be a public.

The word *stakeholder* often substitutes for the word *public,* but the two words aren't interchangeable. Some publics may have no connection with the organization that a public relations practitioner represents. But as we note in Chapter 1, a **stakeholder,** or stakeholder group, has a stake, or an interest, in an organization or issue that potentially involves the organization. For any given organization, then, all stakeholder groups are publics—but not all publics are stakeholders.

Counting all the publics even in just the United States would be like trying to count the stars—an impossible task. So which publics matter in public relations? With which publics do we build and manage values-driven relationships? Certain publics become important to an organization as its values and values-based goals interact with the environment. Those publics become stakeholders. For example, to fulfill its values-driven goal of healing people, a nonprofit hospital must have a good relationship with the community's physicians. The hospital's values somehow must fit comfortably with the values of the physicians if this vital relationship is to work.

Another example: To fulfill its goal of being a clean, attractive facility, that same hospital must have a good relationship with its custodians. The hospital needs to understand the values of the custodians—such as fair wages—to make that relationship work. As an organization's values interact with the values of different publics, relationships—good or bad—are born. In fact, if we know the specific values-driven goals of an organization and we know the environment in which it operates, we can predict with some accuracy the essential relationships that can help the organization attain its goals.

Sometimes, however, a relationship surprises an organization. A public in the organization's environment can discover a relationship before the organization does. Often, a clash of values triggers that unexpected relationship. For example, a Midwestern county government trying to build a highway around a growing metropolitan area was surprised when Native Americans strongly opposed the proposed route. The highway passed too near, they said, to an area they used for worship. A values-driven goal of the county government—easing traffic congestion within the metropolitan area—had clashed with a religious value of Native Americans in the area. As one values system met another, a relationship was born.

Why Do We Need Relationships with Publics?

Now, what about that second word in public relations: *relations*? Why do organizations build and maintain values-driven relationships with a variety of publics? (We're glad that they do: The relationship-management process provides interesting, rewarding jobs for thousands of public relations practitioners.) But, again, it's worth asking: Why do organizations need relationships with different publics? An excellent answer to this question comes from **resource dependency theory,**[1] which consists of three simple beliefs:

1. To fulfill their values, organizations need resources, such as raw materials and people to work for the organization.
2. Some of those key resources are *not* controlled by the organization.
3. To acquire those key resources, organizations must build productive relationships with the publics that control the resources.

Resource dependency theory tells us that, first and foremost, public relations practitioners must build relationships with publics that possess resources organizations need to fulfill their values-driven goals.

Resource dependency theory can even help us determine which publics will receive most of our relationship-management efforts. Clearly, our most important publics are those that possess the resources our organization needs the most. For example, Pitney Bowes, an international message-management company, focuses on resource dependency theory in the first sentence of its values statement: "Pitney Bowes' relationships with our four constituent groups—customers, employees, stockholders, and the communities—are critical to our success and reputation."[2] In public relations, we build relationships with publics to secure the resources our organizations need to survive and fulfill their values.

Resource dependency theory, therefore, helps explain values-driven public relations. As we describe in Chapter 1, values-driven public relations brings the entire public relations process—research, planning, communication, and evaluation—into a framework defined by an organization's core values. In the planning phase, practitioners establish values-driven public relations goals. To reach those goals, practitioners often must acquire resources held by other publics; this is where resource dependency theory meets values-driven public relations. If our goals are values-driven, the resources we acquire from targeted publics bring our organization closer to fulfilling its values.

Resource dependency theory also helps explain the two-way symmetrical model, the most successful of the four models of public relations (see Chapter 1). Two-way symmetrical public relations works best when there is an exchange of resources. If an organization wants to acquire the resources it needs, it must be willing to give the resource holders something they need. For example, news media have resources most organizations need, including fair and accurate coverage. In return, those organizations have resources news media need, including a willingness to respond to journalists' questions promptly and honestly. In a two-way symmetrical relationship, an organization agrees to exchange resources to fulfill its values-driven goals.

The Publics in Public Relations

Publics may be as impossible to count as the stars, but, like the stars, they can be grouped into categories, including

- traditional and nontraditional publics
- latent, aware, and active publics

■ intervening publics

■ primary and secondary publics

■ internal and external publics

■ domestic and international publics

Why bother to group publics into categories? Because knowing which category or categories a public belongs to can provide insight into how to build a productive relationship with it. The thoughtful process of deciding which category or categories a public belongs to can help us learn from our own experiences as well as those of others. So let's examine these categories.

Traditional and Nontraditional Publics

Traditional publics are groups with which organizations have ongoing, long-term relationships. As shown in Figure 4.1, traditional publics include employees, news media, governments, investors, customers, multicultural community groups, and constituents (voters). The fact that these publics are traditional, however, doesn't mean that public relations practitioners can take them for granted. Organizations that ignore the values of employees or of the news media, for example, quickly learn to their sorrow how powerful those publics can be. In Pop Goes Your Wednesday, the scenario that opens this chapter, the investment analyst who e-mails you with a request for information represents a traditional public.

Nontraditional publics are groups that usually are unfamiliar to an organization. For example, in Pop Goes Your Wednesday, the high-tech teenagers constitute a nontraditional public—a group with which Kablooie hasn't had an ongoing, long-term relationship. Nontraditional publics can be hard to study and may lead you to try some innovative relationship-building strategies. Nontraditional publics are often sparked by changes in a society—such as the growth of instant messaging and related technologies.

Nontraditional publics can be new and challenging, but it's possible that one day they'll become traditional publics. For example, women from an impoverished fishing village in Nigeria shut down a nearby ChevronTexaco oil terminal by entering the facility and refusing to leave. They wanted the corporation to help them improve living conditions in the village. In ensuing negotiations, cultures collided as corporate leaders met with village leaders—but a relationship emerged. "We are friends forever," said a satisfied leader of the protesters.[3]

Closer to home, the gradual evolution of gay and lesbian publics from nontraditional to increasingly traditional publics was illustrated by a controversy that embroiled *Grey's Anatomy*, a popular television show. When actor Isaiah Washington used an unflattering term to describe the sexual orientation of a fellow cast member, it was Washington, not his coworker, who suddenly became persona non grata.[4] Washington announced that he would seek counseling in a rehabilitation center,[5] and he filmed a television public service announcement in which he declared, "We have the power to heal and change the world by the words we use."[6] Ultimately, however, Washington's contract with *Grey's Anatomy* was not renewed.

FIGURE 4.1 Traditional Publics in Public Relations
A for-profit organization can have dozens of primary publics. Not pictured in this diagram is the most important public for government public relations practitioners: constituents and voters.

In corporate America, United Airlines, Saturn automobiles, and the San Diego Padres baseball team are among organizations that openly market to gay and lesbian consumers. Other organizations, such as the Walt Disney Company, have extended insurance benefits to the life partners of gay and lesbian employees.[7] But boycotts of Disney products by groups including the Southern Baptist Convention, Focus on the Family, and the American Family Association showed that the terms *traditional* and *nontraditional* are relative.[8] One organization's traditional public can be nontraditional to another.

Latent, Aware, and Active Publics

Public relations scholars often categorize publics as *latent, aware,* or *active.*[9] A **latent public** is a group whose values have come into contact with the values of your organization, but whose members haven't yet realized it; the members of that public

Congresswoman Kay Granger of Texas addresses the Log Cabin Republicans, the nation's largest organization of gay and lesbian Republicans. In presidential elections, the Log Cabin Republicans have been a traditional public for some, a nontraditional public for others. (Courtesy of Log Cabin Republicans)

are not yet aware of the relationship. An **aware public** is a group whose members are aware of the intersection of their values with those of your organization but haven't organized any kind of response to the relationship. An **active public,** however, not only recognizes the relationship between itself and your organization but is also working to manage that relationship on its own terms. In Pop Goes Your Wednesday, the teenagers watching and commenting on the online video are more than just a nontraditional public; they're also an active public.

Intervening Publics

Let's say that in our Kablooie Microwave Popcorn scenario, you wisely keep your promise to the local newspaper reporter who telephoned. You call her back in 15 minutes and report that you've checked with the top five manufacturers of microwave ovens, and none are reporting problems with Kablooie popcorn. In fact, they've said that such a defect in their ovens is impossible. You give the reporter the names of the public relations officials for those manufacturers, and you e-mail her a statement from Kablooie's chief executive officer in which he denies the rumors. You even invite her to come tour your factory's quality-control department.

Why spend so much time with one reporter? You know the answer to that: because she has thousands of local readers to whom you want to send the message that Kablooie popcorn is safe. In public relations, any public that helps you send a message to another public is called an **intervening public.** In the Kablooie scenario, one of your most important publics consists of the people of Kablooie Microwave Popcorn's hometown; they're a high-priority public that you're targeting with a specific message to maintain the good relationship between Kablooie and its hometown. If the local newspaper can help you send that message, it is an intervening public.

Primary and Secondary Publics

Publics can also be divided into primary publics and secondary publics. If a public can directly affect your organization's pursuit of its values-driven goals—if it possesses resources that you must have—that public is definitely a **primary public,** a public of great importance. **Secondary publics** are also important. You want to have a good relationship with them—but their ability to affect your organization's pursuit of its goals is minimal. Because resources such as time and money are scarce, public relations practitioners spend most of their time building and managing relationships with primary publics. If resources permit, they also build and manage relationships with secondary publics.

In Pop Goes Your Wednesday, your company's investors are a primary public; your Statement of Values emphasizes that fact. A bad relationship with investors and the people who advise them could immediately and seriously harm the financial security of Kablooie. In this scenario, a secondary public would be local stores that sell microwave ovens. Because they might have to field a few questions, you might telephone them—if time permits. But you wisely decide first to devote your attention to the primary publics that can influence the success of Kablooie Microwave Popcorn.

Internal and External Publics

Publics are either **internal publics** or **external publics;** that is, either they're inside your organization or outside it. Kablooie's employees are an internal public—as well as a primary public. You'd be smart to inform them of the rumors so that they're not surprised by reports in the news media or by inquisitive friends and neighbors. External publics would include investment analysts, news media, the Boy Scouts, and the online teenagers.

Sometimes, however, the line between internal and external isn't clearly drawn. For example, the alumni of your college or university technically are an external public; they're no longer enrolled, and most have probably moved away. But many of them don't *feel* external—to their dying day, they will be Jayhawks or Tarheels or Longhorns or Terrapins or whatever mascot brings a tear of pride to their eyes. Smart public relations practitioners identify such feelings and, when appropriate, treat such a public as a member of the organization's family. Although the Kablooie Microwave Popcorn Company is a new organization, imagine it 30 years from now. Will its loyal retired employees feel like an internal or an external public?

Domestic and International Publics

Last but not least, publics are either domestic publics or international publics. **Domestic publics** are those within your own country. But proximity doesn't necessarily mean familiarity. As we saw previously, some domestic publics can be nontraditional publics, requiring effective cross-cultural communication efforts.

International publics are those beyond your country's borders. Increasingly, public relations practitioners are dealing with international publics. For example, suppose that the factory that supplies the packages for Kablooie popcorn is in Mexico.

Your Tax Dollars at Work

As you're reading this sentence, the federal government of the United States is collecting information about you, your friends, your family—and millions of other Americans.

Sounds scary, right? But that storehouse of information can be incredibly useful to public relations practitioners. Even better, much of the information is online and can be easily accessed at FedStats (www.fedstats.gov).

Need the ethnic makeup of your county? Try the Bureau of the Census. You can reach it through FedStats.

Need employment projections for the coming decades? Try the Bureau of Labor Statistics. You can reach it through FedStats.

Need data on farmers? Try the National Agricultural Statistics Service. On older Americans? Try the Administration on Aging. On prisoners? Try the Federal Bureau of Prisons.

FedStats can connect you to dozens of federal agencies that gather information on the publics that make up public relations. As a taxpayer, you're footing the bill for all those studies, so get your money's worth: Bookmark FedStats for your web browser.

A variety of cross-cultural considerations now confront you. Do you speak Spanish? Does the factory manager there speak English? If your crisis has occurred on May 5 or September 16, will the factory manager answer a telephone call to his or her office? Probably not: Those days are national holidays in Mexico.

The lines between domestic and international publics also can blur. Perhaps Kablooie has plans for international distribution using a company based in the United States but with worldwide operations. Certainly consumers of the popcorn would include both domestic and international publics.

What Do We Need to Know about Each Public?

No two publics are the same. And yet the kinds of information we need to gather about each public are remarkably similar. To manage a productive, values-driven relationship with a public, we must be able to answer seven questions about it:

1. *How much can the public influence our organization's ability to achieve our goals?* How dependent is our organization on the resources controlled by this public? In other words, is the public a primary public or a secondary public? As much as public relations practitioners would like to have positive, well-maintained relationships with every public, that ideal is simply too impractical; it would stretch their resources too thin. Public relations practitioners must focus most of their attention and efforts on the relationships that spell the difference between success and failure for their organizations.

2. *What is the public's stake, or value, in its relationship with our organization?* As we noted earlier, a relationship between a public and an organization is born when values intersect. What values does the public hold that have brought it into contact with your organization? For example, investors value steady increases in the price of the stock they own. Customers value getting their money's worth. Employees value, among other things, interesting work and good salaries.

Identifying the value or values a public seeks to realize in its relationship with your organization is one of the most important things you can do in public relations. It allows you to explore the possibility of a relationship in which both sides win: The public's values can be recognized and honored, and your organization can achieve its goal for the relationship. That's the heart of values-driven public relations.

3. *Who are the opinion leaders and decision makers for the public?* Members of a public turn to **opinion leaders** for advice and leadership. Stockholders, for example, often turn to successful investment analysts for advice. Employees may turn to union leaders or trusted supervisors. If we can identify the opinion leaders of a public, perhaps we can build a relationship with them that will strengthen our relationship with the entire public.

Not every public has well-defined, easily identifiable opinion leaders, however. For example, in the scenario that opens this chapter, who are the opinion leaders for the millions of teenagers using instant messaging? That particular public is so large that we might be wise to divide it into smaller publics—based on geography or on the particular chat rooms the teenagers frequent—and look for opinion leaders of those smaller groups.

Decision makers are people who have the authority to dictate actions and establish policies for publics. Some publics have easily identifiable decision makers. For example, decision makers for news media are the editors, publishers, directors, and producers who oversee the content of newspapers, magazines, radio programs, television programs, or web sites. The decision maker of a local environmental group probably would be the group's president or board of directors—though any important decision might involve a vote among members. Decision makers can be determined by the goal your organization is trying to achieve. For example, when a company wants to build a new factory, one set of decision makers from which it needs approval may be a local zoning board.

Some publics, however, don't have easily identifiable decision makers. Latent publics or aware publics (as opposed to active publics) may be only loosely organized at best. For example, suppose your organization wants to improve its relationship with local alternative rock musicians. Who are the decision makers for that diverse group—or for the online teenagers? Perhaps the best we can do is to point to opinion leaders for our targeted public.

Even within a single, well-defined public, opinion leaders and decision makers can vary, depending on the issue. For example, a local taxpayers group may have one opinion leader for issues involving sales taxes but a different opinion leader for property tax issues. And on simple matters such as scheduling meetings, the president of the group may be the decision maker. But on more important decisions, such as organizing a protest at City Hall, the board of directors may have to call for a vote among members.

Despite the difficulties, public relations practitioners seek to identify and to build relationships with decision makers and opinion leaders because they often have influence over publics that may be essential to an organization's success.

4. *What is the demographic profile of the public?* **Demographic information** is data about who a public is. For example, besides telling us how many members a public has, a demographic profile of a public might include information about age, gender, income, education, and number of children per family. For each of these characteristics, we would probably want medians and ranges. For example, we probably would like to know the median age of an important public (the age that represents a halfway point, with half the public younger and half the public older than the median age). The range of ages would specify the age of the youngest member of the public as well as the age of its oldest member. Demographic information can help us understand who a public is, how important that public might be to our organization, and what its values might be.

In our Kablooie Microwave Popcorn scenario, we might consider grocery-store chains that carry our product to be a public. Although demographic characteristics such as age and gender might not influence our communications with that large public, we certainly might rank the members of that public by how much Kablooie Microwave Popcorn each company purchases for resale. That information could help us subdivide our grocery-store chain public into smaller publics and provide direction on which chains we might choose to contact first.

5. *What is the psychographic profile of the public?* **Psychographic information** is data about what members of a public think, believe, and feel. For example, are they politically liberal, moderate, or conservative? Are they religious? Agnostic? Atheistic? Do they like sophisticated technology or fear it—or, perhaps, are they indifferent to it? Psychographic information can be harder to collect and measure than demographic information, but it's no less important. Like demographic information, a psychographic profile can help us understand who a public is and what its values might be.

6. *What is the public's opinion of our organization?* Any television sitcom about high school students eventually has a scene in which one student wants to date another and is desperately trying to find out that person's opinion of him or her. It's the same in public relations, though perhaps a little less stressful. A public's opinion of our organization is one of the foundations of our relationship. That opinion tells us whether we approach the relationship as friends, unknowns, or enemies. It would be an embarrassing waste of resources, for example, to create a communications program for a public that we think is hostile—only to discover that that public has a favorable impression of us and is puzzled by our actions.

7. *What is the public's opinion (if any) of the issue in question?* As we've noted before, sometimes a particular issue creates a relationship between an organization and a public. For example, the false stories about Kablooie Microwave Popcorn have suddenly created a relationship between Kablooie and teenagers who post and comment on online videos. We need to learn what the public thinks about the issue; in particular, we need to know which of the public's values are supported or threatened by the issue.

Coorientation

Coorientation is a public relations research process that can help us discover where our organization agrees and disagrees with an important public on a particular issue. Coorientation can eliminate damaging misperceptions about what each side believes. Scholar James Grunig says that coorientation is the "parent" of the two-way symmetrical model of public relations.[10] As you'll see, coorientation can get a little like the comedy routine in which one actor says, "I think that you think that I think. . . ." In part, coorientation involves asking these four questions:

1. What is our organization's view of this issue?
2. What is the particular public's view of this issue?
3. What does our organization *think* the public's view is? (Does this agree with reality?)
4. What does the particular public *think* our organization's view is? (Does this agree with reality?)

Let's apply these four basic questions of coorientation to a portion of our Kablooie popcorn scenario:

1. Our view of the situation is that the video and rumors are provably false—but we're concerned that the rumors could influence investment analysts.
2. Quick research on our part shows that investment analysts aren't worried at all. They've encountered such rumors before, and they're laughing. They still like our stock.
3. More research shows that our organization's leaders believe investment analysts are troubled by the rumors. Our CEO has asked us to initiate an emergency webcast for the analysts. (Our management team's opinion clashes with reality.)
4. Our research has shown that investment analysts don't think our organization is worried. (That's wrong, but perhaps we can learn from it.)

To honor our CEO's request, we may want to develop a ready-if-needed plan for a webcast—but in the Kablooie case, coorientation can help keep our organization from overreacting to the crisis. Letting the analysts laugh may be our best option. Using coorientation to discover the perceptions and misperceptions of two different publics can help public relations practitioners manage the relationship effectively.

As we said in Chapter 1, the public relations process begins with research. Answering, to the best of our ability, the seven questions listed above is one of the most important parts of public relations research.

QUICK CHECK

1. In public relations, what is the definition of the word *public*? Of *stakeholder*?
2. What differences separate latent, aware, and active publics?
3. What are the differences between demographic information and psychographic information?
4. What is resource dependency theory?
5. What is coorientation?

The Traditional Publics in Public Relations

Earlier in this chapter we introduced the term *traditional publics*—that is, publics with which organizations have long-term, ongoing relationships. As we noted, *traditional* can be a misleading word. A group that is a traditional public for one organization might be a nontraditional public for another. Many organizations, however, do have long-term relationships with well-established traditional publics, including employees, the news media, governments, investors, consumers, multicultural community groups, constituents (voters), and businesses. In the next several pages, we'll offer brief descriptions of those publics—and, because they change every day, we'll also offer sources you can consult to update your knowledge of these important publics in public relations.

Employees

As the old joke goes, we have good news and bad news. The good news is that a recent worldwide survey of organization managers shows that they understand the importance of effective employee communication. So what's the bad news? More than 60 percent confess a lack of success in their efforts to communicate basic organizational strategies to their employees.[11] And as organizations become increasingly decentralized through telecommuting and globalization, their leaders say that their greatest challenge is building "a common corporate culture" through communication.[12]

Employees often are the most important publics in public relations. Think about it: If your organization's employees aren't on your side, it doesn't matter how good your

---

Employee Publics: FAQs

1. **What resources do employees have that their organizations need?**
   Primarily commitment. Organizations with committed employees have greater innovation, reduced absenteeism, and significantly greater profits.

2. **What are the greatest challenges to building successful relationships with employees?**
   Poor communication breeds distrust and low morale. Employee publics are more diverse than ever. New communications technologies are replacing face-to-face communication.

3. **Where can I find more information on employee publics?**
   - *Communication World* magazine, published by the International Association of Business Communicators
   - U.S. Bureau of Labor Statistics, online at www.bls.gov
   - Society for Human Resource Management, online at www.shrm.org

The low point of employee relations can be an employee strike. When wage and benefits negotiations between Columbia University and its graduate student teachers broke down, the students went on a five-day strike. (Photo by Librado Romero/*New York Times*. Copyright 2005 The New York Times Company. Reprinted with permission.)

relationships with other publics are. So it's good news that organizations are focusing on this key public. But the challenge of building good relationships with employees has never been greater. Employee publics are changing so rapidly that relationship management can seem like building a car while you're driving it. And yet the stakes are huge: Research indicates that companies with good employee relations return three times more value to stockholders than companies with poor employee relations.[13]

What changes are reshaping the employee public? Management consultant Robert Barner identifies five:[14]

1. *A distributed workforce:* Employees are scattering. Some work at home and communicate with the office through e-mail, instant messaging, and other electronic means. Others work at sites around the world as organizations continue to expand internationally. For generations, studies have shown that employees prefer to get important information about their organizations through face-to-face meetings with their supervisors.[15] Offering that "face time" will become more and more difficult.

Ironically, several important workplace innovations can undermine face-to-face communication. A worldwide survey found that flexible work hours were a popular benefit, preferred by more than 40 percent of employees.[16] But those nonstandard hours can mean less face time with supervisors. Electronic messages also can reduce the crucial personal element in successful employee communication. "The pervasiveness of e-mail and voice mail makes it more important than ever to make time

QUICKBREAK 4.2

Sabotage in the Workplace

Sabotage in the American Workplace: That's the name of a book that caught the public's eye in 1992 with its amazing tales of the destruction committed by bored, unhappy, uninformed employees.[17]

Take Ron, for example, who worked at a well-known chain of toy stores. The job was boring, he said, but he found ways to liven things up for himself and his coworkers:

> One Christmas the store had a Barbie doll house on display. Every night I would create a different scene by dressing the dolls up in strange outfits and setting them in unusual situations. One time I dressed the Ken doll in a clown outfit, tied Barbie against a balcony, and set Ken up so he was whipping her.

And let's not forget Reggie, who worked in the mailroom of a well-known, politically conservative think tank. Reggie was hired without any kind of ori-

entation program, and when he discovered that the think tank's politics were at odds with his own, he—well, let him tell the story:

> People would mail in checks. . . . So I started randomly taking envelopes, opening them, and throwing the checks in the shredder. I started doing it more and more. I could tell if it was a check by holding it up to the light. If it was, I'd toss it or shred it.

Ron and Reggie make a powerful case that values-driven public relations begins with good employee relations. No organization can maintain productive, long-term relationships with important publics if it is crumbling from within. An informed, committed, and respected workforce provides a solid base for all the relationships that an organization must build.

for face-to-face communication in order to maintain morale," says Donald Ness, of RHI Management Resources in Canada.[18]

2. *The increasing use of temps:* Temporary workers have been one of the fastest-growing sectors of the U.S. workforce in the past 15 years. In 1990, temporary staffing agencies supplied just under 1 million workers to the U.S. workforce. By 2006, that number had almost tripled to 2.6 million.[19] "Companies increasingly divide their workforces into a core group of permanent, well-paid employees surrounded by less-skilled, lower-wage workers who can be brought in and sent away as demand fluctuates," concluded the *New York Times.*[20] How will organizations build productive relationships with a workforce that increasingly consists of "here today, gone tomorrow" employees?

3. *The growth of information managers:* A generation ago, most workers built products. Today, a rapidly growing percentage of employees manage information—and they need sophisticated technology to do so. As that technology changes literally from day to day, employees will need continuing education throughout their careers. The American Society for Training and Development (ASTD) reported in 2007 that the nation's top companies were annually spending more than $1,400 per employee on training, for a total of over $1.9 billion.[21] Not surprisingly, ASTD research shows a strong correlation between employee training and financial success.[22] "Those leaders who understand how to drive business results in an increasingly competitive, global environment recognize that a better-trained workforce improves performance," said Ray Rivera, director of ASTD's Workplace Learning and Performance Scorecard.[23]

4. *The growth of diversity:* The U.S. Bureau of Labor Statistics estimates that by 2014, 65.6 percent of the U.S. workforce will be non-Hispanic white employees, down from 70 percent in 2004. Employees from other ethnic groups will increase as a percentage of the workforce: Hispanic employees to 15.9 percent; black employees to 12 percent; and Asian American employees to 5.1 percent. By 2014, female employees will constitute 46.8 percent of the workforce, up from 46.4 in 2004.[24] "Among the factors affecting the composition and growth of the labor force over the next 50 years are the aging of the baby-boom generation, the stabilization of women's labor force participation rates, and increasing racial and ethnic diversity in the workforce," reports the Bureau of Labor Statistics.[25]

5. *The aging of the baby boomers:* As baby boomers near retirement, workers 55 and older will jump to 21.2 percent of the workforce by 2014, up from 15.6 percent in 2004. As fewer workers seek early-retirement options, organizations will need new strategies for motivating and training an aging workforce.[26]

We would add one more significant change shaping the new workforce: the impact of employees from Generation X (born 1961 to 1979) and Generation Y (born 1980 to 1994). Employers have gradually learned that different generations have different motivations in the workplace. *Sales & Marketing Management* magazine offers this analysis of generational differences:[27]

- Employees in their 20s want challenging assignments, new responsibilities, and ample continuing education opportunities. They dislike low-tech environments.
- Employees in their 30s want an entrepreneurial and creative environment. They dislike hearing "no" to new ideas.
- Employees in their 40s want time away from work but, still, a chance to shine in the office. They dislike taking orders.
- Employees 50 and older want to mentor younger employees, though they still want learning opportunities. They dislike being considered old.

Communication will continue to be the key to building successful relationships with diverse and changing employee publics. And that brings us back to coorientation. If we understand employees' values regarding the workplace—not just what we think those values may be—we have a basis for relationship building. A survey of more than 4,000 employees in 21 nations revealed their top workplace values: challenging and interesting work; recognition and rewards for accomplishment; opportunity for rapid growth and advancement; a financially strong and stable employer; and an employer that is people-oriented.[28]

Good news and bad news. More than ever before, public relations practitioners recognize the importance of their employee publics. But the challenges of employee relations have never been greater.

The News Media

The numbers are impressive. In the first decade of the 21st century, the United States has[29]

- more than 10,739 newspapers
- 407 weekly magazines and other periodicals
- 3,636 monthly magazines and other periodicals
- 3,814 quarterly magazines and other periodicals
- 3,766 AM radio stations
- 5,339 FM radio stations
- 1,332 TV stations
- 1,335 cable TV systems

No reliable figures exist for the number of news-related web sites. However, the Pew Internet & American Life Project reports that news consumers still prefer traditional news media to online alternatives: In the 2006 midterm elections that brought Democratic Party majorities to both houses of Congress, for example, only 15 percent of American adults received the majority of their political news from web sites. However, that number more than doubled from the 7 percent who preferred the web in 2002.[31]

Some very important members of those news media are the so-called **gatekeepers:** editors or producers who decide which stories to include and which stories to reject. Without the consent of the gatekeepers, public relations practitioners cannot use the news media as intervening publics. Gatekeepers value news that serves the interests of their audiences. If public relations practitioners can supply that kind of audience-focused news, they should have productive relationships with the gatekeepers of the news media.

Because of the First Amendment and its guarantee of freedom of the press, news media in the United States can, with few limitations, report whatever they perceive to be news. But in emerging democracies around the world, freedom of the press is,

---

News Media Publics: FAQs

1. What resources do news media have that organizations need?
Fair coverage and the willingness to consider news stories offered by public relations practitioners. The relative objectivity and credibility of the news media can provide what is called an **independent endorsement** or **third-party endorsement** of an organization's news.

2. What is the greatest challenge to building successful relationships with news media?
A mutual lack of knowledge. Research shows that journalists and public relations practitioners alike value accuracy and fairness—but neither party believes the other holds those values.[30]

3. Where can I find more information on news media publics?
- American Society of Newspaper Editors, online at www.asne.org
- Poynter Institute for Media Studies, online at www.poynter.org
- *Gale Directory of Publications and Broadcast Media*, published annually by Gale

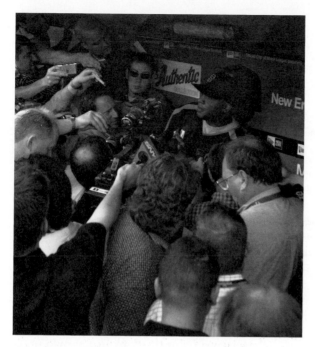

The news media can be an aggressive public, as baseball star Barry Bonds learned when he chased Hank Aaron's home-run record in 2007. (Photo by Barton Silverman/*New York Times.* Copyright 2007 The New York Times Company. Reprinted with permission.)

so to speak, a hotly contested front-page issue. As new freedoms give rise to modern news media, government officials and journalists around the world are debating the limits of freedom.

In the United States, a continuing problem for the news media is the disproportionately small number of minority journalists. In the wake of violent race riots during the struggle for civil rights, the report of the Kerner Commission in 1968 blasted the U.S. news media for their lack of minority journalists. However, in 1998 the American Society of Newspaper Editors conceded that it would not reach its year-2000 goal of having the minority population of newsrooms reflect the actual minority percentages of the U.S. population.[32] In the first decade of the 21st century, diversity in the U.S. news media looks something like this:

- Almost 14 percent of newspaper journalists are members of minority groups: 5.36 percent are black, 4.41 percent are Hispanic, 3.27 percent are Asian American, and 0.58 percent are Native American.[33]

- Some 22 percent of television journalists are members of minority groups: 9.5 percent are black, 9.6 percent are Hispanic, 2.7 percent are Asian American, and 0.5 percent are Native American.[34]

- Almost 6.4 percent of radio journalists are members of minority groups: 2.5 percent are black, 1.9 percent are Hispanic, 0.2 percent are Native American, and 1.8 percent are Asian American.[35]

Any discussion of 21st-century news media must include the concept of **convergence of media**—that is, a blending of media made possible by digital technology (for more on convergence and digital technology, please see Chapter 11). Simply put, digital technology allows journalists to move words, sounds, and images back and forth among radio, TV, newspapers, magazines, and web sites. As a consequence, members of the news media can offer their news in more than one format. Many university newspapers, for example, work closely with affiliated radio and television stations (broadcast and cable) to offer an online edition of the news gathered by all those media. Even the *New York Times,* nicknamed the "Gray Lady" for its stately, traditional nature, has a web site with videos, blogs, classified ads, and a

VALUES STATEMENT 4.1

PepsiCo

Tracing its origins to a popular soda pop first developed in 1898, PepsiCo emerged in 1965 as a corporation that specializes in soft drinks and snack foods. Its headquarters are in Purchase, New York.

PepsiCo's overall mission is to increase the value of our shareholders' investment. We do this through sales growth, cost controls and wise investment of resources. We believe our commercial success depends upon offering quality and value to our consumers and customers; providing products that are safe, wholesome, economically efficient and environmentally sound; and providing a fair return to our investors while adhering to the highest standards of integrity.

—"Mission Statement," PepsiCo web site

list of which articles readers have e-mailed most to others. Public relations practitioners who can offer journalists stories in digital formats suited to several media will thrive in the world of convergence.

No matter what background journalists may have, no matter what news medium they represent, they value one thing that public relations practitioners can supply: information—relevant, accurate, complete, timely information.

Governments

You've probably heard that the nine most feared words in the English language are "I'm from the government, and I'm here to help." Government workers actually *can* help public relations practitioners by providing information and interpreting legislation. But they can also harm a practitioner's organization by adopting unfavorable legislation or regulations. As we note elsewhere in this book, too, a continuing issue in public relations is government licensing of public relations practitioners. That hasn't happened yet, but the debate isn't over.

Who are the members of this influential public? They range from the local chief of police to the president of the United States. Government officials exist at the city/county level, the state level, and the federal level.

The Federal Government. At the federal level, there were 2.7 million nonmilitary employees in the first decade of the 21st century.[36] The U.S. Bureau of Labor Statistics expects that number to increase by 3 percent by 2012, compared with a growth rate of 16 percent for nongovernmental jobs in the United States.[37] Federal employees range from the 535 members of Congress to the 778,360 who work for the postal service and the 4,200 who work in federal libraries.[38]

A 2006 survey revealed that almost 68 percent of federal workers were satisfied with their jobs. Only 46 percent, however, were satisfied with "the information you receive from management on what's going on in your organization," only 40 percent were satisfied with their top leaders, and only 36 percent were satisfied with their chances of a better job within their unit.[39]

By some measures, the federal workforce is more diverse than the private-sector workforce: 17.6 percent of federal employees are black, compared with 10.1 percent in the private workforce; 7.6 percent are Hispanic, compared with 12.8 percent

Government Publics: FAQs

1. *What resources do governments have that organizations need?*

   Fair, nonrestrictive regulations, protection from unfair competition in the marketplace, and interpretations or explanations of existing laws.

2. *What is the greatest challenge to building successful relationships with government publics?*

   The slow growth of the U.S. federal government is increasing the workload of federal employees and transferring new and sometimes unfamiliar tasks to state and local government employees.

3. *Where can I find more information on government publics?*

   - *The Almanac of American Politics,* published by the National Journal Group
   - *Governing: The Magazine of States and Localities,* published by Congressional Quarterly, Inc.; online at www.governing.com
   - FedStats, online at www.fedstats.gov

in the private workforce; 5.2 percent are of Asian/Pacific Islands origins, compared with 4.2 percent in the private workforce; 1.9 percent are Native Americans, compared with 0.6 percent in the private workforce; and 43.9 percent are women, compared with 45.4 percent in the private workforce.[40]

Most visible among these employees, of course, are the members of Congress, each of whom has his or her own values and agendas. An excellent source for studying each member of Congress as well as the top issues among each member's constituency is *The Almanac of American Politics,* which offers state-by-state and district-by-district analyses of senators, representatives, voters, and issues.

Lobbyists who work with federal employees, particularly with elected officials, have at least one bit of advice for public relations practitioners: Be well prepared and work fast.[41] Although 59 percent of federal employees believe their workload is reasonable, only 47.6 percent believe they have the necessary resources to get the job done.[42]

State and Local Governments. At last measurement, there were 5.1 million state government employees and 11.8 million local government employees in the United States—a total of 16.9 million.[43] The U.S. Bureau of Labor Statistics expects that number to increase to 21.9 million by 2014.[44] In this swirl of numbers, public relations practitioners should appreciate an important trend: State and local governments are growing at a faster rate than the federal government—in many cases taking on functions that formerly existed at the federal level.

Diversity figures for individual state governments generally can be found on state government web sites—often in annual reports to the governor and state citizens. In Wisconsin, for example, 8.9 percent of the state's classified employees (nonelected, nonpolitical, usually long-term) belong to recognized minority groups: 4.8 percent are black; 1.8 percent are Hispanic; 1.5 percent are Asian American; 0.8 percent are Native American; 49.5 percent are women; and 7.1 percent are people with disabilities.[45]

The National Association of State Retirement Administrators reports that two-thirds of state and local government employees work in education, public safety, and corrections.[46] A 2005 study predicted that a high level of retirements among state government employees would challenge the quality of "institutional knowledge and leadership" by the year 2010. The study also found that state employees, like most employees, respond positively to praise for a job well done.[47]

Elected officials at all levels of government want to serve their constituents well and be reelected. Public relations practitioners who can help government officials pursue those values will find them to be willing partners in building productive relationships.

QUICK CHECK

1. What do employees around the world value in their jobs?
2. In media relations, what is an independent endorsement?
3. What does the comparatively rapid growth of state and local government workforces mean for public relations practitioners?
4. For public relations practitioners, what essential resources do employee, media, and government publics possess?

QUICKBREAK 4.3

I'll Scratch Your Back . . .

Earlier in this chapter, we noted that resource dependency theory provides an explanation for why organizations form relationships with publics: Those publics have resources the organization needs in order to achieve its goals.

So far, so good. But resource dependency theory is a one-way street: It focuses on one side of a relationship, describing an organization's reliance on resources held by others. Why should those resource-holding publics agree to relationships with the organization? What's in it for them?

We'll answer this question more fully in Chapter 7 in our discussion of "components of relationships." But, for now, **social exchange theory** helps provide a preliminary answer. If resource dependency theory explains our need for relationships, social exchange theory explains why the publics on the other end of those relationships may agree to work with us.

As its name suggests, social exchange theory holds that an exchange of resources occurs in successful relationships: Each party in the relationship gets something that it wants or needs. And as long as both parties believe that the benefits of the relationship outweigh the costs, the relationship continues. On the positive side, we now can improve relationships by understanding how they work. On the negative side, we now have to wonder if key publics may be on the lookout for a better cost–benefit relationship.

"According to social exchange theory, then, unless our expectations are met or exceeded, we will select other viable alternatives if they are available," say public relations scholars John Ledingham and Stephen Bruning.[48]

The two-way symmetrical model of public relations embraces both resource dependency theory and social exchange theory: It acknowledges that organizations need relationships and that win-win relationships are the most productive and successful.

You've probably heard the crude expression "You scratch my back, and I'll scratch yours." If you understand that, you've begun to understand social exchange theory.

Investors

Companies that sell stock have relationships with investors. The investor public encompasses individual stockholders—and much more:

■ Financial analysts study the stock markets to advise investors.

■ Financial news media include the *Wall Street Journal, Business Week* magazine, the *Mad Money* television show, and web sites such as Value Line, at www .valueline.com.

■ **Mutual fund managers** supervise what might be called investment clubs. For a fee, mutual fund managers invest a member's contributions (usually monthly payments) into a diverse collection of stocks and bonds. The popularity of mutual funds has soared in the past 20 years.

■ So-called **institutional investors** are large companies or institutions that generally buy huge amounts of stock. The California Public Employees Retirement System, for example, is the largest public pension plan in the United States. It represents almost 1.5 million state and local government employees in California and has assets of approximately $240 billion.

■ Employee investors are employees of companies, such as Microsoft, that reward employees with stock in the companies they work for.

If you've studied stock markets at all in recent years, you might guess—correctly—that U.S. investors feel as if they've been riding a roller coaster. But studies show that they're not leaving the amusement park. Half of U.S. households now own stocks and bonds, up from 20 percent in the early 1980s.[49]

The UBS/Gallup Index of Investor Optimism (www.ubs.com) measures the confidence of American investors with $10,000 or more in investments and savings. Though the events of September 11, 2001, and the corporate scandals of the early 21st century battered investors' faith in financial markets, they haven't retreated: By 2007, investor confidence had more than doubled since the early-century slump.[50]

"Weathering the market volatility [2001–2004] was no small feat for the individual investor," says Daniel Leemon, chief strategy officer for Charles Schwab & Company, a financial services firm.[51]

Investor Publics: FAQs

1. **What resources do investor publics have that organizations need?**
   Investors purchase stocks. Financial analysts, mutual fund managers, and journalists evaluate stocks and make recommendations to investors.

2. **What are the greatest challenges to building successful relationships with investor publics?**
   Investor publics need information and reassurance as stock markets become increasingly volatile. The growing diversity of investors means that old ways of communicating may not be effective.

3. **Where can I find more information on investor publics?**
   - Securities and Exchange Commission, online at www.sec.gov
   - New York Stock Exchange, online at www .nyse.com
   - National Investor Relations Institute, online at www.niri.org
   - The *Wall Street Journal,* published Monday through Friday by Dow Jones and Company, Inc.

TABLE 4.1   U.S. Investors: Who They Are

- Average age is 51. Most are ages 35–64.
- 56 percent are college graduates.
- 70 percent are married.
- 92 percent are white; 5 percent are black; 3 percent are Hispanic; 2 percent are Asian American (multiple responses are reflected).
- Median annual household income is $65,000.
- 34 percent are willing to take above-average risks to achieve above-average gains.
- 88 percent list retirement plans as a key reason for investing; 60 percent rank it the top reason.

Who are these resilient investors? Not, perhaps, who you might think. Table 4.1 lists data on the investing public.[52]

What about would-be investors—primarily the new college-grad group that many readers of this book hope to enter soon? Studies show that the under-35 age group represents only 15 percent of U.S. investors. A 2007 survey of Americans ages 25–40 found that "younger investors are aware they should be saving for retirement, but face significant challenges like competing spending priorities and a lack of information to make simple investment choices."[53] Although 80 percent of that age group have some form of long-term savings plan, higher priorities include meeting daily living expenses and paying off debts.[54] Most young investors begin investing through retirement plans and mutual funds rather than through purchasing individual stocks and bonds, and they're more willing to consider high-risk/high-return investments than older groups.[55]

Though they are diverse, investors can be stable publics for public relations: 96 percent view their investments "as saving for the long term"; only a small minority buy and sell frequently, trying to beat the daily odds in the stock markets.[56] Gradual changes, however, do occur in investor publics. Investors often diversify their holdings, increasing the mix of mutual funds and individual stock and bonds. They increasingly route their money to non-U.S. investments; more than 60 percent currently own stock in foreign companies. Although almost three-fourths currently use the Internet to study their investments, only 14 percent make online purchases.[57] Overall, investors value profitability and stability.

Consumers/Customers

The people of the United States are consumers—big-time consumers. Monthly consumer spending in the United States could purchase the entire annual goods-and-services output of Finland, Singapore, and Austria combined.[58]

Consumer spending is the most powerful force in the U.S. economy, accounting for two-thirds of all spending in the United States—twice as much as government and business spending combined.[59] In the words of *American Demographics* magazine, the amount of consumer spending "simply boggles the mind."[60]

Consumer/Customer Publics: FAQs

1. **What resources do consumer/customer publics have that organizations need?**
   Loyalty: a willingness to purchase and repurchase an organization's products. Consumers also possess the resource of publicity: Word-of-mouth cheers or jeers are a powerful force in the marketplace.

2. **What are the greatest challenges to building successful relationships with consumer/customer publics?**
   Fifty percent of shoppers report that customer service is "often dreadful." Almost one-third of dissatisfied shoppers tell others.[61] The diversity of consumers is increasing. Also, public relations must learn to coordinate its tactics with the tactics of marketing, and vice versa (see Chapter 13).

3. **Where can I find more information on consumer/customer publics?**
   - *American Demographics,* published by Crain Communications, Inc., online at www.adage.com/americandemographics
   - U.S. Department of Commerce, online at www.commerce.gov
   - U.S. Bureau of Labor Statistics, online at www.bls.gov

Who are these big spenders, and what are they spending all that money on? Some facts:

■ The average U.S. household has a before-tax income of $58,712. Its annual expenditures total $46,409. Where does the money go? Table 4.2 gives a partial breakdown.[62]

■ The biggest spenders are people aged 45 to 54. Households in which the main earner falls into that age bracket spend $58,854 a year. By way of comparison, households in which the main earner is under 25 spend only $27,776 a year. For age 65 and older, the total is $32,866.[63]

■ Annual consumer spending also varies by ethnicity. Black households annually spend $32,849; Hispanic and Latino households (not including blacks and whites) spend $40,123; households of Asian ancestry spend $52,054; and whites (including Pacific Islanders, Native Americans, and Native Alaskans) spend $48,077.

■ Women account for approximately 83 percent of U.S. consumer spending.[64]

■ Generation Y (people born between 1980 and 1994) contributes about 5 percent

TABLE 4.2	How U.S. Households Spend Their After-Tax Income
Food	$5,931
Housing	$15,167
Apparel and services	$1,886
Transportation	$8,344
Health care	$2,664
Entertainment	$2,388
Personal care products and services	$541
Alcoholic beverages	$426
Tobacco products and smoking supplies	$319

QUICKBREAK 4.4

The Customer Is Always Right?

The reigning master of bizarre customer inquiries is the mysterious Ted L. Nancy (who just might be comedian Jerry Seinfeld).[65] Posing as a clueless customer, Nancy bedevils corporate America with inane letters that usually draw painfully serious responses.[66]

To wit: Nancy wrote to San Francisco's Pan Pacific Hotel, asking if it could accommodate his physical abnormality: "I have three legs. . . . I'll need an ottoman I can place next to the bed when I sleep."

The hotel wrote back, politely noting that "our rooms do have ottoman chairs in them."

Nancy also wrote to the Nordstrom department store chain, asking if he might purchase a store mannequin that resembled his dead neighbor.

"Dear Mr. Nancy," replied a Nordstrom representative. "Yours is one of the most interesting requests I have ever received. . . ."

Then Nancy wrote to Hanes about its underwear. . . .

Why do companies reply to such off-the-wall requests? Besides good manners, there's good business: A landmark customer-service study shows that most businesses could increase their profits 25–100 percent simply by retaining just 5 percent more of their current customers every year.[67]

Nancy has published three collections of his letters: *Letters from a Nut, More Letters from a Nut,* and *Extra Nutty! Even More Letters from a Nut.*

of annual consumer spending to the U.S. economy.[68] Survey research indicates that Gen Y'ers have less brand loyalty and are more likely to make impulse purchases than any other age group.[69]

Online shopping, also known as **e-commerce** (for electronic commerce), continues to soar in popularity: In 2006, total U.S. e-commerce spending jumped to $109 billion, a 24 percent increase compared with 2005 spending. Even with that dizzying total, however, e-commerce represented only 2.8 percent of total U.S. sales in 2006.[70] Two-thirds of U.S. consumers say they prefer to buy from traditional, bricks-and-mortar stores—though they do like to go online to research products, locate items, and compare prices.[71] And the increasing threat of online identity theft is dampening the potential of online sales: 46 percent of Americans who use the Internet say that security concerns have affected their online purchasing, driving down e-commerce by $2 billion in 2006.[72]

Regardless of where and how customers do their shopping, what do they value? Any survey gives you the same answer: quality at a fair price. Customers want to get what they paid for—and more.

Multicultural Communities

Public relations professionals must know the so-called movers and shakers in every community in which their organizations do business. Failing to learn who wields

Booklet and Brochures With the assistance of Valencia, Pérez & Echeveste Public Relations, the California Department of Health Services prepares these recipes and good nutrition tips for Hispanic consumers. (Courtesy of Valencia, Pérez & Echeveste Public Relations)

Multicultural Community Publics: FAQs

1. *What resources do multicultural community publics have that organizations need?*
   The willingness to accept an organization as a community member—to be its employees, supporters, customers, and friends.

2. *What is the greatest challenge to building successful relationships with multicultural community publics?*
   The sheer number of such groups. Organizations' resources are limited, and they usually cannot build relationships with every public within a community. Organizations must determine which relationships in a community are most essential to the fulfillment of their values.

3. *Where can I find more information on multicultural community publics?*
   • U.S. Bureau of the Census, online at www.census.gov
   • U.S. Citizenship and Immigration Services, online at www.uscis.gov
   • *American Demographics,* published by Crain Communications, Inc., online at www.adage.com/americandemographics
   • *The Chronicle of Philanthropy,* published weekly; online at www.philanthropy.com

power in a community can have catastrophic results, as the developer of a proposed landfill site once discovered:

One private developer announced a project that soon drew surprisingly intense environmental opposition from local residents. Only months after announcing the planned facility did the developer learn that the town was home to Ralph Nader.[73]

Besides consumer activist and presidential candidate Ralph Nader, who are the influential publics within our diverse communities? Professor Jerry Hendrix of American University offers a useful breakdown, which appears in Table 4.3.[74] Some of the worst, most expensive public relations fiascoes in recent memory have involved companies perceived as being insensitive to racial or ethnic groups. A decade ago, Denny's, the restaurant chain, faced repeated charges of refusing to seat or serve black customers. In fact, the company paid almost $55 million to settle two class-action lawsuits backed by thousands of reportedly mistreated black customers. Denny's had become "synonymous with discrimination" according to national news media. "It was a hard time for the company," said a Denny's representative. "Morale was so low. Something had to be done."[75]

Something was done. In one of the most dramatic rebounds in the history of values-driven public relations, Denny's changed leadership and committed to diversity in the workforce and in clientele. Today, Denny's restaurant managers earn their salaries in part by showing specifically how they honor the value of diversity in their restaurants. In 2006, *Black Enterprise* magazine ranked Denny's one of its "40 Best Companies for Diversity."[76]

More than ever before, public relations practitioners must foster positive relationships with racial and ethnic publics within their organizations' communities. Otherwise, organizations not only may separate themselves from community goodwill, but they also risk separating themselves from potential employees, customers, investors, donors, and other publics that they depend on to survive. Although the racial/ethnic makeup of every community is different, Table 4.4 shows the U.S. Census Bureau's projections for U.S. population totals and percentages for the year 2010.[77]

TABLE 4.3	**Influential Community Publics**

COMMUNITY MEDIA	**COMMUNITY ORGANIZATIONS**
Mass media (such as newspapers and television stations)	Civic
	Business
Specialized media (such as entertainment tabloids)	Service
Online social networks	Social
	Cultural
COMMUNITY LEADERS	Religious
Public officials	Youth
Educators	Political
Religious leaders	Special-interest groups
Professionals (such as doctors and lawyers)	Other groups
Executives	
Bankers	
Union leaders	
Ethnic leaders	
Neighborhood leaders	

TABLE 4.4	**Projected U.S. Population Totals and Percentages for the Year 2010**

TOTAL POPULATION	308.9 million Female: 157.1 million Male: 151.8 million
WHITE POPULATION	250 million (79.3 percent) Female: 123.9 million Male: 121.1 million
BLACK POPULATION	40.5 million (13.1 percent) Female: 21.1 million Male: 19.3 million
HISPANIC AMERICAN POPULATION	47.8 million (15.5 percent) Female: 23.4 million Male: 24.3 million
ASIAN AMERICAN	14.2 million (4.6 percent) Female: 7.5 million Male: 6.7 million
OTHER POPULATIONS, INCLUDING NATIVE AMERICAN	9.2 million (3 percent) Female: 4.6 million Male: 4.6 million

As noted in Chapter 16, immigration is also changing communities in the United States. The foreign-born percentage of the U.S. population recently reached its highest level since 1930: Of today's residents, 11.7 percent were born citizens of other nations—a total of 33.5 million people. Approximately 37 percent reside in the western United States, followed by 29 percent in the South and 22 percent in the Northeast.[78] But even in small communities in southwestern Kansas, the meatpacking industry attracts immigrants from Vietnam and Somalia.

According to the U.S. Census Bureau, 53 percent of today's immigrants came from Latin America, 25 percent from Asia, and 14 percent from Europe. More than one-third arrived in the United States during the 1990s. Though 67 percent have at least a high school education, immigrants are more likely than nonimmigrants to be unemployed and living in poverty.[79]

In short, communities consist of diverse publics—and diversity within each public is probably increasing.

Constituents (Voters)

Not every organization considers voters to be a traditional public, though many organizations try to influence the legislative process by building relationships with eligible voters. But for public relations practitioners employed by democratically elected governments, voters often are the most important public of all.

In a sense, this group includes every citizen of a nation who is of voting age—a huge and diverse public. In countries where voting is compulsory, such as Costa Rica, a description of this public literally would be a description of the country's adult population. In the United States, however, a description of voters is somewhat easier, because not every eligible citizen votes. In the 2006 midterm (nonpresidential) elections, slightly more than 40 percent of eligible voters went to the polls; in modern midterm elections, the 1982 contests set the record with a turnout of 42 percent.[80] In voter turnout, the United States ranks 139th among the world's 170-plus democracies.[81]

What do we know about citizens in the United States who *do* vote? According to the U.S. Census Bureau, the most typical voter is a retired, married female homeowner, 65 or older, with a college degree and an above-average household

Constituent/Voter Publics: FAQs

1. *What resources do constituent/voter publics have that organizations need?*
   Votes and word-of-mouth endorsements. Constituents who approve of their elected representatives can influence the opinions of other constituents.

2. *What is the greatest challenge to building successful relationships with constituent/voter publics?*
   Voter apathy, which is particularly high among voters aged 18 to 24.

3. *Where can I find more information on constituent/voter publics?*
   - The League of Women Voters, online at www.lwv.org
   - *The Almanac of American Politics,* published by the National Journal Group
   - International Institute for Democracy and Electoral Assistance, online at www.idea.int

income. Facts from the bureau's analysis of the 2004 presidential election paint this portrait of American voters:[82]

- *Marriage counts:* 71 percent of married citizens vote compared with 52 percent of single citizens.

- *Education rules:* 78 percent of citizens with a college education vote compared with 40 percent of high school dropouts.

- *Money talks:* 77 percent of citizens with a household income of $50,000 or more vote compared with 48 percent of citizens with a household income of less than $20,000.

The single greatest indicator of regular voting in the United States is age: Voters ages 65–74 are most likely to vote (73 percent). Least likely are voters ages 18–24 (46.7 percent)—the age group of many readers of this book. In 2006, 34 percent of young voters (ages 18–29) identified themselves as liberal; 25 identified themselves as conservative. In the same survey, 33 percent of voters 30 and older identified themselves as conservative; 18 percent identified themselves as liberal.[83]

Although the civil rights movement in the United States increased opportunities for minority citizens to vote, race remains a predictor of voting patterns. White voters have the highest turnout at 67.2 percent. Black voters follow at 60 percent, Hispanic voters (of any race) at 47.2 percent, and Asian American voters at 44.1 percent. As for gender at the ballot box, women are more likely to vote than men by the margin of 65.4 percent to 62.1 percent.

U.S. citizens who *don't* vote offer these Top Eight reasons why they weren't registered to vote (if you're a David Letterman fan, imagine a Top 10 countdown):

8. Not interested in the election or not involved in politics.
7. Did not meet registration deadlines.
6. Didn't know or refused to say.
5. Permanent illness or disability.
4. Did not know where or how to register.
3. Did not meet residency requirements.
2. My vote would not make a difference.
1. Difficulty with English.

Businesses

Organizations have relationships with a variety of businesses. Why? Because those businesses have resources that the organizations need if they are to fulfill their values-driven goals. Such relationships involve **business-to-business communication,** often called **B2B** communication. For example, an organization may have relationships with vendor businesses that supply materials to the organization; distributor businesses that help move the organization's products to consumers; customer businesses that purchase the organization's products; and industry partners, which are in the same type of business and work with the organization to help influence legislative and regulation processes at different levels of government.

Business Publics: FAQs

1. **What resources do business publics have that organizations need?**
   Vendor businesses have supplies and loyalty. Customer businesses have the willingness to purchase and repurchase an organization's products. Direct competitors have the resource of competing fairly.

2. **What are the greatest challenges to building successful relationships with business publics?**
   One surprising challenge may be the reputation of B2B communications. *Marketing* magazine reports that B2B is thought to be "the least glamorous part" of public relations.[84] Also, the sheer number of business relationships that an organization has poses a challenge to relationship building.

3. **Where can I find more information on business publics?**
   • *BtoB* magazine, published monthly by Crain Communications, Inc.; online at www.btobonline.com
   • *Sales & Marketing Management* magazine, published monthly by Nielsen Business, Inc.; online at www.salesandmarketing.com
   • *Business Week* magazine, published weekly by the McGraw-Hill Companies; online at www.businessweek.com

That same organization has sometimes-uneasy relationships with direct competitors. With this wide-ranging focus on relationship building, the management of B2B communications is increasingly known as **partner relationship management (PRM)**.

B2B communication is big business, and it's growing. In 2007, the U.S. Census Bureau reported that business-to-business transactions constituted 92 percent of U.S. e-commerce. In other words, the billions of dollars spent annually by individual online shoppers—at Amazon and iTunes, for example—still amounts to only 8 percent of e-commerce activity.[85] In a 2006 report on partner relationship management, software giant Oracle reported that manufacturers of high-tech equipment sell up to 70 percent of their products to other businesses. In the financial services industry, that figure reaches 80 percent. And as one business sells to another, it often relies on equipment built by a third company and shipping provided by a fourth.

"PRM solutions are becoming increasingly critical as brand owners recognize the tremendous value associated with leveraging their partner relationships," the Oracle report concluded. "PRM has therefore become an imperative for brand owners and partners operating in today's increasingly competitive environment."[86]

QUICK ✓ CHECK

1. What is the demographic profile of people in the United States who invest in the stock markets?
2. What age group in the United States spends the most money on consumer goods and services?
3. What does *B2B* mean? *PRM*?
4. For public relations practitioners, what important resources are possessed by investor, consumer, community, constituent, and business publics?

Summary

A public is a group of people who share a common value or values in a particular situation. In other words, publics unite around their values. For employees, the core value may be job security. For an environmental group, maybe it's clean air and water. An organization forms relationships with publics that have the resources it needs to fulfill its values-driven goals. However, when the values of a public intersect with the values of an organization, a relationship—whether the organization wants it or not—is born. Resource dependency theory and social exchange theory can help explain the why and the how of relationships in public relations.

Traditional publics may vary among different organizations. For many organizations, however, long-established traditional publics include employees, the news media, governments, investors, consumers, multicultural community groups, constituents (voters), and businesses.

Publics can and do change constantly, but the questions a practitioner must answer about each public remain the same. Whether a public is latent, aware, or active, if it has the power to influence an organization, a practitioner must answer these questions:

- How much can the public influence our organization's ability to achieve our goals?
- What is the public's stake, or value, in its relationship with our organization?
- Who are the opinion leaders and decision makers for the public?
- What is the demographic profile of the public?
- What is the psychographic profile of the public?
- What is the public's opinion of our organization?
- What is the public's opinion (if any) of the issue in question?

Not until those questions are answered can public relations practitioners strive to build the relationships that will help an organization achieve its values-driven goals.

DISCUSSION QUESTIONS

1. Your authors state that the most important publics in public relations are employee publics. Do you agree? Why or why not?
2. Can you think of examples of nontraditional publics that have become—or are becoming—traditional publics?
3. Why do public relations practitioners try to identify opinion leaders and decision makers for each public?
4. Why is it important to identify a public's stake in an issue of importance to a practitioner's organization?
5. In our opening scenario, how would you classify the local Boy Scout troops? Are they a primary or a secondary public?

Memo from the Field

A journalism school graduate and former print journalist, Dave Narsavage has been a professional communicator for more than 35 years. Once an Army combat correspondent in Vietnam, he's held communications positions in the U.S. Senate, with a national political party, and as director of employee communications for a 26,000-employee corporation. He now counsels clients of The Aker Partners, a Washington, D.C.–based public affairs firm.

David A. Narsavage; Senior Partner; The Aker Partners, Inc.; Washington, D.C.

It's all about publics, and messages, and desired effects. And the wheelie video. You've got to figure out who you *want* to see the wheelie video. And who you don't.

My teenaged son was lobbying me for a motorcycle. Not *my* kind of motorcycle: low-slung, no plastic in sight, a throaty "potato potato potato" idle note. Now that's a bike. No, his rocket would be clad in fiberglass, sound like a crazed bee, and hit warp speed in a nanosecond.

"Forget it," I told him. "It's a fatal attraction."

But since we were already *in* a motorcycle showroom during this discussion, I agreed there was no harm in looking. We started chatting with a young salesman, making it clear that my son had a fantasy—and I had a fear of him flying.

The salesman smiled and nodded. Knowingly, I thought. "Dudes!" he blurted suddenly, as if just hit with a truly huge idea. "You've *got* to see this video!" And he took us to a monitor, where we watched young men of little brain race my son's fantasy ride on rear wheel only, front wheel only, and no wheels only. "Isn't that *awesome*!?"

My son, no fool, looked at me and smiled. He knew: *This* was a man who had never read a word from Professors Guth and Marsh.

Know the room. Whether you call them a public or a target audience, know who those people are. Know what will move them: the hot buttons that can either bring them closer to your point of view or push them out of sight.

Remember that they'll have some selfish, self-interest issues, because that's how we humans are. But mostly it will come down to emotions.

One of my relics from a previous life as a U.S. senator's press secretary is a treasured copy of a "Shoe" comic strip, personally signed by the much-missed Jeff MacNelly. It shows the editor bird (just go with me on this if you're not a "Shoe" fan) holding up a sheet of paper and asking the professor bird, "Where should I file this urgent press release from Senator Belfry?" The professor replies, "File it under 'W'—for 'Who cares?'"

Who *cares* about your message? Who *doesn't* care now, and what will it take to rouse them? Because no matter how much your client/employer pays you, no matter how much you buy into his or her fervor and embrace that gospel, if your key audiences don't *care*, you're wasting good professional effort.

Public and *relations*. Of the two, I'd worry about relations. That's where the power is, where the blood, and character, and emotions are. Where the *caring* is. As you'll read in this textbook, the value of our profession comes in the building and nurturing of relationships.

You build those relationships by treating audiences with respect and by communicating with them in the same clear and direct way you would in a letter to a friend. Wait, you don't know what a letter is. In an *e-mail* to a friend, OK? But with capitalization and punctuation.

Do the world a favor. Don't let clients insist on corporate-speak, and puffery, and inflated verbiage whose message seems to be "If you can't understand what I'm saying, then I must be *really* smart."

Have a *conversation* with your audiences. Your authors call it two-way symmetrical public relations. We call that communicating. Anything else is what my father used to call—in mixed company—a bunch of padookey dust.

I love these guys, Guth and Marsh. Not just because they gave me a podium, and as a presentation-trainer friend says, *seize* the podium as your own space, but because they share my concern for employees. Talk about an important audience. These are people who will have a long-term influence on putting meaning behind your message and people who represent a built-in grassroots network for your client.

But more than that, it's simply a basic consideration, a courtesy. People shouldn't have to read the paper or watch the news to know about changes in their work home. Bring them into the communications tent. If that helps you achieve your "values-driven goals," peachy. And even if it doesn't, you'll feel better about looking in the mirror.

I'm getting a "cut" signal from the author guys. Wrap it up.

In time, you *will* need to do some honest work. So before you fold up your "College" sweatshirt, pack your street signs, and leave those hallowed halls—why do we never hear of *un*hallowed halls?—I leave you with this:

- Remember that what seems so vital to your client, and thus to you, probably means jack to most everybody else. So find the people who care. It's better to reach the people who count than count the people you reach.

- Don't use *impact* as a verb. Genuflect before the *AP Stylebook* daily.

- You shouldn't expect any audience to understand and retain any more than about three key messages. If you can't state your position during a routine elevator trip, you need help.

- Laugh in the office every day. Avoid agencies and clients who don't know how.

- If you think you're there to do your client's blind bidding, you're in the wrong gig. If you think you're there to be your client's communications *counsel* and *partner,* welcome to the bond.

- Buy quality hand tools. The cheap stuff won't last. Hey, I'm still seizing the podium here.

What we do serves an honorable purpose: We help people tell their stories. We help them be heard. Then the key audiences have what they need to decide whether to print, buy, vote, move, change, eat, love, hate, or yawn. That's a good thing.

And *your* job is to decide: Should I show the wheelie video?

CASE STUDY **4.1**

Criticize Me! Subway and the Crossed-Off Cross-Promotion

The Subway restaurant chain likes to tell its customers to "eat fresh." But in 2004, Subway had to eat something different: a controversial cross-promotional campaign launched by its German franchises.

Cross-promotions occur when two organizations agree to promote each other's products or goals. In the Subway case, the restaurant chain's 100 German franchises contacted the company handling German distribution of *Super Size Me*, a documentary harshly critical of McDonald's, Subway's international rival.[87] To encourage diners to see the film, Subway agreed to use promotional tray liners—ones that featured a chubby Statue of Liberty holding, not a torch and book, but a burger and fries. The liners included the question "Why are Americans so fat?"[88]

"The people in Germany do understand what we want to say and that we do not want to offend anybody," said a representative of the German company that created the liners.[89]

But as Canadian philosopher Marshall McLuhan famously declared, we live in a global village: Unfortunately, a few of Subway's cross-promotional tray liners went cross-country, crossing the Atlantic to the United States, where they made people—well, cross.

"They should feel bad about fanning the flames of anti-Americanism in order to sell more sandwiches," said Jeffrey Mazzella, executive director of the U.S.-based Center for Individual Freedom.[90] The center launched an e-mail campaign, asking supporters to make their feelings known to Subway executives.[91]

"This is every bad stereotype about corporate America come true," railed Tom DeLay, then-majority leader of the U.S. House of Representatives. "I guess for some companies, corporate patriotism is as flexible as Jared's waistline."[92] (Jared Fogle, well known from Subway television commercials, lost 250 pounds on a diet of Subway sandwiches.)

Not all U.S. observers trashed Subway. "This is a gross example of American overreaction," said Alan Hilburg, president of Porter Novelli Consulting.[93]

But just like an extra-value meal, there's more: The crisis supersized when Subway's cross-promo partner, the German film distributor, sent journalists a media kit that contained a startling image: a giant hamburger crashing into skyscrapers, which spew smoke and topple toward the ground. More than one observer noted a strong resemblance to the September 11 terrorist attacks on the World Trade Center.

"That is not our promotion, and the booklet was never handed out at Subway's German franchises," said a Subway representative in the United States, stressing the fact that the media kit belonged to the film distributor alone.[94]

In fact, officials in Subway's international headquarters in the United States disavowed knowledge of the entire campaign. A Subway representative said the company's leaders were as surprised as others at the cross-promotion. "We try not to put too many restrictions on the franchises to keep up the entrepreneurial spirit of the brand," he explained. But he added that, in the future, Subway's top management would take greater control of the company's many regional marketing campaigns.[95]

Subway's cross-promo partner displayed a disturbing lack of knowledge of modern public relations when a representative expressed surprise that the media kit's controversial images had migrated to web sites.[96]

Others knew better. "Because of the Internet, there's no longer a clear delineation between markets," said Ned Barnett of Barnett Marketing Communications. "Everybody working in PR for a multinational needs to realize that what's said to one person is said to everyone."[97]

The Center for Individual Freedom reported that the media kit even found its way into a Subway restaurant in Munich, where a U.S. citizen saw it and delivered it to the center.[98]

The fast food fiasco had a fast ending when Subway's German restaurants agreed to end the cross-promotion early. A representative from Subway's headquarters apologized for the tray liners, adding that the German restaurants had been in daily contact "because they feel bad."[99]

"We're glad they responded," said a representative from DeLay's office. "But [we're] not exactly sure how you undo the damage."[100]

The Center for Individual Freedom termed the apology "unexpected" and said that Subway's statement "left us very satisfied with their response to this whole thing."[101]

But for some, analysis of Subway's cross-promotion had just begun. "Subway's debacle raises several important questions for PR executives to ponder," declared *PR News*. The magazine graded Subway's response to the crisis and awarded the restaurant chain a D.[102]

"This is a classic case—sure to be chewed on for years by the PR industry and academics alike," wrote Katie Delahaye Paine, CEO of KDPaine & Partners.[103]

Let the chewing begin.

DISCUSSION QUESTIONS

1. What do you know about the values of the Center for Individual Freedom? Should it not have respected Subway's freedom to express itself?
2. How many different publics were involved in this incident? What were the values of each? What resources did each possess?
3. Should international companies such as Subway approve and monitor all of their national or regional marketing campaigns? Why or why not?
4. *PR News* wrote that Subway's cross-promotion generated several questions for public relations practitioners. What are some of those questions? What, in your opinion, are the answers?

CASE STUDY 4.2

Swinging for the Wall: Whirlpool Corporation and Habitat for Humanity

Baseball fans know the story well. In the 1932 World Series, Babe Ruth and the New York Yankees faced the Chicago Cubs. In game three of the fall classic, Ruth homered in an early inning. So when he came to the plate again in the fifth, Chicago fans booed mercilessly and jeered as pitcher Charlie Root zipped two strikes past Ruth.

Then Ruth made the gesture.

He pointed to the centerfield wall. And he hit the next pitch over that wall.

Home run.

In the 21st century, the Whirlpool Corporation just might think it's the Babe Ruth of corporate America. One of the world's best-known makers of home appliances, the company generates annual profits of more than $12 billion. Because Whirlpool is an ambitious company—it sells its products in more than 170 countries—it sought an ambitious new goal.[104]

Then Whirlpool made the gesture.

The company committed, in writing, to this pledge: "Every Home . . . Everywhere. With Pride, Passion, and Performance."[105]

Every home. . . . But what about homeowners who simply couldn't afford Whirlpool appliances—or any appliances for that matter? Figuratively speaking, Whirlpool had pointed to the centerfield wall. And now it had to deliver or strike out.

Whirlpool delivered. In 1999, the company vowed to donate a refrigerator and a range to every new Habitat for Humanity house in the United States.[106]

Most college students no doubt are familiar with Habitat for Humanity; many have helped build Habitat homes. Habitat for Humanity International is an organization dedicated to ending substandard housing and the lack of homeownership in low-income families. With local branches in more than 3,000 communities in 92 nations, the organization has built more than 150,000 houses for deserving families.[107]

Since 1999, Whirlpool has donated more than 40,000 appliances to Habitat for Humanity.[108]

"Habitat's mission to provide simple, decent, and affordable housing for economically less fortunate families around the world meshes well with Whirlpool's corporate vision of 'Every Home . . . Everywhere,'" says Whirlpool Chairman and CEO David R. Whitwam.[109]

Whirlpool prides itself on being a values-driven company. One of its core values is integrity—matching its words with actions—and the company clearly addresses values in its statements on *Corporate Responsibility* and *Vision & Strategy*:

> At Whirlpool we strongly believe in the principles of Corporate Responsibility—of achieving success in ways that honor ethical values and respect people, communities, and the natural environment. . . . Supporting those in our communities that need support provides our stakeholders with a real sense of Whirlpool's values. . . . Our employees live by the

values-based strategy that has made Whirlpool the international leader that we are today. Our values represent who we are to our customers, our investors, and to each other.[110]

To help honor its value of community service, Whirlpool assists Habitat for Humanity with more than donations:

- Whirlpool offers substantial price discounts on additional appliances to Habitat homeowners.[111]

- Whirlpool employees around the world volunteer to help build Habitat homes. In 2003, the company built a Habitat house near the main entrance of its corporate headquarters in Benton Harbor, Michigan, and then transferred the house to a new location.[112]

- In 2004, Whirlpool increased its donations to include new Habitat for Humanity homes in Europe.

In working to fulfill its values, Whirlpool believes that it's being more than a good corporate citizen: The company believes it's strengthening its financial future. Whirlpool's *Corporate Responsibility* statement offers this explanation: "Initiatives such as these help ensure the short-term and long-term viability of our company. . . . We firmly believe the socially responsible actions we take today will produce bottom-line benefits tomorrow."[113]

In pursuing its Every Home pledge, Whirlpool encountered a public it might not have anticipated: deserving individuals who couldn't afford their own homes and appliances. Whirlpool could have changed its goal. Or it could have ignored a public that probably wouldn't have fought back. Instead, like Babe Ruth, Whirlpool stood tall and swung for the wall.

Home run.

Or, maybe, just home.

DISCUSSION QUESTIONS

1. Should an organization establish a goal it can never realistically fulfill?
2. Do you agree with Whirlpool that its commitment to Habitat for Humanity can actually help it financially? If so, how?
3. Do you think "cause marketing" works? How can support for a worthy social cause help a company?
4. Can you name other companies involved in cause marketing?

NOTES

1. Larissa Grunig, James Grunig, and William Ehling, "What Is an Effective Organization?" in *Excellence in Public Relations and Communication Management* (Hillsdale, N.J.: Lawrence Erlbaum, 1992), 77, 80.
2. "Pitney Bowes Statement of Value," online, www.pitneybowes.com.
3. Norimitsu Onishi, "As Oil Riches Flow, Poor Village Cries Out," *New York Times,* 22 December 2002, online, LexisNexis.

4. "Exclusive: Isaiah Washington Apologizes," *People,* 25 October 2006, online, www.people.com.

5. "'Grey's' Isaiah Washington Going to Rehab," ABC News, 25 January 2007, online, www.abcnews.go.com.

6. "ABC to Debut Isaiah Washington PSA Today," news release issued by the Gay and Lesbian Alliance Against Defamation, 24 May 2007, online, www.glaad.org.

7. Cherie Jacobs, "More Companies Extend Benefits to Same-Sex Partners," *Tampa Tribune,* 12 August 2001, online, LexisNexis.

8. Alex Johnson, "Southern Baptists End Eight-Year Disney Boycott," MSNBC, 22 June 2005, online, www.msnbc.msn.com.

9. James E. Grunig and Fred C. Repper, "Strategic Management, Publics, and Issues," in *Excellence in Public Relations and Communication Management,* ed. James E. Grunig (Hillsdale, N.J.: Lawrence Erlbaum, 1992), 125.

10. James E. Grunig, "Furnishing the Edifice: Ongoing Research on Public Relations as a Strategic Management Function," *Journal of Public Relations Research* 18 (2006): 156.

11. "Only One-Third of Companies Say Their Employees Understand and Live Business Strategy in Daily Jobs," news release issued by the International Association of Business Communicators, 13 September 2005, online, http://news.iabc.com.

12. "Maintaining Common Corporate Culture Is Chief Concern for Global Executives," news release issued by Accenture, 25 January 2007, online, www.accenture.com.

13. "Effective Employee Communication Linked to Greater Shareholder Returns," news release issued by Watson Wyatt Worldwide, 3 November 2003, online, www.watsonwyatt.com.

14. Robert Barner, "The New Millennium Workplace: Seven Changes That Will Challenge Managers—and Workers," *The Futurist,* March–April 1996, 14–19.

15. "New Frontiers in Employee Communication: 2006," a report issued by Edelman and PeopleMetrics, 16 January 2006, online, www.edelman.com.

16. "Traditional Employer Characteristics Remain Most Popular Among Job Seekers," news release issued by Accenture, 29 August 2006, online, www.accenture.com.

17. Martin Sprouse, ed., *Sabotage in the American Workplace* (San Francisco: Pressure Drop Press, 1992).

18. John Milne, "We Need to Talk," *Canadian Manager* (spring 2000): online, LexisNexis.

19. "Staffing Statistics: American Staffing 2007—Annual Economic Analysis," report issued by the American Staffing Association, 2007, online, www.americanstaffing.net.

20. Louis Uchitelle, "Companies Hold off on Hiring Until Demand Rises," *New York Times,* 6 March 2004, online, LexisNexis.

21. "ASTD Releases New Data on Workplace Learning Investments and Practices," news release issued by the American Society for Training and Development, 12 January 2007, online, www.astd.org.

22. "Federal Reserve Chairman Calls for Enhancing Worker Skills," news release issued by the American Society for Training & Development, 25 February 2004, online, www.astd.org.

23. "ASTD Releases New Data on Workplace Learning Investments and Practices."

24. "Civilian Labor Force by Sex, Age, Race, and Hispanic Origin," U.S. Bureau of Labor Statistics, 11 February 2004, online, www.bls.gov/emp/emplab06.htm.

25. "Labor Force Growth: Past, Present, and Future," report by the U.S. Bureau of Labor Statistics, 4 January 2007, online, www.bls.gov.

26. "Civilian Labor Force by Sex, Age, Race, and Hispanic Origin."

27. Jennifer Gilbert, "Motivating Through the Ages," *Sales & Marketing Management,* November 2003, 34–40.

28. "Traditional Employer Characteristics Remain Most Popular Among Job Seekers."

29. *Gale Directory of Publications and Broadcast Media, vol. 3,* 136th ed. (Farmington Hills, Mich.: Gale, 2002), xxvii.

30. Lynne Sallot, Thomas Steinfatt, and Michael Salwen, "Journalists' and Public Relations Practitioners' News Values: Perceptions and Cross-Perceptions," *Journalism and Mass Communication Quarterly* (summer 1998): 369–370.

31. "The Internet and Campaign 2006," news release issued by the Pew Internet & American Life Project, 17 January 2007, online, www.pewinternet.org.

32. Felicity Barringer, "Editors Debate Realism vs. Retreat in Newsroom Diversity," *New York Times,* 6 April 1998, online, LexisNexis.

33. "Diversity Slips in U.S. Newsrooms," news release issued by the American Society of Newspaper Editors, 26 March 2007, online, www.asne.org.

34. Bob Papper, "Year of Extremes," *Communicator,* July/August 2006, online, www.rtnda.org.

35. Papper.

36. "Federal Government Civilian Employment by Function," U.S. Census Bureau, December 2005, online, www2.census.gov.

37. *The 2006–2007 Career Guide to Industries,* U.S. Bureau of Labor Statistics, 27 February 2004, online, www.bls.gov.

38. "Federal Government Civilian Employment by Function."

39. "Federal Human Capital Survey 2006," report by the U.S. Office of Personnel Management, 17 January 2007, online, www.fhcs2006.opm.gov.

40. "Annual Report to Congress," Federal Equal Opportunity Recruitment Program, January 2007, online, www.opm.gov/feorpreports.

41. James D. McKevitt, "Making Friends on the Hill," *Association Management,* October 1996, online, LexisNexis.

42. "Federal Human Capital Survey 2006."

43. "2006 Public Employment Data: State Governments," U.S. Census Bureau, online, www.census.gov; "2006 Public Employment Data: Local Governments," U.S. Census Bureau, online, www.census.gov.

44. "Employment by Major Industry Sector," U.S. Bureau of Labor Statistics, December 2005, online, www.bls.gov.

45. "Affirmative Action Annual Report for Wisconsin State Government, 27th Edition," State of Wisconsin Office of State Employee Relations, July 2006, online, http://oser .state.wi.us.

46. Maureen Feighan, "Benefit Cuts Hit Public Workers, *Detroit News,* 6 December 2005, online, LexisNexis.

47. "Grading the States 2005," a report by the Government Performance Project, 2005, online, www.gpponline.org; "The Government Performance Project Grades the 50 States," news release issued by the Government Performance Project, 31 January 2005, online, www.gpponline.com.

48. John Ledingham and Stephen Bruning, "Managing Community Relationships to Maximize Mutual Benefit," in *Handbook of Public Relations,* ed. Robert L. Heath (Thousand Oaks, Calif.: Sage, 2001), 530.

49. "Equity Ownership in America: 2005," report issued by the Investment Company Institute and the Securities Industry Association, 2005, online, www.ici.org.

50. "May Investor Optimism Hits Highest Level Since January," news release issued by UBS, 29 May 2007, online, www.ubs.com.

51. "Today's Investor Expresses New Attitudes, New Experiences."

52. "Equity Ownership in America: 2005," Investment Company Institute and the Securities Industry Association, 2005, online, www.ici.org.

53. "Gen-X'ers Facing Significant Roadblocks on the Road to Saving for Retirement," news release issued by Charles Schwab & Company, 20 February 2007, online, www.aboutschwab.com/press/releases.

54. "Gen-X'ers Facing Significant Roadblocks on the Road to Saving for Retirement."

55. "Equity Ownership in America: 2005."

56. "Equity Ownership in America: 2005."

57. "Equity Ownership in America: 2005."

58. "The World Economic Outlook Database," International Monetary Fund, online, www.imf.org.

59. Louis Uchitelle, "Why Americans Must Keep Spending," *New York Times,* 1 December 2003, online, LexisNexis.

60. Christopher Reynolds, "Spending Trending," *American Demographics,* 1 April 2004, online, LexisNexis.

61. Wendy Kaufman, "Poor Customer Service Common, Expensive," *All Things Considered,* 21 May 2007, online, www.npr.org; "Beware of Dissatisfied Customers: They Like to Blab," Knowledge@Wharton, 8 March 2006, online, http://knowledge.wharton.upenn.edu.

62. "Consumer Expenditures in 2005: Annual Report," U.S. Bureau of Labor Statistics, February 2007, online, www.bls.gov.

63. "Consumer Expenditures in 2005: Annual Report."

64. Kristi Turnquist, "Memo to Marketers: Wise Up about Women" (Portland) *Oregonian,* 26 May 2004, online, LexisNexis.

65. Oliver Burkeman, "Is Jerry the Joker?" (London) *Guardian,* 3 July 2002, online, www.guardian.co.uk.

66. All examples are from Ted L. Nancy, *Letters from a Nut* (New York: Scholastic, 1997).

67. Frederick F. Reichheld, *The Loyalty Effect* (Boston: Harvard Business School Press, 1996), 33.

68. James Morrow, "X-It Plan," *American Demographics,* 1 May 2004, online, LexisNexis.

69. Michael J. Weiss, "To Be about to Be," *American Demographics,* 1 September 2003, online, LexisNexis.

70. "Quarterly Retail E-Commerce Sales, 4th Quarter 2006," news release issued by the U.S. Census Bureau, 16 February 2007, online, www.census.gov.

71. "U.S. Consumers Increasingly Going Online," news release issued by Accenture, 4 April 2007, online, www.accenture.com.

72. "Gartner Says Nearly $2 Billion Lost in E-Commerce Sales in 2006," news release issued by Gartner Inc., 27 November 2006, online, LexisNexis.

73. David McDermitt and Tony Shelton, "The 10 Commandments of Community Relations," *World Wastes,* September 1993, online, LexisNexis.

74. Jerry A. Hendrix, *Public Relations Cases,* 4th ed. (Belmont, Calif.: Wadsworth, 1998), 18–19.

75. Tannette Johnson-Elie, "Denny's Turnabout Means Fair Play for Minority Employees," *Milwaukee Journal Sentinel,* 31 October 2000, online, LexisNexis.

76. "Denny's Named Among Top Performers in Black Enterprise List of the 40 Best Companies for Diversity," news release issued by Denny's, 12 June 2006, online, www.dennys.com.

77. "U.S. Interim Projections by Age, Sex, Race and Hispanic Origins," U.S. Bureau of the Census, online, www.census.gov.

78. Luke J. Larsen, "The Foreign-Born Population in the United States: 2003," U.S. Census Bureau, August 2004, online, www.census.gov.

79. Larsen.

80. "Voter Turnout a Tad Higher Than Last Midterm," MSNBC, 8 November 2006, online, www.msnbc.msn.com.

81. "Voter Turnout from 1945 to Date," International Institute for Democracy and Electoral Assistance, 2004, online, www.idea.int.

82. Kelly Holder, "Voting and Registration in the Election of November 2004," U.S. Census Bureau, March 2006, online, www.census.gov. Unless otherwise noted, voting data are from Holder.

83. Scott Keeter, "Election '06: Big Changes in Some Key Groups," Pew Center for the People and the Press, 16 November 2006, online, http://pewresearch.org.

84. "PR League Tables: Why Trade PRs Are Hooked on the Net," *Marketing,* 25 May 2000, online, LexisNexis.

85. "E-Commerce 2005," U.S. Census Bureau, 25 May 2007, online, www.census.gov.

86. "Enabling Partner Value Networks Through Partner Relationship Management," report by Oracle, August 2006, online, www.oracle.com.

87. Nathan Burchfiel, "German Film Defends Subway Restaurant Press Kit," Cybercast News Service, online, www.cnsnews.com.

88. Eric Pfanner, "Subway Stirs the Ire of Patriots," *International Herald Tribune,* 9 August 2004, online, LexisNexis.

89. Burchfiel.

90. "Subway Ends Anti-American Promotion," news release issued by the Center for Individual Freedom, 3 August 2004, online, LexisNexis.

91. John N. Frank, "Subway Under Pressure to Apologize for Insulting U.S.," *PR Week,* 9 August 2004, online, LexisNexis.

92. Pfanner, "Subway Pulls German Promo Featuring Large Lady Liberty," *Los Angeles Times,* 3 August 2004, online, LexisNexis.

93. "Subway's 'Humorous' Promotion Is No Laughing Matter for PR Execs," *PR News,* 23 August 2004, online, LexisNexis.

94. Pam Dawkins, "Subway Disavows 'Fat' Promo" (Bridgeport) *Connecticut Post,* 5 August 2004, online, LexisNexis.

95. "Subway's 'Humorous' Promotion Is No Laughing Matter for PR Execs."
96. Burchfiel.
97. "Subway's 'Humorous' Promotion Is No Laughing Matter for PR Execs."
98. Dawkins.
99. "Subway Pulls German Promo Featuring Large Lady Liberty."
100. Frank.
101. Dawkins.
102. "Subway's 'Humorous' Promotion Is No Laughing Matter for PR Execs."
103. Katie Delahaye Paine, "Image Patrol—Subway/McDonald's," *PR News,* 16 August 2004, online, LexisNexis.
104. "Whirlpool Brand Announces 2004 Reba McEntire Tour Dates," news release issued by Whirlpool Corporation, 10 May 2004, online, LexisNexis.
105. "Vision & Strategy," Whirlpool Corporation, online, www.whirlpoolcorp.com.
106. "Whirlpool and Habitat for Humanity," Whirlpool Corporation, online, www .whirlpoolcorp.com.
107. "Whirlpool Brand to Sponsor Reba McEntire Concert Tour That Will Benefit Habitat for Humanity," news release issued by Whirlpool Corporation, 22 March 2004, online, www.whirlpoolcorp.com.
108. "Whirlpool Brand to Sponsor Reba McEntire Concert Tour That Will Benefit Habitat for Humanity."
109. "Whirlpool Corporation Sponsors Habitat for Humanity Blitz Build on Headquarters' Campus," news release issued by Whirlpool Corporation, online, www.whirlpoolcorp .com.
110. "Our Commitment to Corporate Responsibility," Whirlpool Corporation, online, www.whirlpoolcorp.com; "Vision & Strategy."
111. "Whirlpool and Habitat for Humanity."
112. "Whirlpool and Habitat for Humanity"; "Whirlpool Corporation Sponsors Habitat for Humanity Blitz Build on Headquarters' Campus."
113. "Our Commitment to Corporate Responsibility."

5

Communication Theory and Public Opinion

OBJECTIVES

After studying this chapter, you will be able to

- understand the process of communication and some of the theories of how people react to what they encounter in the mass media

- identify the forces that motivate people

- describe the power of public opinion and the process under which it develops

- recognize the differences between the use of persuasion and manipulation in public relations

KEY TERMS

Growing Pains

The local state university was founded as an agricultural college in the late 19th century. At that time, it was located on farmland several miles from a small town. However, times have changed, and both the school and the community are experiencing growing pains—apparently at each other's expense.

The latest controversy involves the university's purchase of three dilapidated houses on the edge of one of the town's oldest neighborhoods. School administrators want to tear down the houses and build a much-needed residence hall. The neighbors object, saying the structure will increase noise and traffic. Also opposed are members of the local historical society, who believe the dormitory would have a negative impact on a nearby historic site. It seems as if everyone has a dog in this fight, including the university, its students, the neighborhood, the historical society, the local zoning board, and even the governor, who also chairs the state historical commission.

If you were a public relations counselor to one of the many sides in this dispute, how would you proceed?

The Power of Public Opinion

The story of the Allied invasion of France in June 1944 is well documented; lesser known is the tale of a little church, its bells, and their role in the liberation of Europe.

Hermanville-sur-Mer, located near Sword Beach in the British landing zone, was the first village liberated from the Nazis on D-day.[1] The bells of the town's only church rang in celebration, but they gave off an odd sound—German snipers had destroyed the largest of the carillon's three bells just a few hours earlier. With the damaged carillon tolling in the background, BBC radio correspondent Allan Melville reported, "I thought that you would rather hear the bells now, even though the big one has been smashed by the Germans, to let you know that the people of Normandy are celebrating their liberation."[2]

As Allied troops pushed inland, they encountered Nazi propaganda claiming that the invaders (the Allies) had left nothing in the wake of their advance except death and destruction. The German message to the people living in Nazi-occupied Europe was simple: Do not cooperate with the Allies. To discredit the propaganda, the BBC broadcast a mass of liberation from Hermanville's church on June 18. It included the sound of the church's odd-sounding bells, as well as recordings of church bells in other liberated villages. The powerful symbolism encouraged the people of Europe to continue to resist the Nazis. It told them that freedom was in the air—and on the march.

This is not just a war story. It is also about harnessing the power of public opinion. If it is a potent force during war, imagine its power during peace. The very essence of a democratic society is that public policies are created as a result of words, not weapons. Effective communication is a key to success. So is the ability to persuade others to accept or at least respect your point of view. Both are at the heart of the practice of public relations.

As we've said before and will say again, good public relations involves two-way communication between an organization and the publics important to its success. Responding to the concerns and needs of others is a big part of public relations. Ultimately, you want to create a mutually beneficial environment in which both an organization and its publics can flourish. That environment is achieved through the give-and-take that characterizes two-way communication. It is not enough for an organization to be a good listener. It also must be a good communicator. Successful companies and individuals excel in letting others know their values and preferences. And in today's results-oriented environment, success is often measured by one's ability to persuade others to come around to a certain way of thinking.

In this chapter's opening scenario, local residents and university officials are at loggerheads over plans to build a dormitory. School officials see the construction as a good deal for the community. More students on campus means more money for local merchants. Construction would also remove some community eyesores. However, the residents have a different perspective. They fear a dormitory would change the nature of their neighborhood and lower their property values. As a result, each side has certain values it does not want to compromise.

Because public relations focuses on building and maintaining relationships, it is important for practitioners to understand how the processes of communication and persuasion work—and how to use that knowledge to achieve values-driven and mutually beneficial solutions.

A Communication Model

Before we discuss how public opinion is formed, let's look at the process that makes it happen, communication. It is a process familiar to all and completely understood by none. Since Aristotle's day, scholars have tried to figure out how it works. They have developed what are called "communication models," graphic representations helpful in understanding the dynamics of the communication process. Some of these models are simplistic. Others look like the schematic drawing of an MP3 player. For our purposes, we have chosen a model based on the writings of David Berlo.[3] The elegance of this model is its simplicity. It breaks down the communication process into six basic ingredients: noise, source, message, channel, receiver, and feedback (Figure 5.1).

Noise. Sometimes referred to as static, **noise** envelops communication and often inhibits it. Noise can take both physical and intangible forms. It can have a physical quality, such as that experienced when a person is trying to talk with someone in a large crowd. The crowd noise can make it difficult to understand everything being said. However, noise does not have to be audible to inhibit communication. A person's state of mind can also block effective communication. An example is the

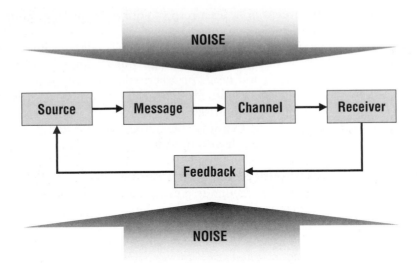

FIGURE 5.1 A Communication Model

mental "static" experienced by a person who is reeling from an emotional event and is not really listening to what is said. There are also times when for a variety of reasons—cultural, religious, and generational among them—we erect barriers to communication. In these instances, we often generate "noise" because we don't like either the message or the messenger.

Source.   The **source** is where a communication originates. The source is also the first part of the coorientation model mentioned in Chapter 4. How a source views its audience—and is viewed by an audience—can help or hinder communication. Source credibility can be influenced by a variety of factors, including reputation, context, and communication ability. For example, a particular elected official was once seen as a leading advocate for strong family values. His subsequent arrest on a morals charge, however, undermined his credibility and ultimately ended his political career.

Message.   The **message** is the content of the communication. To a large degree, successful formation of the message relies on knowledge of both the purpose of the message and its intended receiver. If the message is not relevant or is not in language understood by that receiver, it will probably be misunderstood or ignored. It wouldn't make sense for your professor to speak to the class in French—unless, of course, it was a French class.

Channel.   The **channel** is the medium used to transmit the message to the intended receiver. The selection of the most appropriate channel or channels is a key strategic decision. Like the source, the channel must be relevant and credible to the intended receiver. And much like a broadcast channel on an old-time radio, the channel can

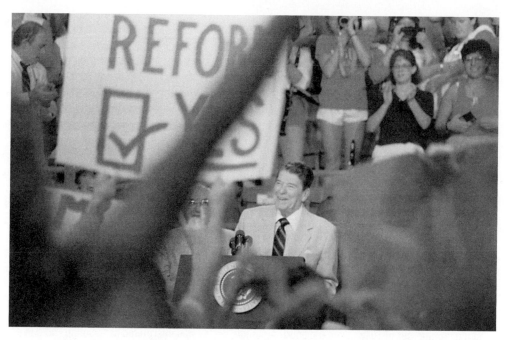

Even Ronald Reagan, considered one of the best communicators to live in the White House, faced the challenge of overcoming noise in the environment when promoting his administration's policies. (Photo by David Guth)

be susceptible to static. In this case, static is defined as physical and psychological forces that can make it difficult for the receiver to acquire the message. For example, many public relations practitioners have had their well-planned efforts at obtaining publicity foiled by breaking news stories that have caused reporters to focus their attentions elsewhere. One of your authors had three painstakingly planned news conferences derailed by attempted political assassinations in the same year.

Receiver. The **receiver** is the person or persons for whom the message is intended. The receiver is also the second part of the coorientation model mentioned in Chapter 4. How the receiver views the source—and is viewed by the source—can help or hinder communication. The most effective communications are those that specifically target the intended receiver. For reasons already stated, the communicator must select the source, message, and channel with the needs of the receiver in mind. That, in turn, requires a thorough knowledge of the receiver, including its needs, values, predispositions, and communication ability. After all, what good does it do to communicate if the intended audience is not listening?

Feedback. **Feedback** is the receiver's reaction—as interpreted by the source—to the message. Without this final step, true communication does not occur. Feedback lets you know whether the message got through and how it was interpreted. Think of a

QUICKBREAK 5.1

Mokusatsu

Communication fails when a source sends a message that cannot be understood or is misinterpreted by the receiver. Never has that fact had more tragic consequences than at the end of World War II, when the decision to use atomic bombs may have hinged on a misunderstanding over the meaning of a single Japanese word.

The decision to use the recently developed bomb against Japanese targets was not an easy one for President Harry Truman. On the one hand, the bomb might shock the Japanese military into surrendering, thus avoiding the bloody consequences of a full-scale military invasion of the island nation. On the other hand, Truman also knew that many civilians would be killed in an atomic attack. However, the signs coming out of Tokyo were not good. Although the Japanese military had been crushed as a result of three years of terrifying and unrelenting warfare, its leaders said Japan would never surrender.

Truman decided to give the Japanese one last chance before unleashing the bomb. In what has become known as the Potsdam Declaration, Truman told the Japanese that they had to surrender unconditionally or face unspecified consequences. Japanese Prime Minister Kantaro Suzuki, an aging civilian

aristocrat, wanted to negotiate peace quickly with the Americans. But Suzuki also knew that the military, which dominated the government, would not let him.

When asked by the military press for his response to the Potsdam Declaration, the prime minister said, "We *mokusatsu* it." Suzuki thought he had been clever. *Mokusatsu* is a Japanese word that has a variety of interpretations, largely dependent on who is perceived as its source. In saying "We *mokusatsu* it," Suzuki was speaking for himself and asking the Americans to keep negotiations open and make another peace offer. However, Truman believed the prime minister was speaking on behalf of the military. In that context, *mokusatsu* was interpreted as meaning "hold in silent contempt."

Believing that the Japanese had rejected the United States' last olive branch, Truman authorized the use of atomic bombs. Hiroshima was attacked on August 6, 1945. An estimated 92,000 people were killed and an unknown number suffered long-term effects from radiation. Another 40,000 people died three days later in the atomic bombing of Nagasaki. One week later, the Japanese surrendered.

stand-up comedian: If the audience laughs, the joke was funny. If there is silence, the joke failed. Good communicators, especially public relations practitioners, actively seek feedback. Feedback, often in the form of telephone calls, e-mails, and letters, can be spontaneous. However, that isn't always the case. Sometimes special mechanisms are established to generate feedback, such as toll-free telephone numbers, interactive web sites, and public opinion polls.

As stated before, social scientists have developed a variety of communication models. However, the models all have something in common: Communication is a lot like an electrical circuit—if a short or break occurs anywhere along the wire, nothing happens. No communication takes place if the source is not seen as credible, the message is not relevant, the channel is filled with static, the receiver is not listening, or feedback is lacking.

A breakdown in the communication process was evident in May 1970, when President Richard Nixon attempted to reach out to anti–Vietnam War protesters. The president made a predawn visit to the Lincoln Memorial, where antiwar activists, mostly college students, were camped out awaiting the start of a major protest rally. The meeting didn't go well. Nixon said he spoke to the students about his and their mutual desire to end the war—but he said they didn't really listen. The students told reporters that the president talked about sports and surfing and "wasn't really concerned about why we were here." Whichever version of the event you accept, the outcome was undeniable: a communication breakdown that reinforced the mistrust that Nixon and the students had of one another.[4] For true communication to take place, it must be a two-way process.

QUICK CHECK

1. What are the six elements of the communication model used in this text?
2. What are some of the things that can block communication?
3. Why is listening essential to good communication and effective public relations?

Mass Communication Theories

Public relations practitioners are, in some respects, the race car drivers of mass communication. Aside from the obvious comparisons—that speed, accuracy, and winning are desired—there's also a critical need to know what makes things work. Drivers know what makes their machines tick. That knowledge gives them the edge they need to gain maximum performance from their cars. For the same reason, practitioners need to understand the processes of mass communication—what makes it tick. Over the past century, a variety of mass communication theories have evolved for just that reason.

The Magic Bullet Theory

World events had a great influence on early theories of mass communications. As you may remember from the history chapter of this book, research interest in persuasion and public opinion heated up in the wake of the use of propaganda techniques during World War I. The growth of fascism in Europe and Asia during the 1930s largely paralleled the growth of the first electronic mass medium, radio. Out of these developments came the first mass communications theory, the **magic bullet theory** of mass communications. This theory, illustrated in Figure 5.2, is grounded in a belief that the mass

FIGURE 5.2 The Magic Bullet Theory of Mass Communications

FIGURE 5.3 Two-Step Flow of Mass Communications

media wield great power over their audiences. It was thought that if a sender developed just the right message, the so-called magic bullet, people could be influenced to do almost anything. The problem with this approach to mass communications is that it supposes that people are weak-willed robots unable to resist finely sculptured appeals.

The Two-Step Theory

By the end of World War II, the magic bullet theory had been largely discredited. Social scientists began to understand better the role of intervening publics in influencing public opinion. From this realization evolved the **two-step theory** of mass communications, the foundation of which is the belief that the mass media influence society's key opinion leaders, who in turn influence the opinions and actions of society itself (Figure 5.3). These key opinion leaders were said to include elected public officials, powerful business executives, and religious figures. Although the opinion leaders were seen as powerful, this theory remained based on the belief that the mass media were powerful forces in molding public opinion.

The N-Step Theory

Recognizing that different people may be credible in different contexts, communication researcher Wilbur Schramm developed the **n-step theory** of mass communications (Figure 5.4). It was similar to the two-step theory in that it stressed the role of

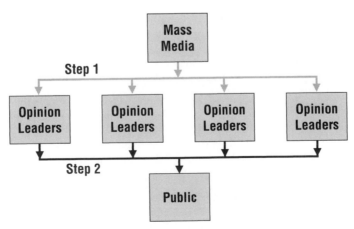

FIGURE 5.4 N-Step Flow of Mass Communications

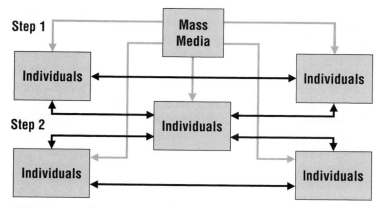

FIGURE 5.5 Diffusion Theory

opinion leaders. However, under the n-step theory, key opinion leaders may vary from issue to issue. For example, you may turn to controversial slugger Barry Bonds if you want to learn how to hit a baseball. However, it is more likely that you would seek insight from a finance expert if you actually wanted to buy some bonds.

Diffusion Theory

Unlike its predecessors, the **diffusion theory** of mass communications was based on a belief that the power of the mass media is not as much to motivate people as it is to inform them (Figure 5.5). Under this theoretical view of mass communications, people have the power to influence members of their own peer groups. Agricultural extension agents have followed this approach for decades. The agents provide farmers with information on how they can improve their crop yields. If a farmer adopts an approach that works, he or she spreads the word of this success to other farmers. In other words, the idea is passed along through a diffusion process. In a sense, everyone can become an opinion leader.

The Agenda-Setting Hypothesis

The most significant and widely accepted view of how the mass media interact with society is currently the **agenda-setting hypothesis.** It is based on the simple principle that the mass media tell people not what to think, but what to think about. In other words, the media set the public agenda (Figure 5.6).

FIGURE 5.6 The Agenda-Setting Hypothesis

Why Public Relations Is Not Propaganda

Few words in the English language are as emotionally and ethically charged as *propaganda*.[5] That's why public relations practitioners bristle when people—especially journalists—suggest that public relations and propaganda are one and the same.

The problem is that propaganda—just like public relations—is hard to define. Historian Brett Gray wrote, "Propaganda as a label suffered (and suffers) from a certain imprecision; it is not unlike Justice Potter Stewart's fabled definition of pornography: 'I don't know how to define it, but I know it when I see it.'"[6]

Many see propaganda as an umbrella covering all forms of persuasive communication, including advertising and public relations. Even the man considered the father of modern public relations, Edward L. Bernays, gave credence to this interpretation when he defined *public relations*—the term he coined in *Crystallizing Public Opinion*—as "the new propaganda."[7]

Some researchers lump all persuasive communication into two broad categories. One is *revealed propaganda*, messages that are overt in their effort to persuade, such as those in conventional advertising. The other is *concealed propaganda*, such as publicity generated from the distribution of news releases. However, if this approach is followed to a logical conclusion, it could be argued that *all* communication is propaganda.[8] One wonders how journalists would feel about that.

Since its earliest days, practitioners have tried to differentiate public relations from propaganda by placing it within an ethical framework. That was certainly the intent of Ivy Lee, whose "Declaration of Principles" in 1906 spoke of providing "prompt and accurate information."[9] But public relations historian Scott M. Cutlip wrote that Bernays' efforts to further define public relations in his 1928 book *Propaganda* served only to muddy the waters and "handed the infant field's critics a club with which to bludgeon it."[10]

Gray argued that propaganda should not be confused with advertising and public relations. "For my part, I try to maintain that distinction by defining propaganda as the organized manipulations of key cultural symbols and images (and biases) for the purposes of persuading a mass audience to take a position, or move to action, or remain inactive on a controversial matter," he wrote.[11]

Propaganda researchers Garth S. Jowett and Victoria O'Donnell prefer an even narrower definition. "Propaganda is the deliberate, systematic attempt to shape perceptions, manipulate cognitions, and direct behavior to achieve a response that furthers the desired intent of the propagandist."[12] In contrast, they argue that persuasion "is interactive and attempts to satisfy the needs of both the persuader and persuadee."[13] These interpretations are in line with more widely accepted definitions of public relations that stress two-way communication, as well as the building and maintaining of mutually beneficial relationships.

As is discussed at the end of this chapter, there's a big difference between persuasion and manipulation. Public relations practitioners know this.

We see examples of the agenda-setting hypothesis at work in every morning's newspaper. Have you ever noticed how one issue can dominate the newspapers—and public debate—for several weeks, only to be replaced by another? Just ask public relations practitioners for Louisville-based Yum Brands. The company's Taco Bell restaurants received intense media scrutiny—and became the target of late night comedians—when an *E. coli* outbreak sickened 71 customers in the northeastern United States during November 2006. This launched a flurry of news stories about food safety. The company engaged in two weeks of damage control, and by mid-December, the media turned their attention to other matters.[14] However, the company returned to the media's crosshairs in February 2007 when a New York television station videotaped dozens of rats running around a Greenwich Village KFC/Taco Bell. Within hours, more than 1,000 blogs had cited the story or posted the video. Food safety was again at the center of public debate.[15]

If you take the agenda-setting hypothesis to its next logical step, it raises an important question: If the media tell us not what to think but what to think about, who tells the media what to think about? Media in democratic societies have the independence to report on any topic they choose, so who sets the media's agenda?

The answer is equally important: Organizations and individuals are free to use public relations techniques to influence the media and thereby to put their imprint on the public agenda. And many organizations and individuals do just that. Historically, presidents of the United States have been particularly good at setting the media's agenda. Because of the power and prestige of the White House, almost anything a president does or says is news. Every president from Washington on has tried to influence news coverage in an attempt to control the public agenda. However, because presidents are not alone in understanding these dynamics, each has enjoyed only mixed success. For example, a CBS News/*New York Times* survey gave President George W. Bush a 90 percent approval rating for his handling of the campaign against terrorism shortly after the 9/11 attacks. However, as the war in Iraq dragged into its fourth year, those ratings dipped to 40 percent in early 2007.[16]

Uses and Gratifications Theory

This brings us to yet another evolution in communications theory. In recent years, theorists have noted that the agenda-setting hypothesis is based on a model in which the receiver is seen as a passive participant in the communication process. If this model is correct, theorists point out, then the source has the ultimate power of persuasion over the receiver. However, this concept of a passive receiver is being challenged by what is known as the **uses and gratifications theory.** The technological advances of recent years have resulted in an explosion of available mass communications channels. Researchers say that the real power now rests in the ability of receivers to pick and choose their channels of information. Although many communicators may seek to persuade the audience to take a particular course of action, the audience serves as a gatekeeper—in effect, deciding to whom it will grant influence (Figure 5.7).[17]

A Two-Way Process

Mass communications theory appears to have undergone a complete reversal. It has evolved from a belief that people are powerless to resist the mass media to an acknowledgment of the public's supremacy over media. This new view suggests that persuasion, like communication, is a two-way street. According to *Excellence in*

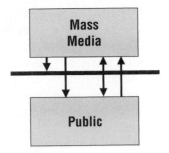

FIGURE 5.7 Uses and Gratifications Theory

Public Relations and Communication Management, a publication of the IABC Research Foundation, "The concept of negotiation, rather than domination or persuasion, is the key to understanding the effects of communication and public relations programs."[18]

Let's go back to the opening scenario of this chapter. Each side of the dormitory debate has its merits. The university says construction will bring important economic benefits to the community as well as remove unwanted dilapidated housing. Opponents of the plan fear it will disrupt the peace and quiet of their neighborhood and possibly harm a historically significant site. If each side enters the debate unwilling to listen to the other, sparks will, no doubt, fly. Eventually, one side will win and the other side will lose. But the controversy will not end there. The lingering effects of the ill will created by such a controversy could have political, social, and economic ramifications for years. However, if the two sides enter the discussion willing to listen to each other's concerns, a compromise is possible. Neighborhood preservation and campus growth are not necessarily mutually exclusive concepts. However, the key to keeping the peace is two-way communication.

Motivation

Having discussed the communication process and the various theories on how mass communications influence people, we now focus on the individual. What motivates a given individual to do something? What forces are in play when we try to influence someone's behavior? What kind of appeals can spark action? These are questions psychologists and sociologists have pondered for centuries.

Although many theories explain why people do the things they do, one simple explanation is best: People usually act in their own self-interests. This may not seem, on the surface, to be an earth-shattering revelation. However, this simple truth is at the heart of molding public opinion. But how do people determine their self-interests? You can look to your own parents for the answer.

As strange as it may seem, your parents were once teenagers. If they grew up in the late 1960s and early 1970s, it is very possible that they owned bell-bottom jeans, wore long hair, and spoke of a desire for a peaceful world governed by a loose-knit

QuickBreak 5.3

Spinning, Framing, and Priming

As already noted several times in this book, many find public relations a difficult concept to define. That's why one often hears practitioners referred to by a variety—and sometimes unflattering array—of nicknames. They have been called press agents, flacks, mouthpieces, fronts, shills—and a few names of which your mother would not approve.

However, public relations practitioners were given a new handle in an October 21, 1984, *New York Times* editorial: **spin doctors.** Editorial writer Jack Rosenthal coined the phrase on the eve of that year's second presidential campaign debate:

> Tonight at about 9:30, seconds after the Reagan–Mondale debate ends, a bazaar will suddenly materialize in the press room of the Kansas City Municipal Auditorium. A dozen men in good suits and women in silk dresses will circulate smoothly among reporters, spouting confident opinions. They won't be just press agents trying to impart a favorable spin to a routine release. They'll be the Spin Doctors, senior advisers to the candidates, and they'll be playing for very high stakes. How well they do their work could be as important as how well their candidates do theirs.[19]

In his book *New Political Dictionary,* political columnist William Safire defined **spin** as "deliberate shading of news perception; attempted control of political reaction."[20] In essence, spin doctors try to influence perceptions by emphasizing certain aspects of events that reinforce their point of view. An example of spin would be the classic difference between a pessimist and an optimist: The pessimist sees the glass half-empty while the optimist sees the glass half-full.

While *spin* is the popular term-of-art, a more appropriate word to describe this kind of activity is **framing.** It is a concept first articulated by Canadian sociologist Erving Goffman in 1974. In his book *Frame Analysis: Essays on the Organization of Experience,* Goffman wrote that all of us "actively classify and organize our life experiences to make sense of them."[21] Researcher Robert Entman has defined framing as communicating an idea in such a way that an audience is influenced, either intentionally or unintentionally, by the way it is expressed.[22]

Regardless of whether it is called spinning or framing, its real purpose is **priming.** According to priming theory, people make judgments about complex issues based on bits and pieces of easily accessible memory. By framing issues in the simplest of terms, politicians and other advocates prime the memories of their audiences, thus leading these publics to see matters in the most favorable light.[23]

At this point, you might question whether spinning, framing, and priming are things ethical public relations practitioners do. The answer is yes—if done in an appropriate manner. Using accurate information within a proper context is no different from articulating mutual interests and values. It is only when one attempts to distort, hide, or mislead that the use of these tactics comes into question.

philosophy known as "flower power." At the center of this popular culture was the most successful rock band the world had ever known, the Beatles. John, Paul, George, and Ringo had a generation believing that if you sought peace and tranquillity, "all you need is love."

If only it were that simple. Unfortunately, the Beatles were wrong.

Maslow's Hierarchy of Needs

Long before the Fab Four sang that love is the central force behind everything, psychologist Abraham Maslow developed a theory to explain how people determine their self-interests: **Maslow's Hierarchy of Needs** (Figure 5.8). The basis of the theory is that some needs are more basic than others and, therefore, must be fulfilled first.[24] On Maslow's list, love comes in only third.

According to Maslow, the lowest (most basic) order of needs is our *physiological* needs. These are the biological demands our bodies make for food, water, rest, and exercise. He included sex among our most basic needs, but only as it related to the continuation of our species. Love and romance had nothing to do with it. By Maslow's way of thinking, if humans do not fulfill their physiological needs, little else matters.

According to Maslow, *safety* is the next order of need. By "safety needs" he means things such as personal security, comfort, and orderly surroundings. To understand Maslow's ranking, assume for a minute that you are in a shelter in the middle of a war zone. Bombs and bullets are flying all around you. The shooting is expected to last for weeks. As long as you stay in that shelter, you are safe. However, suppose that shelter has no food or water. Maslow believed that, eventually, you will leave that shelter and forgo personal safety to fulfill your physiological needs. Otherwise, you will die anyway.

The third order of need is *acceptance,* or what Maslow referred to as love and belongingness. This is where the Beatles come in. At this level, we seek out love, a sense of belonging, an affiliation with others through group memberships. Still, this is only third on the list. Pretend that you have entered our imaginary bomb shelter

FIGURE 5.8 Maslow's Hierarchy of Needs

only to find that it is filled with people you do not like and vice versa. Under Maslow's hierarchy, you are willing to endure any annoyance and indignity that may occur from these uncomfortable arrangements because of the safety the shelter provides.

Next on Maslow's Hierarchy of Needs is *self-esteem,* for which we strive to earn recognition and view ourselves as being successful. Everyone wants to be seen as a winner. However, people are often willing to let their self-esteem suffer if doing so provides some measure of acceptance. That is why some people choose to remain in abusive, unhealthy relationships. It isn't until the victim understands that this isn't true acceptance or that physiological or safety needs are threatened that the abusive relationship ends.

The highest order is *self-actualization* needs. We reach self-actualization when we achieve a goal just for the sake of achieving that goal. Climbing a mountain "because it is there" is an expression of self-actualization. Some people never achieve self-actualization because they haven't fulfilled the requirements imposed by lower-order needs. In some ways, self-actualization is like the Great American Novel that many people say they will write but never do—because their attention is constantly focused on more pressing needs.

Examples of Maslow's Theory at Work

Just a guess: You are not reading about Maslow's Hierarchy of Needs as an expression of self-actualization. Your motivation is probably a result of a need to fulfill your safety needs: Failure to read the material assigned by your professor could well put your grade at risk! However, there is more to this stuff than just passing your next test. Maslow's theory figures prominently in the practice of public relations.

We can see Maslow's theories at work by looking at U.S. politics. The 1980s saw the waning days of the Cold War, a four-decade ideological struggle between western democracies and communist nations. Because of a looming threat of thermonuclear war, national security issues were at the forefront of U.S. elections for nearly 40 years. However, with the fall of the Berlin Wall and the dissolution of the Soviet Union, the threat to survival appeared to dissipate during the 1990s. Voters turned their attention to economic issues, such as rising interest rates, high unemployment, and low wages. However, voter priorities changed on September 11, 2001, when terrorist attacks on U.S. soil made people once again fear for their lives. As a result, national security returned to the top of the national political agenda.

We can see the practical use of Maslow's theory in other ways. When environmental groups such as Greenpeace seek public support, their messages focus on physiological needs—specifically, the survival of the planet. When social service organizations seek additional funding, they realize that an appeal to the public's unfulfilled safety needs will be more effective than one based in either acceptance or self-actualization. By the same token, an appeal to personal self-esteem will have a greater chance of success among affluent audiences, whose physiological and safety requirements have been met, than among lower-income audiences struggling to fulfill basic needs.

QuickBreak 5.4

Monroe's Motivated Sequence

In an era in which change is the only constant, it is refreshing to see an idea that has stood the test of time. In the mid-1920s, Purdue University Professor Alan H. Monroe developed an organizational pattern for persuasive messages that has come to be known as **Monroe's Motivated Sequence**.[25] More than 80 years later, it remains a standard for persuasive communication.

Building persuasive messages using Monroe's Motivated Sequence involves a five-step process. Let's look at that process using a real-world example: a company executive trying to motivate employees to improve quality by reducing workplace errors:

1. *Attention.* Get the attention of the audience through a dramatic story, quote, or statistic. Tell the audience why the topic is important to it.

   "One of our competitors has been forced to cut back production and lay off some of its employees. Its sales have dropped because of consumer complaints of shoddy products. We can't afford to have that happen here."

2. *Need.* Show that a significant problem exists and that it won't go away by itself. Document the need with relevant examples.

   "There is a great deal of competition in today's global economy. Consumers are demanding quality. If they don't get it from us, they have plenty of other options."

3. *Satisfaction.* Now that a need has been shown, offer solutions. They should be reasonable solutions that adequately address the need.

   "By working together, the management and employees of this company can develop

reasonable training programs to improve the quality of our products and reduce production-line errors."

4. *Visualization.* Tell what will happen if nothing is done to solve the problem. Explicitly tell the audience the consequences of its choices.

   "In recent weeks, our research department has noticed an increasing number of consumer complaints. We are headed down the same road as our competition. If we don't make changes, it is likely that some of us will lose our jobs."

5. *Action.* Tell the audience members what they, personally, can do to solve the problem. It is important that the actions requested are explicitly stated.

   "I am asking you to make a personal commitment to quality. Don't be afraid to share your ideas for improving our products. Volunteer to serve on the various committees we are establishing to examine this issue. Help make this company's mission statement—'providing quality products and services'—a reality."

It is not a coincidence that the example cited here is closely linked to the company's mission statement. Values should serve as the foundation of all persuasive communication.

In today's world of the six-second sound bite, the art of persuasive speaking may seem irrelevant. But it is just as important today as it was in Monroe's time. Monroe's Motivated Sequence is a tried-and-true method of making one's points in a logical and persuasive manner.

Do people stop and think, "What would Maslow have me do under these circumstances?" Of course not. However, we instinctively follow Maslow's model. Self-interest is at the heart of motivation. Understanding the needs of the public being targeted is the key to successful communication and persuasion.

Persuasion and Public Opinion

Since the beginning of recorded history, people have pondered the question of how to persuade others to take a desired course of action. And it is a very important question. The persuasion of others and the molding of public opinion are central to our concept of a society, the manner in which people choose to organize themselves.

In democratic societies, we organize ourselves around a core belief in fulfilling the will of the people. However, history has shown us that democratic societies operate best when there is a willingness to seek consensus on matters of importance to all. That, in turn, requires a willingness among the members of these societies to engage in public debate. It is during this debate that we either persuade others to come over to our point of view or are persuaded to accept the opinion of someone else. A measure of these on-going discussions is what we commonly refer to as public opinion.

Persuasion and public opinion are vital elements in the practice of public relations. As has been stressed in many places throughout this textbook, public relations is a two-way process of both communicating and listening. Sometimes the need to convince others about the advisability of a certain course of action arises. In that situation, we try to persuade others to adopt our point of view. However, we must also be sensitive to public opinion and the concerns of others. At its best, public relations is not about winning or losing. Instead, it is about building and maintaining mutually beneficial relationships. That is why understanding the dynamics of persuasion and public opinion is so critical to successful public relations.

Aristotle, Persuasion, and Public Relations

Aristotle said that **persuasion** takes three forms: **logos,** or an appeal to reason; **pathos,** or an appeal to emotions; and **ethos,** or an appeal based on personality or character. He said that a persuasive argument may use one of these forms exclusively or in any combination with the others.

Aristotle believed the decision to choose one form of persuasion over another depended on several factors: the circumstances in which the appeal is made, the specific nature of what is being argued, and the makeup of the audience being addressed.[26] To state this concept in simpler terms: The selection of an appropriate persuasive appeal depends on determining what you are saying, where and when you are saying it, and to whom you are saying it. This concept should sound familiar to you. It is pivotal to the practice of public relations.

Aristotle did believe that ethos, the persuasive value of a communicator's character, is often the most powerful of the three modes of persuasion. In his classic book *Rhetoric,* he says that a communicator's character "may almost be called the most effective means of persuasion he possesses."[27] That's one reason why practitioners should strive to practice ethical, values-driven public relations: Their well-earned good name can help build the relationships that are essential to their organization's success.

Aristotle's analysis of persuasion raises an important question that is currently being debated within professional and academic circles: Is persuasion an appropriate activity for public relations practitioners? Some people believe that the goal of persuasion is inconsistent with the two-way communication requirement for effective public relations. Two-way communication, by definition, implies a willingness to listen to the needs and concerns of the targeted public and act accordingly. Persuasion linked to one-way communication tends to ignore a central tenet of motivation, that people act in their own self-interests. Any effort at persuasion that does not first take into account the public's point of view is poor public relations—and probably won't work. However, when practiced at its highest levels, public relations identifies common interests and promotes actions that are mutually beneficial. Therefore, in that context, persuasion is a **compliance-gaining tactic** appropriate for public relations practitioners.[28]

Public Opinion Defined

In much the same way that an atom is the basic building block of matter, **belief** is the basic building block of public opinion. A belief is one's commitment to a particular idea or concept based on either personal experience or some credible external authority. For example, many people who have traveled to and experienced Paris believe that it is the most beautiful city in the world. However, others who have never been to France may feel the same way because they have heard it from sources they consider credible, such as friends, travel guides, and popular culture.

When a belief starts affecting the way we behave, it creates an **attitude.** To put it another way, an attitude is a behavioral inclination. For example, if a belief that Paris is a beautiful city causes you to start reading about Paris, encourages you to enjoy French cuisine, or just encourages you to look positively upon all things Parisian, you have developed an attitude.

If that attitude is strong and inspires you to share it with others, you have developed an **opinion.** By definition, an opinion is an expressed behavioral inclination. That opinion can be expressed verbally, by telling others how much you admire Paris, or nonverbally, by adopting French fashion as your own preferred style.

That takes us to **public opinion,** the average expressed behavioral inclination. Public opinion takes into account a wide range of positions that people may have on the same issue. For example, a majority of people may feel that Paris is a beautiful city. A small minority may disagree. Yet another group may have no opinion at all. Together, those three groups constitute public opinion on the issue of the beauty of Paris.

As noted in Chapter 4, the publics of public relations can be divided into what are known as latent, aware, and active publics. Which one of these defines a particular public depends on the degree to which the public realizes and cares about the intersection of its values with an issue. The same can be said for public opinion. **Latent public opinion** is the result of people having varying degrees of interest in a topic or issue but being unaware of the interests of others. **Aware public opinion** occurs when people grow aware of an emerging interest. **Active public opinion** occurs when people act—formally or informally, and often not in unison—to influence the opinions and actions of others.

The Evolution of Public Opinion

Although persuading one person to adopt a particular point of view can be difficult, the true challenge is to persuade large numbers of people. That is the essence of decision making in a democratic society—a public debate that leads to a public consensus and, eventually, to public policy. The evolution of public opinion can be outlined as follows:[29]

QuickBreak 5.5

A Public Opinion Checklist

Volumes have been written about how to influence public opinion, but here are 10 key guidelines you should remember:

1. *You may not be the best judge of public opinion.* Don't trust hunches or gut reactions. They could be wrong. Base your decisions on solid research and analysis.

2. *People resist change.* Change is often viewed as a threat. For that reason, do not assume that a targeted public understands the benefits of a proposal. Spell them out.

3. *WIIFM (What's In It For Me?).* Social psychologist Hadley Cantril wrote, "Once self-interest is involved, opinions are not easily changed."[30] Don't tell targeted publics why something is good for you. Instead, describe how the desired action benefits them.

4. *People believe what they want to believe.* When people have their minds made up on an issue, they tend to seek out information that reinforces their position. They also tend to avoid or block out what social scientists call **cognitive dissonance**—the mental disturbance resulting from encountering information that runs contrary to their beliefs.

5. *Plant seeds in fertile ground.* It is easier to provide information than it is to shape an opinion. It is also easier to shape an opinion than it is to change an opinion. You can't afford to waste limited time and resources on those who have

already decided against you. You can achieve greater success by directing public relations efforts to those who are already on your side and those still willing to listen.

6. *KISS (Keep It Simple and Straight).* In the clutter that makes up mass communications, it is the simplest of messages that are most likely to get through and register with a public. Symbolism is often more effective than a complex explanation of concepts.

7. *Demonstrate knowledge of the issue.* When public opinion is undecided or running against you, presenting all sides of the issue tends to be the most effective approach. It also provides an opportunity to demonstrate the comparative strength of your position.

8. *When among friends, preach to the choir.* When public opinion is on your side, stick to your message. In this case usually no need arises to discuss the other side of the issue. Your job isn't so much to change public opinion as to solidify it into action.

9. *Actions speak louder than words.* People are impressed when you actually do what you say you are going to do. Empty promises breed mistrust; keeping your word builds credibility.

10. *Get in the last word.* When there is little to choose from between opposing views, a determining factor tends to be the argument heard last.

1. Public opinion starts with an *already present mass sentiment,* a consensus that developed as a result of earlier public debates.
2. Public opinion begins to evolve when an *issue* is interjected into that consensus. For something to be considered an issue, it has to affect a variety of groups and be seen as evolving.
3. Like-minded individuals coalesce into a *public.* Often these publics can be characterized as being either pro or con. However, many issues are complex and have more than two sides.
4. The various publics engage in *public and private debate* over the issue. This debate can take many forms. It is at this stage that the practice of public relations has its greatest influence among publics that have not yet formed a strong opinion.
5. There is an unspecified period of *time* during which the debate occurs and people make up their minds. The amount of time needed for this to happen varies from issue to issue. With some issues, such as gun control and abortion, the debate seems never to end.
6. Eventually the debate leads to a consensus, which is known as *public opinion.*
7. In turn, that public opinion precipitates some form of *social action,* such as a policy change, an election, or the passing of a new law.
8. At this point the issue evolves into a *social value;* this, in turn, becomes a part of the already present mass sentiment, and the public opinion process begins anew.

You can see the public opinion process at work in the events that followed the death of racing legend Dale Earnhardt at the 2001 Daytona 500. The tragedy reopened a long-simmering conflict between personal privacy rights and the public's right to know (*an already-present mass sentiment*). An Orlando newspaper investigating the accident filed a public records request to view Earnhardt's autopsy photos. The driver's family objected and went to court to have them sealed (*an issue*). This created a legal, political, and ethical debate, with news organizations on one side and victims' rights groups on the other (*like-minded individuals coalesce into a public*).

The two sides sparred in Florida's courts, in the state legislature, and in the court of public opinion (*public and private debate*).[31] Public reaction was swift and decidedly one-sided (*time passes*). There was an outpouring of support for the Earnhardt family—due, in part, to a well-orchestrated campaign created by the Burson-Marsteller public relations agency (*public opinion*). Just 39 days after the Earnhardt crash, the state legislature passed and the governor signed the Florida Family Protection Act, a law restricting access to autopsy photos (*social action*).[32] The U.S. Supreme Court rejected a challenge to the law in December 2003, bringing an end to the debate (*social value*).[33] However, it is a virtual certainty that media groups will continue to pursue public records containing sensitive personal information (*the public opinion process begins anew*).

The dynamics of the public opinion process point out the need for companies and organizations to conduct ongoing programs of public relations. Because public opinion is always evolving, one-shot efforts at influencing it are rarely effective. Sometimes public opinion crystallizes very quickly, as it did in the Earnhardt autopsy photos controversy. Public opinion is also very fluid and can evolve over time, as with the dramatic

VALUES STATEMENT 5.1

APCO Worldwide

APCO Worldwide is a Washington-based global communication consultancy. Listed among its nearly two dozen services are coalition building and grassroots advocacy, communication for governments, crisis management, and issue management and public information campaigns.

CULTURE & VALUES

At APCO we encourage an entrepreneurial spirit where employees have the freedom to push the boundaries of communication and provide innovative solutions for clients.

APCO is a global company providing employees with enriching experiences working with colleagues of diverse backgrounds, both professionally and culturally. Our culture fosters a collegial work environment where everyone feels valued for his or her contributions to client successes and the firm.

Spanning the globe, the glue that binds us is a commitment to living APCO's values. Values are the cornerstone of the company's culture and work environment.

The values provide direction on what is important to the company and to each other, and serve as a guide to how we make business decisions and influence interactions with staff and clients. Our values transcend geographical boundaries and are apparent in any APCO office regardless of city, country or continent.

APCO VALUES

- Client service is our measure of achievement.
- Push the boundaries with innovative solutions.
- Tell the truth.
- Empower great people to do great work.
- Nurture an organization where everyone is valued.
- Rely on one another in achieving our personal potential.
- Provide global service culture by culture.
- Building relationships is the best business development.
- Business success assures our future.

—APCO Worldwide www.apcoworldwide.com

change in public attitudes toward civil rights since the early 1960s. Public relations practitioners need to keep their fingers constantly on the pulse of public opinion. Only then are they properly prepared to guide their organizations through potentially stormy seas.

Persuasion versus Manipulation

Understanding the dynamics of public opinion is essential to the practice of public relations. However, as is true with most things in life, it is possible to get too much of a good thing. Although it is often desirable to win people over to a particular point of view, there is a great temptation to try to manipulate public opinion to achieve one's goals. Such an effort came to light in December 2005, when it was learned that the news articles written by U.S. military public affairs officers had been placed in Iraqi newspapers by Lincoln Group, a Washington-based public relations agency, as paid advertisements. The purpose was to counter negative stories spread by opponents of the U.S. occupation. However, in many instances, the articles were not properly identified as advertisements. Defending the practice, agency spokeswoman Laurie Adler said, "Lincoln

Group has consistently worked with Iraqi media to promote truthful reporting across Iraq." However, Senator John Warner, chairman of the Senate Armed Services Committee, said the disclosure could undermine U.S. efforts in Iraq. Senator Edward Kennedy, another member of the committee, said, "If Americans were truly welcomed in Iraq as liberators, we wouldn't have to doctor the news for the Iraqi people."[34]

This incident illustrates two valuable lessons for public relations practitioners. First, it suggests the need to draw the line between influencing and manipulating public opinion. **Manipulation,** by its very nature, suggests something underhanded. It is true that one may reap short-term gains by telling half-truths or by putting narrow interests ahead of broader ones, but it is also true that those gains are short-lived. Manipulation, whether real or perceived, comes with a cost: credibility. No one likes to feel as if he or she has been used. Manipulation also runs contrary to the ideal of public relations as a problem-solving discipline whose practitioners seek alternatives that are mutually beneficial to all parties concerned.

A second valuable lesson is that those who seek to master public opinion often become a slave to it. This results in a lack of leadership. A common complaint we hear these days about politicians and corporate executives is that they are too often driven by public opinion polls. Instead of acting on what they believe, they seek to do what is popular. Although public opinion is important in democratic societies, so are values. It is often necessary to forgo what is popular for what is right. Think how different human history would be if certain special individuals had not, at critical moments, put their values ahead of public sentiment. Public relations is a values-driven discipline. Those values are determined by what we believe, not necessarily by what is popular.

QUICK CHECK

1. What are the three kinds of persuasive appeals identified by Aristotle?
2. How does public opinion develop?
3. What is the difference between manipulation and persuasion?

Summary

History has shown us that communication is a fragile process. It can fail in a variety of ways, including a lack of source credibility, an irrelevant message, an inappropriate channel, an inattentive receiver, the absence of feedback, or the presence of physical or psychological noise.

With the growth of communications technology in the 20th century, people initially feared that mass media could dominate public opinion. This fear led to the development of what came to be known as the magic bullet theory. However, as the technology of mass communications evolved, so did our understanding of mass media. Now we realize that mass media do not tell us what to think, but rather influence what we think about. That concept is known as the agenda-setting hypothesis.

However, even that theory is evolving. According to uses and gratifications theory, the *real* power to persuade resides with individuals who can pick and choose from thousands of information sources and are driven by their own self-interests—especially their need to survive.

The evolution of public opinion is a dynamic process that never ceases; for this reason, organizations need to stay attuned to changes in public attitudes and conduct ongoing programs of public relations.

Although efforts to win people over to a point of view are legitimate, manipulation of public opinion by underhanded means is counterproductive. Those who engage in manipulation lose credibility and may become slaves to the public mood.

DISCUSSION QUESTIONS

1. Can and should public relations practitioners try to influence public opinion? Should our ability to persuade have any limits?
2. Describe the process of communication. What are some factors that can cause communication to break down?
3. Does an explanation exist for why some things serve as stronger motivations to action than others?
4. To what degree do you think mass media influence you? How does your personal experience relate to the various theories of mass communications?
5. What would be a good example of an issue that has undergone a rigorous public debate and emerged as a social value? Describe the process by which this happened.

Memo from the Field

Jane Hazel, Director General of the Marketing and Consultation Directorate, Health Canada, Ottawa, Ontario

Jane Hazel is the director general of the Marketing and Consultation Directorate of Health Canada. Health Canada is the Canadian federal department responsible for helping the people of Canada maintain and improve their health. Based in Ottawa, Ontario, the Marketing and Consultation Directorate is the departmental focal point for strategic advice; planning and implementation of social marketing; Health Canada's Internet; public opinion research and evaluation; and policy lead for corporate consultation. Hazel's publications include coauthorship of "Social Advertising and Tobacco Demand Reduction in Canada" in the textbook *Social Marketing: Theoretical and Practical Perspectives.*

As a longtime communications professional, I rely heavily on public opinion research (POR) to inform my work. It gives me critical insight into my audience: It helps me understand people's views, attitudes, and perceptions; what they are thinking and feeling and why; what's important to them and how they feel about my organization. This information forms the base of all my communications efforts.

Typically I tend to use POR in 2 specific ways:

1. CAMPAIGN DEVELOPMENT

Working for the health department, a key aspect of my job is to design social marketing campaigns to encourage people to be healthy, e.g., quit smoking, eat better, and be more active. This type of behavior change depends heavily on an in-depth understanding of people's knowledge, awareness, and behaviors. POR helps:

- understand who engages in the behavior
- identify the triggers to starting and the barriers to quitting
- identify role models and credible voices
- determine what information people want and need
- identify where people would go to get information
- determine what would motivate change

We also use POR to pre-test our creative material before production (ads, brochures, posters, and so on) and to evaluate the campaign's effectiveness post launch.

2. ISSUE MANAGEMENT

Another key role POR plays in our organization relates to issue management. Using surveys, we track issues percolating in the media to see if they become part of public debate. This helps us proactively position ourselves to provide accurate information in a timely manner and to plan strategically.

Typically there is a 4-step approach to tracking public opinion to support issue management:

1. First assess the "salience" of the issue.
   - Are people aware of the issue? Have they talked about it in the recent past?
   - Ask "Have you read, seen, or heard anything about X?"

2. Then try to put the issue in context.
   - Issues can be exaggerated if looked at in isolation.
   - Ask "What have you read, heard, seen about X?"

3. Next, assess the impact of what people learn related to your organization.
   - Ask "Did what you read, see, or hear about X leave you feeling (more or less positive) toward organization Y?"

4. Then find out what people think of your reaction.
   - The real question is how well you are seen to be managing the issue.
   - The initial reaction to most issues is negative.

- Ask "Do you (strongly approve, somewhat approve, somewhat disapprove, or strongly disapprove) of the performance of organization Y in responding to issue X?"

This approach worked well in 2003 when SARS hit Toronto. In that case we supplemented tracking with surveys and focus groups to develop, tailor, and adjust our communication strategy. Nightly rolling polling assessed people's evolving understanding of this epidemic, what information they received, and how they received it. This allowed us to tailor our daily media briefings, to ensure that we were providing relevant information, to immediately correct any misinformation, and to use the right channels with our communications strategy overall.

TWO THINGS TO REMEMBER

1. Be survey savvy: In an environment where every newspaper headline proclaims a startling new survey result, take the time to understand and interpret surveys. Methodological rigor and quality control are important, but numbers can also suggest a false or exaggerated sense of accuracy. Be critical.
   - Who sponsored the survey?
   - Examine question wording and where questions are placed in the survey.
   - Compare how many people were asked to participate versus how many did. If the gap is large, is there something different about those who did not respond?
   - How were the data interpreted (was "very good" grouped with "good"?)
   - Remember people are usually doing other things when a survey call comes in. They answer based on their top-of-mind values, core attitudes, and experiences, and usually not on a reflective consideration of all options.

2. Let research be your guide, not your master.
   - Use POR to help your judgment, not as a substitute for it.
   - Plan, plan, plan, and pre-test. Know why you need the data and what you will do with it. The saddest words I hear are "If only I'd asked X!"
   - Find the resources to hire a professional to help you.
   - Leave maneuvering room: Interpret with common sense; don't tie yourself to a decision based on a single source.
   - Seek first to understand. The reasons behind the numbers are more important than the numbers themselves.

All good communication strategies start with a full understanding of the audience. Public opinion research is the first step to that understanding and is critical to anyone working in the field of PR.

CASE STUDY 5.1

I Decide

The Centers for Disease Control and Prevention estimates that on any given day, 4,400 youths age 12–17 will try their first cigarette. That's one every 20 seconds. Of those, one in three will eventually die from a smoking-related disease. That's one every minute.[35]

The problem of teenage smoking is a major concern of the Illinois Department of Public Health (IDPH). According to one study, nearly 36 percent of Illinois high school students (grades 9–12) smoke cigarettes. That is almost eight percentage points above the national average.[36] State health officials have said teenage smoking is part of a much bigger problem. They estimate that tobacco-related illnesses take the lives of more than 16,500 Illinois residents each year and cost the state $6.7 billion annually in medical care and lost productivity.[37]

"Most of these people began using tobacco in early adolescence, typically by age 16," said Dr. John R. Lumpkin, state public health director. "To prevent another generation from being plagued by tobacco addiction, we must try innovative ways to encourage young people not to take up smoking or to quit if they have already started.

"Studies have demonstrated that if young people don't smoke as teenagers, it is unlikely they will ever do so."[38]

Using money obtained as the state's share of a settlement agreement between tobacco companies and 46 state attorneys general, IDPH launched "I Decide," a youth-focused antitobacco organization, in 2000. The effort had two major goals: to reduce smoking rates among teens in a one-county pilot program and "to demonstrate that a comprehensive social marketing campaign aimed at lowering teen tobacco use can be successful."[39] In terms of a long-term strategy, IDPH officials hoped that success of the pilot project would translate into a permanent, statewide effort.

Winnebago County, which includes Rockford and is approximately 80 miles northwest of Chicago, was selected for the program. Focus group and survey research yielded alarming results. Only one-third to one-half of middle and high school students said that they had been taught about the dangers of tobacco in school. An even lower number reported talking about the subject with their parents. An estimated 35 percent of Winnebago County high school students and 15 percent of middle school students smoked.[40]

With the assistance of Golin/Harris International, IDPH launched a $15.5 million peer-to-peer campaign to mobilize teens in their communities. A variety of media and disciplines, including advertising and promotions, were used to achieve campaign objectives.[41]

Inspired by the popular MTV program *TRL: Total Request Live,* campaign officials introduced their own TRL, as in Tobacco Reality Live. It was a traveling event designed to encourage awareness and increase participation in antismoking activities.

These daylong summits featured trained teenagers conducting peer-to-peer presentations on tobacco's manipulative effects. Other peer-to-peer efforts included teen-written articles for the I Decide bimonthly newsletter. Campaign organizers also developed educator kits containing membership cards, teaching materials, brochures, temporary tattoos, book covers, and posters. I Decide organizational information was also available through a campaign web site.

To broaden the reach of the campaign, officials targeted the high-profile state boys and girls basketball tournaments. I Decide rally towels and headbands branded with the names of the qualifying teams were distributed at the arena. Other promotional activities included an overnight lock-in at an athletic center, ice skating events, and movie nights.[42]

Supplementing these public relations efforts was a satirical advertising campaign created by Hadrian's Wall, a Chicago-based advertising agency. A fictitious "All Smoke High"—or A.S.H.—where students were *required* to smoke. Those who rebelled and chose not to smoke were the hip ones. Television ads were broadcast in the Rockford market within programs such as *Friends* and *The Gilmore Girls*.[43] A series of outdoor and local transit bus ads also complemented the campaign.[44]

"We know that teenagers do not react well when told what to do and that, typically, they end up making better decisions than adults give them credit for," said ad writer Kevin Lynch. "So we used a little reverse psychology."[45]

By June 2002, more than 6,000 teens were members of I Decide. The program had expanded to another six Illinois counties. Follow-up studies showed that 78 percent of targeted teens knew about the movement. Among those, 86 percent rated I Decide as "excellent" or "good." More significantly, teenage smoking rates in Winnebago County schools dropped from 35 to 28.5 percent.[46]

However, not everything went as organizers had hoped. Faced with an economic recession, the Illinois legislature voted to cut the program from the 2003 state budget. This action evoked an outpouring of public support for the program. That, in turn, prompted IDPH to look for alternative funding sources and to launch a new, smaller scale teen antitobacco program.

DISCUSSION QUESTIONS

1. Using the theories and issues discussed in the chapter that precedes this case study, why do you think it is difficult to deliver antismoking messages to teenagers?
2. What research was conducted in support of the I Decide campaign?
3. What role did peer-to-peer communication play in this campaign? Why do you think this strategy was used?
4. How was the success of this campaign evaluated? Was it, in your opinion, successful?
5. What would you do differently if the target audience for this campaign were a slightly older group: your college classmates?

CASE STUDY 5.2

Color-Coded Confusion

If then-Homeland Security Secretary Tom Ridge happened to be watching David Letterman's "Top Ten List" on February 20, 2003, it is easy to imagine that he winced when Dave reached item number two.

That evening's category was "Top Ten Ways Dumb Guys Are Preparing for a Terrorist Attack." Number two on that list was "creating elaborate color-code systems to alert citizens to threat levels."[47]

Letterman's jab was aimed at the Homeland Security Advisory System (HSAS), a five-level, color-coded system designed by Ridge's agency to prepare public officials and private citizens for possible terrorist attacks. The comedian's joke came at a time when the nation was under "orange alert," a period in which the nation's security and intelligence agencies rated the threat of a terrorist incident as "high." Many people felt that the terror alert system was a wise precaution. Others ridiculed it as being a counterproductive and costly effort that unnecessarily alarmed the population.

This very easily could have been a "Thumbs Up" case study. The ideas and values behind Homeland Security's efforts were based on sound theory and presented with the best intentions. "The Homeland Security Advisory System is designed to measure and evaluate terrorist threats and communicate them to the public in a timely manner," Ridge said when he introduced the terror threat system on March 12, 2002. "It provides clear, easy to understand factors which help measure threat."[48]

However, it was the last point—that it was "easy to understand"—that drew the most criticism. The HSAS established five terrorist threat conditions: green (low condition), blue (guarded condition), yellow (elevated condition), orange (high condition), and red (severe condition). Each of these levels was accompanied by a list of protective measures that the government and private sectors were advised to take. For example, during an orange alert, public and private agencies were advised to take "additional precautions at public events" and to prepare "to work at an alternative site or with a dispersed workforce."[49]

In announcing the system, Ridge said, "It provides a common vocabulary, so officials from all levels of government can communicate easily with one another and to the public."[50] As noted in Chapter 12, the idea of using a "common vocabulary" is sound crisis management practice. However, the HSAS left unanswered a question on the minds of people outside of the national security and defense establishment: "What is it, *specifically*, that I am supposed to do?"

Government officials tried to answer that question during a February 7, 2003, orange alert announcement. Then-U.S. Attorney General John Ashcroft said that the U.S. intelligence community had concluded that there was an increased likelihood of a terrorist attack coinciding with the end of the Hajj, the annual period of Muslim pilgrimages to Mecca. At the same news conference, Ridge said, "For individual Americans, we ask that you remain aware and remain alert."[51]

With the nation's nerves on edge, officials decided to reassure the American people a couple of days later. They outlined precautionary steps individuals could take to protect themselves. These included storing a three-day supply of food and water, and creating emergency supply kits for both homes and automobiles. The list of materials for the kit included plastic sheeting and duct tape for sealing windows and doors against a terrorist gas attack.[52]

If anything, the attempt to reassure the country appeared to have had the opposite effect. Within hours of the announcement, stores nationwide reported a run on duct tape. A hardware store in Alexandria, Virginia, sold every roll it had in stock. Another Alexandria store announced that its sales of duct tape had tripled. "Everything that was on that newscast, we are selling a lot of it," said one Washington area store employee.[53]

Officials who had sought to prepare the public for possible dangers found themselves trying to avert a public panic and keep people from sealing themselves in their homes with duct tape and plastic. "God forbid, there may come a time when the local authorities or national authorities will tell you that you've got to use them," Ridge said. "But for the time being, we just don't want folks sealing up their doors or sealing up their windows."[54]

Just two days before the February 2003 orange alert, Congress had chided Homeland Security for its flawed warning system. Representative Chris Cox of California, Republican chairman of the House Homeland Security Committee, called it a "senseless, unfocused, nationwide response" too often created by "unspecified threat alerts." Representative Jim Turner, a Texas Democrat, complained "state and local governments spend hundreds of thousands of dollars—perhaps millions—to defend against an amorphous threat." Committee members also scolded the agency for not giving the public information on what it should do when the threat level is raised.[55] Of course, that is exactly what Homeland Security did a few days later—and it prompted a nationwide run on duct tape.

And just in case you are wondering about David Letterman's number one way a dumb guy prepares for a terrorist attack, it was "Taping a duck."[56]

DISCUSSION QUESTIONS

1. Do you agree with the authors that this a difficult case to designate as a definitive "Thumbs Up" or "Thumbs Down"? Why or why not?
2. What do you consider to be the Department of Homeland Security's key failure in explaining the color-coded terror alert system to the public?
3. What communication and persuasion theories discussed in this chapter can explain how this case evolved in the manner it did?
4. What values should government officials consider when weighing a decision to inform the public about potential dangers?
5. What, if anything, would *you* have done differently in this case?

NOTES

1. Personal account of John A. (Tony) Turnbull, "D-Day and Beyond with a Scottish Artillery Regiment: June 6, 1944 to February 27, 1945, revisited," *WW2 People's War,* British Broadcasting Corporation, online, www.bbc.co.uk/ww2peopleswar.

2. "Alan Mellville Broadcasts from a Small Church in Normandy" (CD Track 21), *D-Day Dispatches—Original Recordings from the BBC Sound Archives,* British Broadcasting Corp, 2004.

3. David Berlo, *The Process of Communication: An Introduction to Theory and Practice* (New York: Holt, Rinehart and Winston, 1960).

4. Richard M. Nixon, *RN: The Memoirs of Richard Nixon* (New York: Grosset & Dunlap, 1978), 460–466.

5. This QuickBreak is based on the academic paper "Propaganda v. Public Diplomacy: How 9/11 Gave New Life to a Cold War Debate," by David W. Guth, presented at the annual conference of the Association of Educators in Journalism and Mass Communications, August 2003, Kansas City, Mo.

6. Brett Gray, *The Nervous Liberals: Propaganda Anxieties from World War I to the Cold War* (New York: Columbia University Press, 1999), p. 8.

7. Scott M. Cutlip, *The Unseen Power: Public Relations, A History* (Hillsdale, N.J.: Lawrence Erlbaum, 1994), 82–183.

8. Gayle Mertz and Carol Miller Lieber, *Conflict in Context: Understanding Local to Global Security,* Educators for Social Responsibility, 1991, online, www.esrnational.org/whatispropaganda.htm.

9. Cutlip, 45.

10. Cutlip, 182.

11. Gray, 8.

12. Garth S. Jowett and Victoria O'Donnell, *Propaganda and Persuasion,* 3rd. ed. (Thousand Oaks, Calif.: Sage Publications, 1999), p. 6.

13. Jowett and O'Donnell, 1.

14. Chris Cobb, "Taco Bell *E. Coli* Outbreak: Calming Public Fears during Food-Borne Illness Scares," *Public Relations Tactics,* February 2007, 11.

15. Kate MacArthur, "Taco Hell: Rodent Video Signals New Era in PR Crises," *Advertising Age,* 26 February 2007, 1.

16. CBS News/*New York Times* Poll Results Summary, 27 February 2007, online, http://pollingreport.com/terror.htm.

17. James E. Grunig et al., eds., *Excellence in Public Relations and Communication Management* (Hillsdale, N.J.: Lawrence Erlbaum, 1992), 165.

18. Grunig.

19. Jack Rosenthal, "Spin Doctors," *New York Times,* 21 October 1984, as quoted by "Present at the Creation: Spin," National Public Radio, 4 November 2002, online, www.npr.org/programs/morning/features/patc/spin/index.html.

20. "Present at the Creation: Spin."

21. Erving Goffman, *Frame Analysis: Essays on the Organization of Experience* (New York: Harper & Row, 1974), 21.

22. Robert Entman, "Framing: Toward Clarification of a Fractured Paradigm," *Journal of Communication* 43, no. 3 (December 1993): 51–58.

23. Shanto Iyengar and Donald R. Kinder, *News That Matters* (Chicago: University of Chicago Press, 1987), 63–72.
24. Abraham Maslow, *Motivation and Personality* (New York: Harper & Row, 1954), 9.
25. Raymie E. McKerron, Bruce E. Gronbeck, Douglas Ehninger, and Alan H. Monroe, *Principles and Types of Speech Communication,* 14th ed. (Boston: Allyn & Bacon, 2000), 153–164.
26. Edward P. J. Corbett, *Classical Rhetoric for the Modern Student* (New York: Oxford University Press, 1971), 50.
27. Aristotle, *Rhetoric,* trans. W. Rhys Roberts (New York: Modern Library, 1954), 25.
28. Grunig, 331.
29. Based on Lang and Lang's *Collective Dynamics,* cited in *PRSA Accreditation Study Guide* (New York: Public Relations Society of America, 1993), 38.
30. Hadley Cantril, *Gauging Public Opinion* (Princeton, N.J.: Princeton University Press, 1972), 226–230.
31. "Earnhardt Autopsy Review—A Collision with the Truth," *Salisbury Post,* 13 April 2001, online, www.salisburypost.com/2001april/041301ed.htm.
32. HB 1083, Florida General Assembly, online, www.leg.state.fl.is.
33. Gina Holland, "Florida Newspaper Loses Appeal over Earnhardt Autopsy Photos," *USA Today,* 1 December 2003, online, www.usatoday.com.
34. Eric Schmitt, "Military Admits Planting News in Iraq," *New York Times,* 3 December 2005, online, www.nytimes.com.
35. Centers for Disease Control and Prevention, "Tobacco Use Among Middle and High School Students—United States, 2002," *Morbidity and Mortality Weekly Report,* 14 November 2003, 1096.
36. Centers for Disease Control and Prevention, "Illinois Highlights," online, www.cdc.gov/tobacco/statehi.
37. "Tobacco Kills 16,500 in State; Economic Damage in Billions," Illinois Department of Public Health, news release, 27 May 2004, online, www.idph.state.il.us.
38. "Ryan Proposal Doubles Tobacco Prevention Funding," Illinois Department of Public Health news release, 21 February 2001, online, www.idph.state.il.us.
39. *I Decide, The First Year 2000–2001,* Illinois Department of Public Health, online, www.idph.state.il.us.
40. *I Decide, The First Year 2000–2001,* 3.
41. "I Decide: Illinois Teens Talk Back to Big Tobacco," Silver Anvil award summary 6BW-0301C06, Public Relations Society of America, online, www.prsa.org.
42. "I Decide: Illinois Teens Talk Back to Big Tobacco."
43. Megan Larson, "Hadrian's Wall," *Adweek,* 23 Jun 2003, 18–20.
44. "Anti-Tobacco Bus Ads Unveiled," Illinois Department of Public Health, news release, 17 February 2001, online, www.idph.state.il.us.
45. Megan Larson.
46. "I Decide: Illinois Teens Talk Back to Big Tobacco."
47. "Top Ten Ways Dumb Guys Are Preparing for a Terrorist Attack," *The Late Show with David Letterman,* 20 February 2003, online, www.cbs.com/latenight/lateshow/top_ten/archive.
48. "Remarks by Governor Ridge Announcing Homeland Security Advisory System," White House transcript, 12 March 2002, online, www.whitehouse.gov.

49. "Gov. Ridge Announces Homeland Security Advisory System," White House news release, 12 March 2002, online, www.whitehouse.gov.

50. "Remarks by Governor Ridge Announcing Homeland Security Advisory System."

51. "Homeland Security Threat Level Raised to Orange," White House transcript, 7 February 2003, online, www.whitehouse.gov.

52. "Administration: Prepare, Don't Panic," CNN, 11 February 2003, online, www.cnn.com.

53. Jeanne Meserve, "Duct Tape Sales Rise Amid Terror Fears," CNN, 11 February 2003, online, www.cnn.com.

54. "Ridge Tries to Calm America's Nerves," CNN, 14 February 2003, online, www.cnn.com.

55. Shaun Waterman, "Lawmakers Lambaste Color-Coded Alert System," United Press International, 5 February 2003, online, LexisNexis.

56. "Top Ten Ways Dumb Guys Are Preparing for a Terrorist Attack."

6

Ethics and Social Responsibility in Public Relations

OBJECTIVES

After studying this chapter, you will be able to

- define what is meant by the word *ethics*

- specify categories of ethics codes

- understand the most common ethical challenges

- describe the ethics codes of important philosophers from Aristotle to John Rawls

- use the Potter Box to analyze ethical dilemmas

KEY TERMS

categorical imperative, p. 176
civil disobedience, p. 172
corporate social responsibility (CSR), p. 177
cultural relativism, p. 173
ethical imperialism, p. 173
ethics, p. 166
ethics audit, p. 179
fully functioning society theory, p. 178
golden mean, p. 171
Potter Box, p. 180
transparency, p. 177
utilitarianism, p. 183
veil of ignorance, p. 184
virtual organizations, p. 173

Choose and Lose

You are an upper-level public relations practitioner for an international manufacturing company. Your primary duty is internal (employee) public relations. Three days ago, the CEO of your company told the news media that a much-publicized though minor environmental hazard in your company's production process had been eliminated. The person responsible for eliminating the hazard is one of your best friends. And right now, she really needs your friendship: Because of a death in her family, she's going through a rough time.

As your concern for her grows, you learn, by accident, that she hasn't eliminated the environmental hazard; it still exists. In her distraught condition, she doesn't even realize that she hasn't corrected it. You're afraid that telling her will damage your friendship, one of the few positive things in her life right now. But if the CEO discovers the oversight, he may fire her—which, you fear, would deepen her depression. And, of course, you're concerned that the news media will find out that they were given, albeit unintentionally, false information.

What do you do?

What Are Ethics?

In the 1990s comedy *Bill and Ted's Excellent Adventure,* two young slackers travel through time to learn about history. If you could do the same (not that you're a slacker), you could round up some of the great minds of philosophy to help you learn about ethics. Imagine bringing Aristotle, Immanuel Kant, and John Stuart Mill to your local pizza joint.

"We don't seem to agree on much about ethics," Mill says.

"I disagree," says Kant as Aristotle rolls his eyes. "We agree on a lot."

"The truth is somewhere in the middle," says Aristotle. "We *do* agree that more than anything else, human beings want happiness. Pass the pizza."

"Right," says Kant. "And we agree that unless we're ethical, we can never be truly happy."

"And we agree that being ethical means acting on our values," Aristotle says. "Ethics are values in action."

"Perfect," says Mill. "But we disagree on how to find those values."

"But we agree that Aristotle eats too much pizza," Kant shouts, banging his fist on the table.

And the debate would go on. But you've probably read enough philosophy in your other classes to know that this fantasy is fairly accurate: **Ethics** are values in action. And without ethics, philosophers say, we cannot achieve our goal of happiness. Consider the ethics scandals of the early 21st century: Enron, abuse of congressional pages, steroids in Major League Baseball, and so many more. None seemed to lead to happiness for those involved.

QUICKBREAK 6.1

The Ethics Codes of PRSA and IABC

Members of the Public Relations Society of America pledge to abide by the *Member Code of Ethics 2000*. Based on the values of advocacy, honesty, expertise, independence, loyalty, and fairness (see p. 539), the PRSA ethics code specifies six "Core Principles," including the following two:

- "Free flow of information: Protecting and advancing the free flow of accurate and truthful information is essential to serving the public interest and contributing to informed decision making in a democratic society."

- "Safeguarding confidences: Client trust requires appropriate protection of confidential and private information."

Each core principle includes guidelines that define in greater detail the principle's intent. For example, the following list reproduces the guidelines for the "free flow of information" principle.
A member shall:

- Preserve the integrity of the process of communication.

- Be honest and accurate in all communications.

- Act promptly to correct erroneous communications for which the practitioner is responsible.

- Preserve the free flow of unprejudiced information when giving or receiving gifts by ensuring that gifts are nominal, legal, and infrequent.

Members of the International Association of Business Communicators are governed by the *Code of Ethics for Professional Communicators*. Like PRSA's code, the IABC code specifies guidelines for ethical conduct. Its values echo those of PRSA in many areas, especially in the realms of truth and accuracy. According to the IABC code, "Professional communicators uphold the credibility and dignity of their profession by practicing honest, candid, and timely communication and by fostering the free flow of essential information in accord with the public interest."

The complete text of the PRSA ethics code can be found in the appendix of this book.

Being ethical means identifying our values and acting on them. The late John Ginn, a journalism professor at the University of Kansas, often told his students, "Ethics are not something that we *have*. They're something that we *do*." Ideally, once we decide what our values are, we embrace guidelines for behavior that will help us reach those values. Those guidelines become our ethics code. Our ethics code governs what we're willing to do—and what we're unwilling to do. Ethics aren't something we occasionally think about and then toss into a dark closet. Instead, we use them every day to help us honor and attain our values. In other words, ethical behavior isn't a distant goal. Rather, it's a part of daily life.

Ethics Codes for Values-Driven Public Relations

Ethics codes identify core values. They also specify ways of acting that honor those values. Therefore, ethics codes offer guidelines for values-driven actions. Public relations professionals live their lives under the guidance of several ethics codes: international codes, societal codes, professional codes, organizational codes, and personal codes. Let's look at examples of each.

International Codes. As more organizations build relationships with publics in other nations, international codes of business ethics are emerging. For example, the Global Alliance for Public Relations and Communication Management drafted an outline for an international public relations code in 2003. Members of this consortium of 100,000-plus public relations professionals pledge to act on five key values: advocacy, honesty, integrity, expertise, and loyalty. The Global Alliance's code is online at www.globalpr.org.

Societal Codes. The Ten Commandments, a foundation of Judeo-Christian culture, are an example of a societal ethics code that influences the lives of millions of people throughout the world. Other religions, of course, have codes to help their believers achieve obedience to divine will. Eighteenth-century historian Edward Gibbon said of the Koran, the holy book of Islam, "From the Atlantic to the Ganges, the Koran is acknowledged as the fundamental code, not only of theology, but of civil and criminal jurisprudence; the laws which regulate the actions and property of mankind are guarded by the infallible and immutable sanction of the will of God."[1]

Truett Cathy, founder of the Chick-fil-A restaurant chain, follows his personal ethics code by sponsoring more than 100 foster children. They call him Grandpa. (Courtesy of Chick-fil-A, Inc.)

Professional Codes. Unlike members of some professions, public relations practitioners have no central, binding code of ethics. We're not licensed by a central organization, as are doctors and lawyers. Many public relations practitioners, however, voluntarily join organizations that do have binding ethics codes. The two largest such organizations in the world are the Public Relations Society of America (PRSA) and the International Association of Business Communicators (IABC). Unfortunately, not everyone is familiar with public relations ethics codes. "Recently," say public relations scholars Hugh Culbertson and Ni Chen, "we commented to a journalist friend that we'd been asked to write a paper on public relations ethics. 'There aren't many,' he joked. 'Your paper ought to be quite brief.'"[2] Ouch.

Organizational Codes. Many organizations have written ethics codes that employees are asked to read, sign, and follow. Often, members of an organization's public relations staff are asked to help draft, evaluate, and revise these codes. Facing criticisms of biased coverage of the war in Iraq, the Al-Jazeera news channel—a major news network in the Arab world—announced in 2004 that it would write and follow an ethics code "to uphold journalistic values."[3]

Personal Codes.   Truett Cathy, founder of the Chick-fil-A restaurant chain, closes his 1,500-plus restaurants on Sundays. The company's web site makes it clear that the policy stems from Cathy's personal values:

> Admittedly, closing all of our restaurants every Sunday makes us a rarity in this day and age. But it's a little habit that has always served us well, so we're planning to stick with it.
>
> Our founder, Truett Cathy, wanted to ensure that every Chick-fil-A employee and restaurant operator had an opportunity to worship, spend time with family and friends, or just plain rest from the work week. Made sense then, still makes sense now.[4]

Cathy's son Dan, president of the company, said that his father "didn't want to have to wash dishes on Sunday afternoon like he had to when he was a kid in a boardinghouse, and he didn't want to ask others to do what he didn't want to do himself."[5]

Objectivity versus Advocacy: A Misleading Ethics Debate

In addition to identifying specific ethics codes, we can learn more about ethics in public relations by studying the values of related professions. However, an enduring debate in public relations ethics comes from comparing public relations practitioners with lawyers and journalists. At the heart of this debate lies this question: Are public relations practitioners objective communicators, like journalists, or are we advocates, like lawyers?

Some practitioners charge that total objectivity would lead us to tell the truth but ignore the consequences of what we say. Imagine, for a moment, the consequences of telling every public everything you know about the organization you represent. Surely, not every public has a right to know everything. Legally, some information, such as employee health records, must be confidential. And surely you wouldn't betray strategic secrets that help your organization stay competitive. Advocacy, with its focus on the consequences of communicating, can seem more suitable than objectivity for public relations.

If, however, we choose to operate solely as advocates, we soon encounter the sticky issue of selective truth. In attempting to build relationships with publics, are we allowed to withhold damaging information that certain publics have a right to know? Sometimes we can withhold such information legally—but can we do so ethically? Some scholars actually say yes. They maintain that our society has become adversarial, like a courtroom. Public relations practitioners engaged in a debate, they say, need present only the facts that help them, trusting that opponents will present other facts and that a judge—the public—will decide the truth of the matter.[6]

A Relationship-Management Solution

In recent years, public relations practitioners have worked hard to develop an ethical solution to the misleading "are we journalists or lawyers" question. What if the answer is "neither"? Many practitioners respond to the debate by saying that public relations practitioners are, first and foremost, relationship managers. Their priority is building honorable, ethical relationships between an organization and the publics that are essential to its success. Sometimes relationship management calls for delivering unpopular truths, either to a public or to the organization itself. And sometimes relationship management involves being an advocate—even if that means advocating the viewpoint of an important public within your own organization. In all their actions, however, public relations practitioners are acting for the good of the relationships that sustain an organization.

1. What does the word *ethics* mean?
2. Besides the international level, at what levels do we find ethics codes?
3. What solution does this chapter offer for the misleading "journalist or lawyer" role-model debate?

Challenges to Ethical Behavior

Identifying our values is one thing; acting on them is another. Many kinds of challenges stand in the way of ethical behavior. For one thing, some ethical questions aren't easy. They can keep you lying awake at night, staring at the ceiling and trying to select the right course of action amid four or five unappealing options. Also, overwork sometimes conceals ethical obligations while the damage has already begun. Still another challenge is being aware of the mistaken assumption that something legal is always ethical. Or perhaps the business practices of an international client lead you into unfamiliar cross-cultural ethical territory. Or perhaps the challenge lies in the dangers of short-term thinking, or of working in a so-called virtual organization in which values clash. Let's discuss each of these challenges.

Dilemmas

Some ethical challenges are called *dilemmas*—meaning difficult quandaries in which important values clash and every potential solution will cause pain. A dilemma isn't simply a problem; it's a problem that lacks a good, painless solution. The Choose and Lose scenario that opens this chapter is an example of a dilemma. No matter which course of action you select, you seem to hurt or betray someone who trusts you: your

QuickBreak 6.2

Aristotle, Confucius, and the Golden Mean

Is it all right to tell a lie? If we answer quickly, most of us will probably answer no. Telling a lie, we will say, is wrong. It's unethical.

Let's complicate the situation. Is it unethical to tell a lie to save someone's life? Here's a classic ethical question: If you were hiding an innocent victim of political persecution in your attic and representatives of the corrupt regime asked whether you were hiding that individual, would you lie? Or would you tell the truth and betray an innocent person?

Moral absolutes can be troublesome. We can almost always think of exceptions to the moral guidelines we generally follow. Those exceptions can help us understand the concept of the **golden mean,** developed by the Greek philosopher Aristotle (384–322 B.C.).

Aristotle believed that ethical conduct existed at a point of balance and harmony between the two extremes of excess and deficiency. That point of balance is the golden mean. For example, Aristotle would contend that it's unethical *never* to lie (one extreme), just as it's unethical *always* to lie (the opposite extreme). The challenge of the golden mean lies in answering the crucial question *when:* When is it all right to lie? In what specific circumstances could lying be considered an ethical course of action?

A century before the birth of Aristotle, the Chinese philosopher Confucius (551–479 B.C.) established much the same principle with his *Doctrine of the Mean:* "The superior man . . . stands erect in the middle, without inclining to either side."[7]

Finding the golden mean isn't easy. But as we seek to discover the ethical course between absolutist extremes, we learn more about the values that govern and will govern our lives.

CEO, your friend, the news media, or the publics that might suffer from the environmental hazard.

In real life, PepsiCo, Northwest Airlines, and other large international companies encountered clashing values when the government of Myanmar, a country (formerly known as Burma) in which the companies operated, began a series of increasingly brutal crackdowns on opposition political parties. Should the companies honor the value of justice and leave the country, refusing to help the government through taxes? Or should they honor the value of supporting their local employees, who desperately need their jobs, and stay? By 2007, PepsiCo, Northwest Airlines, Tommy Hilfiger, Wal-Mart, and nearly 100 other international companies had made the difficult decision to leave Myanmar.[8]

Overwork

Is it possible to work too hard? Yes, if doing so clouds your judgment. You, and your organization, have an ethical obligation regarding workload: You should shoulder only the work that you can efficiently handle in a typical 40- to 50-hour workweek. Hard work is probably a value within your organization—but so are quality and accuracy. You have an ethical obligation to control the quality of your work. Over-work can also rob you of time you ideally would devote to self-analysis—that is, to thinking about your organization's values and your own values and checking to see whether all your actions are working toward those values.

Legal/Ethical Confusion

What is legal isn't always ethical—and, to a lesser degree, what is ethical may not always be legal. For example, does any law prevent you from remaining silent when you're mistakenly praised for someone else's work? Your silence wouldn't be illegal—but, by most standards, it would be unethical. Or perhaps your supervisor asks you whether a particular project is done. You're a little behind, but you're certain you can finish it this afternoon; because you know she won't ask for it until tomorrow, you say it's done. The small lie isn't illegal, but is it a breach of your personal ethics code? Probably. Simply following the law isn't enough to guarantee ethical behavior.

When technology giant Hewlett-Packard investigated members of its own board of directors in 2006, it used tactics that may have been legal but were un-ethical according to many critics. To find the source of news leaks, Hewlett-Packard hired an outside agency to conduct pretexting—a deceptive method of gaining access to private telephone records. Experts differ on the legality of pre-texting, but members of a U.S. House of Representatives committee that investi-gated Hewlett-Packard's actions "expressed disbelief that nobody at HP's top level stepped forward to say the practice, legal or not, was unethical and should be stopped."[9]

Can something illegal be ethical? Can doing the right thing involve breaking the law? In 2007, activists ranging from college students to a 90-year-old woman climbed oak trees owned by the University of California, Berkeley, to prevent the trees from being cut down to clear space for a new athletics training center. Said one organizer, "We think a university that has produced 27 Nobel laureates ought to be able to figure out how to build a gym without destroying this precious natural resource."[10] The concept of **civil disobedience** involves peaceful, unlawful actions designed to help change government policies.

Cross-Cultural Ethics

Let's say you're doing business overseas and you're given an expensive vase by one of the many companies seeking to establish a partnership with your organization. Giving gifts to new acquaintances is standard in the culture you're visiting. Can you ethically accept the gift? Or do you reject it as a bribe?

Professor Thomas Donaldson of the Wharton School of Business notes two extremes in the range of your possible responses to the gift: **cultural relativism** and **ethical imperialism**. Both, he says, are wrong. Cultural relativism involves the belief that no set of ethics is superior to any other set. With cultural relativism, you could accept the gift, saying, "It may violate my sense of ethics, but I'm just honoring the ethics of my host nation." Ethical imperialism is the belief that your system of ethics has no flexibility and no room for improvement; your system overrules every other system. With ethical imperialism, you would quickly reject the gift, saying, "Sorry, but this looks like a bribe to me."

Like Aristotle, Donaldson suggests a middle ground:

> When it comes to shaping ethical behavior, companies should be guided by three principles:
>
> - Respect for core human values, which determine the absolute moral threshold for all business activities.
> - Respect for local traditions.
> - The belief that context matters when deciding what is right and what is wrong.[11]

In other words, be clear on your own beliefs but willing to explore the beliefs of others. Is that lavish gift a bribe—or is it a genuine gift of friendship, an important part of the culture you're visiting? If it's clearly a bribe, you politely but firmly explain that you can't accept it. If it's a genuine gift, perhaps your organization's policy allows you to accept it on behalf of the company. Maybe you can donate it to charity when you return home.

Short-Term Thinking

The classic example of someone engaged in short-term thinking is the person who plugs a leaking dam with a lit stick of dynamite. The short-term problem is solved, but at too high a cost. A public relations practitioner who deceives members of any public, from reporters to employees, is guilty of short-term thinking. Eventually, the deception may be revealed, damaging the long-term relationship between the practitioner and the public.

Virtual Organizations

An emerging threat to ethical behavior comes from **virtual organizations,** which are temporary organizations formed by smaller units to complete a specific job. For example, an independent public relations consultant might team up with an architectural agency and a developer to try to persuade a community that it needs a new shopping center. These different units would consider themselves part of one organization for the duration of the project; when the project ends, so does the organization.

Dramatic improvements in communications technology have spurred the growth of virtual organizations, allowing them to include partners from different locations throughout the world. But unfamiliar partners or a lack of internal communication can lead to clashing values and ethics. In *Marketing Ethics: An International Perspective*, Professor Bodo Schlegelmilch writes, "How such organizations can create a sense of shared values and ethics, and how such organizations can be controlled by any external bodies, will constitute one of the key challenges in business ethics in the future."[12]

Specific Ethics Challenges

Studying the specific ethics challenges faced by today's practitioners is another way we can prepare ourselves for an effective career in public relations. To support its Member Code of Ethics, the Public Relations Society of America issues Professional Standards Advisories. PRSA issues a Professional Standards Advisory when a particular ethics challenge emerges as a widespread concern within the profession. From the adoption of its revised Member Code of Ethics in 2000 to late 2007, when this book went to press, PRSA issued seven Professional Standards Advisories. Table 6.1 summarizes those ethics challenges and offers PRSA's recommended solutions.[13]

The Rewards of Ethical Behavior

Let's ask a blunt question: What's the payoff for ethical behavior? What's in it for you?

Payoffs for ethical behavior, of course, are many, but among the most important is simply the deep satisfaction of doing the right thing. As different as Aristotle, Kant, and Mill are, they do agree on one point: You can't be truly happy unless you strive to honor your deepest values. (Unfortunately, they also agree that, though indispensable, ethical behavior may not be enough to guarantee happiness.) Still, this chapter is based on the assumption that you want to be an ethical person who works for an ethical organization.

Besides helping to create a happy life, ethical behavior can have some bottom-line bonuses—compensation, perhaps, for the sheer difficulty of behaving ethically. There's growing evidence that ethical behavior can lead to promotion within your organization. A Harvard University study of successful leaders concluded that a powerful correlation exists between leadership and "strong personal ethics."[14] Many public relations practitioners believe that good ethics positively affect an organization's financial success. A 2006 survey showed that corporations well known for ethical behavior, including Starbucks, Timberland, and Whole Foods, earn profits almost 400 percent higher than companies with average reputations.[15] And ethical companies may have superior employees: One recent survey showed that 65 percent of U.S. employees felt truly loyal to employers who "subscribed to

TABLE 6.1	PRSA Professional Standards Advisories	
ADVISORIES	**ISSUE**	**RECOMMENDED PRACTICES**
Professional Standards Advisory 1 (May 2004)	"Disclosure of employment status of public relations agency staff or independent public relations consultants who work on-site at a client's offices."	"When speaking to the public and/or the media on behalf of a client, agency personnel or independent consultants should uniformly and clearly identify themselves as outside spokespeople, retained by the company."
Professional Standards Advisory 2 (July 2004)	"Overstating charges and/or compensation, financial or otherwise, for actual work performed by a public relations professional."	"PRSA members pledge to adhere to a rigid code of conduct and the highest standards of professional integrity and responsibility. Members and the companies that they represent, including public relations agencies and independent public relations consultants, must bill clients only for services they perform and for expenses they incur on behalf of clients."
Professional Standards Advisory 3 (July 2004)	"Representation of front groups with undisclosed sponsorships and/or deceptive or misleading descriptions of goals, causes, tactics, sponsors or participants."	"PRSA members should recognize that assisting front groups that represent undisclosed sponsorships and/or deceptive or misleading descriptions of goals, causes, tactics, sponsors or participants constitutes improper conduct under the PRSA Member Code of Ethics and should be avoided."
Professional Standards Advisory 4 (August 2004)	"Reporting unethical behavior or unprofessional performance."	"Ethical practitioners have an affirmative obligation to report questionable professional behavior so these situations can be analyzed and helpful explanations developed and guidance provided promptly to all Society members."
Professional Standards Advisory 5 (January 2005)	"Telling the truth, especially in wartime."	"To reduce the confusion inherent in wartime communication, there must be a firewall separation between IO [Military Information Operations] and PA [Public Affairs] and a mechanism based on disclosure, exposure and public discussion to reestablish a basis of truth and trust when situations of honesty, clarity and truthfulness have been breached. Coordination between PA and IO is essential to maintain the firewall."
Professional Standards Advisory 6 (April 2005)	"Disclosure by expert commentators and professional spokespersons of payments or financial interests."	"1. To be proper, commercial relationships must be disclosed in advance or simultaneously in the same public forum to ensure that those affected or influenced can make informed and knowledgeable decisions."
		"2. Every participant in the chain of the financial relationship has an affirmative duty to disclose the relationship. Failure to disclose is improper conduct under the Code."
		"3. PRSA members have important responsibilities in such cases. The Code requires honesty and accuracy in all communications, and requires members to reveal the sponsors for causes and interests they represent and any financial interest they or their clients may have in the outcome of events or individual decisions."
Professional Standards Advisory 7 (October 2006)	"Representation of front groups and individuals using Blogs, Viral Marketing, and anonymous Internet postings with undisclosed sponsorships and/or deceptive or misleading descriptions of goals, causes, tactics, sponsors or participants."	"PRSA members should recognize that assisting front groups and individuals that represent undisclosed sponsorships and/or deceptive or misleading descriptions of goals, causes, tactics, sponsors or participants constitutes improper conduct under the PRSA Member Code of Ethics and should be avoided."

QUICKBREAK 6.3

Immanuel Kant and the Categorical Imperative

The German philosopher Immanuel Kant (1724–1804) contributed the concept of the "categorical imperative" to the study of ethics. Despite the fancy name, the concept is fairly simple. Let's say that you're experiencing an ethical crisis that has several different possible solutions. Kant would tell you to imagine that a universal maxim—a clear principle designed to apply to everyone in the world—will be the outcome of whichever course of action you choose. For example, one course of action might be for you to make a promise that you know you can't keep. Kant would ask you to imagine such an action becoming standard behavior for everyone—and he would ask you to answer two important questions:

1. Could such a world work?

2. Even if such a world could function, would you want to live in it?

In *Fundamental Principles of the Metaphysic of Morals,* Kant writes, "Act only on that maxim whereby thou canst at the same time will that it should become a universal law."[16] When you discover a course of action that could and probably should be a universal law, that is a **categorical imperative.** And a categorical imperative, says Kant, is a course of action that you must follow.

How would you apply Kant's theory of categorical imperatives to the scenario that opens this chapter? You would imagine that each possible course of action created a maxim that everyone in the world would follow. You would then reject any course of action that created a maxim that could lead to undesirable behavior if it were truly adopted by everyone. For example, one such maxim might be "It's all right to deceive the news media to protect our employees." Would that be a categorical imperative you'd want the world to follow every day?

---

ethical practices."[17] However, the 2000 National Business Ethics Survey of U.S. companies concluded that a code of ethics alone has no effect on profits. Instead, values-based ethics must truly be a part of an organization's culture.[18] "If you are going to have a values statement and not follow it," says Shane McLaughlin of the Best Practices in Corporate Communications organization, "it does much more damage to a company than not having a values statement at all."[19]

Not everyone is persuaded by the many studies that tie an organization's profits to its good ethics. "Ultimately, trade-offs must be made between the financial health of the company and ethical outcomes," says Deborah Doane, chair of the Corporate Responsibility Coalition. "And when they are made, profit undoubtedly wins over principles."[20]

At the very least, we can say that good ethics are probably good for business—and that bad ethics are probably bad for business. The odds favor doing the right thing.

QUICK CHECK

1. What is a golden mean? How does that concept apply to ethics?
2. How is a dilemma different from a problem?
3. Is legal behavior always ethical? Is illegal behavior always unethical?
4. In the business world, is ethical behavior financially profitable?
5. What is a categorical imperative?

Trust and Corporate Social Responsibility

The business scandals of the early 21st century damaged an essential ingredient for ethical relationships: trust. Professors Gene Laczniak and Patrick Murphy say trust is the logical outcome of ethical behavior.[21] In a landmark report titled *Restoring Trust in Business: Models for Action,* the PR Coalition—a consortium of more than 20 leading public relations organizations—concluded: "Trust has become an overriding concern for business leadership around the globe. It has been identified as a key factor in successful leadership and management. By contrast, lack of trust in a business is seen as crucially debilitating."[22]

Unfortunately, 80 percent of those responding to a 2006 Gallup poll rated the ethics of business executives as ranging from average to very low.[23] Almost half the respondents in a survey of public relations managers maintain that "the biggest issue facing PR today is credibility/trust."[24]

In its report, the PR Coalition recommended that public relations practitioners help their organizations establish trust with key publics through three values-driven actions:

1. Articulate a set of ethical principles that are closely connected to their core values and business processes and are supported with deep management commitment and enterprise-wide discipline.
2. Create a process for transparency and disclosure that is appropriate for their company and industry in both current and future operations. (**Transparency** involves doing business openly and honestly without hidden agendas.)
3. Make trust and ethics a board-level corporate governance issue and establish a formal system of measuring trust that touches all parts of the organization.[25]

"Trust is built over time, based on what companies do, not say," says Chris Atkins of Ketchum, an international public relations agency.[26]

Corporate Social Responsibility

One way to build trust over time involves a philosophy known as **corporate social responsibility,** or CSR. Organizations that embrace CSR are "a positive force for change to help improve the quality of people's lives" in the words of the International Business

Leaders Forum (IBLF). In other words, such organizations are good corporate citizens. According to the Corporate Social Responsibility Forum, corporate social responsibility strives for high standards in seven areas:

1. human rights, labor, and security;
2. enterprise and economic development;
3. business standards and corporate governance;
4. health promotion;
5. education and leadership development;
6. human disaster relief; and
7. environment.[27]

Public relations agency Cone, Inc., reports that 83 percent of Americans born between 1979 and 2001—the generation of most readers of this book—"trust a company more if it is socially and environmentally responsible." And 89 percent say they will switch from one product to another if "the second brand is associated with a good cause."[28]

Cone's research shows that CSR is more than an ethical imperative; it is a social expectation. Around the world, publics increasingly expect organizations to be good citizens, contributing to the social well-being of their communities—contributing, that is, to a fully functioning society. **Fully functioning society theory** involves the belief that, through public relations, organizations should help address important social needs by using wide-ranging two-way communication to build consensus and discover shared goals. Essentially, in a society that functions at its best, organizations act as citizens who seek the common good. In case this sounds too good to be true, proponents of the theory also point out that a fully functioning society would be good for business.[29]

As a values-driven, relationship-oriented philosophy, corporate social responsibility fits perfectly into the broad profession of public relations. A generation ago, Harold Burson, founder of the Burson-Marsteller public relations agency, offered these thoughts on CSR and public relations in a speech at Columbia University: "My subject pertains to the relationship between public relations and corporate social responsibility. I do not believe there is a relationship between the two. They are not cousins or even siblings. They are even closer than identical twins. They are one and the same."[30]

Beyond CSR: Strengthening Ethical Behavior

Ethical behavior and CSR in an organization must start with top management. Public relations practitioners can monitor and counsel on ethical matters, but ultimately an organization's top managers must lead by example. A whopping 95 percent of respondents to a *Fast Company* magazine survey on business ethics responded "Absolutely" or "Yes" to this question: "Do the ethics of the CEO play a meaningful role in the way the business gets done?" Said one respondent, "Great leaders inspire by example. The behavior of ethical CEOs trickles all the way down into an organization." Another respondent was more concise: "A fish rots from the head."[31]

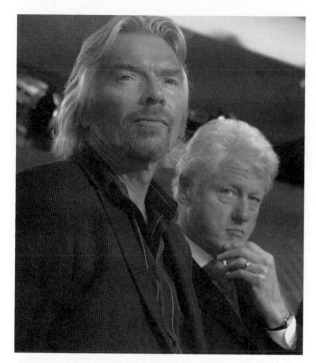

Corporate Social Responsibility Sir Richard Branson, shown here with former U.S. President Bill Clinton, announced in 2006 that approximately $3 billion in profits from his transportation companies would be devoted to developing energy sources that don't contribute to global warming. (Photo by Ruby Washington/*New York Times*. Copyright 2005 The New York Times Company. Reprinted with permission.)

Top executives, with the assistance of public relations counsel, should create an environment that helps the organization to focus constantly on the importance of ethical behavior in its relationships with others. Creating this environment involves CSR and more:

- periodic ethics audits to help you assess the current state of affairs in your organization;

- integration of values into the four-step public relations process (described in Chapter 1); and

- a system such as the Potter Box (see p. 180) for analyzing ethical challenges when they do occur.

Ethics Audits

An audit is a process of examination, evaluation, and recommendations. Most of us, probably, have heard of financial audits, in which a professional auditor examines an organization's income and expenditures and makes recommendations for improvement. In an **ethics audit,** we should ask and answer six basic questions:

1. What is our organization's ethics code?
2. How do we communicate that code to ourselves and others?
3. What do key publics—including employees—know about our ethics code?
4. What successes in ethics have we recently had, and why?
5. What setbacks in ethics have we recently had, and why?
6. What can we do to bolster strengths and reduce weaknesses in our ethics?

Periodically answering these questions and correcting any seeming deficiencies can help your organization build the necessary foundation for ethical behavior.

Integrating Ethics into the Public Relations Process

As we'll discuss in Chapter 12, the best time to solve a problem is before it starts. That's certainly true of challenges to ethical relationships: The best time to solve them is before they become problems. How can you attempt to do that? By ensuring that a focus on values is at the heart of your four-step public relations process.

In the *research* phase, as you scan the horizon searching for issues that may affect your organization, you should be well aware of your organization's written values. When you begin to research a particular issue, you should both remind yourself of those values and gather information on the values of the involved publics. Any clashes among those sets of values should alert you to a potential ethics problem.

In the *planning* phase, you should test every proposed action against your organization's values and against the values of important publics.

In the *communication* phase, you should implement every action with a clear understanding of how it reflects the values of your organization and the involved publics.

In the *evaluation* phase, you should study whether your completed actions were indeed in accordance with your organization's values. You should also consider the impact of the actions on the values of the involved publics. Any lapses or clashes should initiate a study to see whether problems stemmed from the actions or from your organization's values.[32]

The Potter Box

With CSR, periodic ethics audits, and your values-driven public relations process, you've established a foundation. But let's be realistic: Some challenges, like the hypothetical case study that begins this chapter, appear out of the blue. We can't prevent them. All we can do is try to react effectively and ethically. A helpful tool in such situations is the **Potter Box.** Designed by Ralph Potter, a former professor of divinity at Harvard University, the Potter Box helps people analyze individual ethical crises.[33] It derives its name from its boxlike format (see Figure 6.1).

To analyze an ethical problem with the aid of the Potter Box, you follow a six-step process:

1. Define the situation as objectively as possible. What *don't* you know? Would anyone define the situation differently? Who and why? (Definition box).
2. State the different values that you see involved in the situation and compare the merits of the differing values (Values box).
3. Consider traditional ethics principles and approaches from relevant ethics codes and from this chapter's QuickBreak philosophers: Aristotle, Kant, Mill, and Rawls (Principles box). Do these principles suggest any new values?
4. Identify all the stakeholders. What obligations do you have to each? Who most deserves your loyalty? (Loyalties box). Do these loyalties suggest new principles and values that you haven't considered? Are there individuals or groups noted in the definition toward which you feel no loyalty? If so, why?
5. Select a course of action that embraces the most compelling values, principles, and loyalties. Examine it in

FIGURE 6.1 The Potter Box

VALUES STATEMENT 6.1

Goodwill Industries of Orange County

Goodwill Industries of Orange County, California, helps people with disabilities find rewarding employment that benefits employers and employees alike. Founded in 1924, Goodwill Industries of Orange County is accredited by Goodwill Industries of America, Inc.

Mission

The mission of Goodwill Industries of Orange County is to provide people with disabilities the opportunity to achieve their highest levels of personal and economic independence.

Vision

We envision a world where all individuals with disabilities and other barriers to employment will have opportunities to enjoy the full benefits of competitive employment. Goodwill will focus on being the leader in providing quality education, training, and employment services. The core of Goodwill programs will empower individuals to be productive and independent, based on their abilities and interests.

Values

We believe in the inherent value of work; work has a greater value than charity. We trust and respect the dignity and creative potential of every person.
We strive for superior quality in our programs and services.

—Goodwill Industries of
Orange County web site

the light of your definition. If it still seems to be the best choice, implement it. Again, this is not easy. But in each possible course of action, you can now see which values, principles, and loyalties you're honoring.

6. Evaluate the impact of your decision.

This six-step process won't automatically tell you what the most ethical course of action is. But it can help you dissect the situation so that you can examine the relevant values, principles, and loyalties to justify your decision to yourself and to others. The Potter Box can help you practice values-driven public relations.

The Potter Box at Work

Let's apply the Potter Box to Choose and Lose, the scenario that opens this chapter:

1. *Definition box:* Three days ago, the CEO of my company told the news media that a much-publicized environmental hazard in our company's production process had been eliminated. The person responsible for eliminating the hazard is one of my best friends. Right now, she really needs me because she's going through a rough time dealing with the death of her oldest child. Yesterday I learned that she hadn't eliminated the environmental hazard; it still exists. In her condition, she doesn't even realize that she hasn't corrected it. I'm afraid that telling her will damage our friendship, which is one of the few positive things in her life right now. But if our CEO discovers the oversight, he may fire her—which, I'm afraid, could deepen her depression to a dangerous level.

2. *Values box:*
  A. Friendship
  B. Duty to CEO and company

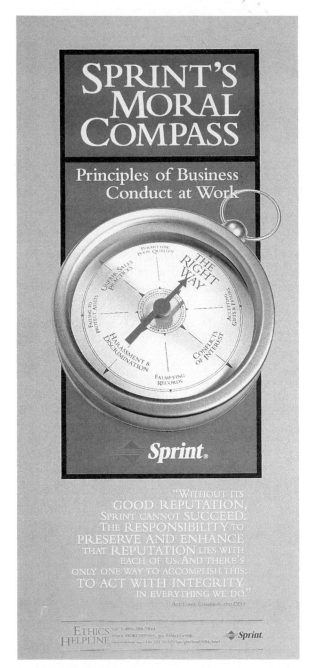

Ethics Helpline Poster Mired in an ethics dilemma? If you're an employee of Sprint Corporation, help—or at least understanding—may be just a phone call away. (Courtesy of Sprint Corporation)

C. Duty to environment

D. Honesty with news media

3. *Principles box:* Using the philosophy of Immanuel Kant, you could turn each value into a possible categorical imperative (see QuickBreak 6.3):

A. Honor friendships. Never damage a friendship.

B. Support the integrity of the CEO and the company in all your actions. Do nothing to undermine the integrity of the CEO and the company.

C. Take every possible action to protect the environment. Do nothing that hurts the environment.

D. Be absolutely truthful with the news media. Never lie to them. Correct every factual error.

Now you ask whether other, standard ethical principles apply. Aristotle's golden mean (QuickBreak 6.2)? Mill's principle of the greatest good for the greatest number (QuickBreak 6.4)? John Rawls' demand for unbiased social justice for all, with special consideration for society's least powerful (QuickBreak 6.5)?

Mill and Rawls help you to realize that you've left out a key value: the health and welfare of people who may be affected by the uncorrected environmental hazard. You now add this as value E, and you add a corresponding principle to the Principles box.

Now you examine the ethics codes of public relations and your organization. Those codes, you decide, strongly emphasize honesty and CSR.

At this point, you may decide that the strongest principles are A, B, D, and E: support of your friend, your CEO/company, the news media, and people at risk from the environmental hazard, respectively. You can think of minor exceptions to C—such

QUICKBREAK 6.4

Jeremy Bentham, John Stuart Mill, and Utilitarianism

The English philosophers Jeremy Bentham (1748–1832) and John Stuart Mill (1806–1873) helped develop the philosophy of utilitarianism. **Utilitarianism** holds that all our actions should be directed at producing the greatest good for the greatest number of people.

The obvious question here is What is the greatest good? According to utilitarianism, the greatest good is the action that produces the greatest happiness. "Actions are right in proportion as they tend to promote happiness, wrong as they tend to produce the reverse of happiness," writes Mill in *Utilitarianism*.[34] Bentham and Mill don't mean cheap, momentary, sensual happiness. They mean profound, lasting happiness, the kind produced by justice and love.

Utilitarianism asks us to consider courses of action that may not benefit us. "As between [a person's] own happiness and that of others," writes Mill, "utilitarianism requires him to be as strictly impartial as a disinterested and benevolent spectator."[35]

You might consider utilitarianism when you face a dilemma—that is, when you face an ethical problem in which every option has a downside. Utilitarianism would suggest that you select the solution that creates the greatest happiness—or perhaps the least unhappiness—for the greatest number of people.

How might you apply utilitarianism to the Choose and Lose scenario that opens this chapter? Simply put (though hard to do), you would examine which course of action creates the greatest good for the greatest number of people.

as damaging the environment slightly by building a new home. As you think more, you begin to wonder about A: Never damage a friendship. Don't you sometimes have to tell a true friend something she doesn't want to hear? Are some values more important than the very important value of friendship? You reluctantly begin to think yes, some are.

Regarding value E, you can think of companies whose processes create environmental hazards, but this doesn't excuse your company's processes because you've pledged to eliminate the hazard in question. You believe you must honor principle E, which might be phrased as *Do not initiate or continue manufacturing processes that injure the health and welfare of others.*

4. *Loyalties box:* Reviewing the situation, you determine that there are six primary stakeholders:
   A. your friend;
   B. the CEO and the company;
   C. the environment;
   D. the news media and their audiences;
   E. people affected by the environmental hazard; and
   F. yourself.

As you seek to determine the most ethical action in this situation, you begin to see that if you remain loyal only to your friend and say nothing, you're damaging the

QUICKBREAK 6.5

John Rawls and Social Justice

What do we owe to those less fortunate than we are? In decision-making processes, who speaks for the powerless who may be affected by the decisions? These questions concern advocates of social justice such as John Rawls.

In his book *A Theory of Justice,* Rawls urges decision makers to recognize and consider the values of all affected publics, not just those who have the power to influence decisions. Rawls recommends two particular techniques for an ethical decision-making process:[36]

1. Rawls suggests that before a decision is made, decision makers figuratively don a **veil of ignorance** that strips away their rank, power, and status. The veil of ignorance strategy asks decision makers to examine the situation objectively from all points of view. In particular, it asks them to imagine lifting the veil of ignorance only to

discover that they are now a member of one of the affected publics instead of the decision maker.

2. Rawls suggests that to redress social injustice, the most disadvantaged publics in a situation should receive the most advantages—with the exception of freedom. Freedom, he says, is an advantage that must be shared equally. All other resources, however, should flow to those who have the least. Power should flow to the powerless, and wealth should flow to the poor.

Rawls' theory of social justice may sound extreme, but it shares some similarities with values-driven public relations. It asks us to identify, respect, and build relationships with the publics whose values come into contact with the values of our organizations.

environment, hurting your company's important relationship with the news media, hurting those affected by the hazard, and perhaps hurting your future with the company. You realize that such damage will affect your organization's ability to reach its goals. Failure to reach those goals will affect your coworkers' ability to send children to college, to plan for retirement, to assist elderly parents, and other important concerns.

Utilitarianism's philosophy of the greatest good for the greatest number of people urges you to act out of loyalty to the environment and three large groups: your company, the news media, and people affected by the hazard. But you still wonder: Now that the choices and consequences are clearer, must you be disloyal to your friend?

5. *Decision and action:* You decide that the highest of the clashing values is honesty and that the most important stakeholders are the environment and the people affected by the hazard. Aristotle helps you realize that you can't always be loyal to friends, and Rawls influences you to consider who has the most to lose. You decide to tell the CEO, help correct the problem, and inform the news media. You approach an official in the company's human resources department with the following plan:

A. You will gently inform your friend of the problem and help her correct it.
B. The human resources official will inform the CEO of the death in your friend's family and the consequent depression your friend is experiencing.

The official will inform the CEO that your friend needs to meet with him on an important matter—but the official will not reveal the failure to correct the environmental hazard. Your friend will do that.

C. Along with the official from the human resources department, you will accompany your friend to the CEO's office, and she will tell him of the omission and of her corrective actions.

D. You will help prepare a news release to be sent to all appropriate news media. In that release, the company will announce the error and state what it is doing to ensure that such temporary inaccuracies never happen again. Your strategy is to explain that the uncorrected problem was the result of an inadvertent human error and that steps are being taken to correct the possibility of a recurrence.

E. You will increase your efforts to support your friend and, with the official from human resources, will explore what company policies and programs are available to help her.

6. *Evaluation:* Most publics—including the news media—are impressed by honesty and will forgive unintended errors. But you'll still evaluate the reaction of important publics such as employees and journalists. You'll also evaluate your friend's progress in dealing with her grief. Your evaluation of this episode will also, no doubt, lead you to establish procedures to verify information before it is distributed throughout your company and to the news media.

QUICK CHECK

1. What is CSR?
2. In the four stages of the public relations process, where should we consider values?
3. What is an ethics audit? What questions should we ask in the course of an ethics audit?
4. What ethical principle is the foundation of utilitarianism?
5. In order, what are the four quadrants of the Potter Box?
6. What is meant by the veil of ignorance? How can it assist ethical decision making?

Summary

No thinking person will ever say that living an ethical life is easy. But the rewards of ethical behavior are substantial. We can attain those rewards by constantly examining our ethics codes and how well our actions live up to our high standards. Sometimes our only reward is the satisfaction of knowing that we analyzed a tough situation and followed the most ethical course of action. Hardly a day goes by, on the other hand, that we read our morning paper without finding evidence of unethical behavior in the business world. The penalties for unethical behavior can be substantial, leading to lost profits and, often, lost jobs. And for public relations practitioners, unethical behavior can mean the loss of credibility, which is one of our most valuable possessions.

The ethics that affect public relations come from five general sources: international codes, societal codes, professional codes, organizational codes, and personal codes. Practitioners must know these codes and should be familiar with ethical decision-making processes such as the Potter Box if they hope to tackle successfully traditional ethical challenges that arise from dilemmas, overwork, legal/ethical confusion, values of other cultures, short-term thinking, and virtual organizations. Practicing CSR and examining your organization's values, as well as those of important publics, at every stage of the public relations process can help you achieve ethical, values-driven behavior.

It's hard to write about ethics and not sound preachy. That's not our purpose in this chapter. But ethical behavior is indispensable in values-driven public relations. For our society, for our organizations, for our important publics, and for ourselves, we should strive for nothing less.

DISCUSSION QUESTIONS

1. Where do you stand in public relations' objectivity–advocacy ethics debate? Should practitioners always tell 100 percent of what they know? Or is selective truth telling acceptable? If so, when?
2. What organizations have news media recently featured for ethical behavior? For unethical behavior?
3. From what you know of Johnson & Johnson's Tylenol crisis, how might that company have applied the utilitarian philosophy? How might it have applied categorical imperatives? How might it have applied the Potter Box?
4. Are John Rawls' theories of social justice unrealistic for profit-making businesses? Why should for-profit businesses care about powerless, disadvantaged publics?
5. What companies are well known for CSR? Do their reputations affect your purchasing decisions?

Memo from the Field

Carol Cone; CEO; Cone, Inc.; Boston, Massachusetts

Carol Cone is nationally recognized for her work in the cause branding and strategic philanthropy arenas. As the CEO of Cone, Inc., she has embraced a steadfast commitment to building substantive and sustainable partnerships between companies and social issues for more than 20 years. Cone has pioneered new alliances for private–public partnerships to create signature programs for a host of Fortune 500 companies, including the Avon Breast Cancer Crusade, ConAgra Foods' Feeding Children Better Program, PNC Grow Up Great Program, the American Heart Association's Go Red for Women Program, Reebok's Human Rights Awards, Rockport's Fitness Walking Program, Gillette Women's Cancer Connection, and Polaroid's Project KidCare, among others. Overall, Cone's signature cause programs have raised more than $500 million for various social causes. Today, Cone, Inc., is acknowledged as the nation's leading cause branding consultancy. A magna cum laude graduate of Brandeis University, Cone has been named one of the "50 Most Powerful Women in Public Relations" by PR Week magazine.

"What do you stand for?"

For over a decade, our Cone research has confirmed the powerful influence of corporate social actions on American attitudes and behavior. "What do you stand for?" is a resounding question asked of corporations by key stakeholders—employees, consumers, communities, governmental officials, and shareholders. The pressure on companies to answer this question has become more intense through a confluence of business challenges. These include ongoing corporate scandals following Enron's demise; a hypersensitive post–September 11 climate in which employees and consumers constantly reevaluate their relationship with the companies they work for and do business with; the need for true organizational and brand differentiation that is long-lasting; and the power of the Internet to unveil corporate operations. In this new reality of conducting business, companies must bring their humanity, indeed their values, to life.

No matter what you call it—strategic philanthropy, corporate citizenship, community relations, corporate social responsibility, cause branding—companies today are strategically approaching their relationship to society in a whole new way. This is an extremely exciting time for public relations practitioners, as the elevation of this practice to strategy brings the function directly into the center of the corporation and into the "C" suite—the office of the chairman and chief executive officer.

Key findings from our ongoing research (the Cone Corporate Citizenship Study) include:

- 78 percent of Americans say that companies have a responsibility to support social issues;

- 89 percent of Americans say that in light of the Enron collapse, it is more important than ever for companies to be socially responsible;

- 85 percent of Americans say that even during an economic downturn, it is important for companies to continue to support causes;

- 77 percent of Americans say a company's commitment to social issues is important when they decide where to work;

- 75 percent of Americans say a company's commitment to social issues is important when they decide which products and services to recommend to other people;

- 84 percent of Americans say a company's commitment to social issues is important when they decide which companies they want to see doing business in their community; and

- 66 percent of Americans say a company's commitment to social issues is important when they decide which stocks/mutual funds to invest in.

How a company brings its values to life depends on how it views its responsibility to society and how it sees this function as a means to deepen its relationships with stakeholders. Early adopters, McDonald's and The Home Depot, had CEOs who keenly understood the social contract—to take from a community, employee, or consumer meant that you also had to give back. From their mission statements, both companies developed operating policies to improve their communities in ways strategically aligned with their businesses: McDonald's provides a myriad of children's programs, from its Ronald McDonald houses to high school scholarships, while The Home Depot rebuilds local neighborhoods hit by disasters or communities in extreme need of physical rehabilitation. Both organizations' CEOs know these efforts tie them to their employees, communities, and customers in highly unique and powerful ways—ways that pay off in hiring and retaining the best employees, customer loyalty, community support, and increased sales.

While McDonald's and The Home Depot were early practitioners of corporate citizenship, today's companies practice a range of actions that fall along the spectrum of corporate social responsibility. These include a variety of strategic internal and external functions, from corporate governance to environmental responsibility, employee and community relations, cause branding, philanthropy, responsible product development, and sourcing.

While select leadership companies have established powerful brands rooted in their values, and many more have implemented corporate citizenship initiatives in the past few years, most are playing catch-up to keep pace with rapidly shifting business and stakeholder pressures. As a public relations practitioner, you can play a leadership role in guiding corporate management toward an understanding of the power of putting values in action, through words, but even more importantly, through credible and lasting deeds.

To do this, you will need a wide range of skills. First, gain a solid knowledge of the public relations profession through school, extensive reading, and internships. Next, gain on-the-job training in a variety of areas from communications (all communications, not just media relations) to community, from employee and investor relations to philanthropy—even spend some time in various business units learning about product development, distribution, marketing, and sales. Then broaden your capabilities beyond work by volunteering for nonprofits.

Concurrently, read, read, read, books and trade publications on business, corporate citizenship, and various social issues of interest to you. A few of my favorites include *Built to Last* by Jim Collins and Jerry Porras, *A New Brand World* by Scott Bedbury and Stephen Fenichel, and *Pour Your Heart into It: How Starbucks Built a Company One Cup at a Time* by Howard Schultz.

Next, get involved in an ongoing corporate citizenship initiative. To eventually earn the mantle of leading a corporate program, you will need to be part of a team executing one or many program elements.

What an exciting journey! Any practitioner who has led this charge has emerged a much more satisfied individual, having brought this critical new business practice into the center of the organization. Recognizing the power of values in action brings a new purpose to the corporation and to each individual the program touches, either internal or external.

Corporate citizenship could indeed become the new golden era for PR professionals, if it is embraced strategically and with deep commitment and honesty to help the CEO and the organization fulfill their mission to their stakeholders.

CASE STUDY **6.1**

Canada's Family Channel Battles Bullies

A recent worldwide survey asked 26,000 adults to name the friendliest nation on Earth. The top answer? Think hockey, maple leaves, and maybe even actors Jim Carrey and Mike Myers. Think Canada.[37]

Even the world's friendliest nation, however, can contain an oddly discordant note: Think bullies. Research shows that 20 percent of Canadian youths ages 4 to 19 have been bullied continually for two or more years.[38]

"Bullying is about behavior," says middle school teacher Bill Belsey, president of Bullying.org Canada. "And we can change behavior."[39]

Although changing a public's behavior may not be as easy as Belsey thinks (see Chapter 8), he has good reason for optimism: His partner in the crusade to end bullying is a media giant—Canada's Family Channel, a subsidiary of Astral Media that reaches more than 5 million homes in that nation.

Why would a for-profit media outlet join a grassroots organization to combat a problem that could hardly affect its bottom line?

In a word, values.

"If it's important to kids, it's important to us," says Joe Tedesco, vice president and general manager of the Family Channel. "The majority of our viewers are Canadian kids, and bullying is an issue that faces every kid at one time or another."[40]

In "The Way We Do Business: Our Guide to Ethical Business Conduct," Astral Media specifies its commitment to corporate social responsibility:

> We are committed to being a responsible corporate citizen of the communities in which we reside. We will strive to improve the well-being of our communities through the encouragement of employee participation in civic affairs and through corporate philanthropy.[41]

In 2005, additional research by the Family Channel and the Canadian Initiative for the Prevention of Bullying noted that the presence of observers can reduce bullying:

- When an observer objects, bullying stops within 10 seconds in 57 percent of incidents.

- In 85 percent of bullying situations, observers are present.

- When observers are present in a bullying situation, they object only 25 percent of the time.[42]

"Family Channel and Bullying.org are trying to change 'bystander' behavior by showing kids examples of how they can act differently and diffuse bullying situations," says Belsey. "We are not asking kids to get involved in a physical way but rather to reach out to victims and show bullies that their actions will not be tolerated."[43]

At the center of the intervention strategy is a pledge that the Family Channel and Bullying.org encourage young Canadians to take:

> This is for me, my friends today, and my friends tomorrow. I think being mean stinks. I won't watch someone get picked on, because I am a do-something person—not a do-nothing person. I care. I can help change things. I can be a leader. In my world, there are no bullies allowed. Bullying is bad. Bullying bites. Bullying bothers me. I know sticking up for someone is the right thing to do. My name is _____. And I won't stand by. I will stand up.[44]

To promote the pledge and encourage intervention in bullying situations, the Family Channel has helped implement the following public relations tactics:

- a National Bullying Awareness Week, launched in 2003;

- a Bullying.org web site where youths can take the pledge and share advice;

- television public service announcements showing youths intervening in bullying situations and taking the pledge;

- a video news release showing the launch of Bullying Awareness Week at an elementary school in Ontario;

- media interviews with young stars of Family Channel shows such as *Radio Free Roscoe*; and

- news releases announcing National Bullying Awareness Week.

In the first National Bullying Awareness Week, 55,000 Canadian youths took the pledge. "The message of the pledge," says Belsey, "is to encourage kids to be leaders and not followers and set an example that bullying is not cool."[45]

In 2005, the Canadian Public Relations Society honored the Family Channel and its anti-bullying campaign with the Award of Excellence for Community Relations.

"As long as they're bringing it to the forefront for people to hear and learn about . . . ," says Ali Mukaddam, a star of *Radio Free Roscoe,* "then it's just a good thing."[46]

DISCUSSION QUESTIONS

1. Family Channel and Bullying.org want to change a public's behavior. What does public relations research say about their chances of success?
2. In addition to the tactics used by the Family Channel to promote the pledge and encourage intervention in bullying situations, what other tactics would you recommend?
3. If you were public relations director of the Family Channel, how would you answer possible stockholder concerns about using corporate resources for charitable activities that don't directly boost the bottom line?
4. Do you believe that ethical companies benefit financially? Do you prefer to do business with ethical companies?

CASE STUDY **6.2**

Appearance of Obfuscation? Digene Corporation and European Women for HPV Testing

Cervical cancer kills. In Europe, it annually takes more than 12,000 lives.[47]

In recent years, Europeans have rallied to conquer the cancer second only to breast cancer in terms of occurrence.[48] They have demanded services for early identification of the disease. In 2001, the European Society for Infectious Diseases in Obstetrics and Gynecology called for improved testing.[49] Nine months later, the European Parliament announced that its insurance program would support screening tests for female members and employees.[50]

Instrumental in both victories was a Brussels-based organization called European Women for HPV Testing. HPV stands for human papillomavirus, which can be an early indicator of potential cervical cancer. Digene Corporation, the U.S.-based manufacturer of a leading test for HPV, acknowledged the support of European Women for HPV Testing in at least two news releases.[51] In one of those releases, Digene reported,

> Women's health advocates throughout Europe today launched European Women for HPV Testing, a campaign that seeks to ensure that all European women have access to HPV testing. The campaign is composed of over 100 high-profile women from the fields of politics, education, media, sports, the arts and entertainment from 11 countries across Europe.

Digene Chairman and CEO Evan Jones added, "The launch of European Women for HPV Testing reinforces the belief that women are interested in knowing if they harbor a cancer-causing virus."[52]

Only one thing prevents this story from being a solid example of a successful third-party endorsement: Digene and public relations agency Burson-Marsteller launched and paid for European Women for HPV Testing. The corporation failed to mention that fact in its early news releases, and critics charge that Digene and Burson-Marsteller disguised their connection to the grassroots lobbying group.

Claims of a "clandestine lobbying campaign" first surfaced in the *Observer*, a British newspaper. In 2004, the *Observer* fired off this headline: "Revealed: How Stars Were Hijacked to Boost Health Company's Profits; Famous Women Have Backed Up [a National Health Service] Screening Test Unaware They Were Being Set Up by a Biotech Corporation and Its PR Agency." In an article even longer than the headline, the *Observer* charged that "celebrities have been duped into supporting a sophisticated lobbying campaign secretly orchestrated from Brussels by one of the world's largest public relations firms."

The *Observer* further reported that an early letter from European Women for HPV Testing was signed by a woman who, the newspaper learned, was an employee in Burson-Marsteller's Brussels office.

In the article, representatives from Burson-Marsteller acknowledged their connection to European Women for HPV Testing. "This is not a cloak-and-dagger operation," said one. "We make sure everything is very transparent, and we clearly state that Digene funds the campaign." But the *Observer* noted a lack of such transparency in documents from Digene and European Women for HPV Testing. The newspaper also reported that celebrities it contacted, women who allegedly endorsed European Women for HPV Testing, "had never heard of the group—let alone . . . being members, as its Web site claims."[53]

In its "Member Code of Ethics 2000," the Public Relations Society of America directs members to "Reveal the sponsors for causes and interests represented." And under "examples of improper conduct," the PRSA Code includes this entry: "Front groups: A member implements a 'grass-roots' campaign or letter-writing campaigns to legislators on behalf of undisclosed interest groups."[54]

Digene Corporation's Mission Statement includes this sentence: "All of our actions are guided by our responsibility to act as good citizens in the global community."[55] Perhaps that declaration led to Digene's eventual decision to post this announcement on all news releases from European Women for HPV Testing as well as on the organization's web site: "European Women for HPV Testing is made possible by an unrestricted grant from Digene Corporation."[56]

As the dust of the controversy settled and Digene publicized its connection to European Women for HPV Testing, *PR Week* magazine wondered why the "duplicitous appearance" occurred in the first place: Why would Digene act as if it had "something to hide" when, in reality, it had developed a popular, life-saving medical procedure? "That's cause for celebration," wrote Paul Holmes, president of Holmes Group public relations agency, "so why even risk the appearance of obfuscation?"[57]

DISCUSSION QUESTIONS

1. If Digene were effectively promoting a test that can save lives, did it really do anything wrong by sponsoring European Women for HPV Testing?
2. Imagine that Digene had asked for your ideas on what advice the great philosophers—Aristotle, Kant, Mill, and Rawls—might have had regarding quiet sponsorship of European Women for HPV Testing. What do you think each would have advised?
3. Were Digene's actions in supporting European Women for HPV Testing consistent with its Mission Statement?
4. What is your personal reaction to the full story of European Women for HPV Testing? Do you agree with Paul Holmes?
5. Can you think of any instances in which a so-called front organization is ethically defensible?

NOTES

1. *New Standard Encyclopedia,* vol. 5 (Chicago: Standard Education Society, 1947).
2. Hugh N. Culbertson, Ni Chen, and Linzhi Shi, "Public Relations Ethics: Some Foundations," *Ohio Journalism Monographs,* no. 7 (January 2003): 2.
3. "Al-Jazeera Pledges 'Truth' in War Coverage" (Kitchener-Waterloo, Ontario), *Record,* 15 July 2004, online, LexisNexis.

4. Chick-fil-A, online, www.chick-fil-a.com.

5. L. M. Sixel, "Five Questions with Dan Cathy," *Houston Chronicle,* 25 June 2004, online, LexisNexis.

6. Ralph D. Barney and Jay Black, "Ethics and Professional Persuasive Communication," *Public Relations Review* 20, no. 3 (fall 1994): 189.

7. Confucius, *The Doctrine of the Mean,* online, http://classics.mit.edu/Confucius/doctmean.html.

8. Free Burma Coalition, online, www.freeburmacoalition.org; John Lanchester, "Walled Off," *The New Yorker,* 11 December 2006, online, LexisNexis Academic.

9. Pete Carey and Therese Poletti, "Incredulous Lawmakers Grill HP Managers," *San Jose Mercury News,* 28 September 2006, online, LexisNexis.

10. Jesse McKinley, "A Dose of Maturity for a California Protest," *New York Times,* 22 January 2007, online, LexisNexis; John Ritter, "Berkeley Protest Branching Out," *USA Today,* 11 January 2007, online, LexisNexis.

11. Thomas Donaldson, "Values in Tension: Ethics Away from Home," *Harvard Business Review,* September–October 1996, online, LexisNexis.

12. Bodo Schlegelmilch, *Marketing Ethics: An International Perspective* (London: International Thomson Business Press, 1998), 11.

13. "Ethics Resources," Public Relations Society of America, online, www.prsa.org/aboutUs/ethics.

14. Shlegelmilch, 145.

15. "Quick Study: PDA Users Report E-mail Overload; Ethical = Profitable; Executive Pay-for-Performance Model PR News," *PR News,* 4 December 2006, online, LexisNexis.

16. Immanuel Kant, *Fundamental Principles of the Metaphysic of Morals,* in *Harvard Classics,* vol. 32 (New York: P. F. Collier and Son, 1910), 352.

17. "National Workplace Study Shows Employees Take Dim View of Current Leadership Ethics," news release issued by Walker Information, 1 September 2003, online, www.walkerinfo.com.

18. Shane McLaughlin, "A New Era for Communicating Values," *The Public Relations Strategist* (winter 2003): 10.

19. Thomas Donaldson, "Adding Corporate Ethics to the Bottom Line," *Financial Times,* 13 November 2000, online, LexisNexis.

20. Deborah Doane, "The Myth of Corporate Social Responsibility," *Stanford Social Innovation Review* 3, no. 3 (fall 2005): 24.

21. Gene Laczniak and Patrick Murphy, *Marketing Ethics: Guidelines for Managers* (Lexington, Mass.: Lexington Books, 1985).

22. PR Coalition, "Restoring Trust in Business: Models for Action," Arthur W. Page Society, 2003, online, www.awpagesociety.com.

23. "Honesty/Ethics in Professions," The Gallup Organization, 14 December 2006, online, www.galluppoll.com.

24. Mark Weiner, "Proving Your Worth," *Communication World,* April–May 2003, 26.

25. "Restoring Trust in Business: Models for Action."

26. Chris Atkins, "Restoring Trust in Business," *The Public Relations Strategist* (winter 2003): 11.

27. Ronald Alsop, "Ranking Corporate Reputation," *Wall Street Journal,* 6 December 2005, online, http://online.wsj.com.

28. "Civic-Minded Millennials Prepared to Reward or Punish Companies Based on Commitment to Social Causes," news release issued by Cone, Inc., 24 October 2006, online, LexisNexis.

29. Robert L. Heath, "Onward into More Fog: Thoughts on Public Relations' Research Directions," *Journal of Public Relations Research* 18, no. 2 (2006).

30. Harold Burson, "Social Responsibility or 'Telescopic Philanthropy': The Choice Is Ours," speech to the Columbia University Graduate School of Business, 20 March 1973.

31. "The 'Fast Track Leadership Survey' on Business Ethics and Integrity," report issued by *Fast Company* magazine, August 2005, 17.

32. For more information on integrating ethics into the public relations process, see Thomas Bivins, "A Systems Model for Ethical Decision Making in Public Relations," *Public Relations Review* (winter 1992): 365–384.

33. See Clifford Christians, Mark Fackler, Kim Rotzoll, and Kathy Brittain McKee, *Media Ethics: Cases and Moral Reasoning,* 5th ed. (New York: Longman, 1998).

34. John Stuart Mill, *Utilitarianism,* ed. Oskar Priest (New York: Bobbs-Merrill, 1957), 10.

35. Mill, 22.

36. John Rawls, *A Theory of Justice* (Cambridge, Mass.: Harvard University Press, 1971).

37. "It's Official—Australia Is All About the Food, Footy, and Fame," news release issued by Global Marketing Insight, 22 February 2006, online, LexisNexis.

38. "Survey Finds That Children Are Often Bullied for an Extended Period of Time," Family Channel news release, 14 November 2005, online, LexisNexis.

39. Todd Saelhof, "Bully Effort Scares Up Help," *Calgary Sun,* 16 November 2004, online, LexisNexis.

40. "Family Channel Takes a Stand against Bullying," Family Channel news release, 8 November 2004, online, LexisNexis.

41. "The Way We Do Business: Our Guide to Ethical Business Conduct," Astral Media, online, www.astralmedia.com.

42. "Survey Finds That Children Are Often Bullied for an Extended Period of Time."

43. "Family Channel Takes a Stand against Bullying."

44. Stephanie McGrath, "Fighting Words," *Toronto Sun,* 21 November 2004, online, LexisNexis.

45. "Family Channel Takes a Stand against Bullying."

46. Saelhof.

47. "Major European Medical Society Includes Broad Use of HPV Testing in Cervical Cancer Screening Guidelines," news release issued by Digene Corporation, 20 September 2001, online, www.digene.com.

48. Digene Corporation, online, www.digene.com.

49. "Major European Medical Society Includes Broad Use of HPV Testing in Cervical Cancer Screening Guidelines."

50. "European Parliament to Include HPV Testing in Its Cervical Cancer Screening Program," news release issued by Digene Corporation, 17 June 2002, online, www.digene.com.

51. "Major European Medical Society Includes Broad Use of HPV Testing in Cervical Cancer Screening Guidelines"; "European Parliament to Include HPV Testing in Its Cervical Cancer Screening Program."

52. "Major European Medical Society Includes Broad Use of HPV Testing in Cervical Cancer Screening Guidelines."

53. Antony Barnett, "Revealed: How Stars Were Hijacked to Boost Health Company's Profits; Famous Women Have Backed Up an NHS Screening Test Unaware They Were Being Set Up by a Biotech Corporation and Its PR Agency," *Observer*, 25 January 2004, online, LexisNexis.

54. Public Relations Society of America, online, www.prsa.org.

55. Digene, online, www.digene.com.

56. European Women for HPV Testing, online, www.womenforhpvtesting.org.

57. Paul Holmes, "Digene's Duplicitous Appearance Counteracts the Accolades Its Cervical Cancer Test Merits," *PR Week*, 2 February 2004, online, LexisNexis.

CHAPTER 7

Research
and Evaluation

OBJECTIVES

After studying this chapter, you will
be able to

- describe the value of research and
  evaluation in the public relations
  process

- recognize the differences between
  formal and informal research

- develop a strategy for conducting
  research

- explain the basics of conducting the
  five most common forms of public
  relations research

- glean valuable information through
  effective analysis of survey results

KEY TERMS

Don't Drink the Water?

You have just had one of those "I can't believe they are asking me to do this" moments. As public information officer for a metropolitan county government, you have communicated with citizens on a wide range of issues. Many times, you have asked the public to take some sort of action to promote the community's best interests. But this one takes the cake: Your boss wants you to convince the people of your county that it is safe to drink sewer water.

To be more accurate, this is recycled and purified sewer water: as clean—if not cleaner—than bottled water found on grocery store shelves. Local water and sanitation engineers developed the idea in response to severe water shortages. The county sits in an arid region subject to drought. Water is pumped in from hundreds of miles away at great expense. As the community's population grows, so does the strain on the region's water supply. In addition to conservation measures, county officials believe that blending the purified sewer water with traditional water sources will significantly ease the problem. However, construction of the water purification plant will be costly and the thought of having people drink recycled sewer water may be one that they find, well, hard to swallow.

Your county is ethnically and economically diverse. Dozens of stakeholder groups regularly lobby county government, many of them in Spanish. Local business and industry groups will likely be heard.

"We need the public's support," your boss says. "The future of our county depends on this."

You ask yourself, "What is the first thing I should do?"

For Love or Money?

Katie Delahaye Paine, a well-known champion of public relations measurement and accountability, once raised a few eyebrows when she asked a room full of PR gurus and research wonks what they thought was more important to measure, love or money? In other words, what's more important, knowing whether public relations added to a client's bottom line or whether it strengthened the client's relationships with key stakeholders?

"The experts were unanimous in their decision that the only thing worth measuring is relationships—i.e., the long-term impact of our efforts on our institutional reputations, the trust of our neighbors, the confidence of our employees and the satisfaction of our customers," Paine said. Then she countered with another provocative question: If measuring relationships is most important, then why are so few doing it?[1]

Paine's questions strike at the heart of what may be the most significant debate in the industry today: How do we measure the value of public relations? At a time when many social institutions are under greater scrutiny than ever before, public relations is no different. Clients and employers are all asking the same question: For what I spend on public relations, am I getting my money's worth?

Here's where many practitioners get into trouble. When they say that you can't measure the value of public relations, their employers ask "why not?" They want hard numbers, much like they get from advertising sales representatives and marketing managers. In response, public relations practitioners and educators have created several complex equations that place a numerical value on intangible concepts such as relationships. However, to many a skeptical client, these formulas seem little more than smoke and mirrors.

As public relations moves well into its second century, the challenge of proving its value is as great—if not greater—than it was in the time of Edward L. Bernays.

Measuring Intangibles

Spurred by organizations such as the Institute for Public Relations (IPR), practitioners have increasingly focused on putting hard numbers into public relations evaluation. IPR cosponsored the Public Relations Evaluation Summit in New York in October 1996. Out of that meeting of leading professionals and academics came a series of guiding principles for public relations measurement and evaluation.[2]

In the past decade, interest in public relations research and evaluation has intensified. You need only look at IPR's web site, www.instituteforpr.org, to see the wealth of public relations research and evaluation literature generated since that summit. Among the most notable papers published on the subject was 1999's *Guidelines for Measuring Relationships in Public Relations* by Linda Childers Hon and James Grunig (see QuickBreak 7.3). It marked the first serious attempt to quantify the strength of the relationships an organization has with its key stakeholders.[3] Recently, much of this academic theory has been put to practical use. Edelman, the world's largest independent public relations agency, announced the development of what it calls the Relationship Index, based on the Hon-Grunig research, in April 2003. Edelman's Bob Kornecki said the new measurement tool will help clients "benchmark, monitor and manage stakeholder relations."[4]

Although measurement and evaluation are hot topics in today's public relations circles, they really aren't anything new. In 2005, Walter K. Lindenmann, one of the industry's leading research experts, noted that the first discussion of communication effectiveness dates back to the 1940s. He also said that the time for talking about evaluation has passed. The time for action is *now*. "We need to more effectively train public relations practitioners and counselors on how to measure and evaluate public relations effectiveness," Lindenmann said. "We need to do a better job of convincing senior management of the importance of allocating appropriate funds to support public relations evaluation efforts."[5]

QUICKBREAK 7.1

ROI and AVE

What is the value of publicity, and how do you know that the public relations budget yielded a favorable financial **return on investment (ROI)**?

Organizations have struggled to demonstrate that their public relations efforts add to their bottom line. Some practitioner associations, such as the Institute for Public Relations, believe that ROI is not the best measure. A 2004 IPR survey showed that a majority of communications directors believe it is possible to show that public relations efforts can make more money for an organization than they cost. However, only one-third of those surveyed said they actually consider public relations budgets in ROI terms.[6]

Facing pressures to demonstrate public relations ROI, many practitioners have turned to **advertising value equivalency (AVE),** a calculation based on advertising rates and the amount of media coverage. For example, suppose a public relations agency distributed a news release that generated a story that took up 10 column-inches of space in the local newspaper. If the newspaper charges $100 per column inch, the math would be simple: 10 inches times $100 equals an AVE of $1,000.

Because of third-party endorsement, some note that publicity is more credible—and therefore more valuable—than advertising. They argue that there should be a multiplier in the AVE formula to account for publicity's added value. For example, the Texas Commission on the Arts advises its stakeholders

that "a good rule of thumb is to mark up the advertising value by a factor of three for a general story."[7] Using this formula, the AVE of our news story would balloon to $3,000.

You may be asking yourself how this credibility multiplier was determined. That's the heart of the controversy. "The weightings for 'third-party' endorsement are totally made up," wrote Professor James Grunig.[8] The Institute for Public Relations Research has gone so far as to suggest that these "arbitrary weighting schemes" are "unethical, dishonest, and not supported by the research literature."[9]

The use of AVE raises other issues. Is a story in a local medium as important as one in a national medium? How do you quantify the value of a story that depicts your organization in a positive, negative, or neutral light? Did the readers, viewers, or listeners take a desired action as a result of the story? As a practitioner, can you ethically tell a journalist that your news release contains news—but then evaluate it using advertising rates?

Gary Getto, vice president of Surveillance Data, embraces AVE. He told one publication that the public relations industry runs the risk of throwing "the baby out with the bath water" by rejecting AVE. Citing research conducted by his and two other firms, Getto said, "We think this study helps to put to rest the claim that AVE is not as valid a tool as audience impressions and article counts."[10]

The Value of Research and Evaluation

The first step in the public relations process is research. The fourth, or last, step is evaluation. Nothing in public relations research could be more important than those two assumptions. Or more wrong.

Some are tempted to view these two steps as necessary "evils" that allow practitioners to get to the "really important" parts of the public relations process—planning (where strategy and tactics are developed) and communication (where plans are executed). Sometimes, we bypass research and evaluation out of a sense of presumed knowledge: We think we already know everything we need to know to act and that we will know whether we have been successful. Other popular excuses for bypassing the research and evaluation steps are lack of time, lack of personnel, lack of money, and lack of how-to knowledge. At face value, these may seem like logical excuses. But that's all they are: excuses. "Clients have difficulty swallowing $20,000–$50,000 on research when most PR budgets are around $100,000 a year," said Paul Owen, president of Seattle's Owen Media. "But $20,000–$50,000 is a drop in the bucket for a $10 million ad campaign."[11]

Research and evaluation are cornerstones of good public relations practice. They lead us to explore two areas essential to success in any public relations effort:

1. *What we think we know:* Do our assumptions hold up under closer examination? If nothing else, research and evaluation can remove lingering doubts by validating the accuracy of information.
2. *What we don't know:* Are pieces missing from the puzzle? By exploring terra incognita—unknown territory—we can open doors of opportunity that may otherwise remain closed.

Why not have separate chapters on research and evaluation? We link those parts of the public relations process in this chapter for two reasons. First, as we noted in Chapter 1, public relations is a dynamic, nonlinear process. The traditional four-step process implies a straight-line approach: research, followed by planning, followed by communication, followed by evaluation. However, public relations does not work that way. The four steps are intertwined. Research and evaluation occur at every phase of the public relations process. It's not unusual for practitioners, in the midst of planning, to decide they need more information. Nor is it unusual for public relations professionals to adjust strategy in the midst of its execution based on either feedback or new information.

The second reason we combine the two steps here is that the processes of research and evaluation are closely related. Both involve using similar methods to gather information. It could be said that research is gathering information before the fact and evaluation is gathering information after the fact. That notion has an element of truth, but it's an oversimplification. Instead, we constantly gather information, evaluate it, and seek new information to test a developing hypothesis. Remember your first school dance? You probably picked a dance partner based on an ongoing process of research and evaluation. At first glance across a dimly lit gymnasium, you may have been interested in dancing with a particular person. However, on closer inspection, appearance and behavior may have changed your mind. You may then have sought new information on someone else. Several cycles of research and evaluation may have occurred before you took that big step and ventured onto the dance floor. Public relations is no different—although it is often less traumatic.

No one, certainly not the authors of this book, expects you to become an expert researcher based on the information you find in this chapter. Later in your career, it may be that you rarely do in-depth research—it may be someone else's job to do it for you. Nevertheless, it is important that you know enough to be a good consumer of research.

QuickBreak 7.2

Issues Management

If you think it is difficult for public relations practitioners to measure what has happened, think of how hard it is for them to predict the future. When they do, they are engaged in **issues management,** a process of predicting and managing *future* issues and concerns.

Issues management often begins with **scanning,** which is short for "scanning the horizon." In the days before satellites and radar, scanning the horizon was the only way to determine if there were any potential threats approaching. This is the concept behind issues management: Through a process of analyzing emerging trends and issues, practitioners can prepare their organizations to respond in a timely and appropriate manner.

That's what the U.S. cattle industry did in 2001 when an outbreak of foot-and-mouth disease in European cattle created a panic among consumers. During that crisis, poor media relations had made a bad situation worse. Learning from Europe's mistakes, Dairy Management, Inc., a marketing coalition created to build demand for U.S. dairy products, launched a proactive campaign of food-safety education and training. Tactics included the creation of a web site, called the Dairy Response Center, designed to go online at a moment's notice.[12] At about the same time, the National Cattlemen's Beef Association conducted its own research and developed a crisis response plan. Much like DMI, the NCBA focused its efforts on creating online resources and conducting extensive media training for staff and industry opinion leaders.[13]

When a single case of mad cow disease was detected in Washington state in 2003, the dairy and beef associations activated their crisis plans. While the industry lost an estimated $1.3 billion because of the outbreak, things could have been much worse.[14] A January 2005 survey showed that consumer confidence in U.S. beef was higher than before the outbreak.[15] Observers credited the cattle industry's proactive crisis planning with softening the blow.[16]

The goal of any issues management program is to scan for issues and trends with a potential impact—either positive or negative—on the organization. Once an issue is identified, active **monitoring** should begin. By keeping track of the latest developments, organizations can plan responses consistent with their values. And this is where the *real* value of issues management is demonstrated: giving an organization time to act in a manner that allows it to dictate its own course rather than having its response dictated by events.

"As communicators, we need to learn how to measure," said Julie B. Chughtai, director, executive communication, DePaul University. "Unfortunately, I had to learn on the job. We should be teaching the next generation of communicators both the art and the science of what we do."[17]

And that's *exactly* what we are going to do.

 QUICK CHECK

1. Why is research an essential part of the public relations process?
2. What are ROI and AVE?
3. What is issues management?

Developing a Research Strategy: What Do I Want to Know?

A quirky but entertaining show called *Mythbusters* premiered on the Discovery Channel in January 2003. The premise of the program involves two former Hollywood special effects artists creatively blending science and show business wizardry to test the validity of urban legends. For example, in episode four they challenged the conventional wisdom that a penny thrown from the top of a skyscraper can kill a pedestrian on the street below. By creating an experiment using a dummy and a staple gun modified to fire pennies, the Mythbusters proved that a penny dropped from a tall building lacks sufficient speed and mass to be lethal. (But it sure can hurt!)

So what does all this have to do with research and evaluation? Perhaps more than you may think. When the Mythbusters designed an experiment to simulate the conditions of a real penny drop, they engaged in a process social scientists call *operationalization*. In effect, they developed a strategy to find out what they wanted to know. The Mythbusters also illustrate another important lesson: Creativity is important at every step of the public relations process.

Getting started in almost any endeavor can be difficult. Research is no different. Before setting out on any journey, it is important to know the destination. A journey into research is no different. That is why the first step when you embark on a research project is to develop a **research strategy.** Just like the Mythbusters, that involves asking yourself two important questions:

1. What do I want to know?
2. How will I gather that information?

By answering these questions, you develop a research strategy. Your research strategy, in turn, begins to lay the foundation for a successful public relations program. Let's take a closer look at how we might answer the first question.

What we need to know in public relations research falls into one of four categories: client research, stakeholder research, problem–opportunity research, and evaluation research. Quite often research findings can fit into more than one category. However, the information itself is far more important than how it is categorized.

Client Research

Client research focuses on the individual client, company, or other organization on whose behalf the practitioner is working. Efforts are geared toward discovering an organization's size; the nature of the products or services it offers; and its history, staffing requirements, markets and customers, budget, legal environment, reputation, and beliefs about the issue in question. It is also essential to understand a client organization's mission and consequent goals. As noted in Chapter 1, an organization's mission statement is based on the organization's core values. Goals are general statements indicating the direction the organization wants to take and are consistent with an organization's values and mission statement.

Stakeholder Research

Stakeholder research focuses on identifying the specific publics important to the success of the client. These various constituencies are known as stakeholders, for each has a different stake in how the organization responds to various issues. The people important to your organization are not a homogeneous mass. They are a wide range of constituencies, each having its own values, attitudes, concerns, needs, and predispositions. How these stakeholders relate to an organization can change from issue to issue. For example, a teachers' union may oppose proposed tax increases for new roads but favor higher taxes for educational programs. Also, people are often members of more than one stakeholder group. Building on the prior example, a member of the teachers' union may favor new road taxes if the funds are earmarked for the area in which that member lives. Stakeholder research helps you better target the message and the media for that message to the needs of each constituency.

VALUES STATEMENT 7.1

Institute for Public Relations

The Institute for Public Relations (IPR) was founded in 1956 as the Foundation for Public Relations Research and Education. Located at the University of Florida, IPR is dedicated to improving the professional practice of public relations around the world and encouraging academic and professional excellence in the field of public relations.

THE INSTITUTE FOR PUBLIC RELATIONS: OUR PURPOSE

No real profession attains that status without a substantial body of codified professional knowledge, as well as educational systems to help create and disseminate that knowledge. This is as true of public relations as it is of medicine, law, accounting or teaching. There is science underlying the art, and it is the working knowledge of that science combined with creativity that marks the best professionals.

The Institute for Public Relations is focused on the science beneath the art of public relations. We exist to expand and document the intellectual foundations of public relations, and to make this knowledge available and useful to all practitioners, educators, researchers and client organizations.

—IPR web site

Problem–Opportunity Research

Put in the simplest terms, **problem–opportunity research** is research designed to answer two critical questions: What is at issue, and what stake, if any, does our organization have in this issue? Problem–opportunity research develops background information on a particular topic or issue. It also identifies related trends that may have developed. Ultimately, problem–opportunity research answers a key question: Why is it necessary—or unnecessary—for our organization to act? Sometimes organizations are reactive, responding to events that could shape their destiny. Other times they are proactive, launching those destiny-shaping events. There are even times when doing nothing is the best course of action. Problem–opportunity research helps the organization decide whether and how to act.

Evaluation Research

Although evaluation is listed last among the four steps in the traditional public relations process, today's climate demands attention to **evaluation research**—procedures for determining the success of a public relations

Measuring Relationships

We bet that you have heard at least one of your professors say something like this: "Your grade is not based on the amount of work you do. It is based on the quality of the work you submit." That's another way of saying that you will be judged by results.

Judging results is a very real-world approach to evaluating success. And it focuses on the most important—and difficult—aspect of evaluation: deciding what constitutes an appropriate measure of success.

For example, how does one measure the success of a news release? Sometimes we measure **outputs,** such as the number of news releases we send to the media. Other times, we measure **outcomes.** Although this could mean the amount of media coverage our news release generates, it is important to remember that we are using the news media as an intervening public. For that reason, a more meaningful measure would be the response of the primary public, the people we are trying to reach through the media. In this case, we may want to measure the number of people who called a toll-free number mentioned in the news release.

Both approaches have their limitations. At best, they measure our public relations activities and the consequent short-term changes in the public relations environment. They also tend to focus only on the target audience's response to a specific program or event. Missing is an understanding of the long-term effects a public relations program has on relationships with key publics.

To address this broader issue, the Institute for Public Relations, based at the University of Florida, established a panel of educators and professionals to search for more meaningful ways to measure the effectiveness of public relations. One of its reports, released in 1999, recommends a process through which practitioners measure the quality of important relationships.

Linda Childers Hon of the University of Florida and James E. Grunig of the University of Maryland wrote that the evaluation of long-term relationships rests on examining six key **components of relationships:**[18]

1. **Control mutuality:** the degree to which parties agree on who has the power to influence the actions of the other. In an ideal relationship, the parties share a degree of control.

2. **Trust:** the willingness of one party to open itself to the other. This depends on perceptions of each party's integrity, dependability, and competence.

3. **Satisfaction:** the degree to which the benefits of the relationship outweigh its costs.

4. **Commitment:** the extent to which each party feels the relationship is worth the time, cost, and effort.

5. **Exchange relationship:** the giving of benefits to one party in return for past benefits received or for the expectation of future benefits.

6. **Communal relationship:** the provision of benefits to each other out of concern and without expectation of anything in return.

Hon and Grunig believe that by administering a questionnaire that includes agree–disagree statements focusing on these six aspects of a relationship, practitioners will have a more meaningful measure of the effectiveness of public relations programs. Grunig has published a follow-up paper in which he said qualitative methods, such as in-depth interviews or focus groups, can sometimes provide more insight into the dynamics of a relationship.[19] In short, it is the difference between generating numbers or intimate detail.

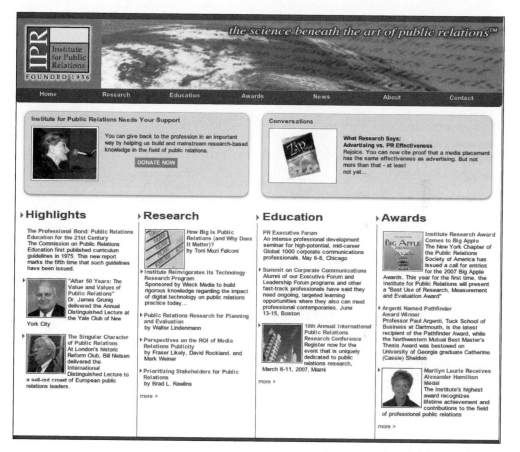

Through its web site (www.instituteforpr.org), the Institute for Public Relations provides both scholars and practitioners with the latest research into a wide range of topics important to the profession. (Used with permission, Institute for Public Relations)

plan—from the very beginning. With practitioners facing greater demands for accountability, every public relations plan must achieve an impact that is measurable.

Just how important is evaluation? According to a 2006 survey of 1,493 public relations practitioners, 39 percent said that "universalizing our ability to demonstrate a clear Return-on-PR-investment, thereby proving the value of public relations" was the greatest challenge facing the profession. That was second only to the 41 percent who said that upholding the credibility of the profession was its greatest challenge.[20] However, these results also show that identifying evaluation standards on which everyone can agree is one of the profession's biggest barriers. As noted in QuickBreak 7.1, the attempt to quantify public relations outcomes through ROI or AVE calculations is controversial.

"Arguments are often made by public relations professionals that articles, with the implied third-party credibility of the publication in which they appear, have a value two or three times that of advertising," write researchers Mark Weiner and Don Bartholomew. "The fact is there is no known objective research to support this claim."[21]

"If we truly want metrics that show public relations has value to an organization, the measures required are deceptively simple," said James E. Grunig, professor emeritus at the University of Maryland. "We should measure the nature and quality of relationships to establish and monitor the value of public relations."[22]

To accomplish this, Grunig, along with fellow researcher Linda Childers Hon of the University of Florida, developed guidelines for measuring relationships (see QuickBreak 7.3). As noted earlier, many within the public relations industry have embraced their approach. However, the Hon-Grunig Relationship Index also has its detractors, mainly among those who believe that the bottom line of a financial statement is the only true measure of value.

Nobody said public relations evaluation is easy. However, evaluation clearly cannot be an afterthought. Practitioners are expected to articulate at the outset of any campaign how success will be defined. A clear understanding of the environment before and after the campaign must be achieved.

1. What are the six key components of relationships?
2. When developing a research strategy, what two questions should you ask yourself?
3. What are the four major categories of public relations research?

Developing a Research Strategy: How Will I Gather Information?

First we asked the initial question, "What do I want to know?" Having done that, our next major strategy decision has to do with the methods we will use to gather information. To a large degree, the answer to the question "How will I gather that information?" depends on the time and resources at our disposal. Those factors, in turn, determine whether the research we are planning to conduct will present a reasonably accurate picture of reality or just a snapshot of some smaller aspect of it.

Using the vocabulary of researchers, this is the essential difference between **formal research** and **informal research.** Formal (also known as quantitative or scientific) research presents an accurate picture. That is because it uses scientific methods designed to create a representative picture of reality. In public relations, formal research generally is used to create an accurate portrayal of a stakeholder group. On the other hand, informal (also known as nonquantitative or nonscientific) research describes some aspect of reality but doesn't necessarily develop an accurate picture of the larger reality as a whole. In public relations, informal research is very useful—but it should not lead us to conclusions about an entire stakeholder group.

Now, back to the question at hand: How will I gather the information I need? Public relations practitioners commonly employ five research methods, some of which are already familiar to you: secondary (library) research, feedback research, communication audits, focus groups, and survey research.

Secondary (Library) Research

Secondary research is probably a research method you know well. It utilizes materials generated by others—sometimes for purposes entirely different from your own. The alternative to secondary research is **primary research,** which is new research you generate from scratch. Sources used in secondary research include

■ *Published materials,* such as newspaper and magazine articles, library references, various directories, and trade association data. This also includes information available through online databases and services such as LexisNexis, Factiva, and various sites on the web.

■ *Organizational records,* such as annual reports, statistics, financial reports, and other disclosures that organizations with publicly held stock are required by law to release. For example, check out the disclosure documents that have been filed with the Securities and Exchange Commission and are available online through the EDGAR search engine, at www.sec.gov.

■ *Public records generated by governments:* With few exceptions, government agencies in the United States are required to operate in the open. These agencies often generate a wealth of useful information, such as the U.S. Census and monthly reports on the nation's economy. Much of this information is available through federal and state depository libraries located in communities and on college campuses around the country. Now that the Internet has gone from being a private tool of researchers to an everyday information source for all, an increasing amount of this information is also available online. For example, check out the FedStats database at www.fedstats.gov.

Secondary research is especially valuable in providing information you might never have the means to gather on your own.

Feedback Research

Feedback research enables an organization to receive tangible evidence—often unsolicited—of stakeholder groups' responses to its actions. This evidence can manifest itself in many forms, most commonly through letters and telephone calls to the organization. For example, every time the president of the United States speaks on television, White House operators keep a running tally of the number of calls expressing support for or disapproval of what was said. Proactive organizations monitor all media, including the Internet, to track what others say about them. Web monitoring products include eWatch, NetCurrents Information Services, CyberAlert, and Canadian-based Bowden's Media Monitoring. Organizations also encourage feedback through a variety of tactics, including point-of-sale surveys and e-mail links on their web sites. Although feedback research is not a formal research method, it can give very strong indications of the public relations environment.

The Communication Audit

Communication audits are research procedures used to determine whether an organization's communications are consistent with its values-driven mission and goals. In completing a communication audit, we review an organization's communications and records, and we conduct interviews with key officials.

A communication audit could have saved Wal-Mart executives from having to explain to the Federal Election Commission why it distributed a company publication to 200,000 North Carolina residents featuring U.S. Senate candidate Elizabeth Dole on the cover just two weeks before the state Republican primary. In an article titled "Elizabeth Dole would like you to read this article," the former American Red Cross president was promoting literacy. Dole wasn't even Wal-Mart's first choice for its annual literacy issue: Oprah Winfrey had declined.[23]

A communication audit should answer five questions:

1. What are the organization's stated goals in relation to its stakeholder groups?
2. What communication activities has the organization used to fulfill those goals?
3. Which communication activities are working well and are consistent with those goals?
4. Which communication activities are not working well toward the achievement of those goals?
5. Given the findings of this audit, what revisions in goals or communication activities are recommended?

The Communications Grid. One illustrative method of conducting a communication audit is a **communications grid.** The various media used by an organization are listed on one axis. Stakeholders important to the organization are listed on the other. An X is placed everywhere a particular stakeholder is reached by a particular medium. This exercise graphically illustrates where efforts have been directed and which stakeholders may have been overlooked.

Figure 7.1 shows a simplified version of a communications grid using the scenario that opened this chapter. Each mark on the grid represents communication between the county and a key stakeholding public. We know from the scenario that county officials need to convince local residents that recycling sewer water for use as drinking water is safe. We also know that the community is diverse and bilingual. For the purposes of this example, we assume that there are only seven stakeholder groups and six channels of communication. In real life, there would be many more of both.

The grid illustrates that all seven publics represented here have access to the county's web site. But this is a passive form of communication—the only people who see it are those who seek it out. (In reality, some residents may not have Internet access.)

	Media Used by County Government					
	Engineering report detailing the sewer water proposal	Media kits	English-language print/TV advertising	Spanish-language print/TV advertising	e-mail	County government bilingual web site
County employees			X		X	X
Local and county officials	X		X		X	X
English-language media		X				X
Spanish-language media						X
English-speaking residents			X			X
Spanish-speaking residents						X
Health care professionals			X			X

County Government's Stakeholders (vertical label at left)

FIGURE 7.1 County Government's Communication Channels

By using only English-language media for publicity and advertising, county officials have ignored the Spanish-speaking community. And while most people may not care to read the county's engineering report, it is likely that health care professionals—an important group of potential opinion leaders—would be *particularly* interested in it, yet didn't receive it. The grid also shows that e-mail is the only direct communication county government has with its employees, another potentially influential group of opinion leaders.

In short, a communications grid is a good way to audit visually whether an organization is reaching all the publics important to its success. However, there is one significant drawback: A grid does not address the messages contained in the various media. Those can be determined only through an analysis of their content.

Focus Groups

Focus groups are an informal research method in which interviewers meet with groups of selected individuals to ascertain their opinions. Although focus group results should not be seen as representative of any particular public, they can indicate a public's knowledge, opinions, predispositions, and behavior.

Focus groups are a popular research method because, compared with survey research (that is, formal questionnaires), they are relatively inexpensive. They also have the advantage of giving the researcher immediate feedback. Focus groups are often used in advance of survey research. The interaction among focus group participants often raises issues that merit further study. Focus groups can even test the clarity and fairness of survey questions.

Focus group research was a key element in a recent award-winning public relations campaign developed by Hill & Knowlton for the Florida Hospital Association. The hospitals wanted state lawmakers to limit the amount of monetary awards in

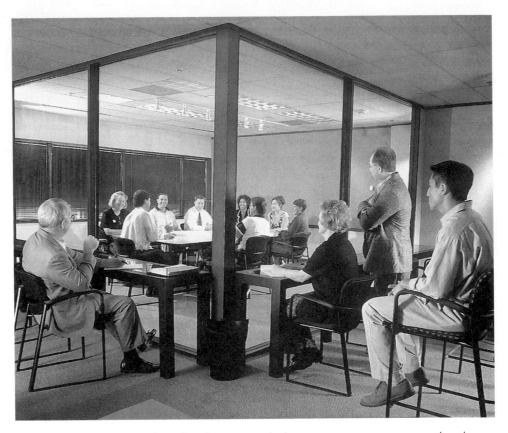

Focus groups are small, informal gatherings in which participants are encouraged to discuss their concerns, attitudes, and predispositions about the subject at hand. (Courtesy of Consumer Research Associates/Dallas, San Francisco)

medical liability lawsuits. Insurance premiums for hospitals had doubled—and for doctors had quadrupled—in just two years. Researchers conducted focus groups among registered voters—people who could influence legislators. They found voters confused by the complexities of tort reform but willing to listen to targeted messages that explained the issue in meaningful terms. By the end of the campaign, newspaper polls showed that 74 percent of Floridians supported some limits. Over well-funded opposition from trial lawyers, the legislature voted to cap noneconomic damages for physicians and hospitals.[24]

How to Conduct a Focus Group.   When preparing to conduct focus group research, we suggest you follow this 10-step process:

   1. *Develop a list of general questions based on information needs.* The questions usually should be open ended, avoiding simple yes–no answers.

2. *Select as a moderator someone skilled in interviewing techniques.* The moderator must be strong enough to keep the discussion on track.

3. *Recruit 8 to 12 participants.* Because of the problem of no-shows (people who promise to participate in the focus group but fail to show up), it is necessary to invite a larger number than you need. You can dismiss any extras with a small reward. As to who should be invited to attend, decide on a selection strategy. From what kind of people do you want to hear opinions? Sometimes a screening questionnaire will narrow the field. Participants are often compensated (with money, a free meal, etc.) for their time. An important rule: Avoid inviting people who have sharply divergent points of view. You are interested in gathering information; you are not interested in conducting a debate. Too much clash can stifle participants who may speak up in a friendlier environment. Even if it means conducting additional focus groups, it is best to keep people with sharply different opinions separated.

4. *Record the session.* Make certain participants know that the session is being recorded. It may be necessary to reassure them that it is being done to provide a record of what was said and will not be used for any other purposes.

5. *Observe the session.* In addition to the moderator, others should watch the focus group. They should record their impressions in notes. They do not participate in the session. Some facilities allow these observers to watch the proceedings from behind two-way mirrors. In many cases, however, observers sit quietly along the wall of the room in which the session is being held.

6. *Limit the discussion to 60–90 minutes.* When the conversation starts repeating itself, that is a sign to wrap it up.

7. *Discuss opinions, problems, and needs—not solutions.* It is very likely that participants are not qualified to discuss solutions.

8. *Transcribe the session.* This makes it much easier to analyze participants' comments.

9. *Prepare a written report on the session.* Identify participants by name, age, occupation, hometown, and any other pertinent information. Where possible, use direct quotations.

10. *Remember that focus groups are informal research.* Opinions stated in a focus group do not necessarily represent everyone else's view. At best, they serve as indicators of public opinion. However, they can be considered even stronger indicators if multiple focus groups yield the same comments.

Although these are the recommended steps for conducting focus group research, we also realize that sometimes it is necessary to bend the rules. For example, time and distance may make it difficult to get everyone together in the same room at the same time. Under those circumstances, the use of teleconferencing technology may provide a viable alternative. How one gathers information isn't really the issue. What matters is whether the information gathered is useful and reliable.

QUICK ✓ CHECK

1. What is secondary research?
2. What is the purpose of a communication audit?
3. What are some of the reasons a researcher may choose to conduct a focus group rather than a survey?

Survey Research

When you are unable to gather the information you need through secondary research or informal research methods, conducting a formal survey may be your best choice. Although **survey research** can be both expensive and time consuming, it can also be a highly accurate way to gauge public opinion. Through the use of specifically worded questionnaires and a carefully selected list of people, researchers are able to make judgments about a much larger population. In essence, surveys provide a snapshot of what people are thinking on a particular subject at a moment in time.

With the practice of public relations becoming more results driven and cost conscious than ever before, surveys are a very useful tool in targeting communications and measuring results. Through computer analysis, survey research makes it easier to select the right target, use the appropriate message, communicate through the most effective channels, and measure the results.

Of course, some surveys are better than others. When the local newspaper asks its readers to vote on a "question of the day," is that a valid survey? When the local television station conducts "person-on-the-street" interviews, do those interviews necessarily reflect the opinions of the larger community? The answer to both questions is no. But if you change the question and ask whether any useful information can be gleaned from those two approaches, the answer is yes.

The degree to which survey results can be seen as an accurate reflection of a larger population depends on two key factors: the composition of the people we are surveying and the structure of the survey instrument.

The Survey Sample

A sample is a portion of a public that we select for the purpose of making observations and drawing conclusions about the public as a whole. In other words, when we question members of a large stakeholder group, we generally don't question every member. Instead, we question a portion, or sample, of that public. A sample is said to be a **representative sample** of a targeted population when it is of sufficient size and when every member of the targeted population has an equal chance of being selected for the sample. Although surveying a representative sample provides a more accurate picture, it is not always practical because of time, cost, and personnel considerations.

QuickBreak 7.4

Worth Every Penny

Although some may question the cost of research in preparing public relations campaigns, they need only look at recent case histories to discover that research is often worth every penny.

One example comes from Down Under, where an extortionist threatened to poison candy bars. Master-Foods Australia New Zealand, which distributes the products in New South Wales, did not waste any time getting a finger on the pulse of consumers. During the seven weeks between the time the candy bars were recalled and later returned to store shelves, MasterFoods and its public relations agency conducted six surveys and 20 focus groups. The research helped them gauge whether the company's key message—that it had acted properly to protect the public—resonated with consumers. When the crisis passed, research showed that 98 percent of consumers thought that MasterFoods acted responsibly. Candy bar sales were 250 percent above average in the week the products went back on sale.[25]

About 17 percent of U.S. children under the age of 18 have a developmental disability. In half of those cases, the problem is not diagnosed until the children enter school. The Centers for Disease Control and Prevention wanted to know why. Working with the Porter Novelli Convergence Group, the CDC surveyed parents and pediatricians nationwide. What they learned was that there was a communications disconnect: The parents didn't know the warning signs, and the pediatricians didn't have the resources necessary for educating parents. The research became the impetus for a campaign called "Learn the Signs. Act Early." As a result, the number of early screenings conducted by pediatricians increased, as did the number of parent inquiries to the CDC.[26]

Sometimes, research is more than just research. It can also be the strategy. That was the case when the Minnesota Chapter of PRSA teamed with local magazine *Twin Cities Business* to conduct a survey and a series of focus groups. The purpose of the research was to engage the business community in a discussion of ethics and reputation management. It resulted in a cover story, "What Business Thinks: Minnesota's Most-Admired Companies—And How They Stay That Way." The survey and focus groups accomplished both of the chapter's goals, to raise the profile of PRSA and to launch a dialogue about reputation and reputation management in the business community.[27]

These are just three examples of why planners should think twice before skimping on the research budget.

For example, which would give you a better picture of U.S. public opinion regarding gun control: an informal poll of your classmates or a formal nationwide survey? Clearly, the latter would provide the more accurate picture. However, the informal poll would at least have advantages in terms of time, money, and effort. And informal results aren't necessarily worthless. To the contrary, they provide an indication of what public attitudes may be—within the limitations of the sample. In this case, those limitations are the size of your sample and the fact that not everyone in the nation has an equal opportunity of being chosen for questioning. You would not be able to say that your classroom poll was an accurate reflection of national opinion. However, if everyone in your class had the same opportunity to express his or her opinion, those results would be representative of the class' views on gun control.

How big should the sample be? No one answer is correct. Nor does a simple explanation exist. At issue here are what statisticians call **confidence levels,** the statistical degree to which we can reasonably assume the outcome is an accurate reflection of the entire population. As a general rule, the larger the sample, the more accurate the outcome is. However, we do come to a point where additional numbers do not significantly improve accuracy. Statistical accuracy within two or three percentage points is usually the best one can hope for.

Developing a Sampling Strategy. Developing a sampling strategy is a step critical to the administration of an accurate survey. Sampling can be as much an act of creativity as writing the survey instrument itself. However, as mentioned earlier, it is not always possible or practical to administer a formal survey. Issues such as cost, time, and staffing often come into play. Before we discuss some of the more common sampling strategies, a few definitions are in order:

■ **Sample:** the segment of a population or public a researcher studies to draw conclusions about the public as a whole.

The U.S. Constitution requires the government to conduct a head count of everyone living in the country at the start of each new decade. The census, named after the sampling technique used in the survey, helps to determine congressional districts and levels of federal funding. Residents are asked to complete a questionnaire that provides a wealth of information about who they are and how they live. Critics claim that many residents, particularly the homeless and undocumented foreign workers, are left uncounted. (U.S. Census Bureau)

- **Sampling frame:** the actual list from which the sample, or some stage of the sample, is drawn. The sampling frame is important because the accuracy of your list will affect the accuracy of the survey. For example, using the local telephone book as a sampling frame may underrepresent the attitudes of either the very rich or the very poor. Survey results should always be reported in the context of the limitations of their sampling frame.

- **Units of analysis:** what or whom you are studying to create a summary description of all such units. It is important to be clear about units of analysis because you don't want to make a common error in analyzing results—comparing apples to oranges. The results of a survey of attitudes of students in your classroom should not be used to describe the attitudes of all students because the units of analysis in your sample were students in your classroom, not all students. The views of students in your classroom may not be representative of those of all students.

- **Probability sampling:** the process of selecting a sample that is representative of the population or public being studied. The sample is considered to be representative when it is large enough and when all members of that population or public have an equal chance of being selected for the sample. Usually within a few percentage points, known as the sampling error, the results of a survey of a representative sample are considered an accurate reflection of the sampling frame.

- **Nonprobability sampling:** the process of selecting a sizable sample without regard to whether everyone in the public has an equal chance of being selected. This sampling technique is often chosen because of time, cost, or personnel considerations. This does not mean that the results are without value. To the contrary, nonprobability sampling results can give researchers an indication of public opinion. However, those results cannot be said to be an accurate reflection of the attitudes of any particular public.

It is important for you to understand these concepts because they are central to your selection of a sampling strategy. The challenge of survey research is to use a sampling technique that serves two masters: a desire for accuracy and a need to achieve it in a logistically realistic and cost-effective manner. Using some techniques, it is possible to be both accurate *and* cost effective.

Nonprobability Sampling. In the real world of public relations, practitioners are often challenged to conduct survey research with little time, money, or staffing at their disposal. This often leads to using a form of nonprobability sampling known as **convenience sampling**—the administration of an informal survey based on the availability of subjects. As the name suggests, this approach has the advantage of being easy to do. However, it also sacrifices accuracy.

The so-called person-on-the-street interviews seen in newspapers and on television are examples of convenience sampling. Reporters often ask a "question of the day" to passersby in an attempt to gauge the mood of their community on a particular topic. But instead of getting an accurate picture of community attitudes, these reporters are only measuring the opinions of the people who happen to be walking by that spot at that time. A reporter standing on an inner-city sidewalk may get answers to questions about the state of the economy that differ greatly from answers obtained in a suburban shopping mall. Even the time of day can make a difference.

Does this mean that data obtained from an informal survey are useless? No, it doesn't. Data obtained from such a survey can provide an *indication* of public opinion. The more indicators you have pointing in the same direction, the greater the chance that your data are accurate.

Probability Sampling. When planning to conduct formal probability sampling, you have a choice of several techniques. All of them have one important element in common: *Every person within the sampling frame has an equal chance of being selected for the sample.* In other words, surveys based on these sampling techniques have a high probability of being an accurate reflection of public opinion. These are some of the most common probability sampling strategies used by public relations practitioners:

■ **Simple random sampling** (Figure 7.2) is the most basic form of probability sampling. But often it is not practical. Simple random sampling involves assigning a number to every person within the sampling frame. By making a random selection of numbers, as in drawing numbers out of a hat, you develop a representative sample. However, think how tedious it would be to assign a number to every name in the local telephone book. Because simple random sampling can be a cumbersome process, especially with large sampling frames, this technique is seldom used in practice.

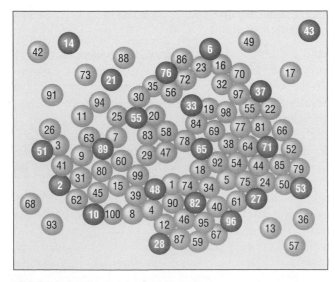

FIGURE 7.2 Simple Random Sampling
In this example, every individual is assigned a number—in this case, a number from 1 to 100. To achieve a sample of 20 individuals, 20 numbers are selected at random.

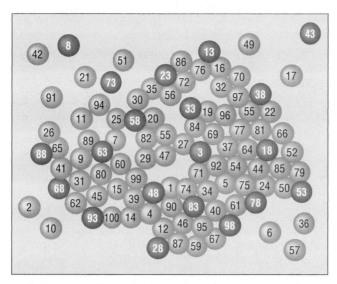

FIGURE 7.3 Systematic Sampling

In this example, we want to achieve a sample size of 20. There are 100 individuals in the sampling frame. The value of K is 100/20, or 5. Therefore, we pick every fifth individual for our sample.

■ **Systematic sampling** (Figure 7.3) is a more practical approach to probability sampling. Through a standardized selection process, it is possible to create a sample that is both representative and easy to develop. At its most basic level, systematic sampling involves the selection of every Kth member of a sampling frame. For example, let us assume that your college or university has 25,000 students. The sampling frame for your survey is a computer printout of enrolled students. If you are seeking a sample of 250 names from a sampling frame of 25,000, then K = 25,000/250, or 100. In this scenario, you would select every 100th name from the enrollment printout for the sample. Compare this with the work involved in simple random sampling, and it is easy to see why many researchers choose to go this route.

■ It is often hard to identify a perfect sampling frame. Although a city telephone directory gives you the names of most city residents, it excludes those who do not have a telephone, who tend to be poor, and those with unlisted numbers, who tend to have higher incomes. In this case, the extremely rich and extremely poor may be underrepresented. One way to overcome a flaw in a sampling frame is by using what is known as **cluster sampling** (Figure 7.4). This technique involves breaking the population into homogeneous clusters and then selecting the sample from individual clusters. For example, pretend that your sampling frame is students enrolled in public relations courses. If your school is typical of the national trend, there is a strong probability that women will easily outnumber men. To achieve a sample that is half men and half women, you group the students' names into different gender pools and

FIGURE 7.4 Cluster Sampling

In an attempt to correct an imbalance in the sampling frame, individuals with similar characteristics are clustered. In this example, systematic sampling is used within each cluster to develop a sample containing 10 from each group.

select an equal number of names from each pool. Cluster sampling is generally not as accurate as simple random sampling or systematic sampling. Under certain conditions, however, it can be the most practical.

■ One way to ensure that a sample is an accurate reflection of a specific population is to survey *everyone*. That is what is known as taking a **census** (Figure 7.5)— that is, surveying every member of the sampling frame. A well-known census is the decennial U.S. Census, in which an attempt is made to count and analyze every person living in the United States. Although a properly done census has the advantage of accuracy, this technique comes up short when it comes to practicality. It may be easy to administer a questionnaire to everyone in your class, but how easy would it be for you to survey everyone in your college or university?

1. What two elements are critical to the administration of an accurate survey?
2. How does a sample differ from a sampling frame?
3. What is the major difference between probability and nonprobability sampling?

FIGURE 7.5 Census

In a census, everyone in the sampling frame is selected.

The Survey Instrument

Creating a good survey instrument is just as important as having a good survey sample. Even if you identify a sample that is representative of the population you want to study, a faulty questionnaire can render your results meaningless. It is not just *whom* you ask, but also *how* you ask the questions that matters.

There are many considerations you need to keep in mind when developing survey questions. The questionnaire should use language that is appropriate for and readily understood by the public for whom the survey is intended. Researchers wouldn't ask elementary school students, homeowners, and nuclear scientists the same questions about nuclear power. Each group has a different level of understanding of the issue; therefore, the questions need to be tailored to the knowledge level of each group. In certain situations it may be necessary to provide background information before asking a question.

Questions asked on surveys cannot be vague if they are to have any real meaning. Questions have to be explicit, not indirect. Ask exactly what you want to know. If respondents are guessing at what a question means, their answers cannot serve as an accurate measure of anything (except, of course, of someone's inability to write clear questions).

Use words that have clear and specific meanings. For example, let's consider a question about presidential job performance. Suppose respondents are given the choice of answering the question using these options: gnarly, groovy, super, cool, and awesome. Can these survey results have any real meaning? The problem is that what may be gnarly to one person could be groovy to another. For the survey results to have real meaning, the words used in the survey must have precise definitions. A

QuickBreak 7.5

Five Ways to Ask Questions

1. **Contingency questions:** Whether a respondent is expected to answer a specific question is often contingent on the answer to an earlier question. For example, if a respondent indicates that he or she doesn't like ice cream, it would make no sense to ask that person in the next question to identify his or her favorite flavor of ice cream. Therefore, the second question is a contingency question. Respondents who answer yes about liking ice cream will answer the next question. Those who answer no will be instructed to skip it.

2. **Dichotomous questions:** These are either/or questions such as true–false, yes–no, and positive–negative. They are sometimes used to set up contingency questions. In the previously cited example, a no answer would make it unnecessary for the respondent to answer the next question about favorite flavor. The respondent would be instructed to skip that question.

3. **Rating scale questions:** These questions measure the range, degree, or intensity of attitudes, something a dichotomous question cannot do. An example of a rating scale question is one that news and polling organizations often ask about the president's job performance. Respondents are asked to respond to the statement "I think

the president is doing a good job." Their options are to strongly agree with the statement, agree, disagree, strongly disagree, or express no opinion. These kinds of questions can give researchers a more detailed read on public opinion than dichotomous questions can provide.

4. **Open-ended questions:** These questions don't define a range of possible answers (called a response set). In other words, the respondent is left to fill in the blank. Answers to these questions can provide detailed information. However, they are the most difficult to analyze because they can't be tabulated as quickly as answers to questions in which the response set is specifically defined.

5. **Closed-ended questions:** These are questions in which the response set is specifically defined. To put it another way, respondents are required to select their answer from a predetermined menu of options. The risk with these questions is that researchers may leave out certain options or may overemphasize other options. Another problem to watch for is answers that overlap slightly. However, these questions are significantly easier to analyze than open-ended questions.

good survey instrument also keeps the questionnaire reasonably short. The longer the survey, the more likely that people will decline to participate because they "don't have the time."

Avoid bias in the wording or ordering of questions. The manner in which a question is worded can influence the response. Even the placement of the question can influence responses to questions that follow. For example, suppose you are answering a survey that poses a series of questions about high taxes, then asks, "What is the most important issue facing government today?" Because of the earlier questions, you may be primed to answer, "High taxes, of course!"

Don't ask objectionable questions. Even the most sensitive information can be obtained if questions are worded tactfully. Also, save the toughest questions for last.

Asking the toughest questions first could abruptly end the process or bias subsequent responses. Demographic questions regarding matters such as age, income, and political affiliation can also be sensitive. Often, researchers place demographic questions at the end of the questionnaire in the belief that members of the sample won't skip them because they've already invested time in filling out the rest of the survey.

A way to avoid problems is to pretest the questionnaire. If the survey instrument has any bugs, it is best to find them before distributing surveys on a large scale. Run a small test first to make sure that the questions are understandable, all biases corrected, and objectionable questions removed.

When it comes time to administer the survey, logistics must be considered as well. Can the personnel requirements be met? Can the survey be administered within the desired time frame? Does the survey plan fit into the budget? The people who administer the survey, the data collectors, must be trained. Will they use the telephone, or meet with members of the sample face to face? Or, as is common, will you simply mail out the survey and dispense with data collectors?

Analyzing Survey Results

Once all the data are collected, the time has come to analyze and report the results. This is a public relations text, not a statistics text, so any attempt at this point to offer a detailed explanation of statistical analysis would not do the subject justice. However, we do not want to ignore the subject entirely. Raw data without structure or purpose are meaningless. Analysis gives data context so that their meaning can be understood.

The truth is that the overwhelming majority of public relations practitioners never conduct survey research. Instead, they pay someone else to do it for them. That's OK. But how do you know whether the research you are buying is good? That's why this discussion of sampling and questionnaire development is important. If you plan to make a career in public relations, you need to be a good consumer of this and all kinds of research.

For the purposes of this discussion, let's start with two basic definitions:

1. **Attributes:** characteristics or qualities that describe an object. In the case of an individual, attributes can be gender, age, weight, height, political affiliation, church affiliation, and so on.
2. **Variables:** a logical grouping of qualities that describe a particular attribute. Variables must be exhaustive (incorporating all possible qualities) and mutually exclusive. For example, the variables associated with the attribute of gender are female and male.

The purpose of analysis is to get a clearer picture from the data. The deeper the analysis, the clearer the picture. The most basic form of analysis is **univariate analysis.** As the name suggests, it is the examination of only one variable. An example of a univariate analysis would be the examination of responses to the question Do you like ice cream? By counting the responses to that question, we would know the total number of people who said yes and the total number who said no. But that is all that we would know.

If we were to examine the same question using two variables, however, the results would become more meaningful. This is what is known as **bivariate analysis.** A bivariate analysis of the question Do you like ice cream? could look at two variables: whether respondents like ice cream and the respondents' gender. We might find that men answer the question differently from women. That, in turn, could affect a variety of marketing decisions.

If we turn to **multivariate analysis,** the examination of three or more variables, our survey results would have even greater depth. Carrying our example to its logical conclusion, let's add the variable of age to our analysis of the ice cream question. Such an analysis could find that younger men and older women like ice cream more than their counterparts in other age groups. If our goal is to promote the sale of ice cream, these results suggest that we need to work harder to attract younger women and older men to the frozen delight. That information is far more valuable to us than only knowing the raw numbers.

The Rest of the Story

If you thought that you would hate to be the county public information officer in the opening scenario of our chapter, think again. The scenario is based on a true story, an award-winning groundwater replenishment system community relations program in Southern California. The Orange County water and sanitation districts, working with Porter Novelli, convinced the residents of a culturally diverse community that a blend of purified sewer water with traditional water supplies was safe. Their communications program was based on solid research, including secondary research, focus group data from the region's different ethnic communities, and a series of surveys. During the four years of the public information campaign, county officials were able to maintain necessary public support for construction of the multimillion dollar treatment facility. The campaign came in approximately 10 percent below its $3.6 million budget. When you think about it, that's not much to pay for providing safe drinking water for the county's nearly 3 million residents.[28]

When confronted with a difficult challenge, the practitioners in Southern California did what any public relations professional should do—they started by developing a research strategy. They asked these two all-important questions:

1. What do I want to know?
2. How will I gather that information?

After developing a research strategy, they conducted client research, stakeholder research, problem–opportunity research, and evaluation research. They used both formal and informal research methods. Eventually, they developed a successful community relations plan—one that served the best interests of both the client and people of Orange County.

That is the essence of good public relations. And it all starts with research.

QUICK CHECK

1. When writing a survey questionnaire, what should you consider in wording questions?
2. What are some of the logistical considerations you should take into account before administering a survey?
3. What are the differences among a univariate analysis, a bivariate analysis, and a multivariate analysis? Why would you want to do any of them?

Summary

There is a huge debate raging in the public relations world: What is the best way to measure effectiveness? While some support controversial methods of linking public relations effects to the cost of advertising, others focus on a less-tangible approach of measuring relationships. Whichever path practitioners follow, one fact is indisputable: Research is critical to the practice of public relations. Research enables a practitioner to understand a client, the problems/opportunities facing the client, and the stakeholders important to the client's success. Evaluation research enables a practitioner to determine the success of communication strategies and the strength of relationships.

Not all research is created equal. Formal research has the advantage of providing a more accurate picture of reality. However, conducting informal research may be necessary because of time, cost, or staffing considerations. Although not as accurate a reflection of reality, informal research results still can help you piece together a picture of the world. Before embarking on research, it is important to have a clear understanding of what kinds of information you are seeking and what is the best way for you to gather it. That is known as developing your research strategy.

The five most common forms of public relations research are secondary (library) research, feedback research, communication audits, focus groups, and surveys. Secondary research is making use of material generated by someone else, sometimes for a purpose other than that for which it was originally intended. Feedback research involves analyzing both solicited and unsolicited communications an organization receives from its stakeholders. Communication audits indicate whether an organization's communications are consistent with its values-driven mission and goals. Focus groups are an informal research method in which a small group of people are brought together to discuss their values, concerns, needs, attitudes, and predispositions. The successful use of survey research depends on both a good sample and a good survey instrument or questionnaire. The value of survey research is that, when properly conducted and analyzed, it provides a reasonably accurate snapshot of reality. That, in turn, provides a solid foundation for a public relations plan.

DISCUSSION QUESTIONS

1. Why do some people believe efforts to base public relations measures on advertising costs are inappropriate? What do you think?

2. Which research should you ordinarily conduct first: primary research or secondary research? Why?
3. How is issues management a part of problem–opportunity research?
4. Why aren't focus groups necessarily representative of a larger public?
5. What is the difference between probability sampling and nonprobability sampling? What is the advantage of probability sampling? Is nonprobability sampling without value?
6. What are some examples of research leading to the success of a public relations campaign?

Memo from the Field

Dr. David B. Rockland, Partner and Global Director of Research, Ketchum, New York, New York

Dr. David B. Rockland is a partner at Ketchum and is that agency's global director of research. In that capacity, he oversees research and measurement in all Ketchum offices in the United States, Europe, and Asia. As of January 1, 2007, he became chairman of the Institute for Public Relations' Commission on PR Measurement and Evaluation.

The career that led me to running research at Ketchum was by no means a straight path. After getting a Ph.D. in economics, I quickly morphed primarily into lobbying in Washington on natural resource issues. I wrote for many top consumer magazines while with Times Mirror Magazines, headed global communications for the world's largest copper mining company, and then eventually sold my own firm, The Rockland Group LLC, to Roper Starch Worldwide in 1998, which is how I started doing research for public relations. At first, Ketchum was a client, and then its leaders asked me to join them to head up a research practice with a great history and an opportunity to build it into the thriving, profitable business it is today. What's neat about a career with many twists and turns is that you learn new things almost every day. Here are some things I've learned at Ketchum:

PR PROGRAMS THAT DON'T SET GOALS AND MEASURES WILL FAIL

Countless times I've had the leader of an account rush into my office asking us to measure their program long after it's done. Their client is demanding to know the results, and while they have a nice stack of clips, the client is using terms like ROI and audience outcomes. If the account leader can't show these kinds of numbers, they'll lose the account.

You have to begin any journey, including a PR plan, knowing where you are going and agreeing with your client on what success looks like. Writing good goals at the start saves lots of heartburn at the end. Answer these questions:

- What needle are you trying to move?
- Among whom?

- By when?
- How much is success?

The needle may be outputs (e.g., reach or impressions); outcomes (i.e., awareness, comprehension, attitude, and behavior) or business results such as sales. Clearly written goals lead you to the right measurement program. And, many times that measurement program already exists at the client such as a brand or advertising tracking system that you can measure your goals against.

PAY ATTENTION TO WHAT PEOPLE SAY

I used to think focus groups were for people who couldn't write good surveys. I was wrong. Focus groups and in-depth interviews often give you very clear signals on what will work and what won't. One time I did focus groups to test a new tagline for a chemical manufacturing company that the CEO loved. And it did sound pretty good. The focus group participants all thought the tagline made great sense, if you were promoting a dating service.

Another time we were testing a new web site about retirement benefits for public employees in Florida. The logo for the program was a road sign showing a fork in the road with one arrow going left and the other right. When we asked the focus group participants to find information on the web site, instead of moving their mouse to the menus on the home page they all moved their arrows to the road sign. Unfortunately the sign or logo was only there for decoration, so nothing happened. In 10 seconds, we knew that the web designers were going to have to change the home page fast.

Sometimes surveys give you insights you really didn't expect. Right before the 2004 presidential elections we did a quick national survey for a new American Kennel Club credit card with Chase Card Services. The key question was along the lines of which breed of dog do President Bush and Senator Kerry most remind you of? The survey resulted in tremendous press coverage for clients. The results (Bush a Rottweiler and Kerry a French poodle), showed Kerry didn't have a chance. Apparently, French poodles don't get elected president.

ADVERTISING CAN BE VERY IMPORTANT

Many in our field think that comparing PR to advertising is wrong. I disagree, assuming you do the math right. Here are things to account for:

- PR results are not always perfect. When you place advertising, you get to say what you want, where, and when. You have to discount the PR value to reflect how good the placement was.
- PR is not necessarily more credible or valuable then advertising. When I wrote for *Field and Stream,* readers were often more interested in the ads for new hunting and fishing equipment than the editorial. Don't mark up the PR value unless you can clearly document that such an increase is warranted.
- Use net ad rates, or the rate the client pays on the open market. Few pay the retail costs on the rate card, and hence those numbers are artificially high.

Many companies have a choice in whether to use their marketing dollars for PR or for advertising. Assuming the cost they would pay for advertising (AVE) has to be worth at least as much to their business, applying such a number to a PR placement with the modifications above can make good sense. Otherwise, what often happens is the person with the marketing budget decides to put all their dollars into advertising. If we can't talk the language of the marketing person, PR usually loses.

TRADITIONAL MEDIA ARE ALIVE AND KICKING

It's early 2007, and the PR world is buzzing about CGM—consumer generated media. Newspapers are dead. Blogs are here to stay. Wrong. We just fielded a national survey of America's media habits. A few things we learned:

- Americans turn to local TV and newspapers over almost anything else to form opinions and decide what to buy. This is also true of younger Americans (ages 18–24). And traditional sources are way more credible than CGM.
- Word of mouth (WOM) is critical. Most people make decisions from talking to friends and family. PR's role in understanding WOM and affecting it is the discipline's next frontier.
- Corporations talk to themselves too much. We feel that corporations place too much emphasis on communicating through their web sites and on their own schedules. A good communicator knows what the audience wants and the best time to reach them.

FINAL WORD

I have two daughters in college (East Carolina and Wisconsin). Both are majoring in communications and public relations. I am very proud of them, but I do hope that they approach this field as a serious discipline that can have a huge impact. Too many PR majors get there because they think "fashion and beauty PR would be so much fun." Three years into their careers, they are still stuffing press kits with perfume samples. With good research and measurement skills, the PR practitioner is taken more seriously, gets a seat at the management table, and has a career that is meaningful and profitable. Otherwise, the field and the people in it will always take a second seat to other types of communications and marketing.

CASE STUDY 7.1

Betting on Terror

"You know, I've been around this building 12 years," the reporter told Defense Department spokesman Lawrence Di Rita. "It seems so absurd that anything like this could ever see the light of day."

"But I just—there's really—I don't think I have much more to say on that," Di Rita responded.[29]

Based on that unusual exchange at a July 29, 2003, Pentagon briefing, you must be wondering what it was that had the reporter so befuddled and the spokesman so rattled? The subject of such confusion and amazement was a tactic in the War on Terrorism that, even today, sounds so outlandish that you may believe it was a hoax. But it wasn't. And some still believe it was a good idea.

What they were talking about was the Policy Analysis Market (PAM), an online trading market designed to help predict terrorist attacks. Speculators could go on the Internet and place wagers on a probability of a wide range of terrorist activities. These included an attack on Western tourists at the pyramids in Egypt, the assassination of Middle East political figures, or even a North Korean missile attack.

PAM was the brainchild of the Defense Advanced Research Projects Agency (DARPA), the Defense Department's Research Arm. According to one of its creators, Robin Hanson of George Mason University, it was based on the same market forces that drive agricultural and financial futures markets.

"Prediction markets are speculative markets created for the purpose of aggregating information on topics of interest," Hanson said on a statement on his web site. "Previous field studies had found that such markets out-predict co-existing institutions regarding the weather, printer sales, movie sales, elections and much more."[30]

Stanford University economics professors Justin Wolfers and Eric Zitzewitz wrote in the *Washington Post* that the concept of a "terrorist futures market" merited public support. "The reason markets work so well is that they reflect our collective wisdom. And your opinion will be reflected only to the extent that you are willing to put your money where your mouth is."[31]

"There is good reason to believe that a market set up to forecast the sort of political instability that leads to terrorism might well work," wrote Information and Management Systems Professor Hal R. Varian of the University of California–Berkeley. "At least, there is enough reason to warrant an experiment, given the high payoff to having better forecasts of these events."[32]

That experiment did not come. It was short-circuited when two U.S. senators highlighted the plan in a congressional budget debate over defense intelligence spending. Senator Ron Wyden, an Oregon Democrat, said, "spending taxpayer dollars to create terrorism betting parlors is as wasteful as it is repugnant. Clearly, this is morally wrong." Senator Byron Dorgan, North Dakota Democrat, called the scheme "incredibly stupid."[33]

Even members of the Bush administration appeared surprised by the plan. "I share your shock at this kind of program," said then-Deputy Defense Secretary Paul Wolfowitz. He told the Senate Foreign Relations Committee that he first learned of PAM by reading his morning newspaper.

"The agency is brilliantly imaginative in places where we want them to be imaginative," Wolfowitz said. "It sounds like maybe they got too imaginative."[34]

In the face of a flood of public criticism, the Pentagon moved quickly to kill the program. "No one from Congress asked us if the accusations were correct, or if the more offending aspects could be cut from the program," Hanson said. "The next morning the secretary of defense announced that [PAM] was cancelled."[35]

Retired Rear Admiral John M. Poindexter, who as head of DARPA's Terrorism Awareness Office had conceived the program, resigned under pressure. Many Washington observers had a sense of déjà vu: Poindexter had been forced to resign as President Reagan's national security adviser over his role in the Iran-Contra "weapons for hostages" scandal nearly two decades earlier.

"The war against terrorism is not likely to be won by hiring more economists," wrote *Washington Post* columnist Steven Pearlstein. "It is going to have to be won the old-fashioned way, improving the government's intelligence network one spy at a time."[36]

DISCUSSION QUESTIONS

1. What does this story have to do with public relations research and evaluation?
2. What values were in conflict in this controversy?
3. What could the Pentagon have done to make this program more publicly acceptable?
4. What do you feel about a terrorist futures market as a means of predicting future terrorist activities?

CASE STUDY 7.2

Big Bang PR

Unless you have been trained in nuclear physics, you might believe that *quark* refers to an alien bartender on the old television series *Star Trek: Deep Space Nine.* You could also be forgiven for thinking *gluon* is something you do when you break the handle on a coffee mug. However, if you have a lot more scientific knowledge than, say, the authors of this textbook, then you know that quarks and gluons are basic particles of atomic nuclei—the building blocks for everything in the universe.[37]

Quarks and gluons may be pretty small stuff, but they are big business at the Brookhaven National Laboratory on Long Island, New York. Operated by the U.S. Department of Energy, BNL has approximately 3,000 permanent employees and hosts more than 4,000 guest researchers each year.[38] From 1993 to 2003, BNL's total local and national spending of $4.76 billion created more than 7,700 secondary jobs in New York state.[39] Because of its huge economic impact, any challenge to BNL's federal funding is viewed as a significant threat.

BNL officials learned in early 2005 that they faced an $18 million cut in the budget for their Relativistic Heavy Ion Collider (RHIC)—basically a giant atom smasher. Ironically, at the same time that they learned that the program would have to be scaled back, researchers using the atom smasher made one of the most significant scientific discoveries in years. To place their findings in laymen's terms: The scientists discovered a new substance that they say resembled the state of the universe in the first 100 millionths of a second after the big bang that created the universe. To their surprise, the matter created in the RHIC—known as quark-gluon plasma—appeared to be more of a liquid than the gas they had expected.[40] In the world of science, this was big news.

It also presented BNL officials with an opportunity and a challenge. The announcement of an important scientific breakthrough would boost the program's image at the same time that their funds were on Washington's chopping block. However, the timing of the release could also be interpreted as a blatant attempt to influence congressional budget negotiations. Their concerns were well founded: Research showed that a 2000 media announcement by a European research laboratory had been widely criticized as being premature and exaggerated. In the current political environment, they could not afford to make the same mistake.

Working with M. Booth & Associates, a New York–based public relations agency, BNL officials devised a strategy for unveiling their remarkable discovery without any hint of ulterior political motives.[41] They started by researching the schedule of upcoming scientific conferences, looking for the right venue in which to make the big announcement. They chose an April meeting of the American Physical Society in Tampa—just five weeks away. They also knew that they would have to broaden the reach of the announcement beyond the Florida meeting. Through a search of national science and consumer media, they identified leading general-science reporters. After a round of telephone calls to gauge the reporters' intentions, they realized that many of the journalists they wanted to target were not planning to attend the conference.

In advance of the big day, an embargoed news release was placed on a password-protected section of BNL's web site. Also available on the site were copies of scientific papers, high-resolution photographs and animation, and links to experts. BNL also reached out to journalists affiliated with media outlets used by influential people who would appreciate the importance of the announcement. These included the *New York Times, USA Today, Science* magazine, and National Public Radio. Media relations experts were assigned to both the Tampa conference and BNL headquarters to handle the anticipated flood of media inquiries. BNL also reached out to members of the nation's scientific community in the belief that they would provide third-party endorsement of the significance of the event.

Following the April 18 announcement, BNL and M. Booth & Associates got all they asked for—and more. The news received widespread coverage, with more than 700 million impressions worldwide. Many of the stories noted the irony of the big discovery coming in the shadow of projected budget cuts. Typical was the story in *USA Today,* which reported, "Despite the success of the experiments, cuts in Energy Department financing will probably reduce the program's operating time from 30 weeks to 12 weeks next year."[42] Only one columnist linked the announcement with an effort to influence the budget negotiations. Congress restored the budget cuts to the program, and President Bush included full funding in the following year's budget request. At a cost of $13,400 for the entire campaign, you would have to say that BNL got a big bang for its bucks.

DISCUSSION QUESTIONS

1. What role did research play in this case study?
2. Who were the targeted publics of this public relations campaign?

3. Would you consider this case to be an example of issues management? Please explain your reasoning.
4. As a practitioner—and as a taxpayer—do you think that Brookhaven National Laboratory officials were ethical in their attempt to influence federal budget decisions?

NOTES

1. Katie Delahaye Paine, "PR's Naked Lust for ROI: Which Do We Value More—Love or Money?" *Bulldog Reporter's Daily Dog*, 27 February 2006, online, www.bulldogreporter.com/dailydog.
2. *Guidelines for Measuring the Effectiveness of PR Programs and Activities*, Institute for Public Relations Commission on PR Measurement and Evaluation, 2002, 1.
3. Linda Childers Hon and James E. Grunig, *Guidelines for Measuring Relationships in Public Relations*, Institute for Public Relations Commission on PR Measurement and Evaluation, 1999.
4. "Edelman Offers New Relationship Index," news release issued by Edelman, 29 April 2003, online, www.edelman.com.
5. Walter K. Lindenmann, "Putting PR Measurement and Evaluation into Historical Perspective," Institute for Public Relations Research, February 2005, online, www.instituteforpr.com.
6. "Return on Investment Is an Inadequate Expression of PR Value," news release issued by the Institute of Public Relations, 19 May 2004, online, www.ipr.org.uk/Nedws/stories/197.htm.
7. "The Power of Public Relations: A Basic Guide to Getting Noticed—Measurement/Evaluation/Wrap-up," Texas Commission on the Arts, 1999, online, www.arts.state.tx.us/news/prpower/measure.htm.
8. James Grunig, "Evaluation," International Public Relations Association e-group, 4 August 2000.
9. *Guidelines and Standards for Measuring and Evaluating PR Effectiveness*, Institute for Public Relations, University of Florida, 2000, online, www.instituteforpr.com.
10. "Ad Value Equivalency Comes Out of the Shadows, but Is It Still Considered 'PR Witchcraft'?" *Ragan Media Relations Report*, 1 October 2001.
11. Sherri Deatherage Green, "Up-Front Research Doesn't Yet Have a Permanent Place in PR," *PR Week* U.S. edition, 4 August 2003, 15.
12. "Maintaining Confidence in Dairy During a Crisis," Dairy Management, Inc., with Weber Shandwick, Silver Anvil Award description, Public Relations Society of America, online, www.prsa.org/_Awards/silver.
13. "Protecting Consumer Confidence in U.S. Beef: A Success Story," National Cattlemen's Beef Association, Silver Anvil Award description, Public Relations Society of America, online, www.prsa.org/_Awards/silver.
14. Alwyn Scott, "Is Beef Industry Reeling? Not Exactly," *Seattle Times*, 29 February 2004, A1.
15. "Protecting Consumer Confidence in U.S. Beef: A Success Story."
16. Greg Hazley, "Beef Industry Passes Its First Run-in with Mad Cow," *O'Dwyer's PR Services Report* 18, no. 2 (February 2004): 1.

17. John Finney, "Assessing the Value of Communication," *Communication World,* January/February 2004, 36–40.

18. Hon and Grunig.

19. James E. Grunig, *Qualitative Methods for Assessing Relationships between Organizations and Publics,* Commission on PR Evaluation and Measurement, online, www.institutefor.pr.com.

20. *2006 State of the PR Profession Opinion Survey,* Public Relations Society of America and Bacon's Information, Inc., 1 February 2007.

21. Mark Weiner and Don Bartholomew, *Dispelling the Myth of PR Multipliers and Other Inflationary Audiences Measures,* Institute for Public Relations, August 2006.

22. James E. Grunig, "After 50 Years: The Value and Values of Public Relations," 45th Annual Distinguished Lecture, Institute for Public Relations, 9 November 2006.

23. "Wal-Mart: Timing of Cover Was Mistake," Associated Press, 31 August 2002, online, LexisNexis.

24. "Help Heal Florida's Healthcare," 2004 Silver Anvil Award summary no. 6BW-0406B11, Public Relations Society of America, online, www.prsa.org.

25. "Mars and Snickers Extortion Threat," 2006 Silver Anvil Award Campaign Profile 6BE-0611 A12, Public Relations Society of America, online, www.prsa.org.

26. "Learn the Signs. Act Early: Educating Parents and Doctors on the Warning Signs of Developmental Problems," 2006 Silver Anvil Award Campaign Profile 6BW-0605B09, Public Relations Society of America, online, www.prsa.org.

27. David Hakensen, "PRSA's Minnesota Chapter Raises Profile of PR Locally," *Public Relations Tactics,* December 2003, 21.

28. "Groundwater Replenishment System Community Relations Program, 2006 Silver Anvil Award Campaign Profile 6BW-0601C08, Public Relations Society of America, online, www.prsa.org.

29. Department of Defense briefing transcript, 29 July 2003, online, www.defenselink.mil.

30. Robin Hanson, "The Policy Analysis Market Archive," 9 January 2004, online, http://hanson.gmu.edu/policyanalysismarket.html.

31. Justin Wolfers and Eric Zitzewitz, "The Furor Over Terrorism Futures," *Washington Post,* 31 July 2003, A19.

32. Hal R. Varian, "A Good Idea with Bad Press," *New York Times,* 31 July 2003, online, www.nytimes.com.

33. Richard Sisk, "Gambling on Terror," *New York Daily News,* 29 July 2003, online, www.nydailynews.com.

34. "Pentagon Axes Online Terror Bets," BBC News, 29 July 2003, online, http://news.bbc.co.uk.

35. Hanson.

36. Steven Pearlstein, "Misplacing Trust in the Markets," *Washington Post,* 30 July 2003, E01.

37. "Ask A Scientist Archives—Physics Index," Argonne National Laboratory, U.S. Department of Energy, online, http://www.newton.dep.anl.gov/askasci

38. "About Brookhaven National Lab," Brookhaven National Laboratory, online, www.bnl.gov.

39. "Gov. Pataki Announces Collaborative Effort to Support Brookhaven National Laboratory," news release, U.S. Fed News, 22 May 2005, via LexisNexis.

40. "RHIC Scientists Serve Up 'Perfect' Liquid," news release, issued by Brookhaven National Laboratory, 18 April 2005, online, www.bnl.gov.

41. "RHIC Results: Perfect Fluid Creates Big Bang for Lab," 2006 Silver Anvil Award Campaign Profile 6BW-0612B01, Public Relations Society of America, online, www.prsa.org.

42. Dan Vergano, "Picking Apart the 'Big Bang' Brings a Big Mystery," *USA Today*, 20 April 2005, 6D.

8

Planning:
The Strategies of
Public Relations

OBJECTIVES

After studying this chapter, you will be able to

- describe the different kinds of public relations plans

- discuss why public relations practitioners create plans

- explain the process of creating a public relations plan

- summarize the qualities of a good plan

- explain where and how values enter into the planning process

The Art of Planning

You're the director of public relations for an art museum in a city in the southwestern United States. Your museum is renowned for its collection of contemporary Native American art, but the museum also has other, diverse artwork and a growing national reputation.

Like many successful public relations operations, your three-person staff has a well-organized issues-management process. You're constantly scanning the environment for potential problems and opportunities. When you spot a potential issue, you monitor it to see whether action is desirable. Last week, you discovered a possible issue: One of your assistants attended a luncheon sponsored by the Hispanic American Leadership Conference. During dessert, a participant asked her why the museum didn't promote Hispanic artists. Another participant overheard the question and agreed that the museum tended to overlook Hispanic artists.

At your weekly issues-management meeting, you and your team discuss that possible perception within your city's Hispanic community. You agree to monitor the situation. Two days later, another staff member shows you an advertisement that a local corporation placed in Hispanic Plus, *a national magazine that targets graduating seniors. The ad boasts of the exciting Hispanic influence on your city's cultural attractions. Your museum is not mentioned in the ad's list of cultural highlights.*

You're puzzled, because the museum recently hosted a very successful exhibition on mid-20th-century Mexican artists Frida Kahlo and her husband, Diego Rivera. But you're also concerned: Almost one-third of your city's residents are of Hispanic origin. If influential members of that broad public believe that your museum is not serving their interests, consequences for future attendance as well as future budgets could be disastrous. Almost 40 percent of your museum's budget comes from city tax revenues.

You assemble a focus group, and a clearer picture of the potential problem emerges. Members of the focus group loved the Kahlo-Rivera exhibition, but they were unanimous in believing that your museum does nothing to promote Hispanic artists now living and working in your city. Additional in-depth interviews with opinion leaders in the Hispanic public echo that belief. One of the opinion leaders says, "Please don't limit yourself to modern Hispanic art—but don't ignore it, either."

More research turns up some startling misperceptions. You learn that almost 65 percent of your museum's small cash grants to up-and-coming artists went to city residents of Hispanic origin—but that you haven't publicized that fact. And you discover another misperception: The head curator of the museum—herself of Hispanic origin—says to you, "No one can say there's a problem here. We're doing more than enough to support Hispanic-influenced art."

On the wall in your office is a poster that contains the museum's statement of values and its mission statement. One of the values is "Diversity." Below that, part of the mission statement says, "This museum will diligently nurture the artistic interests of the residents of our city."

Given your values-based mission and the damaging misperceptions that your research has revealed, you decide that you must address this emerging problem.

What do you do?

The Basics of Values-Driven Planning

Bitter accusations of backroom deals surrounded the O2, formerly known as the Millennium Dome, when the vast arena near London lost a multimillion-dollar bid in 2007 to become England's first Las Vegas–style casino.[1] But controversy was nothing new to the structure, whose debut in 2000 was greeted by the phrases "public relations disaster," "public relations gaffe," "public relations fiasco," and, perhaps worst of all, "bad planning."[2]

Built to host year 2000 celebrations, the Millennium Dome began as an enormous public relations opportunity. As a government project, the arena could not justify a hefty advertising budget. Instead, officials chose to promote the Dome primarily through public relations, particularly media relations. Thus, on opening night—the magical last night of the old millennium—Dome officials invited the United Kingdom's best-known journalists to the festivities. At least, that was the plan. However, Dome officials chose to route the journalists through the crowded London subway system, where, with their families, they were stranded for three hours. They missed most of the Dome celebration and spent much of that memorable night in an underground station.

In retrospect, journalists reported, they should have anticipated the most frustrating evening of their lives. Said one reporter, "[The Dome's] public relations team habitually treated the most innocent inquiry with a combination of paranoia and defensiveness that caused relations with the press to sour long before virtually every national newspaper editor and TV chief was trapped in Stratford station on New Year's Eve."[3]

With that kind of a relationship, media reaction to the Dome's opening-night transportation travesty was predictable:

- "One also marvels at the Dome's public relations, which must have broken the first lesson on day one at PR school: make sure the opinion formers get their tickets on time and get good seats."[4]

- "The organizers could not have planned a worse public relations disaster if they had tried."[5]

Because the Dome consumed substantially more government funding than anticipated, the United Kingdom's National Audit Office investigated Dome finances. The auditors' report took an unusual detour into public relations practices, gently but clearly blaming poor media relations planning for a portion of the Dome's failure. In a section titled "Contingency Planning," the National Audit Office concluded:

- "On any major project managers need as much flexibility as possible to respond if things do not go to plan."
- "Managers may find it difficult to respond to major unforeseen events unless they have already developed crisis plans. This is not planning for failure. It is planning to make the best of a bad situation."

Near the end of its report, the National Audit Office analyzed the impact of the poor media relations planning:

> The [Dome] Company considered that negative media coverage of the Dome . . . had a significant depressing effect on visitor numbers. . . . The Company estimates that each time the Dome received "bad press," sales inquiries dropped by 30 percent to 50 percent in the following week.[6]

The saddest conclusion of all, however, may have come from a Dome public relations official as he led a group of politicians and journalists through the exhibits. "There hasn't been a dull moment at the Dome," he said, "but I think I'll be getting out of public relations after this."[7]

Lessons Learned

Now *there's* an optimistic start to a chapter on planning: prolonged international failure and personal career crisis. But as you've no doubt already realized, the Dome's doom was avoidable. Perhaps you've already considered some key questions: Did the Dome's media relations plan have a goal? Did that goal reflect the government's values? Did anyone measure progress toward the goal? Did the public relations team do *any* research on the values of journalists? Were the tactics realistic? As you know from the basic public relations process, a good plan begins with good research.

Let's look at a public relations challenge that we can still salvage: the Art of Planning, the scenario that opens this chapter. Scanning and monitoring, which are *problem–opportunity research* techniques, have revealed the Hispanic community's belief that the museum isn't supporting local Hispanic artists. *Client research* has shown that the museum is doing a good job of supporting local Hispanic artists—but that the museum isn't publicizing that success. Last but certainly not least, *stakeholder research*—particularly coorientation (p. 101)—has identified disturbing differences in what key publics think of the situation: Leaders of the Hispanic community think there's a problem; the curator of the museum doesn't.

By this point, you (the public relations director) have studied the issue. You know what the important publics think about it. So you're ready to begin planning, right? Wrong. You still need to answer one more question before you begin planning: *What values-based outcome do you seek?* You're about to take action, so what results do you seek? And will those results be consistent with your organization's values, mission, and goals? In the scenario, the outcome you seek is an improved relationship between your museum and the Hispanic residents of your city. Is that outcome consistent with the museum's values? Indeed it is. One of your organization's stated values is "Diversity." Furthermore, the values-based mission statement poster in your office includes these words: "This museum will diligently nurture the artistic interests of the residents of our community." The improved relationship you seek definitely would help your organization fulfill its mission.

Now you're finally ready for some values-driven planning.

Different Kinds of Public Relations Plans

To attain their organizations' public relations goals, public relations practitioners devise different types of plans. These fall into three basic categories: ad hoc plans, standing plans, and contingency plans.

Ad Hoc Plans

The plan you will create to end the misperceptions surrounding your museum will target a temporary (we hope) situation; therefore it's called an **ad hoc plan**. *Ad hoc* is a Latin phrase that means "for this purpose only." When you and your friends make plans for a party, for example, that's an ad hoc plan. Your plan is important, but it's temporary. It's not something you're going to live with for years (unless your party is truly legendary).

Standing Plans

Because many important relationships are ongoing and long term, wise organizations have ongoing and long-term plans to nurture those relationships. A plan of this type is often called a **standing plan.** Your museum, for example, probably would devise a standing plan to maintain a positive relationship with Hispanic residents once your ad hoc plan had succeeded.

A weekly blog that a corporate leader writes for her upper-level managers is part of a standing plan. The blog helps the organization fulfill its values-based goal of maintaining a good relationship with some very important employees. Ideally, another part of that standing plan would be frequent opportunities for those upper-level managers to express their concerns to the corporation's top leadership. Remember: Successful public relations is built on two-way communication and on an organization's willingness to change when necessary.

One danger of standing plans is that they sometimes stand too long. The plan becomes tradition, and we continue carrying out its directives because, we are told, "That's what we've always done." A plan that stands too long can become divorced from its original values-based goal. For example, we may be publishing a great weekly blog for those upper-level managers, but perhaps it's no longer effective because they now need daily, not weekly, updates on some of the topics.

Conducting evaluation research can reduce the danger of obsolete standing plans. As we noted in Chapter 7, evaluation research can help us see whether our plan is meeting its goals. A communication audit, for example, is a form of evaluation research that would examine our organization's communications goals and then check to see how well our communications actions are reaching those goals. An effective communication audit would be the death of an obsolete standing plan.

Contingency Plans

A third kind of public relations plan is called a **contingency plan.** Such plans are used for "what if" scenarios. Through good scanning and monitoring, organizations often spot issues that may require action if they suddenly gather strength. If any such issue has the potential to become powerful, a smart organization prepares a contingency plan. One of the best-known examples of a contingency plan is a crisis communications plan, which is discussed in Chapter 12. Many (though not enough) organizations have a basic crisis communications plan that they practice and can quickly adapt to meet the needs of an emerging crisis.

QuickBreak 8.1

Planning for the Entire Organization

Besides creating ad hoc, standing, and contingency plans, public relations practitioners ideally help create plans at an even higher level: They help determine their organization's values, mission, and specific business goals. In a 2006 survey, corporate chief executive officers reported that they first turn to their public relations departments and their boards of directors for management of the company's reputation.[8] In another 2006 survey, almost 40 percent of practitioners said that their organization's public relations department reported directly to the organization's leader.[9] In its 2006–2007 analysis of the public relations profession, the U.S. Bureau of Labor Statistics reported, "As managers recognize the growing importance of good public relations to the success of their organizations, they increasingly rely on public relations specialists for advice on the strategy and policy of such programs."[10]

Public relations practitioners should contribute to organizational planning for two important reasons:

1. Realistic values, missions, and business goals depend on a clear understanding of relationships with employees, partners, competitors, and other powerful groups. No one has a better understanding of those essential groups than public relations practitioners.

2. A good public relations plan contributes to the fulfillment of an organization's highest aspirations: its values, mission, and business goals. An organization's public relations team, therefore, must thoroughly understand and eagerly accept those aspirations. The best way for public relations practitioners to achieve understanding and acceptance is to help the organization establish those same values, mission, and business goals. Put this in terms of your own life: You're a lot more likely to support a spring break trip if you get to help plan it.

In a well-run organization, public relations practitioners have frequent and easy access to the organization's top management. That access is particularly important when an organization is creating its values, mission, and business goals. "It's not just about creating press releases," says Herbert Heitmann, chief of global communications for SAP, a software maker. "It's about being thought leaders."[11]

For example, KFC Corporation, owner of more than 11,000 Kentucky Fried Chicken restaurants worldwide, has developed a contingency plan to reassure customers about the safety of its products should concerns about bird flu increase in the United States. KFC executives estimate that company sales in China dropped 10 to 20 percent because of fears related to bird flu, which can be fatal. KFC's plan includes news releases, advertisements, talking points for company spokespeople, and even point-of-sale materials for its restaurants. "Hopefully, we'll never have to use any of [those tactics]," said a member of the company's public relations team. "It's a contingency plan."[12]

Despite the different natures of these three kinds of plans—ad hoc, standing, and contingency—they share many characteristics, which we'll discuss next. But one shared characteristic is so important that we'll emphasize it now as well as later: _All public relations plans should be values-driven._ Any public relations plan that you propose should strive to fulfill some area of your organization's values-based mission statement. A good way to win the enthusiastic support of your organization's top managers is to show them exactly how your plan helps to achieve an important business goal. It's not enough to say, "This plan is great! It's going to help us build better relationships with important publics." Instead, show the top managers how those improved relationships help fulfill the organization's values-based mission.

1. How do an organization's values relate to the public relations planning process?
2. What kinds of research should precede the creation of a public relations plan?
3. What are the three kinds of public relations plans? How do they differ?
4. Why should public relations practitioners help an organization establish its values, mission, and related business goals?

Why Do We Plan?

Effective public relations practitioners spend a great deal of their time making ad hoc, standing, and contingency plans. So it's logical to ask _why?_ Why is planning so indispensable to successful public relations? We can think of six good reasons, which we'll detail next.

To Keep Our Actions in Line with Our Organization's Values-Based Mission

As we'll discuss shortly, a good plan is a series of proposed actions designed to produce a specific result. That specific result should advance our organization toward the fulfillment of its values-based mission. Planning prevents random, pointless actions that don't promote our values or our mission. Planning helps us ensure that all our actions are ethical and goal-oriented.

Let's put this same philosophy in terms of your own life. Why are you attending college? Chances are, your presence on campus isn't a random action. Instead, your collegiate studies are part of a plan that's consistent with several values in your life: a good education, a good career, and so on. You wouldn't dream of investing so much time and money in something that took you nowhere. It's the same in public relations. We plan in order to avoid waste as we energetically pursue our broader mission.

To Secure Needed Resources

Remember resource dependency theory from Chapter 4 (p. 93)? A primary duty of public relations practitioners is to build relationships with publics that have the resources an organization needs to achieve its goals. As you know, relationship building usually requires planning. Well-run corporations, for example, have employee relations plans, media relations plans, investor relations plans, government relations plans—in fact, name a public that has desired resources, and a well-run organization will have a relationship-building plan for that group.

To Help Us Control Our Destiny

You have surely heard the sports cliché "We control our own destiny." Athletes say it when their team can make it to the play-offs simply by winning—that is, when they don't need the assistance of losses by other teams in other games. Planning helps an organization control its destiny by proactively managing issues rather than just reacting to them. Planning can help an organization ensure that its relationships with key publics are a source of strength, not of weakness.

To appreciate the link between planning and positive relationships, simply apply the link once again to your own life. Imagine that you'd like to spend more time with a particular someone. Are you going to call that person and, with no warning, ask him or her to go out immediately to who knows where because you haven't yet decided? Or are you going to ask a few days in advance with a specific social agenda? Spontaneity can be fun, but a little planning is indispensable in most good relationships.

Public relations departments that create and implement ad hoc, standing, and contingency plans increase their organization's options in a constantly changing environment. In doing so, they increase their value to the organization.

To Help Us Better Understand and Focus Our Research

Planning puts our research to the test. A detailed plan quickly shows us what we know—and what we don't know. For example, before we plan a specific relationship-building action with an important public, we must know several things:

- Does the relationship really require an adjustment?
- Does our organization want to make the adjustment?
- How will the public probably react to our proposed action?
- Do we have adequate resources to implement the action successfully?

You can probably think of other questions, but note what these have in common: They force us to look closely at our research. Planning helps us ascertain what we truly know, and it identifies areas that require more research.

To Help Us Achieve Consensus

As public relations practitioners transform research into a plan, they seek feedback. Many people, especially an organization's managers, provide input as the plan takes shape. When the planners are satisfied, the plan often goes to the client or top management for formal approval. Thus, when the final plan is drafted, there's a sense of joint ownership and consensus. The organization's decision makers and its public relations team also share a commitment to the success of the plan. Consensus and commitment help an organization avoid misunderstandings regarding relationship-building activities.

To Allow Effective Management of Resources

Resources are finite. (Think of your own entertainment budget, for example.) Public relations managers rarely have enough time, money, equipment, and staff to pursue every public relations issue affecting their organizations. Therefore, any waste of resources is painful. Public relations practitioners create plans because they want every fraction of every resource to move the organization toward its values-driven goals.

VALUES STATEMENT 8.1

Boeing Company

Boeing, based in Chicago, develops and produces aircraft, space systems, and missile systems for commercial and national defense purposes.

In all our relationships we will demonstrate our steadfast commitment to:

- Leadership
- Integrity
- Quality
- Customer Satisfaction
- People Working Together
- A Diverse and Involved Team
- Good Corporate Citizenship
- Enhancing Shareholder Value

—Excerpt from "Vision," Boeing web site

It may seem odd to you that the six reasons for planning don't include the notion that we plan in order to change other people's behavior. In reality, much of public relations planning *does* seek to change the behavior of particular publics. A plan designed to motivate a public to do something that it's predisposed to do may well be successful—but recent research suggests that plans that seek dramatic or rapid behavioral changes rarely succeed. In the mid-1990s, the Research Foundation of the International Association of Business Communicators completed a comprehensive study of effective public relations and came to what may be a disappointing conclusion: "[C]ommunication programs seldom change behavior in the short term, although they may do so over a longer period."[13]

Behavior or even opinions *may* change, then, but it's a long process. So what do public relations practitioners do? Through research and planning, we build relationships to gain needed resources. After all, this profession is called public *relations*. Good relationships, built on trust, cooperation, and two-way communication, can gradually produce the kinds of behavior that an organization desires from its important publics. Those good relationships can even cause our organization to change its own behavior. The IABC study confirmed that when we seek partnerships with particular publics—partnerships in which both sides win—we stand the best chance of gaining those publics' cooperation as we pursue our business goals. As noted in Chapter 1, this win-win philosophy is called two-way symmetrical public relations.

Public relations practitioners may understand the wisdom of this "partnership" approach to planning, but there's no guarantee that the top leaders of an organization will share that understanding. They may still expect practitioners to design and implement plans aimed at producing immediate behavioral changes. When such changes are possible and ethical, we should try to bring them about. But we also need to educate—diplomatically—our organizations' top leaders. We should seek opportunities to inform them about the wisdom and legitimacy of two-way symmetrical public relations.

How Do We Plan?

Public relations planning usually begins after an organization establishes its mission-related business goals. In an ideal setting, public relations managers help establish those business goals. Once those goals are clear, however, the focus of the public relations team shifts to the development of relationship-management plans that help the organization reach its business goals.

A public relations goal is a general statement of the outcome we want a public relations plan to achieve. The goal of our museum scenario, for example, might be *To improve our museum's relationship with Hispanic residents of this city.*

The sections below describe the phases of the planning process, from consensus building to brainstorming to the creation of a written plan.

Consensus Building

Agreement on the need for action must be reached before planning can proceed. In the museum scenario, do museum managers agree with the above goal? Your research has revealed that the head curator doesn't think there's a problem in the museum's relationship with Hispanic residents. Thus, before you can plan for an improved relationship, you need to persuade her, and perhaps other museum officials, that the museum indeed has a problem. Otherwise, you lack agreement on your goal.

Fortunately, you have solid research you can use to show the curator that a growing problem does exist. Is that enough to win agreement on the goal? Perhaps not. You also need to show her that fulfilling this public relations goal will help the museum fulfill its broader goal. When the curator understands that vital connection, you will probably win her enthusiastic endorsement of your goal. Again, public relations practitioners must clearly link their public relations plans to the broader goals of their organizations.

Brainstorming

Once we've achieved consensus on a goal, we move to a speculative phase in which we explore our options for action: **brainstorming**. We ask tough questions about the quality of our research. We ponder what conclusions we can draw. We discuss what specific actions would be the best relationship builders. A good brainstorming session might even prompt us to revise our goal. In short, we have a wide-ranging, no-holds-barred session in which we frequently ask, "Do we know that for sure?" and "What if we tried this?" One Dallas-based agency tries to ensure creative brainstorming sessions by holding them on a basketball court, mixing planning and playing as practitioners work for some slam-dunk ideas.

To guide a brainstorming session, we recommend—in addition to a basketball court—a system based on a planning grid (see QuickBreak 8.2). A planning grid is a tool that public relations practitioners use to develop communication strategies. It's a systematic approach to the planning process. As a prelude to a formal, written plan, a brainstorming grid highlights five areas for discussion:

- *Publics:* Which publics are or must be involved in the issue? For each public, who are the opinion leaders and decision makers?
- *Resources:* To reach our goals, what resources do we require from each public?
- *Values:* What are each public's interests, stakes, or involved values? In other words, why does each public care about this situation?
- *Message:* What message should we send to each public? A successful message addresses a public's values and attempts to get a specified response that would help your organization achieve a particular public relations goal.
- *Media:* Note that the word *media* is plural. You're not limited to just one channel of communication when you send a message to a targeted public.

As a brainstorming session starts to generate ideas, you can write them in a grid. The beginning of a brainstorming grid (p. 244) for our museum scenario would articulate a clear goal:

GOAL: *To improve our museum's relationship with Hispanic residents of this city.*

In our museum scenario, one *public* we could identify would be opinion leaders within the Hispanic community; they hold the *resource* of the potential to influence others. We might decide that from the museum's standpoint, the key *value* held by that group is a strong interest in seeing more support for local Hispanic artists. Our *message* could focus on the little-publicized fact that the museum actively supports local Hispanic artists. Finally, we might discuss using face-to-face meetings and a special event as *media* to send that message.

As you brainstorm and begin to formulate a specific plan, be sure to test all the options against your organization's values-based mission statement and goals. As we've noted before, actions that become divorced from values are counterproductive and a waste of resources.

GOAL: To improve our museum's relationship with Hispanic residents of this city.				
PUBLIC	**RESOURCE(S)**	**VALUE(S)**	**MESSAGE**	**MEDIA**
Opinion leaders in the Hispanic community.	The power to influence members of the Hispanic community.	They want more support for local Hispanic artists.	The museum *is* actively supporting those artists— and it's willing to do more.	Address Hispanic Chamber of Commerce.

The wonderful thing about brainstorming is that you're not yet making firm commitments. Instead, you're just thinking on paper, or on a chalkboard or a flip chart. However, the brainstorming grid does provide the basic information we need for the next step: the written plan, consisting of goal(s), objectives, strategies, and tactics.

QUICK CHECK

1. Should public relations plans focus on quickly changing the behavior of a public or publics? Why or why not?
2. How can public relations practitioners win top management's support for a public relations plan?
3. What is brainstorming? Why is it useful in planning?
4. How does understanding a particular public's values help public relations practitioners create a message for that public?

Goals, Objectives, Strategies, and Tactics: The Written Plan

A written public relations plan consists of four main elements, as shown in Figure 8.1. However, practitioners often disagree on what to call those elements and how to define them. "Practitioners have almost as many different definitions of goals, objectives, strategies, and activities as we have for defining the profession itself," says Tom Hagley, a practitioner with 30-plus years of experience.[14] This book will use four commonly accepted terms:

1. a *goal* or goals,
2. *objectives*,
3. *strategies*, and
4. *tactics*, or recommended actions.

FIGURE 8.1 Goal, Objectives, Strategies, and Tactics
In a public relations plan, a goal determines the necessary objectives, which, in turn, determine the necessary strategies and tactics. In executing the plan, a public relations practitioner first executes the tactics; this leads to the fulfillment of the strategies and objectives, which, in turn, leads to the fulfillment of the goal.

The order of the four is important. Not until you've clearly established the goal and shown that it's consistent with your organization's values can you move to objectives. And not until you've specified the objectives and shown that they, too, are consistent with organizational values can you move to strategies and tactics (recommended actions), which, again, must be consistent with organizational values.

Let's look at goals, objectives, strategies, and tactics in more detail.

Goals. Your starting point, the **goal,** is a generalized statement of the outcome you hope your plan achieves. For example, in our museum scenario, you've diplomatically persuaded the management team that the goal is

To improve our museum's relationship with Hispanic residents of this city.

Goals often begin with infinitives, such as *to improve* or *to increase.* By beginning your plan with a verb, you place an immediate focus on action.

Objectives. Once you have agreement on a well-written goal, you move to the next part of a written plan: the **objectives.** Whereas goals are general statements, objectives define particular ambitions. Objectives, in the words of the PRSA Accreditation Board, are "specific milestones that measure progress toward achievement of a goal."[15] For example, we earlier mentioned an ad hoc plan for a party that you and your friends might throw. Your goal, of course, would be to throw a great party. Your objectives would include activities such as identifying and inviting guests; creating a fun, social atmosphere; and so on. You'd have to meet each of these objectives in order to meet your goal.

According to the Institute for Public Relations, good objectives have five qualities. They must

1. specify a desired outcome (increase awareness, improve relationships, build preference, adopt an attitude, generate sales leads, etc.)
2. directly specify one or several target audiences
3. be measurable, both conceptually and practically
4. refer to "ends," not "means"
5. include a time frame in which the objective is to be achieved, for example, by July 1[16]

In the book *Using Research in Public Relations,* Professors Glen Broom and David Dozier write, "The most frequently asked question in our classes and workshops is 'How much change do you know how to call for in an objective?' The simple response is 'By researching the situation to learn what is possible.'"[17] To that solid beginning, we offer these additional pointers:

- Remember that changing a public's behavior, if it can be done at all, is a long-term process.[18] Measuring resource acquisition or the quality of relationships may be easier (see QuickBreak 7.3, p. 204).

- When appropriate, consider targeting opinion leaders and decision makers with your objectives. It may be easier to create and measure results with a smaller group.

- As you enact your plan, conduct ongoing evaluation to see if your objectives were realistic. You may have time to change course.

In a public relations plan, objectives often focus on the targeted publics. If your plan involves six publics, the plan may well have at least six objectives—because you're seeking to build six different relationships to achieve your goal. However, it is also true that some objectives can serve more than one public. Unfortunately, no magic formula exists that can help you determine the right number of objectives for a goal. The only true test of whether your objectives are sufficient is this question: If I fulfill each objective and manage my resources wisely, will I reach the goal? If the answer is yes, you have the right number of objectives.

In our museum scenario, your objectives might look something like this:

Objective 1: To increase the number of Hispanic artists contacted by 30 percent by November 1.

Objective 2: To increase the Hispanic community's knowledge of the museum's programs by 20 percent by December 1.

Objective 3: To establish a continuing program, by January 1, that informs 100 percent of museum managers of the museum-related values of this city's Hispanic residents.

The PRSA Planning Grid

Ready for a healthy dose of alphabet soup? The Accreditation Board of the Public Relations Society of America recommends that you use PIPP, POST, and TASC grids as part of a three-step planning process.[19]

PIPP, POST, and TASC are memory aids to help you complete three fill-in-the-blank planning grids. The PIPP acronym stands for a process that helps you identify and define the publics your goal-oriented plan may target. It stands for **P**ublic, **I**mportant Segments, **P**rofile, and **P**riority. A PIPP grid looks like this:

Public	Important Segments	Profile	Priority

For each public that you identify, you note the important segments of that public, such as influential members and decision makers, that may require special attention. You then profile each public: You describe its "unique issues, needs, concerns, special demographics, . . . etc."[20] Profile information helps you determine what communication tactics you'll recommend for that specific group. Finally, you assign each public a priority: Which of the identified publics is the most important to your organization? Which is least?

After PIPP comes POST, which helps you develop specific communication actions. The acronym stands for **P**ublic/Segment, **O**bjectives, **S**trategies, and **T**actics. A POST grid looks like this:

Public/ Segment	Objectives	Strategies	Tactics

You begin by naming the identified segments of the key publics. For each segment, you then specify objectives, strategies, and tactics. Objectives are measurable results that you hope to achieve with each public. Strategies are general descriptions of the actions you'll take to reach each objective. Tactics are specific actions that help you fulfill your strategies.

Having worked through PIPP and POST, you're ready to move to the final step of the three-phase process: outlining the logistics of each tactic. The third acronym, TASC, stands for **T**actic, **A**mount, **S**chedule, and **C**oordinator. A TASC grid looks like this:

Tactic	Amount	Schedule	Coordinator

For each tactic, you list the amount it will cost, when it is scheduled to occur, and who will coordinate its implementation.

From the identification of key publics to the naming of a coordinator for a specific action, the three-part PRSA planning grid can help you assemble the information you need for an effective public relations plan.

If you can fulfill these objectives, you'll surely meet your goal. One of your challenges, however, may be measurability. To commit to specific increases, you'll need to know current levels of knowledge and activities. For example, before you plan to increase the Hispanic community's knowledge of museum programs by 20 percent, you'll need to conduct research to specify the current level of knowledge and to understand what degree of improvement is actually possible.

The specificity of your objectives will, in all likelihood, be familiar to top managers within your organization. Many organizations practice a philosophy called management by objectives, or MBO for short. MBO involves having managers commit to specific performance objectives for their particular departments. MBO is also used in performance evaluations for employees. Public relations plans that focus on goals, objectives, strategies, and specific tactics are clearly part of the MBO philosophy favored by many of today's organizations.

Strategies. Strategies help you move from specific objectives to specific recommended actions. Based on good research, **strategies** are general descriptions of the kinds of actions (tactics) you'll implement to fulfill your objectives. Professor Robert Kendall writes that strategies "indicate the conceptual approach in selecting specific actions to be taken to achieve objectives and reach the goal."[21] For example, given our objective of increasing the Hispanic community's knowledge of our museum's programs, our research might show that a strategy of face-to-face communication with community leaders would be best. Our consequent strategy might read: "Seek face-to-face opportunities to demonstrate to Hispanic community opinion leaders how our museum supports local Hispanic artists." Strategies begin with active verbs; they resemble general commands.

Tactics. When you're satisfied with your goal(s), objectives, and strategies, it's time to suggest specific tactics. **Tactics,** or recommended actions, make up the fourth and final part of a written plan; they are how you enact each strategy. To fulfill each objective, you need to take specific actions. Thus, you can list recommended actions under each strategy. That placement is important. You don't gather all your tactics together and place them at the end of the plan. Instead, you put strategies and recommended actions under each objective to show how you plan to achieve that specific ambition.

Unlike goals and objectives, tactics don't begin with infinitives. They begin with active verbs; they're commands. Thus, in the museum scenario, your first tactic under your second objective might be something like this:

Objective 2: To increase the Hispanic community's knowledge of the museum's programs by 20 percent by December 1.

Strategy: Seek face-to-face opportunities to demonstrate to Hispanic community opinion leaders how our museum supports local Hispanic artists.

Tactic 1: Address the November meeting of the city's Hispanic Chamber of Commerce.

That tactic is a good command, but it's not very complete. Who should address the Hispanic Chamber of Commerce? When is the meeting? How can you get on the meeting's agenda? What presentation materials will the speaker use? Besides being expressed as a brief command, each tactic should provide enough specific details to enable someone to implement it. It's common under each tactic to give the following information:

- *Brief description* (specifying only what is essential for the action to be executed)
- *Deadline*
- *Budget*
- *Special requirements* (specifying anything out of the ordinary, such as a need for unusual technology)
- *Supervisor* (name of the person in charge of seeing that the action is executed)

Our tactic might now look something like this:

Tactic 1: Address the November meeting of the city's Hispanic Chamber of Commerce.

Consumer Relations Tactic To promote its energy drink, Red Bull sponsors Flugtag (German for "Flight Day"), an annual "Will It Fly?" competition. At a Flugtag event in New York, the Flying Mozarts proved that pianos don't fly. (Photo by Dith Pran/*New York Times.* Copyright 2003 The New York Times Company. Reprinted with permission.)

- *Brief description:* Request permission for curator to give a 10-minute presentation on the museum's support for local Hispanic artists. Permission is generally granted if we provide two-weeks' advance notice. Use handouts and computer-generated slides to show the scope of the museum's support for local Hispanic artists. To demonstrate our willingness to change and to be accommodating, the curator should begin her presentation in Spanish (which she does speak) before switching to English. Handouts and slides should be in Spanish and English.
- *Deadline:* Contact Hispanic Chamber of Commerce by November 1. November meeting date is November 21.
- *Budget:* $100 for preparation of handouts and computer graphics.
- *Special requirements:* Take grant-application forms to the meeting so that Hispanic Chamber of Commerce members can help distribute them to local Hispanic artists. Ensure that forms are written in Spanish and English.
- *Supervisor:* Public relations director.

Having supplied this much detail, you're ready to move on to your next tactic under your face-to-face strategy.

The SWOT Analysis

Imagine the success you would enjoy as a public relations professional if you could create relationship-building plans that helped your organization or clients

- improve strengths;
- diminish weaknesses;
- seize opportunities; and
- avoid threats.

SWOT analysis can help you achieve that ambition. SWOT is an acronym for strengths, weaknesses, opportunities, and threats. For an organization, those qualities can be internal or external.

- *Strengths* are an organization's current assets, including issues and social conditions, that can help the organization achieve its goals. Strengths can include employee expertise, public opinion, and new legislation.
- *Weaknesses* are an organization's current disadvantages, including issues and social conditions, that can prevent the organization from achieving its goals. Weaknesses can include a lack of internal resources and a public scandal.
- *Opportunities* are emerging assets, issues, and social conditions that, in the future, could help the organization achieve its goals. Opportunities

can include new products and services the organization is developing, pending legislation, and new international markets.

- *Threats* are emerging disadvantages, issues, and social conditions that could prevent the organization from achieving its goals. Threats can include the upcoming retirement of key employees, growing competition in the marketplace, and pending legislation.

A SWOT analysis is a bridge between research and planning. It helps sort out your data about an organization and the social environment in which it operates. Using specific information from a SWOT analysis, public relations practitioners can create plans to boost positives and reduce negatives. A highly focused SWOT analysis that identifies the strengths, weaknesses, opportunities, and threats in a particular situation can serve as a situation analysis for a proposal (page 251).

Whether broad or narrow in scope, a SWOT analysis must be factual. Avoid opinions and the temptation to overstate positives and understate negatives. Be realistic. Be objective.

And be ready to bring SWOT analysis into the planning process.

Fleshing out each tactic helps give us the road map we need to reach our goal. When we're finished, we have a highly detailed, realistic, workable plan—in writing.

Expanding a Plan into a Proposal

Even with your written plan completed, your writing may be unfinished. Some plans exist alone as plans. Sometimes, however, you need to "sell" your plan to a client or a supervisor who may want a greater amount of background information. Often, therefore, a plan is inserted into a larger document called a **proposal**. Agencies often prepare proposals for their clients, and even within corporations public relations practitioners often prepare proposals for top management. A public relations proposal generally contains, in order, these sections:

1. A title page
2. An **executive summary** that briefly, in one page, describes the problem or opportunity, identifies the targeted publics, lists the specific tactics for addressing the situation, and includes a budget summary
3. A **situation analysis** that accurately and fairly describes the current situation in such a way that action seems advisable
4. A **statement of purpose** announcing that the proposal presents a plan to address the described situation
5. A list and description of publics that the plan targets
6. A plan that specifies your goal(s), objectives, strategies, and tactics
7. Other sections as appropriate, such as
   - campaign theme and key messages
   - line-item budget
   - timetable
   - evaluative measures
   - supporting documents (usually in the appendices)

A proposal, as you can see, can be an extensive document. But at its heart is a clear plan consisting of a goal or goals, objectives, strategies, and tactics.

QUICK CHECK

1. How is a goal different from an objective?
2. What are the qualities of a well-written objective?
3. What are tactics? What is their relationship to strategies?
4. How is a plan different from a proposal?

Qualities of a Good Plan

We've covered why we plan and how we plan, and we've seen how a plan can be incorporated in a proposal. Let's turn now to the qualities of a good plan. We've already mentioned some: A good plan seeks measurable results, and it has specific deadlines. What other qualities should a good plan have?

■ *A good plan supports a specific goal of your organization.* As we've said before, don't take for granted that your organization's leaders automatically recognize the value of good public relations. Show them how your plan can help the organization reach a specific business goal.

■ *A good plan stays goal-oriented.* Remember the problem with some standing plans? They stand for so long that we forget why we're following them; instead, we just execute the actions, such as an employee newsletter, because we've always done them. That won't happen if we stay goal-oriented, finding ways to remind ourselves of why we're executing these particular actions.

■ *A good plan is realistic.* Don't promise more than you can achieve. It's OK to dream an impossible dream, but you should plan for an achievable reality. Unrealistic goals and objectives often involve quickly changing a public's behavior. That's not necessarily always impossible, but public relations is much better at building the open and honest relationships that foster gradual changes. Unrealistic tactics include those that require more resources or expertise than your organization can supply.

■ *A good plan is flexible.* Things change. Sometimes important elements of a situation change just as you're launching a plan. If you constantly evaluate the situation, as you should do, you may need to adjust your plan to fit the new circumstances.

■ *A good plan is a win-win proposition.* Whenever possible, the success of your plan should benefit the target publics just as much as it benefits your organization. Forcing a public to change against its will is rarely possible and is almost always bad public relations. A good plan tries to honor each important public's values. When that's not possible, a good plan seeks to minimize damage to important relationships.

■ *Finally, and most importantly, a good plan is values-driven.* As we've noted more than once, if your plan isn't helping your organization achieve its values, it's pointless. It's wasting resources. A good plan resonates with the well-known values of your organization.

Summary

Plans usually fit into one of three categories: ad hoc, standing, or contingency. Successful public relations plans have many qualities, but they share one in particular: They must be clearly tied to an organization's goals. In other words, public relations practitioners must show an organization's top managers how a proposed relationship-building plan aligns with the organization's values and mission. If that connection is not established, the plan will probably die for lack of consensus and approval.

Good public relations plans consist of a general goal or goals; measurable objectives; strategies; and specific tactics, or recommended actions. Often, a written plan becomes part of a larger document called a proposal, which practitioners use to present a plan to a client or to their organization's top management.

Good, creative planning is an art—but it's an art based on science. A good plan is goal directed and research based. It is realistic and flexible, and it aims for a win-win outcome. Above all, a good public relations plan helps an organization fulfill its values.

DISCUSSION QUESTIONS

1. At what specific points do values enter the public relations planning process?
2. What unique characteristics differentiate ad hoc plans, standing plans, and contingency plans from one another?

3. Can you think of examples—in public relations or otherwise—of standing plans that have stood too long?

4. Why should you go to the effort of producing a written plan if you've already completed a planning grid? If you have a written plan, when should you consider expanding it into a proposal?

5. Why are measurable objectives important to the evaluation phase of the public relations process? What are the advantages of measurable objectives? What are the disadvantages?

Memo from the Field

Timothy S. Brown, APR, Ph.D., Director, Corporate Communications, Delmarva Power/ Atlantic City Electric, Newark, Delaware

Timothy S. Brown is an accredited public relations professional with more than 20 years of communications experience in public relations, public affairs, and marketing communications. Brown currently serves as director, corporate communications, for the mid-Atlantic energy companies Delmarva Power and Atlantic City Electric, subsidiaries of Pepco Holdings, Inc. In this capacity, he is responsible for directing all public relations activities of the organization, including strategic communications planning, media relations, crisis communications, and employee communications. Brown also taught a business writing course at Wesley College in New Castle, Delaware. He holds a Ph.D. in English and rhetoric from the University of Maryland at College Park, a master's degree in English from George Mason University, and a bachelor's degree in journalism from Pennsylvania State University. Brown lives in Newark, Delaware—a great college town, he says—with his wife and two children.

When I was in college, sitting where you are, one of my favorite professors began one of my favorite classes by writing a time line on the board. The time line charted the length of time between major technological advances in the history of man—from the invention of simple tools, to the domestication of fire, to the use of the wheel, and so on up to modern times. My favorite professor's point was that the pace of change had accelerated dramatically over time. While it had been thousands of years between the domestication of fire and the invention of the wheel, these days major technological changes are measured in years, if not months or weeks. Such well-known history is behind the well-known maxim that life is change.

This chapter offers a wealth of valuable advice on public relations planning. It explains why planning is important, lays out a sensible approach to planning, offers useful examples of effective plans, and defines the qualities of a good plan. One particular point the authors made in the last section struck a chord with me. They note that "a good plan is flexible" because "things change," making it important for you to "constantly evaluate the situation...[so you can] adjust your plan to fit the new circumstances."

If I were you, I'd underline, highlight, and asterisk that passage. My 20 years of experience as a communications professional has underscored the power behind the simple truth that "things change." I've seen the electric industry where I now work change dramatically with the onset of "deregulation." I've seen dozens of executive leaders come and go. I've seen my latest organization significantly change its business strategy three times in six years. Such experiences have left me convinced that the best public relations plans must both anticipate and accommodate change.

Let me give you an example that illustrates the importance of adapting your public relations plans to accommodate change. It is my good fortune to be able to coordinate the strategic communications planning process for my company, Pepco Holdings, Inc. My colleagues and I ground that planning process in the needs of the business units that we support. We also factor in what is happening in our industry and the broader environment in which we do business. All of these elements are combined in a matrix that identifies the goals, objectives, strategies, messages, and tactics that we will use to execute our plan over the next several years.

I'm sure you can guess the flaw in that process. You got it: Things change. Most recently, for example, our company was hit by a major hurricane that disrupted service to nearly one million of our 1.8 million customers. Those customers had questions and issues that weren't anticipated in our plan. To address those new public relations challenges, we had to adapt our well-established plans.

We followed the basic process that we used in developing the initial plan. We conducted research, including surveys and focus groups with customers that had been hardest hit by the hurricane. Based on that research, we reformulated our strategies and objectives for our matrix communications plan. Those new strategies, in turn, translated into adaptations of previously planned communications tactics. For example, we modified a long-running advertising campaign to reflect the lessons of the hurricanes, including, especially, the desire for more information about when power would be restored, which customers expressed via our research. This process resulted in a "new and improved" version of our matrix communications plan that we are currently implementing.

You will likely find in your career that you will have to accommodate similar new developments. If anything, change will be even more of a constant for you. You will be judged in large part by how well you adapt to such a climate in which change is the norm. It will of course be important for you to follow the sound advice that you have received about planning in this chapter and this course. But it will be equally important for you to be adaptable enough to adjust those plans to the ever-changing conditions that will be a constant reality in your public relations career.

Unfortunately, I can't tell you exactly how to do that. You will need to develop the experience, expertise, and judgment to know when and how to adapt your plans based on changing conditions. Doing so will be one of the most challenging and yet satisfying aspects of your career.

There is, however, one piece of advice with which I would leave you. No matter how much you have to change your *plans* to adapt to new challenges, you should not feel that it is necessary to change your *values*. As the title of this textbook suggests, your public relations practices must ultimately be grounded in the values that define you and your organization. In fact, it is only by identifying the values that most matter to you and your organization that you can decide how to most appropriately adapt existing public relations plans in the face of inevitable changes.

Hopefully, as you look back on your own college experience in the future, you'll consider this class to be part of the formative process of the way you approach public relations. If so, I'll hope you'll agree with the importance of always being ready to change your plans but never being too quick to change your values.

CASE STUDY **8.1**

Grape Expectations: Planning to Save California Wines

If you're a video-gamer, the glassy-winged sharpshooter may sound like one of those archvillains that haunt a game-level's conclusion. One of the sharpshooter's sworn foes, in fact, is the Terminator himself—California Governor Arnold Schwarzenegger. But the sharpshooter isn't a digital fantasy: It's a half-inch long insect that threatens California's $45 billion wine grape industry.

In 2001, California's wine grape growers voted to create the Pierce's Disease and Glassy-Winged Sharpshooter Board to combat the insect. Overseen by the state's Department of Food and Agriculture and funded by mandatory contributions from the state's wine grape growers, the board sought to eradicate Pierce's Disease, spread by the sharpshooter and devastating to vineyards. But authorization for the funding was set to end in 2006. The only way to extend the board's life to 2011 was for growers to vote again to fund its mission. And that was a problem.

"It's tough," said grower Brad Lange, who chairs the board. "Some of my colleagues may feel that they can't afford it, or they may forget to vote. But if we don't continue this, the industry will lose control of the sharpshooter, and [Pierce's Disease] will start showing up in our vineyards."[22]

"We're concerned that the program might become a victim of its own success," added grower Paul Kronenberg. "Growers might say, 'Hey, it's OK. We haven't had a problem in a long time, so why should I pay this?' Things aren't OK."[23]

Concerned that it would lose the vote and its funding, the board turned to Brown-Miller Communications (BMC), a public relations agency based in San Martinez, California. BMC's initial research confirmed the board's fears: Surveys and personal interviews showed that many growers doubted the effectiveness of continued funding. The board's inadequate communications efforts had failed to spread the word of its dramatic successes.[24]

BMC's research also showed that the most credible sources for California's wine grape growers were other growers, not government officials. Based on its research,

BMC crafted a public relations plan with the goal of increasing grower support for the board's continuation. The plan's objectives included:

- increasing grower recognition of the board's identity and messages by at least 25 percent;

- increasing grower awareness and support for the board's goals and activities by 50 percent; and

- securing the support of at least 50 percent of the state's key intervening publics (grower associations and wineries) to echo the board's messages.[25]

BMC recommended an overall strategy of using respected growers who supported the board as the primary spokespeople for the campaign. Particular tactics included speaker kits with talking points for the selected growers, increased involvement in trade shows and special events, a quarterly newsletter to growers, news releases, a news conference, and editorials written by respected growers.[26]

In one such tactic, three respected growers wrote a letter to the editor of the *San Francisco Chronicle* in which they declared, "We urge every grower to demonstrate their support for continuing the research and control efforts by voting 'Yes' on the referendum. For hundreds of thousands of Californians whose jobs or lifestyles are benefited by the wine industry, we hope that you'll work to persuade growers to support continuance of important research and control programs."[27]

BMC's strategy of using respected intervening publics to influence individual growers was also evident in the comments of the president of the Sonoma County Grape Growers Association: "The industry and state have done a remarkable job of containing this threat so far, but we have to remain vigilant and search for an answer. Passage of the referendum is the best way to ensure that."[28]

The growers voted yes in overwhelming numbers: almost 90 percent of the 4,000-plus growers who voted supported the continued funding. Virtually 100 percent of the targeted intervening publics supported the board, and the amount of media coverage of the sharpshooter threat increased by 800 percent.[29]

"Anytime a measure passes with almost 90 percent of folks marking their ballots with a yes vote, you know voters are deeply concerned," said grower Jim Richards.[30]

For its impressive success in helping the board win approval of continued funding, Brown-Miller Communications won a top public relations prize: a 2006 Silver Anvil Award from the Public Relations Society of America.

In honoring the year's many Silver Anvil winners, David Imre, chair of the awards competition, singled out BMC's superior planning. "We congratulate Brown-Miller Communications for its public relations programs that incorporated measurable and sound research, planning, execution and evaluation," he said. "These programs contribute to the best practices of our industry."[31]

DISCUSSION QUESTIONS

1. How does the Brown-Miller Communications plan show a general goal, specific objectives, general strategies, and specific tactics?

2. Besides the ad hoc plan that BMC developed, can you think of a standing plan that it might have developed? Can you think of a contingency plan it might have developed?

3. How does this case demonstrate the value of opinion leaders and intervening publics?

4. Why do you think the Pierce's Disease and Glassy-Winged Sharpshooter Board chose to use public relations rather than advertising?

CASE STUDY **8.2**

Mess at Maryville: A Private Plan Goes Public

Maryville Academy was earning headlines for all the wrong reasons. The Catholic-run institution for troubled youth, the largest such program in Illinois, faced allegations of beatings, sexual misconduct, and suicide among its residents. Investigators cited a lack of cooperation from academy officials and even claimed that Maryville employees had tried to smear their reputations.[32] Unfortunately, an 11-page public relations plan to rebuild key relationships became part of the problem rather than the beginning of a solution.[33]

"Maryville Academy officials have publicly rejected a proposed public relations plan to conduct a smear campaign against critics of the Roman Catholic child-care institution," the *Chicago Sun-Times* reported.[34] Two days earlier, the *Sun-Times* had trumpeted this headline: "Cardinal [Francis George] Rips Maryville P. R. Plan as 'Fiasco.'"[35]

Two passages in the public relations plan, prepared by Serafin & Associates of Chicago, drew fire from client and critics alike: "Conduct opposition research" and "Utilize a third-party organization to question unnamed insiders and sources and their motives in questioning Maryville's leadership."[36]

Reaction to those passages was immediate. "After I read it, I felt like taking a bath . . . ," said Patrick Murphy, a Cook County (Chicago) public official. "It's clear what they're saying. They don't come right out and say 'smear,' but that's what they mean. . . . I don't think that's what the Catholic Church should be all about."[37]

Reaction from within Maryville was equally harsh. "I refused it, and I don't want to discuss it," said the Reverend John Smyth, Maryville's founder.[38]

James Guidi, Maryville's head of operations, added, "I read it and came back the next day, sat with Father Smyth and said, . . . 'Father, as a practicing Catholic, I don't want to be involved in anything like that, and as a Catholic organization, we should not be involved in anything like that.'"[39]

How could a public relations plan designed to improve relationships worsen them? The answers may lie in a lack of research, a lack of clarity, and a lack of confidentiality.

Serafin & Associates had been working with Maryville for less than a year, and a lack of client knowledge may have affected the plan. Regarding planning sessions with top Maryville officials, Thom Serafin, president of Serafin & Associates, said,

"I never had any discussions—no discussions—with anyone."[40] The *Sun-Times* reported that some critics believed that Serafin was trying to protect his client by taking sole responsibility for the plan.[41]

But Guidi also cited a lack of research as a cause for rejecting the plan: "It's unfortunate that the public relations firm has not done their research well enough to realize that as a Catholic institution it would be immoral to do this kind of research."[42]

Lack of clarity may also have hampered parts of the report. Serafin told *PR Week* magazine that, to him, "conduct opposition research" meant that Maryville should study similar institutions to better understand the statewide conditions of child care.[43] But Herbert Simons, a Temple University professor of speech communication, disagreed with that definition: "You find out all kinds of nasty things about your opponents," he said, describing opposition research. "You spread it around."[44]

"The language is wrong, but the intent is good," Serafin said. "One of the problems and the principle issues with Maryville is, organizationally, they need to communicate better. This was an effort to communicate internally so you can communicate better externally."[45]

In addition, Serafin had submitted a confidential draft to Maryville, not a finished product—and the draft had leaked to the media. "I rejected it outright," Smyth reasserted to the *Chicago Daily Herald,* adding that someone must have taken the plan from his desk.[46]

Serafin reacted quickly to the public disclosure of the work in progress. "This draft has been misinterpreted," he said. "[Critics] decided to focus on three words in the report. Full disclosure is always best."[47] To ensure full disclosure and to allow the controversial passages to be seen in context, Serafin posted the entire plan on his agency's web site.

"If you read the entire plan," he said, "it's a great plan to put more scrutiny on Maryville."[48]

One tactic in the plan did call for weekly meetings with area news media to inform them of progress at Maryville.

In the swirl of charges and countercharges regarding the public relations plan, the Maryville–Serafin partnership received a bleak appraisal from Cardinal Francis George of the archdiocese of Chicago. "The very fact that you're hiring people who would think about this is not encouraging," he said. "I think we have to reconsider the whole relationship."[49]

Maryville Academy did reconsider—and chose to retain Serafin & Associates as its public relations agency.[50]

DISCUSSION QUESTIONS

1. How might better knowledge of stakeholder values have prevented this problem?
2. In public relations, is it unethical to conduct research on hostile publics? Why or why not?
3. In your opinion, should Serafin & Associates have shown a draft version—rather than the final version—of its plan to the client?

4. In your opinion, did Serafin & Associates do a good job of responding to the crisis? Why or why not?

NOTES

1. Colin Brown and Ian Herbert, "Despair for Dome as Manchester Wins Supercasino," *The (London) Independent,* 31 January 2007, online, LexisNexis Academic.
2. Patrick Wintour and Anthony Browne, "The Dome: Triumph or Disaster?" *Observer,* 9 January 2000, online, LexisNexis; Mark Fox, "We Need a Moan-Free Zone for the Dome," *Sunday Express,* 9 January 2000, online, LexisNexis; Dominic Kennedy, "Now for a Few Dome Truths," *Times,* 7 January 2000, online, LexisNexis.
3. John Rees, "Doomed Saucer Crashes to Earth," *Sunday Business,* 10 September 2000, online, LexisNexis.
4. David Lister, "Media: The Editors and the Queuing Zone," *Independent,* 11 January 2000, online, LexisNexis.
5. Wintour and Browne.
6. "National Audit Office: The Millennium Dome," 9 November 2000, online, www.nao.gov.uk.
7. John Chapman, "Tory Julie Roams the Dome," *Express,* 25 May 2000, online, LexisNexis.
8. "*PR Week* CEO Survey 2006," report by *PR Week* and Burson-Marsteller, 6 November 2006, online, www.prweek.com/us.
9. "2006 State of the PR Profession Opinion Survey," report by the Public Relations Society of America and Bacon's Information, Inc., 2007, online, www.prsa.org.
10. *Occupational Outlook Handbook 2006–2007,* U.S. Bureau of Labor Statistics, online, www.bls.gov.
11. Andrew Gordon, "SAP Retools Global Comms," *PR Week,* 9 August 2004, 1.
12. Beth Herskovits, "Popeyes, KFC Forge Plans in Case of Bird Flu Outbreak," *PR Week,* 14 November 2005, online, LexisNexis; Kate MacArthur, "KFC Preps Bird-Flu Fear Plan," *Advertising Age,* 7 November 2005, online, LexisNexis.
13. James E. Grunig, "Communication, Public Relations, and Effective Organizations: An Overview of This Book," in *Excellence in Public Relations and Communication Management,* ed. James E. Grunig (Hillsdale, N.J.: Lawrence Erlbaum, 1992), 14.
14. Tom Hagley, "Lead with Integrity," *Public Relations Strategist* (winter 2003): 40.
15. *Accreditation Study Guide, 1993* (New York: Public Relations Society of America, 1993), 81.
16. "Guidelines for Setting Measurable Public Relations Objectives," Institute for Public Relations Commission on PR Measurement and Evaluation, 1999, online, www.instituteforpr.com/printables/objectives.htm.
17. Glen M. Broom and David M. Dozier, *Using Research in Public Relations: Applications to Program Management* (Englewood Cliffs, N.J.: Prentice Hall, 1990), 40.
18. Grunig, 14.
19. *Accreditation Study Guide, 1993,* 89.
20. *Accreditation Study Guide, 1993,* 90.
21. Robert Kendall, *Public Relations Campaign Strategies,* 2nd ed. (New York: Harper-Collins, 1996), 250

22. Jon Ortiz, "Pinot Pest Growers Grapple with Extending a Fee to Fight Vine Infestation," *Sacramento Bee,* 21 March 2005, online, LexisNexis Academic.
23. Ortiz.
24. "Creating an Identity to Rally Winegrape Growers Around," report by the Public Relations Society of America, 2006, online, www.prsa.org.
25. "Creating an Identity to Rally Winegrape Growers Around."
26. "Creating an Identity to Rally Winegrape Growers Around."
27. Ben Drake, Jim Richards, and Bobby Koch, "Pest Requires Vigilance," *San Francisco Chronicle,* 12 May 2005, online, LexisNexis Academic.
28. "Grape Growers Support Referendum," *Western Farm Press,* 7 May 2005, online, LexisNexis.
29. "Creating an Identity to Rally Winegrape Growers Around."
30. "New Report on PD," news release issued by Family Winemakers of California, 25 July 2005, online, LexisNexis Academic.
31. "California Firm Captures Nation's Highest P.R. Honor," Avenue Vine: Wine News and Information Magazine, 19 June 2006, online, www.avenuevine.com.
32. Cathleen Falsani, "Maryville Critics Say They Are Targets of Smear," *Chicago Sun-Times,* 19 August 2003, online, LexisNexis.
33. John N. Frank, "Criticism Forces Firm to Make PR Plan Public," *PR Week,* 25 August 2003, online, LexisNexis.
34. Falsani, "Maryville Critics Say They Are Targets of Smear."
35. Cathleen Falsani, "Cardinal Rips Maryville P.R. Plan as 'Fiasco,'" *Chicago Sun-Times,* 17 August 2003, online, LexisNexis.
36. Falsani, "Cardinal Rips Maryville P.R. Plan as 'Fiasco.'"
37. Amy McLaughlin, "Maryville, Public Guardian Square off Over Report, Fight," *Chicago Daily Herald,* 16 August 2003, online, LexisNexis; Cathleen Falsani, "DCFS Probes Charges of Cover-Up at Maryville," *Chicago Sun-Times,* 16 August 2003, online, LexisNexis.
38. Ofelia Casillas, "Proposed Tactics Deemed Immoral," *Chicago Tribune,* 17 August 2003, online, www.prwatch.org.
39. Falsani, "DCFS Probes Charges of Cover-Up at Maryville."
40. Falsani, "Maryville Critics Say They Are Targets of Smear."
41. Falsani, "Maryville Critics Say They Are Targets of Smear."
42. Casillas.
43. Frank.
44. Casillas.
45. "Critics Say Draft Plan Shows Shelter's Intent to Hide Trouble," *Northwest Indiana News,* 17 August 2003, online, www.thetimesonline.com/articles/2003/08/17/news.
46. McLaughlin.
47. Frank.
48. McLaughlin.
49. Falsani, "Cardinal Rips Maryville P.R. Plan as 'Fiasco.'"
50. "Maryville Officials Stick with PR Firm for Now," *Chicago Tribune,* 19 August 2003, online, www.poynter.org/dg.lts/id.46/aid.44966/column.htm.

Communication: The Tactics of Public Relations

OBJECTIVES

After studying this chapter, you will be able to

■ understand what makes a tactic effective

■ discuss traditional and social media tactics in public relations

■ select tactics that seem particularly appropriate for specific publics

■ describe how to carry out tactics efficiently and effectively

KEY TERMS

Canada to Costa Rica

You are assistant director of public relations for a small but profitable international manufacturing firm based in California. Your company is publicly held; that is, it sells shares of ownership to stockholders throughout the world. Today you helped other members of the management team make a decision that's good news for some of your publics and bad news for others: To save money, your company is going to move a factory from Toronto, Canada, to San José, Costa Rica.

During the decision-making process, you advised the company's leaders about the move's impact on different publics. You suggested specific public relations tactics to be deployed if the company did vote to move the factory to Costa Rica. You even pointed out that some publics would be bitterly disappointed no matter what kinds of relationship-building tactics your company undertook. The best your company could do in those situations, you said, would be to minimize the unavoidable damage to these relationships.

After voting to move the factory, the leaders praised your assistance in helping them understand the wide-ranging impacts of such a decision. Now they've asked you to draw up a plan that recommends specific relationship-building tactics for each affected public. And they've asked you to hurry. The move will be announced next week.

Time to get started. Who are the relevant publics, and what relationship-building tactics do you suggest for each one?

Tactics, Fun, and Values

Let the fun begin.

Actually, we hope the fun already has begun with the challenges and rewards of public relations research and planning. But almost every practitioner loves to create **tactics**—the actions that we devise and undertake to influence relationships with particular publics.

The process of accomplishing the tactics—often called communication—is the third phase of the public relations process, the logical follow-up to research and planning. In public relations, tactics unavoidably shine the spotlight on values. Because people often judge us by our actions, tactics tend to show our true values as well as our knowledge of our targeted publics' values. Therefore, in this chapter, we'll do more than study the traditional tactics in public relations—everything from low-tech bulletin boards to high-tech blogs. We'll also examine *how* you can accomplish values-driven tactics to improve their effectiveness and efficiency. It's hard to have fun standing in the smoldering ruins of poorly executed tactics.

Tactics as Messages and Channels

In Chapter 5, as you'll recall, we presented a basic communication model, which looks like this:

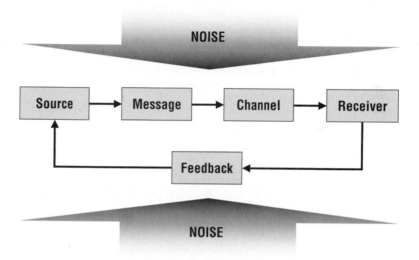

Social media, such as wikis and content communities (see QuickBreak 9.2), can turn this model on its head, with traditional receivers reversing the flow and becoming sources. For example, you've been both a source and a receiver if you've both watched and posted videos on YouTube. But whoever creates public relations tactics, those relationship-building actions enter this communication model as messages and channels. Messages have tactical value because they can influence a relationship. In our Canada to Costa Rica scenario, for example, management (source) could refuse to help (message) the unhappy workers in Toronto (receivers). That message certainly would influence the relationship. On the other hand, management could send a message that it will help the workers find new jobs. That message probably would have a different, more beneficial impact on the relationship. Because public relations tactics are designed to influence relationships, messages definitely are tactics.

More commonly, however, tactics are thought of as channels. A presentation from your company's top official in Toronto to the unhappy workers would be a channel—a tactic—designed to deliver a message and influence the relationship. A brochure that specifies exactly what the company will do for the Toronto workers could be another channel. Sometimes channels and messages are so intertwined that the channel becomes the message. For example, let's say your message to the unhappy workers in Toronto is *We'll help you find new jobs*. One channel for that message could be the creation of a training and placement center to help the employees polish their résumés and brush up on new job skills. In this case, the channel (the training and placement center) is so intertwined with the message (*We'll help you find new jobs*) that the two are indistinguishable.

If this seems overly complicated, let's remember our definition of a tactic: a public relations action designed to have a particular effect on an organization's relationship with a particular public. The messages we create can affect relationships; so can the channels that we use to send messages. Thus, both messages and channels can be tactics. Generally, a tactic is a channel with a message.

Successful messages and channels must respect the receiver's needs and preferences. An effective message, as we noted in Chapter 8, clearly addresses the receiver's values and interests. Likewise, an effective channel is one that appeals to the receiver. We can't rely exclusively on the channels that are cheapest or easiest, though that may be very tempting. Instead, our messages must flow through channels that our targeted receivers prefer.

How do we know which messages to send and which channels to choose? The planning grids discussed in Chapter 8 (Planning: The Strategies of Public Relations) help you create messages and select channels that effectively address targeted publics and their values. This chapter will help you identify traditional and nontraditional channels, everything from news releases to podcasts. Generally speaking, however, three kinds of channels exist: special events, such as open houses or festival sponsorships; controlled media, such as podcasts; and uncontrolled media, such as the news media.

Special Events

You've certainly heard the cliché that actions speak louder than words. That cliché describes the message-sending power of a **special event.** For example, in our opening scenario, you could simply *tell* the upset employees in Toronto that your company cares about them and that the company will help them. But actions speak louder than words—so what "wordless" actions could *prove* that you'll help? You could offer a generous pay package that includes an extra three months of salary after the employees have been let go. And you could establish that training and placement center to help the workers prepare for new jobs with other employers. Those special events would clearly demonstrate that you're not abandoning your former employees. Instead, your special events would send the message that you value those individuals and that you'll help them through this difficult transition. Special events often weave together the message and the channel.

Special events are designed for the participants, of course, but in many cases they're also designed for observers. Your training and placement center in Toronto, for example, is clearly meant for the workers there—but it also sends a powerful message to workers in your other factories throughout the world: Your company takes care of its employees. That reassuring message should help strengthen relationships with the people who are best able to increase your company's productivity.

Another example of a special event that could target both participants and observers would be a student group's sponsorship of a Halloween party for underprivileged children. The party may send a message to the children, though that seems doubtful; they probably will be enjoying themselves too much to find any kind of

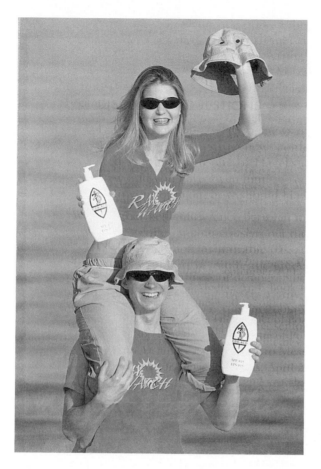

Sponsored by the Canadian Dermatology Association, the Raywatch safe-sun team holds special events on beaches in hopes of reducing the incidence of skin cancer among Canadian teens. (Courtesy of Canadian Dermatology Association and GCI Group)

message in their fun. But with a little help from the news media, the Halloween party definitely can send a message to important observers: potential members of the student group; university officials; and, perhaps most important, community members who may not have realized the contributions that college students can make to the community. One special event can help build relationships with many different important publics.

When public relations practitioners create a special event designed only to attract the attention of the news media, some practitioners call it a **pseudoevent.** However, as we discuss in QuickBreak 9.1, that term may be misleading. Public relations practitioners do not have the final say in what is news. Journalists who cover special events determine what is pseudo and what is not—and what is news and what is not.

Controlled Media

Media channels send words and images to the receiver. Some of those channels, such as newspapers and television news programs, are beyond the direct control of public relations practitioners; we can only give their editors information and hope that

QUICKBREAK 9.1

Kisses, Tea Parties, and Pseudoevents

You may have seen it live: Madonna, Britney Spears, and Christina Aguilera heating up the MTV Video Music Awards when—cover your eyes, grandparents—Madonna kissed Britney on the lips. Uproar ensued, and Fox News quickly labeled the kiss a "pseudoevent."[1]

In recent decades, *pseudoevent* has become a term meaning an activity created solely to generate publicity. Historians have suggested that the Boston Tea Party was an early example of a U.S. pseudoevent. Critics have applied the same term to such activities as marches for and against abortion legislation.

So-called pseudoevents raise at least two interesting questions: What is the dividing line between a "real" event and a publicity stunt? And does it matter?

Regarding the first question, an activity's purpose may help separate the real from the fake. The Miss America pageant began as a publicity ploy to extend the tourist season of Atlantic City. Should

that event, swimsuits and all, be compared to the Boston Tea Party? Surely the goal of the desired publicity can separate one event from another.

But a more important factor may be the news coverage itself: If journalists report an event, they have deemed it newsworthy, nothing pseudo (from the Greek word *pseudes,* or "fake") about it. And this leads to the second question: Does it really matter if we call a public relations tactic a pseudoevent?

It does matter. Credibility is essential to effective public relations. The label *pseudoevent* suggests fakery on the part of public relations practitioners and gullibility on the part of journalists who report such an activity. Those qualities are not the hallmarks of a healthy relationship or a healthy democratic society that relies on the integrity of the two professions.

As more than one scholar has written, news is what journalists say it is. Madonna's kiss made worldwide headlines—nothing *pseudo* about that.

they use it. But with other media channels, such as various forms of advertising, employee newsletters, speeches, podcasts, brochures, and web sites, we control the message. Such media are called **controlled media.** In controlled media, not only do we control the words and images; we also control when the message is sent and how often it's repeated.

Special events often use controlled media to emphasize their main point. For example, you might inaugurate your Toronto training and placement center with a speech from your company's district manager. In that speech, he or she would directly deliver the message to the factory employees: *We appreciate all you've done for us, and we'll help you find new jobs.* You might also produce and distribute a brochure that describes the extended-salary policy as well as the features of the new training and placement center.

You could also use controlled media to manage your relationships with several other affected publics. You could send letters from the chief executive officer to all your stockholders, explaining how they'll benefit from the move. You could place articles in employee newsletters in your other factories around the world, telling employees there that their jobs are not in danger. You could place advertisements in the news media in San José, Costa Rica, notifying residents of the move and seeking employment applications. Such nonproduct advertising is often considered to be part of public relations. You could even create special sections of your web site for different publics. Those messages could help you manage relationships with publics that initiate contact with you, rather than vice versa.

Uncontrolled Media

Not all media, of course, are controlled. We can't tell television and radio stations which news stories to broadcast. We can't tell bloggers what to write about our organization. Yet those media can be valuable channels in our quest to send messages to our targeted publics. By **uncontrolled media,** we often mean the news media: newspapers, radio and television stations, magazines, and online news providers. Each of those news providers employs individuals who act as gatekeepers—that is, editors who decide which stories to include and which stories to reject. Even if the gatekeepers decide to publish or broadcast our story, we can't control exactly what information they'll use or what other sources of information they'll seek out. Nor can we control when or how often they will publish or broadcast our story. In recent years, uncontrolled media have grown to include blogs, content communities, wikis, and social networks (see QuickBreak 9.2).

Furthermore, uncontrolled media can initiate a story against your wishes. For example, perhaps a television station in Toronto has learned about your factory's planned move to Costa Rica before you're ready to announce it. The station sends a camera crew to your California headquarters with a request to interview the CEO. Should the CEO tell the reporters about the move? Ideally, you've planned for this possibility, and you have a tactic ready. For example, the CEO might simply say, "We'll be making an announcement about that in a few days." That won't satisfy reporters, but at least you haven't allowed a definite message to reach your publics ahead of schedule; just as important, you haven't violated your values by lying. Because the reporters will keep digging, you'd be wise to speed up your timetable to make the announcements as soon as possible.

Not every form of media is easily classified as controlled or uncontrolled. Sometimes a channel can be both. For example, suppose that your organization's director of investor relations has a blog that invites readers to post comments. Blogging etiquette would allow her to delete obscene or abusive feedback—but not comments that simply disagreed with her. Although she can control the content of her blog and the wording of her responses to comments, she has chosen not to control the comments. Although her blog is basically a controlled medium, it actually doesn't fit neatly into either category: Some portions are controlled while others are uncontrolled.

Controlled versus Uncontrolled Media

So which are better: controlled or uncontrolled media? Neither. Each has its own advantages and disadvantages. The advantages of controlled media include your ability to select the exact words and images that get sent. A possible disadvantage is a

A Social Media Primer

The newest, hottest tactics in public relations are social media. **Social media,** according to Internet marketing company Spannerworks, are online media that have most or all of these characteristics:

- *Participation:* They encourage feedback, blurring the distinction between source and receiver in the familiar communication model (p. 263).
- *Openness:* They're accessible, with few barriers to participation.
- *Conversation:* They encourage quick, two-way communication.
- *Community:* They facilitate the formation of groups around common interests.
- *Connectedness:* They often link to other social media.

Spannerworks' research indicates that social media include five tactics: blogs, social networks, content communities, wikis, and podcasts. And your authors will add a sixth: social media news releases.[2]

1. Blogs. Short for *web log,* a blog is an online journal that offers the author's opinions about politics, entertainment, marketing—whatever. Most blogs allow and encourage reader comments, which bloggers post below their own comments. Not content with print, some bloggers have moved to video, creating *vlogs.*

2. Social networks. Chances are strong you know all about these: Facebook and MySpace are examples. Social networks link small personal web sites, often called "profiles," within a larger web site.

3. Content communities. YouTube is perhaps the most famous example of a content community. These web sites seek particular kinds of input from individuals or organizations. YouTube seeks videos

and encourages feedback. Digg seeks news stories and encourages feedback.

4. Wikis. Wikis are web sites or online multimedia documents that allow different individuals to contribute and edit the content; they're often perpetual works in progress. The word *wiki* is Hawaiian for "quick."

5. Podcasts. A podcast is a downloadable audio program—a movie review, for example. Video versions are called *vodcasts,* although increasingly *podcast* now covers both audio and video.

6. Social media news releases. Social media practitioners—especially bloggers—have made it clear they have little use for traditional news releases and media kits.[3] Although public relations practitioners can write blogs, they can also seek the third-party endorsements that other blogs and social media offer. Few social media reproduce long narratives; rather, they use snippets—a quote here, a fact there, a brief video and links to more information. Social media news releases, therefore, aren't news stories. They contain enough snippets—quotes, facts, videos, and links—to create a news story, but they leave the selection of snippets to the blogger. In that sense, social media news releases resemble b-roll in a video news release. They supply raw materials for others to arrange. For examples of social media news releases, visit www.edelman.com/news.

"People now have access to so much content and have so many ways to gather news and information that the likelihood of your . . . message penetrating through the clutter is virtually nil," says Katie Delahaye Paine, CEO of KDPaine & Partners. "Instead, if you engage the audience in a conversation and learn what the social community is looking for, you might be able to persuade them to hear your message."[4]

lack of credibility. Receivers know that you're controlling the message, and they may wonder whether you're telling the whole truth. Another disadvantage of controlled media is cost: Generally, you pay for control, especially when using advertising to send a message. Unlike public relations, advertising purchases space or time in the news media; and, within legal limits, advertising controls the content of its messages.

Credibility and costs are lesser problems with *un*controlled media. Receivers know that you're not controlling the message; that key fact tends to give the message more credibility. As we've noted before, one reason media relations is such an important part of public relations is that the news media can provide a **third-party endorsement** or **independent endorsement** of a news story. In public relations, news media are third parties—neither the sender nor the receiver—that can implicitly offer independent verification of a story's newsworthiness.

Sending messages through uncontrolled media usually costs less than doing so through controlled media. Using uncontrolled media may call for a written news release or a time-consuming meeting with a reporter, so it's not fair to say that uncontrolled media are free—but they generally are significantly less expensive than controlled media.

The disadvantage of uncontrolled media is clearly stated in their name: *uncontrolled.* Public relations practitioners can do their best to ethically influence the messages sent through uncontrolled media, but ultimate control of the message rests with others.

Public relations campaigns generally use both controlled and uncontrolled media. The trade-off is that controlled media ensure precise messages; uncontrolled media are less expensive and offer stronger credibility.

Tactics and Traditional Publics

Public relations tactics range from low-tech, such as face-to-face meetings, to high-tech, such as wikis. However, successful public relations tactics have several qualities in common:

- Successful tactics are part of a written, approved public relations plan that is tied to an organization's values-based mission.
- Successful tactics target one public at a time. What works for one public may be completely inappropriate for another. However, if a tactic would be effective with more than one primary public, using it for all the appropriate publics could save time and money. A newsworthy special event, for example, could target event participants while also targeting other publics through the intervening public of the news media.
- Successful tactics are based on research about the targeted public's values, interests, and preferred channels of communication.
- Successful tactics send a clear message that targets a public's values and interests even as it strives to achieve an organization's objective. In other words, successful

tactics try to create win-win situations in which both the sender and the receiver benefit.

■ Successful tactics are specific. As we noted in the previous chapter on planning, a *strategy* is a general description of a group of communications actions—face-to-face meetings, for example. A related *tactic,* however, would propose the details of a specific face-to-face meeting: a question-and-answer session with an employee group, for example.

■ Successful tactics are evaluated as they're performed and after they're executed.

It would be impossible—and unwise—to create a list of standard public relations tactics to fit every situation. Every public relations challenge is different and requires special, even sometimes unique, tactics. But there are traditional tactics that every practitioner should know. Because successful tactics are directed toward specific publics, we'll organize a discussion of traditional tactics around the publics that they might target. Table 9.1 presents a capsule summary of the discussion that follows, beginning with a list of social media tactics.

Employees

We'll start with employees, who usually constitute one of every organization's most important publics. If employees aren't well informed and motivated, the quality of an organization's relationships with other publics may not matter; the organization is in danger of collapse.

Face-to-Face Meetings. Virtually every study of internal communications shows that employees' favorite channel for receiving information about their organizations is face-to-face meetings with their immediate supervisors. To use this channel, you may need to work with your organization's human resources or personnel department to create communication training programs for supervisors. Perhaps your organization could use the approach known as MBWA—management by walking around. Managers who aren't "chained" to their desks can initiate spontaneous face-to-face meetings with employees. However, as more organizations allow employees to work at home and "telecommute" by computer, organizing face-to-face meetings with immediate supervisors is becoming more difficult.

Newsletters. Newsletters are generally inexpensive, and they have the virtue of putting a message in writing so that employees can review it. Newsletters should be frequent; if they appear infrequently, they run the risk of delivering old news—which means, of course, that they won't be read. Newsletters needn't be limited to paper. Online newsletters can include videos, sound clips, links to other sites, and an archive of former issues.

Magazines. Because they're more difficult than newsletters to produce, magazines usually aren't used to communicate breaking news stories to employees. Instead, magazines contain less time-sensitive stories, such as broad overviews of the organization's values and goals, stories about key employees, and updates on continuing issues. Some

TABLE 9.1   Traditional Tactics for Traditional Publics

Social Media

blogs

wikis

content communities

social networks

podcasts/vodcasts

Employees

face-to-face meetings

newsletters

magazines

videos

bulletin boards

speeches

intranets

e-mail

instant messaging

special events

News Media

news releases

media kits

fact sheets

backgrounders

photo opportunity
sheets

media advisories

pitches (letters, e-mail,
and telephone)

video news releases

actualities

news conferences

public service
announcements

guest editorials and
commentaries

letters to the editor

interviews

satellite media tours

stories for trade or association
magazines

Investors

newsletters

magazines

letters

annual meetings

annual reports

web sites

facility tours

conference calls

news releases to financial
news media

media advisories to financial
news media

webcasts

Community Groups

volunteering

donations

sponsorships

cause marketing

speeches

open houses and tours

face-to-face meetings

Governments

lobbies

grassroots lobbying

political action committees

soft money

disclosure documents

Customers

product-oriented news releases

product-oriented media kits

special events

open houses and tours

responses to customer contacts

cell-phone text messaging

Constituents (Voters)

letters

newsletters

news releases

media advisories

news conferences

speeches

face-to-face meetings

web sites

responses to constituent contacts

Businesses

stories in trade magazines

extranets

organizations mail their magazines to employees' homes, often in hopes that other family members will read them and feel goodwill toward the organization. Like newsletters, magazines can also exist online.

Videos. A message-bearing video can be used in several ways. Special videos or video newsletters might be shown on monitors in employee cafeterias and break rooms. Online videos and DVDs can easily reach employees around the world.

Bulletin Boards. Low-tech doesn't mean ineffective. Some organizations use controlled-access bulletin boards—often with the messages under a locked glass cover—to deliver daily news to employees. Some large organizations place the cafeteria's daily lunch menu on the bulletin board. Employees checking out the daily desserts just may stop and read other important announcements. Bulletin boards can help organizations meet legal requirements to post information regarding new labor laws or changes in employee benefits.

Speeches. Employees generally like to see and be seen by the big boss. If an organization's leader is a good speaker, a face-to-face speech containing an important message can be highly effective as well as complimentary to an organization's employees. Such a speech means that the leader cares enough to look employees in the eye and tell them about the future of their organization. Copies of speeches can be distributed to specific employees; short speeches and excerpts of longer speeches can also be reprinted in employee newsletters and posted online.

Intranets. An **intranet** is an organization's controlled-access internal computer network. A well-designed intranet not only provides e-mail processing; it includes an internal web site with department descriptions, links to other web sites, an area for the latest news, and maybe even a social network similar to Facebook. As noted above, it also can contain newsletters, magazines, and videos.

E-Mail. According to recent studies, **e-mail** usage has soared to become organizations' most-used employee communications tactic. However, employees still consider face-to-face meetings more effective.[5] Employees report feeling overwhelmed by the volume of e-mail—and they know that it allows supervisors to relay bad news without the awkwardness of a face-to-face meeting. E-mail's convenience can also be its danger: Misunderstandings—or worse—can arise if one doesn't think before posting a message.

Instant Messaging. As most teenagers and young adults know, **instant messaging** is a network-based computer system that allows several individuals to instantly exchange typed messages with one another. For example, five employees in different locations could conduct an instant messaging meeting on an important project. All five employees could see and respond to messages from one another. As with e-mail, users of instant messaging should not sacrifice clarity and diplomacy for speed and convenience.

Special Events. Special events for employees can range from company picnics to special nights at sporting events to more complex tactics, such as the hypothetical training and placement center for your former employees in Toronto. Remember: controlled media such as brochures can often emphasize the message sent by a special event. For example, a groundbreaking ceremony for your new factory in Costa Rica would be a special event for government officials and the news media. A short speech—ideally in Spanish—by your CEO could be a controlled medium within that special event to help ensure that participants and observers receive the message that your company pledges to be a good corporate citizen.

QUICK CHECK

1. What is a public relations tactic? In what stage of the public relations process do tactics play a role?
2. What's the difference between a message and a channel? When are they the same? When are they different?
3. What are the differences between controlled media and uncontrolled media?
4. What are social media?

News Media

Public relations practitioners generally target the news media as an intervening public—that is, as a go-between public that helps carry a message to a primary public. To place a message in the news media, practitioners use a variety of tactics to appeal to the media's so-called gatekeepers: the editors and producers who decide which stories to report and which to reject.

News Releases. The **news release** is one of the most important yet misused documents in all of public relations. A news release, ideally, is an objective, straightforward,

---

QUICKBREAK 9.3

Beating the Odds: Successful News Releases

Studies show that journalists have a favorite place for 92 to 98 percent of the news releases they receive: their wastebaskets, online or otherwise.

That's the bad news. The good news is that a tiny minority of well-written news releases do succeed. But what makes a good news release?

Journalism professor Linda Morton has conducted several national studies of what journalists seek in news releases, and she offers this advice:[6]

- Write in a simple style. Use short sentences and paragraphs and common words.

- Focus your news release on one of the four topics that succeed best with editors: consumer information, a coming event, interesting research, or a timely issue.

- Localize the news release. Practitioners often call such news releases "hometowners," because they clearly target an editor's specific audience.

- Above all else, serve the editor's audience. Research the information needs of each editor's audience, find a way in which your organization can address those needs, and then write an objective news story on that crucial link.

Morton's research shows that public relations practitioners who follow these basic guidelines place almost one-third of their news releases. That's about 700 percent better than the success rate of practitioners who ignore the needs of journalists and their audiences.

Page 1—or the wastebasket? You can make the difference.

unbiased news story that a public relations practitioner writes and distributes to appropriate news media. For example, in our Canada to Costa Rica scenario, you would issue news releases to news media in Costa Rica, in Toronto, in your hometown in California, and in any other cities where your organization has operations. In addition, because you have stockholders, you would issue news releases to the major financial news media around the world. News-release distribution services such as PR Newswire and BusinessWire could help circulate the news releases, and you could post the stories on your organization's web site as well.

Why do we say that news releases are among the most misused documents in public relations? Studies show that gatekeepers throw away more than 90 percent of the news releases they receive. Many news releases commit one or both of two deadly sins: They have no local interest—that is, no appeal to a particular gatekeeper's audience—and/or they're too promotional; they lack the strict objectivity that characterizes good news reporting. An effective news release uses its headline and first paragraph to show a gatekeeper that it contains local interest. For example, your news release to the Toronto news media would be slightly different from your California news release. And far from being promotional, the information about your organization would sound as if it were written by an objective reporter, not a public relations practitioner.

Though news releases go to print, broadcast, online news media, and social media, such as blogs, most are written in newspaper style. Nonprint news media take such news releases and, if they use them, rewrite them in their own formats (see Chapter 10). The news media rarely publish or broadcast news releases word for word. If they use a news release, they generally rewrite it, often shortening it or including additional sources. Bloggers have expressed their preference for social media news releases (see QuickBreak 9.2) rather than regular news releases.

News releases reach the news media in a variety of ways. They can be mailed, faxed, e-mailed, posted online, or distributed through services such as PR Newswire. One of your authors once received a news release printed on the label of a full bottle of champagne (which gives new meaning to the concept of social media).

Media Kits. Public relations practitioners use media kits to publicize complex stories that have many newsworthy elements. For example, television networks use media kits to publicize their upcoming programming seasons. A **media kit** packages at least one news release with other supporting documents. Two of the most common types of supporting documents are called *fact sheets* and *backgrounders*. A **fact sheet** is usually a what–who–when–where–why–how breakdown of the news release. Unlike the news release, however, the fact sheet is not written as a story; instead, it's just a well-organized list of the facts. Why include a fact sheet when the media kit already has a news release? Some journalists don't want to see your version of the story; they think you're biased. They want just the facts, and the fact sheet delivers those.

A **backgrounder** is a supplement to the news release. It contains useful background information on, for example, a person or organization mentioned in the news release. Like news releases, backgrounders usually are written as stories. Unlike news releases, however, backgrounders aren't news stories. Some feature testimonials from satisfied customers. Many others read like biographies. For example, you might

Media Kit Morningstar Communications created this attention-grabbing media kit for CommunityAmerica Credit Union's "Stuff the Bus" campaign, which donates school supplies to needy children. (Courtesy of Morningstar Communications Company and CommunityAmerica Credit Union)

choose to send media kits to Costa Rican news media so that they can learn more about your company. Your news release might announce a groundbreaking ceremony for the new factory. Your backgrounders might include a short history of the company that expands the brief description contained in your news release. Another backgrounder might be a biography of the CEO that, again, expands the briefer identification of that individual contained in your news release.

Media kits can have other documents. If the media kit is publicizing a visually attractive event, such as a groundbreaking ceremony for your new factory in Costa Rica, you might include a **photo opportunity sheet.** Photo opportunity sheets aren't meant for publication, so they can include a little bit of fact-based promotional writing designed to spark a gatekeeper's interest. Photo opportunity sheets tell what, who, when, and where. They can include special instructions for photographers as well as maps showing the location of the event.

Media kits can also include brochures, product samples, and any other document or item that can help gatekeepers make well-informed decisions about the newsworthiness of the story.

Media kits ordinarily are mailed to the news media. Increasingly, entire media kits—including news releases, backgrounders, fact sheets, videos, and photographs—are placed on **CD-ROMs** or **DVDs** and distributed to the news media.

Media Advisories. Some newsworthy stories take shape so quickly that there's not time to write and distribute a news release. In such situations, public relations practitioners often issue a **media advisory.** Media advisories are also issued to remind the news media about events they may want to cover. Like a fact sheet, a media advisory isn't written as a story; instead, it simply lists the necessary information about what, who, when, where, why, and how. Media advisories are generally faxed or e-mailed to the news media.

Pitches (letters, e-mail, and telephone). Pitches, in certain circumstances, replace news releases. A **pitch** is a persuasive message to a journalist, using a letter, an e-mail, or a phone call to describe an interesting story that may not be important, timely news. Pitches often promote softer, human-interest stories that don't merit the "hard news" approach of a news release yet remain newsworthy and would help make a favorable impression on targeted publics. Unlike news releases, which are sent to several news media at the same time, pitches usually target one news medium at a time. In other words, they offer exclusive stories to an individual news outlet. Building and maintaining good relationships with individual journalists is a key to successful pitches.

Video News Releases. Video news releases, commonly called **VNRs,** are distributed to television stations and online news media. Video news releases are designed to look like television news stories. Like news releases, VNRs ideally are finished products; they're ready to broadcast. However, most VNRs include a section called **b-roll,** which contains unedited video footage of the news story. Many television stations prefer to create their own version of the story, using b-roll instead of the finished VNR. B-roll, they believe, gives them more control over the presentation of the story.

VNRs are distributed via videocassette, DVD, web sites, and satellite. A VNR can be beamed to a satellite at a particular time and downloaded by interested television stations, which have been notified, often by media advisories, about the timing and the correct satellite coordinates. Unlike print news releases, VNRs are expensive to produce and distribute. They should be used only for highly visual, highly newsworthy stories.

Actualities. Actualities are sound bites for radio stations and web sites. They're catchy quotes and sometimes accompany written news releases. Actualities can be distributed via satellite, web sites, CDs, telephone links, and even old-fashioned cassette tapes.

News Conferences. News conferences are like dynamite. They should be used only when necessary—and even then with caution. A **news conference** is a scheduled meeting between an organization's representative(s) and the news media. Your organization should consider scheduling a news conference when—and *only* when—three conditions exist:

1. You have a highly newsworthy breaking story. A breaking story is extremely timely; it can't wait on a news release, media kit, or VNR.
2. It is advantageous to meet with reporters as a group, instead of individually.
3. You know that journalists will be glad they came; the story is that good.

News Conference In the aftermath of the April 2007 campus shootings, Virginia Tech President Charles Steger used a news conference to convey information to a variety of important publics. (Photo by Melanie Blanding/*New York Times*. Copyright 2007 The New York Times Company. Reprinted with permission.)

If your story meets the above three criteria, no problem; your news conference is a productive media relations tactic. But if your story *doesn't* meet those criteria, get ready for trouble: Either journalists will be angry that you didn't use a different communication tactic that shows more respect for their time—or they simply won't come, damaging your reputation as a public relations practitioner. If journalists can get the same information in another form—such as a VNR or a media kit—without being disappointed, use that other form instead of a news conference.

News conferences should be used with caution because they are the ultimate experience in uncontrolled media. You can try to set the agenda with an opening statement, but following that, reporters generally get to ask questions—and there is no guarantee that they'll ask questions that you want to answer or are prepared to answer.

When a news conference definitely is the media relations tactic to use, however, consider these guidelines:

- Invite news media to the news conference with media advisories and follow-up telephone calls.

- Schedule the news conference strategically. By this we mean that you should balance your organization's interests against those of the news media. The news media generally prefer a mid-morning schedule. That's the best time for TV journalists who want to broadcast the story on the evening news, and it also benefits newspaper journalists with late-afternoon deadlines for the next morning's paper. A mid-*afternoon* news conference, on the other hand, limits immediate media coverage of the story to your organization's message; it reduces journalists' time for investigation. In scheduling a news conference, you must balance the needs of your organization against the value of a good relationship with the news media.

- Rehearse your presenters. Ask them the toughest questions that reporters may pose, and help them develop honest, credible answers.

- Have very few presenters—ideally, just one. Don't muddle the news conference with several speakers.

- Hold the news conference in a location that's easily accessible and has plenty of parking spaces.

- Hold the news conference in a room that has plenty of electrical outlets for television crews and photographers.

- Begin with a prepared statement; have copies available. After that, accept questions from journalists. Avoid answering, "No comment." If you can't or won't answer a question, explain why.

- Don't let the news conference run more than one hour.

- Distribute media kits that reinforce and supplement the news story.

- Film and record the conference to provide video- and audiotapes to TV and radio stations that couldn't attend. These recordings also allow you to keep a record of exactly what was said.

Public Service Announcements. **Public service announcements,** often called **PSAs,** are advertisements created by nonprofit organizations to publicize their services. The news media do not charge for PSAs as they do for commercial announcements. PSAs for the broadcast news media exist in a variety of formats. A broadcast PSA might be simply a short script for a radio announcer to read, or it might be produced like a commercial and distributed on CDs or DVDs. Radio and television stations broadcast PSAs to meet legal public service requirements. Just as with news releases, however, there's no guarantee that the media will use your PSA.

PSAs also target the print media, where they're sometimes called *public service advertisements* or *public service messages.* In newspapers and magazines, PSAs are similar to print advertisements. Organizations provide them in standard advertising sizes and "camera ready," which means ready to be downloaded into the digital prepress version of the magazine.

PSAs also exist for web sites. In the United States, the Ad Council, a group of corporations and other organizations that creates and distributes PSAs, offers animated graphics and thin horizontal online advertisements called "banners" that promote Smokey Bear, seat-belt safety, education, and other social needs. Organizations wanting to support those causes can, with permission, download a banner from the Ad Council's web site and place it on their own web site.

Guest Editorials/Commentaries. Most news media, especially newspapers, are willing to consider guest editorials or commentaries on issues important to the medium's audience. In our Canada to Costa Rica scenario, for example, you might want to consider having your chief executive officer prepare an editorial for a Toronto newspaper. The editorial could defend the move, describing the actions your company took to try to stay in Toronto and explaining why those efforts failed. In reality, the CEO might ask you to write the editorial. He or she might then make a few changes, and the editorial would be sent to the newspaper under the CEO's name.

Unlike news releases, guest editorials or commentaries aren't sent to several different news media at once. Instead, news media are approached one at a time and asked whether they would be interested in such an editorial. Editorials are offered as exclusives. Editors and producers can be contacted by a business letter that's quickly followed up with a phone call.

A related tactic involves meeting with a news medium's editorial board. That board doesn't exist to do favors for your organization, but it should be interested in fairness and fact-based opinions. Some news media have community editorial boards in which selected nonjournalists help a news medium formulate the editorials it publishes or broadcasts. Members of such boards occasionally write the editorials themselves.

Letters to the Editor. Like a guest editorial or commentary, a letter to the editor allows a member of your organization to express an opinion on an important issue. Unlike an editorial, however, a letter to the editor doesn't require you to contact the news medium first. You simply send a well-written letter or e-mail message and hope for the best. Though most of us think of sending letters to print media such as newspapers and magazines, radio stations and television stations also sometimes read, on air, letters from members of their audiences. For example, the show *All Things Considered,* on National Public Radio, reads messages from its listeners every Thursday afternoon.

Interviews. Yet another way for your organization to publicize its point of view is to offer a high-ranking official to different news media for interviews. Occasionally, interviews for television stations can involve a tactic called a **satellite media tour** (SMT). During a satellite media "tour," your organization's official actually never leaves a local television studio. Instead, he or she links one at a time, via satellite, with television stations around the world for live or recorded interviews. In the Canada to Costa Rica scenario, for example, your organization's CEO could offer individual interviews to the major television stations in Costa Rica without ever leaving California. Satellite media tours often are publicized by means of media advisories or phone calls to specific television stations.

Stories for Trade or Association Magazines. If your organization is known for its expertise in a particular area, trade or association magazines may well be interested in publishing a story written by one of your experts. **Trade magazines** target members of particular trades and professions: construction companies, farmers, veterinarians, and so on. **Association magazines** are similar, being a benefit of belonging to an organization such as the American Library Association. If your organization offers a product or service that might benefit members of a trade, profession, or association, you can contact these magazines' editors with story ideas. You can also offer your experts should the magazine editors have story ideas for which they're seeking writers. Unlike news releases, such stories are not distributed to several magazines at once. Instead, the story is an arrangement between your organization and one particular magazine.

Investors

Investors are an important traditional public in public relations. By purchasing stock, they represent a source of capitalization for an organization—and because they own stock, they technically are the organization's owners. As we note in Chapter 4, investors include individual stockholders; institutional investors, such as the huge California Public Employees Retirement System; investment analysts; mutual fund managers; and the financial news media. We now know the traditional ways to communicate with the news media, but what are the standard tactics for other members of the investment community? A warning before we proceed: As we discuss in Chapter 15, communications with the investment community are closely regulated by such organizations as the Securities and Exchange Commission and the major stock exchanges.

Web Sites. Web sites are an excellent way for companies to communicate with their investors. Live **webcasts** regarding important announcements can be broadcast. Stock prices can be updated continuously; e-mail links can be provided; news releases can be indexed; video tours can be offered; the text of recent speeches can be featured; and the annual report (p. 281) can be included, as can the quarterly updates filed with the SEC. A good, interactive web site can function as a daily newsletter for investors, investment analysts, and the financial news media.

Newsletters and Magazines. Some companies have periodic publications that they distribute to investors. Such publications can discuss company goals, changes in leadership, new product lines, or anything else that might affect the performance of the company's stock. The publications also can steer investors to the company's web site or its investor relations office for more current information.

Letters. Databases allow companies to send personal letters to stockholders, addressing them by name and noting the number of shares they have as well as how much they're earning in dividends. These letters can be more intimate than comparatively impersonal newsletters and magazines. A company might use personal letters for sensitive situations, as in an effort to get minor shareholders either to buy more of the company's stock or to sell their few shares back to the company.

Annual Meetings. The Securities and Exchange Commission requires every U.S.-based company that sells stock to hold an annual meeting for its stockholders. Most stock exchanges also require annual meetings as a prerequisite for membership. Not only stockholders but investment analysts and members of the financial news media attend annual meetings. The **annual meeting** can be an excellent channel to investors; it allows a company to use controlled media tactics such as speeches, videos, and printed materials.

Not every element of an annual meeting is controlled, however. Question-and-answer periods with investors can rattle even the toughest executives. Some investors, known as gadflies, buy a few shares of a company's stock just to earn the right to attend the annual meeting, where they ask confrontational questions. In the Canada to Costa Rica scenario, for example, you should prepare for the possibility that former employees or other residents of Toronto who own shares in your company may attend your next annual meeting and launch emotional attacks on your rationale for the move.

Annual Reports. Like annual meetings, annual reports are required by the Securities and Exchange Commission and by most stock exchanges. Anyone who owns even a single share of stock in a company receives its annual report, which often looks like a glossy magazine but can also exist in a second, complementary form such as a video, DVD, or web site. By law, an **annual report** features recent financial information, a year-to-year comparison of financial figures, a description of the organization's upper-level management, and a letter from the company's leader that discusses the organization's health and direction.

Annual reports are also sent to investment analysts, mutual fund managers, the major financial news media, and any potential investor who requests a copy. Many organizations post their annual reports on their web sites.

VALUES STATEMENT 9.1

Johnson & Johnson

Johnson & Johnson is a manufacturer and provider of health-care products and services. The company was founded in 1886 and is headquartered in New Brunswick, New Jersey.

Our Credo:

We believe our first responsibility is to the doctors, nurses and patients, to the mothers and fathers and all others who use our products and services. In meeting their needs everything we do must be of high quality. We must constantly strive to reduce our costs in order to maintain reasonable prices. Customers' orders must be serviced promptly and accurately. Our suppliers and distributors must have an opportunity to make a fair profit.

We are responsible to our employees, the men and women who work with us throughout the world. Everyone must be considered as an individual. We must respect their dignity and recognize their merit. They must have a sense of security in their jobs. Compensation must be fair and adequate, and working conditions

clean, orderly and safe. We must be mindful of ways to help our employees fulfill their family responsibilities.

We are responsible to the communities in which we live and work and to the world community as well. We must be good citizens—support good works and charities and bear our fair share of taxes. We must encourage civic improvements and better health and education. We must maintain in good order the property we are privileged to use, protecting the environment and natural resources.

Our final responsibility is to our stockholders. Business must make a sound profit. We must experiment with new ideas. Research must be carried on, innovative programs developed and mistakes paid for. New equipment must be purchased, new facilities provided and new products launched. Reserves must be created to provide for adverse times. When we operate according to these principles, the stockholders should realize a fair return.

—"Our Credo," Johnson & Johnson web site

Other Tactics for Investment Analysts, Mutual Fund Managers, and the Financial News Media. Investment analysts, mutual fund managers, and financial journalists don't like to be surprised. They require current information on a company and immediate updates about any events that might affect the company's financial performance. Investor relations practitioners can ensure rapid, frequent communication through such tactics as live webcasts, factory or other facility tours, telephone conference calls, e-mail updates, and letters. News releases and media advisories can be distributed to the financial news media, often through services such as PR Newswire and BusinessWire, which can electronically transfer these documents to news media throughout the world. Often, news releases regarding important developments are required by the SEC and the major stock markets (see Chapter 15).

1. How is a news release different from a media advisory? From a backgrounder? From a fact sheet? From a VNR?
2. What advice would you have for a friend who wants to hold a news conference?
3. What is an annual report? What publics does it target?

Community Groups

Community groups include churches, schools, professional organizations, clubs, chambers of commerce, and other local groups whose values somehow intersect with those of an organization. Relationship-building tactics for such groups can be high-tech; more often, however, community relations tactics fall into the roll-up-your-sleeves-and-get-involved category.

Volunteering. Many organizations encourage employees to volunteer at schools, churches, hospitals, senior centers, libraries, and other important local institutions. Some organizations allow time off for volunteer activities, and others make cash donations to community groups based on how many volunteer hours their employees donate. Volunteerism is a powerful, rewarding way to build positive relationships with community groups.

Donations and Sponsorships. After organizations have rolled up their sleeves and volunteered, they sometimes open their wallets and donate. Sometimes those donations take the form of sponsorships—for example, paying the bills for a local literacy program's fund-raising carnival. Such generosity can create goodwill for an organization, but letting someone else spend your money sometimes leads to unpleasant surprises. Be sure to specify in writing exactly what the donated money is for, and then monitor the situation to ensure that your donation was spent correctly. Instead of money, some organizations donate goods or services or even the expertise of their employees. For example, a community bank might lend a tax expert to a local nonprofit organization to help it prepare its tax returns.

Cause Marketing. Organizations sometimes devote money, goods, services, and volunteerism to particular social needs, such as literacy or cancer research. In a sense, the organizations adopt a particular social need as their primary philanthropy. Such a community relations tactic is called **cause marketing.** Like special events, cause marketing often addresses more than one public. As a form of social responsibility (Chapter 6), cause marketing certainly addresses people affected by the social need; most organizations that adopt a cause genuinely want to help. But the tactic also is designed to create goodwill among government officials, consumers, current and potential employees, and other important publics that can help the organization achieve its goals.

Speeches. Professional and civic groups such as the Kiwanis Club, the Rotary Club, and the League of Women Voters often seek community leaders to speak on current issues at weekly or monthly meetings. If an organization has a stake in a local issue, a speech followed by a question-and-answer session can promote the organization's point of view and collect information about how other people feel.

Open Houses/Tours. Organizations that produce interesting goods or services can build goodwill in the community by sponsoring open houses and offering tours of company facilities. Open houses and tours often provide opportunities to use controlled media such as speeches, brochures, and videos. They also provide opportunities to distribute so-called specialty advertising products such as coffee mugs, Frisbees, ball caps, and other items that feature an organization's name and logo.

Face-to-Face Meetings. Community groups sometimes are activist groups. For example, an environmental group in Costa Rica may wonder how your company's new factory will dispose of toxic waste. At the first sign that such a group is studying your organization—or even before—it's vital that you open lines of communication with its members, ideally through face-to-face meetings. Many activist groups gather their research before they assume a firm public stance; in other words, they are *aware publics* (p. 96). If you can demonstrate your organization's good intentions before the activist group solidifies its position, you may defuse a crisis before it begins.

In community relations, face-to-face meetings need not be limited to activist groups. An organization can conduct such meetings with a variety of neutral or friendly community groups in hopes of paving the way for alliances or partnerships on future problems or opportunities. Such a process is called **coalition building.**

Governments

Governmental action at any level—federal, state, county, or city—can profoundly affect an organization. Public relations practitioners thus use a portfolio of tactics to make their organizations' voices heard in the halls of government.

Lobbies and Lobbyists. A **lobby** is a special-interest group that openly attempts to influence government actions, especially federal and state legislative processes. One of the most effective lobbies in recent decades, for example, has been AARP, formerly the American Association of Retired Persons, which advances the interests of people age 50 and older. A *lobbyist* is someone who, acting on behalf of a special-interest group, tries to influence various forms of government regulation. Lobbies and lobbyists generally pass persuasive information along to government officials. They host educational events for officials and their staffs, and they often respond to government officials' requests for information on particular issues.

At the federal level in the United States, lobbies and lobbyists are regulated by the Lobbying Disclosure Act, which mandates that people who are paid to lobby Congress or the executive branch of the federal government must register with the government. Paid lobbyists must specify whom they represent and how much they are being paid.

Grassroots Lobbying. Not all lobbyists must register with the federal government. If you write a letter to your congressional representatives asking them to increase funding for student loans, you're acting as a lobbyist for a special interest, but you need not register. Such informal, infrequent, "unprofessional" lobbying is often called **grassroots lobbying,** especially if you're acting with others to show legislators broad support for your opinion. Because grassroots lobbying is the "voice of the people," it can be highly influential with elected government officials.

Political Action Committees. **Political action committees,** often called **PACs,** have one purpose: to donate money to candidates and political parties. Two types of PACS exist: separate segregated funds (SSFs) and nonconnected committees. SSFs are sponsored by corporations, labor unions, special-interest groups, and other formal organizations. They can collect voluntary donations only from members. Nonconnected committees are not sponsored by groups and can collect money from almost anyone. Both kinds of PACs must register with the federal government if they donate to candidates for federal offices. State governments have similar laws.

Soft Money. So-called **soft money** was money donated to political parties to be spent not on individual candidates but on noncandidate projects such as get-out-the-vote drives, voter education, and issues-oriented advertising. Critics of soft money contended that political parties often illegally used it to support candidates. In 2002, Congress passed legislation that stopped the flow of soft money to political parties. Proponents and opponents of soft money alike attacked the legislation. Proponents claimed it violated First Amendment guarantees of freedom of speech. Opponents of soft money claimed the legislation left open many loopholes, including hefty donations to national political conventions, local branches of political parties, and special-interest groups. Proponents and opponents of soft money also agree that the legislation will change in the future. Public relations practitioners who specialize in government relations are well advised to monitor the legality of soft money.

Disclosure Documents. In the United States, companies that sell stock must, by law, communicate with the government. Often, investor relations practitioners help write and file a comprehensive annual report—called a Form 10-K—with the federal

Securities and Exchange Commission. Other SEC forms that practitioners often help prepare or review are the Form 10-Q (quarterly financial report) and the Form 8-K (used to announce an event that might affect the price of the company's stock). Disclosure law is covered more fully in Chapter 15.

Customers

Customer relations is where public relations overlaps with marketing (see Chapter 13). Marketing, simply put, is the process of getting a customer to buy your product or service. Most marketing tactics lie outside the boundaries of traditional public relations; marketing tactics include advertising, direct-mail letters, coupons and other sales promotions, and face-to-face sales encounters. But public relations can add several tactics to what is called the *marketing mix*.

Product-Oriented News Releases and Media Kits. We discussed news releases and media kits earlier in this chapter. When news releases or media kits focus on a newsworthy aspect of a product or service, they target customers and are part of the marketing mix. The news media become an intervening public between an organization and the customers it's hoping to reach.

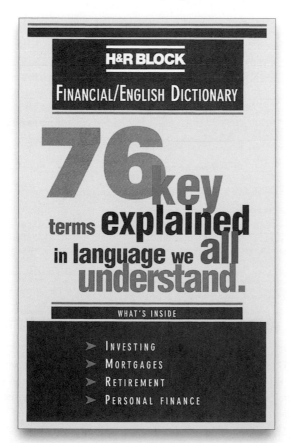

Brochure A popular brochure by H&R Block, a financial services company, builds relationships by addressing customers' often-insufficient knowledge of financial and tax terms. (Courtesy of H&R Block)

Special Events. There's no telling who the next fictional hero for young readers will be. We've already seen a wizard named Harry and a school principal who can become Captain Underpants. One thing is certain: Whoever or whatever the next heroes are, costumed actors who portray them will visit our bookstores. Such a visit is a special event, which is any out-of-the-ordinary occurrence designed to attract customers.

Open Houses and Tours. An organization with interesting products or services or unusual production technology can attract customers by inviting them to tour its facilities. During open houses and tours, customers often get to sample or test products or services. Wineries, for example, often offer tours and free samples to visitors of legal drinking age.

Responses to Customer Contacts. Smart organizations respond quickly to phone calls, letters, and e-mail messages from customers and potential customers. Such two-way communication not only builds customer loyalty; it also helps an organization know what its customers are thinking.

Cell-Phone Text Messaging. Organizations can use **text messaging** to notify customers of special offers—even using global positioning devices and satellites to contact customers as they near favorite stores.

Constituents (Voters)

As we noted in Chapter 4, many organizations try to influence the legislative process by building relationships with eligible voters. But for public relations practitioners

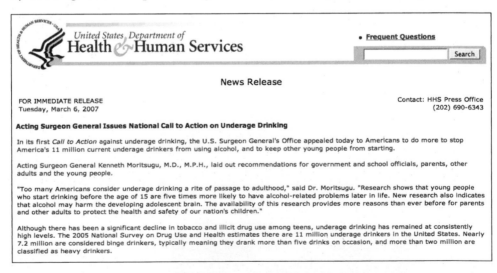

Online News Release The United States Department of Health and Human Services used news releases to help launch its "Call to Action," a program targeting underage drinking. For a Spanish-language version of this news release, see page 453. (Courtesy of the Department of Health and Human Services)

QuickBreak 9.4

Sticky Situations

As we said earlier, a tactic is a fusion of message and channel. Much of this chapter focuses on traditional and social media channels. But what about messages? We know they should be values-driven and goal-oriented. But what makes a message effective? What makes it memorable? What makes it, in a word, "sticky"?

Brothers Chip and Dan Heath, authors of the book *Made to Stick: Why Some Ideas Survive and Others Die,* believe they know the answer. Their research shows that a sticky, memorable concept comes from having one or more of six qualities: simple, unexpected, concrete, credible, emotional, and story. Bonus points if you see the acronym SUCCES(S) there.[7] (Maybe the last "S" can be for *sticky.*)

If that memory trick seems too cute, *Time* magazine noted that the Heath brothers support their

findings with "an avalanche of social-science research."[8] The Heaths maintain that with a little work, you can take your ordinary message and make it sticky by seeking the elements of SUCCESS.

The book illustrates successful stickiness with specific examples, among them the famous anti-litter "Don't Mess with Texas" campaign and presidential candidate Bill Clinton's "It's the Economy, Stupid" sign to help him stay on message. Then there's the stickiest idea of all: Jared, the slim spokesman for the Subway restaurant chain. Jared's tale of weight loss by eating fast food scores a six of six on the SUCCESS scale.

So what makes a message effective? The explanation gets a little sticky.

employed by democratically elected governments, voters may be the most important public of all. We're already familiar with many of the tactics that government practitioners use to build productive relationships between elected or appointed officials and their constituents: interactive web sites; letters and newsletters; news releases, media advisories, and news conferences; speeches; and face-to-face meetings.

Although every organization should respond quickly to letters, phone calls, and e-mail messages from members of important publics, such responses are particularly significant in the relationship between elected or appointed government officials and voters. A quick, personalized reply, even if a more detailed follow-up response is necessary, is one of the most important tactics in constituent relations. These responses encourage constituents to feel connected to and valued by their representatives. Members of Congress, for example, have staff members who spend the majority of their working hours addressing constituent concerns. Contacts from constituents can also be an excellent source of research data regarding issues that concern potential voters.

Businesses

Business-to-business communication is big business. If organizations are to reach their goals, they must use a variety of tactics to build relationships with other businesses that have needed resources: suppliers and business customers, for example. Just like tactics for individual customers, business-to-business tactics sometimes more closely resemble marketing than public relations. Such tactics include personal selling, price discounts, trade shows, and direct-mail advertising. But some business-to-business tactics are pure public relations.

Extranets. **Extranets** are controlled-access computer networks, similar to intranets. At a minimum, they usually include web sites and e-mail capabilities. Unlike intranets, extranets are for businesses outside the host business. For example, winemaker Robert Mondavi purchases NASA satellite photos of vineyards and posts them on its extranet so that its independent grape suppliers can spot problems before they become serious.[9]

Magazines. Businesses that offer products to other businesses sometimes publish glossy magazines with articles that feature product applications. Targeted customers receive the magazines at no charge.

Stories in Trade Magazines. Businesses can attract new customers as well as new suppliers by writing and submitting stories to trade, or professional, magazines. Often, such stories present a company official as an expert on a particular topic. Many magazines focus on trades or professions such as law, carpentry, and farming. Those magazines accept and publish well-written stories of interest to their readers. Such magazines also publish news releases, which generally are shorter than featured stories and do not include a byline.

Accomplishing the Tactics

Most of the research has been done. The plan has been written and approved. Now it's time to carry out the tactics. Though this section appears near the end of the chapter, it is, in reality, the center of gravity, the focus of this chapter. Simply selecting a tactic does not create communication. Rather, communication begins when the tactic is executed. High standards are essential at this point of the public relations process. No amount of research or planning can overcome sloppy communication efforts. Public relations practitioners, therefore, tend to stress six key factors as they execute a plan's tactics: delegation, deadlines, quality control, communication within the team, communication with clients and supervisors, and constant evaluation.

1. *Delegation.* Delegate the responsibility for a tactic's execution to a particular individual. With every tactic in a written plan, include the responsible individual's name. For example, in the Canada to Costa Rica scenario, your plan would charge one individual with the responsibility of creating a job-training and placement center. That individual wouldn't have to act alone—but he or she, ultimately, would bear the responsibility of creating the center. Naming names in this manner helps ensure successful results: No one wants to be the highly visible manager of a failed tactic.

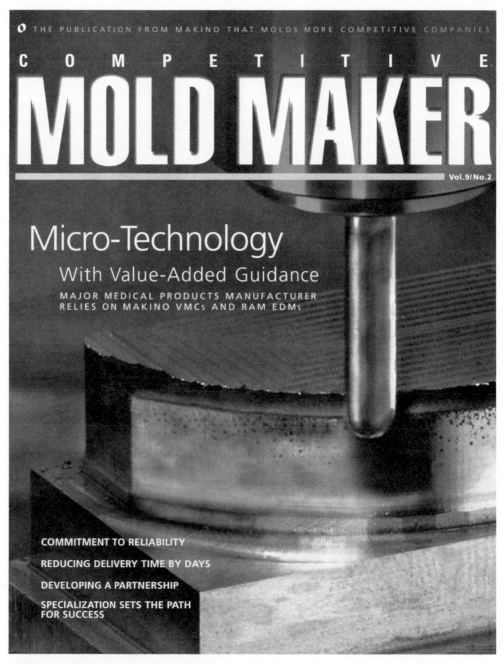

Business-to-Business Magazine Makino publishes *Competitive Mold Maker,* and its accompanying web site, to promote its technological abilities to the die- and mold-making industry. (Courtesy of Makino and HSR Business to Business, Inc.)

2. *Deadlines.* In the written plan, establish a deadline for the completion of each tactic. For example, each local-interest news release necessary in the Canada to Costa Rica scenario would have a distribution deadline. The named manager of each tactic would be responsible for meeting that deadline.

3. *Quality control.* Conduct quality control. Have more than one editor and proofreader examine every document. Attend photo shoots to ensure that photographers are getting the picture you planned. Visit printing companies to ensure that the colors of your brochures and magazines are correct. (You may even get to shout, "Stop the press!") Look over a lot of shoulders as the tactics progress. In public relations for the move to Costa Rica, part of quality control would include double-checking the quality of Spanish-language news releases and podcasts. And because the Spanish of Costa Rica is different from the Spanish of Spain, you would be wise to seek the assistance of native Costa Rican public relations professionals.

4. *Communication within the team.* Encourage communication among the practitioners who are executing the tactics. Frequent short meetings in which teammates update one another can be a good idea. For example, the manager of one of the news releases on the Costa Rica move may need to know that the job-training and placement center will indeed open on a particular date; it may be an important point in her news release. Good communication within your team can ensure that the tactics of your plan complement one another as they are accomplished.

5. *Communication with clients and supervisors.* Communicate frequently with the clients and/or supervisors as the execution of the tactics progresses. Be sure to inform them of any problems, and try to present realistic solutions. In our scenario, perhaps a company executive phones you at the last moment, wanting to change some of the job-training and placement brochures from two colors to full color. You will need to communicate as quickly as possible with your supervisor, detailing the impact of the proposed change on budget and scheduling.

6. *Constant evaluation.* Evaluate the process as it progresses. Are news releases, videos, and web sites professional in every respect? Are people downloading podcasts? Are deadlines being met? Do any sudden changes within your targeted publics or within the social or political environment require a change of tactics? Perhaps a video news release prepared for San José television stations, for example, doesn't run because, as you later discover, the stations wanted a longer Spanish-language question-and-answer session on the VNR's b-roll. If your plan calls for a second VNR, you can remedy that situation in hopes of improved media coverage.

Carrying out the tactics of a public relations plan is exciting. You've worked hard to create a realistic, effective plan, and now you're giving it your best shot. But even after the tactics are completed and you heave a heartfelt sigh of relief, the public relations process isn't over. Now it's time to evaluate the impact of the tactics. It's time to see whether your plan met its objectives and goals.

QUICK   CHECK

1. What is cause marketing?
2. What are the differences between a lobby and a political action committee?
3. What makes a message sticky?
4. What can you include in a written plan to help ensure that tactics are completed on schedule?

Summary

Accomplishing the tactics—often called communication—is the third phase of the public relations process, coming after research and planning. During this phase, practitioners complete well-defined actions to achieve a written plan's objectives. Each tactic targets a particular public and sends a message that does two things: appeals to the receiver's values and promotes the sender's objective. An effective tactic helps build a relationship that benefits a message's receiver as well as its sender.

A wide range of effective tactics can help organizations communicate with their publics: employees, the news media, investors, community groups, governments, customers, constituents (voters), businesses, and others. Ranging from low-tech face-to-face meetings to high-tech wikis, such tactics strive to create win-win situations that benefit both an organization and the targeted public.

As public relations professionals execute the tactics of a plan, they are guided by the principles of delegation, deadlines, quality control, communication within the team, communication with clients and supervisors, and constant evaluation.

Public relations tactics, after all, are values in action. An organization's values lead to a mission statement. That mission statement leads to goals. Those goals lead to objectives. And those objectives lead to strategies and tactics. Tactics are actions that allow an organization to strive toward its highest values.

DISCUSSION QUESTIONS

1. In the Canada to Costa Rica scenario, what publics besides employees, stockholders, investment analysts, and the news media would you target with a public relations plan?
2. What message would you send to each public you identify in your answer to question 1? Can you create win-win messages?
3. What tactics could you use to send the messages that you described in your answer to question 2?
4. Why should tactics be evaluated as they're being implemented?

Memo from the Field

Deborah Charnes Vallejo, Vice President and Managing Director, Bromley Communications, San Antonio, Texas

Deborah Charnes Vallejo is vice president and managing director of San Antonio–based Bromley Communications, one of the nation's top Hispanic-led full-service agencies. Under her direction, the agency has won numerous honors from *PR Week* magazine and the Texas Public Relations Association. She also has won a Silver Anvil Award from the Public Relations Society of America. Before joining Bromley, she served as a vice president with Ketchum Public Relations in Miami.

In her memo, Vallejo offers a series of phrases that can chill the blood of any public relations professional, all of them related to Murphy's Law: If something can go wrong, it will.

"I'M A PEOPLE PERSON"

Please, job applicants, trash that response. Talk about your ability to multitask, prevent gaffes, and respond under fire. Those are critical success factors for this field. PR practitioners must be quick to respond and, ideally, possess ESP.

"DO A PRESS CONFERENCE"

I cringe when I hear this—as if that's all public relations is about. Too many PR folks have been embarrassed with a conference that's attended only by the organizers. So if a client insists, a ghost party must be prevented.

At my last press conference, aside from lining up high-profile speakers to "guarantee" coverage (of course, there are no guarantees in PR), we selected a highly trafficked venue. We bused in schoolchildren to sit in the backdrop and lead a rally. Additionally, we scheduled a radio remote immediately prior to start. The event was a success. We generated good media turnout and great photo ops—no stage-managed "grip and grins."

On the other end of the spectrum, I managed media relations for a concert uniting two singers from diverse genres. The artists arrived late to our press conference (as predicted). They made a few statements, answered a select number of questions and were ready to go. As they filed out of the room, media bombarded them, wanting one-on-one interviews. The artists refused. A fight nearly broke out between aggressive photographers. "People person" to the rescue.

On concert night, some 50 pre-credentialed media were corralled in a holding room and only allowed into the theatre for the few songs the artists performed together. Keeping them happy, confined to the green room while the concert was taking place, required more than the food and drinks we offered. At the same time, it presented a great opportunity to "get closer" to these influential media.

"BROWNIE, YOU'RE DOING A HECK OF A JOB!"

President Bush's compliments to his buddy [FEMA Director Michael Brown] during the Hurricane Katrina fiasco will go down in history as being insensitive and disingenuous. This was likely one rare example when the president strayed from his PR-prepared messages.

Despite a well-oiled team and action plan, the best of professionals cannot always predict a national disaster. But their responses live on forever. The airline industry gets a pass when a delay is due to *force majeure*. Not so in our business. When misfortune strikes, news media focus obsessively on the issue, canceling traditional interviews, programming, or assignments.

I was flying to San Diego for a women's conference when I answered a frantic call. Wildfires that had been incubating in the surrounding forests were now ravaging the city with black ash flying everywhere. The city was under lockdown, and government offices and schools would close the following day—event day.

From the 747, we devised our contingency plan shortly before the San Diego airport closed its runways to arriving carriers. Before take-off, I briefed my office. We repositioned our activity as a safe haven with free lunch for moms and kids when schools and businesses were closed. We salvaged our pre-scheduled media interviews by positioning our event as one of the few activities continuing during the wildfires. We lined up special provisions donated by our client and, in light of the disaster, recognized a team of local firefighters.

In South Florida, hurricane-preparedness is expected. When Hurricane Andrew hit, arguably the worst to affect the region, my office there was inaccessible and inoperable for a week. My apartment was an hour north of the storm's eye, and electricity, water, gasoline, and telephone lines were back within 24 hours. As part of preparedness, I had hard copies of databases and media materials in my possession.

In the end, I was one of only two employees able to conduct business in Andrew's aftermath. To help solidify coverage for a campaign I was promoting in Puerto Rico, I offered the media live updates on Andrew when none of their contacts were reachable. This was a valuable tactic to provide the media with front-page news while getting my story placed in Section B.

"THE SHOW MUST GO ON"

These are just a few examples of how to think quickly and resolve problems, ideally before they occur. Down-and-dirty basics include the following: ship items several days earlier than required; prepare Q&As for all potential scenarios; allow for double the "drive time" stated in map quests; shoot for a dry run drive-around in unfamiliar surroundings; bring presentation materials in multiple formats to allow for tech nightmares; plan travel to allow for flight holdups and traffic jams; prepare for client and spokesperson delays; and finally, always have a personal PR First-Aid Kit containing nutrition bars to replace meals, cell phones, PDAs, GPS, battery chargers, jump drives, and piles of patience.

CASE STUDY 9.1

Fleishman-Hillard Prompts Young Singles to Shout Yahoo!

In retrospect, doing the downward dog in front of national news media and millions of viewers may not have been the best idea, but scheduling nine romantic dates in three days can scramble the best of brains.

The dog (a yoga position) and dates were part of a special event designed to attract media attention to Project: Real People, an advertising campaign for Yahoo! Personals, an online dating service hosted by the popular web portal. The ad campaign would feature 50 real subscribers to Yahoo! Personals. To launch the campaign, public relations agency Fleishman-Hillard helped Yahoo! create a special event: Julie Koehnen, a 39-year-old Hollywood screenwriter and one of the 50 subscribers featured in the ads, would live—and date—for three days under a billboard on Los Angeles' Sunset Boulevard.

While living on an elevated platform beneath the billboard, which featured her photograph and the confession that she was "looking for a few good dates," Koehnen would go online and select eight Yahoo! Personals subscribers for dates, inviting her favorite back for a ninth date. And the world could watch it all via a live webcast on Yahoo!

The Yahoo! team did show some mercy: Koehnen could depart for her real home at night. But from 7 A.M. to 7 P.M. for three days, she would eat, go online, date, work, date, exercise, be interviewed, date, doze, and date for all the world to see.

"The immediate interaction with people was amazing," Koehnen said of her three-day marathon. "They'd e-mail me while I was up there and respond as fast as I read their messages on the web cam. The Internet is so fast and visceral."[10]

If the Internet was fast and visceral, the traditional media weren't far behind. On day one of the special event, TV trucks from local stations and national networks arrived in the predawn darkness. "I got a phone call at 4:30 in the morning that the trucks were there and I had to get ready for interviews right away," Koehnen said. "I thought I'd just be hanging out with the Yahoo! people, but this was really huge."[11]

To promote the special event, Fleishman-Hillard used other public relations tactics. Before the event, it prepared video b-roll footage, distributing it to local and national media via satellite and disk. It also prepared and distributed a media advisory/photo opportunity sheet headlined "Los Angeles Single Searches for Love on Yahoo! Personals atop Sunset Strip Billboard." Finally, the agency helped sponsor a contest on a Los Angeles radio station, with the winner gaining one of the eight dates.

Though it called the special event "a live ad," *Adweek* magazine noted the importance of public relations in attracting news media: "Because PR determines the success of a live ad, novelty and originality are crucial."[12]

Not only did novelty, originality, and romance flourish—among Koehnen's billboard dates were a police officer, a surfer, and a race-car mechanic—so did media coverage and activity on the Yahoo! Personals site. The special event generated almost 350 stories in 100 U.S. media markets, gaining exposure to a potential audience of 126 million. Traffic on the dating web site jumped almost 20 percent from the previous two-week period; subscriptions jumped 27 percent during the same period. The webcast recorded more than 500,000 hits.[13] *Promo* magazine named the billboard extravaganza its Campaign of the Year,[14] and the Public Relations Society of America honored Fleishman-Hillard with a Silver Anvil, the society's top award, in its special events category.[15]

And the downward dog? It was a yoga position that Koehnen assumed during an early-morning workout—a position that involved inadvertently aiming her posterior at the news media. "I don't think I'll do that again," she told a reporter from Reuters, an international news service.[16]

On a brighter note, the story might have a Hollywood ending for screenwriter Koehnen: As this book goes to press, she and the winner of the ninth date are still together.[17]

DISCUSSION QUESTIONS

1. Recall the discussion of special events and so-called pseudoevents. Was the Yahoo! billboard tactic a pseudoevent?
2. *Adweek* magazine called the special event "a live ad." Was the event an advertisement? Would that mean it wasn't public relations?
3. If you had been able to help Fleishman-Hillard promote the special event, what tactics besides the b-roll, media advisory, and radio contest might you have used?
4. Using the communication model described in this chapter and Chapter 5, can you describe source, message, channel, receiver, feedback, and noise for this special event?

CASE STUDY **9.2**

No News at a Senatorial News Conference

If a tree falls in a forest and there's no one there to hear, does it make a sound?

Or, more to the point, if a politician holds a news conference but announces no real news, will journalists listen?

Maybe yes, maybe no—but it's a sure bet they'll be angry about having their time wasted. Just ask Senator Chuck Hagel of Nebraska.

In early 2007, Hagel made it known he was considering a run at the presidency. So when he scheduled a news conference in Lincoln, Nebraska, promising to make a major announcement, reporters arrived en masse: 15 television cameras squeezed into the room, including crews from NBC, CNN, and MSNBC.[18] Newspaper journalists flipped open their notebooks.

Live television coverage began as Hagel stepped to a lectern at the University of Nebraska, looked into the cameras, and delivered his news: "I'm here today to announce that my family and I will make a decision on my political future later this year," he said.[19]

"Now that was peculiar," declared the *Lincoln Journal Star* in a follow-up editorial. "Chuck Hagel left people scratching their heads. . . . [I]f Hagel wants to be president, Monday's news conference was an odd way to go about it."[20]

So peculiar was the tactic of inviting national news media to the middle of the nation to reveal a nondecision that media responded even before the news conference concluded. In the question-and-answer session that followed Hagel's statement, NBC correspondent Michelle Kosinski told Hagel, "Senator, at least one Republican political analyst called your announcement today bizarre just now."[21]

That Republican analyst was Brad Blakeman, part of the MSNBC team reporting on the news conference. In a parting comment as the network quickly broke away from the nonevent, Blakeman said, "That was one of the most bizarre political statements I have ever heard."[22]

Blakeman may have been the first critic, but he was only one of many:

■ "Senator Chuck Hagel came out to a suspense-filled room . . . and didn't announce anything," said CNN correspondent Dana Bash.[23]

■ "I'll bet those television guys are glad they schlepped all the way out there to hear that. . . . That's it? The whole thing? You couldn't have sent an e-mail?" wrote reporter Donald Kaul.[24]

■ "The groans from the reporters in the audience were almost audible," declared an Australian journalist.[25]

■ "Why couldn't the same news, given its modesty, have been presented . . . through a simple press release?" wrote the *Omaha World-Herald*.[26]

Democrats were quick to poke fun at Hagel and even cited Republicans as their sources. A news release issued by the Democratic Senatorial Campaign Committee began "Earlier this week Republican Senator Chuck Hagel called a massive press conference in his home state of Nebraska to announce, well . . . nothing." The release went on to note that even Republicans were amused by Hagel's unusual tactic, citing the comment of Republican representative Roy Blunt, who thwarted reporters' questions about a confidential meeting by responding, "This is like a Chuck Hagel news conference—come back Thursday."[27]

Hagel's response to the media criticism was muted. In response to the "bizarre" charge, he explained that he had promised to announce his presidential plans early in the year:

> Well, I, first of all, told the people of this state, as well as the people of this country, that I would make an announcement, a decision on my political future after the first of the year. It is after the first of the year—before St. Patrick's Day—and that's the first responsibility I have.[28]

Every week, *PR Week* magazine selects one noteworthy public relations action for its "PR Play of the Week." The magazine irreverently describes the action—planned or otherwise—and assigns it one of five ratings: clueless, ill-advised, on the right track, savvy, or ingenious. The Hagel news conference earned "PR Play of the Week" honors, and the magazine offered the Nebraska senator this suggestion: "Reporters need sleep. Don't waste their time." Then *PR Week* delivered its assessment of the Hagel news conference.

Ill-advised.[29]

DISCUSSION QUESTIONS

1. In your opinion, were the news media unfair to Hagel? Why or why not?
2. What alternatives to a news conference might Hagel have used?
3. If you had been one of Hagel's advisers, what advice about news conferences would you have given him?
4. In your opinion, how should Hagel have responded to the negative coverage?

NOTES

1. *Fox News Watch,* 6 September 2003, online, LexisNexis.
2. "What Is Social Media? An E-Book from Spannerworks," report issued by Spannerworks, 16 November 2006, online, www.spannerworks.com.
3. "Blog to the Chief: The Impact of Political Blogs on the 2008 Election," panel discussion sponsored by the Dole Institute of Politics, University of Kansas, 13 February 2007.
4. Katie Delahaye Paine, "How to Measure Social Media Relations," report issued by the Institute for Public Relations, April 2007, online, www.instituteforpr.org.
5. "New Survey Shows High Trust Levels among New Jersey Employees," news release issued by the New Jersey Chapter of the International Association of Business Communicators and Berry Associates Public Relations, 4 December 2003, online, LexisNexis.
6. Linda Morton, "Producing Publishable News Releases: A Research Perspective," *Public Relations Quarterly* 37, no. 4 (22 December 1992), online, LexisNexis.
7. Chip Heath and Dan Heath, *Made to Stick: Why Some Ideas Survive and Others Die* (New York: Random House, 2007).
8. Barbara Kiviat, "Are You Sticky?" *Time,* 29 October 2006, online, www.time.com.
9. Andy Reinhart, "Extranets: Log On, Link Up, Save Big," *Business Week,* 22 June 1998, online, LexisNexis.
10. Betsy Spethman, "Getting Personal," *Promo,* 1 December 2004, online, LexisNexis.
11. Spethman.
12. Joan Voight, "Living It Up," *Adweek,* 26 September 2005, online, LexisNexis.
13. Fleishman-Hillard, "Yahoo! Personals Takes Online Dating to New Heights, Silver Anvil 2005 competition entry, online, www.prsa.org.
14. Spethman.
15. Fleishman-Hillard.
16. "Love Writ Large," *Sydney Morning Herald,* 9 January 2004, online, LexisNexis.
17. Spethman.
18. Dana Milbank, "When No News Is Strange News," *Washington Post,* 13 March 2007, online, www.washingtonpost.com.
19. "Sen. Chuck Hagel Holds a News Conference," *Congressional Quarterly,* 12 March 2007, online, LexisNexis.

20. "Hagel Steps to the Beat of a Different Drum," *Lincoln Journal Star,* 13 March 2007, online, www.journalstar.com.

21. Milbank.

22. Milbank.

23. Dana Bash, "Sen. Hagel Delays Political Announcement," *CNN Student News* transcript, 12 March 2007, online, LexisNexis.

24. Donald Kaul, "Republicans 'Out-Strange' the Democrats," *Springfield (Missouri) News-Leader,* 24 March 2007, online, LexisNexis.

25. Michael Rowland, "Candidates Woo American Public in U.S. Presidential Race," *AM* (Australian Broadcasting Corporation), 13 March 2007, online, LexisNexis.

26. "Hagel's 'Big News,'" *Omaha World-Herald,* 13 March 2007, online, LexisNexis.

27. "Chuck Hagel," news release issued by the Democratic Senatorial Campaign Committee, 14 March 2007, online, http://dscc.org.

28. "Sen. Chuck Hagel Holds a News Conference."

29. Hamilton Noland, "Hagel Gives Press Nothing to Talk About," *PR Week,* 14 March 2007, online, www.prweek.com/us.

Writing and Presentation Skills

OBJECTIVES

After studying this chapter, you will be able to

■ describe and follow the different stages of the writing process

■ describe the fundamentals of writing for the web

■ identify and use techniques that increase the effectiveness of spoken language

■ describe and follow the process of making a successful presentation

KEY TERMS

active voice, p. 312
attribution, p. 320
demographic information, p. 306
inverted pyramid, p. 309
macroediting, p. 314
microediting, p. 315
modifiers, p. 312
passive voice, p. 312
psychographic information, p. 306
transition, p. 320
visual aids, p. 324
writing process, p. 302

Publicizing Volunteer Clearinghouse

A college internship has led to your first job: You're now an assistant account executive with a public relations agency. As an intern, you impressed the agency's partners with your character, work ethic, team spirit, and writing abilities. At the end of your internship, the partners asked you to stay in touch, which you did, occasionally sending them class projects and successful assignments from other internships. One week before you graduated, the partners rewarded your talent and persistence with a job offer, which you accepted.

Your first task at the agency involves writing a news release for Volunteer Clearinghouse, which coordinates volunteer recruitment for nonprofit social-service agencies in your county. Volunteer Clearinghouse is one of your agency's pro bono clients, meaning the agency doesn't charge for its services. Offering unpaid services to Volunteer Clearinghouse helps your agency honor one of its founding values: a commitment to building a better community through social responsibility.

The board of directors of Volunteer Clearinghouse has just named a new executive director. Her name is Elaine Anderson, and she succeeds Phil Connors, who accepted a similar position in another state. The board of directors would like your agency to write a news release announcing Anderson's hiring. The account executive who serves as a liaison to Volunteer Clearinghouse quickly agrees and turns to you.

It's 3 P.M., and the account executive would like the news release by 10 A.M. tomorrow.

It's the first assignment of your new job, and you want to do well. How and where do you start?

The Importance of Writing and Presentation Skills

"Writing is easy," said U.S. journalist and playwright Gene Fowler. "All you do is stare at a blank sheet of paper until drops of blood form on your forehead."[1]

We might update Fowler's description to include a computer screen, but his point remains: Good writing is hard work. In fact, more than one writer has compared the activity to spilling blood. Nobel Prize–winning novelist Ernest Hemingway declared, "Writing is easy. Just open a vein and bleed on paper."[2]

Whew! Tough business, this writing. Could anything be more challenging? Well, how about making a presentation? By yourself. In front of a lot of people. With your reputation and a potential client at stake. According to *The Book of Lists*, public speaking ranks number one on the list of people's greatest fears, ahead of heights, sickness, and even death.[3]

This chapter focuses on spilling blood and tackling terrors worse than death. In other words, this chapter focuses on writing and presentation skills. Why? Because they're at the heart of the practice of public relations. A recent survey of almost 300 diverse business communications professionals found that participants achieved near-unanimity on only one topic: "Writing business communications is 'very or extremely important' to their success on the job."[4] *PR Week* magazine lists both "public speaking" (with an emphasis on "confidence") and "writing" (including "proficiency in spelling [and] grammar") in its list of essential skills for entry-level public relations practitioners.[5] And employers say these qualities apply to all potential hires, not just entry-level applicants. Clearly, writing and presentation skills are prerequisites for success at every stage of a public relations career.

One objective of this chapter is to reduce the stress involved in writing and presenting by dividing those activities into small, achievable steps. Writing and presenting are processes. Rather than approaching them as jagged mountains to be scaled in one leap, we can learn to master writing and presenting by tackling them one step at a time—methodically climbing the mountain, so to speak, instead of trying to reach the top in one doomed jump.

However, this chapter doesn't pretend to tell you everything you need to know about writing and presenting. Those topics consume whole textbooks all by themselves. Instead, this chapter strives to cover the basics of writing and presenting, suggesting their fundamental importance to the profession of public relations. Let's begin with blood-spilling—that is, with writing.

A Context for Public Relations Writing

Journalists write to inform. Advertisers write to persuade. What, then, is the mission of public relations writing? In a sense, that question echoes one posed in Chapter 6: Are public relations practitioners objective communicators, like journalists, or are they persuasive advocates, like advertisers and lawyers? Our answer now—as it was then—is "none of the above." Public relations practitioners are neither journalists, nor lawyers, nor advertisers. They are relationship managers.

The mission of public relations writing is relationship management. Sometimes the ethical management of relationships requires journalistic objectivity; other times, it may require persuasion. Often, it requires a little of both. As a relationship-management strategy, public relations writing should address the values and interests of the writer's organization as well as the values and interests of the targeted public or publics. For example, a well-written news release certainly addresses the interests of the writer's organization: It communicates important information that the organization considers newsworthy. The same news release also addresses the interests of the news media, which rely on news releases to help them identify and communicate the news. Additionally, the news release addresses the interests of targeted publics within the news media's audiences—investors, perhaps, or local environmentalists. By addressing the individual interests of each of those parties, the news release maintains and even strengthens relationships that sustain the organization.

Think of our definition of public relations: *Public relations is the values-driven management of relationships between an organization and the publics that can affect its success.* Public relations writing supports that definition. Whatever the document may be—a speech, an annual report, a blog, or even an in-house memo—its aim is consistent: to be an effective tactic in the management of relationships vital to an organization's success.

The Writing Process

Public relations writing, whether a news release, a podcast script, or something else altogether, can be intimidating. Writers respond to such anxiety in many ways. Sometimes they avoid the challenge by putting the writing task off until the last moment. Or, conversely, perhaps they attack the challenge by flying to their computer keyboards and banging away. Both responses usually lead to frustration, however, not to good writing. Like public relations itself, writing is a process: It can't be started at the last moment, and it doesn't begin with your fingers flying over the keyboard. The **writing process** begins with values and ends with evaluation. Because writing is a process, its first step leads logically to a second step, which leads to a third, and so on.

The writing process, in fact, has something in common with Maslow's Hierarchy of Needs, presented in Chapter 5. As you'll recall, moving too high too fast in Maslow's hierarchy can be disastrous; the needs at each level of that pyramid must be fulfilled before you can move up to the next level. It's the same in the writing process: It's counterproductive to move to the fourth level, for example, when you haven't completed the first, second, and third levels. In fact, if you're stalled at a particular stage of a writing project, you should consider dropping down to the earlier levels. Perhaps a failure to complete one of them has led to your momentary dead end. At the very least, reviewing your progress may reveal a solution to your frustration.

Envisioning writing as a process can help you cope with the intimidation that sometimes accompanies important writing assignments. The writing process can help you avoid procrastination because it eases you into the actual writing; it helps you approach an assignment with confidence. And the writing process prevents you from wasting your time (and others' time) by jumping in too quickly and trying to write without adequate preparation. The writing process helps you tackle a writing assignment in a logical, productive fashion.

So what are the different stages of the writing process? As Figure 10.1 shows, the writing process for public relations consists of 10 stages. These stages, in order, are credibility, research, organization, writing, revision, macroediting, microediting, approval, distribution, and evaluation. Figure 10.1 also suggests that you should communicate with supervisors and/or clients—whoever is appropriate—as your writing assignment progresses. For a short newsletter story, communication with supervisors and/or clients might be brief: checking quotations, confirming deadlines, suggesting a new angle that your research has revealed, and submitting a draft before the deadline. But for a more extensive document, such as major sections of a corporation's annual report, communication might take the form of regularly scheduled meetings or a constant exchange of e-mail messages and rough drafts. Ask supervisors and clients how much communication they would like—and always inform them as new challenges and opportunities regarding an assignment arise.

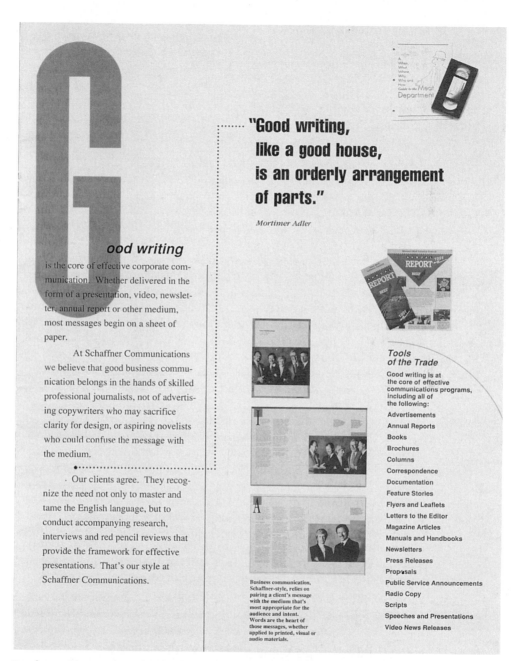

"Good writing,
like a good house,
is an orderly arrangement
of parts."

Mortimer Adler

Good writing is the core of effective corporate communication. Whether delivered in the form of a presentation, video, newsletter, annual report or other medium, most messages begin on a sheet of paper.

At Schaffner Communications we believe that good business communication belongs in the hands of skilled professional journalists, not of advertising copywriters who may sacrifice clarity for design, or aspiring novelists who could confuse the message with the medium.

Our clients agree. They recognize the need not only to master and tame the English language, but to conduct accompanying research, interviews and red pencil reviews that provide the framework for effective presentations. That's our style at Schaffner Communications.

Business communication, Schaffner-style, relies on pairing a client's message with the medium that's most appropriate for the audience and intent. Words are the heart of those messages, whether applied to printed, visual or audio materials.

Tools of the Trade

Good writing is at the core of effective communications programs, including all of the following:

Advertisements

Annual Reports

Books

Brochures

Columns

Correspondence

Documentation

Feature Stories

Flyers and Leaflets

Letters to the Editor

Magazine Articles

Manuals and Handbooks

Newsletters

Press Releases

Proposals

Public Service Announcements

Radio Copy

Scripts

Speeches and Presentations

Video News Releases

Brochure Chicago-based Schaffner Communications wins and keeps clients with its intense focus on good writing. (Courtesy of Schaffner Communications)

FIGURE 10.1 The Writing Process
Successful public relations writing begins with credibility and ends with evaluating the success of the written document. The 10 stages of the writing process should be followed in order: Research comes before organization, which comes before writing, and so on. As the document progresses, the writer should discuss problems or new ideas with supervisors and/or clients.

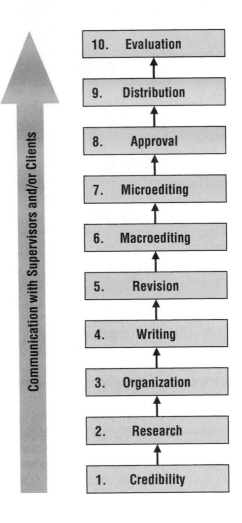

Although our chapter focuses on the writing process within the context of public relations, the process applies to other situations, such as writing an advertisement, a short story, or even a love letter. However, some of the stages are more appropriate for public relations than for other writing situations; these stages include credibility, approval, and evaluation.

Let's now examine the individual stages of the writing process.

Credibility: Stage One of the Writing Process

This is *really* beginning at the beginning, but starting anywhere else would be misleading and counterproductive. As a communicator, you must have credibility, or there's no point in trying to send a message. Clients and supervisors won't give an important writing assignment to an individual they don't trust. Receivers of a message may discount it if they lack respect for the source. As we noted in Chapter 5,

Aristotle believed that the most powerful persuasive strategy of all often is the character of the communicator.

So how can you establish character? Actually, as you know, you've been doing that since you learned to think for yourself and to make your own decisions. But character isn't static. It grows—or diminishes. As a public relations practitioner, you can "grow" and establish your character by testing your actions and those of your employer against your own values, the values of your employer, the values of the public relations profession (as stated in the ethics codes of organizations such as the Public Relations Society of America), and the values of the society in which you live.

Establishing character can't be an occasional thing. The values that surround and help give meaning to your life should be with you every day. One of the many payoffs of values-driven public relations is that it helps make you a credible, trustworthy communicator.

Research: Stage Two of the Writing Process

Different public relations documents require different kinds of research: For example, a CEO's speech to a corporation's stockholders requires different research than an employee relations document on how to apply for a promotion. But regardless of what document they're preparing to write, public relations practitioners ask the following five questions.

1. What Is My Purpose in Writing? In other words, what is the goal of this document? What does your organization hope this document will achieve? You should be able to answer this question with one clear, precise sentence. If that isn't possible, you don't understand the mission of the document, and you shouldn't proceed until you do.

For example, suppose that your supervisor asks you to write an employee newsletter story about your organization's new voluntary long-term disability insurance program. Great; but what's the goal? Should the story just inform employees about the new program? Or should it recruit them? Ideally, your supervisor can answer your questions—but if she can't, your story probably is on hold until you learn more about the story's precise purpose.

2. Who Is My Targeted Public? For most documents, this means *Who are my readers?* For the text of a speech or for a radio public service announcement, it means *Who are my listeners?* In all cases, it means *Who are the receivers of the message I intend to send?*

In Chapter 4 you encountered seven questions that public relations practitioners must answer to build successful relationships with important publics. These seven questions can help you answer *Who is my targeted public?*

■ *How much can this targeted public influence my organization's ability to achieve its goals?* Because resources are limited, public relations practitioners must devote most of their attention and efforts to publics that can help their organization succeed.

Writing for Diverse Publics: Tips for Inclusive Language

Public relations writing builds relationships. The careless use of language, however, can inadvertently exclude valuable members of important publics. To create inclusive documents, consider the following guidelines:[6]

- In documents that cite individuals as sources, draw on diverse individuals. In many organizations and publics, it's easy to rely on a steady stream of white Anglo-Saxon males in their 40s and 50s. Not all qualified sources are of that race, ethnicity, gender, or age.

- Balance personal pronouns. For unnamed, generic individuals such as a supervisor or senator, balance the use of *he* and *she*. Don't, however, include illogical shifts. A hypothetical supervisor shouldn't change gender within a paragraph. Another solution is to use plural nouns—*supervisors* and *senators*—that can be replaced by *they.*

- Avoid words that describe particular relationships: *your wife, your husband, your boyfriend, your girlfriend, your parents, your children.*

Female readers generally are excluded by *your wife,* just as male readers generally are by *your husband.* Let your targeted public be your guide as to what is appropriate.

- Know the dates of major religious holidays. When is Rosh Hashanah? When is Ramadan?

- Don't describe individuals by race, ethnicity, religion, age, sexual orientation, or physical or mental disability unless the information is relevant to your document's purpose. If an individual must be so described, consider applying the same exactness of description to every other individual mentioned in your document.

- If you are responsible for a document's design, apply your quest for inclusiveness to photographs and other visual representations of individuals. Even if you're *not* in charge of the design, don't hesitate to point out lapses of diversity.

Words have power. They can include—or exclude. Use them wisely.

- *Who are the opinion leaders and decision makers in my targeted public?* Can you appeal to those individuals without excluding other members of the targeted public?

- *What is the demographic profile of my targeted public?* What is the age range of its members? The education range? The male–female ratio? In other words, statistically speaking, who is your targeted public? What does **demographic information** say about your public's members?

- *What is the psychographic profile of my targeted public?* Are members of your targeted public politically conservative, liberal, or middle-of-the-road—or is the range too broad to generalize? Are they devoutly religious, assuredly secular, or scattered along the spectrum of religious intensity? **Psychographic information** includes data about what people believe, think, and feel.

- *What is my targeted public's opinion of my organization?* Are you approaching a friendly public, a neutral public, or a hostile public?

■ *What is my targeted public's opinion of the subject I'm addressing?* How much do members of your targeted public already know about the subject you are preparing to address? Do levels of knowledge differ within your targeted public? You don't want to dwell on information they already know well; on the other hand, you don't want to make false assumptions about what you think they know. And beyond the targeted public's knowledge, what do its members *think* about your subject? Do its members agree, or do opinions vary?

These are six of the seven standard questions you can ask to help you answer, *Who is my targeted public?* The seventh question is so important that we reserve it for its own section, which follows.

3. What Are the Values and Interests of My Targeted Public in This Situation? One of the most important research functions in public relations writing is the identification of your targeted public's stake in your subject matter. Determining the targeted public's values and interests helps you do two things. First, you can quickly move to values and interests in your document, ensuring that your targeted public will pay attention (after all, its members have suddenly realized that you're addressing their concerns). Second, knowing your targeted public's values and interests can help you fulfill them, when possible. As you know, the best relationships in public relations are those in which both sides benefit: true win-win, symmetrical situations. You improve the odds of achieving a win-win relationship when you know your targeted public's stake in the relevant issue.

In Publicizing Volunteer Clearinghouse, our opening scenario, your consideration of your targeted public would provide extremely useful information for the news release you're about to write. You know that your immediate targeted public is news media editors, and you know what they value: a newsworthy, objective, unbiased, local-interest story that they can deliver to their own audiences. You also know that they have a good opinion of Volunteer Clearinghouse and probably will use your news release—if you can meet their standards.

4. What Message Should I Send? You can answer this question by combining what you've learned from answering question 1 above (*What is my purpose in writing?*) and question 3 (*What are the values and interests of my targeted public in this situation?*). As you know from Chapter 8, a successful message combines the purpose of your document with the targeted public's values and interests.

Earlier, for example, we looked at a hypothetical situation in which you were asked to write an employee newsletter story on a new voluntary long-term disability insurance program. Your purpose, you learn, is to persuade employees to enroll in the program. But that's not your message; it doesn't yet have any appeal to the targeted public's values or interests. In researching your targeted public, you learn that your organization's employees have a powerful interest in the financial security of their families. *Now* you have a message: *Enroll in the new insurance program to provide additional financial security for your family.* You need not use those exact words, but that message needs to be the unmistakable theme of your newsletter story. (Remember what makes messages "sticky"; see page 287.)

5. What Information Supports My Message? What information does your organization want you to include in the document you're preparing to write? What information does your targeted public hope to learn from reading your document? Answers to those questions will guide you in your search for relevant information. In researching their stories, journalists seek specific information in six broad areas: *who, what, when, where, why,* and *how.* Those questions may not apply to every public relations writing situation, but asking them can help you anticipate the information requirements of your document.

With all this research gathered, you can turn with confidence to the next stage in the writing process: organization.

1. In what way is the writing process like Maslow's Hierarchy of Needs?
2. In the research stage of the writing process, what kinds of information should you gather about your targeted public?
3. In public relations, what qualities are essential in an effective message?

Organization: Stage Three of the Writing Process

The organization of a document should draw the targeted public's attention to the message and to the information that supports and develops it. Often, that means that the document moves gracefully but quickly to the message. Because the message directly targets the readers' or listeners' values and interests, the sooner we reach it, the sooner the targeted public knows why it should be reading, watching, or listening.

There are, however, exceptions to the general rule of moving quickly to the message. In bad-news situations, for example—in which you tell people something they don't want to hear—the message generally comes *after* a concise description of your reasons for the upcoming bad news. In other words, a quick explanation of *why* comes before you announce the bad news. If we simply announce the bad news first, our unhappy targeted public may tune out our explanation, and that could further damage our relationship. In rejecting employment applications, for example, many organizations use business letters that place the *why* before the bad-news message: *Unfortunately, we have no positions open at this time. Therefore, we are unable to offer you a job.* The job applicant may not like the message, but at least he knows why his request cannot be satisfied.

Clearly, different documents are organized in different message-focused ways. But every document, no matter what its organization is, can benefit from an outline. Outlines needn't be the formal Roman-numeral lists that you learned to create in elementary school; a few scribbled notes for each paragraph may work just as well for you. And outlines aren't etched in stone: As you write a document, better ideas—and a better organization—may occur to you. But some form of outline, some written plan of how you're going to get from here to there, is essential. During spring break, for example, you wouldn't drive to some distant, sunny beach without a map. You

United Way of the Plains

245 N. Water
Wichita, KS 67202
Phone: (316) 267-1321
Fax: (316) 267-0937
www.unitedwayplains.org

United
Way

what matters.™

NEWS RELEASE

DATE: May 8, 2007
CONTACT: Delane Butler, Vice President of Marketing, 267-1321

United Way of the Plains accepts Gov. Sebelius' request for statewide coordination

• *United Way of the Plains establishes statewide Green for Greensburg Fund in partnership with United Ways across Kansas*

WICHITA, Kan. — United Way of the Plains announced that it has accepted Gov. Kathleen Sebelius' request to administer the Green for Greensburg Fund. This fund will serve as a central collection point for anyone wishing to make a monetary contribution to help tornado victims in the Greensburg, Kansas, area.

"We've already seen a tremendous outpouring of support for the residents of Greensburg, and I know they truly appreciate the thoughts and prayers of their fellow Kansans and of people all over the world," said Gov. Kathleen Sebelius. "They face a tough road, but if we come together to support them and to provide the assistance they need to rebuild their lives, I know Greensburg will be rebuilt stronger and more vibrant than before. That's why I ask everyone to support United Way in its efforts to help the victims of this horrible storm."

 "The Governor has asked United Way to administer this fund out of concern for coordination of fund-raising efforts," said Patrick J. Hanrahan, president of United Way of the Plains. "We hope that individuals and groups already conducting fund-raising will add

News Release The headline and first words of a news release should quickly satisfy a journalist's desire for specific details about a newsworthy story. (Copyright United Way of the Plains. Reprinted with permission. Copyright 2007.)

might get there without one, but why waste time and risk failure? The same logic applies to writing. Use an outline.

In our Volunteer Clearinghouse scenario, the research you conducted in the previous stage of the writing process can now help you create an outline. You know that your targeted public consists of news editors, and you know that news editors want the news. Therefore, you decide to organize your news release in the **inverted pyramid** style of a traditional news story, with the most important information at the beginning and the least important at the end (see Figure 10.2). You review the most important details in the areas of who, what, when, where, why, and how, and you organize the details in terms of importance. You decide that your first paragraph needs to announce the most important news: The board of directors has hired Elaine

FIGURE 10.2 The Inverted Pyramid

The inverted pyramid represents the traditional organization of a news story. Where the pyramid is widest, the information in the story is most important. The narrowing of the pyramid represents the decreasing importance of information as a new story progresses toward its ending. Thus, a traditional news story places the most important information at the beginning, which journalists call "the lead." In public relations, most new releases use the inverted pyramid organization.

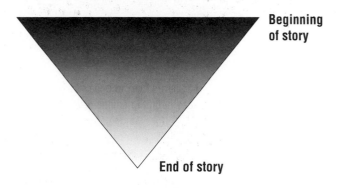

Beginning of story

End of story

Anderson to be the new executive director of Volunteer Clearinghouse. You decide that it's also important to describe briefly who Anderson is and when she'll begin her new job.

In your research you got a quotation about Anderson's abilities from the chairman of the board, but you decide to place that after your lead paragraph. Although it's a good quotation, you decide that it's just not as important as the announcement of Anderson's hiring and the details about her qualifications for this new job.

Your final outline might look something like this:

Paragraph 1:	Anderson hired for new exec director.
	Brief note on who she is.
	Brief note on what Volunteer Clearinghouse is.
	Note when she starts.
Paragraph 2:	Quote from board chairman.
Paragraph 3:	Anderson's biography.
Paragraph 4:	She succeeds Phil Connors. Note where he's gone.
Paragraph 5:	Note that anyone interested in volunteering with community service agencies can call the Volunteer Clearinghouse. List phone number and address.

Now you're organized. You know how to get from here to there. It's time to write.

Writing: Stage Four of the Writing Process

Because you've completed the research and organization stages of the writing process, the question that now faces you isn't *What should I write?* Instead, it's *How should I write what's in my outline?* That difference doesn't make writing easy—but it certainly makes it easier. Having an outline allows you to begin anywhere. If you're intimidated by the importance of the first paragraph, start with the second: Your outline tells you what information to include.

VIAGRA FACT SHEET

Viagra™ (sildenafil citrate), now approved by the U.S. Food and
Administration, is a breakthrough treatment for erectile dysfunction
more commonly known as "impotence."

- Viagra is a tablet that works regardless of the underlying caus
  was shown to be effective in men with ED associated with a
  of medical conditions, including diabetes, a variety of
  neurogenic conditions, and depression.

- Viagra is not an aphrodisiac:
  It enables a man to respond naturally to sexual stimulat

- Viagra is remarkably effective:
  The drug improved erections in approximately four c
  it in clinical trials. Viagra is taken orally in 25-, 50
  about 1 hour before anticipated sexual activity.

- Viagra has been extensively tested:
  In trials worldwide more than 3000 men took
  attempts resulted in successful sexual interco

- Viagra works by increasing the blood flc
  establishing and maintaining an erection:
  The drug accomplishes this by sel
  phosphodiesterase type 5, which
  monophosphate (cGMP), a necessary
  flow into the penis. Viagra helps res
  in response to sexual stimulation.

- Viagra provides men with a marked
  ED: Previous treatments involv
  penis, the use of urethral supp
  surgery, or the use of a vacuum
  While other therapies prod
  Viagra enables a man to res

- The combination of Viagr
  blood pressure. Therefo
  nitrates in any form.

Pfizer Inc
235 East 42nd Street
New York, NY 10017

www.pfizer.com

News

For immediate release
March 27, 1998

Contacts:
Andy McCormick 212-573-1226
Mariann Caprino 212-733-5686

FDA APPROVES PFIZER MEDICINE VIAGRA FOR ERECTILE DYSFUNCTION

NEW YORK, New York -- The U.S. Food and Drug Administration has
approved the breakthrough oral therapy Viagra (sildenafil
citrate) for the treatment of erectile dysfunction, Pfizer Inc
announced today.

Taken about an hour before anticipated sexual activity, Viagra is
a tablet that works naturally with sexual stimulation. Viagra
is effective in most men with erectile dysfunction (ED), the
medical term for impotence, which is associated with a broad
range of physical or psychological medical conditions.

Discovered and c   Viagra is the first in a new
class of medica
that improve bl
has been demons   inhibitors
patients.

"Viagra is a m
treats a medi
quality of li
Steere, Jr.,
innovative t
underscores

ERECTILE DYSFUNCTION PERSPEC

*The following selections are from letters that Pfizer has receive
past three years.*

- "It may be difficult for someone who has not suffered with impo
  fully comprehend the effect of this condition on a person's life, but th
  'devastating' comes close to capturing the feeling..."

- "I suffer from impotence, erectile dysfunction or whatever other n
  you may call it...I'm desperate...I want to walk with my head high ag
  like a whole man, not half of one..."

- "...I would very much like to know if [Viagra] would help a rectal cance
  patient now in remission eight years with a sigmoid colostomy. This type
  of surgery rendered me impotent..."

- "Before I took part in the [Viagra] study I was heavily depressed...The
  feeling of being inadequate, even inferior, let alone impotent, was
  unbearable..."

- "My boyfriend is a 45-year-old healthy male with an undiagnosable
  impotence problem...We are desperately trying to find out if this new
  product is going to be the answer to our prayers, or, if not, he must resign
  himself to the fact that he will never be able to have his manhood back..."

- "...I am a healthy 50-year-old female involved for the past year with a
  healthy 44-year-old male who suffers from impotence. We have been to
  11 doctors...We have had every kind of test imaginable done, and
  suffered through many types of corrective action, none of which have
  worked without great pain to one or both of us..."

- "...I've enjoyed a very active sex life until the past two years. I now feel
  like less than half of a man, embarrassed so many times, actually getting
  out of bed to hide in the bathroom and cry...."

# # #

References available upon request.

NDC 0069-4210-30
30 Tablets

Viagra™ 50
(sildenafil citrate) tablets

50 mg*

Distributed by
Pfizer Pfizer Labs
Division of Pfizer Inc, NY, NY 10017

Media Kit Among the many written
documents in the first media kit for
the anti-impotence drug Viagra were
a news release, a fact sheet, and a
backgrounder that contained
consumer comments about erectile
dysfunction. (Courtesy of Pfizer, Inc.)

VIAGRA
(sildenafil citrate)

VIAGRA
(sildenafil citrate)

QuickBreak 10.2

Ten Tips for Writing Better Sentences[7]

1. *Challenge "to be" verbs.* Challenge *is, are, was, were, will be,* and every other form of the verb *to be.* Often, you can find a stronger, more descriptive verb that might also shorten the sentence.

Original	Revision
He will be a good communicator.	He will communicate effectively.
We are inviting you . . .	We invite you . . .

2. *Use active voice.* In the **active voice,** the subject of the sentence does the action. In the **passive voice,** the subject receives the action.

Passive Voice	Active Voice
Our profits were affected by a sales slump.	A sales slump affected our profits.

Passive voice can seem timid, and it requires a *to be* verb. Active voice is confident and concise.

3. *Challenge modifiers.* **Modifiers** (adjectives and adverbs) can strengthen a sentence by sharpening your meaning. But sometimes they prop up weak words, especially nouns and verbs. A precise, well-chosen word needs no modification.

Original	Revision
We are very happy.	We are ecstatic.
She ran fast.	She sprinted.

4. *Challenge long words.* If a long word or phrase works best, use it. Otherwise, use a shorter option.

Original	Revision
utilize	use
prioritize	rank

5. *Challenge prepositional phrases.* Avoid strings of prepositional phrases:

Original	Revision
We will meet on Thursday in Centerville at the Lancaster Hotel, on McDaniel Street.	We will meet Thursday at the Lancaster Hotel, 1423 McDaniel St., Centerville.

Some prepositional phrases can be tightened into adjectives:

Original	Revision
I will present the report in the meeting on Thursday.	I will present the report in Thursday's meeting.

6. *Challenge long sentences.* How long should a sentence be? Long enough to make its point effectively—and no longer. Challenge any sentence that exceeds 25 words. Eliminate *to be* verbs and tighten prepositional phrases when possible.

7. *Avoid overused expressions.* Clichés such as "It has come to my attention" and "I regret to inform you" lack original thought. They also sound insincere.

8. *Avoid placing important words or phrases in the middle of a sentence.* The beginning of a sentence breaks a silence and calls attention to itself. The last words of a sentence echo into a brief silence and gain emphasis. The middle of a sentence generally draws the least attention.

9. *Keep the focus on the reader.* Tell readers what they want and need to know—not just what you want them to know. Keep the focus on how they benefit from reading your document.

10. *Read your sentences aloud.* Or at least whisper them quietly to yourself. That's the surest way to check for effective sentence rhythms.

Another strategy for getting started is simply to start: Write the first paragraph, no matter how bad it seems. Then stop and evaluate it. If it really is bad, why? What specifically is wrong with it? Are the sentences too long? Does the paragraph fail to move toward the targeted public's values and interests in this situation? Does it not follow your outline? Identifying specific problems helps you fix them.

For example, let's imagine that you roll up your sleeves and, with a quick glance at your outline for the Volunteer Clearinghouse news release, you just start writing:

> *The board of directors of Volunteer Clearinghouse has announced that Elaine Anderson, formerly with the Coxwold County Red Cross, will be Volunteer Clearinghouse's new executive director.*

Not bad. But you quickly identify three points in your lead that you don't like:

1. The sentence seems too long: 26 words. It doesn't move concisely to the announcement of a new director.
2. The lead doesn't include Anderson's starting date (a question of *when*)
3. The lead assumes that readers know what Volunteer Clearinghouse is (a question of *who*).

With the problems identified, you're ready to eliminate them. Your second draft might look like this:

> *The Volunteer Clearinghouse board of directors has named Elaine Anderson the organization's new executive director. Anderson, formerly with the Coxwold County Red Cross, will begin her new duties May 29. Volunteer Clearinghouse recruits and trains volunteers for Coxwold County United Way agencies.*

That's better. There's still room for improvement, but your first paragraph is now good enough to justify moving on to another section of your document. You'll get another chance to polish all sections of the document during the next stage of the writing process: revision.

Revision: Stage Five of the Writing Process

As writers consider revision, a seductive danger confronts them: the euphoria of creation. Good writers work hard to complete their first drafts, and when they're done, they're often relieved, excited, and justifiably pleased with themselves. *I've worked hard,* they think. *I've agonized over every sentence. I'm not going to change a thing, because this document is good!* That's the euphoria of creation: the feeling that your just-finished document is great and needs no revision. One of the few cures is to get away from the document for as long as possible. Put it aside, even if it's for only half an hour. Concentrate on something else. Let the euphoria of creation subside. Finally, reapproach your document with the faith that revision just might make it better.

That's the goal of revision: to make a good document even better. One way to improve a good document is to approach it with the reader's vision. Poet and novelist Robert Graves recommends imagining one of your intended readers leaning over your shoulder and saying, *But what does that mean? Can't this part be clearer? What's in this for me? What do I gain by reading this?*[8] Instead of banishing this annoying reader back to your imagination, do your best to satisfy his or her demands. Engage in a true *re*-vision.

A second method of revision is to test each sentence against the core message of the document. As you reread your document, does *every* sentence work toward the message? Could some sentences work toward the message more effectively? One definition of poetry is "the best words in the best order." That's not a bad definition for a public relations document. Every word should contribute to the document's clear reason for existing.

Let's return again to our Volunteer Clearinghouse scenario. Having put your news release aside for about 45 minutes, you begin to reread it, imagining that the editor of a local newspaper is leaning over your shoulder. Because she's a journalist, she immediately tells you, *Give me specific details. No vagueness!* Your reader's vision leads you to reconsider your second sentence: *Anderson, formerly with the Coxwold County Red Cross, will begin her new duties May 29.*

You're specific about *when,* but Anderson's former job at the Red Cross seems vague. So to satisfy your reader's interest in exact details, you revise the sentence: *Anderson, the former supervisor of the Coxwold County Red Cross, will begin her new duties May 29.*

It's a small change, but it has a big impact: It helps to satisfy the needs of your readers. When you've worked through the entire document with a fresh perspective and tested each sentence against the core message, you're ready for the next stage of the writing process: macroediting.

Macroediting: Stage Six of the Writing Process

You've no doubt heard that a lawyer who represents himself or herself has a fool for a client. The same is partially true of editing: No writer should serve as the only editor of his or her writing. A qualified coworker should edit your document before you submit it to a supervisor or the client for approval. Does that mean that you as writer have no editing responsibilities? No: Your goal is to deliver a flawless document to the editor—and that means completing the first edit yourself. Your own edit should consist of two levels: the macroedit and the microedit.

Macroediting challenges the "big picture" of your document: the meaning, the organization, and the format. Among the important questions in a macroedit are

- Is the message of the document clear?
- Does the document answer a reporter's traditional questions: who? what? where? when? why? how?
- Is the document fair? (You don't have to present other points of view, but your document shouldn't distort reality, present half-truths, or ignore damaging information.)
- Does the document make any claims that seem unsubstantiated?
- Does the organization of the main points follow a logical order?
- Does one paragraph lead gracefully to the next?

- Is the format of the document correct? (For example, does the format of a news release identify a contact person?)
- Does the format assist the meaning? (For example, would internal headlines help?)

The macroediting stage is your last opportunity for significant rewriting before you deliver your document to others. If you are satisfied that the meaning, organization, and format are as good as they can be, it's time for the microedit.

Microediting: Stage Seven of the Writing Process

Microediting means doing a sentence-by-sentence double-check of accuracy, spelling, grammar (including punctuation), and style. But by this point in the writing process, you've probably read your document at least a dozen times; you may even have parts of it memorized. This familiarity makes it hard for you to conduct an effective microedit: You may read what you *meant* to write instead of what you *accidentally* wrote. One way to increase your focus on the actual words in each sentence is to conduct the microedit backward, starting with the last full sentence. Moving through the document backward "defamiliarizes" it, helping you see what you've really written. When you're certain that the last sentence is flawless, move to the second-to-last sentence, and so on. As you might guess, proofreading backward isn't exciting, but it is effective.

To verify accuracy, double-check all names, titles, numbers—any fact that can be confirmed. Also double-check all spelling, punctuation, and common grammatical errors such as disagreements between verbs and their subjects. For style, verify that each sentence follows specific style guidelines preferred by its targeted public. In your Volunteer Clearinghouse news release, you probably would use Associated Press style, which many newspapers use. Most news releases are written in newspaper style, which broadcast media rewrite to their specifications.

Imagine doing the microedit of your news release for Volunteer Clearinghouse. As you'll recall, you had revised your first sentence to this:

> *The Volunteer Clearinghouse board of directors has named Elaine Anderson the organization's new executive director.*

This would be the last sentence to undergo a microedit, because you wisely began at the end of the document and moved backward one sentence at a time. Stifling a yawn, you double-check the spelling of Elaine Anderson's name against her résumé—and your yawn turns into a gasp: Her first name is spelled *Elayne*. As you type in the correction, you're grateful that you edited the document yourself before submitting it to another editor. Good microediting helped save your credibility as a writer.

When the editing process is through, the document is ready for an important test: the approval stage of the writing process.

Approval: Stage Eight of the Writing Process

Oftentimes, many people want to review a document before distribution to the targeted public: your supervisor, your client, anyone who is quoted, anyone who supplied important information, key department heads . . . the list can seem endless. And many

Grammar on the Web

What's the difference between *who* and *whom?* How about *lay* and *lie?* Or *that* and *which?* Should an opening subordinate clause be set off by a comma—and what's an opening subordinate clause, anyway? Now imagine asking such questions in the middle of the night as you toil away at an important public relations document. Who can answer such questions when only you and the bakers in the local doughnut shop are awake?

Let the web come to the rescue. It abounds with sites sponsored by university writing centers, editing professors, and other cyberspace grammarians. Just go to your favorite search engine and type in the key word *grammar.*

Two of the best sites for college students have little in common except clarity and usefulness. The first is the first edition of the famous *Elements of Style* by William Strunk Jr., online at www .bartleby.com/141. Strunk clearly explains the blunt guidelines he offers, such as "Use the active voice" and "Omit needless words." The short, well-organized book closes with the sections "Words and Expressions Commonly Misused" and "Words Commonly Misspelled."

A second highly useful web site is *Guide to Grammar and Writing,* easily accessed with your favorite search engine. This comprehensive, well-organized site can help answer your *who/ whom, lay/lie,* and *that/which* questions. The site also includes quizzes and frequently asked questions. Best of all, as a welcome relief, the entries are informal and reflect a sense of humor.

When questions of grammar arise, help may be only a few keystrokes away.

of these reviewers have the power to insist on changes. In the workplace, your supervisor can assist you in determining which of the requested changes should be made.

Who is in charge of the approval stage? That depends on the company or organization, but in many cases the writer is in charge of securing approvals. The approval process involves knowing who needs to review the document, how soon each reviewer must respond, and who has the final say over requested revisions. Along with the document, each reviewer should receive a memorandum that politely specifies a deadline for response. An important strategy for the approval stage of the writing process is to keep a chart for every document, noting to whom it was sent, when it was sent, when it was returned, what revisions were requested, and what revisions were made.

The approvals list for the Volunteer Clearinghouse news release, for example, probably would include your supervisor, a representative of the clearinghouse's board of directors, and perhaps Elayne Anderson herself. Some documents, such as corporate annual reports, have much longer approval lists; for example, lawyers and accountants read every annual report to ensure that it meets all its legal and financial reporting requirements.

For most public relations documents, a second round of approvals generally is not necessary unless substantial revisions were requested and made. However, be sure your supervisor grants final approval before you proceed to the next stage of the writing process: distribution.

Distribution: Stage Nine of the Writing Process

Distribution differs from document to document. A news release can be hand-delivered, mailed, e-mailed, faxed, posted on a web site, or routed through online distribution services such as PR Newswire. A policy and procedure document telling employees how a certain process works can be placed in employee mailboxes or on desktops, e-mailed, posted on an intranet, placed in a binder in the organization's library, or even tacked onto an old-fashioned wall-mounted bulletin board. The writer may be in charge of all or some of the distribution, or distribution may be delegated to others.

As more and more distribution occurs through e-mail and web sites, however, writers are assuming increasing responsibility for distribution. With improvements in technology, distribution through cyberspace can be triggered by the push of a button. But therein lies a problem for public relations practitioners. Should that message be posted on the organization's public web site—or, perhaps, should it be only on the intranet or extranet site? If the document is to be e-mailed within an organization, should everyone receive it—or just top management? More than one communicator has been embarrassed by accidentally posting a private document to every electronic mailbox within an organization. The ease of online communication is accompanied, unfortunately, by the possibility of instantaneous errors in distribution.

Even when distribution is delegated to others, the writer may want to double-check that it did occur. A sad truth is that the best writer and the most polished document in the world can be defeated by faulty distribution. Many writers, therefore, carefully monitor the distribution stage of the writing process. Double-checking distribution can be as simple as checking a web site or as complicated as driving to different office buildings to ensure that posters are properly displayed.

Despite the countless ways of distributing a document, a few facts hold true for every method: Whenever possible, a document should be delivered in the manner and at the time and in the place preferred by the targeted public. When we're satisfied that our distribution method meets these public-focused criteria, we're ready for the final stage of the writing process: evaluation.

Evaluation: Stage Ten of the Writing Process

In earlier chapters, when we discussed the four-stage public relations process of research, planning, communication, and evaluation, we noted that although evaluation is mentioned last, it actually occurs throughout the public relations process. It's the same in writing: Evaluation is ongoing throughout the process. Above all, however, we evaluate at the end of the writing process to see whether our document succeeded. Did it address the targeted public's values and interests well enough to be read and acted upon? For example, did journalists use the news release we wrote for Volunteer Clearinghouse? If so, which media used it, and how many of our main points did the coverage include? In short, how well did we succeed? If some journalists chose not to use the news release, why not? Without excessively troubling the journalists, can we determine why our news release didn't become news in certain media? In the writing process, evaluation helps us to identify and reinforce what we did well—and to identify and not repeat any errors we may have made.

And now we're at the end of the writing process. At this point, it's only human to ask whether it's really worth working through all these stages. What's the reward for such a meticulous approach to writing? Fortunately, the rewards are many. Adhering to the writing process can help prevent the nausea that comes from staring at a computer screen as a deadline approaches and not knowing what to say. Within the framework of the writing process, should such a moment happen, we can drop back to previous levels, strengthen them, and then move forward again with confidence. Using the writing process can mean job security and promotability. As we note at the beginning of the chapter, public relations relies on skillful, precise use of language. Using the writing process, finally, can earn you respect as a thoughtful, professional writer who knows how to strengthen relationships with the magic of words.

Writing for the Web

One strategy for web writing is simply to move print documents onto web sites, as some newspapers do. However, studies show that we read computer screens up to 50 percent slower than we do ordinary print documents.[9] And most readers have expectations for web writing that don't apply to paper documents—expectations such as links and search options. Just like broadcast writing (or writing for the ear), writing for the web requires special techniques different from those of traditional print. Whether your online writing is for a social media news release, a blog, or copy for a web site page, marketing professional Bonnie Poovey Short recommends these tips:[10]

- Information must be current. Web pages in particular should immediately reflect any changes in important facts and figures.

- Web writing should include highlighted links to other sites or other pages within a web site. Bloggers often link to other blogs. Social media news releases can link to videos and background information.

- Sentences on web pages should be concise, with one idea per sentence. (The conversational nature of blogs can make them an exception to this guideline.) Paragraphs also should be short, rarely running to more than three sentences.

- Successful web pages effectively use headlines and captions. Studies show that readers often examine those items first. Headlines, followed by a brief article summary, often link to the full article located on a separate page.

- Successful web sites incorporate graphics, of course—but eye-movement studies show that readers prefer concise text to graphics.

Finally, web writers and their organizations are accessible. Interactive web sites offer contact information that includes e-mail addresses, telephone numbers, and street addresses. Responding to reader questions and comments should be a priority. Bloggers often acknowledge readers' responses by posting their comments below blog entries.

QUICK CHECK

1. How formal does a writer's outline need to be?
2. What is "the euphoria of creation"? How can its influence be diminished?
3. What questions should a writer ask in the macroediting stage of the writing process?
4. Why and how does a writer move backward in the microediting stage of the writing process?
5. How does writing for web documents differ from writing for paper documents?

Writing for the Ear

We've seen how the writing process works for documents designed to be read, such as news releases. But the writing process works equally well for documents designed to be *heard,* such as speeches and podcasts. Documents designed to be heard, however, require special writing techniques to ensure that targeted publics easily comprehend the speaker's meaning. After all, unlike readers, listeners can't simply reread a paragraph or pause to decipher a challenging passage. Professional speechwriters, broadcast news writers, and other professionals who write for the ear have developed several guidelines for effectively conveying meaning to their listeners:

■ *Remember that the speaker has to breathe.* Use short sentences. Short sentences create frequent pauses, which allow the speaker to breathe. The pauses also give listeners a moment to consider the previous sentence. An average effective spoken sentence contains 9 to 10 words.

■ *Limit each sentence to one idea.* Avoid linking clauses together with coordinating conjunctions such as *and* and *but* or with subordinating conjunctions such as *because* and *although.* By the time listeners receive the closing idea of a multiclause sentence, they may have forgotten the idea at the beginning.

■ *Use concrete words and images, not abstractions.* Clear, explicit language helps your listeners stay focused. They won't pause to try to decipher the meaning of vague, abstract language. Charles Osgood of CBS-TV and CBS Radio so believes in the power of concrete, evocative language that he ends his television broadcasts with these words: "*See* you on the radio."

■ *Use precise nouns and verbs.* An imprecise verb needs an adverb to clarify its meaning. A vague noun needs an adjective to make it accurate. Choosing exactly the right word helps you create short, precise sentences. Avoid excessive use of *to be* verbs such as *am, is, was,* and *were.* Such verbs don't convey precise images to listeners.

■ *Challenge every word in every sentence.* Is each word necessary? Can a more precise noun eliminate the need for an adjective? Can you replace a long word with a shorter word without losing meaning? Spoken language is not the place to impress an audience with your knowledge of sesquipedalian (long) words.

■ *Spell out big numbers and give phonetic spellings for hard-to-pronounce words.* If the speaker stumbles, so do the listeners. Assist the speaker by providing pronunciation cues for big numbers and difficult names or words. For example, broadcast writers often write the number 5,200 as "52–hundred."

■ *Use traditional syntax (word order).* In the English language, the simplest sentences begin with a subject, which is followed by a verb, which in turn is sometimes followed by a direct object and perhaps an indirect object. Traditional word order offers the fewest roadblocks to understanding.

■ *Link sentences and paragraphs with clear transitions.* Often, you can create a clear **transition** by making the direct object of one sentence the subject of the following sentence. Note how objects become subjects in the following example: *In 1863 Abraham Lincoln wrote his greatest speech: the Gettysburg Address. The Gettysburg Address expresses principles that still guide us today. The most important of those principles is contained in the words "government of the people, by the people, and for the people."*

■ *Attribute direct quotations at the beginning of a sentence.* In written English, we often place the **attribution**—the *said Abraham Lincoln*—in the midst or at the end of a direct quotation. But listeners can't see quotation marks. Placing the attribution at the beginning of a quotation is the only way to signal clearly that the speaker is citing someone else's words.

■ *Introduce important points with general, descriptive sentences.* Let listeners know that an important point is coming. If a speaker simply says, *Sixty percent of our employees want better communication with top management,* listeners may not retain the percentage as they absorb the rest of the sentence. We can assist our listeners by writing, *A high percentage of our employees want better communication with top management. Sixty percent of our employees say that top management should communicate with them more often.*

■ *Gracefully repeat main points.* Know the main points that you hope to convey, and seek opportunities to state them more than once.

■ *Avoid closing with "In conclusion."* Readers can see the end of a document coming. But how do listeners identify an upcoming conclusion? A return to the broad theme of the document—a restatement of the main point—can signal that the end is near.

■ *Break any of the above guidelines when doing so will assist the listener.* These are only guidelines, not rigid laws. Usually, these guidelines help convey meaning to the listener. In cases where they interfere with meaning, discard them.

Writing the spoken word well is an art, as is all good writing. Writing the spoken word, in fact, leads logically to our next section. Public relations professionals sometimes stand and deliver the words they have written. Sometimes they make presentations.

DRAFT PUBLIC SERVICE ANNOUNCEMENTS

TITLE: Breathing Year-Round

LENGTH: 60

LIVE READ RADIO PSA

Heart disease claims millions of lives.

Asthma impairs the health of so many children and adults.

Air pollution, especially particles, aggravates heart disease and lung disease. In fact, it can be deadly for some people. And it can be damaging for older adults, and children.

Particle pollution tracking and Air Quality Index forecasts are now available every day throughout the year. It's one of the most effective ways for you to manage your health year-round.

The Air Quality Index is now a "forecast to breathe by."

Want to know more? Check out Air Quality Index forecasts on your local television weathercasts, radio stations, and newspapers, and at this Web site at: www.epa.gov/airnow.

Public Service Announcement Radio public service announcements demonstrate how writing meant to be read aloud differs from ordinary print writing. Note the brevity of the sentences. (Courtesy of the U.S. Environmental Protection Agency)

QUICK   CHECK

1. How many words are in the average effective spoken sentence?
2. In general, do adjectives and adverbs add to or detract from the effectiveness of spoken language?
3. In spoken language, why should an important point be introduced by a general, descriptive sentence?

The Process of Successful Presentations

Comedian Jerry Seinfeld—someone who knows a thing or two about appearing before large groups—has no illusions about the difficulty of public speaking: At a funeral, he says, most of us would rather be the corpse than the person delivering the eulogy.[11] Cicero, the greatest of the Roman orators, wrote, "I turn pale at the outset

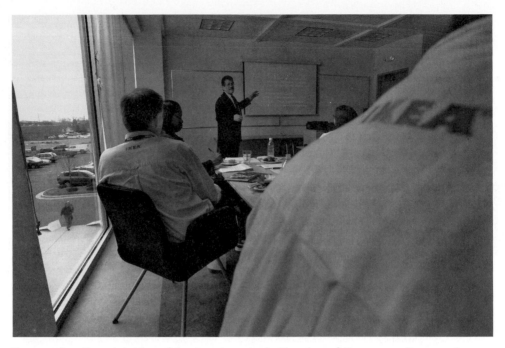

Presentation Fouad Ashkar of the American Arab Chamber of Commerce discusses the subtleties of marketing to Muslim citizens with employees of IKEA USA. (Photo by Fabrizio Costantini/*New York Times*. Copyright 2007 The New York Times Company. Reprinted with permission.)

of a speech and quake in every limb and in all my soul."[12] As we noted earlier, public speaking ranks number one among people's greatest fears.

Why the terror? Often, we fear making fools of ourselves. Other times, we're afraid that the discomfort of being in front of a group will rattle us, making our voices tremble and our hands shake. People will see how nervous we are, and their awareness will intensify our nightmare. Make a presentation? No thanks. We'll schedule a root canal for that day (fear of dentists is not among people's top 14 fears).[13]

Public relations practitioners, however, cannot avoid presentations. Clients want proposals. The news media want statements. Community groups want speeches. The question is not *Will we make presentations?* We will. Rather, the question is *How can we make successful presentations?* Our answer should sound familiar: A successful presentation requires research, planning, communication, and evaluation—the four stages of the public relations process. By the time you actually deliver your presentation, it should be an old friend. It should fit you and your targeted public like a pair of comfortable shoes. With presentations, familiarity doesn't breed contempt. Instead, your familiarity with your presentation, your audience, and even the room in which you'll be speaking breeds confidence and success. And it all starts with research.

VALUES STATEMENT 10.1

Kellogg Company

Based in Battle Creek, Michigan, the Kellogg Company produces breakfast cereals, toaster pastries, frozen waffles, bagels, cereal bars, and other food products. The Kellogg Company values statement includes this passage:

INTEGRITY AND ETHICS

Integrity is the cornerstone of our business practice. We will conduct our affairs in a manner consistent with the highest ethical standards. To meet this commitment, we will:

Engage in fair and honest business practices.

Show respect for each other, our consumers, customers, suppliers, shareholders and the communities in which we operate.

Communicate in an honest, factual and accurate manner.

—Kellogg Company web site

Researching Your Presentation

Presentation research begins with knowing your targeted public. Who are its members? What values and interests unite them? Could cultural differences affect your presentation? What do they want from you? How long do they expect you to speak? If the situation permits such a request, don't hesitate to ask members of your future audience what they hope to learn from you. To create an effective message, you should combine audience research with another area of research: research into what you want to tell the audience. As you know, an effective message combines your purpose with the values and interests of the targeted public. During your presentation, if you consistently address the concerns of your audience, you can expect to be rewarded with eye contact, nodding heads, and attentive listeners.

Another aspect of audience research is identifying the decision makers and opinion leaders within your audience. Of course, you should maintain eye contact with and speak to everyone in the room. But at important moments in your presentation, you may want to focus extra attention on the people who can most help you achieve your goals.

Researching a presentation also involves learning about the room in which you'll be speaking. Is there enough space to allow freedom of movement as you speak? Are there windows that need to be shaded if you plan to project visuals onto a screen? Is there a screen? A projection system? A lectern? Answers to such questions not only improve the technical support of your presentation; they also increase your comfort level as you prepare for the presentation. You won't be walking into unknown territory.

Planning Your Presentation

Begin by planning to be yourself. Trying to be someone else during your presentation is stressful and distracting. You impress your targeted public more by addressing its values and interests than by maintaining icy composure at every moment. Have confidence in the message you create, and relax. Be yourself.

Planning includes message creation. Again, your message should combine your presentation's purpose with your audience's values and interests. Everything in your presentation should support the central, unifying theme of your message. But how long should "everything" be? Your research answers that question: Length is guided by what the audience wants. Ideally, a speech should take no more than 20 minutes and include no more than three main, message-related points. Presentation of a proposal to a client generally should take no more than one hour; anything longer might suggest a lack of respect for the client's time. During that hour, every point you make should be related to the central theme provided by your message. A brief statement to the news media may take only one minute. An educational presentation may take an entire day or two. Again, the ideal length for any presentation is established by the needs of the targeted public.

When you know the message and the length, you're ready to outline your presentation. Unless you're delivering a formal speech or a highly technical performance in which assistants trigger multimedia effects as you say specific words, experts suggest that you not have a word-for-word script. An outline allows you to maintain eye contact and helps you speak with—instead of read to—your audience. Many professionals recommend, however, that you memorize your introduction, your conclusion, and any important anecdotes. At those key moments, you want unflinching eye contact as you dazzle the audience with your sincere, articulate, and polished presentation.

Another aspect of planning for success is practice. And more practice. And even more practice. Practicing not only polishes your presentation; it also helps you become comfortable with it. And being comfortable with your presentation reduces the terror that freezes many of us at the mere thought of public speaking. Being comfortable with your presentation can actually make you eager to deliver it: You know it's good, you know you're ready, and (being human) you're eager for the praise you know you deserve. So practice. And then practice some more.

As you practice, try to duplicate the conditions and environment of the actual presentation. Practice in the room in which you'll make the real presentation. If that's not possible, practice in a similar room. Practice at the scheduled presentation time. If you intend to invite questions from your audience, have friends and coworkers observe your practice presentations and ask questions. Wear the comfortable clothing that you'll wear during the presentation—usually clothing at or just above the level of formality of your audience's attire. Use the technology and visual aids that you'll use in your actual presentation, and practice your solutions to sudden technological failures.

Using Visual Aids. Planned and used wisely, **visual aids** can enhance most presentations. Visual aids range from handouts to flip charts to overheads, slides, and computer projections. Studies show that well-designed visual aids can increase audience learning by 200 percent, increase audience retention of main points by 38 percent, and reduce explanation time by 40 percent.[14] Well-designed visuals are short and have headlines. Because you don't want your audience to read ahead of you, consider using a program such as PowerPoint, which allows you to use a computer projection system to build a visual one sentence or one image at a time. Although it's OK to look at your own visuals, don't turn your back and speak to them. Speak to your audience. If a gap occurs between one visual and the next, consider going to a blank screen—or covering your flip chart—so that an old visual doesn't become a distraction. And absolutely, positively avoid misspellings in your visuals.

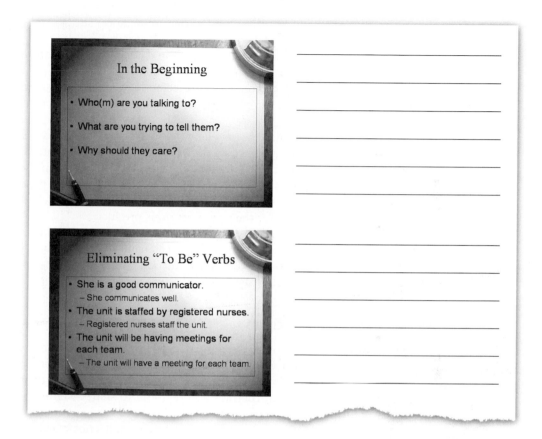

Presentation Handouts Copies of presentation visuals can help audience members take notes and focus on a speaker's message. Most slide-creation programs have special print functions for handouts.

Many audiences will be grateful for photocopies of visuals. Rather than interrupt your presentation to distribute them or make audience members wait until the presentation is over, have the attractively bound photocopies ready as the audience enters the room. Ideally, you have individualized both your visuals and the photocopies for this particular presentation. For example, if you're addressing your local chamber of commerce, the cover sheet of your bound photocopies should acknowledge that.

Planning for Problems. You should also plan for trouble. If you're speaking from a script or an outline, you should have quick access to a second copy in case you misplace yours at the last moment. Ensure that extra lightbulbs are available for the projection system. If you're using a computer projection system, have overhead transparencies and access to an overhead projector in case the system fails. If the journey to your presentation site involves airline travel, carry on—don't check—luggage that includes presentation materials. Otherwise, as you arrive in Barcelona to make your presentation, your visual aids may be 40,000 feet above Honolulu. Consider shipping bulky handouts or technology to the presentation site several days early to ensure that they arrive.

Your final moment of troubleshooting should occur approximately an hour before you start your presentation. Arrive early, and test the technology one last time. Double-check the location of your backup technology, such as an overhead projector and transparencies or a flip chart. Ensure that you have access to two copies of your outline or script.

Preparing for trouble also means being flexible. Know your presentation so well that you can cut it short if your hosts decrease your time allotment. Watch for any changes in your subject matter that might alter the direction of your presentation. For example, a potential client suddenly facing a lawsuit over one of its products may be more interested in crisis communications counseling than in your scheduled presentation on a DVD media kit for the now-notorious product.

Finally, if someone will be introducing you, consider writing a short introduction for that individual to use. He or she may appreciate the assistance, and you won't be surprised by an inadequate or a too-lavish introduction. Be sure to send that introduction to your introducer at least a week before your presentation.

Making Your Presentation

It's the moment of truth. You've been introduced, and you're the center of attention. After thanking the person who introduces you, pause a moment before you begin. Smile. Look at the people in the room. Show them that you're confident, that you're quietly excited about the information you're about to share. Maintain eye contact, and begin your memorized introduction.

Should you begin with a joke? Most experts say no. It's not worth the risk of failing and beginning the presentation with an awkward silence or strained laughter. A more effective opening strategy can be an anecdote with which your audience can identify. Another effective strategy is to begin by targeting your audience's concerns: Tell audience members exactly what you hope they gain from your presentation. After that, you may want to establish the basic guidelines of the presentation, such as when you'll take questions.

As you speak, continue eye contact, looking at one person at a time, gracefully forcing that person to realize that you are acknowledging and valuing his or her presence. Again, single out decision makers and opinion leaders for extra eye contact. Unless you are giving a formal speech, try not to anchor yourself to a lectern or a technology table. A handheld remote control can allow you to project visuals from any point in the room. If you move smoothly about the presentation area, the audience's eyes will follow you, helping everyone stay alert.

If your technology fails—and, eventually, in some presentation it will—don't try to hide the fact. You've prepared for this eventuality, and you're ready to handle it professionally. Acknowledge the failure; after all, everyone can see it. Toss off a quick joke, if appropriate, and move smoothly to your backup solution. Audience members probably are empathizing with you; it could just as easily be one of them suffering the failure. They'll be relieved and pleased to see you avoid panic. Your seamless

QuickBreak 10.4

Conquering the Presentation Jitters

"We have nothing to fear but fear itself," said President Franklin Roosevelt. Of course, Roosevelt referred to fear created by a faltering economy, but his shrewd comment also applies to presentations. Frequently, the presentation itself is not what we fear; instead, we fear appearing nervous and uncertain in front of others. We're unnerved by the fear that our hands will shake and our voices will tremble.

Expert presenters offer this advice about fighting stage fright:

- Practice in front of others. Present to test audiences before you present to the ultimate audience.

- Deliver the goods. If you're conveying useful information to your audience, its members will think you're great.

- As you present, maintain eye contact. Don't think about yourself; think about your audience. Talk to people, not to the walls, floor, or ceiling.

- Channel your nervous energy into movement. If appropriate, walk around as you speak. Address different sections of the room. Use hand gestures that complement your words.

- Realize that you are your own worst critic. Few people in the audience are evaluating your performance. Instead, they're evaluating the quality of the information they're receiving—so, again, deliver the goods.

- After a presentation, reward yourself with a special purchase or some other treat. Be grateful to the presentation for giving you the excuse for a minor extravagance.

One last bit of advice. Attack your fear. Seek opportunities to do presentations. Franklin Roosevelt *didn't* say, "Practice makes perfect"—but, once again, the phrase applies to presentations.

---

move to an alternate plan will impress them, in part because it shows just how seriously you've taken this opportunity to speak with them. As we'll note in Chapter 12, sometimes a well-handled crisis creates a hero.

When possible, close your presentation by calling for questions. A question-and-answer session can emphasize one last time your respect for your audience's particular concerns. Don't finish with an answer, however. Instead, after you answer the final question, deliver a summary statement, a strong, planned "cap" for your remarks. In presentations that are *not* formal speeches, consider this closing tactic: After your final statement, clap your hands once, bow slightly, straighten, and, looking your audience in the eyes, say, with a smile, "Thank you very much." Your own clap and your slight bow just might trigger applause.

Formal speeches generally do not include a question-and-answer session. Instead, if you're presenting such a speech, deliver a strong conclusion and close with a simple "Thank you." Applause automatically follows most speeches.

However you conclude your presentation, keep an eye (subtly) on the clock. No one appreciates a presentation that runs past its allotted time. An overlong presentation can show a serious lack of respect for the audience, undermining the powerful focus you've placed on addressing its values. Presentation coach Karen Susman recommends the following timing strategy: "Know your material and how long it takes to deliver. Follow the 75 percent rule. If you're scheduled to speak for one hour, plan 45 minutes of material. . . . Be so familiar with your presentation that you know where you can cut if you need to."[15]

After finishing your presentation, relax. That wasn't so bad, was it?

Evaluating Your Presentation

Don't bask in glory too long, though: Another presentation looms, and you can help make it great by applying what you've learned from your recent presentation and other past efforts. Wait 24 hours until the euphoria of finishing has passed, and then write yourself a memo, evaluating your recent presentation. What worked well? What didn't work as well as you had planned? How well did the technology perform? Did anything during the presentation surprise you? Was the audience responsive? If so, when? How do you know it was responsive? Did you finish on time? What questions and comments from the audience did you receive? When you've answered such questions, consider giving yourself a grade: A for excellent, B for good, and so on. Try to score a higher grade on your next similar presentation.

The ultimate evaluation, of course, comes from your targeted public. Did it receive and act on the message you delivered? If your presentation was a public relations tactic, did it help you achieve your objective? Ultimately, the success of your presentation must be judged by that standard.

QUICK ✓ CHECK

1. Why is it important to be able to recognize the opinion leaders and decision makers in your audience?
2. Who determines the ideal length of a presentation?
3. Which parts of a presentation should be memorized?
4. What is the 75 percent rule for presentations?

Summary

The difficulty of writing and making presentations is matched by the importance of these two skills: They are core elements in the profession of public relations. Neither will ever be easy, but you can make them easier by following the process that each requires. Those processes are similar, moving through research, planning, implementation, and evaluation. Each stage must be completed before the practitioner can successfully grapple with the next stage. And after the last stage lies success.

As you gain more access to public relations professionals through guest lectures and internships, ask them when they last wrote a document or made a presentation. Their answers will underscore the importance of writing and presentation skills in the practice of public relations.

DISCUSSION QUESTIONS

1. Given what you know of writing for the ear, how would you rewrite the proposed first paragraph of the Volunteer Clearinghouse news release to adapt it to a radio news story? Your final draft of the first paragraph was *The Volunteer Clearinghouse board of directors has named Elayne Anderson the organization's new executive director. Anderson, the former supervisor of the Coxwold County Red Cross, will begin her new duties May 29. Volunteer Clearinghouse recruits and trains volunteers for Coxwold County United Way agencies.*

2. In what ways would a social media news release (page 268) be different from your standard news release for Volunteer Clearinghouse?

3. Why do journalists prefer the inverted pyramid for news stories?

4. What is the difference between macroediting and microediting? Why aren't the two done simultaneously?

5. Can you quote memorable passages from famous speeches? How do those passages support or refute the guidelines for writing for the ear contained in this chapter?

6. Do you fear public speaking? If so, why? Be specific. Do you think the process for successful presentations outlined in this chapter could relieve some of your anxiety? Why or why not?

Memo from the Field

Regina Lynch-Hudson is founder and president of The Write Publicist in Atlanta. Self-described as "the quintessential American mutt," Lynch-Hudson has a 15-year track record of conceptualizing print media campaigns for people, places, products, and performances.

Lynch-Hudson has launched and syndicated columns about public relations, travel, business, and other topics. She has been profiled in the magazines *Entrepreneur* and *Black Enterprise*.

Regina Lynch-Hudson, President, The Write Publicist, Atlanta, Georgia

Admittedly, when I was asked to contribute to this public relations textbook, I wondered what I would communicate to wide-eyed, idealistic students, when my own career path has not been conventional. But then *public relations* is such an ambiguous term.

I regard public relations as an art form, combining some theory and a great deal of impressionism. From the subliminal theatrics required to deliver memorable presentations to the gut spontaneity of merging words that evoke reaction—a wordsmith's success isn't tied to academia alone. My own college years were short-circuited, due to a family tragedy. NEWS FLASH: Kidney dialysis patient brutally murdered leaving hospital. *Victim's daughter turns to writing for solace.*

Ongoing courses in consumer behavior, body language, and psychology melded with world travel, and an oftentimes nontraditional mélange of seminars, workshops, and lectures enhanced my perspective. I relied on creative ripeness and ravenous "literary consumption" to whet my writing skills.

You should also develop a penchant to read anything you can get your hands on—newspapers, magazines, menus, billboards, and direct mail. You never know when you'll be writing about an automotive manufacturer; a software company; a humanitarian organization; or a corporation with international reach. Subconsciously we all plunder our past for material—and in the profoundest, most unexpected way, up pops a tidbit of knowledge precisely when needed. Somewhere between writing's structure, public relations' principles, and imagination's abstractions, you'll discover a definite and confident style.

Be prepared to undergo years of clarifying and deepening your personal vision, of focusing your energies, of developing patience, just to objectively identify where *you* fit. Discovering one's strengths and weaknesses, maintaining one's commitment and capacity for learning, and perfecting one's craft are imperative in this business.

It's been said that life is a costume party and that we keep changing and changing and changing until we find the outfit that fits best. Some public relations practitioners blossom into world-class event coordinators. Many of us PR'ers are the "idea geniuses" who pen attention-grabbing news releases. Other PR-types possess a gift for gab and are better suited to "pitch" to editors or to deliver persuasive speeches. Tailor your career around a specialty that's a "fit," rather than with what the market seemingly needs. The market can be quite capricious. Embracing those skills that spur passion and inner solace, and daringly carving out a niche based on talents and interests, are not only necessary for productivity but are also necessary for longevity.

Poignancy sells. Regardless of the company or target audience, ability to elucidate a client, on paper, verbally, and even in your body language during oral presentations, requires varying degrees of ardor—delivered enthusiastically, succinctly, and with sincerity. Frankly, one must, to a certain extent, psychologically bond with the client's product or service to promote it. Genuineness is not easily feigned—unless you minor in drama and acting. And even then, audiences are not easily fooled over the long haul.

Originality rules. Oftentimes, originality implies being bold enough to go beyond accepted norms. It's how you pen (or peg) your clients as *distinct* that will brand them in the psyche of target audiences. Whether you are penning a proposal to reap sponsorship for an event, a speech to lure voters to a politician, or a script for a videotape to be used as a sales tool for a luxury resort, communicating what's "different" is fundamental. Knowing your clients enables you to gage how demonstrative you can be in your written, verbal, or pictorial personification of them. A bank or a life insurance company may require black-and-white doses of realism, whereas in promoting tourism, the arts, or food, you may add splashes of wit and whimsy.

Don't be afraid to stroke with a broad brush, to try new techniques, to make mistakes. Mistakes are the catalysts that germinate genius. There are no paint-by-number strategies for mastering public relations. The web and the 2000 Census reflect dramatic change in not only *how* we communicate but in the profile of who *we* are.

There's a big canvas out there, and, as Van Gogh illustrated, there is more than one way to paint a sunflower. Whether you work for a *Fortune* 500 giant or as a solo practitioner—it's how you distill millions of ideas and translate them into something cohesive that breathes life into the identity of your clients.

CASE STUDY 10.1

Plastic Couple Splits

Fame can complicate romance. Just ask Jessica Simpson and Nick Lachey, Britney Spears and K-Fed, or Barbie and Ken.

In case you missed the Valentine's Day 2004 news flash, Barbie dumped Ken, her steady guy for 43 years. Toy maker Mattel announced the dolls' breakup with a news release.

"With Ken, everything we did was on display," Barbie confided to reporter Jill Ingram of the *Asheville* (NC) *Citizen-Times*. "I mean, it's awful to have your breakup announced in a press release."

(At the end of her interview with Barbie, Ingram added this note: "Barbie can't converse. This interview is fake. I made the whole thing up. Please, oh please, let this disclaimer save me from the legal wrath of Mattel.")[16]

Executives at Mattel had better things to do than sue Ingram: They were busy counting the avalanche of news stories about Barbie's breakup. *PR Week* magazine estimated that the news release helped generate 500 broadcast stories and approximately the same number of print articles.[17] Internet company Terra Lycos, which monitors online searches, announced that within days of the breakup, *Barbie* had become one of the Internet's top 50 search terms. "Barbie was not even close to the list the previous week, but there she is at number 22 last week," the company reported. "We hope Ken has a good lawyer."[18]

Mattel, with the assistance of the Ketchum public relations agency, distributed the news release February 12, just before Valentine's Day and the American International Toy Fair in New York—an event that helps set trends in the toy industry.[19] Under the headline "The Storybook Romance Comes to an End for Barbie and Ken," the release began, "After more than 43 years together, Hollywood's quintessential 'doll' of a couple, Barbie and Ken, have decided to spend some time apart."[20]

Though journalists generally reject cute leads in news releases, the straight-faced treatment of the dolls as real people overcame journalism's preference for unadorned facts. Russell Arons, Mattel's vice president of marketing, became the celebrity couple's agent in the news release and offered this parody of the usual celebrity-split quote: "Barbie and Ken have always been an extraordinary couple. . . . And now they feel it's time to spend some quality time—apart."[21]

The news release not only made headlines around the world: It became part of the story. The release was discussed in the *New York Times*, the *Sunday Telegraph* of London, and the *Toronto Sun*. The *Post-Crescent* of Appleton, Wisconsin, mentioned the news release five times in one story, and the *Baltimore Sun*, in addition to mentioning the release, labeled the breakup a "pseudoevent" (see p. 266).

Mattel's news release even sparked other news releases that jumped aboard the breakup bandwagon. Reacting within 24 hours, 1-800-FLOWERS.COM issued a news release with this headline: "Ken Lost Barbie . . . Don't Lose Your Love This Valentine's Day." In the release, company CEO Jim McCann continued Mattel's "these are real people" charade: "If Ken had only visited us online or given us a call, we might have been able to help him."[22]

QualiLife Pharmaceuticals had a different romantic suggestion for the couple. Its news release, also distributed within 24 hours of the original, featured this headline: "Barbie & Ken Break Up After 43 Years: Did Her Sexual Dysfunction Play a Role?" In the release's lead, the company offered an alternative to flowers: "As Mattel announces the breakup of Barbie and Ken, QualiLife Pharmaceuticals, developers of the female arousal fluid Zestra for Women . . . mourns what might have been." Noting that Barbie was 43, CEO Martin Crosby said, "Zestra increases and restores sexual pleasure for most women that experience a broad range of sexual difficulties related to perimenopause."[23]

But the Barbie–Ken breakup may have had more to do with sales than romance. Before the Valentine's Day split, business media were reporting that Barbie's sales had been disappointing for years, affecting Mattel's profits and prospects.[24] "We are not pleased," said Mattel CEO Robert Eckert.[25]

London's *Sunday Telegraph* concluded, "It will be . . . interesting to see if Barbie's breakup with Ken falls into the category of publicity stunt—designed to stir up a campaign prior to an imminent but tearful reconciliation and reunification— or whether this storied brand can truly be successfully repositioned for growth."[26]

Could Barbie lose her Malibu beach house and that cool pink car? Is Ken gone forever? And what about Blaine, the Australian surfer introduced in yet another Mattel news release?

At last report, Barbie had no comment.

DISCUSSION QUESTIONS

1. Can we judge the success of the Barbie breakup news release by the amount of media attention it generated?
2. Was Mattel wise to gamble with a "cute" news release?
3. Were the related news releases from 1-800-FLOWERS.COM and QualiLife Pharmaceuticals good for Mattel?
4. Was the Barbie–Ken breakup a pseudoevent? (You may wish to consult Quick-Break 9.1 on page 266.)
5. And, of course, the big question: Should Mattel have Barbie and Ken get together again?

CASE STUDY **10.2**

Ghost Story: A Questionable Tactic Haunts Medical Journals

Professor Adriane Fugh-Berman has encountered a ghost—twice. A professor of physiology and biophysics at Georgetown University School of Medicine, Fugh-Berman received an e-mail from a major international pharmaceutical company in 2004. The message offered her an article, already researched and written, that she could revise, if she wished, and submit to a medical journal under her own name. Journal articles can help professors gain promotion to higher ranks and higher salaries.

The professor looked at the article, which touted one of the company's drugs, but refused to submit it under her name. A short while later, however, she encountered the article again. This time, it carried another medical researcher's name: It had been submitted to a prestigious medical journal, and the journal's editors were consulting Fugh-Berman to see if the article merited publication. Rather than examine the article, she told the editors about the ghost.[27]

The ghost, of course, was a ghostwriter. Ghostwriting is a time-honored activity within public relations: Practitioners write speeches for executives, news releases without personal bylines, and a host of other documents for which others often receive the credit. Such ghostwriting is standard procedure. But some ghosts are scarier than others: Editors of medical journals maintain that ghostwriting in the medical profession, especially when the ghostwriter is paid by a pharmaceutical company attempting to secretly promote its own products, is unethical and dangerous.

"Scientific research is not public relations," explains Robert Califf, vice chancellor of clinical research at Duke University. "If you're a firm hired by a company trying to sell a product, it's an entirely different thing than having an open mind for scientific inquiry. . . . What would happen to a PR firm that wrote a paper that said this product stinks?"[28]

Unfortunately, the ghost that appeared twice before Fugh-Berman may have lots of company. "I believe 50 percent of articles on drugs in the major medical journals are not written in a way that the average person would expect them to be," says David Healy, professor of psychological medicine at the University of Wales. "The evidence I have seen would suggest there are grounds to think a significant proportion of the articles in journals . . . may be written with help from medical writing agencies. They are no more than infomercials paid for by drug firms."[29]

Paraphrasing the charges of yet another angry medical professor who had seen a ghost, a *New York Times* reporter wrote, "Public relations firms hired by drug companies—furtive spin doctors—are ghostwriting articles in the journals to suit clients' interests."[30]

A survey published in the *Journal of the American Medical Association* found that ghosts had written at least 11 percent of articles in the top U.S. medical journals.[31] "It introduces another bias into the whole clinical drug trial picture," says Professor Thomas Bodenheimer of the University of California at San Francisco.

"The American public and the physicians in the United States are not going to know, really, the true facts about the drugs."[32]

To combat ghostwriting, medical journals and medical researchers have enlisted their own writing skills: They are asking pharmaceutical companies and their ghostwriters to follow a written ethics code known as *Good Publications Practice: Guidelines for Pharmaceutical Companies*. In part, that document states:

- The Acknowledgments section of a paper should list those people who made a significant contribution to the study but do not qualify as authors. It should also be used to acknowledge the study's funding and the [pharmaceutical] company's involvement in the analysis of the data or preparation of the publication. . . .
- The named author(s)/contributors should approve the final version of the manuscript before it is submitted.
- The contribution of the medical writer should be acknowledged.[33]

By listening to their target audience—medical editors—and following the provisions of such ethics codes, public relations practitioners can help lay this ghost to rest.

DISCUSSION QUESTIONS

1. Is it ethical, in your opinion, for public relations practitioners to ghostwrite articles that tout a pharmaceutical company's product?
2. Is all ghostwriting in public relations unethical? Is it unethical for a public relations practitioner to write a speech for which another individual receives credit?
3. The vice chancellor of clinical research at Duke University suggests that a public relations agency that ghostwrote an honest article about a defective drug would lose its pharmaceutical client. What should public relations practitioners do when their research reveals that a pharmaceutical client's drug may have defects?
4. Would it be ethical for a public relations practitioner, in the employ of a pharmaceutical company, to openly assist a professor in writing a journal article about one of the company's products?

NOTES

1. Writerly Things, online, www.ecentral.com/members/writers/quotes/writers.html.
2. Nexxus: A Place for Poetry, online, www.sage.net/~sgreene/nexxus.
3. David Wallechinsky, Irving Wallace, and Amy Wallace, *The Book of Lists* (New York: William Morrow, 1977), 469–470.
4. "Information Mapping Inc. Survey Reveals the True Impact of Ineffective Business Communications," news release issued by Information Mapping, Inc., 7 December 2006, online, www.infomap.com.
5. "*PR Week* Career Guide," report issued by *PR Week*, 2006, online, www.prweek.com/us.
6. Adapted from Charles Marsh, David W. Guth, and Bonnie Poovey Short, *Strategic Writing* (Boston: Allyn & Bacon, 2005).
7. Adapted from Marsh, Guth, and Short.

8. Robert Graves and Alan Hodge, *The Reader over Your Shoulder,* 2nd ed. (New York: Vintage Books, 1979).
9. Marsh, Guth, and Short, 95.
10. Marsh, Guth, and Short, 95–97.
11. Rowena Crosbie, "Speak Your Way to Success," *Canadian Manager* 22, no. 4, 1997, online, LexisNexis.
12. Cicero, "Of Oratory," in *The Rhetorical Tradition*, eds. Patricia Bizzell and Bruce Herzberg (Boston: Bedford Books, 1990), 217.
13. Wallechinsky et al., 469–470.
14. Crosbie.
15. Karen Susman, "Six Key Indicators Guaranteed to Reduce Audience Stress and Increase Your Applause," *Records Management Quarterly* 31, no. 3, 1997, online, LexisNexis.
16. Jill Ingram, "What a Doll!" *Asheville* (N.C.) *Citizen-Times,* 5 March 2004, online, LexisNexis.
17. John N. Frank, "Mattel Makes Most of Barbie-Ken Breakup," *PR Week,* 23 February 2004, online, LexisNexis.
18. "The Passion of Christ Makes Top 10 Web Searches," news release issued by Terra Lycos, 24 February 2004, online, LexisNexis.
19. Holly Mullen, "Solo Barbie Makes Left, Right Happy," *Salt Lake City Tribune,* 17 February 2004, online, LexisNexis.
20. "The Storybook Romance Comes to an End for Barbie and Ken," news release issued by Mattel, 12 February 2004, online, LexisNexis.
21. "The Storybook Romance Comes to an End for Barbie and Ken."
22. "Ken Lost Barbie . . . Don't Lose Your Love This Valentine's Day," news release issued by 1-800-FLOWERS.COM, 13 February 2004, online, LexisNexis.
23. "Barbie & Ken Break Up After 43 Years: Did Her Sexual Dysfunction Play a Role?" news release issued by QualiLife Pharmaceuticals, 13 February 2004, online, LexisNexis.
24. Richard Siklos, "How the Marketing Men Destroyed a Profitable Romance" (London) *Sunday Telegraph,* 25 April 2004, online, LexisNexis.
25. Siklos.
26. Siklos.
27. Anna Wilde Mathews, "At Medical Journals, Writers Paid by Industry Play Big Role," *Wall Street Journal,* 13 December 2005, A1.
28. Mathews.
29. Antony Barnett, "Revealed: How Drug Firms 'Hoodwink' Medical Journals," *The Observer,* 9 December 2003, online, http://observer.guardian.co.uk.
30. Lawrence K. Altman, "The Doctor's World: Some Authors in Medical Journals May Be Paid by 'Spin Doctors,' " *New York Times,* 4 October 1994, online, LexisNexis.
31. Melody Petersen, "Madison Ave. Has Growing Role in Business of Drug Research," *New York Times,* 22 November 2002, online, LexisNexis.
32. Mathews.
33. Elizabeth Wagner, Elizabeth A. Ford, and Leni Grossman, "Good Publication Practice for Pharmaceutical Companies," *Current Medical Research and Opinions* 19, no. 3 (2003): 153.

CHAPTER 11

Cyber-Relations in the Digital Age

OBJECTIVES

After studying this chapter, you will be able to

- describe the changes occurring through the development of digital communications technology, as well as the implications of those changes

- recognize the opportunities and challenges confronting public relations practitioners in the Digital Age

- identify the challenges and opportunities facing practitioners with the creation of social media and nontraditional online social networks

- appreciate that "new" doesn't always mean "better" and that in certain situations, traditional channels of communication are preferable to new high-tech ones

KEY TERMS

Differing Designs for the Future

Olds Young and Associates is one of the community's oldest architectural firms. One of the co-owners is Bud Olds, who founded the firm nearly three decades ago. The other owner is Betty Young, whose late father formed the original partnership with Olds.

In the five years since her father's death, Young has redirected the focus of the firm. Once known only as a local business, the firm has become nationally known for its designs of sports venues such as stadiums and arenas.

Because of increasing competition, your public relations agency has been asked to develop a public relations plan for Olds Young and Associates. As part of your initial research, you conducted separate interviews with the co-owners. It didn't take you long to discover a generation gap.

"We didn't use fancy public relations firms in the old days," said Olds. "If you wanted to generate new business, you went door-to-door and pressed the flesh. Who needs fancy PowerPoint presentations when a handshake and a smile will do the job? Don't let Betty talk you into proposing something as silly as podcasts and blogs. Most people in this town have never even heard of digital whatevers."

"Bud Olds has been like a second father to me," said Young. "But we need to bring this firm into the 21st century. The days of Magic Markers and flip charts are gone forever. I want to see us on YouTube and Second Life. We have potential customers that we need to reach."

"I think this firm is getting too big for its britches," said Olds.

"I have some big plans for our firm's future," said Young.

You have a problem. You have asked for a joint meeting with Olds and Young. What are you going to tell them?

It's All about You

Bree, the 16-year-old home-schooled daughter of strictly religious parents, posted her first video blog on YouTube in June 2006. The videos were secretly filmed on a web cam in her bedroom and posted under the username *lonelygirl15*. In the months that followed, Bree told anyone who would listen about her life as a young woman coming of age. And a lot of people did listen—her videos received an estimated 2 million views in their first two months.[1] However, it wasn't long before the truth behind *lonelygirl15* was revealed. Bree was identified as Jessica Rose, whom the *New York Times* described as "a twentyish resident of New Zealand and Los Angeles and a graduate of the New York Film Academy." Working with a couple of filmmakers and a software engineer, Rose and a handful of other actors created the hoax in the hope of eventually attracting a movie deal.[2]

The story of *lonelygirl15* tells us a lot about life in the Digital Age. Software engineer Grant Steinfeld said he helped to perpetrate the hoax because he came to believe that it was something new and important and that the team of YouTube conspirators had become "the new Marshall McLuhan."[3] This reference was to the Canadian philosopher who wrote in 1964 that we are living in a **global village,** where everyone can share simultaneous experiences. McLuhan said, "In our time, we have devised ways of making the most trivial event affect everybody."[4] Keep in mind that his observations came almost three decades before the advent of the **World Wide Web.** Pop artist Andy Warhol added his own twist to the concept of celebrity in highly mediated societies in 1968 when he said, "In the future, everyone will be world-famous for 15 minutes."[5] It appears as if the predictions of both men have come true: *lonelygirl15* is where Andy Warhol meets Marshall McLuhan.

In so many ways that we are still trying to discover, the emergence of **digital** technology has transformed society. It is easy for today's college students to take computer-readable communication for granted. However, prior to 1990, the **Internet,** as you know it, did not exist. In less than a generation, a digital revolution has affected almost every aspect of the ways we live, work, and play. This is especially true in the practice of public relations, where growth in the profession has paralleled growth in communications technology. Practitioners have always been among the first to adapt technological advances to their needs. Digital technology contributes to every step of the public relations process: research, planning, communication, and evaluation. With the advances in wireless technology, a world of information and opportunity is at our fingertips any time and any place we choose.

Web 2.0

Time magazine's decision to name *You* as its Person of the Year for 2006 was an acknowledgement of the power of **Web 2.0,** what the magazine described as "a tool for bringing together the small contributions of millions of people and making them matter."[6] The term *Web 2.0* was coined by a group of Silicon Valley consultants in 2004 to describe a new generation of Internet services that emphasize online collaboration and sharing. YouTube, the popular video-sharing service, and Wikipedia, the free—and not always accurate—online encyclopedia, are well-known examples of this phenomenon. Both are made possible through the voluntary efforts of thousands of contributors. Web 2.0 has unleashed a new force in mass communication: **social media.** *Time's* editors said they decided to recognize the online individual "for seizing the global media, for founding and framing the new digital democracy, for working for nothing and beating the pros at their own game."[7]

To put this another way, the Digital Revolution has helped to create new **social networks,** the often-informal structures through which individuals and/or organizations maintain relationships. Social networks can operate on many levels, such as families, civic organizations, trade associations, and neighborhoods. As a result of advances in communication technology, the number of these social networks is growing exponentially. This has resulted in a power shift, in which the ability to frame public debate is no longer the exclusive domain of the rich, the powerful, and the well connected.

"Whatever language we use to describe it, the beating heart of the Internet has always been its ability to leverage our social connections," wrote Pew Internet & American Life Project researchers Mary Madden and Susannah Fox. "Social networking sites like MySpace, Facebook and Friendster struck a powerful social chord at the right time using the right technology."[8]

Web 2.0 has made it possible for almost everyone to join the conversation. Granted, not everyone has something worthy to say. However, the debate is nothing if not lively. More important, these nontraditional online social networks have forced organizations to focus on new issues. Traditional media organizations, as well as the disciplines of public relations, advertising, and marketing, have had to reexamine how they reach targeted publics.

The reality of Web 2.0 comes down to this: It is all about you.

A Double-Edged Sword

Considering that the purpose of public relations is to build and maintain mutually beneficial relationships with publics critical to an organization's success, it is easy to see why practitioners have been at or near the cutting edge of the digital revolution. They are excited about the possibility of tapping into these online social networks and, in some cases, creating their own. Social networks also represent an opportunity to bypass traditional gatekeepers, such as those in the news media, to directly reach targeted publics.

However, the digital revolution can cut both ways. In a postmodern world, the impulse of many within these social networks is to redefine public policies and issues in a whole new narrative. They are not bound by traditional relationships and do not necessarily use traditional strategies and tactics. They also are adept at converting latent publics into active publics within a relatively short time frame. The challenge for the practitioner is to identify, monitor, and, if necessary, engage these nontraditional social networks. The failure to do so could negatively impact an organization.

"Modern information technology is creating a new corporate communication landscape," said researcher Augustine Ihator. "Computer technology has altered the power structure and relationship between corporations and their publics, stakeholders and the media."

"There is an emerging power sharing," Ihator wrote in *Public Relations Quarterly*. "Publics now have ready access to the mass media to tell their story from their own perspective and complain vehemently if necessary."[9]

Recent elections in the United States provide examples of the power of these nontraditional web-based social networks. During the 2004 presidential campaign, CBS News broadcast a story critical of President George W. Bush's National Guard service during the Vietnam War. Within hours of the *60 Minutes* segment, bloggers questioned the authenticity of documents on which the report was based. Less than two weeks after the report aired, the network apologized, with network anchor Dan Rather telling viewers that the report "was a mistake which we deeply regret."[10] CBS fired several staffers, with Rather eventually accepting early retirement.

Another example comes from the 2006 midterm elections, when U.S. Senator George Allen appeared headed for easy reelection and a possible White House bid. However, a combination of poor judgment and YouTube proved to be the Virginia senator's undoing. Spotting Ramanuja Sidarth, one of his opponent's campaign workers, at a campaign stop, Allen took a verbal jab at Sidarth, who is of Indian descent, by twice referring to him as "macaca," a class of monkey. Many people interpreted the statement as a racial slur, which Allen later denied. Unfortunately for the senator, the exchange was videotaped and posted online. A YouTube clip of the "macaca incident" played more than 320,000 times. Following Allen's defeat, many pundits cited the clip as the turning point in the campaign.[11]

Though certain online social networks such as MySpace and Facebook are successful, some social scientists have cautioned that their popularity may be fleeting. Marketing Professor David Bell at the Wharton School of Economics at the University of Pennsylvania believes the long-term success of these sites depends on their ability to retain the interest of their members. "There is a fad or fashion component to all of these networks," Bell said. He cited the social network site Friendster as an example. It dropped from 20 million visitors a year to under a million when newer sites with better music and video capability came online. "If another community shows up that has better functionality in some way, there can be a mass migration," he said.[12] A challenge for public relations practitioners hoping to tap into these networks is to remain sensitive to the fluid nature of the online environment.

Media, Messages, and Values

For many, the selection of the medium has become an even more important decision than the content of the message to be delivered. However, even the best communications medium needs content. While it is true that the medium can alter the perception of a message, the reverse also holds true. An appropriate message delivered via an inappropriate medium is just as ineffective as an inappropriate message delivered via an appropriate medium. Message and medium must be equal considerations in communication. If not, true communication will not occur.

More to the point, the selection of both message and medium is closely tied to the values of the communicator, as well as to those of the targeted public. Those values are not linked to changes in technology. Instead, they are expressions of who we are and who we want to be. The first book ever produced in mass quantities was the Bible. Since the days of Gutenberg, millions of copies of the Bible have been produced using an increasing variety of media, including audiocassettes, videotapes, CD-ROMs, DVDs, and web sites. Despite the many advances in communications technology, the values expressed in the Bible have not changed.

For an example of how values dictate the message and the medium, let's revisit the architectural firm of Olds Young and Associates mentioned in this chapter's opening scenario. At the heart of the dispute between Olds and Young are conflicting values. Olds sees the firm as one with strictly local clientele. Young has a different vision—that of a firm competing on a global scale. Before any decisions can be made on *how* to communicate, the two partners must first reach a consensus on *what* to communicate and to *whom*. Only when those issues are decided is it appropriate to discuss messages and media.

Part of your job with Olds Young is to help the partners reach that consensus. Fortunately, you don't have to choose one option over the other. It is commonplace for different divisions within the same company to target different publics. If the architectural firm is willing to commit the necessary resources, *both* partners can have their way. Bud Olds can focus on local customers, using more personalized communication channels. At the same time, Betty Young can use more technologically advanced methods to reach out to clients more accustomed to communicating at that level. This is one generation gap that the sound application of public relations practices can close.

The point of this chapter is to put cyber-relations and the Digital Age in perspective. Advanced technology is a useful tool in the practice of public relations. However, it is only a tool. Ultimately, the expression of our values determines how we use all the tools available to us.

QUICK ✓ CHECK

1. What is Web 2.0 and what makes it different from the Internet of the 1990s?
2. Why do the authors of this book say practitioners may find the growth of social media and social networks "a double-edged sword?"
3. What role do values play in media selection in the Digital Age?

The Digital Revolution

At the center of the explosion in communications technology is the *bit*, the basic element of transmission in digital communications. Nicholas Negroponte, cofounder of the MIT Media Laboratory, calls the bit "the smallest atomic element in the DNA of information."[13] Our increasing ability to transfer thoughts, images, and sounds into bits is changing the way we interact with our world.

The communications revolution of the late 20th century was a result of the ability to convert analog communication into digital formats. **Analog** communication relays all information present in the original message in the form of continuously varying signals. Those variations correspond to the changes in sound or light energy coming from the source.[14]

The conversion of analog communication into a digital format—into computer-readable bits—makes it possible to filter out unwanted information. Analog communication is like talking to a friend while seated in the stands of crowded Analog Stadium. You have to strain to hear your friend above the cheering of the crowd and the noise of the game. At Digital Stadium, however, you would have no trouble hearing your friend. The ambient noise in the stadium would disappear, leaving only the sound of your friend's voice.

Digital communication also permits the simultaneous transfer of more information. Analog technology severely limited the number of calls a telephone company could transmit at any given moment. Essentially, telephone calls were handled one at a time along a vast copper wire network. With the introduction of digital communications and fiber optics, the capacity of telephone communication systems dramatically multiplied.

QuickBreak 11.1

The Internet by the Numbers

In December 1990, there was only one **web site** in the world, located at CERN, the European Laboratory for Particle Physics, in Switzerland. By the start of 2007, that number had risen to more than 101 million web sites.[15] And there doesn't appear to be an end in sight to the web's phenomenal growth. The Internet, which started as a rudimentary computer network linking military and academic researchers in the 1960s, has become a major force in 21st-century society.

Based on the results of a December 2006 survey, the Pew Internet & American Life Project estimates that 70 percent of U.S. adults—about 141 million people—go online.[16] Nearly two-thirds of the adult users access the Internet daily.[17] A gender gap that once existed has virtually disappeared, with 69 percent of adult women on the Internet compared with 71 percent men. More than 80 percent of people younger than 50 surf the web, compared with 70 percent for ages 50–64 and 33 percent for people 65 and older. Race appears to influence Internet use, as 72 percent of white, non-Hispanic adults go online, compared with 58 percent for black, non-Hispanic adults. The Pew study also suggests that higher household income and educational attainment increase the level of Internet use.[18]

What are people doing when they go online? Among adults who go online daily, just over half of them send or read e-mail, 41 percent use a search engine to find information, 31 percent get the latest news, and 22 percent check the weather. Twenty-eight percent of those surveyed by Pew said they surf the web daily just for fun.[19]

A place where the Internet is really making its mark is business, where the level of **e-commerce** continues its steady rise. The U.S. Census Bureau estimates that e-commerce retail sales (business-to-consumer) during 2005 were $86.3 billion dollars, a nearly 25 percent increase over the previous year. That represents 2.3 percent of total U.S retail sales—a relatively small percentage, but four times greater than it was just five years earlier.[20] Although the growth of retail sales online is impressive, the real action is in business-to-business, B2B, which accounted for more than 93 percent of e-commerce activity—$1.82 trillion—in 2004.[21] Another sign of the web's growing economic clout: For the first time, employers spent more money online for employment recruitment advertising than in newspapers—$5.9 billion to $5.4 billion— in 2006. Market research firm Borrell Associates, Inc., which conducted the study, said it expects Internet job-listing revenues to hit $10 billion in 2011.[22]

Back at Analog Stadium, imagine what it would be like if thousands of people on one side of the field tried to communicate with a counterpart on the opposite side. It would be impossible to distinguish any one conversation in that din. However, it is a different story at Digital Stadium. Everyone on the east sideline would clearly hear their west sideline counterpart—and no one else!

We see this principle at work in television, through which it has become possible to transmit multiple programs on a cable TV or satellite channel that previously carried only one. Digital technology also makes it possible to store a remarkable amount of data in a relatively small space. For example, the typical music CD holds

783 million bytes of information.[23] A DVD of your favorite movie holds about seven times more data than a CD.[24]

To take it one step further, digital communication makes it possible for many to simultaneously share information from a single source. This capability has evolved into an on-demand delivery system, which allows consumers to choose what they want, whenever they want. Instead of waiting around all day for your favorite movie to be broadcast at a specific time, you can download it from a programming source just as the pizza arrives!

Convergence and Hypermedia

Perhaps the most important consequence of the digital revolution is a **convergence of media.** As different media adopt digital technology in their production and distribution, barriers that have traditionally stood between them are tumbling down. Practically every medium we interact with now is digital, from our telephones, to our MP3 players, to the web. The television signal you receive in your home is very likely digital. And before long, all television signals will be digital. The newspaper, seemingly an artifact of 18th-century technology, is currently produced—and may soon be delivered to your "electronic doorstep"—digitally.

A more dramatic development is the convergence of traditionally distinct media into one form. Integrated multimedia—called **hypermedia**—incorporate digital audio, visual, and text information. To see hypermedia in action, one need only log on to the web site maintained by the Cable News Network, one of the web's most popular sites. CNN.com combines text from magazines such as *Time* and *Sports Illustrated* with video and audio supplied by CNN. The site also provides links to other sites where more information on subjects of personal interest can be found.

The potential application of hypermedia goes beyond the Internet. Think of what the week before the start of each school year is like. You have to run to the bookstore to purchase the textbooks you need for the coming semester. Depending on how many classes you take, this errand can bring new meaning to the idea of "carrying a full load." In the future, however, it may not be necessary to leave home. You will be able to download the contents of all your texts into a single device, a digital book. These textbooks will be unlike any you have ever seen. You will be able to highlight a word and have its definition appear. Instead of footnotes, links will take you to vast quantities of background information. Video and audio will be inserted to complement the text. When you finish your assigned reading, you will be able to use the same electronic book to download the daily newspaper or one of the bestselling novels of the day.

However, students have been slow to embrace e-texts. Despite savings of nearly half the price of a printed book, the Government Accountability Office reports students "may run into technical difficulties" and "may not have the option at the end of the term to keep the textbook." Studies have also shown that words on a page are easier to read than those on a computer screen. The GAO noted that "according to publishers, electronic textbooks have not caught on with students, and sales of these products have been unsuccessful."[25]

Wireless Digital Communication

Another area in which technological advancements have had a tremendous impact on the practice of public relations is wireless technology. Our ability to communicate with others over great distances is no longer restricted by the length of a wire. The ability to communicate from anywhere using a variety of communication devices—telephones, computer modems, radios, video, facsimile (fax) machines, and satellites—has made us more mobile, responsive, and cost effective. Through the use of miniature transmitters and global positioning satellites, it is possible to locate the exact position of anyone and anything on the planet—particularly important in both commerce and travel. And what may have been the most important social, economic, and technological development of the 20th century, wireless communications technology, such as television, makes it possible for people in all corners of the world to share simultaneously in a common experience—in much the way the world watched in horror as terrorists attacked the World Trade Center and the Pentagon on September 11, 2001.

Look at what has happened in just the past few years. Because of the growth of the Internet, advancements in digital communications, and the availability of less expensive and more compact portable telephones, the demand for telephone service has exploded. Cellular telephones are ubiquitous, and palm-sized computers, which serve as both portable telephones and Internet connections, have become standard equipment for executives on the move.

Just as important, the growth in cheaper, more accessible wireless communication is making the world a smaller place. Globally, there are telephone lines for only one person out of every eight. Most of these lines are located in the developed nations of the Western world. However, access to phones will change dramatically over the next quarter-century as developing nations embrace wireless communications technology. Frances Cairncross, senior editor of *The Economist*, has written that this change will have significant geopolitical consequences. In her book *The Death of Distance*, Cairncross argues that the expansion of wireless technology will remove one of the Western world's key competitive edges, the vast superiority of its communications system. The worldwide economic impact of this shift in competitive equilibrium, she believes, will rival that of the collapse of communism.[26]

The rapid growth of wireless communication has revolutionized the practice of public relations. With their activities no longer restricted to office settings, practitioners can communicate with colleagues and key stakeholders wherever they are. This development has sparked the practice of virtual public relations. (Photo by Peter DaSilva/*New York Times*. Copyright 2007 The New York Times Company. Reprinted with permission.)

Social Ramifications

Although digital technology opens up a world of possibilities for the 21st century, progress does not come without its price. Only now are we beginning to understand the social ramifications of this new digital world. New communications technology has raised numerous issues for public policy makers and individuals to address. Among these are questions about media mergers, personal privacy, job security, and intellectual property rights.

A New Town Commons. In the days before the Internet, television, and the telephone, people gathered in their community's main public square—the town commons—to hear the latest news. Arguably, the Internet has become the 21st-century town commons. This was dramatically demonstrated on September 11, 2001. According to one study, the total number of people online temporarily dropped during the three weeks following the attack. However, the number of site visits increased 240 percent during the same period—an indication that people were surfing the web more intensely to find information about the attacks and their aftermath. The Internet also became a place for people to console one another about the tragedy. The report said, "Nearly three-quarters of Internet users (72 percent) have used e-mail in some way related to the events—to display their patriotism, contact their family and friends to discuss events, reconnect with long-lost friends, discuss the fate of friends, and share news."[27]

Redefined Communities. For those concerned that the Internet will destroy social relationships and a traditional sense of community, have no fear. "Instead of disappearing, people's communities are being transformed," conclude researchers for the Pew Internet & American Life Project. According to their analysis, "The traditional human orientation to neighborhood- and village-based groups is moving toward communities that are oriented around geographically dispersed social networks." However, the researchers also conclude, "People's networks continue to have substantial numbers of relatives and neighbors—the traditional bases of community— as well as friends and workmates."[28]

The effect of this redefinition means that public relations practitioners must learn the values and preferences of nontraditional online communities if they want to build and maintain mutually beneficial relationships. Though this may make strategic communication more challenging, it also opens new doors of opportunity in the form of access to highly defined social networks.

Mergers of Media Companies. The convergence of communications technology has brought about a convergence of media companies; that is, media companies have merged for competitive reasons. These new giant media conglomerates now own the means of production and distribution of a wide spectrum of media. One of the largest is Time Warner, which reported $43.65 billion in revenues during 2005. Its vast corporate umbrella includes CNN, HBO, AOL, *People, Time, Sports Illustrated,* and Time Warner Cable. The company also produces and distributes films, such as *The Lord of the Rings* trilogy and the *Harry Potter* series, and television programs, including *ER* and *Two and a Half Men*.[29] Although a seemingly efficient arrangement, the concentration of numerous powerful channels of mass communication into the hands of a few corporations has caused some to worry about the loss of journalistic independence.

Preservation of Personal Privacy. The digital revolution has made it easier for people to gather, store, and transmit personal information. This is a matter of convenience for individuals as well as corporations. But there are risks. Even with sophisticated safeguards, digital information is not entirely secure. Privacy concerns extend to personal messages, whether sent via e-mail or wireless telephones. At a time when computer hackers are at least as knowledgeable as computer programmers, you never know who is accessing your private conversations. In the highly competitive economy of the 21st century, new technology opens the door to commercial espionage on an alarming scale.

However, there's an even darker side. The growth of online social networks has led to personal safety concerns. The Center for Missing and Exploited Children reported in 2006 that there had been more than 2,600 incidents of adults using the web to target children to engage in sexual activity. There are also the unintended consequences of posting personal information on the Internet. In one instance, a gay student at a religious college was expelled when he inadvertently outed himself in a Facebook posting.[30]

Job Security. The good news is that improved technology can make people more productive in the workplace. The bad news is that increased ability to do more with less lowers the demand for highly skilled workers. New communication technology allows many industries to outsource corporate functions. We have seen this in public relations, where many corporate public relations offices have been downsized. Much of the slack has been picked up on a per-job basis by independent consultants who do not receive any of the traditional corporate benefits (e.g., health coverage, retirement plans, or stock options).

Then too, technological advances often disrupt successful companies, a phenomenon Clayton M. Christensen of the Harvard Business School has called "the innovator's dilemma" and about which he has written a book of the same name. The digital revolution has led to simpler, cheaper, and more user-friendly ways of doing things that can squeeze out the products of older companies. Although not a direct threat to public relations, these so-called disruptive technologies can threaten the organizations in which it is practiced.[31]

Protection of Intellectual Property. The fact that digital copies are both identical to original works and easy to alter poses a huge problem in the Information Age. A person's intellectual property has value. When others ignore copyright law (see Chapter 15) and use someone's intellectual property without permission or compensation, it is tantamount to theft. Today's digital technology makes it easier to copy and distribute the results of someone else's labors. This is a particular problem in the music and film industries, where the performances of top artists and actors can be rapidly duplicated for illegal sale or downloaded illegally. And the problem is not limited to consumer goods. Specialized business software is also a prime target. In some instances, this piracy has national security implications.

1. How are digital media different from analog media?
2. What are the implications of the growth of wireless communication?
3. What are the social ramifications arising from the digital revolution?

The Birth of Cyber-Relations

In many ways, the Internet has helped to reduce the psychological distance that exists between an organization and the publics important to its success. Instead of being seen as a distant and obscure entity, the organization is now as close as the nearest Internet connection. It is as if the Internet has become the organization's new front door and its web site the digital equivalent of the lobby, from which visitors are directed to various information sites within the organization.

Interactive web sites allow visitors to communicate directly through e-mail links with key personnel within the organization. Through the integration of audio and video technology, visitors may be personally welcomed by the company CEO. For those looking for specific information, many web sites are equipped with search engines that allow visitors to browse the entire site as well as company archives. It is even possible to take a virtual tour of an organization's facilities without leaving one's home. Add to this the role of corporate intranets and extranets (discussed in Chapter 9). Because of these innovations, once seemingly distant companies are now only a mouse click away.

This has led to what we call **cyber-relations,** the use of public relations strategies and tactics to deal with publics via and issues related to the Internet.[32] Although cyber-relations does not exclude other forms of public relations, we use it to describe what has become a dynamic aspect of the practice of public relations with unquestionable social ramifications. With the rapid growth of the Internet over the past generation, practitioners have discovered that the web is often both the cause of and the solution to the challenges they face.

Because the Internet is practically everywhere, it is an ideal medium for public relations practitioners. But the web's omnipresence is also a challenge when it comes to targeting a specific audience. That's because different people use it in different ways. In its 2005 study of how men and women use the Internet, the Pew Internet & American Life Project acknowledged that though men dominated web use in its early days, since "2000 and continuing on to today, the user population has been evenly divided between men and women." However, the study found that men and women use the Internet in very different ways. For example, younger women are

QUICKBREAK 11.2

Making a Good First Impression

First impressions, it is said, are lasting. The first contact many people have with companies and organizations is on the Internet. Unfortunately, some of these web sites do their creators more harm than good.

A problem with many well-intentioned web sites is that their purpose is not well defined. A great advantage of the Internet is that it allows the delivery of multiple messages to multiple audiences. But who are these audiences, and what do you want to say to them? Unfortunately, many web designers skip this crucial step. Internet researchers Candace White and Niranjan Raman have concluded that, in many cases, "web site planning is done by trial and error, based on intuition, with little or no formal research."[33]

Web sites can also assist in building and maintaining important relationships—especially in the area of media relations. However, an analysis of *Fortune* 500 company web sites revealed that most were not being used to their full potential. Researcher Coy Callison said that journalists often complain that they can't find information they want, and that "a few have even suggested that their coverage of companies with poor Web presence is skewed negative, if they cover these companies at all."[34]

This brings us to an important rule of web design: Web sites must be user-friendly. Just ask anyone who has spent time twiddling his or her thumbs waiting for a graphics-heavy page to download. Visitors should be able to easily find the information they want. Organizing the homepage by audience-specific categories is one way to achieve this. Another is to design pages that do not require the user to scroll down for additional information.

The web site's hyperlinks should be carefully planned. "Developing your links strategy is one of the most crucial elements involved in Internet marketing," said Susan Sweeney, author of *101 Ways to Promote Your Web Site.* "Appropriately placed, links can be a real traffic builder."[35] Exchanging links with professional, business, and trade associations can help drive new visitors to your site.

Good writers always consider the medium. According to a study by Sun Microsystems, individuals take 50 percent longer to read from a computer screen than from a printed page.[36] Web writing consultant Sara Means Geigel noted, "You don't curl up with a web site on your favorite chair or sofa or in bed to read it like a good book."[37]

Once the web site is up and running, let people know about it. Place its address on all company communications. The site should also include easily accessible contact information. A good web site that leaves a favorable first impression should be an integral part of an organization's branding.

---

more likely to be online than younger men, but older men are more likely to be online than older women. Unmarried men are more likely to use the Internet than unmarried women. Men go online more frequently than women, "pursue and consume information more aggressively," and tend to be more interested in the web's technical aspects. However, women are more enthusiastic online communicators and use e-mail in a more robust way. The report said, "Men and women both appreciate e-mail for its efficiencies and convenience, but women are more likely to feel satisfied with the role of e-mail in their lives, especially when it comes to nurturing their relationships."[38]

For an example of cyber-relations, you need look no further than one of the most basic tools on the public relations workbench, the news release. Not only has the method of distribution changed—e-mail versus so-called snail-mail—the structure is also changing to take advantage of digital technology. John Guiniven of Elon University wrote in *Public Relations Tactics* that reports of the death of the traditional news release "are greatly exaggerated." However, Guiniven also cautioned, "Social media releases are preferred by a growing number of journalists, particularly younger journalists in all media and practically all journalists in new media."[39] Examples of social media releases include imbedded hyperlinks that take the reader to supplemental information, such as backgrounders, photographs, and video. "Including links to third-party sources does more than make life easier for reporters," writes Guiniven. "It adds credibility to your release and helps you control the debate over the issue that is the subject of the release."[40]

As mentioned in QuickBreak 11.1, the development of the Internet sparked the rapid growth of e-commerce, online financial activity. However, the use of the web for commercial transactions is not limited to big business. Many small businesses believe that having a presence on the web is important. More than half of small business owners surveyed in 2003 agreed with the statement that their web site primarily provides company credibility. Two out of three small and medium-sized businesses with web sites regularly use e-mail to communicate with their customers.

"This research reinforces the growing importance of web sites to small business," said Joel Kocher of the online service company Interland. "As more and more consumers connect using the web, it's vital that small businesses gain an effective online presence."[41]

Virtual Public Relations

Another byproduct of the digital revolution is the emergence of **virtual public relations,** the networking of small, independent public relations consultants. Linked by telephones, fax machines, and the Internet, these informal practitioner networks successfully compete for business against traditional public relations agencies.

Here's how it works. A public relations consultant in Cincinnati has a client who needs to improve internal communications. This may require the services of a publications designer in Toronto, a freelance writer in London, a web developer in Sacramento, and an event planner in Charlotte. In many cases, these consulting arrangements are made on a project-by-project basis. However, in some virtual firms, such as INK, Inc., of Kansas City, Missouri, these widely scattered practitioners are full-time employees of an agency, with its scattered operations linked by a secure intranet.

A reason for the growth of virtual public relations is its cost. "You can keep your overhead lower and pass that savings on to your clients," said Dick Grove of INK, Inc. Virtual agencies offer client discounts of up to 40 percent over traditional firms by sharing the money they save on office space. When Internet security company nCipher Corp. Ltd. switched to a virtual agency, public relations manager Claire Collins said, "It was not important to us to see what kind of desks they had or what their lobby looked like to gauge the level of their work as PR professionals."[42]

VALUES STATEMENT 11.1

INK, Inc.

INK, Inc., is a virtual public relations agency with its headquarters in Kansas City, Missouri—or wherever it chooses.

WE DO THE JOB OTHERS CAN'T

INK Inc. is a different kind of public relations firm. We don't bill by the hour, and we don't wax on for weeks about strategic positioning and research capabilities. We don't care about being the biggest firm with offices around the globe. We do care first and foremost about one thing above all else: achieving measurable results for clients.

Staffed exclusively by senior media professionals with actual newsroom experience, INK Inc. focuses on generating mainstream press coverage and placing stories in top-tier, national and international media. While we do offer a full range of services including broadcast production, writing, media training and special events, our specialty—and our bottom-line objective for every client—is publicity, or to put it bluntly, "getting ink."

—INK, Inc., web site

Another reason virtual agencies are becoming more attractive is the freedom they give to practitioners. "I've never been very good in the corporate structure," said Grove. "People are not geographically dependent."[43]

QUICK ✓ CHECK

1. What is cyber-relations?
2. What are the challenges of targeting specific publics on the Internet?
3. What is virtual public relations?

Life in a Digital World

As anyone who has bought a new computer knows, technological change is so rapid that the computer is already outdated by the time you remove it from the box. During the digital revolution, change is the only constant. If public relations practitioners are to achieve success in this brave, new world, they must embrace and understand the changing environment. But this is about more than understanding technology. It is also about understanding the political, social, legal, and ethical ramifications of this change.

Whenever we change the way we communicate with one another, that decision creates ripple effects that can change relationships. In a sense, we have to be more self-aware than ever before. How do these technological advances influence our messages? When we adopt new technology, we need to reevaluate whose needs are being

Viral Marketing

In word-of-mouth advertising, one person receives a tidbit of information and passes it along to a friend. Before you know it, the message has spread like wildfire.

That is essentially how **viral marketing** works. The thing that makes it different is that the information exchange takes place on the Internet. Much like a virus, it is spread via e-mail from person to person. Unlike a virus, the spread of information is intentional. Each person passes the information along to many people. The information quickly multiplies and, so to speak, infects a large population.

Marketing Week has identified three basic types of viral e-mail. The first is the kind that no one wants to receive: from an antisocial prankster containing a computer-contaminating virus. The second is a genuinely noncommercial—sometimes anticommercial—message. For example, the magazine cited a June 2004 e-mail campaign to boycott several oil companies in protest of high gasoline prices. The third form of viral e-mail, one that appears to be growing in popularity, is the e-mail campaign that is ultimately commercial in intent.[44]

Pete Snyder, of the online marketing firm New Media Strategies, wrote that viral marketing brings great promise:

> Whether we call it buzz, peer marketing, chatter or online posting, [viral] marketing provides marketers with one-of-a kind, real-time, dynamic access to users who are discussing a multitude of issues, products and services in their own unvarnished terms. More so, it allows what in the past was "the nameless, faceless corporation" to have real, honest and open exchanges with consumers and build valuable relationships for the future.[45]

Government and industry officials in Toronto, Ontario, launched a viral marketing campaign to counter a serious drop in tourism during 2003. Earlier that year, the region had a widely publicized outbreak of severe acute respiratory syndrome, SARS, a pneumonia-like illness that claimed 40 lives in Canada and 916 worldwide. One official estimated that fears aroused by the epidemic cost the Toronto tourism industry $500 million in just a matter of months.[46]

In addition to regional advertising and special promotions that included a Rolling Stones concert, Toronto launched a viral marketing campaign—although, for obvious reasons, no one referred to it as such. It incorporated a promotion called the Kids Summer Road Trip. Canadian sports, media, and political celebrities sent e-mail postcards to potential visitors. The recipients were told that children 12 and younger would receive free admission to several popular Toronto attractions. They were also encouraged to act as ambassadors and send the e-mail invitations along to friends and family.[47]

While viral marketing has great potential, it also has its critics. The European Commission adopted a Privacy and Electronic Communications Directive in 2003. Under these rules, commercial e-mails can be sent within the European Union only to consumers who request them.[48] President George W. Bush signed similar legislation into law later that same year. The U.S. legislation prohibits senders of unsolicited commercial e-mail from disguising their identities by using false return addresses or misleading subject lines. The law also prohibits harvesting of e-mail addresses from web sites.[49]

However, these restrictions do not mean an end to the practice. Companies can still engage in viral marketing as long as they ask their customers' permission. As British online marketer Richard Bush noted, "We'd rather do a viral campaign that generated 1,000 qualified, opted-in e-mail addresses from 100,000 viral hits than have to deal with the 100,000 unqualified e-mail addresses."[50]

served—ours, those of the targeted public, or both? How does the manner in which we communicate reflect our values? These are the questions we need to answer to live in a digital world. As always, the first step to finding answers is also the first step of the public relations process: research.

Individuals as Gatekeepers

In Chapter 5 we discussed the evolution of communication theory. As you may remember, theorists once believed that mass media could control the public opinion process. They thought that editors at newspapers, magazines, and radio stations dictated what information people received and when they received it. However, the growth in communications technology changed all that. The magic bullet theory evolved into uses and gratifications theory—the belief that each person is his or her own information gatekeeper and picks and chooses from a wide variety of information sources.

What does this mean for public relations? For starters, **push technology**—a term that often means different things to different people—allows information to be automatically delivered or "pushed" directly to a user. By subscribing to various push services, individuals receive downloads of customized information. This can include news stories covering specific topics, sports scores, or the latest from the financial markets. If you represent a client that caters to people who travel extensively, a push service providing the latest in travel news and tips would be a cost-effective strategy for reaching this audience. What makes it most attractive is that it automatically delivers the information to an already receptive audience.

However, this also is an example of how communications innovations can mean both good news and bad news for public relations. Push technology may make it harder to get the attention of certain individuals. In the mass media, editors serve as information gatekeepers. But with push technology, individuals become their own editors. That can make reaching targeted publics more difficult. Opportunities for exposing your message may lessen, which, in turn, means making the best of the chances that remain.

Individuals as Publishers

Not only have individuals become information gatekeepers, they have also become self-publishers. Digital communications technology has made it possible for people to communicate more effectively and efficiently than ever before. In the past, if your campus organization wanted to typeset and print a meeting notice to post around campus, it was necessary to employ the services of a designer and the local photocopy shop. Today, those tasks can be accomplished by only one person using a laptop computer and a printer. In the past, if your organization wanted to contact a large number of people off campus, the job might require the use of direct mail, advertising, or telephone solicitations—expensive and time-consuming procedures. Today, e-mail and faxes can do the job cheaper and quicker, though they would reach smaller, more targeted publics. In the past, only media moguls had the resources necessary to reach a worldwide audience. Today, all you need is your own web site.

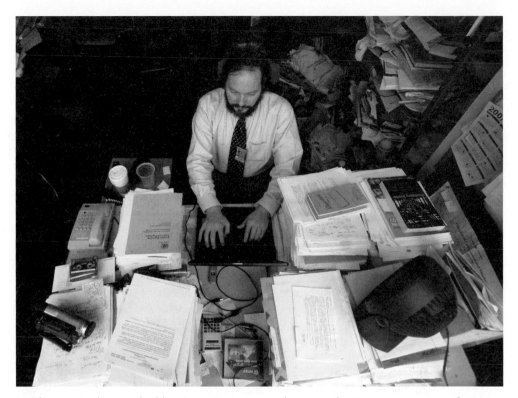

Matthew Lee, who runs the blog innercitypress.com, has accreditation as a correspondent at the United Nations. The UN was one of the first institutions of its size and importance to allow bloggers not affiliated with larger, more traditional media companies into the permanent press corps. (Photo by Shiho Fukada/*New York Times*. Copyright 2007 The New York Times Company. Reprinted with permission.)

Another popular form of Internet self-publishing is the **blog,** a regularly updated online diary or news forum that focuses on a particular area of interest. At first, most blogs were created by web fanatics who had a story they wanted to tell. Blogs started catching on when reporters covering the Iraq war began posting their personal experiences. Employers have also begun to recognize their value as a communications tool. "Employer interest currently is the highest that I've ever seen it," said Google's Jason Shellen. "The interest is mainly in developing blogs as external communication tools with customers and clients, though some employers are beginning to consider ways they can use blogs internally."[51]

One reason practitioners find blogs attractive is that they target specific audiences. Some practitioners have begun pitching stories to bloggers with similar interests. However, before taking the plunge, practitioners should do their research, read through the blog, and determine whether its environment is right for their message.

A significant development in self-publication has been the introduction of wiki software that makes it easy for multiple people to author, edit, and remove online information. That's where Wikipedia, an online encyclopedia that contains articles from a community of contributors, gets its name. While this collaborative authoring software has obvious advantages for internal communication, it has been the use of **wikis** to create online social networks that has had the most profound effect.

Podcasts are another popular form of self-publication. They are audio and video files published online and downloaded by subscribers. (Video versions of podcasts are often referred to as *vodcasts*.) One of the most popular examples of a podcast service is iTunes, the Internet music and video provider. As noted at the beginning of this chapter, *lonelygirl15* is another example. Podcasting sources range from individuals with something to say to giant corporations with something to sell (see Case Study 11.2). The value and technical quality of podcasts are as varied as the people who create them. Think of podcasts as online radio and television programs. The distribution of these programs is made possible through *RSS* (Really Simple Syndication), a computer programming language that simplifies downloading. In some instances, all the user has to do is connect an MP3 player to the computer—the software does the rest. A number of podcasts target public relations practitioners, including *PR Quest* (http://podcast.prtopics.com), an educational project of AuburnMedia; *Inside PR* (www.insidepr.ca), a podcast targeting Canadian practitioners; and *PRWeb* (www.prwebpodcast.com), a user-supported news-release distribution service.

The dramatic growth in social media has resulted in a new phenomenon, the **citizen journalist.** Armed with cell phone cameras, wireless laptops, and wikis, ordinary people are changing the way news is covered. Though these citizens may not have been trained as journalists, the new technology allows them to bear witness to events that reporters often cannot.

This was made tragically apparent in April 2007, when a deranged gunman killed 32 students and professors on the Virginia Tech campus before turning the gun on himself. The most vivid images of that terrible day came from the cell phone camera of graduate student Jamal Albarghouti, who entered campus just as the shooting began. "His material is still the best of the day in terms of capturing on video what took place there," said Nancy Lane, CNN's vice president of domestic news.[52] The *San Francisco Chronicle* called the Virginia Tech shooting "the first major news story in which traditional media and new-media technologies became visibly interdependent."[53] When Virginia Tech students were not serving as the eyes and ears of an anxious world, they turned to social media such as Facebook and MySpace to console one another and let others know they were safe. Within 24 hours of the shootings, a Facebook group set up as a tribute to the victims had more than 130,000 members and 10,000 comments.[54]

As you can imagine, self-publication has a downside. The fact that everyone can become his or her own publisher doesn't necessarily mean that he or she should. It only takes a few minutes of web surfing to realize that there are a lot of people on the Internet with nothing to say. And sometimes what they have to say is downright vicious. Numerous organizations, the subjects of grievances imagined or real, have been victims of what one author has called **cybersmears**—the use of the Internet to attack the integrity of an organization and/or its products and services.[55]

Cybersmear tactics include the creation of what are called **gripe sites.** One example is now defunct "chasemanhattansucks.com," established by a disgruntled bank customer who said he had trouble removing an erroneous charge on his credit card account. What harm can one guy do? In its first two years of existence, that site recorded 300,000 hits.[56]

Perhaps an even bigger problem is that much of what is self-published, electronically or otherwise, does not go through the scrutiny that an editor applies to more traditional publications. Many self-published materials are inaccurate, incomplete, or biased—not to mention poorly written. Even Wikipedia acknowledges that information it receives from contributors may be inaccurate or open to substantially different interpretations.[57] Because of this, the need for constant monitoring of the Internet is growing. Organizations, especially publicly held companies, have a lot to lose from inaccurate information being flashed globally. The ease of self-publishing also brings into focus the need for rapid response plans to counter false or negative information on the Internet.

Internet researcher Michael Dertouzos has written that new communications technology will dramatically affect human behavior within organizations. With an increased ability to monitor all aspects of the organization, executives will be able to hold their employees more accountable for their actions. Dertouzos said this "will improve a firm's efficiency, even though its employees may be unhappy to have their individual work so open to inspection and critique."[58] Dertouzos also said the new technology will shift responsibility further down the corporate ladder, thus creating a greater need for employees to understand and embrace their organization's goals and values:

> For an organization to extract this increased decision power from its people, it will have to provide them with more knowledge about why some things are done and who does them, and why certain decisions are made and who makes them.[59]

With this growing reliance on employee communications, public relations will remain an important management responsibility in the 21st century.

1. What are the benefits and risks of having individuals act as their own gatekeepers?
2. What are the benefits and risks of having individuals self-publish?
3. What are blogs? What do public relations practitioners see as their benefits?

Other Internet Issues

For all of the possibilities created by the Internet, it is still not the answer to all of the problems that public relations practitioners face. Let's look briefly at a variety of Internet-related issues a practitioner should consider.

QuickBreak 11.4

Flogging Wal-Mart

The practice of using front organizations to hide the true source of communications goes back to the days of Edward L. Bernays (see QuickBreak 3.1). Unfortunately, a 21st-century version of this controversial and ethically questionable strategy has shed an unfavorable light on the world's largest retailer and one of the world's largest public relations agencies.

Wal-Mart is unquestionably a financial success, with 1,092 discount stores, 2,195 Supercenters, 576 Sam's Clubs, and 110 Neighborhood Markets in 14 nations at the start of 2007.[60] During fiscal 2006, the company's net sales were a record $312.4 billion.[61] However, in its climb to the top, Wal-Mart has made enemies. Complaints against the retail giant include low wages, the company's adverse effect on local retail stores, and the importation of cheap overseas products at the expense of U.S. manufacturing jobs. Legislators in Maryland passed a first-of-its-kind law in 2006 that would have forced Wal-Mart to spend more on employee health care. Although the law was eventually struck down in two federal courts, the company knew it could be the target for further legislative assaults.[62]

Wal-Mart launched a grassroots campaign to blunt its critics. Working with Edelman, a Chicago-based public relations agency, the company created Working Families for Wal-Mart. Edelman Vice President Kevin Sheridan said WFWM would be "independent of the company" and "very transparent" in its dealings with the public and press.[63] When critics launched a bus tour publicizing their grievances against Wal-Mart in 2006, WFWM launched its own bus tour. Using a recreation vehicle, "Laura" and "Jim" visited with Wal-Mart shoppers from Nevada

to Georgia. They kept company supporters abreast of their adventures with a blog.[64] Soon thereafter, a second blog, known as "Paid Critics," joined in the pro-Wal-Mart chorus.

In one posting about the Maryland health-insurance controversy, blogger "Brian" wrote, "All across the country, newspaper editorial boards—no great friends of business—are ripping the legislation."[65]

To some, this kind of third-party endorsement seemed too good to be true. As things turned out, it was. Laura, Jim, and Brian were all Edelman employees. They had engaged in what critics call *flogging,* or false blogging. By failing to identify themselves as Edelman employees, they undermined the credibility of the company they were trying to help. The disclosure also hurt the reputation of Edelman, which was roundly criticized nationwide by public relations practitioners. CEO Richard Edelman apologized for what he said was an "error in failing to be transparent."[66]

"The shame is that if they'd been a little more up-front about the financial details of the [bus] trip, the integrity of the idea might have been protected," wrote Paul Parton of *Media Magazine.* "The thing I find staggering is that anyone really believed the ruse wouldn't eventually be uncovered."[67]

In its review of this and similar online deceptions, *Advertising Age*'s Noelle Weaver wrote, "The consumer is smarter than you think. Alternative marketing tactics must be genuine, authentic and in today's world, transparent."[68]

The Online Generation Gap. The next time someone says "everyone's on the Net," you should politely beg to differ. Although the number of senior citizens using the Internet is rising rapidly, the fact remains that most still are off-line. As already noted in QuickBreak 11.1, only one-third of U.S. adults 65 years and older use the Internet. "The best place to reach someone age 70 or older is still offline," according to

Susannah Fox of the Pew Internet & American Life Project. Fox notes that only 26 percent of Americans age 70–75 and 17 percent of those age 76 and older go on-line.[69] However, she also notes that as today's Internet users in their 50s get older, "they will be unlikely to give up their wired ways."[70]

The Global Digital Divide. Although English-speaking people constitute only 8 percent of the world's population, they represent 35.2 percent of its Internet users. According to Global Reach, a global online marketing firm, Chinese-language users are second at 13.7 percent, followed by Japanese at 8.4 percent, Spanish at 9.0 percent, and German at 6.9 percent. This uneven Internet access is known as the **digital divide,** and it has great social and economic ramifications for the future. In addition to access, cultural considerations exist. "[A] low context society, such as the United States, wants the essence of a message clearly and quickly," wrote researcher Augustine Ihator, "while [a] high context society, as in the Arab countries, appreciates the nuances and uses the physical context of the message to attribute meaning."[71]

Internet Research Problems. As a research tool, the Internet is, in many ways, a mile wide and an inch deep. For all the information readily available online, the total represents only a small fraction of what can be gathered through more traditional forms of research. For example, many libraries do not have the necessary resources to digitize everything in their archives; a lot of vital information exists in print and on the shelves, but not online. Also, more can be learned through a personal examination of historical artifacts than by looking at digitized pictures of them. In addition, while an overwhelming majority of investors turn to company web sites to gather corporate information, a Burson-Marsteller study found that only one in five believes what he or she reads. Almost half of those polled said they considered newspapers and magazines to be the most credible source of information.[72]

Unwelcome Visitors. Do you dread opening your e-mail in-box? Many do because of unsolicited **spam** e-mail, the cyberspace equivalent of junk mail. Spam has become so prevalent that it has created problems for legitimate web users. For example, spam-filtering software can't always differentiate a mailing from an unwelcome marketer and one's own student organization. And who hasn't heard from a grieving relative of a former African ruler wanting to use your bank account number to move gold out of the country? Spamming doesn't build relationships—and can actually harm them. The Associated Press banned one public relations agency for sending too much "spam-like" e-mail.[73]

Another new headache is **spim,** the unwelcome commercial use of instant messaging. We must also guard against even more sinister visitors: **hackers,** who try to break into networked computer systems to either steal confidential information or just create mischief. And let's not forget the ever-dangerous **computer viruses** that can attach to a person's e-mail address book and spread to computers around the world attacking data and causing incalculable personal and global economic damage.

Passive Communication. It is important to remember that the Internet is a passive way for an organization to communicate. People have to go to a web site; it does not automatically come to them. Although push technology allows organizations to send information via the Internet to subscribers, users must first sign up for the service. This is one of the reasons why the Internet is best used as a component of a larger integrated marketing communications plan (see Chapter 13).

Career Implications. The rapid growth of the Internet has created a demand for college graduates capable of serving as web masters. However, before you are tempted to skip all your other studies to focus on developing web site programming skills, let us sound a cautionary note. One of the consequences of the advancement of technology is that, with the passage of time, it becomes more user-friendly. Because of advances in software, almost anyone can create his or her own web site, thus pulling the rug out from under those who have only technical skills. Those who are more well rounded will be able to cope with this change and thrive. They are the folks who will be able to give web sites substance. Therefore, the bottom line is that you should not give up on your studies quite yet.

QUICK CHECK

1. When someone tells you that "everyone is on the Net," what can you say in response?
2. What is the global digital divide?
3. Why should you use other sources in addition to the Internet when conducting research?

Why New Isn't Always Better

The introduction of new communications technology does not automatically spell doom for the old. Let's go back to Gutenberg's invention of the movable-type printing press in 1455. Many at the time predicted that it would mean the end of handwritten text. However, it had just the opposite effect. As vast quantities of inexpensive reading materials became more accessible, literacy rates grew; and, in turn, so did the calligraphic arts. Similarly, audio books and downloadable digital books have not destroyed book sales. One book publishing trade association estimated U.S. book revenues at $34.6 billion in 2005 and projected them to rise to $40.4 billion by the end of the decade.[74]

The reason older technologies are able to survive the onslaught of newer technologies is that they are able to develop a niche in the New World Order. Despite their use of 18th-century technology, newspapers continue to publish in the 21st century. Why? Because they deliver something of value that consumers can't get elsewhere—in this case inexpensive and comprehensive coverage of local, regional, national, and global news. Similarly, although many people thought radio would fade into oblivion after commercial television was introduced to the United States in 1947, it didn't;

instead, radio evolved from a national source of entertainment programming into a local source of music and information. And the beat goes on.

In a public relations context, the introduction of new communications technology has created new ways of reaching and being reached by targeted publics. It is hard to imagine what life for the public relations practitioner was like without fax machines, cell phones, e-mail, and satellite media tours. But even in this age of technological wonders, it is equally difficult to envision the practice of public relations without some of the old standbys, such as brochures, and good old-fashioned face-to-face communication. Dertouzos wrote, "The Information Marketplace must be supported with all the traditional methods for building human bonds, including face-to-face, real-life experiences, if it is to serve organizations as more than a high-tech postal system."[75] The real challenge for the future is to stay up to date on what is new without forgetting what has worked well in the past.

As with all communication, the choice of communications technology ultimately comes down to recognizing one's audience and purpose. Public relations practitioners must understand their audience and its values: What are its needs, what is its level of knowledge, and what are the best ways to reach it? Practitioners must also be clear about their values and purpose—especially because some media are better suited for certain purposes than for others. The choice of which technology to adopt rests more on whether the technology works than on whether it is new.

Summary

The digital revolution has profoundly affected our personal and professional lives. It has resulted in the advent of nontraditional online social media. It has also enabled a convergence of messages and images in multiple media. Web 2.0, a recent software advance that permits online collaboration of multiple users, has created new social networks. The revolution has also forced traditional media to reinvent themselves and has had a profound effect on the practice of public relations. It has led to the creation of virtual public relations agencies that provide the same services as those of traditional agencies but at a fraction of the cost. For practitioners, the creation of new social networks brings both benefits and risks. The challenge for the practitioner is to identify, monitor, and, if necessary, engage these networks.

While the technology has brought many benefits, it also has raised a number of serious questions. Powerful channels of mass communication are being concentrated in the hands of relatively few corporations. In addition, issues of privacy, job security, and protection of intellectual property have come to the forefront. And while it is important to keep up with technological advances, it is also important to remember that when it comes to deciding strategies and tactics, new doesn't always mean better. Regardless of advances in technology, the decision about which message to deliver or which medium to use depends largely on the communicator's intended audience, purpose, and values.

DISCUSSION QUESTIONS

1. What are Web 2.0 and social media? How have they influenced the way people communicate?
2. In what ways has the introduction of digital communications technology influenced the practice of public relations?
3. What are some of the social ramifications of the digital revolution?
4. Name some considerations cyber-relations practitioners face when deciding whether to adopt new communications technology over more traditional channels.

Memo from the Field

**Craig Settles,
President,
Successful.com,
Oakland,
California**

As president and founder of Successful.com, Craig Settles helps organizations develop effective strategies for using Internet and wireless technology to make money, save money, and run a better business operation. His current focus is helping local governments implement municipal wireless network projects. He has developed and implemented innovative marketing campaigns for more than 21 years.

As we wrap up the new millennium's first decade, managing effective PR efforts will be akin to taming wild broncos rather than riding herd on button-down business processes dominated by predictability and a well-populated media contact database. This truly isn't your parent's PR profession.

Luckily, ye of the YouTube, MySpace, and iPhone generation are better prepared than many PR veterans to capitalize on the profession's New World Order.

The Internet at the turn of the century redefined "late-breaking news" to mean "news online, viewed worldwide, minutes after a story breaks." News production shifted from being the total domain of professional journalists, influenced significantly by PR pros, to one heavily influenced by anyone with a brain, a blog, and some time on their hands. PR pros tried to catch up with their own blogging tactics and dynamic web pages, but the universe shifted again. And here is where the PR class of '09 holds the upper hand.

YouTube puts the power of video broadcast into the hands of the masses. Podcasts likewise turn anyone into a radio broadcast maven. MySpace is the digital printing press the common man and woman can master. All of these deliver information worldwide at Internet speed. Smarter cell phones, iPhones, and the surge of iPhone wannabes enable average people to capture (or create) news, then immediately post on the aforementioned newest news media outlets. Instant news production couples with instant news broadcasts to millions.

How do you know this changes the business of news generation and management? Look around you.

National and international media outlets use video captured from cell phones as major segments of their news stories. A mayoral candidate in a major metropolis, written off in a crowded field, aggressively rides YouTube and MySpace to help stage a major upset. Feature stories from major media quote individuals' MySpace pages. People immediately become online celebrities—sans PR agents—and have larger subscriber bases than some prominent national publications.

The burning question in some executive circles, then, might be "Do we still need PR people?" If any random soul with a cell phone and laptop potentially can break a story, cover it, or analyze it later directly to our markets, how do we run an effective PR campaign when we can't control the message and we can't manage our brand?

As you strike out in your PR career, meet this question with a very simple statement—"We helped make this newest media what it is. Who better to help make this media work for you?" Then lay these four points out there to make your case.

1. *We're in the communication business.* Politely inform your future employers that the world is shifting, regardless of demographics the organization is targeting, and their PR has to change how it communicates or it will become increasingly irrelevant. One of the most popular videos on YouTube in 2006 was from an elderly gentleman that garnered over 2 million views, many from other seniors! Online PR tactics that looked dated at the turn of the century will be outright medieval if we don't get on top of the tech tools at hand.

2. *The power of one is increasing.* Everything about social networks, instant messaging, and a slew of techie tools and toys is spiraling rapidly toward giving the individual—customer, prospect, boss, employee, journalist, whomever—more control over who they communicate with, how, and when. PR must likewise shift from communicating to the masses to communicating with masses of individuals.

3. *As you gain control, you lose control.* Though counterintuitive, this is the stark reality of this newest media. The more organizations try to control vehicles such as blogs and social network pages, the faster people will abandon them in droves.

4. *The new PR has to live on the edge.* As the vanguard of a new generation of PR professionals, advocate that strategy plans incorporate the range of social networking, video sharing, and other online communication tools. Communicate to maximize individual input and creativity from target audiences, including journalists.

Be ready to move at Internet speed. Whether you're prepping media alerts, announcing new products, promoting feature stories, capitalizing on "late breaking news," or deflecting a crisis, use every Internet vehicle to mouse click your way to more effective media coverage.

With your smart phone and digital video camera handy, plunge into the thick of things.

Either strangers and bloggers you don't know are going to directly influence coverage and public opinion of your organization, or you're going to be the big influencer. You know firsthand how to use all of this technology. So just do it.

CASE STUDY 11.1

Big Mama Is Watching

With more than 87 million of its citizens surfing the Net, China became the world's second-most wired nation in 2004, moving ahead of Japan and trailing only the United States. While that figure represents less than 7 percent of China's estimated 1.3 billion people, it is still an impressive 140 times higher than it was only six years earlier.[76]

The dramatic growth of the Internet is just one example of that ancient nation's push to become a world economic power in the 21st century. China stood for centuries as one of the world's leading civilizations. However, political and economic unrest in the 19th and 20th centuries slowed its progress and isolated it from much of the outside world. The communist takeover of China in 1949 placed the nation under the dictatorship of Mao Zedong, who imposed strict controls on everyday activities and cost the lives of tens of millions of people. His successor, Deng Xiaoping, gradually introduced market reforms that loosened the central government's control over the economy. Within two decades, China's economy quadrupled.[77]

According to the CIA's *World Factbook,* "Beijing says it will intensify efforts to stimulate growth through spending on infrastructure—such as water control and power grids—and poverty relief through rural tax reform aimed at eliminating arbitrary local levies on farmers."[78] The communist hierarchy also recognized the value of the World Wide Web in spurring economic growth. Chinese officials launched a Government on the Net program in 1999, in which 40 government agencies established an Internet presence. To promote Internet use, China's largest telecommunications provider launched a program that same year to provide higher-speed data lines and to reduce dial-up fees.[79]

"The government sees [Internet technology] as a driver of China's global competitiveness and a key to gaining international recognition," said Jay X. Hu, managing director of the U.S. Information Technology Office in Beijing.[80] In February 2002, Chinese Premier Zhu Rongji said, "The use of information technology is vital for the world economy and social development."[81]

Those efforts appear to have paid dividends. After 15 years of trying, China was finally admitted as a member of the World Trade Organization in 2001. Shanghai hosted the Asia-Pacific Economic Cooperation Leaders summit that same year. China also won the highly coveted right to host the 2008 Olympic summer games.[82] However, these expressions of global recognition did not come without strings attached. To win approval from its critics, most notably the United States and the European Union, China promised to reform its economy, making it more open to the outside world. For the first time, the communist leadership had to pay heed to opinions of people outside their own regime.

This is where the Chinese leaders find themselves on the horns of a dilemma—a desire to introduce what is known as transparency into the nation's economy while maintaining tight controls over personal freedoms. The Internet has become a focal point of this conflict.

At the same time the communist regime has been encouraging its citizens to join the global Internet community, it has aggressively restricted what they can read or say about their government. Under regulations issued in 2000, Internet service and content providers are required to provide detailed records about their subscribers, including records of all web sites visited. The government prohibits the posting of "information that goes against the basic principles set in the Constitution" and "information that is detrimental to the honor and interests of the state." The measure also prohibits "information that undermines the state's policy for religions or that propagates heretical organizations or feudalistic and superstitious beliefs"— specifically targeted against Falun Gong, a spiritual movement that the Chinese government has systematically suppressed.[83]

China employs an estimated 40,000 censors—derisively known as "Big Mamas"— to police the web.[84] They monitor web sites, chat rooms, and private e-mail. Much of the government's attention has focused on Internet cafes. Under the pretense of health and safety concerns, the government shut down 150,000 unlicensed cafes in 2003. Those remaining were required to install software that blocks 500,000 banned sites. That software also records attempted hits on banned sites and automatically forwards that information to Big Mama.[85]

The crackdown continued into June 2004 when the Ministry of Information Industry unveiled a series of measures designed to control online chat rooms and bulletin boards. According to the government's official news agency, Xinhua, the measures aimed at "information threatening national security or social stability." The government also launched the Illegal and Harmful Content Reporting Center, a web site (http://net.china.cn) for people to complain to if they have seen something online that they believe is unlawful.[86]

"The public will be mobilized to supervise content on the Internet," Xinhua said. In a separate article, Chinese Internet service providers were encouraged to police themselves. "The basic principles of self-discipline for the Internet industry are patriotism, observance of the law, fairness and trustworthiness," the official news agency said.[87]

How serious is China about controlling Internet content? The Supreme People's Court has said, "In cases of a gross violation of law and where especially serious harm is caused to the state and people, law offenders may be sentenced to death and their properties will be confiscated by the state." The human rights organization Amnesty International reported that two members of Falun Gong imprisoned for Internet-related crimes have died in custody.[88]

The great unanswered question is whether China can manage the difficult balancing act of providing its citizens with economic freedom while depriving them of their basic human right to self-expression.

"Online freedom fighters—loose connections of Chinese dissidents and 'hacktivists' outside China—will continue to test the censors' ingenuity, while at home, Chinese 'netizens' will continue to push the envelope," wrote Beijing-based freelance writer Paul Mooney. "In the end, the Internet could prove too big to control."[89]

DISCUSSION QUESTIONS

1. Why should anyone outside of China be concerned about that government's attempts to control Internet content?
2. What are some of the tactics the Chinese government uses to try to control the Internet?
3. What are some of the contradictions in Chinese public policy that are pointed out in this case?
4. What do you believe is the answer to the "great unanswered question"—whether China can establish a free market economy while repressing political debate?

CASE STUDY 11.2

Corporate Podcasting

If you were web surfing on February 10, 2005, and happened across the Oregon-based *Northwest Noise,* you might have thought that the end of the world was near. The editor of the popular blog proclaimed, "Just now, as I look out my window and, yes, yes, there are pigs flying and a fat lady is singing,"[90]

What, you may ask, provoked such a reaction? That was the day General Motors entered the world of podcasting and, in turn, transformed what many saw as a vehicle for counterculture into a mainstream medium.

Podcasting, both as a term and practice, emerged in 2004. It is a marriage of the words *iPod,* Apple's revolutionary digital audio player, and *broadcasting.* Podcasts are audio files that sound like radio programs downloaded to computers or portable digital devices for on-demand listening. At the outset, podcasting was the domain of the eclectic, including what the *New York Times* described as "programs of weird monologists and couples capering, complaining and exposing their personal lives in ostentatiously appalling ways."[91] However, by April 2005, it was estimated that more than 6 million U.S. adults had downloaded podcasts—and that number was expected to rapidly grow.[92] The practice had become so prevalent that the editors of the *New Oxford American Dictionary* named *podcast* their Word of the Year for 2005.[93]

General Motors, for many a symbol of staid, conservative corporate values, entered the world of podcasting in connection with the 2005 Chicago Auto Show. In a five-minute presentation, GM North America President Gary Cowger introduced the 2006 Cadillac DTS and Buick Lucerne sedans. It was a no-frills production absent of music and sound effects.[94] Many in the podcast community were not impressed.

"Kinda looks like the time when ol' Dad put on the gangsta wear and hoodie, and tried to bust a rhyme," wrote software developer Dave Ritter. "You had to give him points for trying, but no matter how hard he tried to be hip, it wasn't going to fly."[95]

Despite the initial criticism of GM's first efforts in the new medium, the company logged approximately 10,000 downloads of the podcast within the first month of its release.[96] As the company increased both the quality and quantity of its podcast offerings, the number of downloads soared, an estimated 75,000 during August 2005.[97]

While these figures look impressive, what do they *really* mean? As is often a challenge with many public relations tactics, the tangible impact of podcasting is difficult to measure. How can one equate downloads to sales figures, especially with high-end purchases such as automobiles? And as is true with any individual tactic that is part of an integrated marketing communications campaign, how does one measure its effectiveness in motivating the consumer when working in combination with other tactics?

"No one knows the impact of podcasts, or even how many hits constitute a success," said Travis Austin, director of creative services for the Washington-based Strat@comm agency. "Finding the right length and frequency to hold an audience in this format has not been established."[98]

Even with a lack of measurement, podcasts offer companies something they lack in traditional broadcast media. "Companies are completely losing control of their messages, and one way to get into the game is by blogging and podcasting," said GM Director of New Media Michael Wiley. "The companies that are early adopters stand tremendous opportunity to be winners in the long run."[99]

Other advantages to podcasts are that they are relatively inexpensive and that their audience is self-selecting, meaning that people are already interested in the topic when they choose to download. "It is an interesting way to connect with niche audiences," Wiley said.[100]

Within a year of GM's first podcast, some of the biggest names in business and industry had jumped on the bandwagon. Disneyland celebrated its 50th anniversary with a series of podcasts recorded in the amusement park. The major broadcast networks began offering downloads of audio and video versions of their news and entertainment programming. IBM uses podcasts as an internal communications tool, one that reaches 7,000 employees weekly at an annual savings of $700,000 in conference-call costs.[101]

Some bloggers—including some on GM's *FastLane Blog*—said they feared the introduction of corporate marketing messages into what they saw as an alternative to commercial broadcasting. In other words, they were concerned that corporations will dominate the new medium. GM's Wiley's dismisses that argument, noting that the audience has ultimate control.

He said, "If you don't want to listen to it, don't."[102]

DISCUSSION QUESTIONS

1. What are the advantages and disadvantages of podcasting?
2. Does a traditional company such as General Motors take a risk in adopting cutting-edge communication tactics such as podcasting?
3. What differentiates a good podcast from a poor one?
4. Is podcasting a suitable tactic for both internal and external publics?

NOTES

1. Adam Sternbergh, "Hey There, Lonelygirl," *New York Magazine,* 28 August 2006, online, www.nymag.com.
2. Virginia Heffernan and Tom Zeller, " 'Lonely Girl' (and Friends) Just Wanted Movie Deal," *New York Times,* 12 September 2005, online, www.nytimes.com.
3. Ibid.
4. Gerald E. Stearn, *McLuhan Hot & Cool* (New York: Dial, 1967), cited online, www.beaulieuhome.com/mcluhan/stearn.html.
5. Justin Kaplan, ed., *Bartlett's Familiar Quotations,* 16th ed. (New York: Little, Brown, 1992), 758.
6. Lev Grossman, "Time Person of the Year—You," *Time,* 25 December 2006, 38–41.
7. Ibid.
8. Mary Madden and Susannah Fox, "Riding the Waves of 'Web 2.0,'" Pew Internet & American Life Project, 5 October 2006, online, www.pewinternet.org.
9. Augustine Ihator, "Corporate Communication: Challenges and Opportunities in a Digital World," *Public Relations Quarterly* 46, no. 4 (winter 2001): 15–18.
10. "CBS Ousts Four over Bush Guard Story," CNN, 10 January 2005, online, www .cnn.com.
11. "S. R. Sidarth—The Accidental Assassin," *Time,* 25 December 2006, 47–48.
12. "MySpace, Facebook and Other Social Networking Sites: Hot Today, Gone Tomorrow?" Knowledge@Wharton, 3 May 2006, online, http://knowledge.wharton.upenn.edu.
13. Nicholas Negroponte, *Being Digital* (New York: Knopf, 1995), 14.
14. Joseph Straubhaar and Robert LaRose, *Communications Media in the Information Society* (Belmont, Calif.: Wadsworth, 1996), 16.
15. Robert H. Zakon, "Hobbes' Internet Timeline v8.2," online, www.zakon.org/robert/ internet/timeline.
16. "Demographics of Internet Users," Pew Internet & American Life Project, 11 January 2007, online, www.pewinternet.org/trends.
17. "Daily Internet Activities," Pew Internet & American Life Project, 11 January 2007, online, www.pewinternet.org/trends.
18. "Demographics of Internet Users."
19. "Daily Internet Activities."
20. "Quarterly Retail E-Commerce Sales—4th Quarter 2005," news release issued by U.S. Census Bureau, 17 February 2006.
21. *E-Stats,* U.S. Census Bureau, 25 May 2006.
22. Mark Walsh, "Online Job Ad Revenues Surpass Print, *Online Daily Media,* MediaPost Publications, 20 December 2006.
23. Marshal Brain, "How CDs Work," How Stuff Works, online, http://electronics .howstuffworks.com.
24. Karim Nice, "How DVDs Work," How Stuff Works, online, http://electronics .howstuffworks.com.
25. *College Textbooks—Enhanced Offerings Appear to Drive Recent Price Increases* (GAO-05-806), United States Government Accountability Office, July 2005.

26. Frances Cairncross, *The Death of Distance: How the Communications Revolution Will Change Our Lives* (Boston: Harvard Business School Press, 1997), 28.

27. Lee Rainie and Bente Kalsnes, "Commons of the Tragedy—How the Internet Was Used by Millions after the Terror Attacks to Grieve, Console, Share News, and Debate the Country's Response," Pew Internet & American Life Project, 10 October 2001, online, www.pewinternet.org.

28. Jeffrey Boase, John Horrigan, Barry Wellman, and Lee Rainie, "The Strength of Internet Ties," Pew Internet & American Life Project, 25 January 2006, online, www.pewinternet.org.

29. Time Warner, Inc., Form 10-K/A (Amended Annual Report) for Period Ending 12/21/2005, 13 September 2006, 7.

30. "MySpace, Facebook, and Other Social Networking Sites: Hot Today, Gone Tomorrow?"

31. Paul T. Hill, review of *The Innovator's Dilemma, Education Week on the Web*, 14 June 2000, online, www.edweek.org/ew/ewstory.cfm?slug=40hill.h19.

32. David W. Guth and Charles Marsh, *Adventures in Public Relations: Case Studies and Critical Thinking* (Boston: Allyn & Bacon, 2005), 320.

33. Candace White and Niranjan Raman, "The World Wide Web as a Public Relations Medium: The Use of Research, Planning, and Evaluation in Web Site Development," *Public Relations Review* 25, no. 4 (winter 1999): 405–419.

34. Coy Callison, "Media Relations and the Internet: How *Fortune* 500 Company Web Sites Assist Journalists in News Gathering," *Public Relations Review* 29 (2003): 29–41.

35. Joe Dysart, "Making the Most of Promotional Links," *Public Relations Tactics,* November 2002, 21.

36. Sara Means Geigel, "Web Writing That Wows," *Public Relations Tactics*, February 2003, 15.

37. Geigel.

38. Deborah Fallows, "How Women and Men Use the Internet," Pew Internet & American Life Project, 28 December 2005, online, www.pcwinternet.org.

39. John Guiniven, "Getting Social with Press Releases," *Public Relations Tactics*, November 2006, 6.

40. Ibid.

41. "Survey Finds Web Sites Are Key in Driving Credibility, Marketing, for Small Business," *Public Relations Tactics,* November 2003, 18.

42. Steve Jarvis, "Virtual Firms Win Respect for Performance, Savings Virtual Agencies Deliver Tangible Results," *Marketing News,* 8 July 2002, 4–5.

43. Dick Grove, telephone interview, 2 August 2004.

44. Robert Dwek, "Viral E-Mails Fast Becoming Marketing Tool of the Future," *Marketing Week,* 24 June 2004, 19.

45. Pete Snyder, "Wanted: Standards for Viral Marketing," *Brandweek*, 28 June 2004, 21.

46. Guth and Marsh, 312–316.

47. Guth and Marsh, 312–316.

48. "Special Report—Viral Marketing: Viral Strains," *Precision Marketing*, 9 July 2004, 17–18.

49. "Bush Signs Anti-Spam Legislation," Associated Press, 16 December 2003, via the *Baltimore Sun,* online, www.sunspot.net.

50. "Special Report—Viral Marketing: Viral Strains."

51. Bill Leonard, "Blogs Begin to Make Mark on Corporate Communications," *HRMagazine* 48, no. 4 (September 2003): 30.

52. David Zurawik, "Eyewitness Testimonies and Footage Dominate News; Citizen Journalists, Online Communities Give Unique Perspective," *Baltimore Sun,* 17 April 2007, 8A.

53. Joe Garofoli, "Virginia Tech Massacre: New-Media Culture Challenges Limits of Journalism," *San Francisco Chronicle,* 20 April 2007, A1.

54. Mathew Ingram, "In a Crisis, a Wave of 'Citizen Journalism,' " *The Globe and Mail* (Canada), 18 April 2007, A15.

55. Nicole B. Cásarez, "Dealing with Cybersmear: How to Protect Your Organization from Online Defamation," *Public Relations Quarterly* (summer 2002): 40–45.

56. Cásarez.

57. Wikipedia: About, online, http://en.wikipedia.org/wiki/Wikipedia:About.

58. Michael Dertouzos, *What Will Be: How the New World of Information Will Change Our Lives* (New York: HarperCollins, 1997), 210–211.

59. Dertouzos, 211–212.

60. Investor information on the Wal-Mart web site as of 2 December 2006, http://investor.walmartstores.com.

61. *Building Smiles—2006 Wal-Mart Annual Report,* 14.

62. Michael Barbaro, "Appeals Court Rules for Wal-Mart in Maryland Health Care Case," *New York Times,* 18 January 2007, C4.

63. Marilyn Geewax, "Spinning Wal-Mart—Retailer, Union Activists Wage High-Stakes PR Battle," *Atlanta Journal-Constitution,* 26 November 2006, 1C.

64. Geewax.

65. Michael Barbaro, "Wal-Mart Enlists Bloggers in P.R. Campaign," *New York Times,* 7 March 2006, online, www.nytimes.com.

66. Geewax.

67. Paul Parton, "The Consumer: Reining in the Flog," *Media Magazine,* December 2006, online, http://publications.mediapost.com.

68. Noelle Weaver, "What We Should Learn from Sony's Fake Blog Fiasco," *Advertising Age,* 18 December 2006, online, http://adage.com.

69. Susannah Fox, "Generations Online," Pew Internet & American Life Project, December 2005, online, www.pewinternet.org.

70. Susannah Fox, "Older Americans and the Internet," Pew Internet & American Life Project, 25 March 2004, online, www.pewinternet.org.

71. Augustine Ihator, "Corporate Communication: Challenges and Opportunities in a Digital World," *Public Relations Quarterly* 46, no. 4 (winter 2001): 15–18.

72. Howard Stock, "Web Site Users Don't Trust Corporate Content," *Investors Relations Business,* 27 October 2003, 1.

73. Susanne Fitzgerald, "Predictions for the New Millennium—Have They Come True?" *Public Relations Quarterly* 48, no. 4 (winter 2003): 28–30.

74. "*Book Industry Trends 2006* Shows Publishers' Net Revenues at $34.59 Billion for 2005," news release issued by Book Industry Study Group, 22 May 2006, online, www.bisg.org.

75. Dertouzos, 205.

76. "China Now Second-Most Wired Nation on the Globe," *China Daily,* 21 July 2004, online, LexisNexis.

77. *The World Factbook,* Central Intelligence Agency, online, www.odci.gov/cia/publications/geos/ch.html.

78. *The World Factbook.*

79. David James, "China's Love-Hate Affair with the Net," *Upside* 11, no. 8 (August 1999): 52–55.

80. James.

81. "State Control of the Internet in China," Amnesty International, November 2002, online, http://web.amnesty.org/web/content.nsf/pages/gbr_china_internet.

82. "China Issues More Internet Regulations."

83. "State Control of the Internet in China."

84. Paul Mooney, "Beijing's Internet Dilemma," *South China Morning Post,* 14 April 2004, online, LexisNexis.

85. Alfred Hermida, "Behind China's Internet Red Firewall," BBC News, 3 September 2002, online, http://news.bbc.co.uk/1/hi/technology/2234154.stm.

86. "China Issues More Internet Regulations," Agence France Presse—English, 19 June 2004, online, LexisNexis.

87. "China Issues More Internet Regulations."

88. "State Control of the Internet in China."

89. Mooney.

90. "GM Starts a Podcast," *Northwest Noise,* 10 February 2005, online, www.northwestnoise.com.

91. Virginia Heffernan, "The Podcast as a New Podium," *New York Times,* 22 July 2005, E1.

92. "Data Memo: Podcasting," Pew Internet & American Life Project, April 2005, online, www.pewinternet.org.

93. Nathan Bierma, "At Random—'Podcast' Is Word of the Year," Knight-Ridder/Tribune Business News wire, 28 December 2005, LexisNexis.

94. John Couretas, "Podcast Is New GM Marketing Tool," *Automotive News,* 14 March 2005, 25.

95. Jamie Smith Hopkins, "Corporations Podcast Their Marketing Nets," Knight-Ridder/Tribune Business News wire, 11 December 2005, LexisNexis.

96. Couretas.

97. Hopkins.

98. John Guiniven, "Podcast as a PR Tool: What Do You Need To Know?" *Public Relations Tactics,* September 2005, online reprint, www.prsa.org.

99. Hopkins.

100. Couretas.

101. Hopkins.

102. Couretas.

12

Crisis Communications

OBJECTIVES

After studying this chapter, you will be able to

- understand what crises are and how they develop

- recognize that crisis situations often create opportunities

- appreciate the importance of anticipating crises and planning for them before they happen

- explain the elements of an effective crisis communications plan

KEY TERMS

The Rumor

You are the head of corporate communications for a company that produces one of the nation's most popular snack foods. The company prides itself on making products that are both delicious and nutritionally sound. In your advertising you brag of using only natural ingredients with no artificial flavorings or other additives.

Recently a rumor cropped up on the Internet asserting that a leak from a nearby nuclear power plant has made most of your company's snack foods radioactive. Officials at the nuclear power plant say there has been no such leak. Despite this reassurance, the company has noticed a small decline in sales. To make matters worse, a producer from a nationally syndicated tabloid television show has called and wants to know whether it is true that the company's snack food products glow in the dark.

What are you going to do?

The Storm before the Storm

It was the disaster everyone feared. The massive hurricane slammed the Louisiana coast with sustained winds of 120 miles per hour and up to 20 inches of rain. The storm surge topped levees in low-lying New Orleans, leaving portions of the city under 10–12 feet of water and thousands of people stranded on rooftops or trapped by floodwaters. Transportation in and out of the city was severely restricted by flooding or a shortage of fuel. Hospitals and other medical services were closed or cut off by the rising tide. Usually reliable communications networks failed.[1] New Orleans was dying, and there was little anybody could do about it.

While this may sound like Hurricane Katrina, which ravaged much of the U.S. Gulf Coast in late August 2005, it is not. This is the scenario for Hurricane Pam, a fictitious storm simulation created by Baton Rouge–based Innovative Emergency Management, Inc., for a five-day training exercise for 270 representatives of local, state, and federal agencies. The purpose of the exercise was to learn what might happen if the much-feared "big one" made a direct hit on the Crescent City. More important, officials hoped to learn the steps they could take to minimize, if not eliminate, the threats posed by a Hurricane Pam–like storm.[2] The simulation occurred almost one year to the day *before* Katrina.

IEM consultants developed a 109-page report, "Southeast Louisiana Catastrophic Hurricane Functional Plan," within a few weeks of the exercise. In it, they described a scenario that eerily paralleled the human tragedy that played out in the streets of New Orleans less than a year later. In an ironically accurate prediction, state and federal officials concluded "the gravity of the situation calls for an extraordinary level of advance planning to improve government readiness to respond effectively to such an event." However, Katrina struck before the officials put the plan into action.

"We were still fairly early in the process," said IEM President Madhu Beriwal. "This was part of FEMA's initiative for doing catastrophic disaster planning. New Orleans was picked as the first place to be studied."[3]

A FEMA Urban Search and Rescue task force member rescues a New Orleans resident from his flooded neighborhood. Despite this and countless other acts of heroism, emergency response officials were widely criticized for what many viewed as an inadequate response to Hurricane Katrina. (Courtesy of Jocelyn Augustino, Federal Emergency Management Agency)

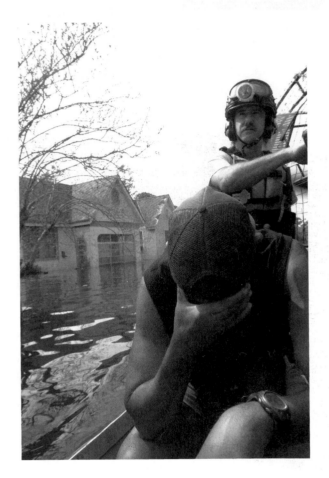

Not Just Bad Luck

Hurricane Katrina was the worst natural disaster in U.S. history. It is easy to rationalize that people have no control over the forces of nature. It is also tempting to suggest that the onset of Katrina before officials had time to implement their newly minted emergency response plan was just a stroke of bad luck. But was it?

The dangers confronting New Orleans, much of which is situated precariously below sea level, had been well known for decades. Even in the days before the deadly storm made landfall, Dr. Max Mayfield, director of the National Hurricane Center, warned Federal Emergency Management Agency (FEMA) and Department of Homeland Security officials of the potential for a catastrophe. "It's not like this was a surprise," Mayfield said. "We had in the advisories that the levee could be topped."[4]

What happened next—as documented in Case Study 1.2—has been the subject of rancorous political debate, heated recriminations, and a slew of investigations. Local, state, and federal emergency management officials often took actions that were either too little or too late to make a difference. Although the death toll from

Katrina was a fraction of that predicted by the Hurricane Pam scenario, it still exceeded 1,800 throughout the region. While the media had a difficult time separating fact from fiction, the lasting image of the government's response was thousands of people stranded on rooftops or at the battered Louisiana Superdome pleading for help five days after the storm had passed. Regardless of whose version of the events one may choose to believe, there is an undeniable fact: a widespread belief that people charged with the responsibility of protecting their fellow citizens had failed in their duties when they were needed most.

The Katrina fiasco was not just an emergency management failure. It was a public relations failure. Central to the Gulf Coast tragedy was the failure to manage relationships among key stakeholders, including other public and private response agencies, the residents of the region, and the news media. "Communications is the glue that holds a crisis response together," said Kathy Baughman of HLB Communications in Chicago. "Without it, chaos quickly ensues, which, of course, was the case in the immediate aftermath of Katrina."[5]

"When action and communications are inconsistent, credibility goes out the door, and the public's trust disintegrates," said Dan Keeney of Texas-based DPK Public Relations. "You can't say that everything that can be done is being done while failing to deliver basic necessities to crowds of people."[6]

Part of the failure can be blamed on the reorganization of the federal government's emergency response apparatus following the terror attacks of September 11, 2001. Prior to that date, FEMA was a stand-alone agency with established relationships with other public and private agencies. That changed in 2002 with the creation of the Department of Homeland Security, an umbrella agency designed to coordinate the government's response to all public safety threats, especially terrorism. Several experts have said that this reshuffling of the federal bureaucracy disrupted long-existing relationships, many of which had not been adequately reestablished by the time of Katrina.

The reorganization also had another unintended consequence: a failure of values. Christopher Cooper, a *Wall Street Journal* reporter who has coauthored a book highly critical of the federal government's response, said that Homeland Security officials, who he said had a mind-set that "natural disasters are for pansies, and real men handle the terrorist stuff," undervalued FEMA's mission.[7] Michael Brown, the ex-FEMA director who many see as a central villain in the Katrina drama, has since told audiences that Homeland Security Secretary Michael Chertoff was "clueless" and that President Bush had turned "a deaf ear" to his concerns about FEMA's ability to handle major disasters.[8]

It is unfair to say that emergency management officials were totally unprepared for Hurricane Katrina. Nor would it be fair to suggest that they didn't do anything right. The truth is that they did a lot of things right: sheltering and feeding hundreds of thousands of evacuees, rescuing countless others, and mobilizing the largest relief effort in the nation's history. However, the storm exposed serious weaknesses. There was a failure of planning, evidenced by the slow response to the recommendations arising from the Hurricane Pam exercise. There was a failure to build and maintain relationships among the members of the emergency response community. Local, state,

FEMA Undersecretary Michael Brown and Louisiana Governor Kathleen Blanco were among the local, state, and federal officials severely criticized for the government's inadequate response to Hurricane Katrina. (Courtesy of Jocelyn Augustino, Federal Emergency Management Agency)

and federal officials should have spent less time pointing fingers of blame and more time talking to one another. There was also a failure of values. It didn't matter whether the threat came from Al Qaeda or Mother Nature, the priority for government officials was to protect their people. Unfortunately, on that count, they fell short.

Crises Can Happen to Anyone

The unforgiving truth is that bad things do happen to good people. When we hear of misfortune happening to others, we may easily rationalize that "it couldn't happen here." However, recent history suggests otherwise:

- H&R Block, a leading tax-preparation service, announced in June 2005 that it had made a $19 million error in its favor in its financial statements. Two months later, the company revealed that it found another $77 million error—this time in the other direction.[9]

- Hundreds of JetBlue passengers were stranded in parked aircraft for up to 11 hours because of a snow and ice storm in New York in February 2007. The airline refused to let the passengers return to the terminal, a decision that prompted a congressional investigation and an apology from the CEO.

- To promote a new show on the Cartoon Network, a marketing company placed 40 laptop-size devices along key transportation routes in the Boston area in

January 2007. Unfortunately, the devices were mistaken for bombs, sparking a terrorism alert.[10]

- Three people died and more than 200 fell ill because of an *E. coli* outbreak at Taco Bell restaurants in the United States and Canada during late 2006. Company officials first blamed green onions but later recanted when it was learned that tainted lettuce had been the source of the outbreak.

- ChoicePoint, an identification verification service, mistakenly sold the personal data of 145,000 people to an identity-theft ring and then charged the victims to see the information it provided to the criminals. The blunder eventually cost the company $21 million.[11]

If anything, these and other incidents testify to this reality: Anything can happen. However unexpected, the sad truth is that most crises are not wholly unpredictable. Perhaps even sadder is the fact that many, if not most, are avoidable. By identifying and analyzing potential risks, we can eliminate many crises before they ever happen. With crisis planning we can mitigate the damage when crises do occur.

QUICK ✓ CHECK

1. Since people have no control over the forces of nature, is it fair to criticize public officials for the problems they had responding to a massive storm like Hurricane Katrina?
2. Was there a failure of values in governmental responses to Hurricane Katrina?
3. Are most crises unpredictable and therefore unavoidable?

The Anatomy of a Crisis

"If economics is the dismal science," disaster recovery consultant Kenneth Myers writes, "then contingency planning is the abysmal science. No one likes to look into the abyss."[12] But like it or not, crisis planning has become an imperative in the 21st century for big and small organizations alike. "Any small business owner who doesn't have a crisis management plan is derelict in his duties," says Martin Cooper of Cooper Communications in Encino, California.[13] As researchers Donald Chisholm and Martin Landau have pointedly noted, "When people believe that because nothing has gone wrong, nothing will go wrong, they court disaster. There is noise in every system and in every design. If this fact is ignored, nature soon reminds us of our folly."[14]

A series of surveys over the past two decades has unearthed a surprising pattern: Despite warning after warning, many organizations remain unprepared for crises and their consequences. In research conducted in the 1980s and 1990s, just over half of the organizations surveyed said they had written crisis plans. Only one-third of them said they had practiced them.[15]

One could logically assume that the 2001 terror attacks would have been a wake-up call. However, that does not appear to be the case. In a survey of IABC members

Textbook Examples: Exxon and Tylenol

Whenever people discuss the right way and the wrong way to conduct crisis communications, two names inevitably enter the conversation: Exxon and Tylenol.

Although both incidents date back to the 1980s, their lessons stand the test of time. In fact, much of the growth in the science and practice of crisis communications can be traced to the spectacular successes and failures of these two companies. They constitute what we call—somewhat apologetically—textbook examples of crisis communications.

No one wants to be remembered for being the poster child for how *not* to act during an emergency, but that is the woeful legacy of Lawrence G. Rawl. He was chairman and chief executive officer of the Exxon Corporation when one of its tankers, the *Exxon Valdez,* spilled 11 million gallons of crude oil into the pristine waters of Alaska's Prince William Sound. Oil contaminated shorelines nearly 600 miles from where the tanker ran aground just after midnight on March 24, 1989.

Rawl declined to go to the accident site. Critics said he should have gone to Alaska and personally taken charge of the cleanup. "From a public relations standpoint, it probably would have been better if I had gone up there," Rawl later told *Fortune.* "But I would have used up a lot of people's time."[16]

Rawl waited one week before making his first public comment, in which he blamed U.S. Coast Guard and Alaskan government officials for holding up the cleanup. He came across in television interviews as combative, ill at ease, and unprepared. Exxon newspaper advertisements apologized for the oil spill but did not take responsibility for it. When the company announced that it would pass along spill-related expenses to customers as a "cost of doing business," angry consumers returned more than 45,000 credit cards.[17]

In an interview two months after the accident, Rawl said the spill and subsequent lawsuits would cost Exxon less than $1 billion.[18] In fact, a federal judge in Anchorage imposed $4.5 billion in punitive damages against Exxon in January 2004 on behalf of 32,000 fishermen and residents who had sued

the company 15 years earlier. Exxon said it would appeal the decision.[19]

The actions of James E. Burke stand in sharp contrast to those of Rawl. Burke was CEO of Johnson & Johnson when one of its most successful products, Tylenol, was involved in deadly product tampering crises in 1982 and 1986. On both occasions, Tylenol capsules were laced with cyanide by unknown perpetrators and placed on store shelves. Seven people died in the two incidents.

Within two weeks of the first Tylenol tampering incident, the value of Johnson & Johnson stock dropped $657 million. It was also estimated that the company had received as much as $300 million worth of negative publicity.[20]

The Food and Drug Administration advised against a massive product recall out of fear that doing so might spawn "copycat" crimes. However, Johnson & Johnson officials said they had no choice but to demonstrate their concern for consumer safety by recalling their product: Their values statement placed customer safety above all else. To further calm an uneasy public, Tylenol capsules were placed in triple-sealed safety packaging after the first incident. After the second, Johnson & Johnson replaced the capsule with tamper-proof caplets.

Burke took another important step to maintain his company's credibility. Early Johnson & Johnson statements indicated that there was no cyanide present in its manufacturing plants. However, that statement was wrong. Rather than risk discovery of this potentially damaging fact, the company immediately issued a news release correcting the error.

The textbook lessons of Exxon and Tylenol are clear. Companies that communicate quickly and compassionately with their stakeholders during crises have a far greater chance of saving their reputation—and their bottom line—than those that don't. People are more forgiving of those who admit their mistakes and move quickly to correct them than those who refuse to be held accountable and try to blame others. When the heat is on, success goes to those who keep cool and adhere to their values.

conducted in December 2005, one in three of the respondents indicated that they had no crisis communications plan in place at the start of the year. Almost half of those who said they had been unprepared reported being forced to quickly cobble a plan together when a crisis struck. According to Robert J. Holland and Katrina Gill, the study's authors, "54 percent of the communicators who work in organizations without a crisis communications plan said it is because senior management there does not consider it a priority."[21]

What Is a Crisis?

The word *crisis,* just like the term *public relations,* is often misused by those who do not know it has a specific meaning. Everyone instinctively understands that flash floods, hurricanes, and earthquakes can usually be classified as crises. But what about a flat tire, missed homework, or being stood up on a date? Are these crises, too?

The difference between a **problem** and a **crisis** is a matter of scope. Problems are commonplace occurrences and fairly predictable. They usually can be addressed in a limited time frame, often without arousing public attention or without draining an organization's resources. On the other hand, crises tend to be less predictable. They require a considerable investment of time and resources to resolve and often bring unwanted public attention. And more than problems, crises can challenge an organization's core values.

Researchers Thierry C. Pauchant and Ian I. Mitroff have written that a crisis is "a disruption that physically affects a system as a whole and threatens its basic assumptions, its subjective sense of self, its existential core."[22] According to Pauchant and Mitroff, crises can threaten the legitimacy of an industry, reverse the strategic mission of an organization, and disturb the way people see the world and themselves.[23]

Steven Fink, a noted crisis consultant, has characterized crises as being prodromal situations (situations often marked by forewarning) that run the risk of

- escalating in intensity;
- falling under close media or government scrutiny;
- interfering with the normal operations of business;
- jeopardizing the positive public image enjoyed by a company and its officers; and
- damaging a company's bottom line.[24]

Laurence Barton refines the terminology even further, describing a crisis as a major event that "has potentially negative results. The event and its aftermath may significantly damage an organization and its employees, products, services, financial condition, and reputation."[25]

Crisis Dynamics

As you might imagine, crises come in many shapes and sizes. They can also influence public perceptions of organizations in vastly different ways. Some crises cast organizations in the role of *victim.* In other crises, organizations may be seen as the *villain.*

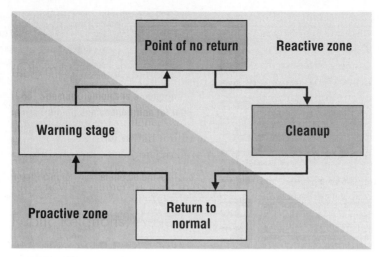

FIGURE 12.1 Crisis Dynamics

And in a few cases, well-prepared organizations have emerged from crises in the role of *hero.*

Most people would rather be seen as a hero than as either a victim or a villain. At the same time, many people operate under a false assumption that crises and their consequences are unavoidable. However, public relations practitioners can do much to influence events before they happen and, in some instances, to avert crises altogether. That role of public relations is a focus of this chapter.

But before trying to change the course of events, we should understand the dynamics of a crisis. It is a mistake to believe that crises operate as randomly as next week's lottery. In fact, they follow predictable patterns. Although various researchers have adopted different terminology to describe these patterns, there is general agreement that crises tend to develop in four stages (Figure 12.1):

1. **Warning stage:** In reality, most crises don't "just happen." Usually, there are advance signs of trouble. At this stage, it may still be possible to avoid trouble, but the clock is ticking. This is a period in which we have an ability to be proactive and control events *before* they happen. However, one of the greatest challenges in crisis communications is to recognize the potential for danger and then to act accordingly.

2. **Point of no return:** At this moment, the crisis is unavoidable, and we are forced to be reactive. Some damage will be done. How much remains to be seen and depends, to a large degree, on the organization's response. This is often the time when most of the stakeholders critical to the success of the organization first become aware of the crisis. And from this point on, they are watching very closely.

3. **Cleanup phase:** Even when the point of no return has been reached and the public spotlight shines upon the organization in crisis, an opportunity to minimize the damage remains. How long this period will last depends on how prepared the organization is to deal with the crisis. The cleanup phase is also a period of recovery and

investigation, both internal and external. Fink says this is often the point at which the "carcass gets picked clean."

4. Things return to normal: If *normal* is defined as returning to the way things were before the crisis, then things probably will never be normal again. Following a crisis, operations may differ radically from before. New management may be in place. In addition to these changes, it is very likely that the organization learned valuable lessons. A vigorous evaluation of the organization's performance in dealing with the crisis can result in plans for coping with—or avoiding—the next crisis.

This brings us to an important point: The crisis dynamics model implies that this is a cyclical process, one in which we automatically move from one crisis to another. However, that doesn't have to be the case. Management has at least two opportunities to take steps to minimize or eliminate crises. One is identifying the warning signs of a looming crisis and taking forceful action before reaching the point of no return. The other comes after the crisis, when things return to normal. Management should then take the time to evaluate its performance and apply the lessons it learned. But if no such evaluation occurs, management runs the danger of making the same mistakes and creating a new crisis. After all, history has a tendency to repeat. Just ask NASA.

A Tale of Two Shuttle Disasters

Two dates are forever burned into NASA's collective consciousness: January 28, 1986, and February 1, 2003. On the first date, the space agency experienced its first fatal in-flight accident when seven astronauts died in the explosion of the space shuttle *Challenger* shortly after liftoff. Seventeen years and four days later, another seven astronauts were lost when the space shuttle *Columbia* disintegrated during reentry following what had been a successful 17-day mission in Earth orbit.[26]

While both tragedies came as a complete surprise to most people, a handful of NASA insiders knew that both shuttles had experienced problems that could lead to a catastrophe. Investigations of both accidents would attribute the failures, in part, to a NASA corporate culture known as "go fever": a strong desire to accomplish mission objectives on schedule without regard to NASA's long-standing value of putting safety first. In its report, the *Columbia* Accident Investigation Board said the disaster was "likely rooted to some degree in NASA's history and the human space flight program's culture."

However, from a public relations perspective, major differences separated the *Challenger* and *Columbia* accidents. Let's compare the two events and NASA's response to them during each of the four stages of crises.

Warning Stage

- *Challenger:* The explosion was caused by a failure of O-rings that sealed sections of the shuttle's solid-rocket boosters. The escaping propellant had the same effect on the shuttle's external fuel tank as a blowtorch on a gas tank. Engineers had identified the problem six months earlier and debated it as late as 12 hours before launch.

- *Columbia:* The shuttle's fate was sealed during liftoff when a chunk of insulating foam broke off the external fuel tank and struck the orbiter's left wing at almost 600 mph. It damaged some of the external tiles designed to protect the shuttle from the searing heat of reentry. NASA officials knew of the incident. After an internal debate, they decided that it did not pose a threat to the shuttle and its crew.

Point of No Return

- *Challenger:* The shuttle exploded 71 seconds into the flight. The explosion was witnessed by millions on live television—including thousands of schoolchildren following the exploits of Christa McAuliffe, the first participant in NASA's Teacher in Space program.
- *Columbia:* The first signs of trouble appeared when temperature gauges on the left wing failed during reentry. Within a few minutes, all voice contacts and data were lost. Simultaneously, people on the ground watched a blazing trail of debris following the shuttle's flight path. Television cameras captured the disintegration of the orbiter over Texas.

Cleanup Phase

- *Challenger:* Despite a crisis plan that required an announcement of an in-flight death or injury within 20 minutes, NASA was silent for five hours. When officials held their first postaccident news conference, they promised a thorough investigation. But even then, they gave no information on the fate of the crew. That was left to President Ronald Reagan, who addressed a grief-stricken nation more than five hours after the explosion.
- *Columbia:* Within 15 minutes of the loss of shuttle data, NASA declared a "Shuttle Contingency" and posted an announcement on the agency's web site. Within 30 minutes, NASA spokesman Kyle Herring told NBC, "Obviously it is the break-up of something, and based on the timing it is more than likely that, yes, that is the shuttle."[27] Within four hours, President George W. Bush spoke to the nation, followed by NASA Administrator Sean O'Keefe. NASA then began a series of technical briefings on the accident.

Things Return to Normal

- *Challenger:* NASA's poor response to the crisis and subsequent loss of public confidence led to a White House decision to take the investigation out of the space agency's hands. An independent panel sharply criticized NASA management, resulting in the premature end of many promising careers.
- *Columbia:* NASA's quick response won it public praise. More important, it was allowed to conduct its own investigation of the accident. While the investigating board criticized NASA for "cultural traits and organizational practices detrimental to safety," the agency avoided the traumatic restructuring it had faced 17 years earlier.

That NASA won public praise for its response to the *Columbia* tragedy brings us to what may be the most important lesson in crisis communications: Not all

NASA Administrator Sean O'Keefe briefs reporters on the investigation into the loss of the space shuttle *Columbia* and its seven-person crew. The agency's handling of media relations during this crisis contrasted sharply with relations following the *Challenger* accident. (Courtesy of NASA)

outcomes of crises have to be bad. In fact, when managed properly, crises can bring opportunity.

Crises Can Bring Opportunity

Gerald C. Meyers, a former automobile industry executive who has written and lectured extensively on the subject of crisis communications, says a "window of opportunity" opens during the warning and point-of-no-return stages of crises.[28] During these stages key stakeholders tend to sit back and withhold their judgment while placing the organization in crisis under close scrutiny. How long the window of opportunity remains open depends on the organization's reputation.

Meyers says seven potential benefits can be reaped from a crisis:[29]

1. *Heroes are born.* Crises can make people the focus of public attention. Those who respond well to that scrutiny are often seen as heroes.

2. *Change is accelerated.* People and organizations resist change. When change is suggested, you often hear, "But we have always done it this way." Crises often finally compel organizations and individuals who have lagged behind various social and technological trends to change the way they do things.

3. *Latent problems are faced.* When things are going well, it is easy to ignore some problems. This fact is reflected by the "if it ain't broke, don't fix it" mentality. During

QuickBreak 12.2

Are You Ready?

While recent world events remind us of our own vulnerability, dozens of organizations have turned to the Internet to help people deal with whatever Mother Nature or people of ill will may throw in their direction.

The growth of the World Wide Web has created a cost-effective way to help public and private organizations reach large audiences with detailed emergency preparedness information. But like any other form of communication, the content of each organization's web site is determined by its mission and intended audience.

When the Department of Homeland Security introduced its "Ready" campaign, the major focus of the campaign's web site, www.ready.gov, was terrorism. Because of the criticism DHS received following Hurricane Katrina, the web site has toned down its terrorism emphasis and dealt more broadly with all kinds of disasters. The web site urges visitors to "Prepare. Plan. Stay Informed." In the "Ready America" section of the web site, DHS provides information on how to create a household disaster kit, how to develop a family emergency plan, and how to remain informed of potential threats. The web site also has special sections for businesses, kids, older citizens, persons with disabilities, and pet owners.

"Emergency preparedness is no longer the sole concern of earthquake prone Californians and those who live in the part of the country known as 'Tornado Alley,'" the Ready America web site warns. "For Americans, preparedness must now account for man-made disasters as well as natural ones."[30]

There have also been post-Katrina changes on the Federal Emergency Management Agency's web site. While terrorism remains an area of concern, it is now listed as just one of 17 potential hazards. In addition to disaster-specific information, the web site includes a section of "Mitigation Best Practices and Case Studies," a collection of stories and

information on how people can take proactive steps to protect themselves and their property before a crisis strikes. The web site also has specifically targeted information for businesses, emergency personnel, other government agencies, institutions, kids, and the news media. Visitors can also download "Are You Ready? An In-depth Guide to Citizen Preparedness."[31]

The American Red Cross is a private volunteer organization. As such, its disaster services web site (www.redcross.org) tends to have a more personal focus. While covering many of the same topics found on the DHS and FEMA sites, the Red Cross site also includes information on how to help children cope with disaster, animal safety tips, and how to minimize property damage and financial risks. It also contains a key message that the Red Cross constantly stresses: You have to be prepared to help yourself.

"Local officials and relief workers will be on the scene after a disaster, but they cannot reach everyone right away," the web site states. "Therefore, the best way to make your family and your home safer is to be prepared before disaster strikes."[32]

The Boy Scouts is a private organization created nearly a century ago to instill character and citizenship for boys growing into manhood. Its web site (www.scouting.org) is geared to the interests of its members and volunteers. Visitors to "Emergency Preparedness BSA" are told that "the emergencies of today's world demand more than ever that our young people and adults be trained as individuals and units to meet emergency situations."

In a reaffirmation of the organization's values, readers are told, "the basic aims of Scouting include teaching youth to take care of themselves, to be helpful to others, and to develop courage, self-reliance, and the will to be ready to serve in an emergency."[33]

And as you might expect from the Boy Scouts, a clear message to be prepared.

crises, however, organizations often have no choice but to tackle these problems head-on.

4. *People can be changed.* This item has a double meaning. On the one hand, it means that the attitudes and behavior of people can be changed, as has been dramatically demonstrated by society's loss of patience with sexual harassment in the workplace. However, "changing people" can have a pragmatic meaning: Sometimes it is necessary to replace some people with others who have a fresh perspective and new ideas.

5. *New strategies evolve.* Important lessons can be learned from crises. We often discover a better way of doing things or perceive new paths to opportunity.

6. *Early warning systems develop.* Experience is a wonderful teacher. If we know what the warning signs are, we can recognize a crisis on its way. As a child, you may have been told never to touch a pan on the stove without first checking to see whether the stove was hot. The same principle applies here.

7. *New competitive edges appear.* It has been said that nothing is more exhilarating than having someone shoot a gun at you and miss. Organizations and individuals often feel like this after surviving a crisis. The sense of teamwork and accomplishment that comes with a job well done often carries over to the next challenge. Because of the various changes that occur during the crisis cleanup, organizations are often better equipped to compete in the new environment.

1. What is the difference between a problem and a crisis?
2. Do crises follow a predictable pattern?
3. Are the outcomes of crises always negative?

Crisis Communications Planning

Public relations, which by definition is a management function, plays a critical role during times of crisis. In an ideal setting, practitioners should be in a position to advise management before, during, and after each incident. Mayer Nudell and Norman Antokol, veterans of the U.S. Foreign Service, have written that communications specialists should be involved in every aspect of crisis communications.[34] Robert F. Littlejohn, who has experience in both academic and emergency management communities, favors the inclusion of a good communicator on a crisis management team, saying that strong communication skills are an essential quality of the team leader.[35]

Nobody likes to think about the consequences of disasters. However, the stark reality is that no one is immune to their effects. As the events of recent years have shown, crises can strike at any time and place. Public relations practitioners owe it to themselves, to their employers, and to all of their stakeholder publics to confront these unpleasant issues head-on and map out a course of action for dealing with crises that is consistent with their organization's values. In the final analysis, planning for a hurricane while it is still out at sea is a lot easier than when you are in the eye of the storm.

Effective crisis communications, like the public relations process as a whole, involves four steps: *risk assessment, crisis communications planning, response,* and *recovery.* Let's look more closely at each of these phases in turn.

Step One: Risk Assessment

At the heart of proactive crisis communications is **risk assessment:** the identification of the various threats under which an organization operates. Some potential crises are common to most organizations. These include problems created by bad weather, fires, financial difficulties, and on-the-job accidents. Other crises are more closely related to the specific nature of the product or service a given organization provides. These can include dangers inherent in the product/service itself (e.g., accidents involving public transportation or contamination of a food product) and toxic by-products from manufacturing processes (e.g., radiation from a nuclear power plant). Compared with private companies, publicly owned companies operate in an environment in which their crises are often more visible. The same holds true for well-known as opposed to lesser-known organizations. Sometimes crises have to do less with *what* business you are in than with *where* you are doing business. For example, the location of an office within a floodplain or in a country with an unstable political environment entails risks not faced elsewhere.

But the goal of risk assessment is not just the identification of potential hazards. Once a threat is identified, steps should be taken to eliminate or lessen it. The wisdom of this can be seen in the experiences of Nokia Corporation of Finland and Telefon AB L.M. Ericsson of neighboring Sweden. Both were leaders in the sale of mobile telephone handsets. Both relied on the same New Mexico semiconductor plant to supply them with computer chips. A March 17, 2000, lightning strike caused a fire that dramatically reduced the plant's ability to produce the critical components. Without the chips, neither company would be able to make its products. Because of more aggressive monitoring and better internal communication, Nokia officials recognized the crisis first. They immediately began working with the supplier on developing alternative sources of the computer chips. Ericsson officials were slower to react to the news out of New Mexico. By the time they realized the problem, it was too late. Nokia had effectively cornered the supply of the critical component and became the market leader. Ericsson's sales plunged. Remember: The best crises are those that are averted.

Many organizations can avert crises by clearly articulating and actively implementing their core values. By doing so, they can make all aware of the legal and ethical limits under which they choose to operate. This is much easier to do during a period of relative calm than it is during the heat of a crisis. Decisions made during a crisis without consideration of organization values can have long-term ramifications that can eventually trigger new crises.

A U.S. senator cited such a failure of values in describing the crisis that enveloped the Enron Corporation, which filed for bankruptcy in 2001. Accounting irregularities at the Houston-based energy company led to thousands of lost jobs, billions of dollars in investor lawsuits, prison terms, and the eventual collapse of the company. But Enron's persistent refusal to answer questions during the crisis also troubled affected publics. "It's taken a silent posture and is hiding at precisely the wrong time," said one investment analyst.[36] After his conviction for aiding and abetting fraud, Enron's chief of investor relations said, "I definitely did not make the right choices in my last year at Enron. I am profoundly sorry for that."[37] Senator Carl Levin of Michigan concluded, "What happened at Enron wasn't a failure of regulations and law. It was a failure of corporate culture, a failure of values, a failure of heart."[38]

When undertaking a program of risk assessment, organizations can choose either to hire outside consultants or to perform an in-house evaluation. Some organizations, in fact, choose to do both. Often, outside consultants assume a training role after the planning is complete. These consultants can be expensive, but worth every penny.

For those who decide to do in-house planning and training, the development of a broad-based **crisis planning team** (CPT) is a logical step. The makeup of these teams varies. According to a National Association of Manufacturers study, the chief legal counsel is the company official most often assigned to the CPT, followed by the director of public affairs, the director of security, and the chief operating officer.

It is not enough for the management to dictate a crisis response to the rank and file. The plan will be more successful if employees have some ownership of it. For this reason, employees at all levels of the organization should take part in the risk assessment process. This brings different and valuable perspectives to the process. If two heads are better than one, think how much better the risk assessment can be if many heads contribute to the final product.

QUICK ✓ CHECK

1. What are the four steps of the crisis communications process? Do these remind you of any other process you have seen?
2. What is risk assessment?
3. What role do values play in crisis communications?

Step Two: Developing the Plan

Crisis communications planning means developing communications strategies for identified risks—making as many decisions and taking as many steps as you possibly can *before* a crisis occurs. The best decisions are usually made when you have time to think through their ramifications.

Because crises vary in their scope and nature, it is best to have a flexible crisis plan that is not event specific. The contents of such a plan include crisis definitions, a list of crisis managers, stakeholder communication strategies, planned coordination and information sites, and an employee training program.

QUICKBREAK 12.3

The Crisis Plotting Grid

Steven Fink is a public relations and management consultant who has firsthand knowledge of crises. During the Three Mile Island nuclear power plant crisis in 1979, Fink provided valuable advice to Governor Richard Thornburgh of Pennsylvania that, in the long run, helped prevent public panic. In his book *Crisis Management: Planning for the Inevitable,* Fink developed a useful tool for risk assessment: the **crisis plotting grid** (Figure 12.2). By placing every potential crisis on the grid, an organization can easily identify the areas where its crisis planning is most needed.

The vertical axis of the grid, which runs from 0 to 10, represents the **crisis impact value (CIV).** Fink says you should respond to the following five questions for each potential crisis on a scale of 0 to 10, with 0 being the lowest level of impact on your organization and 10 being the highest:

1. If the crisis runs the risk of escalating in intensity, how intense can it get and how quickly can it escalate?

2. To what extent will the crisis fall under the watchful eye of key stakeholders, including the media, regulators, shareholders, and so on?

3. To what extent will the crisis interfere with the organization's normal operations?

4. To what degree is the organization the culprit?

5. To what extent can the organization's bottom line be damaged?

Add up the total from the five questions (maximum 50 points) and divide by 5. The resulting figure is the CIV for that potential crisis.

The horizontal axis represents the **crisis probability factor (CPF).** Determine the CPF for the crisis in question by estimating the probability of the crisis on a scale of 0 percent (absolutely no likelihood that the crisis will occur) to 100 percent (the crisis is an absolute certainty).

The CIV and CPF axes intersect at their midpoints (5 and 50 percent). Fink says the grid now becomes a barometer for crises facing an organization. Potential crises whose scores place them in the red zone are ones that present an organization with the greatest danger and require immediate attention. The next priority is to address crises that fall in the amber and gray zones. Potential crises located in the green zone shouldn't be ignored altogether but require less of your attention.

FIGURE 12.2 The Crisis Plotting Grid

Crisis Definitions. Different people conjure up different images when they hear the phrase *public relations,* and the same is true when the word *crisis* is mentioned. A good crisis plan eliminates the guesswork as to whether something is "an incident" or "a crisis." One pharmaceutical manufacturer has a "decision tree" on the first page of its crisis communications plan in which a series of questions helps gauge the nature and intensity of each situation. Developing a common language is also critical for interactions with those outside an organization. Electric utilities with nuclear generators are required to ensure that public agencies, as well as people residing within 10 miles of these facilities, are familiar with terminology that relates to various emergencies and the possible responses to those emergencies.

A List of Individuals Who Will Manage the Crisis Response. When possible, crises should not be allowed to keep an organization from conducting its daily operations. A special **crisis management team (CMT)** should be assigned the responsibility for monitoring and responding to any crisis. These people should be identified by their job titles, not by name—who knows whether Frank Jones will be working here two years from now? Backup persons should also be identified. Ideally, this team should consist of the following members:

■ *The CEO or a designated crisis manager.* Deciding whether the CEO should head the CMT depends on the nature of the crisis. Sometimes no one else will do. In other instances, however, someone who has the CEO's confidence can head the team. If the presence of the CEO inhibits frank discussion among the CMT members, it is better to appoint a **crisis manager,** someone who represents the interests of the CEO and to whom is delegated decision-making authority.

What is not as clear is *when* the executive should publicly leap into the fray. A misjudgment can be very damaging. As noted in QuickBreak 12.1, Exxon Chairman Lawrence Rawl waited one week to comment on the *Exxon Valdez* oil spill in Alaska. He believed that public opinion issues should take a back seat to more important issues relating to the cleanup. "We thought the first task should be to assist our operating people to get the incident under control," Exxon President Lee Raymond told reporters. Based on public reaction, that was a mistake.

"When a major crisis occurs, the CEO must step out immediately into the glare of TV lights and tell the public what is being done to fix the problem," said Andy Bowen of Atlanta-based Fletcher Martin Ewing Public Relations. "The CEO can't wait until all of the information is in."[39]

■ *Legal counsel.* Lawyers often present business communicators with their most difficult challenges during crises. Gerald Meyers, a veteran of many skirmishes with attorneys while he was head of American Motors, believes that the best advice is often to "cage your lawyers." He wrote, "Smart executives are not intimidated by lawyers who do not have to run the business once the legal skirmishing is over."[40]

This is not suggesting that legal counsel should be excluded from CMTs. Even their critics, including Meyers, say lawyers have an important role in crisis discussions and can provide valuable legal advice. But it is important to remember that the organization must answer to more than just a court of law. It also answers to the court of public opinion, where the judgment can be more devastating. That is why the legal and public relations counsels must have a good working relationship.

■ *Public relations counsel.* Public relations is a management function. In this capacity, the practitioner advises how best to communicate with important stakeholders and, when necessary, represents these stakeholders' views to the CMT. The public relations counsel also advises the CMT on public opinion and potential reactions to the proposed crisis responses. The public relations practitioner is also responsible for serving as the organization's conscience, making certain the organization's actions square with its stated values.

■ *Financial counsel.* Many crises have the potential for severely damaging the company's bottom line. Someone with hands-on knowledge of organization finances can be a valuable asset to the CMT.

■ *Appropriate technical experts.* These people may vary from crisis to crisis. After identifying the various threats to the organization, the crisis communications plan should then identify experts who can assist in the resolution of each type of crisis.

■ *Support personnel.* The CMT may require any of a variety of support services, including people with secretarial skills, people with computer skills, and artist/illustrators.

Stakeholder Communication Strategies. The plan should identify the various stakeholders who must be contacted and should provide appropriate telephone numbers, fax numbers, and e-mail addresses. Given adequate warning of a potential problem, some organizations prepare news releases and other stakeholder communications in advance.

The value of communicating with key stakeholders was demonstrated in October 2003, when destructive wildfires erupted throughout Southern California. San Diego Convention Center Corporation (SDCCC) officials realized that negative publicity could cause 15 groups to cancel multimillion-dollar trade shows and conventions. They moved quickly to reassure meeting planners through a series of telephone calls and e-mail updates. SDCCC also reassured the members of the American Society of Plastic Surgeons, which had already opened its meeting when the fires erupted. By keeping these stakeholders informed, SDCCC ensured that none of the conventions were canceled.[41]

Key stakeholders with whom organizations need to communicate during crises include the following:

■ *Employees.* This may be the most important group. Too often, employees are overlooked. Long after the reporters have left, these people remain. The plan needs to outline how employees will be notified of an emergency on short notice. It should also include plans for providing employees with updated information on a regular basis.

■ *The media.* It is critically important that an organization speak with one voice during a crisis. The plan should designate an official spokesperson. A procedure should be established for the timely release of information through news releases or regularly scheduled briefings. The plan should also include provisions for monitoring media reports. The establishment of a media information center (MIC) is discussed below.

■ *Other key stakeholders.* The plan should designate the individual or individuals responsible for serving as liaisons with people who require "special" attention. These

Relatives of miners trapped in the Sago coal mine comfort each other outside the Sago Baptist Church. False reports indicated that all but one of the 12 men trapped in the West Virginia mine had been saved. However, news later arrived that all but one had died, further compounding the tragedy (see Case Study 12.1). (Photo by Tyler Hicks/*New York Times.* Copyright 2006 The New York Times Company. Reprinted with permission.)

key stakeholders include members of the board of directors, major stockholders, financial analysts, regulators/public officials, unions, and community leaders.

■ *The curious public.* Some crises attract a lot of public attention. In those cases, it is a good idea to have a rumor control center where people can telephone and have their questions promptly answered. This is a very useful mechanism for tracking down the source of erroneous information and squelching false rumors before they spread.

Where the Response Is Coordinated. The CMT meets in what is called the **emergency operations center (EOC).** The EOC is the command post for the organization's crisis response; therefore, it should be in a secure location. That doesn't mean that the meetings need to be held in Fort Knox. However, CMT members should be free to do their work without interruption and without the peering eyes of reporters, curious employees, and other rubberneckers. The meeting place should have adequate communications capabilities, including televisions and radios for monitoring the media (see Figure 12.3). It should also be close to the place where the media are briefed.

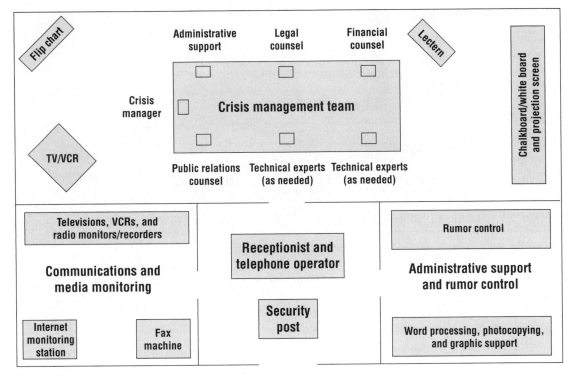

FIGURE 12.3 Emergency Operations Center Layout

Where Reporters Can Go to Get Information. The place set aside for meeting with reporters covering your crisis is the **media information center (MIC).** The most important goal in its operation is to make the MIC the only place journalists can go for information during a crisis. When it comes to interagency and multiorganizational communication with the media, this is the place where all responding organizations ensure they are "singing off the same sheet of music." The MIC has to be close enough to the action to satisfy reporters, but far enough away to prevent journalists from getting in the way. A procedure for verifying the identity of working reporters, known as **credentialing,** should be established. Reporters and officials should have separate entrances into the building. Furnishings for the MIC should include a lectern or table capable of handling many microphones, adequate lighting and background for photography, tables and chairs for writing, access to telecommunications, and a place for distributing and posting news releases (Figure 12.4). The MIC should also be staffed at all times with a media center coordinator who can assist reporters in getting their questions answered.

The Role of the Internet. Organizations in crisis are increasingly turning to the Internet as a means of outreach. A web site can serve several audiences, including news media, employees, and others affected by a crisis. American Airlines made extensive

FIGURE 12.4 Media Information Center Layout

use of the Internet in the months following the 9/11 terrorist attacks. Facing possible bankruptcy, the world's largest airline used a special web site and e-mail to communicate with its employees—including 20,000 who had been laid off because of the attacks—and investors. When a would-be terrorist attempted to ignite a bomb hidden in his shoe on a Paris-to-Miami flight, the airline used the Internet in an unusual way. The FBI had imposed a news blackout. However, it allowed American to tell its employees that the security breach was the fault of French officials—not a result of the airline's actions. American posted the news on an employee web site, knowing that the news media were monitoring it and would report what it said.[42]

Employee Training. Crisis communications training should occur as a normal part of employee orientation. Periodic reminders of each person's responsibilities also are in order—even if those responsibilities consist of nothing more than referring a matter to someone else. Mid- to upper-level managers should have more rigorous training, including tabletop exercises and role-playing scenarios. Part of this training should also focus on the language used and the information gathered when managers report

QuickBreak 12.4

Hard to Say I'm Sorry

The year was 1982, a few years before many readers of this book were born. The rock group Chicago was topping music charts with "Hard to Say I'm Sorry." The song was part rock, part ballad, and all about the use of apology to mend fractured love. Although the music may seem outdated to today's college students, the sentiment of the song—the use of apology to salvage an important relationship—remains a strategic option for crisis communicators.

In fact, apology is just one of the strategies in **apologia,** which has been defined as "the speech of self-defense."[43] However, it should not be confused with *apology,* although it may include one.[44] Organizations engage in apologia as a way of presenting their side of the story in the face of negative events or to repair damaged reputations and limit losses.

Crisis communications experts don't agree on exactly how many apologia strategies exist. One of the dominant theories is known as **Image Restoration Discourse,** developed by communications professor William Benoit. He identified five apologia strategies: denial of wrongdoing, evasion of responsibility, reduction of the perceived offensiveness of the act, promise to take corrective action, and mortification, when one admits responsibility and seeks forgiveness.[45]

Benoit also notes that an apologia can involve more than one of these strategies and can progress from one strategy to another as events change. We saw that in the first Tylenol tampering incident in 1982—the same year Chicago was singing its apologia tune. While Johnson & Johnson was not

responsible for the lacing of Tylenol capsules with cyanide, the tampering incident could have had a catastrophic effect on the company's financial stability (see QuickBreak 12.1).

CEO James E. Burke moved quickly to counter the damage using two apologia strategies: by denying any wrongdoing and taking corrective action. Going against the government's advice, the company pulled 22 million bottles of Tylenol off store shelves. "We value that trust too much to let any individual tamper with it," Burke said in a television advertisement. "We want you to continue to trust Tylenol."[46] At another point in the crisis, Burke erred when he told reporters that there was no cyanide in company manufacturing plants. In fact, cyanide was used in the quality control process. After learning of his error, Burke employed the apologia strategy of mortification and admitted he had misspoken. In the end, these strategies helped to save the Tylenol brand—and possibly the company.[47]

Apologia as a strategy has its risks. While a well-framed apologia can moderate stakeholders' anger, it can also strengthen negative associations between the company and the problem. Because of the diverse composition of an organization's stakeholders, not everyone requires an apology or an explanation.[48] "An admission of guilt could exacerbate legal difficulties stemming from the offensive act," said Benoit. "But I cannot recommend that an organization attempt to deny an accurate accusation."

He added, "Tylenol's response to the poisoning was exemplary."[49]

a potential crisis. Inaccurate language and incomplete information can lead to misunderstandings that could cause an organization either to over- or underreact.

Every employee needs to know what to do when disaster strikes. Since Hurricane Andrew in 1992, one Miami law firm has issued a disaster-preparedness manual to all its employees. The manual includes emergency contacts, evacuation procedures, and instructions on what to do in the event of a variety of calamities. The firm has also set up an emergency telephone contact system so it can keep track of employees and their needs during crises.[50]

Everyone needs to know whom they should call at the first sign of a crisis. The most important person in a crisis is often the first person to recognize it as such. That person's actions (or inactions) go a long way toward dictating the nature and quality of an organization's response. Employees should feel comfortable reporting trouble if even the slightest thing seems amiss. If the culture of the organization discourages such feedback, the organization may end up missing early warning signs that, if acted on, could have averted trouble.

QUICK ✓ CHECK

1. What are the advantages of designating a crisis management team? Who should be in charge of it?
2. Why must a good working relationship exist between an organization's legal counsel and its public relations counsel?
3. What is apologia?

Step Three: Response

Crisis **response** is the execution of crisis communications strategies. If all the necessary steps have been taken, this is where the organization is rewarded for its hard work. Critical decisions on whom to call and how to respond have already been made. In some cases, actions may have already been taken to avert or minimize the crisis.

At the risk of being repetitive, the response phase is when employee training provides its greatest dividends. Employees who have been trained in how to respond—even if the preferred response is to defer to someone else—are less likely to make critical errors that compound a crisis. That is why it is important that every employee know what he or she should do.

However, just as with any public relations plan, a crisis communications plan must be flexible. Every crisis is unique. And although most crises are predictable, some are not. A crisis communications plan should guide, not dictate, the organization's response. It may be that because of some unanticipated factors, the organization's planned response may be inappropriate. The crisis in question could involve a group of stakeholders with whom the organization has little or no experience. And in some circumstances, such as the case of a catastrophic explosion, some of the response mechanisms anticipated in the plan may no longer be available.

Does this mean that a crisis communications plan is useless? Of course not. Think of a crisis communications plan in the same way a coach sees his or her game plan. Like a good game plan, a good crisis communications plan lays the foundation for success. All the training has been geared toward successful execution of the plan. However, both coaches and crisis managers can face circumstances that force them to change their plans. In sports, a key player may get hurt. In crisis management, some key decision makers may be unavailable. That may force some changes in the original plan, but the changes will be based on options and resources provided for in the plan. Even when one is forced to improvise, good planning can mean success.

Step Four: Recovery

When the immediate threat of a crisis ends, the natural instinct is to relax and to return to a normal routine. However, it is important to resist that temptation. There is an important final step: **recovery,** in which the organization should evaluate the quality of its response and take appropriate actions on the basis of lessons learned. The questions asked at the end of one crisis may make the difference in averting or minimizing the next crisis. Some questions that need to be asked are

- Were our actions during and after the crisis consistent with our organization's values?
- What aspects of the crisis did our plan anticipate? How can we build on these successes?
- What aspects of the crisis did our plan fail to anticipate? What changes do we need to make?
- How well did our employees perform? Were they adequately trained?
- What are the lingering effects of the crisis? Are there follow-up actions we should take?
- How have our stakeholders' views of the organization changed since the onset of the crisis?
- What actions can either take advantage of new opportunities created by the crisis or repair damage created by it?

Not every crisis response is successful. Some organizations are better prepared for crises than others. Some events are more unexpected than others. However, there is little sympathy or tolerance for those who fail to learn the lessons of the past. That is why a period of honest evaluation is absolutely essential. Xerox CEO Anne Mulcahy said that crisis response is a lot like a farmer with a cow stuck in a ditch: The farmer has to get the cow out of the ditch, understand how the cow got into the ditch, and make changes so she never gets stuck again. Mulcahy said, "Do we really understand where we are, how we got there and how not to make the same mistakes in the future?"[51]

Crisis Planning Ethics

At a time when "big government" and "big business" are under increasing attack for being out of touch with the people, proactive crisis communications planning can be critical to an organization's continued success. Through this approach, many

VALUES STATEMENT 12.1

Department of Homeland Security

Created in 2002, the Department of Homeland Security mobilizes and organizes efforts to secure the United States from terrorist attacks. A major reason for the establishment of the department was to unify a vast national network of organizations and institutions involved in efforts to protect the nation. Its headquarters are in Washington, D.C.

Vision: Preserving our freedoms, protecting America . . . we secure our homeland.

Mission: We will lead the unified national effort to secure America. We will prevent and deter terrorist attacks and protect against and respond to threats and hazards to the nation. We will ensure safe and secure borders, welcome lawful immigrants and visitors, and promote the free-flow of commerce.

—DHS Vision and Mission Statements, DHS web site

crises that confront organizations can be averted or, at least, minimized. However, many organizations' lack of planning for crises is a cause for great concern. Crises, as well as inappropriate responses to them, pose societal threats on a variety of levels. There are tangible losses associated with them, such as damage to property and financial setbacks. There are also intangible losses, as evidenced by the psychological damage to crisis victims and a loss of public confidence in organizations. Even more, who can determine a value and assess the cost when the outcome of a crisis is the loss of human lives?

Is crisis communications planning an ethical imperative? In the minds of researchers Pauchant and Mitroff, the answer is a resounding yes. Although they have a certain degree of "empathy" for those caught in the vortex of a crisis, they also express "moral outrage" when crises and their subsequent fallouts are preventable.[52] Although PRSA's *Member Code of Ethics 2000* does not specifically mention crisis communications planning, one of the professional values it identifies is honesty. "We adhere to the highest standards of accuracy and truth in advancing the interests of those we represent and in communicating with the public," the code states.[53] That wording prompts the question "Can one claim to have acted in such a manner when one has failed to take reasonable precautions against predictable crises?"

It is not enough to develop technical contingencies to meet the logistical needs of an organization in crisis. Developing plans for communicating during times of stress is critical to the success, if not the very survival, of organizations. As one postmortem of Exxon's Alaskan oil spill noted,

> The *Exxon Valdez* spill clearly shows the penalty for perceived unreadiness in the face of an environmental disaster. But it also shows the importance of having insurance for when things go wrong. It would be unthinkable to go without liability insurance against claims for loss or negligence. Why then do some companies fail to take out strong public relations "insurance" for claims against image?[54]

Although ethical arguments might move some of the unconcerned and unprepared to action, tangible evidence of the consequences of such failures may prove more convincing.

BE INFORMED
BIOLOGICAL THREAT

1. A biological attack is the release of germs or other biological substances. Many agents must be inhaled, enter through a cut in the skin or be eaten to make you sick. Some biological agents can cause contagious diseases, others do not.

2. A biological attack may or may not be immediately obvious. While it is possible that you will see signs of a biological attack it is perhaps more likely that local health care workers will report a pattern of unusual illness.

3. You will probably learn of the danger through an emergency radio or TV broadcast.

4. If you become aware of an unusual or suspicious release of an unknown substance nearby, it doesn't hurt to protect yourself.

5. Get away from the substance as quickly as possible.

6. Cover your mouth and nose with layers of fabric that can filter the air but still allow breathing.

1

Poster The Department of Homeland Security provided this example of citizen preparedness information on its special web site www.ready.gov. (Courtesy of the Department of Homeland Security)

Summary

Crises don't just happen. Usually warning signs indicate that trouble is on the way. Too often, however, people fail to recognize the signs. When this failure occurs, a considerable amount of an organization's time and resources must be spent dealing with a crisis.

Crises tend to develop in four stages: a warning stage, a point of no return, a cleanup, and a return to normalcy—although crises can alter what normalcy means for an affected organization.

Crises don't have to have exclusively negative outcomes. Good things can come out of a crisis—if an organization is prepared. But the sad truth is that most organizations are not. Many do not even have a written crisis communications plan. Among those that do, many have not properly trained their employees in its use.

Crisis communications planning is one of the most proactive things a public relations practitioner can do. However, it is not something he or she does alone. A good crisis plan is one that has been developed in collaboration with people throughout the organization *and* has the wholehearted support of top management. A good crisis plan also reflects an organization's values—and there is usually no more important time for communicating those values than during a crisis.

Good crisis communications planning begins with an honest assessment of the potential risks an organization may face. It follows with a plan that identifies the members of the crisis management team, key stakeholders, and the logistics necessary for a swift and appropriate response. The training of all employees is the key to a good response. Although the organization should be guided by its crisis communications plan, its response should not be dictated by it. As is the case with all plans, it should be flexible enough to address unanticipated circumstances. As the crisis ends and the organization moves into the recovery phase, it is important to evaluate what happened and why. This is the first step in preparing for—and possibly preventing—future crises.

DISCUSSION QUESTIONS

1. Can you name a crisis and identify how it proceeded through its four stages?
2. What lessons can be learned from the government's badly handled response to Hurricane Katrina?
3. What do you think are some excuses organizations may proffer for not having adequate crisis communications plans? How would you counter those arguments?
4. Identify some crises that officials at your college or university might face. Where would you place each on Steven Fink's crisis plotting grid?
5. What role do organizational values play in crisis planning?

Memo from the Field

Wayne Shelor, Civilian Public Information Officer, Police Department, Clearwater, Florida

Wayne Shelor is the civilian public information officer for the Clearwater (Florida) Police Department and former president of the 700-member National Information Officers Association (www.nioa.org), the nation's preeminent training organization for public safety spokespersons. Shelor's memo was written just days after his agency responded to its second hurricane in a month—and while he was closely monitoring the progress of a third storm. He proudly notes that he was a Boy Scout. And he certainly was prepared.

Time and tide wait for no man.
    —William C. Somerville, English poet (1675–1742)

After a quarter-century in the field of information dissemination—10 years as a newspaper reporter and editor, and the past 18 as the spokesman for a metropolitan police department—I've found my strongest professional trait is that of crisis communications.

When the world is at its worst, I've discovered, I am at my best.

And, I learned early on, there's no time in the midst of a crisis to research or prepare. When a crisis unfolds, the media are *always* close behind, rolling in like an unstoppable hurricane-driven tide. And those who wisely took the time to *prepare* for worst-case scenarios will avoid drowning in the sometimes suffocating publicity that is . . . public relations.

The media—particularly with the advent of cable news and satellite television trucks and the ubiquitous presence of the Internet—is a voracious beast that must be fed. Constantly.

When events break and a crisis looms, there's no time to stop and retreat, pause and prepare. If you don't feed the media beast, it will feed on you. Time is a media commodity that must be filled; if a public relations specialist doesn't supply pertinent, accurate, topical facts in a timely fashion, then the media will find someone, somewhere, to fill the time with speculation, opinion, and innuendo.

That's when reputations are ruined, careers are lost, and situations spiral out of control. Once that control is lost, it's rarely recovered.

As a Police Public Information Officer (PIO), I prepare constantly for the worst that can happen to my public safety agency. I read constantly (everything from newspapers and profession-related periodicals to myriad media Internet web sites and news portals), and I research what worked—and what failed—in high-profile cases around the nation.

Then I apply the lessons learned to the demographics and capabilities of my agency, its employees, and its policies and procedures. And my research and preparation have served me well:

- When a police officer shot dead an unarmed man at a wedding rehearsal dinner, the expedient, timely dissemination of factual information was handled so well that the region's "newspaper of record" wrote a positively glowing editorial about how the police dealt with an ugly situation.

- During a two-year, high-profile death investigation that garnered constant media scrutiny from around the globe, the sensitive case was protected—and the agency's sterling reputation left unsullied—because of the way information was (and was not) released.
- After Hurricane Andrew destroyed south Florida, we had a team dissect the public safety preparation and response policies of agencies across America and then develop what has been held out as the nation's most sophisticated and detailed disaster response and recovery plan.

There's no way anyone can ever anticipate every possible problem facing a business, organization, or public agency. Even plans such as our much-heralded Hurricane Response and Recovery policy are subject to changes in geography, manpower, funding, laws, infrastructure, government, and the strength and angle of attack of these unpredictable storms.

But we are *prepared* to address bad and sensitive situations.

Preparation involves everything from knowing the wants, needs, habits, styles, personalities, and practices of your various local media to anticipating and preparing for an eventuality that may not be likely, but is certainly possible. (I've never had one of my officers killed in the line of duty; it's really quite unthinkable within the law enforcement community. But it's a daily possibility, and as the PIO, I am prepared for everything from working with a mourning community to detailing for the family the scope and specifics of survivor benefits to the most minute details of orchestrating a police funeral, including how to best accommodate the media. Were I to wait until it happens, I—and the entire department—would be overwhelmed.)

I learned long ago that the best public relations practitioners prepare themselves for the worst and invariably discover they're ready when the bad-but-not-the-worst unfolds. Every event and crisis situation "seasons" public relations specialists, and in time, they discover that panic and confusion are something they see only in the eyes of others, never in the mirror.

I've always found a healthy measure of comfort in that hard-earned self-confidence.

I've been practicing public relations for more than 15 years now and teaching the mechanics of media relations and crisis management for almost as long.

And my first admonition to those new to the profession is something I learned when I was but a lad: Always be prepared.

CASE STUDY 12.1

False Hope

An explosion rocked a Sago, West Virginia, coal mine on the morning of January 2, 2006. Thirteen miners were trapped 260 feet below ground. Company, local, state, and federal authorities immediately began a frantic effort to rescue the men.[55] The mine's owner, International Coal Group (ICG), also activated its crisis communications plan. Company officials conducted regular news briefings, counseled the miners' families, and cooperated with state and federal regulators. The company received high marks for its initial crisis response.[56]

That changed just before midnight on Wednesday, January 3. Within a three-hour period, the families experienced the joy of being told that 12 of the 13 miners had survived—only later to suffer the shock and grief of learning that 12 of the 13 had died. Like the mining families who had just realized their worst fears, people around the world began asking the same question: How could this miscommunication have happened?[57]

A visibly shaken ICG President Ben Hatfield met with reporters on the day after the disaster and explained how poor communications conspired with good intentions. By the early evening hours of Wednesday, rescuers had already found the body of one of the miners near the site of the initial blast. The fate of the remaining 12 miners was unknown. Shortly before 11 P.M., rescue workers wearing full-face oxygen masks radioed the rescue command center that they had found the missing miners.[58]

In a muffled, barely audible voice over a crackling radio, a member of the rescue team announced that they had found the missing men. Six minutes later, an emergency medical technician radioed the rescue team and asked, "And what am I telling them?" The rescuer replied, "Twelve, and they're bringing them out." When the EMT said, "And they're all alive," the rescue worker replied, "Uh, as far as I know."[59]

According to Hatfield, this exchange was heard on an open speakerphone in the command center. And as might be expected after 36 hours of nearly unbearable tension, the place erupted into a spontaneous celebration of joy and relief. Several people in the command center—exactly who is not known—could not wait to share the good news with the anxious families. In violation of the ICG's crisis response plan, they pulled out their cell phones and announced that the miners had been rescued.

The news spread like wildfire to the nearby Sago Baptist Church, where most of the trapped miners' families and friends had waited for news. According to media reports, a man burst through the front door of the church and screamed, "They've found them! All 12 are alive!" The church bell tolled as the crowd cheered, wept, prayed, and sang the hymn "How Great Thou Art." A friend of three of the trapped men proclaimed, "There still are miracles!"[60]

Back at the command center, a different picture emerged. The rescuers had initially thought that the miners were unconscious but alive. However, 45 minutes later, the rescue team radioed that only one of the miners appeared to be alive. The company immediately dispatched more medical teams to the mine.

Hatfield was aware of the premature celebration back at the church and did not want to confuse matters by releasing unverified information. He decided to wait until he was certain of his facts. Three hours after the first erroneous report, Hatfield went to the church to tell the crestfallen families that only one of the 12 miners had survived.

Hatfield later said that he asked a state trooper to call the church and warn the families that the company had to sort out conflicting information. However, that was not done. If he had to do it all over again, Hatfield said that he, personally, would have gone to the church sooner and warned the people. "In the process of being cautious, we allowed the jubilation to go on longer than it should have," Hatfield said.[61]

While ICG rightfully accepted blame for what turned out to be a cruel mistake, it shares the blame with others. The news media quickly accepted as fact unverified reports from unofficial sources. West Virginia Governor Joe Manchin, who first questioned the validity of the reports, admitted that he "got caught up in the euphoria" and helped to spread the false rumor.[62]

The fact is that people heard what they desperately wanted to hear. No one wanted to compound the families' grief with a glimpse of false hope. But that's what happened when some well-intentioned people failed to follow the company's crisis communications plan.

DISCUSSION QUESTIONS

1. The case suggests that some of the families' heartache could have been avoided if "well-intentioned" people had followed the company's crisis communications plan. Where, specifically, did they fail to follow the plan?
2. How could ICG have improved its communications with the families?
3. Should ICG seek to share the blame with the news media for spreading the false rumor?
4. Knowing what you now know about the events at the Sago Mine, what would you have done differently had you been in charge of crisis communications?

CASE STUDY 12.2

Embedded Journalists

In no other time are values in greater conflict than during war. This is especially true in democratic societies, where the act of waging war is an expression of national policy. In open and free societies, people have a right to know how the conflict is going and about the manner in which it is being fought in their name.

The U.S. military has long struggled with the dual values of transparency and security. To put it another way, no one wants the enemy to see what troops are doing before they do it. Journalists, to their credit, understand this and are willing to work under some rules. However, the degree to which these restrictions are applied is often a flash point of conflict between the media and the military. During the Vietnam War, journalists had virtually unrestricted access to the battlefields. After U.S. troops withdrew from South Vietnam and it fell to the communists, many in the military blamed the news media for undermining American public support for the war.

"This opinion that the media lost the Vietnam War became deeply engrained in some of these officers and stayed with them as they rose through the ranks," wrote Robert S. Pritchard, former director of public affairs for the U.S. European Command.[63] As a result, tight restrictions limited journalists' access to future military operations, such as in Grenada in 1983 and during the first Gulf War in 1991.

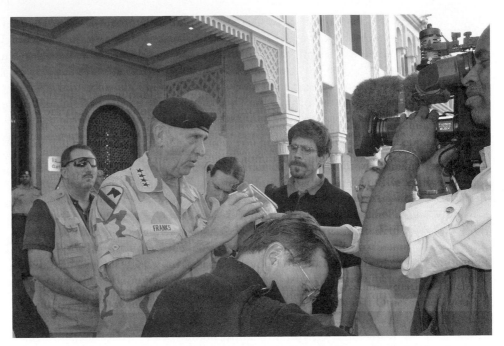

U.S. Commanding General Tommy Franks meets with reporters during Operation Iraqi Freedom. The Pentagon increased media access to the battlefield during the war to counter Iraq's propaganda and to garner public support. (Courtesy of the U.S. Department of Defense)

During the buildup to the 2003 invasion of Iraq—the nation's most controversial war since Vietnam—Pentagon officials were concerned about public opinion both in the United States and abroad. Taking a page out of its own history—World War II, to be exact—the U.S. military agreed to give journalists largely unfettered access to the front lines by "embedding" them in individual units. This meant journalists would live and travel with the troops. It also meant that they would share the same dangers.

"The official rationale for the new policy is that the war in Afghanistan convinced the military brass that the best way to counter enemy propaganda about things like civilian casualties is to let credible reporters see for themselves," reported the *Columbia Journalism Review.*[64]

Victoria Clarke, the person most often credited with creating the embedded journalists policy, also wanted to show the human side of the armed forces. "It's a fundamental belief that the more news and information we provide, through a variety of media, the better off we are," said Clarke, who served as spokesperson for the Defense Department during the invasion. "Anytime you can give people an up-close and personal look at the U.S. military, you're having a good day."[65]

Though the notion of "bringing journalists along" was something untried during the Digital Age, it was hardly something new. It even predates World War II, when journalists reported from the front lines. "The strategy is simply classic public relations, the kind espoused by Ivy Lee," wrote *Public Relations Review* editor Ray E. Hiebert. "In the Rockefeller conflict with striking coal miners in Ludlow, Colorado, in 1913, with public opinion thoroughly against the Rockefellers and other mine owners, Lee invited reporters to come inside, talk to any officials, examine any documents, and observe the conflict firsthand.

"That proved to be the decisive strategy, gaining Rockefeller a rare sympathetic press, although pro-labor forces continued to castigate Lee for decades as a result."[66]

As the prospects for war in Iraq increased, the Pentagon announced its new policy to an appreciative, but skeptical, media. Journalists would be allowed to report events in "real time" without censorship. More than 600 journalists underwent a week of physical and procedural training—a sort of reporters boot camp. There were a handful of restrictions, such as not reporting specific locations and troop movements. Otherwise, reporters from around the world—even Al-Jazeera—were free to report as they pleased.

It was "old-fashioned war reporting, but with razzle-dazzle technology that brings it to our living room in real time," said *Washington Post* columnist Howard Kurtz.[67]

With the outbreak of war, the world witnessed events as never before. Viewers watched "live" as U.S.-led coalition forces raced across the Iraqi desert toward Baghdad. They saw troops battle for small towns, villages, bridges, and airfields. It was history as it was happening.

The first real test of the Pentagon's new openness came from an unanticipated event—a disgruntled U.S. soldier tossing hand grenades into the tents of officers in his own unit. "But the story behind the story was that as the first real test of the embedding process, it did work," said CBS embedded correspondent Mark Strassman. "The communication from them to us in terms of what was happening was great."[68]

While the embedding process appeared to work well, it wasn't without its critics. "You were put in a position where you would certainly not be antagonistic to the kids that you were involved with and admired," said embedded journalist George C. Wilson of the *National Journal*. "In effect, I was putting myself in a position to be a propagandist, which was great for the Pentagon, but not so great for the readers."[69]

There were other issues, as well. Because reporters covered the war from a limited perspective, that of the unit to which they were assigned, it was hard for them to see the big picture. Small victories or defeats were blown out of proportion. The speed of the invasion and earlier U.S. military operations may have also led to an unrealistic expectation that wars are won in a few days or weeks. President Bush fed this misconception when he declared the end of military operations on May 1, 2003. Continuing violence and mounting U.S. troop casualties dogged the president and brought his approval ratings to near-record lows.

"Embedding in the Iraq war raised a host of arguments and controversies among journalists, but it succeeded beyond doubt as public relations," wrote Hiebert.[70]

"When a crippling public relations battle looms, the first issue is not who spins best, gets the best stories and wins the week," said Clark S. Judge, managing director of the White House Writers Group. "The issue is who becomes the standard of truth."[71]

DISCUSSION QUESTIONS

1. On what values do the U.S. military and media agree during a time of war? On what do they disagree?
2. From the Pentagon's perspective, what were the advantages and disadvantages of the policy of embedding journalists during the Iraq war?
3. Although many people disagreed with the decision to go to war with Iraq, does that make the policy of embedding journalists with the troops unethical?
4. What are some of the issues that arose out of the embedded journalist experience?
5. Can you describe the stages of crisis communications planning that went into the development of the embedded journalists policy?

NOTES

1. Mark Schleifstein, "FEMA Knew Storm's Potential, Mayfield Says," *New Orleans Times-Picayune,* 4 September 2005, via NewsBank, online, http://infoweb.newsbank.com.
2. John McQuaid, "Before Katrina, There Was Pam," *New Orleans Times-Picayune,* 10 September 2005, via NewsBank, online, http://infoweb.newsbank.com.
3. McQuaid.
4. Schleifstein.
5. Ed Cafasso, "Going Back to Basics: Hurricane Katrina Illustrates the Importance of Aligning Action and Communications," *Public Relations Tactics,* October 2005, 12.
6. Cafasso.
7. Eric Weslander, "Speaker: Government Compounded Disaster of Hurricane Katrina," *Lawrence Journal-World,* 15 March 2007, online, www.ljworld.com.
8. Steve Vockrodt, "Ex-FEMA Director: Nation Still Isn't Prepared for Major Disaster," *Lawrence Journal-World,* 5 April 2007, online, www.ljworld.com.
9. "101 Dumbest Moments in Business—2005," *Business.20,* online, http://money.cnn.com.
10. Paul J. Gough, "Boston Terror Scare Sparked by Cartoon Net Ad Lighting," *The Hollywood Reporter,* 1 February 2007, online, http://hollywoodreporter.com.
11. "101 Dumbest Moments in Business—2005."
12. Kenneth N. Myers, *Total Contingency Planning for Disasters* (New York: Wiley, 1993), 2.
13. Jane Applegate, "Why Crisis Management Plans Are Essential," *Los Angeles Times,* 29 December 1989, D3.
14. Donald Chisholm and Martin Landau, "Set Aside That Optimism if We Want to Avoid Disaster," *Los Angeles Times,* 18 April 1989, sec. II, 7.
15. "Many Still Aren't Prepared," *Public Relations Journal,* September 1986, 16; David W. Guth, "Organizational Crisis Experience and Public Relations Roles," *Public Relations Review* 21, no. 2 (summer 1995): 123–136.
16. "In Ten Years You'll See Nothing," *Fortune,* 8 May 1989.
17. Allanna Sullivan and Amanda Bennett, "Critics Fault Chief Executive of Exxon on Handling of Recent Alaskan Oil Spill," *Wall Street Journal,* 31 March 1989.

18. Sullivan and Bennett.

19. Adam Liptak, "$4.5 Billion Award Set for Spill of *Exxon Valdez*," *New York Times*, 29 January 2004, online, www.nytimes.com.

20. "Tylenol Tries for a Comeback," *Newsweek*, 1 November 1982, 78.

21. Robert J. Holland and Katrina Gill, "Ready for Disaster?—A New Survey of IABC Members Reveals That Crisis Communications Are Not as Widespread as Expected," *Communication World*, March–April 2006, 20–24.

22. Thierry C. Pauchant and Ian I. Mitroff, *Transforming the Crisis-Prone Organization* (San Francisco: Jossey-Bass, 1992), 12.

23. Pauchant and Mitroff, 15–16.

24. Steven Fink, *Crisis Management: Planning for the Inevitable* (New York: AMACOM, 1986), 15–16.

25. Laurence Barton, *Crisis in Organizations: Managing and Communicating in the Heat of Chaos* (Cincinnati: South-Western Publishing, 1993), 2.

26. Except where otherwise noted, facts and figures about the *Challenger* and *Columbia* disasters come from the report of the *Columbia* Accident Investigating Board, issued August 2003.

27. NBC coverage, approximately 9:30 A.M. EST, 1 February 2003.

28. Heather Dewar, "Officials to Improve City Emergency Plan," *Baltimore Sun*, 27 July 2001, online, www.sunspot.net.

29. Gerald C. Meyers with John Holusha, *When It Hits the Fan: Managing the Nine Crises of Business* (Boston: Houghton Mifflin, 1986), 28.

30. Ready America web site, U.S. Department of Homeland Security, online, www .ready.gov.

31. Federal Emergency Management Agency, online, www.fema.gov.

32. "Disaster Services," American Red Cross, online, www.redcross.org/services/disaster.

33. "Emergency Preparedness BSA," Boy Scouts of America, online, www.scouting.org/ pubs/emergency.

34. Mayer Nudel and Norman Antokol, *The Handbook for Effective Emergency and Crisis Management* (Lexington, Mass.: D.C. Heath, 1988), 36.

35. Robert F. Littlejohn, *Crisis Management: A Team Approach* (New York: American Management Association, 1983), 18–32.

36. "Is Enron's IR Hobbled by Its Lawyers?" *Investor Relations Business*, 21 November 2001, online, LexisNexis.

37. Kristen Hays, "Ex-Enron Executive Starts Prison Term," *Houston Chronicle*, 25 January 2007, online, www.chron.com.

38. Felix Pomeranz, "Ethics: Toward Globalization," *Managerial Accounting Journal* 19 (2004): 8.

39. Andy Bowen, "Crisis Procedures That Stand the Test of Time," *Public Relations Tactics*, August 2001, 16.

40. Meyers, 232–236.

41. "San Diego Convention Center Corp: San Diego Wildfires 2003," Silver Anvil Award Profile No. 6BW-0411B02, Public Relations Society of America, online, www.prsa.org.

42. David W. Guth and Charles Marsh, *Adventures in Public Relations: Case Studies and Critical Thinking* (Boston: Allyn & Bacon, 2005), 307–311.

43. B. L. Ware and W. A. Linkugel, "They Spoke in Defense of Themselves: On the Generic Criticism of Apologia," *Quarterly Journal of Speech* 59 (1973): 273.

44. K. M. Hearit, "Apologies and Public Relations Crises at Chrysler, Toshiba, and Volvo," *Public Relations Review* 20 (1994): 115.

45. William L. Benoit, "Image Repair Discourse and Crisis Communication," in *Responding to a Crisis: A Rhetorical Approach to Crisis Communication,* eds. Dan P. Millar and Robert L. Heath (Mahwah, N.J.: Lawrence Erlbaum, 2004), 263–280.

46. "Tylenol Tries for a Comeback," *Newsweek,* 1 November 1982, 78.

47. Bill Powell, "The Tylenol Rescue," *Newsweek,* 3 March 1986, 52–53.

48. Barbara Kellerman, "When Should a Leader Apologize—and When Not?" *Harvard Business Review* 84, no. 4 (April 2006): 72–81.

49. Benoit, 280.

50. Sharon Nelton, "Prepare for the Worst," *Nation's Business,* September 1993, 22.

51. "The Cow in the Ditch: How Anne Mulcahy Rescued Xerox," *Knowledge@Wharton,* 16 November 2005, online, http://knowledge.wharton.upenn.edu

52. Pauchant and Mitroff, 5–6.

53. *Public Relations Society of America Member Code of Ethics 2000,* online, www.prsa.org.

54. E. Bruce Harrison with Tom Prugh, "Assessing the Damage: Practitioner Perspectives on the *Valdez,*" *Public Relations Journal,* October 1989, 42.

55. Vicki Smith, "12 Miners Found Dead after Rescue Effort," *Lawrence Journal-World,* 5 January 2006, 1.

56. Jim Jordan, "Mining Company Lost Control, Experts Say," Knight Ridder Newspapers, 4 January 2006, online, www.charlotte.com.

57. Bob Dart, "Company Knew Report Was Wrong," *Kansas City Star,* 5 January 2006, 1.

58. Allen G. Breed, "Answers to Foul Up in Mine Disaster Sought," Associated Press, online, http://abcnews.go.com, 6 January 2006.

59. "Sago Mine Emergency Call Transcripts," ABC News, online, http://abcnews.go.com, 5 January 2006.

60. Breed.

61. Breed.

62. Breed.

63. Robert S. Pritchard, "The Pentagon Is Fighting—and Winning—the Public Relations War," *USA Today* (supplement), July 2003, 14, online, LexisNexis.

64. Andrew Bushell and Brent Cunningham, "Being There," *Columbia Journalism Review,* March/April 2003, 18–21.

65. Dale Eisman, "Clarke Discusses Revolution in War Reporting," *Virginian-Pilot,* 3 June 2003, A5, online, LexisNexis.

66. Ray Eldon Hiebert, "Public Relations and Propaganda in Framing the Iraq War: A Preliminary Review," *Public Relations Review* 29, no. 3 (summer 2003): 243–255.

67. Pritchard, 14.

68. *The NewsHour with Jim Lehrer* transcript, 21 April 2003, online, LexisNexis.

69. *The NewsHour with Jim Lehrer* transcript.

70. Hiebert, 249.

71. Hiebert, 249.

13

Public Relations and Marketing

OBJECTIVES

After studying this chapter, you will be able to

- describe recent changes in marketing

- define integrated marketing communications

- explain the differences between public relations, advertising, and marketing

- describe marketing public relations

- summarize the process of integrated marketing communications

KEY TERMS

Face the Music

What a dream job. You've just been appointed marketing director for a new chain of music stores that feature hard-to-find alternative rock CDs and discounts on downloads. Your company has opened stores in 12 major college cities around the United States.

Unfortunately, you've been hired only two months before the stores open. Now your associates are asking you for a marketing plan that will bring students flocking into the stores. Some associates want advertising; others prefer public relations. But, fortunately, you soon determine that everyone is flexible and eager to be innovative in the company's marketing efforts.

You have an adequate marketing budget but not enough money to advertise on national television or in magazines such as Spin.

What do you do?

Public Relations and Marketing

Let's begin by addressing a question you may be asking right now: *Why am I reading about marketing in a public relations textbook?*

Good question. Here are some answers:

- Marketing focuses on consumers, as does consumer relations, or customer relations, which is part of public relations. Traditional consumer relations tactics, such as product-oriented news releases, can work hand in hand with marketing tactics such as direct mail and in-store displays.

- Other areas of public relations, such as government relations and employee relations, can affect the success of marketing programs—and vice versa. Some of the biggest headaches in public relations, in fact, come from mishandled marketing programs that damage important relationships. For example, Major League Baseball struck out with a key public—baseball fans—during a joint-marketing agreement with makers of the movie *Spider-Man 2*. Fans tolerated ballpark signs and scoreboard movie clips—but they cried foul when promoters planned to put the Spider-Man logo on the bases. The webslinger who whipped the Green Goblin and Doc Ock couldn't conquer outraged fans of the national pastime. Major League Baseball retreated, and the games proceeded with web-free bases.[1]

- Marketing in the 21st century is undergoing dramatic changes. Far from just persuading consumers to buy products *now*, new marketing strategies seek to build long-term, productive relationships with consumers. That should sound a lot like public relations to you. These new relationship-oriented marketing theories signal a profound shift from the mass-marketing programs of the past.

The Decline of Mass Marketing

Life seemed easier when professionals in public relations and advertising believed they could rely on the awesome power of the mass media. When Company X wanted to sell its new and improved gizmo to millions of eager customers, it simply bought ads on the right TV and radio shows and did the same with a few newspapers and magazines that delivered huge audiences. Company X often tried to place news releases in the same media. With the boom of network television in the mid-20th century, such a marketing plan really seemed to work . . . for a while.

However, we're now witnessing the weakening of the mass media. In a world with hundreds of cable and satellite channels, the traditional television networks (ABC, CBS, NBC, and Fox) can no longer automatically deliver a mass audience. In addition, thousands of specialized blogs, e-mail newsletters, web sites, and other online media have helped plow over the few broad paths that once reached millions of consumers. No longer can public relations and advertising professionals reach a mass audience of consumers simply by placing news releases and ads in a few national print media and on the television networks your parents watched.

"It's time that public relations, advertising, sales promotion, and marketing pause for a reality check," says public relations professor E. W. Brody.[2]

And what does our reality check reveal? These facts, says Brody:

- Mass media continue to proliferate (which leads to the next point).
- Audiences continue to fragment.
- New media, sometimes beyond practitioners' reach, are supplanting the old.
- Media that reach individuals one at a time with personalized messages are growing in efficiency and effectiveness.

The Growth of Consumer-Focused Marketing

In this new reality, many organizations are decreasing their reliance on mass marketing. Instead, they are embracing what we will call consumer-focused marketing. Consumer-focused marketing uses a variety of media to build relationships with individual consumers. Since the 1990s, one of the most popular forms of consumer-focused marketing has been **integrated marketing communications (IMC)**. Almost two-thirds of marketers in a national survey reported that they planned to spend more time developing IMC strategies in 2007 than they had in 2006.[3]

IMC differs from mass marketing in five respects:

1. IMC practitioners focus on individual consumers. Products are developed to fill consumers' specific needs, and sales messages are created to target specific consumers' self-interests. (Because IMC targets consumers, not all of public relations is part of IMC. Public relations, of course, targets other publics as well: employees, government officials, and stockholders, to name just a few.)
2. IMC practitioners use **databases** to target individual consumers rather than mass audiences. These databases contain a wealth of information on individual consumers' wants, needs, and preferences.
3. IMC practitioners send a well-focused message to each consumer through a variety of approaches: advertising, public relations, direct marketing, and all other forms of marketing communications, including packaging and pricing.
4. IMC practitioners use consumer-preferred media to send their marketing messages.

5. IMC practitioners favor interactive media, constantly seeking information from consumers. Thus, media such as interactive web sites can be ideal for IMC.

Just as public relations has evolved over the decades, consumer-focused marketing is growing and changing. Although IMC is the best-known form of consumer-focused marketing, other forms exist, and they are helping to shape the future of marketing. IMC was preceded by database marketing, which helped turn marketing away from mass audiences and toward individuals. Other approaches that can be grouped under the broad umbrella of consumer-focused marketing include relationship marketing, customer relationship management (CRM), and integrated brand communication (IBC). QuickBreak 13.1 discusses similarities and differences among these new consumer-focused marketing approaches.

Public Relations, Advertising, and Marketing

The three main pillars of IMC, as we said in Chapter 1, are public relations, advertising, and marketing. Although these three disciplines have much in common, much also differentiates them (Figure 13.1). Let's quickly review the definitions we established previously for each discipline:

Advertising is the use of controlled media (media in which one pays for the privilege of dictating message content, placement, and frequency) in an attempt to influence the actions of targeted publics.

Marketing is the process of researching, creating, refining, and promoting a product or service and distributing that product or service to targeted consumers. Marketing promotion disciplines include sales promotions (such as coupons), personal selling, direct marketing—and, often, aspects of advertising and public relations.

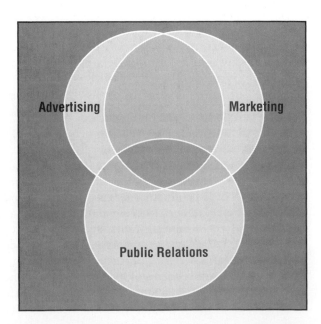

FIGURE 13.1 The Relationship among Advertising, Marketing, and Public Relations
Advertising, marketing, and public relations are three distinct professions with important areas of convergence. But not all advertising is marketing; nor is all public relations marketing.

QuickBreak 13.1

IMC and More

Databases and new methods of communication have revolutionized marketing. In the 1990s those two developments came together in integrated marketing communications (IMC), probably today's best-known consumer-focused marketing philosophy. But consumer-focused marketing includes other, closely related philosophies that you should know: database marketing, relationship marketing, customer relationship management (CRM), and integrated brand communication (IBC).

Database marketing. The new consumer-focused marketing philosophies began with database marketing. A computerized database can store vast amounts of information about individual consumers: what they buy, when they buy, how often they buy, how much they spend, how and how often your organization contacts them, and much more. "Database marketing," says management consultant Mindi McKenna, "involves the collection, storage, analysis, and use of information regarding customers and the past purchase behaviors to guide future marketing decisions."[4]

Relationship marketing. John Dalla Costa, president of the Centre for Ethical Orientation, says that the true value of modern organizations "involves a return on relationship. . . . The worth of companies depends more and more on the worth of [their] varied relationships."[5] Relationship marketing looks beyond profits to individual relationships with specific consumers, all in the belief that if the relationships are good, profits automatically follow.

Customer relationship management (CRM). The Conference Board, a U.S.-based business-research association, defines CRM as "the business processes an organization performs to identify, select, acquire, develop, retain, and better serve customers. These processes encompass an organization's . . . engagement with its customers and prospects over the lifetime of its relationship with them."[6] CRM combines the technology of database marketing with the philosophy of relationship marketing to develop lifelong relationships with individual customers. Applied to business-to-business relations, CRM becomes **partner relationship management.**

Integrated brand communication. According to marketing professors Don Schultz and Beth Barnes, integrated brand communication goes beyond IMC, which focuses on sales. It goes beyond CRM, which focuses on relationships between organizations and customers. Instead, IBC focuses on relationships between consumers and brands. Schultz and Barnes define brand as "the bond between the buyer and the seller."[7] In IBC, a brand is an individual consumer's perception of his or her relationship with a product or an organization. The goal of IBC is to discover each consumer's view of the brand and to align it with the organization's view. To do so, the organization must identify and integrate all forms of communication, sending one, clear message—just as in IMC.

These consumer-focused marketing strategies, including IMC, are closely related to one another. And with their increasing focus on building two-way, win-win relationships with important publics, they are closely related to public relations.

Public relations is the values-driven management of relationships between an organization and the publics that can affect its success.

Advertising, marketing, and public relations follow the same process: research, planning, communication, evaluation. But unlike marketing, public relations focuses on many publics, not just on consumers. And unlike advertising, public relations doesn't control its messages by purchasing specific placements for them.

The Impact of Consumer-Focused Marketing on Public Relations

Consumer-focused marketing makes so much sense that some practitioners say, "We've been doing this for years. There's nothing new here." And, to some degree, they're right. Although certain aspects of IMC, for example, are relatively new, including the extensive use of databases and the use of new and innovative communications technologies, IMC is still based on a traditional commonsense approach familiar to most practitioners of good public relations: focusing on the values of a particular public and responding with a clear message.

But consumer-focused marketing *is* changing some aspects of public relations. The growing number of mergers of advertising and public relations agencies is evidence of this change. A generation ago, public relations constituted only a small portion of the activities of advertising agencies—almost an afterthought. But in recent years ad agencies have widened their range of services to better serve clients and to counter a decline in advertising's share of marketing budgets. Some agencies are expanding through mergers. Others are forming strategic partnerships with public relations agencies. Still others are building public relations departments from scratch. In some agencies, advertising and public relations divisions act as separate profit centers, partnering only when circumstances dictate the need for an IMC approach.

Consumer-focused marketing also is changing **marketing public relations**, the part of our profession that exists to promote organizations' products. More practitioners are learning—or at least learning about—disciplines such as direct marketing, product packaging, and other forms of advertising and marketing. IMC, for example, is increasing the communications options of marketing public relations practitioners.

The Impact of Public Relations on Consumer-Focused Marketing

But the influence flows both ways: Public relations has also had a profound influence on consumer-focused marketing. Public relations professionals have always believed in breaking down publics into their smallest units, just as consumer-focused marketing does. And good public relations has always been two-way; the best practitioners have always listened—not just talked—to their publics. Two-way symmetrical public relations by definition seeks to identify and honor the values and interests of important publics. Critics of traditional marketing communications charge—perhaps not altogether fairly—that consumer values and interests were left out of the traditional marketing process. Those critics say that companies designed products and sent marketing messages with very little analysis of what individual consumers really wanted. Whether or not that's true, it is undeniable that consumer-focused marketing is increasing the power of the consumer in the marketing process.

Public relations practitioners seek communication with publics through media that those publics prefer; consumer-focused marketers do the same. Two-way symmetrical public relations involves the notion that sometimes an organization has to change to meet the needs of its publics, just as consumer-focused marketing involves

VALUES STATEMENT 13.1

J.M. Smucker Company

The J.M. Smucker Company manufactures jams, jellies, preserves, ice cream toppings, and natural peanut butter. The company was founded in 1897 and is based in Orrville, Ohio.

Quality applies to our products, our manufacturing methods, our marketing efforts, our people, and our relationships with each other. We will only produce and sell products that enhance the quality of life and well-being. These will be the highest quality products offered in our respective markets because the Company's growth and business success have been built on quality. We will continuously look for ways to achieve daily improvements which will, over time, result in consistently superior products and performance.

At the J.M. Smucker Company, quality comes first. Sales growth and earnings will follow.

—Excerpt from "Our Basic Beliefs,"
J.M. Smucker web site

realizing that a product may need to change. In fact, modern marketing's basic philosophy of respecting and listening to consumers may well be a contribution from the practice of successful public relations.

Differences between Public Relations and Consumer-Focused Marketing

A problem with some interpretations of consumer-focused marketing is the mistaken belief that all public relations is part of marketing communications. Knocking down that idea is easy. Marketing focuses on a very important public: consumers. But that's only one public. Public relations must focus on developing healthy long-term relationships with employees, stockholders, news media, and any other public essential to an organization's success. Certainly the two professions need to work together. But as Figure 13.1 indicates, public relations and marketing are distinct, complementary professions.

In *Excellence in Public Relations and Communication Management,* a landmark study on how award-winning public relations works, Professor Emeritus James Grunig of the University of Maryland declares, "The public relations function of excellent organizations exists separately from the marketing function, and excellent public relations departments are not subsumed into the marketing function."[8] Nearly 20 years ago, a panel of public relations and marketing experts concluded that the two professions were "separate and equal, but related functions."[9] Jack Bergen, senior vice president of corporate affairs and marketing for Siemens, a multinational corporation, says, "PR people understand the richness of audiences that have an interest in a company; advertisers just focus on customers."[10]

Public relations isn't advertising or marketing. But public relations and consumer-focused marketing certainly share important values. Both focus on the needs and interests of a public or publics. Both try to listen as much as they speak. And both act to strengthen an organization.

QUICK ✓ CHECK

1. How does consumer-focused marketing differ from mass marketing?
2. How and why does consumer-focused marketing use databases?
3. What are the differences among public relations, advertising, and marketing?

A Closer Look at Marketing

Before beginning this chapter, you probably had a basic understanding of marketing. After all, you encounter it every day. And earlier in this chapter, we defined marketing. But as you might suspect, we're about to tell you even more. Understanding how marketing works can make you a better public relations practitioner.

At its core, marketing means making the consumer want to buy your product. The so-called **marketing mix** consists of everything from product research and design to packaging, pricing, and product demonstrations. It even includes selecting the product's name. Years ago, marketing professors Jerome McCarthy and Philip Kotler defined the marketing mix with what they called the four P's of marketing:

1. *Product* (including name, design, and packaging)
2. *Price*
3. *Place* (where, exactly, can the customer buy it?)
4. *Promotion*

Public relations usually enters the marketing mix in the promotion category, and its importance is growing. Studies at Procter & Gamble, for example, have shown that public relations tactics earn the highest return on financial investment of all the different tactics in P&G's diverse marketing mix. "This could be the best thing to happen to the PR business in decades," reported *Advertising Age*.[11]

One of IMC's greatest contributions to marketing is the belief that every bit of the marketing mix communicates to consumers. A product's name sends a message to the consumer, as do design, packaging, price, the place consumers purchase the product, and the promotions that publicize the product. Humor columnist Dave Barry accurately reported that North Dakota was considering a name change because the word *North* suggests cold, snow-swept plains to potential tourists. Barry then stretched the truth—but illustrated the communicative power of names—by adding, "In contrast, SOUTH Dakota is universally believed to be a tropical paradise with palm trees swaying on surf-kissed beaches."[12] Like names, price and place also can send consumers a message. A lavishly packaged product that sells for an eye-poppingly high price at the most exclusive store in town has a different image in consumers' minds than a product sold for 25 cents at the town's grungiest gas station.

One problem with traditional marketing, some critics say, is that these various forms of communication may be sending different messages about the same product. And if consumers don't have a clear vision of the product, they won't buy it. For example, consumers may easily be confused by a product whose advertising suggests exclusivity and luxury—yet whose price suggests availability and cheapness.

"Most marketers send out a communications hodgepodge to the consumer, a mass message saying one thing, a price promo creating a different signal, a product label creating still another message, sales literature having an entirely different vocabulary, a sales force pitching nothing but 'price,' 'price,' 'price' to the retailer," say the authors of *Integrated Marketing Communications,* an excellent book on IMC. "Mixed-up, mass-directed, incompatible communication stems from the manufacturer's wishes rather than from customer needs."[13]

IMC tries to end that hodgepodge of messages by ensuring that every aspect of the marketing mix sends the same clear message to highly targeted consumers.

Marketing Public Relations

Before we take a closer look at how IMC in particular works, let's look at marketing public relations, which is the part of public relations that fits into marketing. Marketing public relations focuses on building relationships with consumers, with the intent, of course, of persuading them to buy a product.

Revlon, an international cosmetics company, uses marketing public relations, together with other IMC tactics, to gain competitive advantage in the multibillion-dollar beauty-aids market. For example, knowing the power of celebrity, Revlon signed Grammy-award winner Sheryl Crow as spokesperson for its new line of Colorist hair-color products in 2006. Three months later, when she appeared on the *CBS Evening News* to discuss her successful battle with breast cancer, she prominently mentioned her gratitude to Revlon for helping to lobby the federal government for increased cancer research.

How much did Revlon pay CBS for such a positive, prominent mention? Zero.

Grammy-award winner Sheryl Crow has helped Revlon gain international exposure through media appearances in which she mentions her partnership with the cosmetics giant. (Photo by Vincent Laforet/ *New York Times*. Copyright 2003 The New York Times Company. Reprinted with permission.)

Zip. Nada. Crow's appearance on the program was a form of media relations—of providing interesting information that news media want and need. And because her appearance promoted both cancer research and Revlon, it became a form of marketing public relations. "We are very excited to have someone of Sheryl's great beauty, both inner and outward, as the new spokesperson for our company," said Revlon CEO David Kennedy. "Sheryl will not only be a terrific partner in our business but she will be invaluable to us in supporting our various initiatives in women's cancer research and treatment."[14]

Other tactics in marketing public relations include:

- product- or service-oriented news releases and media kits;
- video news releases (VNRs) featuring newsworthy products or services;
- news conferences to announce significant new products or services;

- blogs, interactive web sites, messages in social networks such as MySpace, and other social media;
- satellite media tours (SMTs), in which a spokesperson for a newsworthy product or service gives individual interviews to local television stations via satellite;
- displays at trade shows, where industry analysts and interested consumers gather to examine new products and services;
- special events designed to attract media attention to a particular product;
- spokesperson appearances in the media (including Internet chat rooms) and at special events; and
- communication efforts that target employees, investors, government regulators, and other publics besides consumers that can influence the success of marketing campaigns.

Marketing public relations can work alone or, better, as part of a marketing campaign. Marketing public relations targets consumers, sometimes gaining independent endorsements by working through intervening publics such as the news media. Although all of an organization's relationships can have marketing implications—after all, everyone is a consumer—other areas of public relations work less directly with marketing, focusing instead on publics such as employees, government units, and investors.

A Closer Look at IMC

Enough background. Let's jump into a deeper definition of integrated marketing communications. IMC, say the authors of *Integrated Marketing Communications,* is "planned, developed, executed, and evaluated with affecting one specific consumer behavior in mind, the process of making purchases now or in the future."[15]

Focusing on Individual Consumers

In IMC, individual consumers are the focus of thematically consistent messages sent through a variety of media. In fact, marketing professor Robert Lauterborn suggests that the traditional four P's of marketing have become the consumer-driven four C's:[16]

1. *Product* has become *consumer wants and needs:* These shape every aspect of the marketing process.
2. *Price* has become *consumer's cost:* For example, a price of $500 is a higher cost to a college student than it is to a movie star.
3. *Place* has become *convenience to buy.*
4. *Promotion* has become *communication:* This is two-way communication that actively seeks consumer input.

Sending thematically consistent messages through a variety of media may sound familiar. In Chapter 1, we discussed how an organization must identify its values and then ensure that all its actions, including its communications, are consistent with those values.

As we said earlier, IMC recognizes the ineffectiveness of trying to use only the old mass media to affect masses of people. Instead, IMC uses a variety of media to communicate with small groups and, ideally, individuals. For example, a combination of satellites, global positioning devices, and cell phones can allow marketers to send text messages to consumers as they near a favorite store. The messages can even offer discounts. "It drove me into the shop," said one recipient of such a message.[17]

IMC tactics can include rebate offers or other consumer-response promotions that gather information for databases. Databases are an indispensable element in IMC campaigns. As we've noted, computerized databases do more than record names, locations, phone numbers, and e-mail addresses; they can record when, where, and how a product was purchased. Databases also can record when and how consumers were contacted, when and how they responded, and what the organization and the consumer said. Every contact with a consumer becomes a chance to refine the database.

Sending One Clear Message

If the database lies at the heart of successful integrated marketing communications, so does the philosophy of sending one clear message—or, at least, thematically consistent messages—to consumers. Generally, marketing public relations helps send that one consistent message. However, with its expertise in supplying newsworthy stories to the news media, on some occasions marketing public relations may send a slightly different message than do the other tactics in an IMC campaign.

A classic example of how public relations can lead a campaign occurred when First Alert, Inc., maker of First Alert smoke detectors and carbon monoxide detectors, first prepared to market its carbon monoxide detectors. The marketing message of the First Alert carbon monoxide detector was simple: This product can save your life. But research revealed a problem: Wheatley Blair, Inc., the public relations agency assisting in the launch of First Alert's new detector, discovered through research that the U.S. public didn't understand how dangerous carbon monoxide gas is.

"Most people didn't realize that every appliance in their home that runs on combustible fuel produces carbon monoxide every time it operates," said Bob Wheatley, a partner in Wheatley Blair. "They didn't understand that if appliances such as gas stoves, driers, fireplaces, furnaces, and water heaters aren't functioning properly, they can release into the home a gas that is odorless, colorless, and highly toxic."[18]

The bottom line of Wheatley Blair's research was this: Consumers might not respond to a marketing message stressing safety—because they didn't know that they were in danger.

Wheatley Blair and other members of the First Alert marketing team consequently crafted the following timetable and strategy. First, a public relations campaign targeting the news media would roll out. Mention of the First Alert carbon monoxide detector would be secondary; the campaign's primary goal would be to emphasize the threat of carbon monoxide poisoning. The detector itself then would be shipped to ensure availability. Finally, the advertising campaign would roll out in October, the beginning of the home heating season.

The Fall of Advertising?

Give a book a provocative title, and readers will come. For example, who wouldn't at least pick up a copy of author James Lee Burke's *In the Electric Mist with Confederate Dead*?

As noted in Chapter 1, the most provocative title in recent years for IMC practitioners may be Al and Laura Ries' *The Fall of Advertising and Rise of PR*. The father–daughter team of marketing consultants has made headlines with this claim: Public relations is more successful than advertising in introducing new brands.

"We're beginning to see research that supports the superiority of PR over advertising to launch a brand," the Rieses say. "A new study of 91 launches shows highly successful products are more like to use PR-related activities."[19] According to the Rieses, public relations tops other IMC disciplines for building credibility and generating word-of-mouth publicity; advertising is most successful in maintaining awareness of established brands.

Recent IMC research shows that marketing agencies are increasing the amount of time they spend seeking alternatives to advertising.[20] In a 2006 study of traditional marketing communication functions, marketing executives believed public relations was the most effective discipline in five of eight key areas (product launches, generating word of mouth, building corporate reputation, managing a crisis, and changing perceptions); direct marketing was most effective in three (ongoing product promotion, targeting niche audiences, and increasing sales); and advertising was most effective in none.[21]

"Like Ries, I believe advertising has its place," says John Shattock of Shattock Communications and Research of New Zealand. "It should be a reminder of a perception that has already been established by more credible means. Public relations should come first, establishing perceptions and credibility."[22]

"For the ads to really work well, you needed to have a basic knowledge of what carbon monoxide is, where it comes from, and why it's bad for you," said Wheatley. "Otherwise, you're not going to get it. What we did was to generate newspaper and TV stories all over the country on carbon monoxide poisoning. A lot of the headlines were 'Silent, deadly killer is invading your home.' "

Radio and TV placements were also key to the public relations campaign. Wheatley Blair helped generate stories on CBS, NBC, and CNN network news.

Wheatley Blair's campaign included personal calls to science and home products editors, a comprehensive media kit, video news releases, sponsorship of interviews with scientists and medical personnel, and a toll-free information number.

Wheatley Blair's news-media strategy succeeded in raising public awareness of the dangers of carbon monoxide from 2 percent of consumers to 75 percent, and the entire First Alert IMC campaign was a success. Representatives of Wal-Mart told the makers of First Alert that the new carbon monoxide detector was the most successful new product introduction, up to that time, in the history of Wal-Mart's hardware/ home products department. For its role in the First Alert campaign, Wheatley Blair won a Silver Anvil, the highest award bestowed by the Public Relations Society of America.

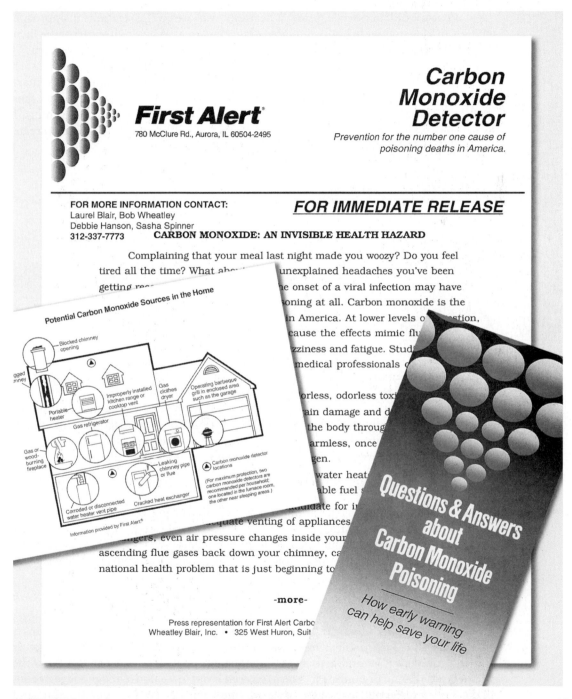

First Alert
780 McClure Rd., Aurora, IL 60504-2495

Carbon Monoxide Detector
Prevention for the number one cause of poisoning deaths in America.

FOR MORE INFORMATION CONTACT:
Laurel Blair, Bob Wheatley
Debbie Hanson, Sasha Spinner
312-337-7773

FOR IMMEDIATE RELEASE

CARBON MONOXIDE: AN INVISIBLE HEALTH HAZARD

Complaining that your meal last night made you woozy? Do you feel tired all the time? What about the unexplained headaches you've been getting rec... the onset of a viral infection may have ...soning at all. Carbon monoxide is the ... in America. At lower levels o... stion, ...cause the effects mimic flu... ...zziness and fatigue. Studi... ...medical professionals c...

...orless, odorless toxi... ...ain damage and d... ...the body throug... ...armless, once ... ...gen.

...water heat... ...able fuel ... ...ndidate for i... ...quate venting of appliances... ...gers, even air pressure changes inside your... ascending flue gases back down your chimney, ca... national health problem that is just beginning to...

-more-

Press representation for First Alert Carbo...
Wheatley Blair, Inc. • 325 West Huron, Suit...

Potential Carbon Monoxide Sources in the Home

Blocked chimney opening
...gged ...mney
Portable heater
Improperly installed kitchen range or cooktop vent
Gas clothes dryer
Operating barbeque grill in enclosed area such as the garage
Gas refrigerator
Gas or wood-burning fireplace
Leaking chimney pipe or flue
Carbon monoxide detector locations
(For maximum protection, two carbon monoxide detectors are recommended per household; one located in the furnace room, the other near sleeping areas.)
Corroded or disconnected water heater vent pipe
Cracked heat exchanger
Information provided by First Alert.®

Questions & Answers about Carbon Monoxide Poisoning
How early warning can help save your life

Media Kit Materials Before safety-oriented advertisements for First Alert carbon monoxide detectors could work, consumers needed to learn of the dangers of the odorless, colorless, lethal gas. First Alert used media kits containing news releases, brochures, charts, and other material to inform news media about the dangers of carbon monoxide poisoning. (Courtesy of Wheatley Blair, Inc.)

"What we did, in essence," said Wheatley, "was use public relations to approach media vehicles that were highly credible. And that created an environment in which the advertising could work harder and be more effective than it might have been."

In most IMC campaigns, public relations sends the same message that other elements of the marketing process send. But, as the First Alert example shows, marketing public relations is flexible. Using the tactics of public relations—or any other IMC profession—to help develop a market is called **premarket conditioning**.[23] By sending a slightly different preliminary message, public relations can help create receptivity for a subsequent IMC campaign.

1. What do public relations and IMC have in common? Is all of public relations part of IMC?
2. What are the four P's of marketing? What are the four C's of IMC?
3. What are some of the traditional tactics of marketing public relations?

How IMC Works

Professor Tom Duncan, author of *Principles of Advertising and IMC*, recommends starting an IMC campaign with an **IMC audit.** An IMC audit is similar in intent to the ethics audit (Chapter 6) and the communication audit (Chapter 7) we examined earlier in this book. As with all audits, the goal is to determine where an organization stands right now—and, perhaps, to make recommendations for future actions. Again and again, it's worth noting that the public relations process begins with good research.

Duncan recommends an IMC audit that consists of five steps:[24]

1. Analysis of the communications network used to develop marketing communications programs
2. Identification and prioritization of key stakeholder groups
3. Evaluation of the organization's customer databases
4. Content analysis of all messages (ads, public relations releases, packaging, video news releases, signage, sales promotion pieces, direct response mailings, social media, and so on) used within the past year
5. Assessment of knowledge of, and attitudes toward, IMC on the part of marketing managers, top management, and key agency managers

With the information a marketing team gathers from an IMC audit, it forms a good idea of the environment from which it intends to launch an IMC campaign. If that environment is favorable to an IMC campaign, great! Full speed ahead. But if the audit shows that an organization has no customer database and a hodgepodge of contradictory marketing messages, then it must make some technological and philosophical changes before it can launch a successful IMC campaign. Perhaps the organization must even reexamine its core values in light of the proposed IMC campaign.

IMC Tactics To familiarize consumers with the new $50 bill, the U.S. Bureau of Engraving and Printing communicated through a variety of media, including an interactive web site and, pictured here, news releases, school lesson plans, and cashier posters. (Courtesy of the U.S. Bureau of Engraving and Printing)

The New Color of Money: Safer. Smarter. More Secure.

The United States government continues plans to issue currency with enhanced designs and security features. The government introduced a new $20 note design in 2003 and will continue with other denominations.. A new $50 note will be introduced in late 2004, followed later by a new $100 note.

The new $50 design retains three of the most important security features that were first introduced in the 1990s and are easy to check: **a watermark, security thread and color-shifting ink.**

The New Color of Money
Safer. Smarter. More Secure.

News Release

www.moneyfactory.com/newmo...

FOR IMMEDIATE RELEASE
TUESDAY, SEPTEMBER 28, 2004

CONTACTS:
Dawn Haley or Claudia Dickens, 202/874-3019
Bureau of Engraving and Printing

Rose Pianalto or Susan Stawick, 202/452-2955
Federal Reserve Board

Penny Kozakos, 202/530-4887
New Color of Money Media Support

Safer, Smarter, More Secure $50 Bill Issued
Banks to Begin Distributing the Redesigned Note Today

...SHINGTON – **September 28, 2004** – Newly redesigned $50 notes arrive at banks ...ing today ready to make their way into circulation and consumer wallets. Today marks ...the Federal Reserve System distributes the new note to banks and thus into the public's

...sion, officials from the U.S. Department of the Treasury, Federal Reserve ...Secret Service were on hand for the first transaction using the newly ...ing homage to the symbol of freedom featured in the note's new ...fficials used one of the first new $50 notes to buy an American flag ...Washington, D.C.'s Union Station.

...ecurity features, subtle background colors of blue and red, ...d a small metallic silver-blue star. The new design is part ...ts to stay ahead of counterfeiting and protect the

...cy is something the U.S. government takes ...ary for Domestic Finance at the Department ...rency regularly and enhancing security ... from would-be counterfeiters."

The New Color of Money
Safer. Smarter. More Secure.

Current Changes in Currency Design
Why a Newly Redesigned $50 Note?

LESSON PLAN

This lesson plan is designed to teach students about the features of the newly redesigned $50 note and offers educators the opportunity to teach U.S. history and economics at the National Standard level.

Reproduction is permitted and encouraged.
Available for download at www.moneyfactory.com/newmoney

Creating an IMC Campaign

With an IMC audit completed, we now know where we are. But how do we get to where we want to be? Using our knowledge of current resources and attitudes, how do we build a successful IMC campaign? The following seven strategies are among several recommended by Matthew P. Gonring, vice president of marketing and communication for Rockwell Automation:[25]

1. *"Create shared performance measures. Develop systems to evaluate communications activities."* Recall Chapter 8 on planning: We need to have a goal and measurable objectives to prove to others the effectiveness of our program. Setting precise sales goals may be too ambitious—but we can certainly specify the number and nature of relationships that we intend to create.

2. *"Use database development and issues management to understand your stakeholders."* Here's another expert telling us that a database is essential to a successful IMC campaign. A database details the individual consumer wants and needs that have been identified through interactive communication with consumers. Issues management, as we noted in Chapter 7, is a process of identifying and managing emerging issues that can affect your organization and the publics important to your organization.

3. *"Identify all contact points for the company and its products."* Some experts recommend an even broader look at contact points, or **contacts.** *"Contacts* will likely be a new term for many advertising and promotion people, particularly the way it is used in IMC," say the authors of *Integrated Marketing Communications.* "We define a contact as any information-bearing experience that a customer or a prospect has with the brand, product category, or the market that relates to the marketer's product or service."[26]

4. *"Create business and communication plans for each local market."* As your IMC program improves, you may want to strive for the goal of developing a plan for every individual customer within your database. Ideally, all those messages to slightly different publics must be consistent with one another.

5. *"Create compatible themes, tones, and quality across all communications media."* Remember: All elements of the marketing process need to send consistent messages about your product.

6. *"Hire only team players."* Jealousy and insecurity can destroy an IMC campaign. Public relations practitioners can't always insist on using public relations tactics, nor can advertisers always insist on using advertising. Members of the IMC team must agree to use the messages and the media that consumers prefer.

7. *"Link IMC with management processes."* Robert Dilenschneider, the former head of Hill & Knowlton, one of the world's largest public relations agencies, offers solid advice: "Think in terms of what the manager wants to achieve, and tie everything you suggest to a financial or business result."[27]

If clearly identified consumer values, wants, and needs are shaping each step of your marketing process, from product design to follow-up after a purchase, the odds are good that you have a successful IMC campaign.

Applying IMC

Let's return to our music store scenario for a moment. What sorts of strategies and tactics might an IMC campaign include? After doing an IMC audit and learning that your organization will support an integrated marketing approach, you gain agreement on a consistent message to be sent to potential customers: "Hard-to-find music at hard-to-beat prices." A quick scientific survey of potential customers shows that this is an effective message. Your mission now is to deliver that message effectively and to bring buyers into your stores. Among the tactics you might consider are

- developing a web site with blogs, podcasts, and a few free downloads, all of which gather information for your database.
- placing ads in student newspapers, both print and online. The ads include your web address and a discount coupon that requests names and e-mail addresses for free drawings. The coupons provide more information for your database.
- sponsoring alternative rock concerts and passing out flyers with coupons.
- offering your store managers to local media as experts on little-known but high-quality bands. You particularly try to place the managers on call-in radio shows, where direct interaction with potential customers is possible.
- sending e-mail newsletters to customers who request them through your web site. You could simply spam everyone in your database, but you wisely decide not to.
- launching a direct e-mail and text-messaging campaign that lets customers know when one of their favorite bands has released a new CD. You know each customer's favorite bands because that information is in your database. You use e-mail and text messaging because students move so often that street addresses are unreliable. And, of course, you send such messages only to students who agree, in advance, that they want them. In those messages you ask students to let you know whether they're interested in other bands as well.

For each of the above tactics, you also would establish some measures of evaluation. Evaluation of your tactics would help you determine which are most successful in helping your company achieve its marketing goals.

You can probably think of more and better ideas, but note what the tactics mentioned here have in common: They deliver approximately the same consumer-focused message, they tend to target individuals rather than mass audiences, they're not limited to traditional public relations and advertising tactics, they're interactive, and they seek information for an increasingly detailed database.

Hey, give yourself a raise.

QUICKBREAK 13.3

DM: The New Kid in Town

Direct marketing isn't really new, but recent techno-logical advances have helped make DM the hottest thing in IMC.

In the words of the Direct Marketing Association, DM is "any direct communication to a consumer or business recipient that is designed to generate a response in the form of an order (direct order), a request for further information (lead generation), and/or a visit to a store or other place of business for purchase of a specific product(s) or service(s) (traffic generation)."[28] To that definition and its many parentheses, we would add that DM can use several different media for direct communication, including e-mail, postal mail, cell phone text mes-saging, and telephone calls. In direct marketing, a company usually contacts a specific individual, by-passing all intervening publics such as retail stores or magazine advertisements.

As IMC practitioners seek cheaper, more effec-tive alternatives to advertising (see QuickBreak 13.2), DM has come on strong. "Advertising's usage [has] slumped, largely at the expense of direct marketing's rise," *PR Week* magazine concluded in a study of IMC tactics.[29] Market-ing executives report that DM measures and documents its success better than either public relations or advertising and is superior to both of those disciplines for sustaining current product promotions, targeting niche audiences, and increasing sales.[30]

In cyberspace, particularly e-mail, the laziest form of DM is called **spamming,** which involves sending the same promotional message to a long list of receivers, whether they're interested or not. Ferris Research of San Francisco estimates that more than 1 billion telephone text spams were sent in 2007, up 38 percent from 2006.[31] Although legislation to can spam is on the rise, some experts predict that the tactic eventually will self-destruct.

"The last time I checked," says marketing pro-fessor Stephen Hoch, "irritating people doesn't have a long-term benefit for anybody."[32]

Problems with 21st-Century Marketing

We hope you're excited about IMC, CRM, and the other approaches to consumer-focused marketing. However, we also hope that you're realistic. These relatively new approaches to marketing still face problems that can limit their effectiveness.

We've already hinted at one: jealousy, or so-called turf battles, with every member of the marketing team promoting only his or her own area of expertise. Only 18 percent of marketers say their IMC programs are "seamlessly integrated."[33] Bob Seltzer, head of IMC programs at public relations agency Ruder Finn, says, "Everyone understands that integration is smarter than isolation, but the desire to integrate hits the wall when one discipline has to fight the other for what they want."[34] Two tactics described earlier in this chapter—conducting an IMC audit and hiring only team players—can help eliminate this problem.

A second problem in consumer-focused marketing involves measuring results. The different professions of IMC tend to measure success differently. "One of the biggest obstacles to working with other disciplines is that we do not share a common ROI [return on investment] measurement vehicle," says Richard Mintz of public

QUICKBREAK 13.4

Data Danger: Kids and Europeans

With its many divisions such as IMC, CRM, and IBC, consumer-focused marketing can certainly seem complicated. But we can console ourselves by remembering that one constant is the database, right?

Wrong, in some cases—particularly in marketing to U.S. preteens and marketing in Europe.

With the passage of the Children's Online Privacy Protection Act of 1998, the U.S. Congress and the Federal Trade Commission placed significant restrictions on database marketing to preteens. To gather and store data on children younger than 13, web site operators must, in most cases, get verifiable consent from the children's parents, allow parents to request that such information not be disclosed to third parties, allow parents to examine stored information on their children, and allow parents to delete any stored information and opt out of future collection of such data. In addition, web site operators must maintain the security of collected information and cannot make data collection a condition for entry into their web sites.[35]

Ditto for Europe—for consumers of all ages. The Data Protection Directive of the European Union specifies that database marketers must have a consumer's permission to gather and store data on that individual; must allow consumers to review and correct database information; can use a database for one purpose only; and must get each consumer's permission to use a database for anything other than the original, single purpose.[36] Organizations that do not meet these requirements cannot use any form of database marketing in European Union nations.

A small loophole exists for U.S.-based companies doing business in the European Union. A so-called safe harbor agreement with European officials allows U.S.-based companies to import information from their European databases and use it according to U.S. laws—if they provide European consumers a chance to "opt out" of the new databases. U.S.-based high-tech giants such as Microsoft, Apple, IBM, and Oracle have sailed into the safe harbor.[37]

In case you're thinking you can't operate a database without enough lawyers to start a beach volleyball team, here's a contrarian opinion from marketing professor Peter Fader: You don't need all that information anyway. "I have heard industry professionals say that they have this huge data warehouse and 600 different measures," he says. "I say, 'Big deal, 595 of them are useless.'"[38]

Feel free to disagree—and think of a team name for those lawyers.

relations agency Burson-Marsteller.[39] However, marketing executives do give higher marks to public relations professionals than to advertisers for their efforts to document success or failure.[40]

A third problem in consumer-focused marketing is privacy. As noted in Quick-Break 13.4, the United States and the European Union have different standards regarding consumers' rights to privacy. And within the United States, concern for individual privacy increases as marketers seek more and more information on individuals. A survey of marketing professionals in the midwestern United States found that 74 percent favored government intervention to ensure additional privacy for consumers; only 7 percent strongly opposed government intervention. The authors of the study concluded, "The respondents . . . want legislation to protect privacy even though it might encroach upon their professional activities, partially to suppress their culpability and also because they desire such protections in their own lives."[41]

Finally, the very nature of consumer-focused marketing can be a problem. Excessive focus on consumers' desires could pull a company away from its core values. An organization that lives only to satisfy the whims of consumers may well lack the deeply felt, enduring values that characterize successful organizations. Consumer-focused marketing will succeed best when it operates on a solid foundation of organizational values. "The integrity of the corporation that stands behind the brand is even more important than the marketing or promoting of the brand itself," says Frank Vogl, president of Vogl Communications in Washington, D.C. "So many people involved in the integrated marketing and communications of corporate brands have not paid adequate attention to the values that should be seen at the core of the brand itself."[42]

No one can deny that consumer-focused marketing faces serious challenges. However, at the beginning of the 21st century, the new, database-driven approaches to marketing offer significant opportunities for public relations practitioners.

QUICK ✓ CHECK

1. What is an IMC audit? What steps does it involve?
2. In marketing, what is a contact or contact point?
3. Why are team players essential to a successful IMC campaign?

Summary

Consumer-focused marketing is not a passing fad. It's a growing reality for organizations that want their products to have clear, consistent, appealing images in the marketplace. It's also a growing expectation on the part of consumers, who seek more and more individual attention from organizations as new technologies make such communication possible. Unlike mass marketing, consumer-focused marketing begins not with a public but with an individual. Products are designed to accommodate, as much as possible, individual needs and desires. Sales messages focus on those same individual self-interests, which are discovered through two-way communication and are recorded in databases.

Integrated marketing communications unites a variety of communications disciplines to address individual self-interests: advertising, public relations, marketing promotions, packaging, pricing, direct marketing, and any other approach that can send an effective message to a potential customer. Despite the wide array of available tactics, the messages in an IMC campaign are integrated: Consumers should receive a consistent message about an organization's product or service. The message of an advertisement, for example, should be consistent with the message of the price and of a product-oriented news release.

Not all of public relations is part of consumer-focused marketing, of course. Marketing addresses one very important public: consumers. Public relations builds relationships with any public that can affect an organization's success, including employees, stockholders, and government regulators. But one of the most exciting areas in the future of public relations is its role in consumer-focused marketing. In the

21st century, marketing means building relationships with individual consumers, and that's good news for public relations.

DISCUSSION QUESTIONS

1. How are the philosophies of public relations and consumer-focused marketing similar? How are they different?
2. What is "integrated" about integrated marketing communications?
3. What are the benefits of using consumer-focused marketing instead of mass marketing?
4. Does IMC, as it is currently practiced, have any problems or potential problems?
5. How is an IMC audit similar to an ethics audit and a communication audit?

Memo from the Field

Vin Cipolla, President and CEO, National Park Foundation, Washington, D.C.

Vin Cipolla is president and CEO of the National Park Foundation, a private philanthropy dedicated to preserving, protecting, and improving U.S. national parks. He also led the integrated marketing agencies HNW, Inc., and Pamet River. He is a Phi Beta Kappa graduate of Clark University.

There's a very good reason why integrated marketing has become so popular lately. Basically, without it, we marketers are doomed. In fact, when a company doesn't present a consistent marketing message to the public, it not only wastes a lot of money, it also risks its own reputation.

But that's not all. These days it's not enough for marketing functions like advertising, PR, and direct mail to work together. Now, marketing needs to be integrated throughout the entire company—with departments like customer service, sales, distribution, and manufacturing all working together on corporate objectives. The goal today is to make certain that everyone in the company is conveying the same message. Not just the marketing department.

Not convinced? Think about it. Imagine watching a heartwarming television advertisement promoting a particular airline's commitment to friendly service. Now, the next time you fly, you certainly expect that airline's in-flight personnel to be extra friendly, right? You certainly expect that airline to have spent as much effort maintaining high customer service standards as it did creating that expensive television advertisement.

The fact is, we expect more now as consumers than we did a few years ago. Interactive technology, web sites, and sophisticated database marketing have all raised the standard of customer service by facilitating dynamic two-way communication between business and consumers. Today it's not enough simply to sell products; companies must also build relationships with customers if they want to compete.

For example, consumers like to feel remembered and appreciated. That's one reason why some mail-order companies have started to track customer orders more effectively. Perhaps the next time you call, they may thank you for your repeat order and ask if you'd like the same size as before. It's that type of personal attention that is becoming the new norm.

That level of integration isn't easy to achieve. It requires a centralized database in which every customer contact position (e.g., billing, marketing, and service) is integrated so that valuable customer data is captured, analyzed, and maximized fully. That's a challenge. Maybe that centralized customer data isn't available yet. Or maybe it is, but the company doesn't know how to interpret it so the data provides valuable insight.

Another problem may be the company's own staff. Internal power struggles are responsible for the failure of many integrated marketing programs. Unfortunately, many employees aren't trained to work in cross-departmental partnerships. Finance managers speak a different language than marketing managers. Customer service has different priorities than sales. And rarely is there a company incentive for these disparate employees to work together in teams on company goals.

That's why the most successful companies have strong leadership at the top. Only the CEO or president has the authority to cross so many departmental borders. Without that senior-level support, a truly effective integrated marketing program will remain a distant dream.

So what does all this mean for you? It means your job just became a lot more difficult. Now you don't just need to work well with other marketing divisions. You also need to work well with customer service, billing, and distribution too.

The more you understand how the entire company functions, the better you'll perform your own job. The more you understand what these various managers consider important, the easier a time you'll have working with them on the corporate goals. And, finally, the more you understand how emerging technology is impacting marketing, the more successfully you'll play by today's new marketing rules.

As you take on the challenge, I wish you all the luck in the world.

CASE STUDY **13.1**

Dove Soars with Real Beauty

Chances are, you've done it. After all, more than 3 million have.

If you haven't, go ahead: Direct your browser to YouTube and search "Dove Evolution." Push play, and, for one minute and 14 seconds, watch one of the most famous integrated marketing tactics of recent years.

The Dove Evolution viral video—in which a young woman digitally transforms into an impossibly perfect supermodel—is part of the award-winning Campaign for

Real Beauty, sponsored by Dove, Unilever's line of cleansing and personal-care products. The goal of the Campaign for Real Beauty is impressive: "to help widen the definition of beauty and offer a more diverse representation than the stereotypical images that women and girls are bombarded with every day."[43] To achieve that goal, Unilever, ad agency Ogilvy & Mather, and public relations agency Edelman have worked together to create an array of integrated, on-message tactics.

Before the planning and tactics, however, came the research. Edelman surveyed more than 10,000 women worldwide and discovered that only 2 percent describe themselves as beautiful. Almost 80 percent wish that the media could do "a better job of portraying women of diverse physical attractiveness—age, shape, and size."[44] A subsequent survey on age and beauty found that "91 percent of the women surveyed believe the media and advertising need to do a better job of representing realistic images of women over 50."[45]

"Without having a foundation in the global research study, which showed that the image of beauty was unattainable, we wouldn't have had the credibility in creating the materials," said Larry Koffler, Edelman's senior vice president for consumer brands. "The research was critical."[46]

To build on that credibility, Unilever wanted a campaign that went beyond advertising. "We had advertising, public relations, customer marketing and consumer promotions sit down at the table at a very early stage and all think about the entire marketing communication architecture, not just our channels," Koffler recalled.[47]

The Dove Evolution viral video, for example, earned coverage on TV programs *The View, Entertainment Tonight,* and *The Ellen DeGeneres Show,* and it generated three times more visits to the IMC campaign's web site than did an earlier Super Bowl commercial.[48]

Other campaign tactics included

- print, television, and billboard advertisements featuring "real women [with] real bodies and real curves."[49]
- a "Self-Esteem Fund" and "Uniquely Me!" programs that target girls ages 8 to 17 with the aim of "educating and inspiring girls who believe in a definition of beauty that doesn't include them."[50]
- the CampaignForRealBeauty.com web site, which includes news releases, the Dove Evolution video, self-esteem kits for mothers and daughters, Real Beauty e-greeting cards, online discussion forums, news about the Self-Esteem Fund, and other initiatives.
- photography and essay competitions on real beauty for young girls.
- the Campaign for Real Beauty Tour, a traveling photography exhibition, featuring photographs of women by women. According to an accompanying news release, "The images, which depict confidence, individuality and character, are accompanied by an anecdote or quote that explains the photographer's vision."[51]

Advertising has played a major role in the Campaign for Real Beauty, but the success of the public relations tactics has won admiration even from advertising media. Fernando Acosta, the senior vice president of Dove, told *Advertising Age* that "although the ads are eye-catching and thought-provoking, public relations is used as the lead medium in all countries" in which Dove has launched the Campaign for Real Beauty.[52] *Advertising Age* also reported that "so powerful was the [campaign's] public relations effort that paid media was light."[53]

Media response to the advertisements—a success for both advertising and public relations—has helped Dove become the leading brand in promoting realistic images of beauty. As early as 2005, *PR Week* reported that "Dove's 'Real women, real curves' campaign has had so much press that Unilever could justifiably claim stewardship of the real women demographic that everyone is now talking about."[54]

Dove may have lost count of how many national and international marketing awards the Campaign for Real Beauty has won, but to date the list includes the Silver Anvil Award from the Public Relations Society of America and the Golden World Award from the International Public Relations Association.

Perhaps the greatest testament to success, however, came from a woman who wrote to the Campaign for Real Beauty web site after seeing a Dove commercial in which young girls discussed insecurities about their appearances. "I want to hug every single one of them," she wrote, "and tell them how beautiful I think they are."[55]

DISCUSSION QUESTIONS

1. Before reading this case, were you aware of Dove's Campaign for Real Beauty? If so, where have you encountered it? What are your impressions?
2. What were the advantages of doing Dove Evolution as a viral video rather than a television commercial?
3. Dove doesn't try to sell its products on the Campaign for Real Beauty web site. Is that a mistake?
4. If Dove asked you to help brainstorm new integrated tactics for the Campaign for Real Beauty, what might you suggest?

CASE STUDY **13.2**

Flunking History: Umbro and the Holocaust

Reebok, a manufacturer of athletic shoes and apparel, won a place in marketing's mythical Hall of Shame in 1997 when the company named a women's running shoe the Incubus.

Reebok representatives said they chose Incubus because it sounded like *incubate*. The name, they hoped, would evoke images of warmth and rebirth.[56]

They should have checked a dictionary. Here's how the *American Heritage Dictionary* defines *incubus:* "an evil spirit believed to descend upon and have sexual intercourse with women as they sleep."

The marketing misfire earned international headlines, gained a spot on several "year's dumbest ideas" lists, and even became a staple in college textbooks. Shoe marketers probably scared their new employees with the story, right?

Not at Umbro, apparently. In 2002, the British manufacturer of sports gear attracted international notoriety for naming a running shoe the Zyklon. In German, *zyklon* means *cyclone*—but during World War II, Zyklon B was the name of a gas used to murder millions of Jews and other prisoners in Nazi concentration camps. The deadly brutality of the camps and their gas chambers became known as the Holocaust.

When the Simon Wiesenthal Center, an international Jewish human rights organization, expressed outrage, Umbro quickly confessed ignorance. "The naming of the shoe is purely coincidental and was not intended to communicate any connotations," said an Umbro representative.[57]

"Umbro dropped the name but had no explanation," reported a columnist for United Press International. "It probably sounded cooler than their original choice, Black Plague #7."[58]

Other observers were equally stunned:

- "It's sick when you think about it," said a 78-year-old concentration camp survivor whose mother and two younger sisters died in Nazi gas chambers. "It is also very unprofessional."[59]

- "Considering the care with which companies normally choose titles for their products, I also find it hard to believe Umbro's assertion that the naming of the shoe was 'purely coincidental,'" said a Wiesenthal Center representative. "Any investigation of the word, on the Internet for example, quickly reveals its links to the Holocaust."[60]

- "How on earth did Umbro's marketing people, who are paid a fortune to think up new product names, fail to realize that this one could cause massive offense?" asked a London newspaper. "Do they know nothing about history?"[61]

Umbro lacked a good explanation. "I don't think the person who named them knew what it would mean to some people," said an Umbro representative. "We are currently looking at who chose it, but I can tell you it wasn't chosen deliberately for its unfortunate meaning. I think in the future, we will be checking the names we use more carefully."[62]

To that last comment, an Australian newspaper responded, "Too bloody right."[63]

If Umbro decides to learn from history, it might want to study Reebok's response to the Incubus debacle. Reebok may have helped restore its reputation by accepting responsibility and truly apologizing. "We apologize," said a Reebok representative in response to the crisis. "Certainly it is very inappropriate."[64]

In contrast, Umbro seemingly chose to apologize not for its action but, rather, for the offense its action "may" have caused. "I would like the opportunity to express our sincere regret that the Zyklon name may have upset someone," said an Umbro representative.[65]

College students generally take two or three history courses during their undergraduate years. Umbro and the ill-fated Zyklon provide an example of why those courses matter.

DISCUSSION QUESTIONS

1. How is a product's name part of an integrated marketing communications campaign?
2. What is your opinion of Umbro's response to the disaster?
3. If you had been an Umbro official at the time, what actions, if any, would you have suggested to end the problem and repair the damage?
4. What stories have you heard about other badly named products?

NOTES

1. "Spider-Man Can't Steal Bases," *Promo*, June 2004, 11.
2. E. W. Brody, "PR Is to Experience What Marketing Is to Expectations," *Public Relations Quarterly* 39, no. 2 (1994), online, LexisNexis.
3. "Marketing Management Survey 2006," report issued by *PR Week* and Manning, Selvage & Lee, 22 May 2006, online, www.prweek.com/us.
4. "Will Database Marketing Work in Health Care?" *Marketing Health Services* (fall 2001): online, LexisNexis.
5. John Dalla Costa, *The Ethical Imperative* (Reading, Mass.: Addison-Wesley, 1998), 178.
6. "Customer Relationship Management Programs: New Hot Business Issue," news release issued by PR Newswire, 28 August 2001, online, LexisNexis.
7. Don E. Schultz and Beth E. Barnes, *Strategic Brand Communication Campaigns* (Lincolnwood, Ill.: NTC Business Books, 1999), 44.
8. William P. Ehling, Jon White, and James E. Grunig, "Public Relations and Marketing Practices," in *Excellence in Public Relations and Communication Management,* ed. James E. Grunig (Hillsdale, N.J.: Lawrence Erlbaum, 1992), 390.
9. Glen M. Broom, Martha M. Lauzen, and Kerry Tucker, "Public Relations and Marketing: Dividing the Conceptual Domain and Operational Turf," *Public Relations Review* (fall 1991): 224.
10. "The Route to the Consumer," *PR Week*, 17 May 2004, online, www.prweek.com.
11. Jack Neff, "Bottom Line on PR," *Advertising Age*, 7 November 2005, online, LexisNexis.
12. Dave Barry, "North Dakota Name Change Lacks Direction," *Lawrence Journal-World*, 12 August 2001, 9B.
13. Don E. Schultz, Stanley I. Tannenbaum, and Robert F. Lauterborn, *Integrated Marketing Communications* (Chicago: NTC Business Books, 1993), 22.
14. "Sheryl Crow Launches New Revlon Colorist," news release issued by Revlon, 31 January 2007, online, LexisNexis.
15. Schultz, Tannenbaum, and Lauterborn, 107.
16. Schultz, Tannenbaum, and Lauterborn, 12–13.
17. Patricia Odell, "Text Messaging Gets a Cautious Reception in the U.S.," *Promo*, May 2003, 25.
18. Bob Wheatley, telephone interview by author, 24 March 1994.
19. Al Ries and Laura Ries, "Part 1: The Fall of Advertising," Ries & Ries Focusing Consultants, online, www.ries.com.
20. "The Route to the Consumer."

21. "Marketing Management Survey 2006."
22. John Shattock, "The Fall of Advertising and the Rise of PR," Shattock Communications and Research, online, www.shattock.net.nz.
23. "The Route to the Consumer."
24. Tom Duncan, "Is Your Marketing Communications Integrated?" *Advertising Age,* 24 January 1994, online, LexisNexis.
25. Matthew P. Gonring, "Putting Integrated Marketing Communications to Work Today," *Public Relations Quarterly* 39, no. 3 (1994), online, LexisNexis.
26. Schultz, Tannenbaum, and Lauterborn, 51.
27. Cliff McGoon, "Secrets of Building Influence," *Communication World,* March 1995, 18.
28. "What Is 'Direct Marketing'?" Direct Marketing Association, online, www.the-dma.org.
29. "The Route to the Consumer."
30. "Marketing Management Survey 2006."
31. Dan Frommer and Lisa Lerer, "Spam Could Spell Trouble for Wireless Industry, MSNBC, 12 October 2006, online, http://msnbc.com.
32. "State-of-the-Art in Direct Mail: Getting Ever Closer to the Customer," Knowledge @Wharton, 24 March 2004, online, www.knowledge.wharton.upenn.edu.
33. "Marketing Management Survey 2006."
34. "Working with Ad Agencies," *PR Week,* 19 July 2004, online, LexisNexis.
35. U.S. Federal Trade Commission, "You, Your Privacy Policy, and COPPA," U.S. Federal Trade Commission, online, www.ftc.gov.
36. Eve M. Caudill and Patrick E. Murphy, "Consumer Online Privacy: Legal and Ethical Issues," *Marketing and Public Policy* (spring 2000): online, LexisNexis; Ross D. Petty, "Marketing without Consent: Consumer Choice and Costs, Privacy, and Public Policy" (spring 2000): online, LexisNexis; Bodo Schlegelmilch, *Marketing Ethics: An International Perspective* (London: International Thomson Business Press, 1998), 100.
37. "Blueroads Granted the European Union Safe Harbor Privacy Seal," news release issued by Blueroads, 21 March 2007, online, www.blueroads.com.
38. "State-of-the-Art in Direct Mail: Getting Ever Closer to the Customer."
39. Sherri Deatherage Green, "PR Leads the Way," *PR Week,* 21 June 2004, online, LexisNexis.
40. "Marketing Management Survey 2006."
41. Stuart L. Esrock and John P. Ferré, "A Dichotomy of Privacy: Personal and Professional Attitudes of Marketers," *Business and Society Review* (spring 1999): 113, 121, 123.
42. "Enviro Activists Use Ethics to Drive Powerful PR Strategies," *PR News,* 12 March 2001, online, LexisNexis.
43. "Dove Campaign for Real Beauty Press Statement," news release issued by Unilever, 22 December 2006, online, LexisNexis.
44. Taylor Simmons, "Real Women, Real Results," *The Strategist,* August 2006, online, LexisNexis.
45. "Too Old to Be Young," news release issued by Unilever, 8 February 2007, online, LexisNexis.
46. Simmons.
47. Simmons.
48. Jack Neff, "A Real Beauty," *Advertising Age,* 30 October 2006, online, LexisNexis.

49. Simmons.
50. Laurel Wentz, "Real Beauty Gets Global Breakout via Evolution," *Advertising Age,* 8 January 2007, online, LexisNexis.
51. "Get the Picture!" news release issued by Unilever, 11 March 2005, online, LexisNexis.
52. Wentz.
53. Randall Rothenberg, "Dove Effort Gives Package-Goods Marketers Lessons for the Future," *Advertising Age,* 5 March 2007, online, LexisNexis.
54. Eleanor Trickett, "When Marketing Directly Reflects Everyday Women, Brands Take on Real-Life Credibility," *PR Week,* 22 August 2005, online, LexisNexis.
55. Campaign for Real Beauty, online, www.CampaignForRealBeauty.com, posted 13 April 2007.
56. "Foot in Mouth," *Financial Times,* 24 February 1997, online, LexisNexis.
57. Jonathan Petre, "Protests by Jews Halt the Zyklon Sports Shoe" (London) *Daily Telegraph,* 29 August 2002, online, LexisNexis.
58. Joe Bob Briggs, "Joe Bob's Week in Review," United Press International, 16 January 2003, online, LexisNexis.
59. Graham Hiscott, "Umbro Drops Name after 'Nazi Gas' Blunder," Press Association, 28 August 2002, online, LexisNexis.
60. Hiscott.
61. Victor Lewis-Smith, "Sporting Soles of Indiscretion" (London) *Mirror,* 14 September 2002, online, LexisNexis.
62. "Fury Over Nazi Gas Sports Shoe Name," BBC, 29 August 2002, online, www.news.bbc.co.uk.
63. David Moore, "Fascist Fashion Fad Flops," *Townsville* (Australia) *Sun,* 31 August 2002, online, LexisNexis.
64. Helen Kennedy, "Reebok Exorcises Its Shoes" (New York) *Daily News,* 20 February 1997, online, LexisNexis.
65. Tovah Lazaroff, "Zyklon Beige Sport Shoe Renamed," *Jerusalem Post,* 29 August 2002, online, LexisNexis.

Cross-Cultural Communication

OBJECTIVES

After studying this chapter, you will be able to

- describe broad areas that historically have distinguished one culture from another

- explain the differences between a culture and a public

- discuss traditional obstacles to successful cross-cultural communication

- describe a nine-step process organizations and individuals can use to achieve effective cross-cultural communication

KEY TERMS

communication, p. 445
communication model, p. 445
cross-cultural, p. 445
culture, p. 437
decoding, p. 446
demographics, p. 437
encoding, p. 446
geodemographics, p. 437
globalization, p. 437
Hofstede's cultural dimensions, p. 451
psychographics, p. 437
stereotyping, p. 447

East Meets West

You are the new senior communications specialist for a multinational producer of breakfast cereals. Your company is based in the United States, and you are eager to begin traveling internationally. You've been to Mexico and Canada but have never been overseas. The director of corporate communications has just asked you to launch an internal social network—a kind of in-house MySpace—and a related magazine for employees in the three countries in which your company operates: the United States, Spain, and Japan.

You quickly learn the names of the company's senior communications officials in Spain and Japan and, with the director's permission, invite them to the United States to help plan the network and magazine. You know that a lot rides on the success of these meetings. You're new with the company, and you want to impress your employers. Your guests from Spain and Japan report to you, and you don't want them to entertain doubts about their new boss. And you know that the director of corporate communications wants a great project that will impress the company's chief executive officer.

As the three-day meeting approaches, you're excited as you review the preparations. You've scheduled a comfortable meeting room, reserved tables in your city's best restaurants, and arranged entertainment for two evenings. You're startled, however, when a colleague asks about cultural differences.

Cultural differences? You will be dealing with individuals from highly developed economies who, in addition to their native languages, speak fluent English. Could there really be important cultural differences? And could those differences affect the success of your project?

That's a risk you must avoid, but what can you do? How do you cope with the challenges of cross-cultural communication?

Cultures: Realities and Definitions

The job seemed easy for the U.S.-based poultry company: It wanted to translate its English-language slogan—"It takes a tough man to make a tender chicken"—into Spanish. But the Spanish rendition may have startled Hispanic consumers: "It takes a sexually aroused man to make a chick affectionate."[1]

Affection was in short supply in 2006 when retail giant Wal-Mart fired its new senior vice president of marketing communications, advertising superstar Julie Roehm. "In retrospect, Julie Roehm working at Wal-Mart looks like a match made in hell," declared *Advertising Age*. "Wal-Mart and its culture rejected her like a bad kidney."[2] Recruited to enliven Wal-Mart's lackluster marketing campaigns, Roehm reportedly irritated the retailer's leaders with a flashy management style ill-suited to the Arkansas-based company. "Her style and marketing ideas were too much for the company's culture, and she rubbed people the wrong way," concluded *Business Week*.[3] When Roehm sued for wrongful termination, Wal-Mart filed a countersuit that included allegations of broken rules, poor ethics, and an "inappropriate romantic relationship."[4]

Promoters of a Seattle-area rave—a huge, uninhibited dance party—unintentionally offended Muslims when they lifted Arabic passages from the Koran, the holy book of Islam, to decorate a brochure. Devout Muslims honor the Koran so much that they wash their hands and mouths three times before touching and reading from the book.

"This is a disgrace to Islam," said a spokesman for a Seattle mosque. "The activities in raves are totally immoral."

The brochure's designer apologized and confessed that he found the passages in a school textbook. "We had no idea what any of it meant," he said. "It looked good on [the brochure]. It is a beautiful language. And we had a desert and a camel in there. It was a theme."[5]

The theme of these three anecdotes is cross-cultural communication. Each of these damaging mishaps occurred when different cultures intentionally or unintentionally met. In each case, important values were at issue. Those values grew, in part, out of **demographics** (nonattitudinal characteristics), **psychographics** (attitudinal characteristics), and **geodemographics** (characteristics based on where a person or group lives). But the values grew from more than these three "graphics." The values shaped and were shaped by unique cultures.

The term **culture,** in the sense of a group of people unified by shared characteristics, defies precise definition. "It seems obvious from the use of the word in our everyday language that it is impregnated with multiple meanings," says Anindita Niyogi Balslev of the Center for Cultural Research in the Netherlands.[6] In fact, as early as 1952 scholars had identified more than 150 definitions of *culture.*[7] The *Dictionary of Anthropology* defines a culture as "a social group that is smaller than a civilization but larger than an industry,"[8] with *industry* being an anthropological term for a small community. A culture, therefore, is usually larger than a public. In fact, a culture may consist of countless different publics, all of which are influenced by the traits of that culture. As if that weren't enough, the concept of culture can transcend a group of people: Culture is also the set "behavior patterns, arts, beliefs, institutions, and all other products of human work and thought" characteristic of that group.[9]

Why study cross-cultural communication? "Now, more than ever before in human history, more people are coming into contact with people from cultures other than their own," says Robert Gibson, author of *Intercultural Business Communication.* Gibson cites several reasons for the growth of cross-cultural contacts, including improved travel methods, the Internet, and increasingly diverse workforces.[10] To that list, we might add the increasing number of mergers and acquisitions in the business world, the growth of democratic governments around the world, and the consequent increase in international trade. Many of these forces help fuel **globalization,** the growing economic interdependence of the world's people.

Relationship-building errors such as those of the poultry company, Wal-Mart and Roehm, and the Seattle rave occur because, in the words of Stephen Banks, author of

Multicultural Public Relations, "scant attention is paid in research or practice to the predicaments of culturally diverse populations and the necessity for learning to communicate effectively across cultural differences."[11] Recently, a representative of the National Association of Corporate Directors recommended that, to negotiate successfully with diverse cultures throughout the world, each U.S. business should create an Office of Foreign Affairs to study trends, politics, moods, and opinions in regions where the business wishes to operate.[12] The authors of this book respectfully suggest that such an office should already exist: the organization's public relations department.

International Public Relations

Not all cross-cultural communication involves relationships between two nations. For example, the Wal-Mart–Roehm situation involved the awkward marriage of two business styles. And the wealth of ethnic groups within the United States, Canada, and other nations can make cross-cultural communication an everyday occurrence. In the current global economy, however, when public relations practitioners study unfamiliar cultures, they often are studying consumers and business partners in other nations. "Cultural diversity and identity," says the author of *Multicultural Public Relations,* "tend strongly to conform to national borders."[13] For example, a recent survey of European tourists found that 25 percent of visitors to Italy went there hoping for a love affair with an Italian male. Only Italy's natural beauty scored higher; the lovers outscored museums and other attractions. Right or wrong, a large percentage of European tourists believe that romance, passion, and availability are cultural characteristics of Italian males.[14]

Musician Randy Newman has a satirical song that envisions the world becoming "just another American town"—a humorously offbeat premise for a song but a disastrous notion for international public relations. If the world were a town, it would be stunningly diverse—not at all a representation of a culture familiar to most students. A popular children's book, *If the World Were a Village,* shows that if Earth were a village of 100 people, current demographic ratios would make the village look like this:[15]

- 24 residents would have no electricity; most of the others would use it only at night to light their homes.
- 22 would speak Chinese; 9 would speak English; 7 would speak Spanish.
- 20 would earn less than a dollar a day.
- 17 would not be able to read or write.
- 10 would be younger than 5 years old; 39 would be younger than age 19; 1 would be older than age 79.
- 7 would own a computer.

Successful international public relations recognizes such diversity. Successful international public relations attempts to create harmonious, productive relationships through well-researched cross-cultural communication.

ТОРГОВЛЯ С АМЕРИКОЙ

СПРАВОЧНИК ПО ПРОГРАММАМ ПРАВИТЕЛЬСТВА США

Публикация BISNIS -
Службы деловой информации о странах Содружества независимых государств
Министерства торговли США

Business Guide An indication of the increasing importance of cross-cultural communication is this U.S. Department of Commerce Russian-language publication, *Doing Business in America.* (Courtesy of the U.S. Department of Commerce)

Cultural Attributes

Without a research strategy, studying a different culture can seem impossible. Where do we start? What information should we gather? Fortunately, social scientists and business experts have created systems for categorizing important cultural attributes. One of the best-known systems was created by marketing professional Marlene Rossman.[16] Rossman's system distinguishes among cultures by analyzing attitudes regarding eight characteristics. Let's examine each to see how it can differ from culture to culture.

Attitudes about Time

Different cultures have different attitudes about time. In some Latin American nations, a dinner party scheduled for 8 P.M. may not really begin until near midnight. In other cultures, arriving later than 8 P.M. would insult your hosts. In some cultures, a designated time is a flexible guideline; in others, it is a specific target. On a working vacation in Zurich, Switzerland, one of your authors was warned by Swiss colleagues to avoid the center of the city on a particular Thursday afternoon; college students would be holding a spontaneous demonstration at that time, he was told. A scheduled spontaneous demonstration: something to be expected from a nation famed for making clocks and other timepieces.

In a study of national attitudes toward time, *American Demographics* magazine reported that, of 31 nations studied, Switzerland ranked first in terms of a rapid, time-oriented pace of life. The United States ranked in the middle at number 16, and Mexico ranked last. In general, Japan and Western European countries had the fastest pace of life. Developing nations in Africa, Asia, the Middle East, and Latin America had the slowest, most flexible pace.[17]

In our East Meets West scenario, differing attitudes toward time could affect the success of your meetings. Japanese tend to be punctual about business meetings. If a meeting is scheduled for 9 A.M., businesspeople in Japan and the United States generally are ready to sit at the table and begin at that hour. In Spain, however, businesspeople are more casual about specified starting times. Roger Axtell, author of *Do's and Taboos around the World,* says that in Spain "the only time punctuality is taken seriously is when attending a bullfight."[18] Is that wrong? No: It's just different.

And how about early-afternoon meetings? No problem for your Japanese guest, but will your Spanish guest expect a traditional siesta at that time? In Spain and several other nations in Europe and Latin America, businesses often close from lunch until late afternoon.

Attitudes about Formality

Should you address a new business associate from another nation by his or her first name? Should you hug? Bow? Shake hands? The answers depend, of course, on cultural preferences. As a rule, however, formality is safer than informality in new business relationships.

A Quieter Quack When AFLAC, a leading international insurance company, recently cast its famous duck in Japanese TV commercials, the company introduced a kinder, gentler quack. Japanese culture frowns on yelling, an AFLAC representative explained. (Courtesy of American Family Life Assurance Company of Columbus—AFLAC)

Syrians often embrace new acquaintances. Pakistanis shake hands, though rarely a man with a woman. Zambians shake hands with the left hand supporting the right. Norwegians rarely use first names until relationships are well established. Japanese almost never use first names in business settings.

What do cross-cultural experts say about the visitors you're expecting for your project planning meeting? A warm handshake and even an accompanying pat on the back would be acceptable as you greet your Spanish visitor. The Spanish make no distinction about shaking hands with men or women. With your Japanese guest, however, be prepared to bow, even though he or she may offer to shake hands. You can flatter your Japanese guest by bowing first. In Japan, the person who initiates a bow is acknowledging the high social status of the other person. If you exchange business cards with your Japanese visitor, bow slightly and extend yours with both hands. You should accept your visitor's card in the same manner and should look at it respectfully after receiving it.[19]

Attitudes about Individualism

People in the United States pride themselves on the rugged individualism that turned a diverse group of immigrants into a powerful nation of highly mobile individuals. It's comparatively rare in our society to live one's life in the town of one's birth surrounded by family. Other cultures, however, especially those of Asian and Hispanic origin, often place more emphasis on preserving extended families. Chinese names, for example, place the family name before the individual name.

Japanese businesspeople in particular see themselves as part of a team; in fact, only 8 percent of Japanese adults say they respect entrepreneurs.[20] An individual may speak on behalf of an organization, but not until he or she has painstakingly built consensus on the issue under discussion. The Japanese call the consensus-building process

VALUES STATEMENT 14.1

Special Olympics

Founded in 1968, Special Olympics is a nonprofit program of sports training and competition for individuals with mental retardation.

SPECIAL OLYMPICS OATH

Let me win. But if I cannot win, let me be brave in the attempt.

—Special Olympics web site

nemawashi; it precedes virtually all important organizational decisions. "As a result," says Sanae Kobayashi, an executive with LBS Company in Tokyo, "decision making in Japanese organizations usually takes more time than it does in the West. However, as compensation, in Japan the execution is made with more speed and completeness."[21]

Because of the importance of *nemawashi* throughout their culture, the Japanese are reluctant to say no. In your project planning meeting, for example, it would be unusual for your Japanese guest to veto a particular proposal. Instead, he or she might meet the idea with thoughtful silence and a polite "If only . . ."

Attitudes about Rank and Hierarchy

In cultural terms, rank and hierarchy extend beyond organizations: They exist within society itself. India, for example, still struggles to overthrow a traditional caste system of Brahmans—often Hindu priests—at the top and so-called untouchables at the bottom. Knowing the social status of a business associate and understanding the consequent signs of respect he or she expects can be essential to successful cross-cultural communications. For example, your Spanish guest would be honored to be seated at your right during meals—a sign of respect in Spain. And when you initiate a bowing sequence with your Japanese guest, you courteously suggest that he or she outranks you.[22]

Attitudes about Religion

Knowing the religious conventions and traditions of a culture can help prevent unintended errors that can hamper cross-cultural communication. For example, Muslims fast from dawn to sunset during the holy month of Ramadan. Inviting an Islamic business associate to a working lunch during that time could inadvertently suggest a lack of respect for his or her religious beliefs. The Jewish Sabbath extends from Friday evening to Saturday evening and, in Judaism, is a day of rest. Scheduling a Friday evening business dinner in Israel, where Judaism is the dominant religion, could be a serious cultural faux pas.

Cultural differences regarding religion became starkly apparent in 2005 when a Danish newspaper published editorial cartoons depicting the Islamic prophet Muhammad. Many Muslims feel that images of Muhammad are blasphemous, and riots broke out in Syria, Iran, Lebanon, and other nations. Meanwhile, believing the controversy threatened freedom of the press, newspapers throughout North America and Europe reprinted the cartoons. As different groups—religious and otherwise—clashed worldwide, the death toll exceeded 100.[23] An apology from the Danish newspaper failed to end the violence, and bloodshed continued for months.[24]

QuickBreak 14.1

The Melting-Pot Myth

Much of this chapter focuses on cultures beyond the borders of the United States. Can we assume, then, that the United States is a uniform hot-dogs-and-apple-pie culture? Hardly.

In *America's Diversity*, a study of 200 years of U.S. Census data, the Population Research Bureau reported, "Residential separation of the races continues to be so pronounced that sociologists Douglas Massey and Nancy Denton have called it 'American Apartheid.' "[25] (Apartheid is the former South African policy of enforced separation of races.) A national survey of U.S. citizens indicates that *apartheid* may be too strong a word for some: 38 percent want a more uniform culture; 31 percent want cultural differences to remain; and 29 percent lack strong opinions on the matter.[26]

But can culture and race really be linked? Studies show that race can indeed be an indicator of a unique culture. A recent survey of racial and ethnic groups within the United States, for example, concluded that blacks, Asians, Hispanics, and non-Hispanic whites (a U.S. Census Bureau designation) spend their time in different ways. Asians spend more time each week on education than do blacks, Hispanics, or whites. Blacks devote more time to religion each week than do the other racial and ethnic groups. Hispanics spend more time caring for their children than do the other groups. Whites spend more time at work than Asians, blacks, or Hispanics.[27]

"The trend in every aspect of American life is toward greater cultural, ethnic, and linguistic diversity," says marketing expert Marlene Rossman. "Not only are minority groups increasing in size, they are also not assimilating the way many minority and ethnic (especially immigrant) groups did in the past. . . . Our cultural model is becoming the mosaic, not the melting pot."[28]

Attitudes about Taste and Diet

For many public relations practitioners, cuisine is the reward for mastering the subtleties of cross-cultural communication. Perhaps it's arroz con pollo (chicken with rice) in Costa Rica or couscous in Algeria or bratwurst in Germany or grits in the southern United States. The culinary diversity of the world's cultures is dazzling and gratifying—but also rife with opportunities for serious blunders. Religion and other cultural influences often prohibit the consumption of certain foods. Hindus don't eat beef; cattle are exalted in that religion, which encompasses the belief that souls return to Earth again and again as different life forms. Strict Judaism forbids the consumption of pork products and shellfish, which are considered unclean.

Attitudes about Colors, Numbers, and Symbols

What's the unlucky number in mainstream U.S. culture? Thirteen, of course. How about in Japanese culture? It's four. One of your authors learned that the hard way when he titled an article for a multinational corporate magazine "Four from Japan." Every culture develops an unofficial language of colors, numbers, and symbols that often speaks louder than words. "It's worth knowing that the color white denotes death, to the Chinese," *New Zealand Management* magazine cautioned readers who do business in China. "So no gift should ever be wrapped in white paper. Similarly a bouquet of white lilies would be a definite no-no."[29]

Symbols can be just as fraught with meaning as colors and numbers. For example, most of us interpret the thumbs-up symbol used for case studies in this book as a sign of approval. In Australia and Nigeria, however, the symbol and the gesture mean anything but approval. In those societies, the upward thumb is an obscene sign of disrespect.[30]

Attitudes about Assimilation and Acculturation

How quickly can members of one culture adjust to the traditions of another? How accepting are people of new ideas and nontraditional thinking? Such flexibility can help characterize a culture. The more a culture resists outside influences, the more powerful its own traditions can become. The French Academy, for example, which is the legal watchdog of the French language as it's spoken in France, has officially banned English terms such as *hot dog* and *drugstore*. Russian President Vladimir Putin has begun a similar anti-English campaign, instituting fines and even imprisonment for Russians who used English derivatives such as *biznismeni* for *businessmen*.[31] More tolerant is the attitude of former South African President Nelson Mandela, who drew cheers from young adults attending a rock concert in London by declaring, "I am now almost 100 years old, but I am so proud because my roots are in South Africa but my gaze reaches beyond the horizon to places like Britain where we are tied together by unbreakable bonds."[32]

Sometimes assimilation and acculturation occur so gradually that the process escapes our notice. More than one observer, for example, has noted that U.S. dominance of the technology and content of the Internet is subtly piping U.S. influences into offices and homes around the world. Says Andre Kaspi, a professor at the Sorbonne in Paris, "You have to know English if you want to use the Internet. . . . The main difference now in favor of American culture is the importance of technology—telephone, Internet, films. . . . American influence is growing. It's so easy to get access to U.S. culture; there are no barriers."[33]

No doubt true. But any public relations practitioner who assumes that the world has become one big U.S.-based culture runs the risk of studying a different phenomenon: the culture of the unemployment line.

To Rossman's list of eight characteristics, we might add one more: attitudes about business communication. For example, although executives in the United States and Canada frequently use voice mail and e-mail, executives in European nations generally prefer "real-time," simultaneous communications; thus the use of cell phones in Europe exceeds usage in United States and Canada. Executives in France and Germany, however, prefer paper-based communications to other forms; their use of postal services and fax machines exceeds usage rates in other nations.[34] Part of successful cross-cultural communication involves learning how members of other cultures prefer to receive their business messages.

QUICK CHECK

1. What is the purpose of the analytical system created by Marlene Rossman?
2. Would it be fair to say that the United States is all one culture? Why or why not?
3. What is the difference between a culture and a public?

Cross-Cultural Communication: Definitions and Dangers

Clearly, this chapter uses the term *cross-cultural communication* to refer to exchanges of messages among the members of different cultures. But it's worth stopping to ask what, exactly, is meant by **cross-cultural.** Many sociologists and communication specialists use the term *intercultural* to denote exchanges of various kinds between cultures. Your authors, like many public relations practitioners, prefer the term *cross-cultural* because it prompts an image of crossing a border, of going into partially unknown territory. *Cross-cultural* urges caution and encourages you to stay constantly aware of the obstacles to successful communication between members of different cultures.

And what do we mean by **communication**? We mean more than words can say. In Chapter 13, for example, we noted that every aspect of a product sends a message to consumers. Besides the verbal messages of news releases and advertisements, a product's price, packaging, and distribution all send nonverbal messages to potential purchasers. Consumers in West African communities were horrified when one U.S. company tried to sell its popular brand of baby food in their stores. The labels featured a smiling baby—very popular in the United States, but intensely disturbing in a culture that relies on pictures to identify the contents of jars and cans.[35] Briefly, by *communication,* we mean any exchange of information—verbal and/or nonverbal—between the sender and the receiver of a message.

Encoding and Decoding

In Chapter 5 we examined a basic **communication model,** which, as you'll recall, looks like this:

More complex versions of this basic model include two elements that become particularly important in communication between cultures: encoding and decoding. **Encoding** involves the sender's selection of words, images, and other forms of communication that create the message. **Decoding** involves the receiver's attempt to produce meaning from the sender's message. With those additional elements, the communication model looks like this:

In successful cross-cultural communication, senders must understand how a message will be decoded before they can effectively encode it. The perils of encoding errors are illustrated by yet another U.S. company's adventures abroad. When the Coca-Cola Company translated its name into Chinese, the phonetic version—KeKou Kela—instructed Chinese consumers to "Bite the wax tadpole."[36] It's hard to guess who was most surprised by that particular cross-cultural encoding–decoding glitch.

Even though an organization's message may need different encodings for different cultures, the message should ideally remain shaped by the values that unite the organization. A successful organization cannot embrace one set of values with the elderly in South Africa, a different set of values with women in China, a third set of values with Russian immigrants in Australia, and so on. Such duplicity would be more than dishonest; maintaining so many different personalities would be exhausting. In successful organizations, all messages emanate from a set of clearly understood core values, as well as from the business goals that grow out of those values. Says Jean-Louis Tronc, director of human resources and corporate communications for DuPont de Nemours of France, "There are a certain number of global values within a company which must remain the same everywhere."[37] As we note many times throughout this book, successful public relations is a values-driven process.

Gestures and Clothing

Our broad definition of communication also applies to interpersonal communication. Our gestures, clothing, and expressions can be every bit as communicative as our words. In Taiwan, blinking at someone is considered an insult. In the Islamic faith, shoes are absolutely forbidden on the grounds of mosques. In many Asian cultures, shoes are removed and left at the front doors of residences. The A-OK expression made by forming a circle of the thumb and forefinger and raising the other three fingers is, like thumbs-up, a sign of approval in the United States. But in Japan it's a symbol for money. In Australia and some Latin American nations, it's an obscene gesture. During a 1950s visit to a Latin American country, Vice President Richard Nixon grandly made the A-OK gesture—and was stunned by an immediate chorus of boos.[38]

Because people from almost every culture use their hands when they speak, gestures—more so than clothing or expressions—can send unintended messages during cross-cultural communication. Speaking to a group of journalists in the Central Asian nation of Kyrgyzstan, one of your authors illustrated a point by bringing one fist down on top of the other two or three times. Halting in midsentence, his shocked interpreter leaned over and hissed in his ear that he was signaling, in the crudest possible way, that he wanted to make love to his audience. Fortunately, your author's stricken expression led his audience to forgive him with friendly laughter. That story has two morals: Cross-cultural mistakes can be very embarrassing—and people can be very forgiving if they sense your good will.

Stereotyping

Another sure ticket to failure in cross-cultural communication is **stereotyping:** the assumption that all members of a particular culture act, think, feel, and believe in the same way. Are all Hispanics family-oriented? Are all Swiss punctual? Are all Japanese polite? Are all U.S. citizens blunt? Do all teenagers like loud music? Do all baby boomers like the Beatles? Cultures *do* exist, but they consist of individuals, none of whom are exactly alike. "After all," says Harvard Professor H. L. Gates Jr., "culture is always a conversation among different voices."[39]

Finally, public relations practitioners should be prepared for the distinct possibility that their colleagues from different cultures *also* are studying cross-cultural communication. Your Japanese guest, for example, may insist on shaking hands rather than bowing. Your Spanish guest may ask for an early-afternoon meeting to show his or her willingness to adapt to your culture. So who prevails in such complicated situations? Often, it's easiest to follow the culture of the host, but the host still should seek opportunities to honor the cultures of his or her guests. An abundance of courtesy is a good beginning for cross-cultural communication.

Cross-cultural communication has become an unavoidable challenge for the public relations profession. One recent study shows that two-thirds of international business mergers fail because "cultures and people are often incompatible, national differences emerging."[40] Says Elizabeth Howard, principal partner of an international consulting firm, "Today it is difficult, probably impossible, to find a business that has not been affected in one way or another by the new global economy." Indeed, it's not unusual for farmers from the midwestern United States to find themselves part of trade delegations in Asia or Latin America, seeking new markets for

U.S. agricultural products. And those farmers, like others engaged in cross-cultural business discussions, constantly confront the question posed by sociologist and anthropologist David Howes: "What happens when the culture of production and the culture of consumption are not the same?"[41]

These cultural gulfs must be bridged if the producers and the consumers are to achieve their goals. In the next section we offer a nine-step process that can help organizations and individuals achieve successful cross-cultural communication.

QUICK CHECK

1. What do *encoding* and *decoding* mean?
2. Should an organization's core values change as it communicates with different cultures?
3. What does *stereotyping* mean? How can it threaten successful cross-cultural communication?

Achieving Successful Cross-Cultural Public Relations: A Process

At this point in our chapter, two facts are clear: Cross-cultural communication can be difficult—and it is inevitable. Painstaking encoding and decoding of cross-cultural messages have become everyday challenges. Given that reality, how can public relations practitioners in the 21st century become effective cross-cultural communicators? We recommend a process consisting of nine stages: awareness, commitment, research, local partnership, diversity, testing, evaluation, advocacy, and continuing education. We begin with awareness. If public relations practitioners aren't sensitive to the presence or potential difficulties of a cross-cultural encounter, they have little hope of communicating effectively.

Stage One: Awareness

You can start enhancing your awareness of cross-cultural situations right now—by studying a foreign language and enrolling in liberal arts courses that allow you to explore the traits and traditions of other cultures. If your college or university has an international students association, consider joining it. If it has a study abroad program, plan to spend a semester in another country. Higher education offers you rare opportunities to discover that the rest of the world doesn't think, act, dress, eat, and communicate as you do.

Achieving fluency in a foreign language can keep you from being the butt of an old joke that remains all too current. As the joke goes, someone who speaks three languages is trilingual; someone who speaks two languages is bilingual; someone who speaks one language is a U.S. citizen. English indeed has become the language of international commerce, but learning to speak the language of a foreign business acquaintance—even if you master only a few key phrases—may heighten your

QuickBreak 14.2

Diversity in Public Relations

"To be more effective in our increasingly socially complex society," says Reed Byrum, former president of the Public Relations Society of America, "achieving diversity is more than just a matter of inclusiveness. The public relations profession needs to vigorously recruit minorities into the profession and into leadership positions."[42]

So is public relations an ethnically, culturally diverse profession? In a word, no.

The table below shows the percentages of traditional minority groups in public relations compared with their percentages in the U.S. population:[43]

Group & U.S. Percentage	PR Agencies	Corporate Departments
Black: 12.8	4.8	7.4
Asian/Pacific Islander: 4.4	3.7	4.0
Hispanic: 14.1	6.2	4.2
Native American: 1.0	0.4	0.3

In public relations, minority-group practitioners fill 3.9 percent of senior management positions and 13 percent of nonmanagerial positions. Though not a minority group in public relations, women fill only 38 percent of senior management positions.[44] The Public Relations Coalition reports that percentages for other historically disadvantaged groups, including disabled and gay or lesbian practitioners, are too underreported to calculate accurately.[45]

Despite those less-than-satisfactory percentages, the diversity outlook in public relations does contain some bright spots. PRSA's National Diversity Committee offers diversity speakers and "Diversity Tool Kits" to local chapters.[46] And since 2003, *PR Week* magazine and public relations agency Hill & Knowlton have published the annual *PR Week* Diversity Survey, which details minority-group percentages within the profession as well as efforts to improve those numbers.

"If we're supposed to be communicating with the public, surely we have to be reflective of the population and understand how to communicate with them," says MaryLee Sachs, chairman of Hill & Knowlton USA. "I cannot imagine why PR pros wouldn't see this as a critical aspect of doing business."[47]

---

sensitivity to cross-cultural issues. More important, perhaps, learning a second language can improve the success of your cross-cultural communication by creating good will. On business in Paris, one of your authors was able to persuade a new acquaintance to work late by using his shaky knowledge of French, gained in college. When the Parisian apologized, in English, for missing a deadline, your author was able to respond *C'est la même chose pour tout le monde, n'est-ce pas?*—roughly, "It happens everywhere, doesn't it?" The Parisian was surprised that an American could speak even bad French. The conversation sputtered along in French until the amused Parisian switched back to English and agreed to stay late to finish the project.

Organizations throughout the United States are imitating the college experience by sponsoring courses in multiculturalism and cross-cultural communication. Chicago-based Edelman, one of the world's largest public relations agencies, prides itself on the rigor and comprehensiveness of its diversity "boot camp" for managers. "For us, diversity isn't just about what color you are or what gender you are," says

Michelle Deese, Edelman's senior manager of diversity and talent development. "[Diversity] includes everyone, even the white folks."[48]

Another powerful way to increase awareness is to diversify the workplace, bringing multiculturalism and cross-cultural communication into the everyday business of the office. This strategy will be discussed in greater detail below.

Stage Two: Commitment

Reporters have a technique called "parachute journalism"—dropping into a locality the reporter doesn't know well to write a quick story about that same little-known locality. Journalists aren't proud of parachute journalism. Nor should public relations practitioners be proud of using a similar strategy in their profession: parachuting, so to speak, into a little-known culture to do some hit-and-run relationship building. Successful cross-cultural communication requires personal commitment, as well as commitment from an organization's highest levels, to doing the arduous background work that allows the effective encoding and decoding of messages to and from another culture.

Stage Three: Research

Commitment implies a willingness to do the research demanded by successful cross-cultural communication. Standard reference sources for this research include magazines such as *Communication World* and the *American Demographics* web site at www.adage.com; books such as Roger Axtell's *Do's and Taboos around the World* and *Gestures: The Do's and Taboos of Body Language around the World;* and online resources such as the web site sponsored by the International Trade Administration, a division of the U.S. Department of Commerce. The ITA web site includes information on business etiquette in almost every nation around the world. Hosting a meeting for colleagues from Botswana? Confirm your meeting 24 hours ahead of time, and don't be offended if your guests arrive late. Don't call them by their first names until they initiate that practice, and don't schedule the meeting for September 30: That's Botswana Day. Need more information? See ITA's Market Research Library at www.export.gov.

Believe it or not, the Central Intelligence Agency also makes available some of its highly detailed data on different nations around the world. Check out the CIA's *World Factbook* at www.cia.gov.

A good reference librarian can steer you to other current sources. Such research might help you remember to take off your shoes when you enter the hotel room of your Japanese guest in our East Meets West scenario.

Stage Four: Local Partnership

No matter how much research you conduct, you'll never know as much about a foreign culture as does someone reared in it. When an organization begins a long-term cross-cultural relationship, it should consider bringing members of that culture into its communications team. "You must have representation on the ground in different

QuickBreak 14.3

Hofstede's Cultural Dimensions

Among the strategies for analyzing cultural diversity, the gold standard may well be **Hofstede's cultural dimensions.** In the 1970s, Dutch sociologist Geert Hofstede analyzed cultural information gathered by the multinational corporation IBM, which was trying to learn why particular employee relations strategies worked in some countries but failed in others. Hofstede's extensive research identified five "dimensions" that distinguish one culture from another:[49]

1. *Power distance* measures how tolerant a society is about unequally distributed power. Countries with a high acceptance of power distance include Mexico and France. Countries with a low acceptance include Austria and the United States.

2. *Individualism versus collectivism* contrasts loyalty to oneself with loyalty to a larger group. Countries in Asia and Latin America gravitate toward collectivism, while the United States, Canada, and most European nations gravitate toward individualism.

3. *Masculinity versus femininity* contrasts competitiveness with compassion and nurturing. Mas-

culine nations include the United States, Germany, and Japan. Feminine nations include Sweden and Spain.

4. *Uncertainty avoidance* measures how well a society tolerates ambiguity. Nations that avoid uncertainty include Germany and Japan. Nations that tolerate ambiguity include Great Britain and the United States.

5. *Long-term orientation* measures a society's willingness to consider the traditions of the past and carry them into the future. China and other East Asian nations have a long-term orientation, while the United States has a short-term orientation.

Hofstede's national profiles, included in his 1991 book *Cultures and Organizations: Software of the Mind,* may be able to help you with the scenario that opens this chapter. For example, your Japanese associate comes from a masculine culture, while your Spanish colleague comes from a feminine culture. Several web sites, including www.clearlycultural .com, also include Hofstede's national profiles.

---

parts of the world, but you should be extremely cautious about hiring a major global PR agency," says Robert Wakefield, former chairman of the International Section of the Public Relations Society of America. "Instead, tap into the worldwide network of small local agencies or talented native PR consultants who can guide you through the maze of PR issues in their own country."[50]

Stage Five: Diversity

Not all different cultures are beyond the borders of the United States. As QuickBreak 14.1 notes, the United States is hardly a melting pot; instead, it's a mosaic of different cultures. Diversity within an organization's public relations team can help ensure successful cross-cultural communication at home. Furthermore, it can increase an organization's awareness of cultural differences, which benefits communication both at home and abroad. Pitney Bowes, a multinational message-delivery company, believes that a diverse workforce boosts company profits.[51]

Stage Six: Testing

As every actor knows, it's better to bomb in rehearsal than on opening night. When possible, test your relationship-building tactics on trusted members of the culture you plan to address. For example, in this chapter's East Meets West scenario, you could show a detailed itinerary of your business and entertainment plans to natives of Japan and Spain. You just might learn, for example, that Spanish business dinners don't begin until late evening—often past 9 P.M.—and that Japanese business dinners can go on for hours and often end in nightclubs.[52]

Stage Seven: Evaluation

A constant goal in public relations is to learn from our successes as well as from our mistakes. As soon as possible, public relations professionals should evaluate the effectiveness of completed cross-cultural communication efforts, seeking ways to reinforce the good and revise the bad. In the East Meets West scenario, for example, did your Japanese guest wince when you offered her a gift as you met her at the airport? Your consequent research might show that although the Japanese enjoy receiving

QuickBreak 14.4

Double-Whammy Culture Clash

Merging two company cultures into one new business can be tough. But when those two companies come from different nations, the merger faces a cultural double-whammy. A classic corporate culture clash occurred when German car manufacturer Daimler-Benz bought U.S.-based Chrysler Corporation in 1998.

"These two cultures . . . were bound to collide," said a former U.S. auto executive.[53]

"Problems are caused when an acquirer's corporate culture fails to mesh with that of its new subsidiary," wrote a British business analyst. "That's the biggest single risk in all cross-border acquisitions."[54]

Still, optimism abounded when the two companies joined forces. "The merger of Daimler and Chrysler was hailed as a marriage made in heaven," reported a British financial analyst. "But the honeymoon was shortlived."[55] Within three years, the new DaimlerChrysler was worth only half its initial value, key Chrysler executives had resigned, and the new company was preparing to close six

Chrysler factories.[56] Observers inside and outside the company knew what to blame: clashing cultures.

"[Germans] can't understand this cultural mentality that is forever focusing on the bottom line and quarterly results," said an industry consultant.[57]

"German workforces expect to be consulted at all stages of any strategic deal, while at Chrysler the unions aim to beat down the management and vice versa," said another.[58]

"In the case of DaimlerChrysler, there was a total clash of cultures," said a British business professor.[59]

All sides should have listened to an investment banker who had worked with both companies before the merger. "It could take them at least a year to learn each other's true character and identity," the banker warned. "That's why these transatlantic mergers are always trickier than they look on paper."[60]

DaimlerChrysler ended the clash when it sold Chrysler in 2007.

gifts, they often are embarrassed if they cannot reciprocate immediately.[61] The gift may have been a blunder, but it was a valuable misstep: It taught you to be sensitive to the intricacies of offering a gift to a member of another culture.

Stage Eight: Advocacy

Cross-cultural communication works best when an entire organization commits to it. Commitment requires a persistent focus, and a persistent focus requires an advocate. Perhaps that advocate can be you. Says international communication consultant Mary Jo Jacobi:

> No matter where a multinational company operates, it must remain conscious of the fact that it has audiences in many other parts of the world and that whatever its executives do and say locally could have far-reaching ramifications and business implications. As a result, we must seek to ensure that we communicate a consistent message worldwide, particularly on sensitive matters. Getting this clearly in the minds of colleagues is one of the most important roles that we, as professional communicators, must undertake.[62]

Stage Nine: Continuing Education

The diversity boot camp at the Edelman agency is an example of continuing education, as are exchanges of executives between local branches of multinational companies. Other forms of continuing education can be as simple as reading international

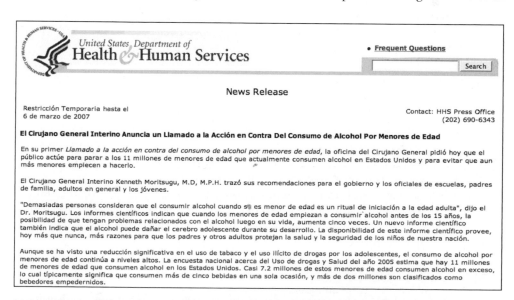

News Release The growing importance of Hispanic publics in the United States has led progressive organizations such as the U.S. Department of Health and Human Services to issue news releases in Spanish. For an English-language version of this news release, see page 286. (Courtesy of U.S. Department of Health and Human Services)

publications, watching international television programming, attending lectures, or—gasp!—returning to a university for an occasional night course on a foreign language or an unfamiliar culture. Fortunately, learning doesn't stop at graduation. It's a big, exciting world out there, burgeoning with opportunities for anyone who can cross its boundaries with knowledge, diplomacy, and confidence.

QUICK CHECK

1. In the nine-step process for successful cross-cultural public relations, what does local partnership mean? Why is it necessary?
2. What sources could you consult for information on the cultures of other countries?
3. Specifically, how does cross-cultural communication mean more than international communication?

Summary

As we noted in Chapter 11, a generation ago Canadian philosopher Marshall McLuhan argued that the world was becoming a "global village." In many ways, he was right. Modern technology can make communication between Kenya and China faster and easier than the task faced by a 19th-century Toronto resident who simply wanted to deliver a message across town. Yet the global village is hardly a community in the traditional sense. Every street has its own customs, biases, traditions, fears, religion, diet, and language. Every street, in other words, has its own culture.

If the global village is to thrive, those streets need to learn to communicate with one another. The conversations won't be easy. We need only to read a daily newspaper to see that the conversations often fail. We can increase the chances of success, however, by learning a process for effective cross-cultural communication—a nine-step process that begins with awareness and includes commitment, research, local partnership, diversity, testing, evaluation, advocacy, and continuing education. That process needs well-educated, talented, versatile communicators. In fact, the process of cross-cultural public relations needs you.

Cross-cultural communication is so essential to the present and future of public relations that we're not yet ready to put the subject aside. We will return to it in Chapter 16, in which we'll examine predictions for the increasing diversity of publics around the world.

DISCUSSION QUESTIONS

1. Besides the gaffes mentioned in this chapter, what cross-cultural communication errors have you heard of? Have any happened to you?
2. What is a culture? What other definitions besides those offered in this chapter can you find? How do *you* define a culture?

3. How might you respond to a colleague who makes the following statement: "You're wasting your time with that cross-cultural stuff. We're all humans, and we're a lot more alike than we are different."

4. In the East Meets West scenario, would it be smarter to meet separately with your international visitors from Japan and Spain? Why or why not?

5. What cross-cultural educational opportunities exist at your college or university? Are you taking advantage of them?

Memo from the Field

Bill Imada, President, IW Group, Los Angeles, California

Bill Imada is the president and founder of IW Group, a Los Angeles–based advertising and public relations agency specializing in the Asian American market. The agency represents a variety of major corporations and governmental agencies, including AT&T, Wal-Mart, Merrill Lynch, Washington Mutual, Comcast, and McDonald's.

Values play a critical role in the way people think, react, relate, communicate, and make decisions. As a student of public relations, take a moment to think about the values that shape your own personality and the way you make decisions in life. As the authors of this book clearly note, there are a host of common values that people around the world share. When you walk into a room filled with nationals from Japan, Spain, or any other country in the world, consider all of the values you might share first. You will be pleasantly surprised by the number of values you have in common with your colleagues from another country or even another neighborhood or community. Your efforts to communicate will be made easier and more enjoyable when you find the values that bring you together. Afterwards, take time to discover the things that make you different and unique. Celebrate what you have learned from one another, and share what you have learned with others.

As you move forward with your studies in public relations and communications, take a moment to think about some of the values you may take for granted. In this chapter, the authors talk about the concept of time. Many people from Western countries often talk about the lack of time we have to accomplish things. Americans, for instance, often say "time flies." On the contrary, many Latin American and Asian cultures may say "time walks." From a cultural point of view, which phrase is right? Both are right. How might this concept of time influence the way you interact and negotiate with your counterparts from Japan and Spain?

Now think of some other values that shape your views on life and ask yourself and your classmates to evaluate how these values might influence the way you think, react, relate, communicate, and make decisions. What thoughts come to mind when you think of these values: independence, family, sales, and equality.

Now ask people from other cultures to talk with you about their views on these values. I think you will find their answers enlightening and thought-provoking.

The authors also talk about the significance of gestures in other cultures. It is important to note that gestures are an important method of communicating in many cultures around the world. In Japan, public relations professionals often say that the Japanese can say "no" 40 different ways without even uttering the word. Facial expressions, hand movements, and body positions can signal a variety of different messages. As public relations practitioners, it is essential for you to learn how gestures can and will play a role in cross-cultural communication.

Lastly, think about what you have learned in the past about getting from one point in life to another. What did your teachers, professors, and parents tell you about getting from point A to point B? You and your classmates may say that the best way to get from point A to point B is a straight line. Why? Because it is considered the most efficient, cost-effective, and timely way to reach your desired destination. As you move forward in your public relations career, remember that there can be many different and unique ways to get from one point to another—and not necessarily by taking the direct approach. The most effective public relations practitioners will recognize early on that there are a myriad of different ways to reach where you'd like to go. Take time to explore each route. You'll be pleased that you did.

CASE STUDY 14.1

Pro Bono: Bridging the Cultures of Rock and Politics

The world's news media call him "a political coalition builder" and a "hyperagent."[63] The *New York Times* credits him with spearheading "a worldwide public relations campaign."[64] A reporter on the CBS program *60 Minutes* said, "He gets a lot of credit for lobbying President Bush. They've met several times."[65]

Oh, and he also performs with a band. He's Bono, lead singer and songwriter of U2, the Irish rockers who rival Madonna for creative longevity.

Bono as a public relations practitioner? Maybe not quite—but to fight AIDS and poverty in developing nations, Bono has crafted a variety of relationship-building tactics to win resources from wealthy nations. He has hosted special events, held meetings with world leaders, and created photo opportunities by telephoning a U.S. president live from stage and by lending a pope his ever-present sunglasses. And he uses the language of his target publics: "When I'm speaking to corporate America," he says, "I always talk about countries being brands."[66]

For helping to raise billions of dollars for the world's poor, Bono and Microsoft's Bill and Melinda Gates were named *Time* magazine's 2005 Persons of the Year. So you'd think Bono's life, to quote a U2 song, might be "the sweetest thing." But you'd be ignoring the perils of cross-cultural communication.

In a scathing article titled "Saint Bono the Martyr," London's *Daily Mail* underscored the challenge of living on stage and in the corporate boardroom: "His obsession with changing the world has alienated both band-mates and fans. Could it now spell the end of the U2 singer's career?"[67]

Even less tolerant of Bono's cross-cultural odyssey was the *Ottawa (Canada) Sun*: "We resent spoiled brat rock stars . . . trying to dictate government policy decisions and telling us how to spend federal dollars."[68]

Less inflammatory critics still note the improbable clash of Bono's two worlds. CNN labels Bono and President George W. Bush the "odd couple."[69] The *New York Sun* calls Bono and a leading economist "an unlikely pair."[70] Melinda Gates herself said, "We'd certainly never had a rock star to the house before . . . but the whole reason we got together is because we have this joint cause."[71]

Bono himself tackles the cultural divide by confronting it head-on. In a meeting with President Bush and congressional leaders, he said, "I'm the first to admit that there's something unnatural, unseemly, about rock stars mounting the pulpit and preaching at presidents. . . . Talk about a fish out of water. . . . Yes, it's odd having a rock star here—but maybe it's odder for me than for you."[72]

Bono is quick to admit that he sometimes stumbles in the alien cultures of world politics and corporate boardrooms. In one of his first meetings with President Bush, he says he pushed so relentlessly for more AIDS-relief money that Bush finally pounded the table to silence him. "He banged the table to ask me to let him reply," Bono recalls. "I was very impressed that he could get so passionate. And let's face it: Tolerating an Irish rock star is not a necessity of his office."[73]

An entire nation may have wanted to pound a collective fist when Bono—still seeking funds for the world's poor—declared, "Ireland is now the richest country in the European Union, second only to Luxembourg—and Luxembourg isn't really a country."[74]

To critics in Luxembourg and elsewhere, he concedes, "I'm sick of Bono—and I'm Bono."[75] He says he worries that his bandmates are "sick of the sight of me shaking hands with politicians."[76] Ironically, just as some scorn a rocker turned lobbyist, others decry the president's pal who still rocks: "He has courted ever greater risks to his street reputation," notes the *International Herald Tribune*.[77]

Why invite such culture clashes? One answer might be his success: "Bono charmed and bullied and morally blackmailed the leaders of the world's richest countries into forgiving $40 billion in debt owed by the poorest," *Time* declared in its story naming him one of its 2005 Persons of the Year.[78]

Bono himself believes that, if world poverty declines, he'll be remembered for his communications in just one culture: rock and roll. "Oddly enough," he says, "I think my work, the activism, will be forgotten. . . . I hope it will because I hope those problems will have gone away. But our music will be here in 50 years' and 100 years' time."[79]

DISCUSSION QUESTIONS

1. Do you agree with the *New York Times* that Bono's fund-raising efforts can be called public relations? Why or why not?
2. Are the worlds of rock and roll and of politics and corporations really different cultures? Why or why not?

3. As Chapter 14 notes, stereotyping can interfere with successful cross-cultural communication. In what ways, if any, has stereotyping hurt Bono's fund-raising efforts?

4. Before reading this case study, what were your impressions (if any) of Bono? Do his relationships with Bill and Melinda Gates and George W. Bush hurt his credibility as a rock star?

CASE STUDY 14.2

Zakazukha!

Two cheers for *Expert,* the magazine named Russia's best business periodical by the Russian Managers Association. *Expert* has more than 70,000 readers in Moscow alone, and it won top honors for "brand awareness, authority, inspired confidence, and depth of analysis."[80]

But why not three cheers? In a word, *zakazukha.*

Zakazukha is the Russian word for payments to journalists—often from public relations practitioners—to win favorable or prevent negative news media coverage. "In a study on business and the media published this year [2003]," wrote the *Moscow Times,* "the [Russian Managers Association] estimated that *zakazukha* articles account for about 30 percent of all stories published."[81]

Recent news reports suggest that *zakazukha* is a standard tactic in Russian media relations:

- In Moscow, an investigative journalist has been charged with blackmailing a local business leader. Pay $100,000, she allegedly told the man, or she'd feature him in a devastating exposé.[82]

- A Russian journalist has admitted accepting money for a favorable article on a fitness club owner—and accepting a 30 percent discount for illegal, unlicensed cosmetic surgery at the club to repair his broken nose (broken by the angry target of a non-*zakazukha* story). The journalist alleges that when he later wrote about the illegal surgery, thugs hired by the club owner beat him (no report on whether they rebroke his nose).[83]

- To test journalists' willingness to be partners in *zakazukha,* a Russian public relations agency sent a bogus news release, detailing the opening of new business, to Moscow news media. "More than half of the publications that received the release initiated negotiations to run the story in exchange for cash," reports *PR Week* magazine.[84]

The prestige of Russian news media has sunk so low that when a Russian pulp mill hired public relations agency Fleishman-Hillard to help thwart a violent hostile takeover, the agency decided to target the most credible news media in Russia: foreign media. "We determined [the Moscow bureaus of foreign media] to be a potentially potent counterweapon because those Western institutions had a much greater degree of credibility and authority not only here in the West but also in Russia," said Andrew Kattel, senior vice president of international business communications at Fleishman-Hillard.[85]

In 2002, the International Public Relations Association conducted a survey of public relations professionals in 52 nations—and learned that *zakazukha* had spread throughout Eastern Europe. "*Zakazukha* is a common practice," said a Ukrainian practitioner. "We have the law on advertising which directly forbids [publishing] materials paid for by an advertiser without making it clear that it was paid. This law is widely ignored."[86]

Said a Croatian practitioner, "Some journalists openly demand goods or services in exchange for not publishing negative stories (even made-up negative stories) about the company/organization."[87]

The IPRA survey revealed these discouraging facts about *zakazukha* and media relations in Eastern Europe:[88]

- Only 13 percent of Eastern European practitioners believe that journalists are not influenced by *zakazukha*.

- 41 percent of Eastern European practitioners believe that journalists often accept money in return for publishing news releases. In contrast, no North American practitioners in the survey—literally 0 percent—believed that North American journalists often accept money to do so.

- Eastern European practitioners believe that their regional news media are less reliable than news media from other regions.

By participating in *zakazukha*, practitioners undermine the credibility of the news media, damaging an important part of democracy and eliminating news media's ability to supply reputable third-party endorsements. "The credibility of any publication can only be based on its independent objectivity," says Frank Ovaitt, of the U.S.-based Crossover International agency. "As long as the practice of illicit paid-for editorial continues in any marketplace, the local public can never have confidence in what they read."[89]

Russian journalist Alexei Pankin sees the damage of *zakazukha* firsthand. "This total lack of trust on all sides," he says, "has become a heavy cross to bear today, at a time when business is taking its first steps toward social responsibility and the demand for reliable information, whether it be positive or negative, is very much on the rise."[90]

DISCUSSION QUESTIONS

1. What do you know of the history of journalism in Russia? Could that history help explain *zakazukha*?
2. If you had a Russian client and a journalist in that nation demanded *zakazukha* to prevent a negative story, what council would you offer your client?
3. What do you know about the values of the U.S.-based Society of Professional Journalists? What is its stance on *zakazukha*?
4. What international public relations practices besides *zakazukha* concern the International Public Relations Association? (A visit to the organization's web site, www.ipra.com, can help you answer this question.)

NOTES

1. Marlene Rossman, *Multicultural Marketing* (New York: Amacom, 1994), 6.

2. Matthew Creamer, "Unruly Julie and the Scandal That Rocked the Ad World," *Business Week,* 8 December 2006, online, www.adage.com.

3. David Kiley, "An Open Letter to Wal-Mart, Julie Roehm, and Draft/FCB," *Business Week Online,* 14 December 2006, online, www.businessweek.com.

4. *Julie Roehm, Plaintiff, v. Wal-Mart Stores, Inc., Defendant: Countersuit.* Case No. 2.07-cv-10168. United States District Court in the Eastern District of Michigan, Southern Division, 19 March 2007.

5. Mike Lindblom, "Muslims Protest Koran Use in Rave Ad," *Seattle Times,* 10 February 2001, online, LexisNexis.

6. Anindita Niyogi Balslev, ed., *Cross-Cultural Conversation* (Atlanta: Scholars Press, 1996), 10.

7. Stephen P. Banks, *Multicultural Public Relations,* 2nd ed. (Ames: Iowa State University Press, 2000), 9.

8. Charles Winick, *Dictionary of Anthropology* (Totowa, N.J.: Littlefield, Adams, 1972), 144.

9. *American Heritage Dictionary of the English Language,* 4th ed. (New York: Houghton Mifflin, 2000), online, www.bartleby.com.

10. Robert Gibson, *International Business Communication* (Oxford: Oxford University Press, 2000), 3.

11. Banks, ix.

12. John Budd Jr., "Opinion . . . Foreign Policy Acumen Needed by Global CEOs," *Public Relations Review* (summer 2001): 132.

13. Banks, 105.

14. "Italian Stallions," *Times* (of London), 1 May 2001, 17.

15. David J. Smith and Shelagh Armstrong, *If the World Were a Village* (Toronto: Kids Can Press, 2002).

16. Rossman.

17. Robert Levine, "The Pace of Life in 31 Countries," *American Demographics,* November 1997, 20.

18. Roger Axtell, *Do's and Taboos around the World,* 3rd ed. (New York: Wiley, 1993), 68.

19. Much of the information in this section comes from two excellent books by Roger Axtell: *Do's and Taboos around the World* (note 18) and *Gestures: The Do's and Taboos of Body Language around the World* (New York: Wiley, 1991).

20. Budd, 131.

21. Sanae Kobayashi, "Characteristics of Japanese Communication," *Communication World,* December/January 1996–97, 15.

22. Axtell, *Gestures,* 150.

23. Lydia Polgreen, "Nigeria Counts 100 Deaths Over Danish Caricatures," *New York Times,* 24 February 2006, online, www.nytimes.com.

24. Colin Nickerson, "Danish Paper's Apology Fails to Calm Protests," *Boston Globe,* 1 February 2006, online, LexisNexis Academic.

25. Daphne Spain, "America's Diversity: On the Edge of Two Centuries," *Reports on America* 1, no. 2 (Washington, D.C.: Population Reference Bureau), 7.
26. Spain, 7.
27. John Robinson, Bart Landry, and Ronica Rooks, "Time and the Melting Pot," *American Demographics,* June 1998, 20.
28. Rossman, 6, 12.
29. Colin Taylor, "Great Gifts or Gifts That Grate?" *New Zealand Management,* August 2003, online, LexisNexis.
30. Axtell, *Gestures,* 50.
31. Alice Lagnado, "Putin to Purge Russian Tongue of Foreign Elements," *Times,* 1 May 2001, 16.
32. Adam Sherwin, "Mandela Steals Show in Trafalgar Square," *Times,* 30 April 2001, 8.
33. Mark Rice-Oxley, "The American World," *Seattle Times,* 18 January 2004, online, LexisNexis.
34. "Pitney Bowes Messaging Study Reveals Hidden Cultural Pitfalls for Communicating with Colleagues and Customers outside the United States," news release issued by Pitney Bowes, 31 July 2000, online, www.PitneyBowes.com.
35. David Howes, ed., *Cross-Cultural Consumption* (London: Routledge, 1996), 1.
36. Naseem Javed, "Naming for Global Power," *Communication World,* October/November 1997, 33.
37. Maud Tixier, "How Cultural Factors Affect Internal and External Communication," *Communication World,* February/March 1997, 25.
38. Information in this paragraph comes from Axtell's *Do's and Taboos* and *Gestures* (notes 18 and 19 above).
39. Henry Louis Gates Jr., "Whose Culture Is It, Anyway?" *Cast a Cold Eye* (New York: Four Walls Eight Windows, 1991), 263.
40. Budd, 126.
41. Howes, 2.
42. "Public Relations Society of America Finds Progress of Industry in Diversity Efforts 'Mixed' in Landmark Survey," news release issued by the Public Relations Society of America, 22 August 2003, online, www.prsa.org.
43. "Diversity Survey 2006," report issued by *PR Week* and Hill & Knowlton, 11 December 2006, online, www.prweek.com/us; "Race and Hispanic Origin 2005," report issued by U.S. Census Bureau, February 2007, online, www.census.gov.
44. "PR Coalition Diversity Tracking Survey," report issued by BPRI Group and the Public Relations Coalition, 2005, online, www.prfirms.org.
45. "PR Coalition Diversity Tracking Survey."
46. "PRSA National Diversity Committee," Public Relations Society of America, online, www.prsa.org.
47. "Diversity Survey 2006."
48. Hamilton Nolan, "The Agency Business: Diversity Training Evolving to Be All-Inclusive, *PR Week,* 25 September 2006, online, LexisNexis.
49. The following description of Hofstede's cultural dimensions draws from Marieke de Mooij, *Global Marketing and Advertising: Understanding Cultural Paradoxes* (Thousand

Oaks, Calif.: Sage Publications, 1998); and Geert Hofstede, *Cultures and Organizations: Software of the Mind* (New York: McGraw-Hill, 1991).

50. Cynthia Kemper, "Challenges Facing Public Relations Efforts Are Intensified Abroad," *Denver Post,* 1 March 1998, online, LexisNexis.

51. Pitney Bowes, online, www.pitneybowes.com.

52. Axtell, *Do's and Taboos,* 68, 89.

53. Peter Jennings, Bob Jamieson, and Bob Woodruff, *ABC World News Tonight,* 25 January 2001, online, LexisNexis.

54. Peter Martin, "Shoals across the Pond," *Financial Times,* 2 June 2001, online, LexisNexis.

55. Widget Finn, "Mind the Culture Gap," *Daily Telegraph,* 14 June 2001, online, LexisNexis.

56. Jennings, Jamieson, and Woodruff; William Drozdiak, "Alacatel Aims to Purchase Lucent," *Washington Post,* 29 May 2001, online, LexisNexis; "When Business Pops the Question," *Engineer,* 18 May 2001, online, LexisNexis.

57. Jennings, Jamieson, and Woodruff.

58. Finn.

59. Andrew Leach, "DaimlerChrysler Just the Latest Example of a Merger Most Foul," *Daily Mail,* 21 January 2001, online, LexisNexis.

60. Drozdiak.

61. Axtell, *Do's and Taboos,* 90.

62. Mary Jo Jacobi, "Communications without Borders: Thinking Globally While Acting Locally" (speech delivered to the 1998 annual meeting of the International Public Relations Association, London, 17 July 1998).

63. Eric R. Danton, "The Many Faces of Bono," *Hartford (Connecticut) Courant,* 1 December 2005, online, LexisNexis; Alexandra Marks, "Celebrity Hyper-Agents Transform Philanthropy," *Christian Science Monitor,* 19 September 2005, online, LexisNexis.

64. Richard W. Stevenson and Alan Cowell, "Bush Arrives at Summit Session, Ready to Stand Alone," *New York Times,* online, LexisNexis.

65. Transcript, *60 Minutes,* CBS, 5 February 2006, online, LexisNexis.

66. Joel Selvin, "U2's Bono Makes Fiery Case," *San Francisco Chronicle,* 11 November 2005, online, LexisNexis.

67. Paul Scott, "Saint Bono the Martyr," *Daily Mail,* 24 December 2005, online, LexisNexis.

68. "Act Like Pro, Bono," *Ottawa Sun,* 7 July 2005, online, LexisNexis.

69. Transcript, "The Situation Room with Wolf Blitzer," CNN, 2 February 2006, online, LexisNexis.

70. John P. Avlon, "The Rock Star and the Economist," *New York Sun,* 7 October 2005, online, LexisNexis.

71. Jamie Wilson Washington, "Melinda, Bill and Bono Are Time's People of the Year," *The Guardian,* 19 December 2005, online, LexisNexis.

72. Bono, "Bono's Prayer for Africa," *The Record* (Kitchener-Waterloo, Ontario), 18 February 2006, online, LexisNexis.

73. George Rush and Joanna Molloy, "When Dubya Silenced Bono's Vox," *New York Daily News,* 26 January 2005, online, LexisNexis.

74. Richard Kay, "Bono's Little Bit of Bother," *Daily Mail,* 23 February 2006, online, Lex-isNexis.

75. "They Said What?" *The Journal* (Newcastle, England), 31 December 2005, online, Lex-isNexis.

76. "The Lobbyist Rock Star," CNN.com, 16 April 2004, online, LexisNexis.

77. Brian Lavery, "The Irish Love U2, Except When They Don't," *International Herald Tribune,* 28 June 2005, online, LexisNexis.

78. Desmond Butler, "Bill and Melinda Gates, Bono Named *Time*'s Persons of the Year for Work on Poverty," Associated Press, 18 December 2005, online, LexisNexis.

79. *60 Minutes.*

80. Igor Semenenko, "Expert Gets Top Spot in Business Media Survey," *Moscow Times,* 23 July 2003, online, LexisNexis.

81. Semenenko.

82. Frank Brown, "A Free Press for Sale," *Newsweek,* 28 June 2004, online, LexisNexis.

83. Brown.

84. Ian Hall, "Ceyda Aydede, IPRA—IPRA Chief Aydede's on a Global Mission," *PR Week,* 13 December 2002, online, LexisNexis.

85. "Navigating the Rough-and-Tumble World of International PR," *PR News,* 22 September 2003, online, LexisNexis.

86. "Examples of Unethical Media Practice," International Public Relations Association, online, www.ipra.org.campaigns/icmt/examples.htm.

87. "Examples of Unethical Media Practice."

88. "IPRA Campaign for Media Transparency," International Public Relations Association, online, www.ipra.org.

89. "Unethical Media Practices Revealed by IPRA Report," news release issued by the International Public Relations Association, online, www.ipra.org/campaigns/icmt/docs/press2.htm.

90. Alexei Pankin, "No Foothold for Trust in Vicious Media Circle," *Moscow Times,* 27 May 2003, online, LexisNexis.

CHAPTER

15

Public Relations
and the Law

OBJECTIVES

After studying this chapter, you will
be able to

- understand the differences between
  and the regulation of political and
  commercial speech

- appreciate how privacy and
  copyright laws affect the practice of
  public relations

- identify the higher burden of proof
  public officials and public figures
  have in libel cases

- recognize the increasing role public
  relations has in the judicial system

KEY TERMS

SCENARIO Working in a Minefield

It has been a bad day at the Ferndale Corporation's investor relations office, and it almost got worse.

Your headache began when the corporate attorneys called and said that you would have to prepare a news release announcing the chief executive officer's sudden, unexpected resignation. Ferndale's revenues have fallen dramatically in recent months, and the board of directors wants to move in a new direction before the next annual meeting.

When you go to brief the staff on what is happening, you find a colleague illegally downloading music from the Internet. She tells you "downloading music doesn't hurt anybody." But you know differently.

As you sit down to write the news release about the CEO's departure, a number of questions come to mind. What should I say? What can I say? What must I say? Three questions similar in structure, but entirely different in their legal ramifications.

On top of everything, the timing for this could not be worse. The annual report is due at the printer this afternoon. Can you delay it?

It's times like these that everyone needs to talk to a friend. Your best friend from college is an investment analyst at a local stock brokerage firm. But before you start dialing, you suddenly hang up the telephone. You realize that you almost made the biggest mistake of your life, one that could have landed you in prison.

You think to yourself, "It's like working in a minefield."

The Statue of Responsibility

Freedom of expression is easily taken for granted—unless you don't have it.

In adopting the *Universal Declaration of Human Rights* in 1948, member states of the United Nations agreed that "Everyone has the right to freedom of opinion and expression."[1] Now, six decades later, nearly every nation has a free speech provision in its constitution. However, these are empty words in many places. According to the U.S. State Department, "In every region of the globe in 2006, there were governments that responded to the growing demands for personal and political freedom not by accepting their obligations to their people but by oppressing those who advocated for human rights and who exposed abuses."[2]

Fortunately, democratic nations are built on a free speech tradition. However, even in those countries, there are limits. While the government enforces some of these restrictions, limitations on speech are often self-imposed. The First Amendment of the U.S. Constitution severely restricts the *government's* ability to regulate speech. However, those same rules often do not apply to *individuals*.

What is—and is not—considered acceptable speech is often affected by the ebb and flow of public opinion. For example, nearly half of those surveyed by the First

Amendment Center in 2002 said they agreed with the statement that the First Amendment goes too far in the rights it guarantees. However, only 18 percent of respondents agreed when asked the same question four years later. In that same 2006 survey, 58 percent said that newspapers should be allowed to criticize the military, 63 percent said musicians should be allowed to sing songs with offensive lyrics, and 55 percent said people should be allowed to say things that might be offensive to religious groups. However, when asked if people should be allowed to say things in public that might be offensive to racial groups, 55 percent said they should not.[3]

This brings us to radio shock jock Don Imus, a broadcasting legend who fell from grace in just a matter of days during April 2007. When Imus, described by *Time* as a "66-year-old white male country music fan," used racially and sexually offensive slang to describe the Rutgers University women's basketball team, he torpedoed his career.[4] Within days, MSNBC and CBS stripped him of his television and radio shows. Were the shock jock's First Amendment rights violated? The answer, in a word, is no. The government didn't deprive Imus of his public platform. Public opinion did. In free societies, free expression is self-regulating.

Don Imus, behind the microphone, speaks with the Rev. Al Sharpton, right, during an appearance on Sharpton's radio show in April 2007. CBS fired Imus from his radio show following a public outcry over the shock jock's use of racial and sexual slurs to describe the Rutgers University women's basketball team. (Photo by Jeremy M. Lange/*New York Times*. Copyright 2007 The New York Times Company. Reprinted with permission.)

"The messier the speech, the louder the clamor for government to clean up the mess," wrote Charles C. Haynes, senior scholar of the First Amendment Center. "The only thing worse than an uncivil society is a society where government legislates what is civil."[5]

Where does public relations fit into this debate? Do practitioners have a responsibility to engage in civil discourse—even when others do not? As noted in Chapter 3, free expression and First Amendment protections are foundations of public relations practice. We have also noted that practitioners have a boundary-spanning role between their organization and the many publics important to their organization's success. Their goal is to build and maintain strategic relationships.

Some forms of speech are regulated with well-defined boundaries. However, most speech is not. It is difficult for practitioners to identify the fine line between good and bad speech. To paraphrase the movie *Broadcast News*, "they keep moving that sucker."

Viktor E. Frankl, a holocaust survivor who went on to author *Man's Search for Meaning,* one of the most influential books of the 20th century, believed that freedom must be linked to personal responsibility. "Freedom is in danger of degenerating into arbitrariness unless it is lived responsibly," Frankl wrote. "That is why I recommend that the Statue of Liberty on the East Coast be supplemented by a Statue of Responsibility on the West Coast."[6]

Fund-raising is under way to build Frankl's monument. Meanwhile, public relations practitioners are challenged every day to balance the benefits and responsibilities of free speech.

Public Relations, the Law, and You

In Chapter 6, we discussed ethical issues facing 21st-century public relations practice. We also noted the difference between conduct that is legal and ethical. There are times an action may be legal but not ethical and vice versa. That is the nature of the complex and diverse society in which we live. However, there are many times when legal and ethical considerations *are* the same. Sometimes the world *is* black and white. That is why this chapter focuses on the legal environment in which public relations practitioners operate. And as anyone who has watched any television crime drama knows, ignorance of the law is not an excuse.

We live in a litigious society. According to the U.S Justice Department, civil lawsuits outnumber their criminal cases by nearly 2 million cases annually. This high level of legal activity is clogging the court system. The department says there are other effects, including massive punitive damage awards, a glut of frivolous lawsuits, and large settlement awards in medical malpractice lawsuits.[7] In today's legal environment, everything organizations do is under intense public scrutiny. The message is unmistakable: If you screw up, there is a good chance you are going to court.

This fact should not be lost on public relations practitioners. They are often thrust into the limelight when their employer's actions face legal challenges. Practitioners also require an intimate knowledge of the laws governing what they may or must say or do in a variety of situations. For example, a certain degree of exaggeration is perfectly acceptable at times. However, at other times it is not. Depending on whom the practitioner is representing, some information can be considered public (for all to see) or very private.

The challenge for public relations practitioners is to understand the many laws and regulations that govern or, at least, influence their practice. Unfortunately, at least one study suggests that many practitioners do not have a good understanding of the laws and regulations governing the public relations profession. More than half the practitioners questioned in one survey indicated they had no familiarity with Securities and Exchange Commission regulations. In the same survey, more than 48 percent said they were not familiar with laws relating to professional malpractice, 45 percent were not familiar with laws governing financial public relations, and 40 percent were not familiar with laws pertaining to commercial speech. These responses led the author of the study to this conclusion:

> The finding that most practitioners are only somewhat or not at all familiar with important legal issues, combined with the finding that most of their work is either not reviewed or subject to limited review by legal counsel, suggests that many public relations practitioners may be placing both themselves and their clients at risk of legal liability.[8]

Attorney Morton J. Simon said that public relations practitioners "can and have cost companies millions of dollars. While the incidence of legal implications [to the practice of public relations] may vary, their importance when they exist cannot be minimized."[9]

Unfortunately, there are recent examples of practitioners who crossed the line. Douglas R. Dowie, a Fleishman-Hillard executive in Los Angeles, was sentenced to federal prison in 2007 for defrauding taxpayers by padding his bills.[10] Commentator Armstrong Williams, who concealed he had been paid to promote the No Child Left Behind Act, agreed to return $34,000 to the U.S. Education Department for work not performed.[11] Not even the British royal family is immune: RJH Public Relations, owned by the Countess of Wessex—wife of Prince Edward—was taken to court in 2006 for a string of unpaid debts.[12]

Public Relations and the First Amendment

As noted in Chapter 3, the most important event in the development of public relations in the United States was the adoption of the **First Amendment** to the Constitution. The freedoms guaranteed by the First Amendment provide the framework for the nation's social, political, and commercial discourse:

> Congress shall make no law respecting an establishment of religion, or prohibiting the free exercise thereof; or abridging the freedom of speech, or of the press, or the right of the people peaceably to assemble, and to petition the Government for a redress of grievances.[13]

In the more than two centuries since its adoption, a great deal of thought and debate has surrounded what the First Amendment does and does not guarantee. There have been many instances in which free expression has come in conflict with other social interests. Does a person's First Amendment right to freedom of speech supersede someone else's Sixth Amendment right to a trial by "an impartial jury"? Does freedom of expression allow one to yell "fire" in a crowded theater? Clearly, the freedoms embodied in the First Amendment are not absolute. It has been left up to the courts, and, ultimately, the Supreme Court, to decide on the amendment's limits.

Political versus Commercial Speech

Although public relations enjoys certain protections under the First Amendment, these rights are not without some limitations. The practice of public relations often falls into a gray area between what the law characterizes as political speech and commercial speech. **Political speech** is defined as expression associated with the normal conduct of a democracy—such as news articles, public debates, and individuals' expressions of their opinions about the events of the day. In general, the U.S. Supreme Court has been reluctant to limit political speech. Justice William Brennan wrote in 1964 that there is a "profound national commitment to the principle that debate on public issues should be uninhibited, robust, and wide-open, and that it may well include vehement, caustic, and sometimes unpleasantly sharp attacks on government and public officials."[14]

Commercial speech, which is defined as expression "intended to generate marketplace transactions," is more restricted.[15] In fact, for much of the nation's history, commercial speech has been treated by courts as if it were unprotected by the First Amendment. In 1976, however, the Supreme Court ruled that a Virginia law prohibiting pharmacists from advertising prescription drug prices was unconstitutional. In doing so, the court recognized limited First Amendment protection for "pure commercial speech":

> Generalizing, society also may have a strong interest in the free flow of commercial information. Even an individual advertisement, though entirely "commercial," may be of general public interest. . . . And if it is indispensable to the proper allocation of resources in a free enterprise system, it is also indispensable to the formation of intelligent opinions as to how that system ought to be regulated or altered. Therefore, even if the First Amendment were thought to be primarily an instrument to enlighten public decision making in a democracy, we could not say that the free flow of information does not serve that goal.[16]

Supreme Court Justice Harry Blackmun also wrote in *Virginia State Board of Pharmacy v. Virginia Citizens Consumer Council Inc.,* "In concluding that commercial speech, like other varieties, is protected, we of course do not hold that it can never be regulated in any way. Some forms of commercial speech regulation are surely permissible."[17] Two years later, in *First National Bank of Boston v. Bellotti,* the Court also affirmed that corporations do enjoy some rights of political speech.

The Supreme Court further defined the limits of commercial speech in the 1980 case *Central Hudson Gas & Electric Corp. v. Public Service Commission of New York.* In that case, Central Hudson Gas & Electric successfully challenged a state ban on promotional advertising by electric utilities. The Court said that there are times when restrictions on commercial speech are justified because they serve certain social interests. In *Central Hudson,* however, the justices felt that the regulation in question was "more extensive than necessary to serve that interest." The Court sided with the utility, saying that the government interest could have been accomplished with less restrictive regulation.[18] The Court clarified what it meant by "not more extensive

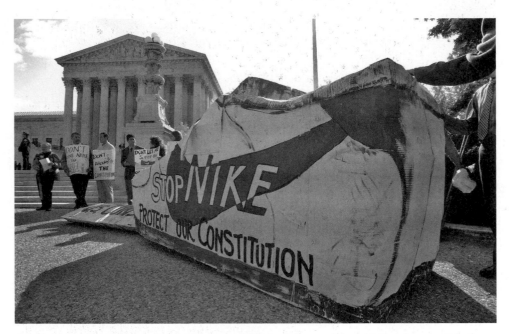

Antiglobalization demonstrators stand alongside a giant cardboard Nike shoe outside the U.S. Supreme Court in 2003. The court briefly considered *Kasky v. Nike,* an important free-speech case for businesses, before sending it back to the California courts for further deliberation. Nike was accused of using false publicity to defend itself against accusations that Asian sweatshops made its footwear. (Photo by Doug Mills/*New York Times*. Copyright 2003 The New York Times Company. Reprinted with permission.)

than necessary" in 1989, when it ruled that the government can "reasonably" restrict commercial speech, even when other means can achieve the "substantial governmental interest" involved.[19]

Is public relations considered political speech, or is it considered commercial speech? The answer largely depends on the public being targeted, the purpose of the message, and the court's interpretation. Despite this somewhat murky answer, two things are very clear. First, there are limits to both political and commercial speech. And second, public relations practitioners need to know what those limits are.

QUICK ✓ CHECK

1. Do public relations practitioners have a responsibility to engage in civil discourse—even when others do not?
2. What is the difference between the ways the U.S. Supreme Court has treated cases involving political speech and those involving commercial speech?
3. Is public relations considered political speech, or is it considered commercial speech?

Kasky v. Nike

When California antiglobalization activist Marc Kasky sued Nike and five of its corporate officers under the state's Business and Professional Code in 2000, he launched a battle that threatened to shake the foundations of corporate speech law and the practice of public relations.

Kasky claimed that Nike had made false and misleading statements in a public relations campaign that answered critics of its overseas labor practices. In response to charges that Nike products were being produced by underage, unpaid workers in harsh conditions, the company retained GoodWorks International, cochaired by former U.S. United Nations Ambassador Andrew Young. The consulting firm found no evidence of widespread abuse of workers. When Nike publicized these findings, Kasky sued. The activist not only wanted the corporation to "disgorge all monies" received through the allegedly illegal practices, but he wanted Nike to undertake "a court-approved public information campaign" to correct the record on its overseas practices.[20]

Nike argued that the First Amendment protected its public relations campaign. It said companies must be free to explain their actions to customers, investors, and anyone else. The case drew little attention when two lower courts sided with Nike. However, when the California Supreme Court said that the messages in question were "made in the context of a modern, sophisticated public relations campaign intended to increase sales and profits by enhancing the image of a product or of its manufacturer or seller," the court, in essence, ruled that

Nike's public relations campaign did not have First Amendment protection and was subject to state law.[21]

What had been a fairly obscure legal matter was suddenly on everyone's radar screen. Public relations, advertising, media, and business organizations filed legal briefs urging the U.S. Supreme Court to overturn the decision. Among the public relations organizations that entered the fray were the Public Relations Society of America, the Council of Public Relations Firms, the Arthur Page Society, the Public Affairs Council, and the Institute for Public Relations.

"Those of us who assist companies in gathering and disseminating information related to their businesses have always relied upon the same First Amendment protections as those who openly criticize Nike and other corporations," said PRSA President and CEO Reed Bolton Byrum. "Without that protection, there will be a serious impact on all aspects of corporate communications."[22]

At first, the U.S. Supreme Court agreed to hear the case. Then the justices sent it back to California. Before a final decision was rendered, the two sides settled out of court. The company agreed to pay $1.5 million in workplace program investments and to continue existing after-hours worker education programs.[23] While the legal precedent still stands in California, for the rest of the country, nothing—at least from a legal standpoint—has changed. However, most observers agree that *Kasky v. Nike* muddied the waters of corporate speech law for years to come.

The Key: Know Your Own Business

It is not suggested here that every public relations practitioner should be ready to take the state bar exam. However, you don't have to be a lawyer to have a good working knowledge of the law. And that understanding should begin in the workplace. All public relations professionals need to know the laws and regulations that govern their organization.

Many of these laws and regulations relate to the handling of private information. For example, hospital public information officers need to know the rules pertaining to the confidentiality of patient records. Most of the information found in a patient's file is considered private. An improper release of that information could open the practitioner and the hospital to civil or criminal litigation.

The actions of practitioners can also be controlled by the legal status of the organizations they represent. Government practitioners must learn that all their records are open to public inspection, except records specifically exempted by law. The best-known federal law guaranteeing access to government information is the **Freedom of Information Act (FOIA)**. The FOIA applies to all federal agencies and departments except the president and his advisers, Congress and its subsidiary committees and agencies, and the federal judicial system.[24] Although there are specific exemptions to the FOIA, a vast majority of federal government records are available for anyone to inspect. Similar laws covering records held by state and local governments have been enacted nationwide. State and federal "sunshine" laws also require that meetings of government agencies at which official decisions are made must be open to the public. However, as is the case with open records laws, specific exemptions permit some government business to be conducted in private.

Practitioners employed by nongovernmental organizations enjoy a much greater degree of privacy than do their government counterparts. However, even they may be governed by state and federal requirements relating to disclosure (a concept that we discuss later in greater depth), taxation, and ethical conduct. For example, people hired for the purpose of influencing the actions of state and federal officials must register as lobbyists. Practitioners representing the interests of governments or organizations based outside the United States must also register as foreign agents. Both lobbyists and foreign agents must file periodic reports on their activities with designated agencies.

Federal Agencies That Regulate Speech

The federal government does not license public relations practitioners. Several federal agencies, however, do have a major impact on the practice of public relations. These agencies create and enforce regulations designed to protect the public's best interests. These rules often cover company or organization communications, especially in areas considered to involve commercial speech. Four of the most prominent of these agencies are the Federal Trade Commission, the Securities and Exchange Commission, the Federal Communications Commission, and the Food and Drug Administration.

The Federal Trade Commission

When public relations practitioners promote a particular product or service, their actions may fall under the watchful gaze of the **Federal Trade Commission (FTC)**. The FTC was established in 1914 "to ensure that the nation's markets function competitively . . . are vigorous . . . and free of undue restrictions."[25] The commission is the source of most federal regulation of advertising. However, it also has jurisdiction over product-related publicity generated by public relations practitioners.

The Federal Trade Commission Act empowers the FTC to "prevent unfair methods of competition, and unfair or deceptive acts or practices in or affecting commerce."[26] This includes advertisements and publicity that may be considered false or misleading, including claims that are unsubstantiated, ambiguous, or exaggerated. The FTC is especially sensitive when the product or service being promoted may adversely affect personal health or when it requires a considerable investment of money before the consumer can determine its effectiveness.

If the FTC believes a violation of the law has occurred, it may obtain voluntary compliance through what is known as a **consent order.** However, if such an agreement cannot be reached, the commission can take a complaint before an **administrative law judge.** This person hears testimony and reviews evidence, much like the judge and jury in a civil or criminal case. An administrative law judge can issue a **cease and desist order.** This decision can be appealed to the full commission, then to the U.S. Court of Appeals, and ultimately to the U.S. Supreme Court. If the FTC's ruling is upheld, it can then seek **injunctions, consumer redress,** and **civil penalties** through the federal court system. In the case of ongoing consumer fraud, the FTC can go directly to federal court in an effort to protect consumers.[27]

An area in which you may have had direct contact with the FTC is the National Do Not Call Registry (www.donotcall.gov). By registering online, consumers can block most telemarketers from calling their home telephones for five years. Charities, survey researchers, and political campaigns are among those exempted by the law. More than 132 million telephone numbers were registered by the end of 2006. Telemarketers face civil penalties of up to $11,000 per violation.[28]

The Securities and Exchange Commission

As a result of the 1929 stock market crash that triggered the Great Depression, the federal government closely monitors the financial affairs of publicly traded companies. Congress created the **Securities and Exchange Commission (SEC)** in 1934 to "administer federal securities laws and issue rules and regulations to provide protection for investors and ensure that the securities markets are fair and honest."[29] In other words, the SEC's job is to see to it that everyone is operating on a level playing field. It does so by ensuring that investors can base their decisions on timely and accurate information.

The concept of **disclosure** is the foundation of SEC regulation. Under the Securities Act of 1933, publicly held companies—companies that issue financial securities, such as stocks and bonds, for public sale—have an obligation to disclose frankly, comprehensively, and immediately any information that is considered important to an investor's decision to buy, sell, or even hold the organization's securities.

Corporate disclosure—or a notable lack of it—was at the heart of several corporate scandals in the early 2000s. Companies such as Enron, WorldCom, and Adelphia focused intense public scrutiny on corporate disclosure. Before it issued

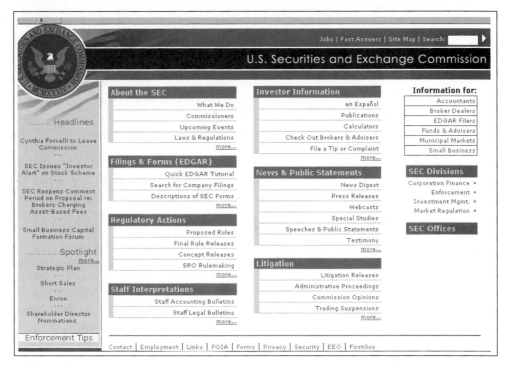

Web Site The Securities and Exchange Commission operates a web site that provides access to a variety of public records and updated information on federal regulations. (Courtesy of the U.S. Securities and Exchange Commission)

Regulation FD (Fair Disclosure), companies often provided selective tidbits of information to favored analysts and money managers to curry favor among major investors. These companies may have been operating within the *letter* of existing disclosure law, but they were clearly outside of its *spirit*. However, Regulation FD, along with amendments to the SEC's disclosure rules, tightened disclosure loopholes. When the new rules were adopted, the SEC announcement said, "We believe that the practice of selective disclosure leads to a loss of investor confidence in the integrity of our capital markets."[30]

Congress further tightened disclosure rules in 2002 by passing the **Sarbanes-Oxley Act.** Under its provisions, CEOs and CFOs are held personally accountable for the truthfulness of corporate financial statements. Violators face up to 20 years in prison and a $5 million fine. The law limits the ability of company officers and their families to sell stock when employees are blocked from doing so. It created new laws against destroying, altering, or falsifying records in an attempt to impede investigations. It also required companies to annually publish a code of ethics.[31]

Although companies are required to file a large variety of reports with the SEC and other federal agencies, the most recognizable channels of disclosure are Form 10-K to the SEC and the annual report to shareholders. Publicly held corporations annually file a **Form 10-K** with the SEC. In it, a company is required to disclose specific information

QuickBreak 15.2

SEC Rule 10b-5

Any practitioner engaged in financial public relations must study SEC Rule 10b-5, which prohibits fraudulent or misleading corporate communications in matters that could affect investment decisions. Rule 10b-5 states that it is illegal "to make any untrue statements of a material fact or to omit to state a material fact necessary in order to make the statements made, in light of the circumstances under which they were made, not misleading." The rule also prohibits "any act, practice, or course of business which operates or would operate as a fraud or deceit upon any person, in connection with the purchase or sale of any security."[32]

One area in which this rule has a major impact on the practice of public relations is insider trading. That was the issue in 1985, when the SEC filed charges against Anthony M. Franco, the owner of a Detroit public relations firm and national president-elect of the Public Relations Society of America. The SEC complaint stemmed from a news release Franco had prepared in which his client, Crowley, Milner and Company, announced its intentions to buy another firm, Oakland Holding Company.

The SEC suit claimed that Franco purchased 3,000 shares of Oakland Holding Company stock in anticipation of making a sizable profit upon the public announcement of the proposed buyout. When the unusual transaction caught the attention of American Stock Exchange officials, Franco rescinded the trade. He claimed that his stockbroker had acted without his authorization. The SEC suit was resolved when Franco signed a consent decree, in which he did not acknowledge any wrongdoing but promised to obey the law in the future. When the affair became public knowledge in 1986, *after* he had

assumed the PRSA presidency, Franco was forced to resign that post. Threatened with action by the PRSA Board of Ethics, he also resigned his membership in October 1986.[33]

Rule 10b-5 is also important in the area of timely and accurate disclosure. This was a central issue in a 1968 landmark case involving the Texas Gulf Sulfur Company. TGS geologists discovered a major deposit of valuable minerals in eastern Canada in November 1963. During the five months between the discovery and its public announcement, a handful of TGS executives—the few people who knew the secret—bought more than 20,000 shares of company stock. To squelch rumors of a major ore strike, TGS issued a news release on April 12, 1964, that said, in part, "The drilling done to date has not been conclusive."[34] Four days later, a second news release announced a major ore strike. An appeals court eventually ruled that the April 12 news release was misleading and a violation of Rule 10b-5. Many of the TGS executives involved in the incident were fined and ordered to repay profits made as a result of the inside information.

PRSA's *Member Code of Ethics 2000* addresses these issues under the section dealing with the disclosure of information. It lists among its guidelines that members shall "be honest and accurate in all communications" and "investigate the truthfulness and accuracy of information released on behalf of those represented." The code cites as an example of improper conduct "Lying by omission: A practitioner for a corporation knowingly fails to release financial information, giving a misleading impression of the corporation's performance."[35]

about its financial health and direction. This includes annual and multiyear reports on net sales, gross profit, income, total assets, and long-term financial obligations. The 10-K report also includes a management discussion and analysis of the company's financial condition.

United States Securities and Exchange Commission
Washington, D.C. 20549

FORM 10-K

☒ ANNUAL REPORT PURSUANT TO SECTION 13 OR 15(d) OF THE SECURITIES
EXCHANGE ACT OF 1934
FOR THE FISCAL YEAR ENDED JUNE 30, 2006

OR

☐ TRANSITION REPORT PURSUANT TO SECTION 13 OR 15(d) OF THE SECURITIES
EXCHANGE ACT OF 1934
FOR THE TRANSITION PERIOD FROM _____ TO _____

COMMISSION FILE NUMBER 0-14278

MICROSOFT CORPORATION

WASHINGTON 91-1144442   (STATE OF INCORPORATION)(I.R.S. ID)   ONE
MICROSOFT WAY, REDMOND, WASHINGTON 98052-6399

(425) 882-8080

Securities registered pursuant to Section 12(b) of the Act:
COMMON STOCK

Securities registered pursuant to Section 12(g) of the Act:
NONE

Indicate by check mark if the registrant is a well-known seasoned issuer, as defined in Rule 405 of the Securities Act. Yes ☒   No ☐

Indicate by check mark if the registrant is not required to file reports pursuant to Section 13 or Section 15(d) of the Exchange Act.   Yes ☐   No ☒

Indicate by check mark whether the registrant (1) has filed all reports required to be filed by Section 13 or 15(d) of the Securities Exchange Act of 1934 during the preceding 12 months (or for such shorter period that the registrant was required to file such reports), and (2) has been subject to such filing requirement~~s~~ ~~90 days   Yes~~

Form 10-K Publicly held corporations such as Microsoft are required to file a Form 10-K every year. Data from the form also have to be included in the company's annual report, which must reach shareholders within 15 days of the annual meeting. (Courtesy of the U.S. Securities and Exchange Commission)

Form 10-K usually provides the basis for the more familiar corporate **annual report,** which has to be in the hands of shareholders no less than 15 days before the corporate annual meeting. Typically, these annual reports are written and designed to make the investor feel good about his or her decision to own stock in the company. But serious investors and analysts look beyond the color pictures printed on glossy paper. They focus on Form 10-K, which is often inserted at the back of the annual report and printed on plain paper. All the small print may seem like gobbledygook, but it *is* necessary; and the information required in Form 10-K also has to be included in the annual report. Among the SEC requirements for an annual report are

- audited financial statements;
- supplementary financial information, such as net sales, gross profits, and per-share data based on income or loss;

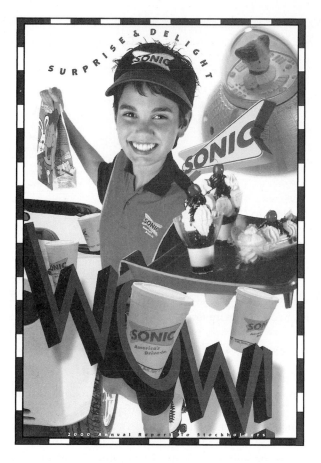

Annual Report Publicly held businesses such as the Sonic restaurant chain are required by law to inform shareholders about the company's financial health and other issues that could affect the value of the shareholders' investments. (Courtesy of Sonic, America's Drive-In)

- management discussion and analysis of the company's financial condition and any unusual events, transactions, or economic changes;
- a brief description of the company's business (products and/or services);
- the identities of company directors and executive officers; and
- a description of any significant litigation in which the company or its directors or officers are involved.

This is only a thumbnail sketch of SEC annual report reporting requirements.[36] It is a good idea to check with the SEC each year to keep up with changes in disclosure requirements.

Another SEC regulation that every practitioner needs to know is SEC Rule 10b-5, which prohibits, among other things, **insider trading** (see QuickBreak 15.2). Indirectly, that is what got Martha Stewart into trouble in 2004. A person violates insider trading rules if he or she buys or sells securities on the basis of insider information not available to other investors. Stewart was convicted of misleading federal investigators about selling shares of ImClone, a pharmaceutical company—just before the government announced an unfavorable ruling on one of the company's

Web Site In an effort to encourage more transparent government, the Marion Brechner Citizen Access Project has created a web site where visitors can research and compare local, state, and federal open records and meetings laws. (Courtesy of the Marion Brechner Citizen Access Project)

experimental drugs. An investigation alleged that inside information may have come from ImClone founder Samuel D. Waksal, a close friend.[37]

If the public is to have confidence in the nation's financial institutions, everyone has to play by the same rules. People in responsible positions, including public relations practitioners, have to be willing to do the right thing. "If you see something that you think is seriously wrong you should do more than just cross your fingers and sign on to it," said business ethics expert Thomas Dunfee. "You have to have a real commitment to the values."[38]

The Federal Communications Commission

Public relations practitioners who work for political candidates or whose clients may be subject to public criticism should be familiar with the federal agency that has regulated the nation's broadcast media since 1934, the **Federal Communications Commission (FCC).** Originally created as the Federal Radio Commission in 1927, the FCC has the primary responsibility for ensuring the orderly use of the nation's airwaves in the public interest. Because a finite number of radio wave frequencies are available for public use, radio and television stations operate under licenses granted by the federal government. In contrast, print media face relatively little government oversight because of historic precedents and First Amendment protections. Since the Telecommunications Act of 1996, broadcast licenses are granted for a period of eight years and may be renewed after a review of the licensee's performance.

VALUES STATEMENT 15.1

Federal Communications Commission

The FCC was established by the Communications Act of 1934 and is charged with regulating interstate and international communications by radio, television, wire, satellite, and cable. Its five commissioners are appointed by the president and confirmed by the Senate for five-year terms. Only three commissioners may be representatives of the same political party, and none may have any financial interest in commission-related business.

It is the mission of the Federal Communications Commission to ensure that the American people have available—at reasonable costs and without discrimination—rapid, efficient, nation- and world-wide communication services; whether by radio, television, wire, satellite, or cable. *47 U.S.C. §151—Title 1, Section 1 of the Communications Act of 1934, as amended.*

—Strategic Plan FY 2003–FY 2008
Federal Communications Commission

Public relations practitioners representing political candidates should also be aware of section 315 of the 1934 Communications Act, better known as the **equal opportunity provision.** Whenever a legally qualified candidate for public office appears in a radio or television broadcast, all other candidates for that office must be afforded equal opportunities for access. It means that if a candidate appears in a broadcast at no cost, all other qualified candidates for that office must be offered the same opportunity. Under another provision of the law, legally qualified candidates must be allowed to purchase commercials at the station's lowest advertising rate.

Section 315 is usually applied to political advertising but can also be triggered by the appearance of a qualified candidate in a product commercial, a public service announcement, or entertainment programming. However, there are exemptions to the rule. The equal time provision does not apply when a candidate appears in a bona fide newscast, news interview, news documentary, or on-the-spot coverage of a bona fide news event.

Under what is known as the **personal attack rule,** stations are required to provide free air time to persons who have been the subject of a broadcast character attack. Unlike section 315, the personal attack rule does not necessarily require equal air time. The station is obliged only to offer a "reasonable" opportunity for response.

An ongoing controversy facing the FCC is the proposed easing of broadcast ownership rules. Under the old rules, media companies were not allowed to own broadcast stations that reached more than 35 percent of the U.S. audience. They also faced limits on how many stations they could own in the same market. The broadcast networks said that they needed wider audience access to compete in today's media-rich environment. However, a large coalition of opponents that cut across the political spectrum opposed the change. Those groups, including PRSA, said this growing media concentration threatened to reduce the diversity of voices in the media.[39] After high-level bargaining, Congress eventually agreed in 2003 to raise the cap to 39 percent. However, in June

2004, a federal appeals court struck down a proposed rule change that would have allowed companies to own more stations in the same market.[40]

Another hot-button issue involving the FCC is a regulation making it unlawful to send an unsolicited advertisement to a facsimile (fax) machine without prior written permission from the recipient. Fines could range up to $500 for each violation.[41] The Junk Fax Prevention Act went into effect in 2005. It has been opposed by a variety of business interests, especially professional associations such as PRSA that use fax messages to communicate with their members.[42] This regulation has also been the target of lawsuits. But unlike the broadcast ownership rules, opponents have not been successful in striking down the junk fax rule.[43] The FCC defines an unsolicited advertisement as "any material advertising the commercial availability or quality of any property, goods, or services which is transmitted to any person without that person's prior express invitation or permission, in writing or otherwise."[44] A similar law, the CAN-SPAM Act of 2003 (Controlling the Assault of Non-Solicited Pornography and Marketing Act), prohibits unwanted commercial messages to e-mail accounts and cell phones. The FTC can levy a fine of up to $11,000 for each violation.

The Food and Drug Administration

As public relations ventures deeper into the integrated marketing of products and services, practitioners are having to familiarize themselves with the regulations of yet another federal agency, the **Food and Drug Administration (FDA)**. The FDA was created to "protect, promote, and enhance the health of the American people." The agency has responsibility for ensuring that "foods are safe, wholesome, and sanitary; human and veterinary drugs, biological products, and medical devices are safe and effective; cosmetics are safe; and electronic products that emit radiation are safe."[45]

The area in which public relations practitioners are most likely to encounter this agency is in the promotion of products or services that are regulated by the FDA. The FDA enforces laws and regulations designed to ensure that regulated products are "honestly, accurately, and informatively represented."[46] FDA rules include restrictions on the labeling and promotion of prescription drugs. Both advertising and public relations professionals working in the health-care field must be aware of these limitations.

The FDA's Division of Drug Marketing, Advertising, and Communications (DDMAC) oversees prescription drug promotional labeling and advertising. Advertising includes commercial messages broadcast on television, radio, or the Internet, communicated over the telephone, or printed in magazines and newspapers. According to regulations, drug ads or promotions cannot be false or misleading and cannot omit material facts. Companies are required to submit their direct-to-consumer (DTC) ads to the FDA at the time they begin running. However, some companies seek prior approval.

"We look at a lot of DTC ads before they run," says Kathryn J. Aikin, of DDMAC. "Manufacturers typically want to be sure they're getting started on the right foot."[47]

QUICK ✓ CHECK

1. Why is it important for public relations practitioners to understand the laws and regulations that govern their organizations?
2. Which federal agency serves as a watchdog against false and misleading advertising claims?
3. What does *disclosure* mean, and why are disclosure rules so vigorously enforced?

Libel

Another area in which public relations practitioners may be restricted in their use of free expression involves **libel,** which is loosely defined as "a false communication that wrongfully injures the reputation of others."[48] To put it another way, when you bad-mouth someone, you had better have your facts!

There are two major reasons why public relations practitioners need to have a good understanding of libel law. First, they need to know that there are limits to free speech, especially when it involves another person's or company's reputation. They also need to understand that the courts have—under certain circumstances—given people great latitude in expressing their opinions on matters of public concern.

The Burden of Proof in Libel

Before 1964, people seeking damages under a claim that they had been libeled needed to prove five things: defamation, publication, identification, damage, and fault. These five things are known as the **burden of proof.**

Defamation. **Defamation** is any communication that unfairly injures a person's reputation and/or ability to maintain social contacts. Untruthful allegations that someone is a Nazi or has AIDS are examples of defamatory statements. It is also possible to defame a company, product, or service. In determining whether defamation has occurred, the court takes into account the context in which the statement was made, asking questions such as whether a reasonable person would understand the comment to be a parody or a joke. A truthful statement cannot be considered defamatory. Also, under the law you cannot defame a dead person.

Publication. **Publication** is the communication of a defamatory statement to a third party. Don't let the term *publication* fool you. This burden of proof is not restricted to print media; it is met regardless of the communication channel used. Another important concept closely related to this is the *republication rule.* If you repeat a defamatory statement made by someone else, *you* can be subject to a separate libel claim, even if you accurately quoted the original source. However, there are exceptions to the republication rule. For example, you may accurately repeat a defamatory statement contained in an official court document or during a meeting of an official governmental body such as Congress.

Identification. **Identification** is the requirement that the person or organization alleging libel has to be identified in such a way that a reasonable person could infer that the defamatory statements applied to the plaintiff. This is easy to prove when names are used. However, this requirement can also be satisfied when no names are mentioned, if the defamatory statement provides information that can lead a reasonable person to believe it describes a particular individual or organization. It is even possible to defame members of a group. An allegation that someone at your college is a crook probably does not satisfy this burden. However, an allegation that someone in your family is a crook probably does.

Damage. There has to be evidence that the person or organization suffered injury or **damage** as a result of the defamation. This is not limited to financial injury, such as the loss of a job. Damage can also consist of loss of social esteem, such as losing all of your friends. Although this kind of damage may be intangible, juries have been known to give out some very high monetary awards as compensation for loss of social esteem.

Fault. A plaintiff can demonstrate **fault** by proving that the defamatory statement is untrue. (Remember, a truthful statement is not defamatory.) Before 1964, the burden was on the defendant to show that the statement was true. Even if the statement was made as a result of unintentional error, the fact that an error was made was all that really mattered. However, it is on this burden of proof—fault, or falseness—that in 1964 the Supreme Court made what many have argued was one of its most significant rulings involving freedom of expression. In that ruling the Court articulated the doctrine of *actual malice,* to which we now turn.

Actual Malice

In the case of ***The New York Times v. Sullivan,*** the Court set a higher burden of proof in libel cases involving public officials. It also shifted the burden of proving the falsity of a statement to the plaintiffs. In essence, the justices said public officials had to show not only that the statements made about them were not true but that the source of those statements knew—or should have known—they were not true. This higher burden of proof is known as **actual malice,** which the Court defined as knowing falsehood or reckless disregard for the truth.

Why did the Supreme Court make it harder for public officials to sue for libel? The case came out of the civil rights struggle of the 1960s. A civil rights group had run a full-page advertisement titled "Heed Their Rising Voices" in the *New York Times*. In the ad the group accused Montgomery, Alabama, officials of illegally suppressing lawful dissent. The basic thrust of the advertisement was accurate. However, some of the statements made in it were not—such as the number of times Martin Luther King Jr. had been arrested (four, not seven as stated in the advertisement). Because of the republication rule, Montgomery Police Commissioner L. B. Sullivan decided to sue the newspaper for libel. The purpose of this tactic was clearly understood by all: to make the nation's news media think twice before accepting the word of civil rights advocates. A jury awarded Sullivan $500,000 in damages, and the Alabama Supreme Court upheld the ruling. The U.S. Supreme Court, however, overturned the decision in a 5–4 vote.

In writing for the Court, Justice William Brennan said this higher burden of proof was necessary to guarantee healthy public debate:

> A rule compelling the critic of official conduct to guarantee the truth of all his factual assertions—and to do so on pain of libel judgments virtually unlimited in amount—leads to . . . "self-censorship." Allowance of the defense of truth, with the burden of proving it on the defendant, does not mean that only false speech will be deterred. . . . Under such a rule, would-be critics of official conduct may be deterred from voicing their criticism, even though it is believed to be true and even though it is in fact true, because of doubt whether it can be proved in court or fear of expense of having to do so. . . . The rule thus dampens the vigor and limits the variety of public debate. It is inconsistent with the First and Fourteenth Amendments.[49]

Subsequent court decisions have defined a **public official** as a person elected to public office (and potentially criticized in that role) or anyone who has significant public responsibility and is engaged in policy making. In another decision, *Gertz v. Robert Welch, Inc.,* the Supreme Court extended the actual malice burden to libel cases involving **public figures**—people who have widespread notoriety or have injected themselves into a public controversy in an attempt to influence its outcome. The Reverend Jesse Jackson may not be a public official, but when it comes to civil rights, he is considered a public figure.

This takes us back to something we stated earlier: People are often given great latitude in expressing their opinions on matters of public concern. As hard a pill as it may be to swallow, there is often little that public relations practitioners can do when they or their bosses are harshly criticized in the media. If a boss qualifies as either a public official or a public figure, then he or she is part of the public discourse and must meet a higher burden of proof, actual malice, to sue successfully for libel. Although a few public officials and public figures have won libel cases, most have not.

Other Forms of Libel

In the mid-1980s the courts handled two libel cases under common law rules. Common law consists of legal rules and principles that originate from judicial decisions, as opposed to those that are enacted by legislators or regulatory agencies.[50] The nature of these **common law libel** cases raises a red flag for business communicators because both cases involve everyday business practices in which human nature can lead to "mistakes." Several elements of these cases are of particular note. First is the lack of constitutional protection. Communication of "a private matter" is not protected by the First Amendment; in these cases, therefore, the plaintiff needed to show only negligence to win punitive damages. Second, in one of the cases the plaintiff won damages on defamatory but true information that exceeded the company's privilege to share such information.

The first case involved the credit reporting firm Dun & Bradstreet, which had issued an erroneous credit report on Greenmoss Builders, a building contractor. The

Supreme Court ruled that this was a "private matter" not involving "matters of public concern" and permitted Greenmoss to recover $50,000 in presumed damages and $300,000 in punitive damages.[51] Although a complicated decision, the ruling appears to exclude nonmedia defendants from constitutional protection.

The second case involved a DuPont company memo following the firing of an employee for sexual harassment. The memo referred to the recent firing and then restated company policies and procedures regarding the issue. Eventually word of the firing, including the identity of the former employee, spread through the community. The former employee sued DuPont for common law libel and won. The court ruled that the company had gone too far in identifying the ex-employee to those who did not need to know his name. The ruling came despite the fact that the information about the employee was true, and despite the company's recognized privilege to pass that information around on a need-to-know basis. Thus, in this common law libel case, truth was *not* a defense. True information that exceeds privilege, in this case someone's legitimate need to know, can cost your company in libel damages.

A recent addition to libel law is **food disparagement laws**—known informally as "veggie libel laws." Although these laws may sound somewhat frivolous, the reason for their creation is not. They are the outgrowth of aggressive news reporting that has had a negative effect—sometimes fair, sometimes unfair—on the marketplace. In the most famous of the veggie libel cases, talk show host Oprah Winfrey successfully defended herself against a suit brought by the cattle industry in 1996. Winfrey had suggested on her show that U.S. beef was not safe to eat. When beef prices fell as a result of what has been called "the Oprah effect," the Texas beef producers sued. However, they lost in the courts as well as in the court of public opinion.[52]

Privacy

Libel is not the only area of the law to distinguish between truly private individuals and persons in the limelight. This distinction is also evident in privacy law. The legal debate over an individual's right to privacy is very complicated and, in many instances, unresolved. It often surprises people to discover that the U.S. Constitution does not specifically mention an individual's right to privacy. However, such a right has developed over the years through the passage of laws and through judicial decisions. As a general rule, private individuals have an easier time suing for invasion of privacy than do public figures.

The Four Torts of Privacy

Although the word *privacy* has one meaning in common everyday usage, it carries a different meaning when used in a legal context. *Black's Law Dictionary* has defined **privacy** as "the right to be left alone; the right of a person to be free from unwarranted publicity."[53] The law recognizes four torts, or wrongful acts, that constitute an invasion of privacy: intrusion, false light, publication of private facts, and appropriation.

QuickBreak 15.3

The Pursuit of Privacy

The *right* to privacy and the *reality* of privacy are two very different concepts in the Digital Age. In a world with a 24-hour news cycle and thousands of reporters needing to fill news holes, woe to anyone who unwittingly becomes a subject of media attention. It can be a suffocating experience.

This was the fate of the late Richard Jewell. He worked as a security guard in Centennial Park during the 1996 Summer Olympics in Atlanta. On a Friday night during the games, Jewell spotted a green backpack, suspected that it was a bomb, and helped hurry enough people from the scene that only one person was killed when it exploded. At first he was hailed as a hero. But when the media identified him as a suspect, he and his family suffered 88 days of unrelenting scrutiny.

"He would appear to be the victim of the beast that the media can turn into when there is blood in the water," *USA Today* reported years later. "The images of Jewell wading through the world press to get to an FBI interview never die."[54]

Jewell was eventually cleared of wrongdoing in the Centennial Park blast. Someone else was arrested. Several media organizations chose to settle libel suits brought by Jewell. Jewell died of natural causes in August 2007. He was 44 years old.[55]

The lines between legitimate news interest and prurient curiosity are often blurred. Consider the matter of Dale Earnhardt's autopsy photos.[56] When the racing legend tragically died from injuries received in the last lap of the 2001 Daytona 500, questions arose about NASCAR's official explanation for the driver's death, a seat belt failure. The

Orlando Sentinel had reported that four drivers had recently died as a result of violent head whip, a preventable injury. In an effort to confirm its suspicions, the newspaper submitted a public records request for Earnhardt's autopsy photos. Although the *Sentinel* said it would not publish the photos, the family fought the request out of a fear that the photos would wind up on the Internet.

What followed was a flurry of legal and legislative activity. In court, the newspaper won a partial victory when it agreed to the selection of an independent medical doctor to examine the photographs under court supervision. The expert confirmed the newspaper's suspicion that violent head whip, not seat belt failure, was to blame. As a result, NASCAR reversed an earlier decision and required head and neck restraints for drivers.

However, in the court of public opinion, the Earnhardt family was a clear winner. Because of an outpouring of public outrage, state lawmakers passed the Florida Family Protection Act within 39 days of the crash. The bill severely restricts media access to autopsy photos. A Florida student newspaper challenged the constitutionality of the law all the way to the U.S. Supreme Court and lost.

And we haven't even begun to discuss hackers and eavesdropping technology that invade our privacy in ways we can't even imagine. The right and reality of privacy continues to evolve in the Digital Age. As with most other social conflicts, the issues will eventually boil down to a question of values.

Intrusion. **Intrusion** is defined as an improper and intentional invasion of a person's physical seclusion or private affairs. This area of privacy law hinges on whether a person has a reasonable expectation of privacy. Examples of intrusion involve trespassing on private property and illegally bugging telephone conversations. But if a television crew positioned on a public sidewalk photographed you inside your home through an open window, that would not, in a legal sense, be considered intrusion.

False Light. You can be sued if you present someone in a **false light,** even if the communication in question isn't defamatory. For example, a picture of a man holding a mug of water in his hand is not, in and of itself, defamatory. But if the man is a member of a religion that prohibits its followers from drinking alcohol, and if the picture's caption implies that he is enjoying a beer, that could result in a claim of false light invasion of privacy. Categories of false light are distortion (the unintentional distortion of reality), fabrication (knowing falsehood perpetrated through alteration or embellishment of the facts), and fictionalization (publication of something, usually a book or movie, that is presented as fiction but closely mirrors real life).

Publication of Private Facts. **Publication of private facts** involves the public disclosure of true personal information that is embarrassing and potentially offensive. The courts have ruled, in essence, that we are entitled to keep some secrets about ourselves. However, to make a successful claim under this tort, a plaintiff must show that the information is neither newsworthy nor from a public record. If an ordinary person drinks too much in the privacy of his or her home and doesn't break any laws, it is likely that the courts will consider this private information. However, if this same person is an elected official and gets picked up for drunken driving, his or her drinking problem becomes a public matter.

Appropriation. **Appropriation** is defined as the commercial use of someone's name, voice, likeness, or other defining characteristics without consent. For example, entertainer Bette Midler was once forced to tone down her stage act because she too closely mimicked the voice and mannerisms of legendary actress Mae West. "The Divine Miss M" herself later successfully used this aspect of privacy law to prevent a Midler sound-alike from appearing in an advertisement. The commercial use of a person's likeness without consent is often referred to either as *misappropriation* or as infringement of an individual's *right of publicity.* This right does not necessarily end with a person's death. In several states, California among them, the deceased's heirs retain the "right of publicity." However, the courts have said that in some circumstances a claim of misappropriation is not valid. For example, news content is not considered a commercial use. Nor is it considered a commercial use when a media outlet uses a likeness in promoting itself. Written consent is the best protection from a claim of misappropriation.

Privacy Issues in Public Relations

Privacy issues can arise in countless aspects of the practice of public relations. Practitioners routinely prepare news releases, publicity photos, videos, newsletters, annual reports, brochures, posters, and web sites for public dissemination. An invasion of privacy suit can originate from any of these communications.

One area in which the practitioner has to be especially sensitive to privacy rights is employee relations. "It should not be assumed that a person's status as an employee waives his/her right to privacy," writes Frank Walsh, an expert in public relations law. "However, there are circumstances in which the employment relationship may provide an implied consent or waiver sufficient to invalidate an invasion of privacy suit."[57]

Privacy concerns also come into play when reporters make inquiries about employees. There are restrictions on the kinds of employee information that can be made public. The laws vary by location and profession. Typically, practitioners are limited to confirming a person's employment, job title, job description, date hired, and, in some cases, date terminated. A good guideline to follow: Check first with the personnel or human resources department about what is considered public or private employee information.

The growth of the Internet has raised many workplace questions. For example, the degree to which an employer may monitor an employee's e-mail may depend on whether a reasonable expectation of privacy exists. In some corporations employees are told that their e-mail will be monitored. Other companies, in search of time-wasting and inappropriate behavior, regularly review printouts of the web sites their employees visit while on the job.

Copyright

Although privacy protections are not specifically mentioned in the U.S. Constitution, **copyright** protections are. Copyrights protect original works from unauthorized use. Central to any discussion of copyright protections is the concept of **intellectual property,** which federal law defines as "original works of authorship that are fixed in a tangible form of expression." Copyrights cover seven forms of expression: literary works; musical works; dramatic works; pantomimes and choreographic works; pictorial, graphic, and sculptural works; motion pictures and other audiovisual works; and sound recordings.[58] Because the development of digital technology has made it nearly impossible to tell a copy from an original, the protection of intellectual property is a legal area of vital importance.

Copyright concerns about protecting one's own property and respecting the rights of others are a common issue for public relations practitioners. Copyright law confronts us all in many different ways every day. Is it all right to take a funny editorial cartoon published in the morning newspaper and reprint it in the company newsletter? Can someone use one company's products to promote another's without permission? Is it legal to take an image off a web site and use it in another medium? Are you allowed to photocopy this book?

Copyright Guidelines

As is true with other aspects of public relations law, the best place to get answers to these and other questions about copyrights are people who have expertise in this area—in this case, copyright lawyers and the U.S. Copyright Office. That said, some general rules of copyright are worth remembering:

- Copyright protection exists from the moment a work is created in a fixed, tangible form. In other words, the law presumes that a work becomes the intellectual property of the author at the moment of its creation.

- Copyrights do not protect works that have not been fixed in a tangible form of expression. Although it is possible to copyright an author's written description of a particular location, that does not prohibit someone else from offering a different description of the same setting.

- If a work is prepared by someone within the scope of his or her employment, it is considered **work for hire** and becomes the intellectual property of the employer. The work belongs to the employer if it was produced while the employee was "on the clock." Even after hours, the employer retains the rights if company resources (such as computers or copiers) were used.

- It is possible for the copyright owner, such as a photographer or writer or artist, to grant limited use of the work while retaining copyright ownership.

- Copyrights do not protect ideas, methods, systems, processes, concepts, principles, and discoveries. They do, however, protect the manner in which these are expressed.

- Government documents and other publicly owned works may not be copyrighted.

The Digital Millennium Copyright Act

The ability to make exact copies of digital files without any measurable decline in quality is one of the great blessings of the Digital Age. However, in the view of copyright holders, it is also one of the great curses.

As noted in Chapter 11, digital technology has made it easier to copy and distribute the fruits of someone else's labors. This is of particular concern to the entertainment and computer software industries, which have seen their intellectual property rights eroded by the manufacturing and distribution of illegal copies.

These industries use special technology designed to foil piracy. For example, when a Hollywood movie studio distributes its latest movie on DVD, it encrypts the data on the disk to prevent unauthorized copying. That should be enough. However, in a world in which the frontiers of computer knowledge are breached every day, it is not. To use an analogy, locksmiths would face the same problem if every time they built a better lock, someone came along behind them and built an even better key.

In an effort to address this problem, the U.S. Congress passed the **Digital Millennium Copyright Act** (DMCA) in 1998. The DMCA established new rules for downloading, sharing, and viewing copyrighted material on the Internet. It made it a crime to circumvent antipiracy measures built into most commercial software, videos, and DVDs. It also outlawed code-cracking devices used to copy software illegally. Violators can be fined up to $2,500 for each violation.

The law has its critics. Academics, computer researchers, and librarians argue that DMCA limits their right to copy and share a limited amount of material for

QuickBreak 15.4

Online Music Piracy

Of all of the issues discussed in this chapter, the one that strikes closest to home for many readers is the battle over intellectual property. Of course, it is not often thought of in those terms. Many young people see it as the clash between the music industry and consumers over downloading music on the Internet. To some, this issue is nothing more than an attempt by the rich to get richer. But the music industry sees it as theft and estimates annual losses from piracy at $4.2 billion worldwide.[59]

In many instances, the law on intellectual property is clear. According to the U.S. Copyright Office, "Copyright is a form of protection provided by the laws of the United States (title 17, U.S. Code) to the authors of 'original works of authorship,' including literary, dramatic, musical, artistic, and certain other intellectual works. This protection is available to both published and unpublished works."[60]

Protection of intellectual property was included in the original draft of the U.S. Constitution. But that was before the Digital Age, the Internet, and the creation of technology that makes it easy to create and globally distribute perfect reproductions.

This is where the legal waters are muddy. At first, the music industry targeted file-sharing services such as Napster. The courts ruled that these services were guilty of abetting copyright infringement because they operated from a central server. However, when companies such as Grokster, KaZaA, and Morpheus moved to more decentralized peer-to-peer (P2P) technology, the music industry hit a snag. Citing the so-called 1983 Betamax case, the courts ruled that these P2P companies have no more control over the actions of consumers than manufacturers of home video recorders.[61]

That legal setback forced the music industry to take the controversial step of suing its own customers. The Recording Industry Association of America filed 261 copyright infringement lawsuits in September 2003.[62] RIAA claimed its lawsuits targeted people who illegally distributed, on average, more than 1,000 music files for millions of other P2P network users.

This tactic brought the music industry both scorn and embarrassment—especially when the media learned that one defendant was a 12-year-old New York honors student.[63] RIAA has targeted college students in recent years, issuing 14,646 notices of illegal downloading on university computer networks during the first half of the 2006–2007 school year. Some schools suspend or dismiss multiple offenders.[64]

educational and noncommercial purposes. However the law provides some exemptions to some of these same groups, including limited institutional liability for violations committed by college faculty and students. While several attempts have been made to amend DMCA, those efforts have been successfully opposed by the music and movie industries.[65]

Fair Use

The courts have said it is all right to use copyrighted works without their owners' permission in some circumstances. These instances fall under the concept known as **fair use,** which the law has said is the use of copyrighted material "for purposes such as criticism, comments, news reporting, and teaching."[66] Again, fair use is a very complex area of the law. However, it is usually considered fair use if the copyrighted work is used for an educational as opposed to a commercial purpose.

The degree to which the copyrighted material is copied and the effect on its potential market value also affect whether a claim of fair use is valid. It is probably safe for professors to photocopy a paragraph from a book and distribute the copies to their classes. Copy shops have stopped reproducing book chapters for professors using course packets, however, because the courts have ruled that this practice harms the book's potential market value.

In a ruling that further defined fair use rights, the U.S. Supreme Court strengthened the rights of freelance writers in 2001. The court ruled by a 7–2 margin that major publishing companies may not reproduce the work of freelancers in electronic form without their consent. The effect of the ruling was to give the writers a voice in whether their work, originally published in one form, could be electronically published in an online database. As a practical matter, the Court's ruling largely affects only that material produced in the pre-Internet era—before freelance contracts specified whether the material could be used online.

Public relations practitioners often claim fair use when taking a quotation from a copyrighted publication for use in a news release, brochure, report, or speech. (For example, we have engaged in this practice in writing this book.) However, a claim of fair use cannot be made without appropriate attribution of the copyrighted material to its owner. As your writing and editing teachers will remind you, this is just one more reason why it is necessary to use quotation marks and to properly cite sources of information.

Protecting Your Intellectual Property Rights

To assert a right of copyright protection, the work in question should bear a copyright notice that cites the year of the copyright and the name of its owner. An example: Copyright © 2008 Joan Q. Public. An even more complete way of securing copyright protection is to register a work within three months of its creation with the U.S. Copyright Office, Library of Congress, 101 Independence Ave. S. E., Washington, D.C. 20559-6000. There is a $45 nonrefundable fee for basic registrations. Although registration is not required to claim ownership, it is required to bring an infringement of copyright lawsuit.

As a result of legislation proposed by the late Congressman Sonny Bono, a California Republican—the guy from Sonny and Cher for those who know pop music history—the owners of copyrighted works retain their rights longer than in the past. According to the U.S. Copyright Office web site: "As a general rule, for works created after January 1, 1978, copyright protection lasts for the life of the author plus an additional 70 years. For an anonymous work, a pseudonymous work, or a work made for hire, the copyright endures for a term of 95 years from the year of its first publication or a term of 120 years from the year of its creation, whichever expires first."[67] The U.S. Supreme Court upheld the change in 2003. That decision relieved executives at the Walt Disney Corp., who were in danger of losing control over their most identifiable icon, Mickey Mouse.[68]

Similar to copyrights are trademarks and service marks. Both protect intellectual property rights. **Trademarks** (™) protect names, designs, slogans, and symbols that are associated with specific products. When you see the symbol ®, that indicates that the trademark is registered with the U.S. Office of Patents and Trademarks. For example, pick up a 12-ounce can of Coca-Cola®. Both the name Coca-Cola® and its derivative, Coke®, are registered trademarks. So is the design of the can and style of the lettering. When organizations want to protect names, designs, slogans, and designs associated with a particular service, they apply for a **service mark,** indicated by the symbol ℠.

1. What is the higher burden of proof that public officials and public figures must meet to make a claim of libel?
2. In terms of privacy law, what is appropriation?
3. What steps have been taken to protect intellectual property rights on the Internet?

Litigation Public Relations

If you are an expert in movie or television trivia, you probably know about Dr. Richard Kimble. He was the lead character in the popular 1993 movie *The Fugitive* and the 1960s television series of the same name. What you may not know is that Kimble, a respected doctor on the run after his wrongful conviction for the death of his wife, is based on a real person. Dr. Sam Sheppard was convicted in 1954 of killing his pregnant wife. Twelve years later, the U.S. Supreme Court threw out Sheppard's conviction on the grounds that he had been denied a fair trial because of sensational media coverage before and during the trial.

The Sheppard case is often evoked when the conflict between a free press and a fair trial is debated. As a result of the Supreme Court's ruling, cameras and microphones were briefly barred from U.S. courtrooms. By the 1980s, they returned to most courtrooms—but not federal courts—under tight restrictions. This coincided with the growth in the number of media outlets, notably cable television and the Internet, and a series of highly publicized trials, particularly the 1995 double-murder trial of football legend O. J. Simpson. As lawyers for both sides played to the cameras, the battle for hearts and minds extended beyond the courthouse to the people on the streets. It is in this context that the controversial practice of **litigation public relations (LPR)** was born.

Litigation public relations is the use of mass communication techniques to influence events surrounding legal cases. Although it often focuses on lawyers' dealings with reporters, including preparation of news releases, coaching for interviews, and monitoring media, LPR can also involve the use of other public relations practices. These include focus groups and surveys as well as courtroom exhibit preparation.

Free Press versus Fair Trial

A clash of values is at the heart of the controversy surrounding LPR. The First Amendment guarantees freedom of speech and of the press. The Sixth Amendment guarantees fair and open trials. In this age of pervasive media, these two social interests often come into conflict.

While serving as chairman of the Criminal Justice Standards Committee of the American Bar Association (ABA), William Jeffress Jr. said, "A lot of us think defense attorneys and prosecutors shouldn't be playing to the press and becoming public relations agents for their clients."[69] One New York judge complained, "Lawyers now feel it is the essence of their function to try the case in the public media."[70]

Not surprisingly, some lawyers vigorously defend the use of public relations in connection with their practices. The late William M. Kunstler, who served as defense counsel in some of the most controversial trials of the past generation, believed that the use of pretrial publicity was necessary to balance scales of justice he thought were tipped unfairly toward the prosecution. "Whenever and wherever practicable, fire must be met with fire," Kunstler wrote.[71]

Because few states have laws that limit what prosecutors and defense attorneys can say before trial, it is generally left to state bar associations to regulate pretrial comment.[72] Most of these regulations mirror Rule 3.6 of the ABA's Model Rules of Professional Conduct. The rule states that "a lawyer shall not make an extrajudicial statement that a reasonable person would expect to be disseminated by means of public communication if the lawyer knows or reasonably should know that it will have a substantial likelihood of materially prejudicing an adjudicative proceeding."[73] However, this rule is rarely enforced.

The waters were muddied even further by the U.S. Supreme Court in June 1991, when the Court reversed sanctions against a Nevada attorney who had conducted a news conference to counter negative publicity about his client. In *Dominic P. Gentile v. State Bar of Nevada,* the Court said the rule, as interpreted by the Nevada state bar, was too vague. In his opinion for the majority, Justice Anthony M. Kennedy wrote, "In some circumstances press comment is necessary to protect the rights of the client and prevent abuse of the courts."[74]

"The stakes are inevitably high in litigation public relations situations," writes Dirk C. Gibson of the University of New Mexico. "At the least, your financial well-being may be affected by the outcome in a civil action, while in a criminal action a trial outcome may literally be a matter of life or death, or the deprivation of personal liberty and freedom."[75]

The Use of LPR Tactics

One survey of trial lawyers suggests that although most do not, as a rule, use mass communication techniques in their practices, a majority approve of their use. Nine out of 10 litigators surveyed said that in certain circumstances it is appropriate to speak to the media on behalf of a client. And by more than a 2–1 ratio, those who were surveyed and expressed an opinion said they thought the media had been fair

Media Analysis Report A media analysis report can help litigation public relations practitioners show clients the effectiveness of media relations strategies and tactics. (Courtesy of Levick Strategic Communications)

in reporting cases in which they had personally been involved. Still, most lawyers appear to be uneasy about being under the media spotlight.[76]

When public relations practitioners are engaged in LPR, they usually work for the lawyer, not the client. LPR practitioners often aid in pretrial research by using public opinion polls and focus groups to determine the mood of the jury pool. Lawyers sometimes use this information to test specific approaches that may be employed in court. Practitioners often coach both lawyers and clients on how to deal with the media, how to be interviewed, and how to be proactive in defending their reputation. A practitioner's roles also may include preparation of courtroom exhibits;

service as a contact point for the media; and, in the most controversial aspect of LPR, assistance in efforts to influence the jury pool before a trial ever takes place.

Even when the practitioner works independently of a lawyer, it is often the lawyer who has the closest access to the client. The reason for this is simple: The lawyer, not the practitioner, has legal immunity. One very public example of this surfaced in 1998, when then–presidential spokesman Mike McCurry told reporters that he had not asked President Clinton about his relationship with a White House intern. McCurry said he did not want to be subpoenaed by the special prosecutor investigating the allegations surrounding Clinton:

> On matters like this that are going to be under investigation, I think it could conceivably jeopardize the legal representation the president is entitled to, so I choose not to ask him directly about these things and rely on what counsel tells me. And then we work with the president to figure how we're going to respond to questions.[77]

For any practitioner, the reality of this lawyer–client **privilege** issue can be difficult to swallow—especially when it runs counter to the professional need to have direct access to management. It was especially frustrating for McCurry, who told reporters at one White House briefing, "I think you all know the constraints that I'm laboring under here, and I don't want to belabor the pain and anguish I feel."[78] However, as a general rule, courts have treated attorney work products—including case-specific public relations activity done under contract to an attorney—as privileged communication.

Is LPR in Society's Best Interests?

Is LPR a good thing for our society? No pun intended, but the jury is still out. On the one hand, people and companies should have every right to defend their reputations in the court of public opinion. However, many are bothered by attempts to use extrajudicial statements (statements made outside a court) to influence proceedings inside the court.

One place where this happens with increasing regularity is the Internet. According to a study released in 2004, a growing number of defendants are taking their side of the story to the web.[79] For example, when Michael Jackson was arrested on child molestation charges in November 2003, his publicist posted his defense on MJJSource.com, "The Official Source for Michael Jackson News and Information." The site contained an open letter to his fans, news releases, background materials, and downloadable court documents. According to the authors of that study, "The analysis revealed that standard litigation public relations standards transfer well to the Internet and suggests that such web sites are a promising means for disseminating and controlling a client's message."[80]

It all comes down to the difficult balancing act left us by the framers of the Constitution. A built-in conflict exists between the First and Sixth Amendments. Judges, lawyers, and public relations practitioners must carefully navigate these uncharted waters. We must also remember that, as public relations practitioners, we have our own codes of ethics to uphold. The PRSA *Member Code of Ethics 2000* says that practitioners must "serve the public interest by acting as responsible advocates for those we represent." The code also says that "a member shall preserve the integrity of the process of communication." Though not explicit statements on LPR, they do, nevertheless, provide meaningful guidance.

QUICK ✓ CHECK

1. What is litigation public relations?
2. Why must litigation public relations practitioners sometimes deal only with lawyers instead of the lawyers' clients?
3. What are the arguments for and against the use of litigation public relations?

Summary

At a time when many mourn a lack of civility in society, public relations practitioners face pressure to operate within both the letter and the spirit of the laws governing their profession. Practitioners must follow a wide array of rules and regulations that cover practically every aspect of their professional responsibilities. Unfortunately, many appear woefully ignorant of these laws.

First Amendment protection for the practice of public relations lies in the gray area between political and commercial speech. The underlying purpose of each communication determines the degree of constitutional protection it enjoys. In addition to constitutional issues, laws govern various aspects of specific businesses. Among the most notable of these are disclosure laws pertaining to publicly held companies. Practitioners also are often confronted by a need to understand libel, privacy, and copyright laws. In the case of libel and privacy laws, they also need to understand the different burdens of proof for public and private individuals. The growth of the Internet and digital technologies has triggered legal issues undreamt of a generation ago.

Public relations is having a growing—and not necessarily positive—effect on our civil and criminal justice systems. The practice of litigation public relations is expanding dramatically—thanks in part to the built-in conflict that exists between our constitutional freedom of expression and our constitutional right to a fair and open trial. Here, as in other areas of public relations, we should be guided by our values.

DISCUSSION QUESTIONS

1. Devise a response to this statement from a fellow public relations practitioner: "This is the United States. I have freedom of speech. I can say whatever I want on behalf of my clients."
2. How do federal agencies regulate commercial speech?
3. What is the burden of proof for libel? Are all persons treated the same under libel law?

4. How do privacy rights affect the practice of public relations?
5. What are some tasks undertaken by a practitioner of litigation public relations? Under what constraints do LPR practitioners operate?

Memo from the Field

James F. Haggerty, Esq.; President; The PR Consulting Group, Inc.; New York, New York

James F. Haggerty, president and CEO of The PR Consulting Group, is an attorney with more than 20 years of experience in marketing, public relations, and public affairs. Among the nation's best-known experts in litigation communications, Haggerty has also earned a national reputation in professional services marketing, public affairs, and crisis management.

The intersection of public relations and law continues to widen, as interest in legal matters and legal media coverage grows. Unfortunately, the intersection is often littered with blind spots, potholes, and other hazards. For the PR practitioner with the right skills, however, it can be an avenue to a unique public relations career, combining media, law, regulation, government affairs, and public opinion in a way that is fast-paced, challenging and, in the end, extremely satisfying.

Law now permeates most aspects of our lives, and media and news coverage are no exception. Watch CNN, MSNBC, or Fox News long enough and you begin to appreciate just how much legal news coverage is a part of our lives. A Court TV producer recently told me that the network became so successful that *all* news is now Court TV. She wasn't very far from the truth.

The ramifications for the public relations field are enormous. You don't have to be a lawyer to excel in this field, but nearly all PR practitioners at some time in their careers will now find themselves immersed in legal issues—or butting heads with the lawyers representing their client. Lawyers who still feel "no comment" is always the best response.

My company spends 70–80 percent of its time advising clients in the relatively new public relations specialty called litigation public relations. It combines the best elements of crisis communications, public affairs, and litigation strategy. In litigation public relations, it is not enough to deliver media coverage or other PR "results"—you've got to deliver coverage that helps to meet the client's litigations goals: whether it is discouraging legal action before it is filed, creating the proper atmosphere for a beneficial settlement, or controlling the effect on the client's reputation as a case moves to trial and beyond.

You need the ability to sift through 100-page legal filings for the sentence or two that catches the real "story" behind the case. You need the confidence to deal with lawyers and argue for a communications strategy that will enhance the litigation strategy. And you need to pick your media targets carefully: Giant media lists and mass-produced press kits are usually the exception rather than the rule.

But here's a fact most lawyers won't tell you: Sometimes what happens in the court of public opinion can be more important than what happens in the court of law.

An example: We recently worked with a client who spent eight years tangled in oppressive litigation with a large multinational corporation. Although the company's lawyers were doing an excellent job, the legal wrangling seemed endless. The other side's strategy was to bury the company in legal filings and discovery requests until virtually all of the defendant's resources were focused on fending off what was, at best, a very weak case. The litigation was sapping the lifeblood of a company that didn't have the resources to match the much larger multinational.

Then we got involved. Six months later, the case was withdrawn, with a simple joint statement that the parties would "agree to disagree."

How did this happen? In looking at the situation, we reasoned that the one thing that would stop the multinational plaintiff from continuing its frivolous litigation was a severe blow to the company's reputation. They needed to look not just wrong on the law but foolish for continuing what was obviously a mean-spirited, vindictive lawsuit designed to crush a smaller competitor. So we worked with thousands of pages of legal documents to assemble the kind of information that would convince an influential columnist to write an opinion piece exposing the true story of the case. Then we showed the column to an Associated Press reporter, who wrote a story on the column itself. The AP story was picked up in about a half-dozen cities nationwide. An editorial writer in one of the key trade publications covering the industry saw the AP story and wrote a very damaging editorial exposing the company's tactics. And so on.

It wasn't long before the multinational began to see that continuing the lawsuit was getting in the way of its own business goals. At that point, the plaintiff realized it was far easier to quit than to fight!

This is the value of litigation public relations. And while we usually can't have that kind of impact on every case, we can ensure that we create the kind of positive conditions that facilitate the best possible result for our clients: allowing them to get the litigation behind them and get back to the *real* work of their company or organization.

CASE STUDY 15.1

Higher Standards?

The theme of the Bank of America's 2002 annual report was "Higher Standards." Chairman, CEO, and President Kenneth D. Lewis said it reflected the "company's commitment to the idea that in every endeavor, there is always an opportunity to raise the bar, to do something better than has ever been done before."[81]

In his letter to shareholders, Lewis took note of what he called "a crisis of public confidence in the ability of American corporations to govern themselves effectively and ethically." He said that Bank of America (BA) would aggressively promote its core values and its recently updated code of ethics.

"But we also know that actions speak louder than words," Lewis wrote. "And so, we foster a culture of openness, in which healthy debate is encouraged and associates are expected to blow the whistle on improper activity."[82]

Unfortunately for BA, someone had already blown the whistle. The Securities and Exchange Commission (SEC) received an anonymous letter during the summer of 2001 accusing BA of improper late-day trading and improper market timing.[83] In simpler terms, the complaint boiled down to giving a handful of investors an unfair advantage.

The timing of the transaction is critical. When someone purchases mutual fund shares after 4 P.M. Eastern U.S. Time—when the New York markets close—the law requires that they be priced at the *next day's* closing value. What the anonymous letter alleged—and the SEC later confirmed—was that BA allowed certain preferred customers to buy mutual fund shares at *that day's* closing price. That means that if the price went up overnight, the buyer got a bargain not available to all investors.[84]

With the anonymous letter were copies of e-mails that documented BA's actions. In November 2001, SEC staff asked BA to turn over the e-mails of seven senior managers from the previous three years. One e-mail in particular, which the bank's director of marketing had sent via blind copies to other senior executives, was of special interest.[85] To put it simply, it was the smoking gun.

What the SEC staff did not know was that BA had also received a copy of the anonymous letter. The company knew exactly what the SEC investigators sought.[86] What followed was a series of stalling and delaying tactics that, in the end, backfired.

BA responded to the government's document request by saying that it could produce e-mails for the previous five months, but that the restoration of earlier e-mails from backup tapes would incur an "unreasonable amount of time, labor, and expense."[87] The company did not disclose that it had already restored the critical e-mail exchange, the so-called smoking gun. The e-mail was retrieved from the backup tape and then deleted.[88]

After receiving only a fraction of what it had requested by May 2002, the SEC again directed BA to turn over all documents in a timely matter. By October, the bank's attorney announced that the firm had fully complied with the government's request. However, it had not—the smoking gun e-mail was still missing. The SEC staff questioned a former company official under oath on October 28 and learned that BA did, in fact, have copies of the missing e-mail, as well as a copy of the anonymous letter that triggered the investigation. Bank officials later blamed "a technical glitch" for the failure to produce the documents.[89]

This pattern of delay continued. In December, the SEC again ordered BA to turn over the documents—only to learn a month later that some of them had been destroyed.[90] Another handover of additional documents in early February 2003 was still incomplete. As if to add insult to injury, SEC auditors flew from Washington to San Francisco later that month to examine what they had been led to believe were the remaining documents. Only after the auditors arrived from their cross-country trip did they learn that the company had known for months that hundreds of documents the auditors had expected to examine were "missing."[91]

To make a long story short, it wasn't until December 23, 2003—more than two years after the initial SEC staff request—that BA handed over all of the pertinent e-mails, including the smoking gun. BA fired several employees who had been embroiled in the scandal.[92] Armed with the evidence, the SEC began to piece together the whole story—not only the improper late-day trading that sparked the investigation, but also the subsequent cover-up.[93]

On May 10, 2004, the SEC announced that Bank of America had agreed to an official censure and a $10 million civil penalty as part of an out-of-court settlement. The commission found that BA "repeatedly failed to promptly furnish documents requested by the staff, provided misinformation concerning the ability of production status of such documents, and engaged in dilatory acts that delayed the investigation."[94]

The other shoe fell a few days later, when BA announced that it agreed to pay $375 million in shareholder repayments and civil penalties to settle impending securities fraud charges. Eight members of the bank's board of directors were also required to leave their positions within a year.[95]

"I believe that we will be judged not by the actions of a few of our associates, but rather by the way we responded as a team to a violation of our shared values," Bank of America CEO Lewis told shareholders in the company's 2003 annual report. "We will have no tolerance for decisions or actions that fail to put the interests of our customers, associates, and shareholders first."[96]

DISCUSSION QUESTIONS

1. From both legal and ethical perspectives, what did Bank of America do wrong?
2. What is the harm in a publicly held company like Bank of America giving its best customers an advantage in stock market transactions? Doesn't a special relationship deserve special treatment?
3. What is your reaction to statements made in Bank of America's 2002 and 2003 annual reports?
4. This case study does not mention the actions of any public relations practitioners. Why do you think the authors chose to include it?

CASE STUDY **15.2**

In Search of Sunshine

One of comedian George Carlin's characters from his classic standup routines is "Al Sleet, your hippy-dippy weatherman." Al, it seems, is just a few fries short of a Happy Meal. So it comes as no surprise when the hippy-dippy weatherman says, "Tonight's forecast: Dark. Continuing mostly dark through the night. Turning to scattered light at dawn."[97]

However, when University of Florida Professor Bill Chamberlin tells you that the forecast for accessing public records in a particular state is "dark," he is not joking. Instead, he and other like-minded individuals are making a statement about the value of citizen access to public records in a democracy.

Chamberlin is the director of the Marion Brechner Citizen Access Project (MB-CAP), a research unit of the Brechner Center for Freedom of Information at the university's College of Journalism and Communications. According to the MBCAP's web site, its goal is "to allow citizens and public officials to better understand public access to local government information in all 50 states."[98] The project is named for Marion B. Brechner, a central Florida broadcasting executive and philanthropist who contributed $600,000 for its creation in 1999. She and her late husband, Joseph L. Brechner, long active in press freedom causes, had given more than $1 million for the creation of the Freedom of Information Center in 1985.[99]

"Any element of government control over information flow means that the coyote is in charge of the chicken barn," Chamberlin said. "Any government control over what information governments disclose and do not disclose to the public means a serious risk to our representative democracy."[100]

Brechner Center personnel often answer queries from the public, journalists, officials, and policy advocates. Chamberlin said that many of these questions in the early 1990s centered on which states had the best and worst laws granting public access to government records. With the help of Brechner's contribution and early support from the Knight Foundation, MBCAP was born and a massive research effort was launched.

Under Chamberlin's direction, UF graduate students examined public records and open meetings laws nationwide. "For the research, we used only graduate students with legal research training, given the sensitivity of putting legal material on the web," Chamberlin said. This involved research of each state's constitutional provisions and laws. It will eventually include reviews of relevant appellate court decisions.

The MBCAP's Sunshine Advisory Board evaluated this information in a variety of categories. For each, the 11-member board rated various state laws on a 7-point scale developed by Chamberlin and several research consultants. The highest ratings went to the states with the fewest barriers to public access to government records. Each of the scale's seven rating points is represented with a weather icon.

For example, the MBCAP staff researched the number of hours public records are available for citizen inspection. None of the states earned either a "sunny" (7), or completely open, rating. Nor did any receive a "mostly sunny" (6), or mostly open, rating. Fourteen states were rated as "sunny with clouds" (5), meaning that public records in those states are somewhat open. Nearly half of the states were rated as "party cloudy" (4), meaning the public records are "neither more open nor more closed." MBCAP rated record access in three states and the District of Columbia as being "cloudy" (3), or somewhat closed. Nine states were rated as "nearly dark" (2), or mostly closed. No states received a "dark" (1), or completely closed, rating.[101]

Each state's ratings are entered into an interactive database on MBCAP's web site. Visitors can study the transparency of individual states or compare ratings among states. The site also serves as a clearinghouse of freedom of information research from other organizations with similar interests, such as the Reporters Committee for Freedom of the Press and the Society of Professional Journalists.

"We are regularly called by freedom of information activists, journalists, and state legislators interested in changing the law in their state," Chamberlin said. "They are anxious to learn what other states are doing and which states have the laws that most encourage access."

Chamberlin said that the MBCAP has focused its attention in recent years on the impact the War on Terrorism has had on state public records law. Democracies have had to strike a delicate balance between two of their core values, public safety and open government, he explained.

"Scholars and FOI activists have found that in the face of terrorism threats, state lawmakers from many states are shutting down access to a wide range of information, including security response plans and criminal investigations," Chamberlin said. "It may seem intuitively responsible to protect information that would assist terrorists."

However, Chamberlin added that shielding the public from the actions of government officials "may do more harm than good" because the public can't pressure officials to correct security flaws if it doesn't know about them.

Despite having relatively modest resources for the pursuit of its vital mission, the MBCAP continues to operate from its Florida office with one goal in mind: to make every state a sunshine state.

DISCUSSION QUESTIONS

1. Why is access to government information important to public relations practitioners?
2. Identify the four steps in the public relations process as they relate to the Marion Brechner Citizen Access Project.
3. What role do values play in this case study?
4. Given what has been described as "relatively modest resources," how would you promote the mission of the MBCAP?

NOTES

1. *Universal Declaration of Human Rights,* United Nations General Assembly resolution 217 A (III), 10 December 1948, online, www.un.org/Overview/rights.html.
2. *Country Reports on Human Rights Practices—2006,* U.S. Department of State, 6 March 2007, online, www.state.gov.
3. *State of the First Amendment 2006,* First Amendment Center, 11 November 2006, online, www.firstamendmentcenter.org/sofa_reports/index.aspx.
4. James Poniewozik, "Who Can Say What?" *Time,* 23 April 2007, 35.
5. Charles C. Haynes, "Imus, Coulter, and the Marketplace for Offensive Speech," First Amendment Center, 15 April 2007, online, www.firstamendmentcenter.org.
6. Viktor Frankl, *Man's Search for Meaning* (New York: Pocket Books, 1984), 119–157.
7. "Criminal Justice Roundtable Discussion," Bureau of Justice Statistics, U.S. Department of Justice, 22 April 2004, online, www.ojp.usdoj.gov/bjs/pub.
8. Kathy R. Fitzpatrick, "Public Relations and the Law: A Survey of Practitioners," *Public Relations Review* (spring 1996): 1–8.
9. Morton J. Simon, *Public Relations Law* (New York: Meredith, 1969), 4.
10. John Spano, "Dowie Gets 3 1/2 Years in U.S. Prison," *Los Angeles Times,* 31 January 2007, B1.

11. "Pundit Williams to Pay Back $34,000," United Press International, 21 October 2006, online, LexisNexis.

12. Andrew Pierce, "Sophie's PR Firm Taken to Court over Bad Debts," *The Times* (London), 3 July 2006, 3.

13. *The Constitution of the United States and The Declaration of Independence* (Commission on the Bicentennial of the United States Constitution, 1992).

14. *The New York Times Co. v. Sullivan,* 376 US 255, 270 (1964).

15. *Virginia State Board of Pharmacy v. Virginia Citizens Consumer Council, Inc.,* 425 US 764, 765 (1976).

16. *Virginia State Board of Pharmacy v. Virginia Citizens Consumer Council, Inc.*

17. *Virginia State Board of Pharmacy v. Virginia Citizens Consumer Council, Inc.*

18. *Central Hudson Gas and Electric Corp. v. Public Service Commission of New York,* 447 US 557, 100 S. Ct. 2343 (1980).

19. John D. Zelezny, *Communications Law: Liberties, Restraints, and the Modern Media* (Belmont, Calif.: Wadsworth, 1997), 361; based on *Board of Trustees v. Fox,* 492 US 469, 480 (1989).

20. Karla K. Gower, "*Kasky v. Nike, Inc.:* The End of Constitutionally Protected Corporate Speech?" paper presented at the Association of Educators in Journalism and Mass Communications Annual Conference, Kansas City, Mo., August 2003.

21. Gower.

22. "PRSA Presses Supreme Court to Protect Free Speech Right for American Business," news release issued by the Public Relations Society of America e-mailed to its membership, 3 March 2003.

23. "Nike, Inc. and Kasky Announce Settlement of *Kasky v. Nike* First Amendment Case," news release issued by Nike, 12 September 2003, online, www.nikebiz.com.

24. David W. Guth and Paul Wenske, *Media Guide for Attorneys* (Topeka: Kansas Bar Association, 1995), 28.

25. Federal Trade Commission, online, www.ftc.gov.

26. FTC web site.

27. FTC web site.

28. *Annual Report to Congress for FY 2006 Pursuant to the Do Not Call Implementation Act on Implementation of the National Do Not Call Registry,* Federal Trade Commission, April 2007.

29. Securities and Exchange Commission, online, www.sec.gov.

30. Final Rule: Selective Disclosure and Insider Trading, 17 CFR Parts 240, 243, and 249; release Nos. 33-7881, 34-43154, IC-245999, File No. S7-31-99. RIN 3235 AH82, online, www.sec.gov.

31. "The Laws That Govern the Securities Industry," Securities and Exchange Commission, online, www.sec.gov/about/laws.shtml.

32. Zelezny, 331; 17 C.F.R. §240.10b-5 (1992).

33. Dennis L. Wilcox, Phillip H. Ault, and Warren K. Agee, *Public Relations Strategies and Tactics,* 3rd ed. (New York: HarperCollins, 1992), 142–143.

34. *Securities and Exchange Commission v. Texas Gulf Sulfur,* 446 F. 2nd 1301 (2nd Cir 1966).

35. Public Relations Society of America, *Member Code of Ethics 2000,* online, www.prsa .org/codeofethics.html.

36. Robert W. Taft, "Discretionary Disclosure," *Public Relations Journal,* April 1983, 34–35.

37. "A Chronology of ImClone and Martha Stewart," *Washington Post,* 8 July 2004, online, www.washingtonpost.com.

38. "Thomas W. Dunfee on the Enron Verdict," Podcast transcript, 30 May 2006, Wharton School of the University of Pennsylvania, online, http://knowledge.wharton.upenn.edu.

39. "Public Relations Society of America Strongly Supports the Overturning of FCC Ownership Rules by the U.S. Third Circuit Court of Appeals," news release issued by the PRSA, 25 June 2003, online, www.prsa.org.

40. Seth Sutel, "Court Throws Out FCC's Media Ownership Rules," Associated Press, 24 June 2004, online, LexisNexis.

41. "Unwanted Faxes: What You Can Do," Federal Communications Commission, online, www.fcc.gov.

42. "FCC Delays Amended Fax Advertisement Regulations," news release issued by the PRSA, 19 August 2003, online, www.prsa.org.

43. Penny Brown Roberts, "Judge Rules Junk Faxes Not Protected Speech," *The Advocate* (Baton Rouge, La.), 6 August 2004, 1A, online, LexisNexis.

44. "Fax Advertising: What You Need to Know," Federal Communications Commission fact sheet, 28 March 2007.

45. Food and Drug Administration, online, www.fda.gov.

46. FDA web site.

47. Carol Rados, "Truth in Advertising: Rx Drug Ads Come of Age," *FDA Consumer,* July–August 2004, online, www.fda.gov.

48. Zelezny, 519.

49. *The New York Times Co. v. Sullivan,* 376 US 254, 279 (1964).

50. This information on common law libel has been graciously supplied by Associate Professor Thomas W. Volek of the University of Kansas.

51. *Dun & Bradstreet v. Greenmoss Builders,* 472 US 749 (1985).

52. "Texas Jury Has No Beef with Oprah," Associated Press story reported in the *Lawrence (Kansas) Journal World,* 27 February 1998, 3A.

53. *Black's Law Dictionary,* 5th ed. (St. Paul: West, 1979), 1075.

54. Mike Lopresti, "Eight Years After Atlanta, Closure Difficult for Jewell," *USA Today,* 17 August 2004, 11D.

55. "Wrongly Suspected Richard Jewell," Court TV, online, www.crimelibrary.com.

56. David W. Guth and Charles Marsh, *Adventures in Public Relations: Case Studies and Critical Thinking* (Boston: Allyn & Bacon, 2005), 283–286.

57. Frank Walsh, *Public Relations & the Law* (New York: Foundation for Public Relations Education and Research, 1988), 15.

58. I. Fred Koenigsberg, *How to Handle Basic Copyright and Trademark Problems, 1991* (New York: Practising Law Institute, 1991), 31.

59. Anti-Piracy Update, Recording Industry Association of America, n.d., online, www.riaa.com.

60. "Copyright Basics," U.S. Copyright Office, online, www.copyright.gov/circs/circ1.html.

61. Mark Thyer, "Understanding and Dealing with Common Peer-to-Peer (P2P) Application Security," *Information Systems Security,* Nov./Dec. 2003, 42–51.

62. "64 Individuals Agree to Settlements in Copyright Infringement Cases," news release issued by the Recording Industry Association of America, 29 September 2003, online, www.riaa.com.

63. "Downloading Girl Escapes Lawsuit," Associated Press, as reported on CBSNews.com, 9 September 2003, online, www.cbsnews.com.

64. Andrew Eder, "Music Plunderers," *Knoxville News-Sentinel,* 21 February 2007, online, LexisNexis.

65. Andrea Foster, "Library Groups Join Effort to Ease Copyright Law's Restrictions on Digital Sharing," *Chronicle of Higher Education,* 9 July 2004, 31.

66. Walsh, 61.

67. "Copyright Basics."

68. Gina Holand, "High Court Backs Longer Copyrights," *Kansas City Star,* 16 January 2003, C1.

69. B. Drummond Ayres, "Simpson Case Has California Debating Muzzles for Lawyers," *New York Times,* 21 August 1994, sec. 1, 40.

70. Hoffman.

71. William M. Kunstler, "The Lawyer: 'A Chill Wind Blows,'" *Media Studies Journal* (winter 1992): 79.

72. Ayres.

73. Rule 3.6 (subsection a), *American Bar Association Rules of Professional Conduct,* 1983.

74. *Dominic P. Gentile, Petitioner v. State Bar of Nevada, U.S. Supreme Court Reports,* 115 L Ed 2nd, 888–912.

75. Dirk C. Gibson, "The Paradoxical Nature of Litigation Public Relations," *Public Relations Quarterly* (spring 2003): 32–34.

76. David W. Guth, "The Acceptance and Use of Public Relations Practices among Kansas Litigators," *Public Relations Review* (winter 1996): 341–354.

77. White House press briefing, 23 January 1998, 1:35 P.M.

78. Karen Tumulty, "Caught in the Town's Most Thankless Job," *Time,* 9 March 1998, 68.

79. Bryan H. Reber, Karla K. Gower, and Jennifer A. Robinson, "The Internet and Litigation Public Relations," paper presented to the Public Relations Division, Association for Education in Journalism and Mass Communications, Toronto, Canada, August 2004.

80. Reber, Gower, and Robinson.

81. *Bank of America 2002 Annual Report,* 1.

82. *Bank of America 2002 Annual Report,* 2.

83. "In the Matter of Banc of America Securities LLC," Admin. Proc. File No. 3-11425, Securities and Exchange Commission, 10 March 2004, 2, online, www.sec.gov.

84. Adam Shell, "Anatomy of a Trick Trading Scheme," *USA Today,* 5 September 2003, 1B.

85. "In the Matter of Banc of America Securities LLC," 3.

86. "In the Matter of Banc of America Securities LLC," 3.

87. "In the Matter of Banc of America Securities LLC," 4.

88. "In the Matter of Banc of America Securities LLC," 4.

89. "In the Matter of Banc of America Securities LLC," 4.

90. "In the Matter of Banc of America Securities LLC," 5.
91. "In the Matter of Banc of America Securities LLC," 6.
92. *Bank of America 2003 Annual Report,* 3.
93. "In the Matter of Banc of America Securities LLC," 8.
94. "SEC Brings Enforcement Actions Against Banc of America Securities for Repeated Document Production Failures During a Pending Investigation," news release issued by the U.S. Securities and Exchange Commission, 10 March 2004, online, www.sec.gov.
95. "SEC Reaches Agreement in Principle to Settle Charges against Bank of America for Market Timing and Late Trading," news release issued by the U.S. Securities and Exchange Commission, 15 March 2004, online, www.sec.gov.
96. *Bank of America 2003 Annual Report,* 3.
97. George Carlin, *George Carlin/FM & AM,* from the comedy routine "The 11 O'clock News," Little David Records, 1972.
98. Marion Brechner Citizen Access Project, online, www.citizenaccess.org.
99. Marion Brechner Citizen Access Project web site.
100. All direct quotes from Bill Chamberlin come from an e-mail exchange on 27 August 2004 unless otherwise noted.
101. Marion Brechner Citizen Access Project web site.

16

Your Future in Public Relations

OBJECTIVES

After studying this chapter, you will be able to

■ understand better the forces that are shaping the future of society

■ recognize the trends that are changing the practice of public relations

■ recognize the leadership role women and minority practitioners are playing and will play in public relations

■ pinpoint steps you can take today to secure a successful future in public relations

KEY TERMS

The Government Contract

The excitement of your agency's winning a big contract from a new client has begun to wear off. As the reality of this opportunity settles in, you realize you need to hire four more people to handle the increased workload.

Besides you, the agency that you head has 10 people: three white females, two Hispanic females, three white males, one black female, and one black male. Your new client, a government agency, requires that its contractors have diverse workplaces that mirror the gender and racial makeup of society at large.

After advertising the positions in local and professional publications, you have determined that only four of the applicants meet your highly technical minimum education and experience requirements. However, all four finalists are white.

You are committed to cultural diversity in the workplace; you were particularly hoping to hire an Asian American practitioner. Both your client and various community groups are closely watching your hiring practices and insist on diversity. However, you have conducted what you considered an open and fair recruitment process. You also have four qualified applicants ready to go to work and a bunch of work piling up. What are you going to do?

What's Next?

Public Relations Tactics, a monthly publication of the Public Relations Society of America, celebrated its 10th anniversary in July 2004 by boldly predicting what the profession would look like in the year 2014. However, in a strategically wise move, the editors also reminded their readers of some past predictions that didn't pan out:

- "This 'telephone' has too many shortcomings to be seriously considered as a means of communication. The device is inherently of no value to us."—*Western Union internal memo, 1876*

- "This wireless music box has no imaginable commercial value. Who would pay for a message sent to nobody in particular?"—*NBC founder David Sarnoff's associates in response to his pushing for investment in radio in the 1920s*

- "Who the hell wants to hear actors talk?"—*H. M. Warner, cofounder and president of Warner Bros., 1927*

- "We don't like their sound, and guitar music is on the way out."—*Decca Recording Company rejecting the Beatles, 1962*

- "There is no reason anyone would want a computer in their home."—*Ken Olson, founder and chairman of Digital Equipment, 1977*[1]

Oops!

Obviously, there is peril in predicting the future. But everybody does it because we all have a stake in it. No one has a greater personal interest in your future than you. After all, isn't going to college about getting yourself ready for the challenges of the future? (OK, at least *one* of the reasons?)

How does one go about predicting the future, especially the future of a dynamic profession such as public relations? We'd hope that by this point of the semester—assuming that you haven't been reading this book backward—you would understand that the answer to any question about how anyone gets started doing anything has a one-word answer: *research*. Understanding the past and the present is the key to predicting the future. Social forces shaped public relations during its first century and will continue to do so in its second.

Social Forces and Public Relations

Public relations—now and in the future—cannot operate in a vacuum. Just as its practitioners seek to exert influence on various aspects of society, social forces are at work that influence the profession. Understanding those forces is a key to unlocking the mysteries about the future of public relations.

The Global Spread of Democracy

One powerful social force is the global spread of democracy. Much of the history of the 20th century centered on the worldwide struggle against forces of tyranny and oppression. Most of that century's wars and great social movements grew out of a desire either to gain or to protect individual freedoms. With the end of the Cold War between democracy and communism, many nations embraced democratic institutions and ideas for the first time.

The changeover from an authoritarian to a democratic society is not easy. Democracy is more than just a set of rules. It is a way of life. Imagine what it would be like to live in a society where the government watched over every aspect of your life. For as long as you can remember, someone was always telling you what you could do, think, or say. Now imagine what it would be like to have all those restrictions suddenly lifted. After the euphoria of liberation had dissipated, you would confront the cold reality of your new way of life. Before, someone else made your decisions for you. Now, you have to make your own choices and live with the consequences of those choices.

To ease this transition, many public and private agencies have engaged in aggressive programs of education and technical support in the newly emerging democracies. At the forefront of these efforts have been journalists, marketers, and public relations practitioners teaching the virtues of free expression. By the thousands, these professionals have crisscrossed the globe in an effort to instill democratic values and traditions in places where historically there have been none. The challenge is to do so in a culturally sensitive manner. The fact that something works well in the United States does not necessarily mean it will work somewhere else. The most successful efforts at spreading democracy have been those mindful of local traditions and values.

QuickBreak 16.1

GUNGGONGGUANXI

No discussion of the globalization of public relations is complete without focusing on the People's Republic of China. The profession is beginning to blossom in what most Western practitioners view as a contradictory and complicated environment.

First, some background on China may be helpful. Slightly smaller in landmass than the United States, China has more than four times the population. Communists under Mao Zedong seized control of China after World War II. This brought the political repression resulting in the loss of tens of millions of lives (see Case Study 11.1). Mao's successor, Deng Xiaoping, introduced market-based reforms and decentralized economic decision making. As a result, the Chinese economy quadrupled in size during that last two decades of the 20th century.[2]

China is engaged in a very difficult balancing act. On the one hand, its communist leaders want to maintain strict political control over the people. However, they also see the growth of a free-market economy as the answer to the many problems that plague the world's most-populous nation. In this environment, the recently introduced profession of public relations—what the Chinese call *gunggongguanxi*—is developing.[3]

According to the China International Public Relations Association and *PRWeek* magazine, annual public relations revenues in China grew by 33 percent in 2006 to an estimated 8 billion yuan ($1 billion in U.S. currency). With demand for practitioners increasing at an annual rate of 30 percent, the number of Chinese agencies stands at 2,000 and is growing. The average practitioner works 47 hours a week and is 29 years old.[4]

One sign of the emergence of Chinese public relations was the creation in 2003 of Xinhua PR Newswire. A joint venture of the Xinhua Financial Network (XFN)—a Hong Kong–based financial services and media company—and the London-based PR Newswire Association, Xinhua PR Newswire assists companies in writing and distributing financial news releases within China and around the world. This first-of-its-kind network serves 500 newspapers and 1,500 specialized industry publications throughout China.[5]

Because of the communist regime's desire to maintain tight social controls, the government closely regulates public relations activities. An example was the release of industry guidelines by the China International Public Relations Congress in 2004. Under the "Service Guidance of the PR Industry," Chinese agencies are required to have standard service procedures and provide clients with standard proposals within certain fee limitations.[6] And as noted in Case Study 11.1, the government's control of the information flow extends to the Internet, where misuse could result in the death penalty.

Beyond political considerations, Chinese public relations practitioners also face cultural hurdles. The very concept of *gunggongguanxi,* which loosely translates into penetrating one's personal networks, clashes with another Chinese value, *guanxi,* defined as obligations associated with close personal relationships. The difference in the two concepts amounts to doing business based on *what* you know versus doing it based on *whom* you know.[7] There is also a Chinese cultural need for modesty that stems from Confucius' belief that people lose stature by promoting their own accomplishments.[8] If you are someone who believes that, then publicity, a favorite tactic in public relations, is one of the last things you want to do.

QUICK ✓ CHECK

1. What is *gunggongguanxi*?
2. What are some challenges facing the development of public relations in the People's Republic of China?
3. How has the end of the Cold War influenced the global growth of public relations?

Globalization

Another major social force influencing the future of public relations is **globalization.** The United Nations Development Program defines globalization as "the growing interdependence of the world's people through shrinking space, shrinking time, and disappearing borders."[9] With each passing day, the peoples of the Earth are being drawn closer together by a vast array of forces. We live in a world where the economies of different nations are inexorably linked. Advances in communications technology have made it possible for us to know what is happening on the opposite side of the world instantaneously. Improvements in transportation have made it possible for you to travel in mere hours distances that took your grandparents weeks and months to cover.

Working in combination, these forces have given us a sense of **interconnectedness** and created a world of opportunities for public relations practitioners. Marshall McLuhan's global village (which we discussed in Chapters 11 and 14) has, in many ways, become a reality. Targeting certain audiences and effectively reaching them are, in many ways, easier than ever. But as we already have discussed in Chapter 11, these advances have also forced practitioners to face serious challenges and make some difficult choices. Thanks to the global reach of digital telecommunications, crises can now spread at the speed of light. And in a world in which the Internet makes it possible for anyone with a "cause" to become a self-publisher, it is becoming more difficult for organizations to identify potential threats.

Although some see globalization as an opportunity, others see it as a threat. Still others see it as both. Antiglobalization forces are concerned that the world's richest nations exploit the poorest in the name of economic development. They are concerned about the relocation of manufacturing jobs to poorer countries where laborers receive only a fraction of pay and have fewer human rights protections than their counterparts in industrialized nations. The exploitation of natural resources and the resulting damage to the environment are also a concern. In addition, technology and knowledge gaps are widening between rich and poor nations. Although it is difficult to gauge the strength of antiglobalization forces, they have made their voices heard. Massive protests in cities hosting international trade meetings have become commonplace in recent years.

The Changing Face of the United States

It is easy to think of globalization in simply economic terms. However, this increasing interconnectedness is changing society, itself. This is especially true in the United

Hundreds of thousands of immigrants and their supporters marched in more than 100 cities in April 2006, casting off the old fears of their illegal status to assert that they have a right to a humane life in the United States. The intense public debate over U.S. immigration policy is a sign of the growth in the numbers—and political clout—of Hispanics/Latinos. (Photo by Stephen Crowley/*New York Times*. Copyright 2006 The New York Times Company. Reprinted with permission.)

States, where the nation's population is undergoing a dramatic demographic shift. According to the 2000 Census, 69.4 percent of the U.S. population was "white alone, not Hispanic." (The U.S. government treats Hispanic origin and race as separate and distinct concepts.) By 2050, that figure is projected to drop to just 50.1 percent. Compare that with persons of Hispanic or Latino origin, who totaled 12.6 percent of the U.S. population in 2000 and are projected at 24.4 percent in 2050. The number of "black alone, not Hispanic" residents will grow from 12.7 percent in 2000 to 14.6 percent in 2050.[10]

These figures also reflect a shift in traditional immigration patterns. In 1990, three out of four people living in the United States were of white European ancestry. However, with the growth of immigration from Latin American and the Pacific Rim, that group is expected to shrink to just over half the U.S. population by 2050.[11]

"These numbers provide further evidence of the increasing diversity of our nation's population," said Census Bureau Director Louis Kincannon.[12]

In an ideal world, public relations should mirror the societies it serves. However, several studies have all come to the same conclusion: People of color are underrepresented in the profession. This issue confronts you as the head of the fictional agency in the opening scenario of this chapter: You are being torn by competing values. On the one hand, you believe in the value of a multicultural workplace and know that the client and community expect it. On the other hand, you question the fairness to the four individuals who followed the rules you established and emerged as finalists. And not to be forgotten is the competing value of getting the job done.

This is a very real-life scenario; it has no easy answers. The choices are difficult:

- You could turn down the contract and avoid the hassles. But this could have a devastating effect on employee morale and could damage your agency's ability to compete for major contracts in the future.

- You could hire the four white males and defend the decision on the basis of sticking by the rules you established at the outset. However, you would do so at the risk of alienating the community and, possibly, losing the contract.

- You could reopen the search from scratch and expand the geographical area in which you advertise the positions. This might bring in more qualified candidates who are women or persons of color. But it might not, and you would run the risk of losing the candidates you have already identified.

- You could hire one or two of the finalists and expand the search for the remaining positions. This might ease the immediate situation; but, for reasons already mentioned, there is no guarantee that this course will lead to a long-term solution.

There is no one correct answer. It all comes down to which value you hold highest. The first option seems the least viable: You wouldn't have sought the contract if you didn't value entrepreneurship and the business it would bring to your agency. The second option indicates that the integrity of the process you established is your highest value. The third option places multiculturalism at the top of your list of values. Many would choose the fourth option because it has the appeal of addressing all three values: entrepreneurship, fairness, and multiculturalism. Of course, it is a compromise without any permanent guarantees. But it still has the advantage of leaving your options open.

The Growth in World Population

If you think dramatic social change is limited to the United States, consider this: By the time you finish reading this sentence, 21 babies will have been born into our global society. According to the U.S. Census Bureau, that's the rate of 4.2 births per second.[13] By most estimates, the world's population passed the 6 billion mark sometime during 1999. Experts predict it will pass 7 billion in 2012, 8 billion in 2026, and 9 billion in 2042.[14] It doesn't take a math major to understand that the world's population is growing at an astounding rate.

According to the Census Bureau, the U.S. population passed the 300 million mark in 2006. By the year 2050, that number is expected to climb to 420 million, a 40 percent increase. In comparison, the world population, estimated at 6.5 billion in 2006, is projected to reach 9.4 billion in 2050, a 45 percent increase.[15]

There is another way to look at this. See Table 16.1 for a list of the 10 most populated nations on Earth in 2010. Now compare those rankings with the projections for the year 2050 in Table 16.2 (page 514). You may be thinking to yourself, "That's interesting. But what does it have to do with me?" In a word: Plenty.

TABLE 16.1	The Ten Most Populated Nations on Earth in the Year 2010	
RANK	**COUNTRY**	**POPULATION**
1	China	1,347,563,498
2	India	1,184,090,490
3	United States	309,162,581
4	Indonesia	242,968,342
5	Brazil	195,579,661
6	Pakistan	179,592,311
7	Bangladesh	159,765,367
8	Nigeria	145,032,482
9	Russia	139,390,205
10	Japan	127,194,656

With the world's population growing rapidly—especially in nations outside the industrialized West—the competition for Earth's limited resources is becoming more vigorous. In the best of all possible scenarios, this means increased economic trade and international cooperation—activities that the practice of public relations can help foster. However, in the worst of all possible scenarios, the intense competition for Earth's dwindling resources could lead to wars, terrorism, and other forms of social unrest. The constructive application of public relations in its role as a catalyst for consensus is critical in helping human populations avoid these dire outcomes.

The growth in world population also foreshadows future environmental problems. The air we breathe, the water we drink, and the land on which we depend for our food are all threatened by an encroaching human population. One of the most immediate concerns is the loss of tropical rain forests, which are being clear-cut and burned to make way for people, animals, and crops. By destroying these rain forests, humanity is losing an irreplaceable source of numerous species of health-giving herbs and flowers, not to mention oxygen. Many of the people who clear-cut and burn the rain forests are not evil. They are just poor and looking for a way to improve their lives. Many companies, such as McDonald's, have developed partnerships that promote alternatives to the destruction of the environment. These and other public relations activities can serve as models for future environmental cooperation.

In addition to these global trends, major changes are taking place within the United States that will have a dramatic impact on future public relations practitioners in this country: the aging of the U.S. population. The **baby boom generation,** born between 1945 and 1964, will place a tremendous strain on the generations that have followed. Baby boomers will start reaching retirement age in 2010. Between 2010 and 2030, the percentage of people age 65 and older will grow from 13 percent to almost 20 percent. During that same time frame, the number of people age 85 and older living in the United States will grow from 6.1 million to more than 9.6 million.[16] From a political and social standpoint, this means that issues important to older citizens—issues such as Social Security, health care, and the stability of personal investments—will take on increasing importance.

TABLE 16.2	The Ten Most Populated Nations on Earth in the Year 2050	
RANK	**COUNTRY**	**POPULATION**
1	India	1,807,878,574
2	China	1,424,161,948
3	United States	420,080,587
4	Nigeria	356,523,597
5	Indonesia	331,020,847
6	Pakistan	294,995,104
7	Bangladesh	279,955,405
8	Brazil	228,426,737
9	Congo (Kinshasa)	183,177,415
10	Mexico	147,907,650

However, the graying of America will have an even deeper impact on today's college students. The percentage of **breadwinners,** people between the ages of 18 and 65 who typically make up the nation's labor pool, is declining. The U.S. Census Bureau estimates that breadwinners will constitute 60 percent of the U.S. population in 2010. By 2030, that estimate dips to 57 percent.[17] In other words, a smaller percentage of breadwinners will carry most of the tax burden for the rest of the nation. That trend, in turn, has a variety of implications for the future—including the likelihood that cost-effective public relations will become increasingly important.

QUICK CHECK

1. Why is an increasing marketing focus being placed on the Hispanic community in the United States?
2. What are the implications of the higher population growth rate in non-Western nations?
3. What effect will the aging of the baby boom generation have on society?

Feminization of the Workplace

The most significant change in the U.S. economy since the 1970s has been the dramatic rise of women in the workplace. The U.S. Labor Department estimates that nearly 60 percent of women 16 years of age and older were in the labor force in 2004, compared with 43 percent in 1970. "Along with the rising labor force participation, women also made substantial inroads into higher-paying occupations," concludes *Women in the Labor Force: A Databook,* a Labor Department publication updated in 2005. "In 2004, half of all management, professional, and related occupations were held by women." The report also notes that women's earnings relative to men's have risen from just 62 percent in 1979 to 80 percent in 2004. The report

The Hispanic and Latino Factor

There's a quiet revolution under way in the United States, one that moves to a decidedly Latin beat.

"The immense buying power of the nation's Hispanic consumers continues to energize the nation's consumer market," reports the Selig Center for Economic Growth. Its study on minority buying power estimated that the economic clout of the Hispanic–Latino community will reach $1.09 billion by 2010—a 413 percent increase from 1990. That compares to a 177 percent increase in the buying power of all consumers during the same period. The report also noted that the number of Hispanic–Latino firms "is growing more than four times faster than the number of all U.S. firms, and that their receipts also rose more quickly than all firms."[18]

The growing influence of the Hispanic and Latino community has caught the attention of the public relations industry. Practitioners are adjusting their approach to a rapidly diversifying marketplace. "It's not do-goodism," said Ofield Dukes, chairman of the Public Relations Society of America's National Diversity Initiative. "It's a matter of economics."[19]

Diversity is often easier said than done. Something as simple as assigning an adjective to describe this community is fraught with peril. While many use *Hispanic* and *Latino* as if they are interchangeable, they are not. *Latino* refers to the Spanish- and Portuguese-speaking people of the western hemisphere. *Hispanic* is associated with Spain and the Iberian Peninsula.[20] The distinction is important to many.

"People from Latin America have immigrated to the U.S. because of hardships, dictatorships, drugs, poverty and the search for the American dream," said Venus Gines, founder of a Latino health awareness group. "Immigrants from Spain, a European, industrialized nation, usually don't come to this country hungry."[21]

Targeting this public is very complicated. It includes people from many countries and cultures. Mexican Americans constitute nearly three-quarters of the Hispanic and Latino population in the United States. Another 11 percent are of Puerto Rican heritage. Seven percent come from Central and South America. Five percent have ties to Cuba.[22]

There is also the language barrier. Not every word easily translates from English into Spanish. For example, Bayer Corporation executives trying to promote an antacid product were surprised to learn that Spanish has no word for heartburn. "We had to define what heartburn was," said one Bayer official.[23]

Then there is the challenge of adapting to cultural nuances. "When you're scheduled to be at a 2:30 meeting, it's OK to show up at 2:55," said account planner Sharon Brunot-Speziale, an Anglo American working at a Chicago Hispanic–Latino advertising agency. "I don't have that sense of urgency and Type A behavior that I've had in other positions."[24]

Many experts agree that success in communicating with a diverse audience starts with a diverse workforce. "Having a team of people with diverse backgrounds and perspectives is a business mandatory," said Kathy Bremer of Porter Novelli. "Effective communication begins with understanding the client's business and target audiences."[25]

links this rise in salaries to the growing number of women attaining college degrees—nearly 33 percent in 2004 compared with just 11 percent in 1970.[26]

It is easy for today's students to take for granted something that was relatively new just a generation earlier: the presence of women in the workplace. This movement—what some have called the **feminization** of the workplace—has dramatically changed our social and political landscapes. Women constitute more than 51 percent

QuickBreak 16.3

An Inconvenient Truth

When an organization attempts to focus public attention on its concern for the environment, this is called **green public relations.** However, skeptical environmental activists call it by another name, **greenwashing.** How an organization's actions are perceived often hinges on its credibility and motivations. These tactics may reflect an organization's values or an attempt to fend off public criticism and government regulation. Many times, they are a mixture of both.

Much environmental debate focuses on the issue of global warming. According to a *Los Angeles Times*/Bloomberg Poll in July 2006, 43 percent of those surveyed said they thought global warming is a "very serious problem." Another 31 percent said it was a "somewhat serious problem."[27] However, it wasn't always this way. A survey conducted in 1981 indicated that only 14 percent of respondents had heard or read "a great deal" or "a fair amount" about the "greenhouse effect," a build-up of carbon dioxide in the atmosphere.[28]

The public relations battle over global warming is reminiscent of the profession's association with the controversy surrounding tobacco. During the early stages of the global warming debate, well-funded corporate practitioners—representing those who feared the economic impact of stiffer environmental regulations—appeared to have the upper hand. Much like the tobacco companies in the early days of public relations, corporations came together to form front organizations to refute the scientific research as nothing more than an unproven theory.

One of those organizations was the Information Council for the Environment, created in 1991. ICE was run by a Washington-based public relations agency and funded by several energy-related corporations, including the National Coal Association, the Western Fuels Association, and the Edison Electrical Institute. It launched a $500,000 campaign targeting "older, less-educated males from larger households who are not typically active information-seekers" and "younger, lower-income women."[29]

In later years, global warming skeptics and their practitioner allies helped to block U.S. ratification of the Kyoto Protocol to the United Nations Framework Convention on Climate Change, an international treaty assigning mandatory limits for greenhouse gas emissions. Under intense political pressure, both the Clinton and Bush administrations declined to send the Kyoto Protocol to the Senate.

As reputable scientific evidence mounted and global warming activists became better organized, public opinion on global warming began to shift. (You can read about the evolution of public opinion in Chapter 5.) This, too, parallels the tobacco debate. *An Inconvenient Truth,* a documentary about global warming produced by former Vice President Al Gore, received widespread acclaim and won two Academy Awards. Gore also received the 2007 Nobel Peace Prize. A year earlier, the Ad Council released two television spots urging citizen action to reduce greenhouse gasses. "In one, a man stands in the path of a speeding train, symbolizing the threat of global warming," reported *Newsweek.* "When he realizes the danger is decades away, he steps safely off the tracks—revealing a young girl standing behind him."

As *Newsweek* noted, "What's significant is that the issue now has the high-minded imprimatur of the Ad Council, which gave the world Smokey Bear."[30]

of the nation's population. They are an increasingly powerful political force. Despite these positive trends, there is still need for improvement in significant areas such as workplace sexual harassment and **salary equity,** equal pay for equal work.

A 2007 report released by the American Association of University Women Educational Foundation showed that just one year out of college, women working

The election of Nancy Pelosi (D-Calif.) as the first female speaker of the U.S. House of Representatives in 2007 had both political and social significance. Since the 1970s, women have entered the workforce in record numbers. They have also exercised their political clout by reshaping public debates and electing more women to public office. (Photo by Doug Mills/*New York Times*. Copyright 2007 The New York Times Company. Reprinted with permission.)

full time earn 20 percent less than their male colleagues doing the same jobs. "These employees don't have a lot of experience and, for the most part, don't have caregiving obligations, so you'd expect there to be very little difference in the wages of men and women," said AAUW Director of Research Catherine Hill. "Unfortunately, we find that women already earn less—even when they have the same major and occupation as their male counterparts." The AAUW report, *Behind the Pay Gap*, also said that 10 years after graduation, women graduates get only 69 percent of the salary paid to their male counterparts.[31]

Findings in a 1986 study commissioned by the International Association of Business Communicators suggested that the field was becoming a **velvet ghetto**—an employment area in which women hold the numerous lower-paying technical positions and men predominate in the few high-paying managerial positions.[32] As one researcher noted:

> This "feminization" of the field has been heralded by some. Women, they argue, are uniquely suited for public relations because of their natural orientation toward "relationships" and their facility with verbal tasks. More often, though, women's entrance into public relations has been viewed with concern. People worry that so many women in the field will lower salaries and frustrate public relations' efforts to be taken seriously as a management function. These fears are bolstered by extensive research that shows women lag behind their male peers in salary and advancement. And this gender gap cannot be explained by age, level of education, or years of experience.[33]

Nearly two decades later, the IABC Research Foundation revisited its velvet ghetto study. While some of the fears raised in the earlier report did not come to pass, researchers said there were still economic and social barriers for women in public relations to overcome:

- While women continued to dominate the public relations industry, evidence suggested that the feminization of the field may have peaked in the 1990s and that the percentage of male practitioners was beginning to slowly build by approximately one-half a percent per year.

- The velvet ghetto predicted that the feminization of public relations could lead to salary declines. That did not happen. But, as we have already shown, women continue to make less than their male counterparts.

- Access to senior management by women practitioners appears to have declined over the past two decades. In the velvet ghetto report, half of the respondents said they reported directly to the CEO. However, *IABC Profile 2002* placed that figure at only 35 percent.[34]

PRSA conducted a similar inquiry. In its *Year 2000 Gender Study*, researchers concluded that men averaged about $17,000 more in annual salary than women, "even after years of experience, age, job interruptions and education were accounted for." However, in terms of promotion, the researchers said "participants are more unsure now than they were five years ago about the existence of a glass ceiling for women."[35]

VALUES STATEMENT 16.1

League of Women Voters of the United States

The League of Women Voters encourages informed and active participation of citizens in government and influences public policy through education and advocacy.

The goal of the League of Women Voters of the United States is to empower citizens to shape better communities worldwide. We are a nonpartisan political organization.

We:

- act after study and member agreement to achieve solutions in the public interest on key community issues at all government levels.
- build citizen participation in the democratic process.
- engage communities in promoting positive solutions to public policy issues through education and advocacy.

We believe in:

- respect for individuals.
- the value of diversity.
- the empowerment of the grassroots, both within the League and its communities.
- the power of collective decision making for the common good.

We will:

- act with trust, integrity and professionalism.
- operate in an open and effective manner to meet the needs of those we serve, both members and the public.
- take the initiative in seeking diversity in membership.
- acknowledge our heritage as we seek our path to the future.

—"Vision, Beliefs and Intentions," LWV web site

QuickBreak 16.4

Sexual Harassment

According to the U.S. Equal Employment Opportunity Commission (EEOC), sexual harassment is a form of sex discrimination that violates Title VII of the Civil Rights Act of 1964. The EEOC defines workplace **sexual harassment** as "unwelcome sexual advances, requests for sexual favors, and other verbal or physical conduct of a sexual nature . . . when submission to or rejection of this conduct explicitly or implicitly affects an individual's employment, unreasonably interferes with an individual's work performance or creates an intimidating, hostile or offensive work environment."[36]

According to the EEOC, 12,025 sexual harassment cases were filed with federal, state, and local agencies during fiscal year 2006. The good news: That's a 32 percent decline over the past decade and the sixth consecutive year that figure has declined. The agencies found "no reasonable cause" in 47 percent of the cases. Another 21.9 percent involved settlements or withdrawals with benefits. Nevertheless, sexual harassment is expensive. Victims were awarded $48.8 million in benefits in FY 2006—and that doesn't include any monetary awards obtained through litigation.[37]

Although there are legal remedies for dealing with blatant sexual harassment, many victims are reluctant to report it because of a fear of damaging their careers. Then there is a more covert form of harassment, dubbed by some as **lookism,** which is defined as a tendency to focus more on a woman's appearance than on her job performance. In one focus group a female practitioner complained that she had to fight the perception of some of her older male colleagues that a woman traveling by herself or out alone after dark is "available."[38]

Sexual harassment in the workplace threatens more than just employees. Companies that do not take steps to enforce sexual harassment policies face increasing risk of stiff financial penalties. In an effort to force companies to take this problem more seriously, Congress amended the Civil Rights Act in 1991. The amendment made it possible for successful plaintiffs to collect not only lost wages but also up to $300,000 in punitive damages against offending companies.[39] The U.S. Supreme Court has also weighed in on this issue. The court said an employer is responsible for sexual harassment committed by a supervisor even if the employer was unaware of the supervisor's behavior. The Court also ruled that workers can still file sexual harassment charges against supervisors even in the absence of adverse job consequences.[40]

It should be noted that sexual harassment is not just about men acting inappropriately toward women. According to the EEOC, men filed 15.4 percent of sexual harassment claims in FY 2006. The U.S. Supreme Court has also recognized that illegal harassment can occur between people of the same sex.[41]

Public relations practitioners will play a critical role in eliminating this offensive behavior from the work environment—both inside and outside their profession. As the EEOC has noted, employers "should clearly communicate that sexual harassment will not be tolerated."[42] That's one of the jobs of public relations.

The only way to rid the workplace of sexual harassment is to create a company culture that makes it taboo, said Naomi Earp, chair of EEOC. She believes that antiharassment-policy education should be a part of every employee's regular training.[43]

"Management should talk about [the antiharassment policy] the way they talk about productivity and attendance," says Michael Fetzer of the EEOC's Cleveland office. "Otherwise, people won't think it's really that important to the company leadership."[44]

As we near the end of the first decade of a new century, the salary gap persists. A 2006 *PR Week* survey showed that women practitioners earn less than their male counterparts at every stage of their careers and constitute only 25 percent of senior management. It prompted Jim Sinkinson, editor of a PR industry newsletter, to write, "An intellectual property business like ours, which depends on hard work and creativity, cannot prosper when women professionals are treated as second-class workers."[45]

While many agree that gender discrimination exists, finding a solution has been elusive. Some argue that women should seek out more professional expertise—that improving their strategic and professional skills will allow them to compete at the same level as men. Others argue that women should push for **empowerment**—not only ensuring that they have the tools for success, but also demanding to be included in decision making.[46] Although sincere people may argue about which is the best path to take, none disagrees on the common goal: equity.

A hopeful sign can be found in a gender study on job satisfaction among public relations practitioners. Although men and women viewed job satisfaction from decidedly different perspectives, evidence supported a growing respect for each other. "Both groups appear to be willing to respect the other, and, perhaps more importantly, to engage in dialogue on the issues in ways that will result in collaboration and benefits for both," the study said. "The willingness on both sides to work toward just solutions is especially critical at this point in the evolution of a workplace where people can be satisfied."[47]

QUICK CHECK

1. What is the meaning of the phrase *velvet ghetto*?
2. What are the differing views on how to level the playing field for men and women in public relations?
3. What is workplace sexual harassment?

Where Public Relations Is Headed

As modern public relations moves into its second century, the signs are generally positive. As it did during its first century, the profession of public relations has to adapt to a changing social environment. However, not everything will change. There will be a continuing need for the profession to address some of the same old questions, including those relating to its ethical standards and its social value. Let's survey briefly some of the key trends for the future of public relations.

Growth. According to the Bureau of Labor Statistics, "Keen competition will likely continue for entry-level public relations jobs, as the number of qualified applicants is expected to exceed the number of job openings." However, before you start rethinking your career choice, you should know that the bureau reports in its *Occupational Outlook Handbook, 2006–07* that "opportunities should be best for college graduates who combine a degree in journalism, public relations, advertising, or another communications-related field with a public relations internship or other related work experience. Employment of public relations specialists is expected to increase faster than the average for all occupations through 2014."[48] Increasingly, this growth is being reflected in boardrooms, as more and more organizations recognize the profession's role in enhancing and maintaining relationships with key stakeholders.

The Struggle for Credibility. After 100 years, the modern profession still isn't sure what it wants to call itself. Because people who do not understand the profession have used *public relations* as a pejorative term since the time of Edward Bernays, many organizations have shied away from that phrase. Others have said the term is too broad or too narrow, depending on the context. By one accounting, "corporate communications" and "communications departments" outnumbered "public relations departments" at *Fortune* 500 companies by a 2–1 margin.[49] Concerns about the profession's credibility may be at the heart of this issue. The Public Relations Society of America Foundation created the National Credibility Index to track the way U.S. citizens perceive information sources. The good news: Many public relations tactics received a high index rating. The bad news: Public relations practitioners were rated near the bottom—below student activists, candidates for public office, and famous athletes.[50] Despite this apparent ambivalence, signs indicate that the profession is earning respect in surprising places. When Al and Laura Ries wrote *The Fall of Advertising and the Rise of PR* in 2002, they challenged the conventional wisdom that public relations plays second fiddle to advertising when it comes to launching or repositioning brands. They cite the Internet as proof of the power of public relations. "Amazon, eBay, Yahoo!, Priceline and even AOL benefited from enormous amounts of publicity," Al Ries said. "Sure, they may have done some advertising, but it was PR that built those brands."[51]

Greater Integration. Public relations activities are being more closely aligned with those of marketing and advertising. As we discussed in Chapter 13, the concept of integrated marketing communications (IMC) is the current rage. But as we also discussed, differences of opinion exist regarding just where public relations fits in the mix. Some see public relations as an element under a broad marketing umbrella. Others (your authors among them) see public relations practitioners as using a separate management discipline whose values often coincide with those of marketers. Regardless of one's point of view, one fact is undeniable: Today's clients are demanding more than just the persuasive messages of advertising and marketing. They also want the credibility that comes through third-party endorsement. For that, they need public relations. This is especially true when it comes to cause-related marketing, something for which public relations is well suited. According to New Jersey public relations executive John Rosica, "Cause-related marketing can increase brand equity, create a more positive image for corporations and establish a preferred brand name with customers and potential customers."[52]

Greater Accountability. Public relations professionals and the organizations they represent are under greater scrutiny than ever before. Practitioners have always faced pressure to show tangible results as well as how they enhance revenue. Katie Paine of KDPaine & Partners, a public relations measurement and analysis firm, said, "I don't think that there's a program proposed any more that doesn't have a measurement element."[53] However, accountability now extends beyond an organization's bottom line. Ever since Ralph Nader's assault on General Motors in the mid-1960s, the public has expected organizations to value public interest as well as profitability. The role of public relations practitioners is well suited for monitoring the conduct of organizations. At the same time, however, practitioners must hold themselves to those same high standards. Failure to do so has often given the profession a bad name. Accountability in public relations also requires that practitioners enthusiastically embrace equal opportunity without regard to gender, race, religion, national origin, or sexual orientation. That aspect of accountability will require aggressive recruitment of a more inclusive workforce, one that mirrors the diversity of society.

Targeting. As a result of social and technological changes, we are living in a world of increasingly fragmented values and desires. Public opinion and public policies are being ruled by ever-shifting and constantly self-defining coalitions of interests. At the same time, the explosion in the number of communication channels has dispersed audiences. The challenge for public relations practitioners is clear: Reaching key publics in the future will require more targeted approaches. Designing those approaches, in turn, requires a greater precision in research methodologies and planning strategies.

Rapid Response. In the race to influence public opinion, time is an enemy. President Abraham Lincoln concerned himself with stories that appeared in the daily newspaper. President Franklin Roosevelt had to respond to stories on hourly radio newscasts. Today the president is confronted with second-by-second developments in stories on 24-hour news channels and the Internet. The window of opportunity for getting across one's point of view is narrowing. By implication, this means that public relations practitioners must plan even further ahead. They must do a better job of anticipating events that could shape the public view of their organization. For that reason, issues management skills will in all likelihood become increasingly important.

A Nontraditional Workplace. While it is doubtful that a government agency has done a survey to support this hypothesis, it is very likely that there has been a sharp increase in the number of people wearing fuzzy slippers to work. That's because more than 20 million people spend some time every week working in the comfort of their own homes. According to the latest government figures, 15 percent of U.S. workers do some work at home as part of their primary job. While half of those surveyed were wage and salary workers who took work home on an unpaid basis, 24 percent said they had a formal arrangement to be paid for work they did at home.[54] *PR Week* reports that telecommuting has become a popular solution for public relations agencies looking to keep employees who have undergone a change in lifestyle, such as having a baby or moving to a rural area. "You have to accommodate talent," explained New York public relations executive Kimberley White. "That often means putting up with where that talent decides it wants to live."[55] However, telecommuting is not the only change in the workplace. As already noted, the labor pool is becoming more diverse in its gender and racial composition. By the time your children graduate from college, the workplace will have a very different look and feel.

Vision. The demands of a rapid-paced society tend to focus on the problems of the moment and to ignore the potential challenges of the future. The charge of short-term thinking is often leveled against business and industry in the United States. Public relations practitioners share responsibility for this state of affairs. With public relations practitioners being held more accountable for a company's bottom line, many move from one planning cycle to another without having a real sense of direction. What organizations—and practitioners—need is a sense of vision. They need to have a sense of where they want to be 5, 10, and 20 years down the road. Here is where values, research, and strategic planning pay dividends. A longer-term outlook also requires practitioners to demonstrate that they have what is commonly referred to as "backbone"—the courage to stand by their vision. Backbones do have flexibility, however; visions can change.

QUICK CHECK

1. What trends are influencing the future of public relations?
2. In what ways will public relations practitioners be held more accountable in the future?
3. What is meant by the need for "vision"?

Your Future in Public Relations

By now it should be obvious that modern public relations is a profession that continues to evolve as it moves into its second century. That is what makes it both challenging and exciting. Every day in public relations brings with it a new adventure. Are you ready for it? The short answer is no—at this stage of your academic and professional life, you probably are not quite ready. But the good news is that if you continue doing the right things, you will be.

Your decision to earn a college degree was the first big step in the right direction. Although exceptions to the rule exist, a college diploma is usually necessary if you are going to make the first cut in the employment process. As to what kind of degree you obtain, that is probably less important than what you studied in earning the degree. Not everyone in the profession has received a degree in public relations. And although the study of public relations is traditionally centered in either journalism or communications studies programs, degrees from other departments can also lead to successful public relations careers.

So what constitutes a good educational foundation for the practice of public relations? In a November 2006 report, the Commission on Public Relations Education said, "Public relations education should be interdisciplinary and broad,

You Are the Future

You are the future of public relations.

As you make the transition from college life into a career in this dynamic profession, it is OK to pause for a moment and take a deep breath. After all, you are about to embark on a wonderful journey—but to where? No one knows for sure. But some pretty smart people have put some thought into what your future will hold. And they see a world of both opportunities and challenges.

"The PR industry has the chance to become the communications tool of choice in the next decade," said Richard Edelman, president and CEO of Edelman. "The opportunity for PR stems from the absence of trust in institutions and the splintering of audiences among various forms of media."[56]

Edelman based his prediction on the fragmentation of media, which he said has led to "information overload" and the creation of "individual webs of trust and triangulation among multiple sources of information." His reasoning: If organizations can establish credibility, they could become a part of these "webs of trust." That, he said, is the opportunity and challenge facing public relations.[57]

And how can future practitioners help establish this credibility? Mark Weiner, senior vice president of global research at Ketchum, said, "Match ethics with the delivery of meaningful business outcomes, and you'll earn credibility."[58]

According to a study of future trends conducted on behalf of the IABC Research Foundation, "An opportunity exists for communication professionals to change their roles. Communication officers are in the best position to provide information for leaders that flags new trends and anticipates potential changes on the horizon." This prediction was based on interviews with more than 30 senior practitioners and survey responses from more than 1,000 IABC members.[59]

However, with this shot of optimism comes a dose of reality. "Communication professionals need to increase their ability to measure results more concretely," the study said. "Proving the economic value of the communication function is becoming increasingly important." But that's the rub: Only 17 percent of the survey participants said they use before and after assessments to gauge communication performance.[60]

Gary Grates, vice president of communication at GM North America, wrote in *Public Relations Quarterly* that practitioners must learn to sense and respond to changes in the environment: "In a way, we must become social scientists in our jobs, able to discern what people are looking at, listening to, and believing in."[61] Practitioners need to focus on problem solving, he said. "The wise firm will, in the long run, achieve greater profitability and stronger relationships by focusing on finding the solution instead of packaging the sell."[62]

The values and lifestyles of today's college graduates will also shape the future. According to Mike Marino, former head of human resources for Burson-Marsteller/New York, new practitioners are already beginning to question the traditional workweek and workplace. "In order to be able to effectively attract and retain this segment of the population," he said, "employers—including agencies—will need to adopt more flexible work arrangements."[63]

See, you are already molding the future of public relations.

particularly in the liberal arts and sciences." In *The Professional Bond: Public Relations Education for the 21st Century,* the commission said, "A minor or a double major is recommended to broaden students' education and knowledge base."[64] The report also said that a strong public relations education is intertwined with business, language, social science, and other disciplines. While the commission's recommendations echoed those of earlier years, the 2006 report also stressed the need for educators to focus on developing positive personal traits in tomorrow's practitioners:

> It continues to be crucial that graduates be responsible, flexible and professionally oriented self-managers. For communication to occur with and among diverse audiences, individuals must be able to respond and adapt to new and changing situations and to feel comfortable in having to make such adjustments without giving up personal identity. Students must have intellectual curiosity and be able to think conceptually. They must have positive attitudes and be able to take criticism. They must be organized self-starters who take initiative to solve problems. They must be both creative and pragmatic, and they must have integrity as team participants and leaders. Students should be able to demonstrate respect and empathy; even if practitioners do not belong to a group or agree with it, a practitioner must be able to show appreciation for those who are different and able to understand others' cultures and perspectives.[65]

The report also identified 22 essential skills that create a foundation for a successful public relations career. They included research methods and analysis, mastery of language in written and oral communication, problem solving, informative and persuasive writing, fluency in a foreign language, technological and visual literacy, and ethical decision making.[66]

Internships—supervised workplace experiences—also figure prominently in public relations career preparation, especially in light of corporate downsizing and the growth of virtual public relations. More than ever, internships give students the opportunity to get hands-on experience in a wide range of public relations activities. Think of internships as an extension of a college education—with one major difference: The "classroom" is the real world. If you are not certain what kind of public relations you want to practice—agency, government, nonprofit, or corporate—having several different internships during college can give you a taste of the different aspects of the field.

Internship experience can be crucial in getting that first job. "Internships are becoming vital to obtaining employment," reports the Bureau of Labor Statistics. "Employers seek applicants with demonstrated communication skills and training or experience in a field related to the firm's business—information technology, health, science, engineering, sales, or finance, for example."[67]

Membership in student public relations organizations also provides a good foundation for a public relations career. Some schools have **Public Relations Student Society of America (PRSSA)** chapters, which are affiliated with PRSA. IABC also sponsors student organizations. Other student groups operate independently. Whatever route one chooses, these student organizations can provide valuable job/internship information, networking opportunities, and professional experience that can be listed on a résumé. Some professional organizations give students who were active in their school's public relations organization a membership discount upon graduation. These student groups also offer opportunities for getting together with people who share common career interests. However, as with other student organizations, what you get out of any such group largely depends on what you put into it.

The Future of Values-Driven Public Relations

Some view the future with hope. Others fear the future. Either way, like it or not, the future is coming.

What kind of future lies ahead? At best, we can only make educated guesses. In QuickBreak 16.5, we choose to leave the prognostications to others. Perhaps our time is better spent on the present and on the things we can do today to prepare ourselves for tomorrow.

Each of us perceives the future in different ways. That's because we are unique individuals who view the world through different prisms. For that reason, the best preparation for the future is getting to know the one individual who will exert the most influence over the future as you will know it. In other words, the person you most need to get in touch with is yourself.

At the risk of being too philosophical, what is life but a series of choices? Some choices, such as what to have for lunch or what color socks to wear, are not particularly challenging. Other times we are confronted with choices that can quite literally mean the difference between life and death. The funny thing about choices, however, is you can't always know the ultimate outcome of what may seem at the time to be the most trivial of decisions. Those are the decisions that steer us to unexpected paths in our lives. The best we can hope for is developing the habit of making good decisions.

That is why values are important. Values are the road map by which we, both as professionals and as individuals, chart a course into the future. Having values alone is not a guarantee of taking a smooth road. In fact, sticking to values can lead to a more treacherous road than traveling down the path of least resistance. But at least when we stick to our values we *know* we may be headed down a bumpy road. Often the path of least resistance does not turn out to be as smooth as it looks.

After a century of modern public relations, it is somewhat disheartening to know that practitioners are still compelled to demonstrate their worth to employers, clients, coworkers—and even to themselves. In the words of a Public Relations Society of America report on the stature of the profession,

> Public relations has evolved from a fringe function to a basic element of society in a comparatively short period of time, despite a number of handicaps. One of the greatest of these is the field's failure to act according to its own precepts. It has allowed prejudices against it to persist, misconceptions to entrench themselves and weaknesses within the field to be perceived as endemic. Public relations, like most elements of society, is now confronted with critical questioning. Its practitioners are questioning its stature and role as pointedly as outsiders. Like other elements of society, it must respond to its challengers or lose even its present stature and role. That role must be clarified; its goals must be set;

its practitioners must earn optimal stature; means to achieve the goals must be established.[68]

In its own way, this report, prepared by PRSA's College of Fellows, is a plea for the very same concept advocated throughout this book: *values-driven public relations*. It is a recognition—and a warning—that until practitioners fully embrace the relationship-building values on which this profession was supposedly built, our period of self-doubt will continue.

Granted, that's a heavy load to place on the shoulders of someone still in college. However, real change can occur if we remember that 21st-century public relations will be built one person at a time.

As you ponder the many choices that await you, here are some guidelines to help you steer down the uncertain paths of the future:

- *Be true to your values.* If you can't be true to yourself, then to whom can you be true? If something doesn't pass the "Can you look at yourself in the mirror?" test, don't do it.

- *Pay your dues.* No one is going to hand you the keys to the executive washroom—at least not yet. Hard work and personal commitment are your investments in the future. Your time will come.

- *Make your own luck.* A wise person once said that luck is where opportunity meets preparation. Circumstances may place you in the right place at the right time. But it will be your talent and professionalism that will keep you there.

- *Learn from your mistakes.* Mistakes are often more instructive than successes. If you are willing to look objectively at a situation and, when necessary, shoulder the blame, it is unlikely that you will make the same mistake again.

- *Celebrate victories.* Just as it is important to learn from mistakes, it is important to accept credit when credit is due. You want to encourage success, not ignore it. Life is too short not to enjoy the good times. Don't take them for granted.

- *Keep learning.* Your education is just beginning. The world is rapidly changing, and you need to keep up with it. Don't pass up opportunities to learn something new; you never know when this knowledge will come in handy. Knowledge is power.

- *Command new technology—and don't let it command you.* Technological advances offer new and exciting ways to reach out to targeted publics. However, having the ability to use a new technology doesn't mean we should. Values, audience, and purpose should govern our decisions on which channels we choose.

- *Pass it on!* It is very likely that you will owe some aspect of your career advancement to mentoring from a more experienced practitioner who took you under his or her wing. The best way you can honor that special person is to become a mentor yourself and show someone else the ropes.

- *Maintain perspective.* Former University of North Carolina basketball coach Dean Smith retired, at the time, with the most victories in the history of major college basketball. But he lost quite a few games as well. That's why he once told a reporter that he didn't treat every game as if it were a life-or-death situation. "If you do," Smith said, "you will be dead a lot."

- *Exercise your rights as a citizen—especially your First Amendment rights.* Freedom can't be taken for granted. It must always be defended and used responsibly. That's why it is important that you vote and speak out on important issues. That is also why you should resist anyone who tries to curb someone else's freedoms. How do you know that your freedoms won't be next on someone's hit list?

One practitioner at a time. That is how values-driven public relations will be established during the modern profession's second century.

Summary

As modern public relations moves into its second century, it has the potential to do both good and harm in society. Its good rests in the profession's ability to bring people together to reach consensus. However, some applications of public relations have been used to block consensus.

Major social forces are shaping the future. Among them are the global spread of democracy, the economic and cultural effects of globalization, the growth in world population, and the increasing feminization of the workplace. The growing presence of women has had and will continue to have a dramatic effect on the field of public relations. Although women in public relations continue to face the same challenges as women everywhere, there appears to be a consensus for addressing salary equity and sexual harassment issues in the industry.

The growth of public relations is expected to continue in the foreseeable future. Public relations will continue to work closely with other marketing disciplines—all of which will be held more accountable. Many of the old problems of the past, such as the search for respect, credibility, and ethics, will continue. Although the workplace in which public relations is practiced may change, the profession's need to adhere to enduring values remains constant.

DISCUSSION QUESTIONS

1. What social, political, or demographic trend will have the most significant impact on the practice of public relations in the 21st century? Please explain your reasoning.
2. How will world and national population trends affect public relations?
3. What steps do you think are necessary to make the profession of public relations more inclusive and representative of the population as a whole?
4. What steps are you taking to prepare for a career in public relations?
5. In a constantly changing world, what role will values play in the future of public relations?

Memo from the Field

**Kevin J. Saghy,
National President,
PRSSA 2006–2007;
Account Coordinator,
Ketchum**

Kevin J. Saghy served as 2006–2007 national president of the Public Relations Student Society of America (PRSSA) while a senior at Ohio Northern University. Saghy received both the Lawrence G. Foster Award for Excellence in Public Relations and the National President's Citation in 2005. He joined PRSSA as a freshman and immediately became an active member. In 2005, he was awarded the DeBow Freed Award for Outstanding Leadership, given by ONU to one male and one female in each class. At the time of publication, Saghy was an account coordinator at Ketchum.

Throughout your collegiate career, you'll read many suggestions about how to succeed in public relations. The authors of this text have cited several outstanding examples, such as the highly desired qualifications according to prospective employers (writing skills, ambition, and critical thinking). As you begin to explore the field, however, keep two simple rules in mind.

1. *Be original.* You're in a crowd of peers that claims quite the creative identity. Figure out a way to stand out, but do so with the second rule in mind. . . .

2. *Relate to the public.* This should be common sense in public relations, but you'll find that many students completely miss the mark. Whether your public is a prospective employer, a staff of employees, or an external client, be sure that the message is catered directly to their needs.

Following these rules will remain a challenge throughout your professional career; however, the rewards are great when you can accomplish them both.

The 2006 Dove Campaign for Real Beauty is one example. Dove launched a campaign for its new line of beauty products that featured "real women with real curves" instead of prototypical, thin models. The campaign generated plenty of hype with advertisements and accompanying public relations activities that positioned Dove as a friend of the everyday woman. Dove was original, related to its public, and enjoyed great success as a result.

Here are some other key elements to this field that will help you as both a student and a young professional:

Current Events. The most knowledgeable PR practitioners and students follow current events. How do some of the busiest people in the industry have time to check the news? Easy—don't give yourself a choice. At the very least, set your online home page to a news site. Sign up for daily news feeds so you have to look at the headlines. Turn to a news station on TV while you're cooking dinner. You can't relate to society if you're not aware of what's happening to it.

Industry Knowledge. Current events will keep you well rounded, but knowledge of the industry will propel your job performance. *PRSA Tactics*, *PR Week*, and several other publications make it very easy to track award-winning campaigns by publishing informative summaries after the fact. Take note of what's done right, so you can reference proven accomplishments that might be similar to your suggestions.

Quality. My first boss in public relations told me a quote I'll never forget: "Make every piece of work that leaves your desk the very best it can be at that moment." His point is simple, but so many people lose sight of quality when deadlines are approaching. Sure, your work will be edited, but treat every item you produce as if it's your sole opportunity to impress. Clients won't tolerate work that is admittedly sub par. Bosses and coworkers shouldn't have to either.

Network. Once you establish a reputation for quality, make sure people know about it! If you're good at what you do, people love to help. After all, it makes them look smarter for referring you. By joining organizations such as PRSSA, you gain access to over 32,000 students and professionals combined. You can bet you'll see some of these faces in the field.

Follow Up. The value of a thank you card cannot be overstated. In some situations, such as a job interview, following up with a kind note is an absolute must. Other times, you can really stand out above your peers by showing unexpected thoughtfulness. Send a card for New Year's to be different during the holidays. Better yet, send one for St. Patrick's Day with a clever message. That simple card adds you to a short list of easy-to-remember names.

Your future in public relations doesn't begin at graduation. From the moment you opened this textbook, you began to learn and understand what it takes to work in the profession and establish yourself as a unique asset. Use those skills now in classes, internships, and volunteer organizations such as PRSSA. Soon enough, you'll be in the field and ready to mentor the next generation of students in your seat.

CASE STUDY 16.1

Shared Sacrifice?

It takes only one misstep to undo months of hard work. Just one miscalculation, regardless of intentions, can turn a hero into a heel overnight. And as frustrating as it can be, it remains a hard fact of life that the management of relationships also requires the management of perceptions.

Just ask American Airlines.

Few companies have faced the trauma the world's largest airline confronted in autumn 2001. The trouble started on September 11, when two of the airline's flights were hijacked and turned into weapons of mass destruction. American Flight 11 out of Boston was deliberately crashed into the North Tower of the World Trade Center in New York. American Flight 77 was flown into the Pentagon near Washington. All civilian air traffic was grounded for four days. Many airlines already faced economic strife. With flights being curtailed and travelers frightened of what might happen next, the airline industry teetered on the brink of financial ruin.

But then came more. In October, flight attendants on a Los Angeles to Chicago flight subdued a disturbed man who tried to break into the cockpit. On November 12, American Flight 587 crashed shortly after takeoff from New York's John F. Kennedy International Airport. Though not terrorism-related, the crash rattled an already nervous nation.

And then came even more. Passengers and crew aboard an American flight from Paris to Miami subdued a man trying to ignite a bomb hidden in this shoe. Just a few days later, a U.S. Secret Service agent of Arab American descent was removed from a flight at Baltimore-Washington International Airport after the crew accused him of being hostile.[69]

Despite this unprecedented series of crises, American successfully navigated through the storm. Less than two weeks after the terrorist attacks, the company and other airlines successfully lobbied Congress for $5 billion in direct federal aid and another $10 billion in loan guarantees. While some in Congress expressed concerns about bailing out an industry that had faced financial problems before the attacks, the overwhelming consensus was that the nation's economy was at risk. "If planes don't fly, the whole economy shuts down," said Senator Jay Rockefeller, a West Virginia Democrat.[70]

Even with the bailout, American faced some hard choices. The company was forced to lay off 20,000 of its 128,000 employees and to reduce the size of its fleet.[71] To ease the burden, American Chairman and CEO Don Carty announced on October 4 that he and the airline's board of directors had offered to serve without compensation through the end of the year. "Perhaps no group is more keenly aware of our problems than our Board members," Carty said. "It is particularly meaningful for them to forgo compensation for the remainder of the year."[72]

The airline also created a special "American Heroes" web site through which employees could make payroll deductions or contribute lump-sum donations to the families of those killed in the attacks and to assist employees who had been laid off. Carty said the web site was established after he had received thousands of e-mails from employees volunteering to take pay cuts.[73]

The company struggled through 2002 and 2003. AMR, the airline's parent company, reported total losses of $5.8 billion during that period. Some 7,000 more employees were laid off.[74] In its 2002 annual report, American said it had to reduce its annual operating costs by $4 billion "in order to become competitive and sustain its operations." Half of those cuts came through a series of cost-reduction measures.[75] Once again, American turned to its employees for help. It asked its unions and employees for approximately $1.8 billion in permanent annual savings through "a combination of changes in wages, benefits, and work rules."[76] At first the airline's three major unions agreed. Then the wheels almost fell off the deal.

Shortly after the unions had agreed to the concessions, published reports indicated that the airline had given seven of its executives bonuses of up to twice their annual salaries during 2002. The airline had also started putting money into a trust fund to protect the pension benefits of 45 executives.[77] The company said the actions were necessary "to retain key executives" and ensure American's stability. The leaders of two unions threatened to reopen the contract vote. American Airlines officials had no choice but to cancel the executive bonuses.[78]

Carty admitted that he had given misleading information to his management team, including communications employees. "I fell short in conveying to my management team and our spokespeople that I had not fully briefed our union leaders on my discussions," he said.[79]

"Mr. Carty's strength is that he is an honest man," American corporate spokesman Gus Whitcomb said. "Now we hope that we have enough time to allow individuals who are understandably angry to set emotion aside and realize that bankruptcy is as ugly an alternative today as it was a week ago."[80]

"No reasonable person can blame the union members for being outraged," editorialized the *Buffalo News*. "Carty has apologized, but an apology is not the same as accountability. His indefensible action has endangered the airline's survival. Is this really the man who should be running the business?"[81]

Apparently not. The leaders of the unions decided to stick with the original labor agreement on April 25, 2003—one day after Carty resigned as chairman and CEO.

DISCUSSION QUESTIONS

1. Were American Airlines executives wrong to take steps to ensure the stability of the company's leadership? What, if anything, should they have done differently?
2. Carty apologized for his actions. In light of his leadership of the company through perilous times, shouldn't that have been enough to save his job?
3. At the start of this case study, the authors write that "the management of relationships also requires the management of perceptions." Do you agree with this statement? Why or why not?
4. If you were in charge of the airline's corporate communications office, what actions would you have recommended to repair the damage to relationships created by the dispute over executive bonuses? Which relationships, in particular, needed attention?

CASE STUDY 16.2

Guns and Greens

During the fall of 2004, a common complaint was heard throughout the Minnesota wetlands. "You can ask people from Baudette to Winona; Worthington to Ely," said Minneapolis *Star Tribune* columnist Dennis Anderson. "There were no ducks."[82]

A decline in the duck population in the "Land of 10,000 Lakes" brought more than 40 hunting, fishing, and environmental groups—a marriage of "guns and greens" as some called it—into an unusual coalition designed to pressure Minnesota's legislature to preserve the state's natural resources and outdoor heritage. What makes this unusual is that hunters and environmentalists are usually at cross-purposes. However, with the U.S. Environmental Protection Agency rating 40 percent of the state's lakes and rivers as "impaired," the guns and the greens found a common cause. Minneapolis-based public relations agency Carmichael Lynch Spong helped them find their voice.[83]

It was Anderson, the *Star Tribune*'s outdoors columnist, who set events into motion. In a December 2004 column, he called for a rally at the state capitol to demand that legislators protect Minnesota's environment. Following the columnist's lead, the guns and greens came together to organize a "Rally for Ducks, Wetlands, and Clean Water." As a popular columnist at one of the Midwest's largest newspapers, Anderson had a ready-made pulpit from which to promote the cause. However, it wasn't long before organizers realized more expertise was needed. With only six weeks to marshal public opinion before the scheduled rally, CLS volunteered its services to the coalition on a pro bono basis.

The agency immediately embarked on primary and secondary research. This included a series of interviews with sportsmen and environmentalists who said they were frustrated by the manner in which state government funded and managed Minnesota's natural resources. Secondary research was used to identify key elected officials who wielded the greatest influence over environmental legislation—with special emphasis on locating those likely to support the coalition's cause. Perhaps most important, research helped to identify issues in which the groups—often at loggerheads with one another—could find common ground. From this research came the coalition's rallying cry and positioning statement: "One voice, many votes." Three goals also emerged: to raise public awareness of the issues facing Minnesota's ducks, wetlands, and waterways; to attract a large crowd to the rally; and to secure passage of coalition-supported legislation.

For the campaign to achieve success, CLS had to convince the guns and the greens that they, literally, had to follow their positioning statement and speak with one voice. To that end, David Zentner, a key rally organizer and prominent conservationist, was selected as the coalition's spokesman. Zentner was quoted in all news releases and offered to media outlets for interviews. Three other individuals were selected as alternate spokespersons. Zentner and the alternates received media coaching from CLS.

A variety of channels were used to attract people to the April 2, 2005, rally. Weekly news releases were distributed to more than 200 media outlets. Key elected officials received letters inviting them to the event. CLS created a special web site, www.wetlandsrally.org, to inform both the news media and sympathetic citizens. The agency distributed more than 5,000 posters to outdoor retailers, bait shops, sporting clubs, and civic organizations throughout the state. Promotional efforts also included radio public service announcements and billboards donated by outdoor advertising companies. To defray costs, bumper stickers, sweatshirts, T-shirts, and baseball caps bearing the "one voice, many votes" tagline were sold on the Internet and at the rally. According to CLS, the campaign generated an estimated 14 million impressions—the number of times people were exposed to the coalition's message.[84]

On the day of the rally, approximately 5,000 people gathered at the steps of the state capitol in St. Paul. All the Twin Cities' network-affiliated television stations, as well as most of the state's major newspapers, covered the event. It even caught the attention of Sierra Club members, who named it as their favorite Earth Day story in an online poll.

The Rally for Ducks, Wetlands, and Clean Water also appeared to grab the attention of its most important target audience, Minnesota's politicians. "One of the most powerful forces in politics is a coalition with people from different viewpoints coming together," Minnesota Governor Tim Pawlenty told the gathering. "I think we are witnessing a historic birth of a powerful coalition for water, wetlands, and wildlife."[85]

While the campaign achieved the first two goals, raising public awareness and attracting a large crowd to the rally, the outcomes for the third goal, changing public policy, were mixed. The 2006 legislature enacted a cornerstone of the coalition's legislative package, the Clean Water Legacy Act. It was designed to help restore the state's impaired lakes and rivers. However, lawmakers allocated only $15 million to enact the measure—well short of the $80 million supporters said was needed to do the job.[86] Another measure supported by the greens and the guns, a state sales tax dedicated to conservation and the arts, eventually passed both houses of legislature in May 2007. However, in what the bill's supporters must have felt was a cruel twist of fate, the clock literally struck midnight and the legislature adjourned for the year before the final version of the measure came to the floor for a vote.[87]

Despite the setback, the guns and the greens are unlikely to quit. As one Minnesota lawmaker said, "If this is going to be an outdoor legacy, and my grandkids ask me years from now whether I supported it, I want to say I did."[88]

DISCUSSION QUESTIONS

1. Who are the "guns and the greens," and why is the coalition they built unusual?
2. Why do public relations agencies such as Carmichael Lynch Spong donate their services to organizations such as the Rally for Ducks, Wetlands, and Clean Water?
3. What steps were taken to ensure that the messages delivered by the guns and greens coalition were consistent?
4. Was the Rally for Ducks, Wetlands, and Clean Water a success?

NOTES

1. Reid Goldsborough, "Unpredictions," *Public Relations Tactics*, July 2004, 25.
2. *The World Factbook,* Central Intelligence Agency, 18 December 2003, online, www.odci .gov/cia/publications/factbook.
3. David Weiner, "Can Canadian PR Help China Break into the World Market?" *Strategy*, 20 October 2003, online, LexisNexis.
4. "High Turnover Troubles Public Relations Agencies," *Financial Times* Global News Wire, 20 April 2007, online, LexisNexis; "Opportunities and Interests Rising in Emerging Markets," *PR Week*, 24 April 2006, online, LexisNexis.

5. "Xinhua PR Newswire Launches Corporate Information Distribution Network to Reach over 2,000 Chinese Media Outlets," PR Newswire, 22 July 2003, online, LexisNexis.

6. "New Guidance to Standardize China's Public Relations Industry," *China Daily*, 26 June 2004, online, LexisNexis.

7. Weiner.

8. Weiner.

9. *Human Development Report 1999*, United Nations Development Program, online, www.undp.org/hdro.

10. "Projected Population of the United States, by Race and Hispanic Origin: 2000 to 2050," U.S. Census Bureau.

11. Alejandro Portes, ed., *The New Second Generation* (New York: Russell Sage Foundation, 1996), 54–81.

12. "Nation's Population One-Third Minority," news release issued by U.S. Census Bureau, 10 May 2006.

13. "World Vital Events per Time Unit: 2007," U.S Census Bureau, online, www.census.gov.

14. "Total Midyear Population for the World: 1950–2050," U.S. Census Bureau.

15. International Data Base, U.S. Census Bureau, updated 24 August 2006.

16. "Resident Population Estimates by Sex and Age 2010–2050," U.S. Census Bureau, online, www.census.gov.

17. U.S. Census Bureau.

18. Jeffery M. Humphreys, "The Multicultural Economy 2005: America's Minority Buying Power," Selig Center for Economic Growth, University of Georgia, *Georgia Business and Economic Conditions* 65, no. 3 (Third Quarter, 2005): 6–7.

19. Leon Stafford, "Missing Out on the Trend; Diversity Focus Can Open Doors," *Atlanta Journal-Constitution,* 27 October 2002, 1F, online, LexisNexis.

20. Yolanda Rodriguez, "Hispanic or Latino? It All Depends," *Atlanta Journal-Constitution,* 10 December 2003, 6F, online, LexisNexis.

21. Rodriguez.

22. Linda P. Morton, "Targeting Hispanic Americans," *Public Relations Quarterly* 47, no. 3 (fall 2003): 46–48.

23. Stafford.

24. Mindy Charski, "Crossing Cultures," *AdWeek*, 3 May 2004, online, LexisNexis.

25. Stafford.

26. *Women in the Labor Force: A Databook*, U.S. Department of Labor, Report 985, May 2005, 1.

27. *Los Angeles Times*/Bloomberg Poll conducted July 28–August 1, 2006, reported by the Roper Center for Public Opinion Research, University of Connecticut, online, www .ropercenter.uconn.edu.

28. Opinion Research Corporation survey conducted March 26–31, 1981, reported by the Roper Center for Public Opinion Research.

29. Bob Burton and Sheldon Rampton, "The PR Plot to Overheat the Earth," *Earth Island Journal* 13, no. 2 (spring 1998): 29.

30. Jerry Adler, "The New Hot Zones; Books, Films, and a Slick Ad Campaign Make Global Warming the Topic du Jour," *Newsweek*, 3 April 2006, 42.

31. "Pay Gap Exists as Early as One Year out of College, Says New Research Report," news release issued by American Association of University Women, 23 April 2007, online, www.aauw.org.

32. L. L. Cline et al., *The Velvet Ghetto: The Impact of the Increasing Percentage of Women in Public Relations and Organizational Communications* (San Francisco: IABC Research Foundation, 1986).

33. Linda Hon, "Feminism and Public Relations," *The Public Relations Strategist* 1, no. 2 (summer 1995): 20.

34. Heidi P. Taff, "Times Have Changed? IABC Research Foundation's 'The Velvet Ghetto' Study Revisited," *Communication World,* February/March 2003, 10–11.

35. Elizabeth L. Toth and Linda Aldoory, *Year 2000 Gender Study,* Public Relations Society of America, 2001, online, http://PR-education.org/prsa2000genderstudy.htm.

36. "Facts about Sexual Harassment," U.S. Equal Employment Opportunity Commission, online, www.eeoc.gov/facts/fs-sex.html.

37. "Sexual Harassment Charges EEOC & FEPAs Combined: FY 1997–FY 2006," U.S. Equal Employment Opportunity Commission, 31 January 2007, online, www.eeoc.gov/stats/harass.html.

38. Linda Hon, "Toward a Feminist Theory of Public Relations," *Journal of Public Relations Research* 7, no. 1 (1995): 33–34.

39. Barry S. Roberts and Robert A. Mann, "Sexual Harassment in the Workplace: A Primer," *University of Akron Law Review,* online, www.uakron.edu/lawrev/robert1.html.

40. The applicable cases are *Faragher v. City of Boca Raton*, 118 S. Ct. 2275 (1998) and *Burlington Industries Inc. v. Ellerth,* 118 S. Ct. 2257 (1998).

41. The applicable case is *Oncale v. Sundowner Offshore Services, Inc.,* 118 S. Ct. 998 (1998).

42. "Facts about Sexual Harassment."

43. Candace Goforth, "Changing the Workplace Culture Can Help Stop Sexual Harassment," 5 November 2003, *Akron Beacon Journal,* online, LexisNexis.

44. Goforth.

45. Jim Sinkinson, "Women in PR: When Will They Get a Fair Shake?" *Bulldog Reporter's Daily Dog,* 10 March 2006.

46. Hon.

47. Shirley A. Serini et al., "Watch for Falling Glass . . . Women, Men and Job Satisfaction in Public Relations: A Preliminary Analysis," *Journal of Public Relations Research* 9, no. 2 (1997): 116–117.

48. *Occupational Outlook Handbook, 2006–07 Edition*, U.S. Department of Labor, Bureau of Labor Statistics, online, http://stats.bls.gov/oco/ocoso086.htm.

49. Cynthia Fritsch, researcher, " 'Communications' Tops 'PR' by 2–1 Margin at Fortune 500," *O'Dwyer's PR Services Report*, February 1996, 1.

50. National Credibility Index, Public Relations Society of America, online, www.prsa.org.

51. Sean Callahan, "B to B Q&A: Proclaiming the 'Fall of Advertising'; Controversial New Book Argues That Public Relations Is the Best Way to Launch a Brand," *BtoB,* 14 October 2002, 3.

52. "Targeting, Relationship-Building Define Marketing Today," *PR News,* 25 March 1996, online, LexisNexis.
53. "Measurement Driving More PR Programs," *PR News,* 18 March 1996, online, LexisNexis.
54. "Work at Home in 2004," news release by U.S. Department of Labor Bureau of Labor Statistics, 22 September 2005, online, http://stats.bls.gov.
55. Paul Cordasco, "Telecommuting Helps PR Firms Keep Their Top Talent at Home," *PR Week—U.S. Edition,* 20 October 2003, 10.
56. Paul Holmes, "Embracing the Paradox of Change," *The Holmes Report,* 12 March 2001, online, www.holmesreport.com.
57. Holmes.
58. Mark Weiner, "The External Factors Shaping Public Relations in 2014," *Public Relations Tactics,* July 2004, 29.
59. Katherine Woodall, "What Will the Future Hold? Study Reveals Opportunities for Communicators," *Communication World,* February/March 2003, 18–21.
60. Woodall.
61. Gary F. Grates, "Through the Look Glass. Seeing the Future of Public Relations Relevance," *Public Relations Quarterly* (fall 2003): 15–19.
62. Grates.
63. Mike Marino, "Questions Abound for the PR Office of 2014," *Public Relations Tactics,* July 2004, 24.
64. *The Professional Bond: Public Relations Education for the 21st Century,* Commission on Public Relations Education, November 2006, 43.
65. *The Professional Bond,* 44.
66. *The Professional Bond,* 43–44.
67. *Occupational Outlook Handbook, 2006–07 Edition.*
68. "Excerpt from Report on Stature of PR: Factors Inhibiting Stature and Role of PR," *O'Dwyer's PR Services Report,* March 1992, 31.
69. David W. Guth and Charles Marsh, *Adventures in Public Relations: Case Studies and Critical Thinking* (Boston: Allyn & Bacon, 2005), 307–311.
70. "Bush Signs Airline Bailout Package," CNN, 23 September 2001, online, www.cnn.com.
71. Guth and Marsh.
72. "Employees of American Airlines, American Eagle, TWA and AMR Board of Directors Chip In to Help American Through Financial Crisis," news release distributed via PR Newswire, 4 October 2001, online, www.prnewswire.com.
73. "Employees of American Airlines, American Eagle, TWA and AMR Board of Directors Chip In to Help American Through Financial Crisis."
74. Guth and Marsh.
75. AMR Corporation Form 10-K for the Fiscal Year Ended December 31, 2002, U.S. Securities and Exchanges Commission, file number 1-8400, online, www.sec.gov.
76. AMR Corporation Form 10-Q for the Quarterly Period Ended March 31, 2003, U.S. Securities and Exchanges Commission, file number 1-8400, online, www.sec.gov.
77. "American Airlines Blunder," editorial, *Buffalo News,* 24 April 2003, B10, online, LexisNexis.

78. AMR Corporation Form 10-Q for the Quarterly Period Ended March 31, 2003.

79. "Comms Team Trying to Help American Avoid Chapter 11," *PR Week—U.S. Edition*, 28 April 2003, 2.

80. "Comms Team Trying to Help American Avoid Chapter 11."

81. "American Airlines Blunder."

82. Lorna Benson, "Hunters and Environmentalists Rally for Ducks and Their Habitat," Minnesota Public Radio, 1 April 2005, online, http://news.minnesota.publicradio.org.

83. "Uniting Guns and Greens to Improve Minnesota's Environment," Silver Anvil Campaign Profile # 6BW-0603D07, Public Relations Society of America, online, http://prsa.org.

84. "Uniting Guns and Greens."

85. Dennis Anderson, "Progress Seems to Be on Horizon," *Star Tribune*, 8 April 2005, 5C.

86. Pat Doyle, "What Passed, What Failed in the Final Hours," *Star Tribune*, 22 May 2006, 3B.

87. Pat Doyle, "Time Runs Out for Outdoors-Arts Plan," *Star Tribune*, 22 May 2007, 8A.

88. Dennis Anderson, "House Vote Creates Capitol Drama," *Star Tribune*, 24 May 2007, online, www.startribune.com.

Appendix

Member Code of Ethics 2000
Approved by the PRSA Assembly, October 2000

Preamble

Public Relations Society of America Member Code of Ethics 2000

> Professional Values
>
> Principles of Conduct
>
> Commitment and Compliance

This Code applies to PRSA members. The Code is designed to be a useful guide for PRSA members as they carry out their ethical responsibilities. This document is designed to anticipate and accommodate, by precedent, ethical challenges that may arise. The scenarios outlined in the Code provision are actual examples of misconduct. More will be added as experience with the Code occurs.

The Public Relations Society of America (PRSA) is committed to ethical practices. The level of public trust PRSA members seek, as we serve the public good, means we have taken on a special obligation to operate ethically.

The value of member reputation depends upon the ethical conduct of everyone affiliated with the Public Relations Society of America. Each of us sets an example for each other—as well as other professionals—by our pursuit of excellence with powerful standards of performance, professionalism, and ethical conduct.

Emphasis on enforcement of the Code has been eliminated. But, the PRSA Board of Directors retains the right to bar from membership or expel from the Society any individual who has been or is sanctioned by a government agency or convicted in a court of law of an action that is in violation of this Code.

Ethical practice is the most important obligation of a PRSA member. We view the Member Code of Ethics as a model for other professions, organizations, and professionals.

PRSA Member Statement of Professional Values

This statement presents the core values of PRSA members and, more broadly, of the public relations profession. These values provide the foundation for the Member Code of Ethics and set the industry standard for the professional practice of public relations. These values are the fundamental beliefs that guide our behaviors and decision-making process. We believe our professional values are vital to the integrity of the profession as a whole.

ADVOCACY

We serve the public interest by acting as responsible advocates for those we represent.

We provide a voice in the marketplace of ideas, facts, and viewpoints to aid informed public debate.

HONESTY

We adhere to the highest standards of accuracy and truth in advancing the interests of those we represent and in communicating with the public.

EXPERTISE

We acquire and responsibly use specialized knowledge and experience.

We advance the profession through continued professional development, research, and education.

We build mutual understanding, credibility, and relationships among a wide array of institutions and audiences.

INDEPENDENCE

We provide objective counsel to those we represent.

We are accountable for our actions.

LOYALTY

We are faithful to those we represent, while honoring our obligation to serve the public interest.

FAIRNESS

We deal fairly with clients, employers, competitors, peers, vendors, the media, and the general public.

We respect all opinions and support the right of free expression.

PRSA Code Provisions

Free Flow of Information

CORE PRINCIPLE

Protecting and advancing the free flow of accurate and truthful information is essential to serving the public interest and contributing to informed decision making in a democratic society.

INTENT

To maintain the integrity of relationships with the media, government officials, and the public.

To aid informed decision-making.

GUIDELINES

A member shall:

Preserve the integrity of the process of communication.

Be honest and accurate in all communications.

Act promptly to correct erroneous communications for which the practitioner is responsible.

Preserve the free flow of unprejudiced information when giving or receiving gifts by ensuring that gifts are nominal, legal, and infrequent.

EXAMPLES OF IMPROPER CONDUCT UNDER THIS PROVISION:

A member representing a ski manufacturer gives a pair of expensive racing skis to a sports magazine columnist, to influence the columnist to write favorable articles about the product.

A member entertains a government official beyond legal limits and/or in violation of government reporting requirements.

Competition

CORE PRINCIPLE

Promoting healthy and fair competition among professionals preserves an ethical climate while fostering a robust business environment.

INTENT

To promote respect and fair competition among public relations professionals.

To serve the public interest by providing the widest choice of practitioner options.

GUIDELINES

A member shall:

Follow ethical hiring practices designed to respect free and open competition without deliberately undermining a competitor.

Preserve intellectual property rights in the marketplace.

EXAMPLES OF IMPROPER CONDUCT UNDER THIS PROVISION:

A member employed by a "client organization" shares helpful information with a counseling firm that is competing with others for the organization's business.

A member spreads malicious and unfounded rumors about a competitor in order to alienate the competitor's clients and employees in a ploy to recruit people and business.

Disclosure of Information

CORE PRINCIPLE

Open communication fosters informed decision making in a democratic society.

INTENT

To build trust with the public by revealing all information needed for responsible decision making.

GUIDELINES

A member shall:

> Be honest and accurate in all communications.
>
> Act promptly to correct erroneous communications for which the member is responsible.
>
> Investigate the truthfulness and accuracy of information released on behalf of those represented.
>
> Reveal the sponsors for causes and interests represented.
>
> Disclose financial interest (such as stock ownership) in a client's organization.
>
> Avoid deceptive practices.

EXAMPLES OF IMPROPER CONDUCT UNDER THIS PROVISION:

Front groups: A member implements "grass roots" campaigns or letter-writing campaigns to legislators on behalf of undisclosed interest groups.

Lying by omission: A practitioner for a corporation knowingly fails to release financial information, giving a misleading impression of the corporation's performance.

A member discovers inaccurate information disseminated via a web site or media kit and does not correct the information.

A member deceives the public by employing people to pose as volunteers to speak at public hearings and participate in "grass roots" campaigns.

Safeguarding Confidences

CORE PRINCIPLE

Client trust requires appropriate protection of confidential and private information.

INTENT

To protect the privacy rights of clients, organizations, and individuals by safeguarding confidential information.

GUIDELINES

A member shall:

Safeguard the confidences and privacy rights of present, former, and prospective clients and employees.

Protect privileged, confidential, or insider information gained from a client or organization.

Immediately advise an appropriate authority if a member discovers that confidential information is being divulged by an employee of a client company or organization.

EXAMPLES OF IMPROPER CONDUCT UNDER THIS PROVISION:

A member changes jobs, takes confidential information, and uses that information in the new position to the detriment of the former employer.

A member intentionally leaks proprietary information to the detriment of some other party.

Conflicts of Interest

CORE PRINCIPLE

Avoiding real, potential, or perceived conflicts of interest builds the trust of clients, employers, and the publics.

INTENT

To earn trust and mutual respect with clients or employers.

To build trust with the public by avoiding or ending situations that put one's personal or professional interests in conflict with society's interests.

GUIDELINES

A member shall:

Act in the best interests of the client or employer, even subordinating the member's personal interests.

Avoid actions and circumstances that may appear to compromise good business judgment or create a conflict between personal and professional interests.

Disclose promptly any existing or potential conflict of interest to affected clients or organizations.

Encourage clients and customers to determine if a conflict exists after notifying all affected parties.

EXAMPLES OF IMPROPER CONDUCT UNDER THIS PROVISION:

The member fails to disclose that he or she has a strong financial interest in a client's chief competitor.

The member represents a "competitor company" or a "conflicting interest" without informing a prospective client.

Enhancing the Profession

CORE PRINCIPLE

Public relations professionals work constantly to strengthen the public's trust in the profession.

INTENT

To build respect and credibility with the public for the profession of public relations.

To improve, adapt, and expand professional practices.

GUIDELINES

A member shall:

> Acknowledge that there is an obligation to protect and enhance the profession.
>
> Keep informed and educated about practices in the profession to ensure ethical conduct.
>
> Actively pursue personal professional development.
>
> Decline representation of clients or organizations that urge or require actions contrary to this Code.
>
> Accurately define what public relations activities can accomplish.
>
> Counsel subordinates in proper ethical decision making.
>
> Require that subordinates adhere to the ethical requirements of the Code.
>
> Report ethical violations, whether committed by PRSA members or not, to the appropriate authority.

EXAMPLES OF IMPROPER CONDUCT UNDER THIS PROVISION:

A PRSA member declares publicly that a product the client sells is safe, without disclosing evidence to the contrary.

A member initially assigns some questionable client work to a non-member practitioner to avoid the ethical obligation of PRSA membership.

PRSA Member Code of Ethics Pledge

I pledge:

To conduct myself professionally, with truth, accuracy, fairness, and responsibility to the public; To improve my individual competence and advance the knowledge and proficiency of the profession through continuing research and education; And to adhere to the articles of the Member Code of Ethics 2000 for the practice of public relations as adopted by the governing Assembly of the Public Relations Society of America.

I understand and accept that there is a consequence for misconduct, up to and including membership revocation.

And, I understand that those who have been or are sanctioned by a government agency or convicted in a court of law of an action that is in violation of this Code may be barred from membership or expelled from the Society.

_____

Signature

_____

Date

Glossary

Terms in the Glossary match those of the Key Terms section in each chapter and reflect the usage in the text. Thus, some entries in the Glossary are singular and others are plural.

account executive A supervisory individual at a public relations agency who assists the account supervisor in the management of a client's account.

account supervisor The individual at a public relations agency with the responsibility for managing a client's account and the people working on that account.

Accredited Business Communicator (ABC) Designation given to accredited members of the International Association of Business Communicators.

Accredited in Public Relations (APR) Designation given to accredited members of the Public Relations Society of America.

active public A group whose members understand that they are united by a common interest, value, or values in a particular situation and are actively working to promote their interest or values.

active public opinion Expressed behavioral inclination exhibited when people act—formally and informally—to influence the opinions and actions of others.

active voice A grammatical term designating that, within a sentence, the subject does the action denoted by the verb (see *passive voice*). In most grammatical situations, writers prefer active voice to passive voice.

actualities Recorded quotable quotes or sound bites supplied to radio stations on cassette tape or via a dial-in phone system or a web site.

actual malice The higher burden of proof that public officials and public figures must satisfy in libel cases: In addition to showing that a defamatory statement is false, a public figure must also show knowing falsehood or reckless disregard for the truth.

ad hoc plan A plan created for a single, short-term purpose; from the Latin phrase meaning "for this purpose only."

administrative law judge The presiding officer in hearings about alleged violations of government regulations. This person hears testimony and reviews evidence, much like the judge and jury in a civil or criminal case. If federal regulations are at issue, this judge's decision can ultimately be appealed in the federal court system.

advertising The process of creating and sending a persuasive message through controlled media, which allows the sender, for a price, to dictate message, placement, and frequency.

advertising value equivalency (AVE) A calculation of the value of publicity based on the advertising rates and the amount of media coverage received.

agenda-setting hypothesis The idea that the mass media tell us not what to think, but what to think about. This hypothesis is the most widely accepted view of how mass media interact with society.

analog Transmitted in the form of continuously varying signals. Those variations correspond to changes in sound and light energy coming from the source.

annual meeting   A once-a-year informational conference that a publicly held company must, by law, hold for its stockholders.

annual report   A once-a-year informational statement that a publicly held company must, by law, send to its stockholders.

apologia   A speech of self-defense. People and organizations engage in it as a way to present their side of the story in the face of negative events or allegations as a means of repairing damaged images and/or reputations.

appropriation   A tort in libel law. In this context, it is the commercial use of someone's name, voice, likeness, or other defining characteristic without the person's consent.

association magazines   Magazines for members of associations, such as the American Library Association.

attitude   A behavioral inclination.

attributes   Characteristics or qualities that describe an object or individual, such as gender, age, weight, height, political affiliation, and religious affiliation.

attribution   The part of a sentence that identifies the speaker of a direct quotation. In the sentence *"Public relations is a values-driven profession," she said,* the words *she said* are the attribution.

aware public   A group whose members understand that they are united by a common interest, value, or values in a particular situation but who have not yet formed plans or acted on their interest or values.

aware public opinion   Expressed behavioral inclination that occurs when people grow aware of an emerging interest.

baby boom generation   People born between 1945 and 1964. The name comes from the record post–World War II surge in population. As the baby boomers reach retirement age early in the 21st century, they are expected to place a tremendous strain on services geared toward the elderly.

backgrounder   A document that supplies information to supplement a news release. Written as publishable stories, backgrounders are often included in media kits.

belief   A commitment to a particular idea or concept based on either personal experience or some credible external authority.

Bernays, Edward L.   The man often acknowledged as the "father of public relations"—a notion he openly promoted. In his landmark 1923 book *Crystallizing Public Opinion,* Bernays coined the phrase "public relations counsel" and first articulated the concept of two-way public relations. Bernays was a nephew of noted psychoanalyst Sigmund Freud.

bivariate analysis   Analysis of research data that examines two variables.

blogs   Regularly updated Internet journals or news forums that focus on a particular area of interest.

boundary spanning   The function of representing a public's values to an organization and, conversely, representing the values of the organization to that public.

brainstorming   A collaborative and speculative process in which options for possible courses of action are explored.

branding   The process of building corporate and product identities and differentiating them from those of the competition.

breadwinners   People between the ages of 18 and 65 who typically constitute the labor force. As the so-called baby boom generation reaches retirement age, the percentage of breadwinners relative to the total U.S. population will decline.

b-roll   Unedited video footage that follows a video news release. Rather than use the VNR as provided, some television stations prefer using b-roll footage to create their own news stories.

B2B   Abbreviation for business-to-business.

burden of proof   The legal standard a plaintiff must meet to establish a defendant's guilt. For example, to prove a case of libel, the plaintiff must show defamation, identification, publication, damage, and fault or actual malice.

business-to-business communication The exchange of messages between two businesses, such as a manufacturer and a distributor.

business-to-business relations The maintenance of mutually beneficial relations between two businesses, such as a manufacturer and a distributor.

categorical imperative A concept created by Immanuel Kant; the idea that individuals ought to make ethical decisions by imagining what would happen if a given course of action were to become a universal maxim, a clear principle designed to apply to everyone.

cause marketing A concerted effort on the part of an organization to address a social need through special events and, perhaps, other marketing tactics.

CD-ROM The acronym for "compact disc–read-only memory," a medium for storage of digital data. It is a popular format for storage of music, computer software, and databases. CD-ROMs are increasingly popular among public relations practitioners for the distribution of multimedia and interactive communications.

cease and desist order An order issued by an FTC administrative law judge upon a ruling that a company or individual has violated federal laws governing marketplace transactions, including advertising.

census Survey of every member of a sampling frame.

channel The medium used to transmit a message.

citizen journalist Individuals not formally trained as journalists, but who through the use of digital technology assist in the traditional newsgathering and reporting process.

civil disobedience Peaceful, unlawful action designed to affect social discourse and/or change public policy.

civil penalties Penalties imposed under civil law for the violation of government regulations. These penalties usually involve the levy of a fine or placement of certain restrictions against the individual or organization found to be in violation.

cleanup phase The third stage of a crisis. During this stage, an organization deals with a crisis and its aftermath. How long this period lasts is influenced by the degree to which the organization is prepared to handle crises.

client research The gathering of information about the client, company, or organization on whose behalf a practitioner is working. Typically, this information includes the organization's size, products or services, history, staffing requirements, markets and customers, budget, legal environment, reputation, and mission.

closed-ended questions Questions for which the response set is specifically defined; answers must be selected from a predetermined menu of options.

cluster sampling A sampling technique used to compensate for an unrepresentative sampling frame. It involves breaking the population into homogeneous clusters and then selecting a sample from each cluster.

coalition building Efforts to promote consensus among influential publics on important issues through tactics such as face-to-face meetings.

cognitive dissonance The mental discomfort people can experience when they encounter information or opinions that oppose their opinions.

commercial speech Expression intended to generate marketplace transactions. The U.S. Supreme Court has recognized a government interest in its regulation.

commitment The extent to which each party in a relationship thinks that the relationship is worth the time, cost, and effort.

Committee for Public Information (CPI) Committee created by President Woodrow Wilson to rally public opinion in support of U.S. efforts during World War I. Often referred to as the Creel Committee, it was headed by former journalist George Creel and served as a training ground for many early public relations practitioners.

common law libel Libel defined by judicial rulings rather than by legislators or regulators; can occur in private communications, such as internal business memoranda.

communal relationship A relationship characterized by the provision of benefits to both members of the relationship out of concern and without expectation of anything in return.

communication The exchange of information, verbal and nonverbal, between individuals. Also the third step in the four-step public relations process. Because the process is dynamic, however, communication can occur at any time.

communication audits Research procedures used to determine whether an organization's public statements and publications are consistent with its values-driven mission and goals.

communication model A diagram that depicts the elements of the process of communication.

communications grid A tool used during communication audits to illustrate the distribution patterns of an organization's communications. The various media used are listed on one axis, stakeholders important to the organization on the other.

communications specialist Job title given to some public relations practitioners, whose jobs usually entail the preparation of communications.

community relations The maintenance of mutually beneficial contacts between an organization and key publics within communities important to its success.

compliance-gaining tactic An action designed to influence the behavior of a person or public. Ideally, the action is consistent both with an organization's goals and values and with the person's or public's self-interests and values.

components of relationships As defined by researchers Linda Childers Hon and James E. Grunig, the six key components that should be used in measuring the strength of a relationship: control mutuality, trust, satisfaction, commitment, exchange relationship, and communal relationship.

computer viruses Software programming that attaches to a computer user's e-mail address book and is spread to computers around the world. Often the product of mischief, they have been known to erase or damage data on the computers they infect.

confidence levels The statistical degree to which one can reasonably assume that a survey outcome is an accurate reflection of the entire population.

consent order Ruling issued by the FTC when a company or individual voluntarily agrees to end a potentially unlawful practice without making an admission of guilt.

consumer redress Compensation for consumers harmed by misleading or illegal marketplace practices. Under federal law, consumer redress can be sought by the Securities and Exchange Commission.

consumer relations The maintenance of mutually beneficial communication between an organization and the people who use or are potential users of its products and/or services.

contacts In marketing, all informative encounters, direct or indirect, that a customer or potential customer has with an organization's product or with the organization itself.

content communities In social media, web sites that seek particular kinds of input, such as videos or news stories, from individuals and organizations. Content communities also encourage comments on the content.

contingency plan A plan created for use when a certain set of circumstances arises. Crisis communications plans are examples of contingency plans.

contingency questions Questions that are asked on the basis of questionnaire respondents' answers to earlier questions.

controlled media Communication channels, such as newsletters, in which the sender of the message controls the message as well as its timing and frequency.

control mutuality The degree to which parties in a relationship agree on and willingly accept which party has the power to influence the actions of the other.

convenience sampling The administration of a survey based on the availability of subjects without regard to representativeness.

convergence of media A blending of media made possible by digitization. As different media adopt digital technology in their production and distribution processes, the differences among them become less apparent, and various media begin to incorporate one another's characteristics.

coorientation   A process in which practitioners seek similarities and differences between their organization's opinions regarding a public and that public's opinion of the practitioners' organizations.

copyright   A legal designation that protects original works from unauthorized use. The notation ©, meaning copyright, indicates ownership of intellectual property.

corporate social responsibility (CSR)   An organizational philosophy that emphasizes an organization's obligation to be a good corporate citizen through programs that improve society.

credentialing   A process for establishing the identity of people working in an otherwise restricted area. Usually used in connection with reporters, credentialing involves issuing passes or badges that give access to an area such as a media information center.

crisis   An event that if allowed to escalate can disrupt an organization's normal operations, jeopardize its reputation, and damage its bottom line.

crisis communications planning   The second step in effective crisis communications. In this step practitioners use the information gathered during risk assessment to develop strategies for communicating with key publics during crises; they also train employees in what they are supposed to do in a crisis.

crisis impact value (CIV)   The vertical axis on Steven Fink's crisis plotting grid. Specific questions are used to measure the impact a given crisis would have on an organization's operations.

crisis management team (CMT)   An internal task force established to manage an organization's response to a crisis while allowing other operations to continue.

crisis manager   The person designated as the leader of a crisis management team. When this person is not the chief executive of an organization, he or she is usually someone appointed by the chief executive.

crisis planning team (CPT)   A broad-based internal task force that develops an organization's crisis communications plan.

crisis plotting grid   A risk assessment tool developed by crisis planning expert Steven Fink for prioritizing crisis communications planning needs.

crisis probability factor (CPF)   The horizontal axis on Steven Fink's crisis plotting grid. It is an estimate of the probability that a given crisis will occur.

cross-cultural   Occurring between members of different cultures.

Crystallizing Public Opinion   Book authored by Edward L. Bernays in 1923, in which the term *public relations counsel* first appeared. In the book Bernays also became the first to articulate the concept of two-way public relations.

cultural relativism   The belief that no culture or set of cultural ethics is superior to another.

culture   A collection of distinct publics bound together by shared characteristics such as language, nationality, attitudes, tastes, and religious beliefs.

customer relationship management (CRM)   The use of individual consumer information, stored in a database, to identify, select, and retain customers.

cyber-relations   The use of public relations strategies and tactics to deal with publics via and issues related to the Internet.

cybersmears   Instances of using the Internet to unfairly attack the integrity of an organization and/or its products and services.

damage   A burden of proof in libel. In that context, to prove damage is to demonstrate that the person or organization claiming libel suffered injury as a result of defamation.

database marketing   The use of individual consumer information, stored in a database, to help plan marketing decisions.

databases   Structured data storage and retrieval systems. In certain situations, such as with commercial online databases, these systems can be accessed by multiple computer users simultaneously.

decision makers Any persons or group of people who make decisions for publics.

"Declaration of Principles" Ivy Ledbetter Lee's 1906 articulation of an ethical foundation for the yet-to-be-named profession of public relations. In his declaration Lee committed his publicity agency to a standard of openness, truth, and accuracy—one that was not, unfortunately, always met.

decoding The process of deriving meaning from a message.

defamation A burden of proof in libel. In that context, defamation is any communication that unfairly injures a person's reputation and ability to maintain social contacts.

demographic information Data on nonattitudinal characteristics of a person or group, such as race, gender, age, and income.

dichotomous questions In a questionnaire, either/or questions such as yes/no and true/false items.

diffusion theory A belief that the power of the mass media rests in their ability to provide information; individuals who act upon that information then influence the actions of others in their peer group or society.

digital Transmitted in a computer-readable format. Digital information is easy to use in a variety of media.

digital divide The term used to describe the uneven distribution of Internet access along geographical and socioeconomic lines.

Digital Millennium Copyright Act A federal law enacted in 1998 that established rules for downloading, sharing, or viewing copyrighted material on the Internet. It also makes it a crime to circumvent antipiracy and code-cracking measures.

direct marketing The delivery of individualized advertising to consumers one at a time, as opposed to mass advertising.

disclosure The full and timely communication of any information relevant to investors' decisions to buy or sell stocks and bonds; a legal obligation of publicly held companies.

domestic publics Groups that are united by a common interest, value, or values in a particular situation and that exist primarily within an organization's home country.

downsizing Reduction in an organization's workforce. Because of economic globalization and technological advances during the last quarter of the 20th century, organizations were forced to do more with fewer employees to remain competitive.

DVD (digital video—or versatile—disc) A computer disk that stores multimedia messages in a digital format.

e-commerce Financial activity conducted on the Internet.

e-mail A process by which a written message is sent electronically via computer to a receiver or receivers.

emergency operations center (EOC) The place where a crisis management team meets to develop its response to a crisis. It is in a secure location, one where the CMT can work free from interruptions.

employee relations The maintenance of mutually beneficial relations between an organization and its employees.

empowerment The process through which an individual or a public gains power and influence over personal and/or organizational actions.

encoding Selecting words, images, and other forms of communication to create a message.

equal opportunity provision The requirement that legally qualified candidates for public office be afforded equal access to broadcast media. This provision does not apply if a candidate's appearance is in the context of news coverage.

ethical imperialism The belief that a particular set of ethics has no flexibility and no room for improvement.

ethics Beliefs about right and wrong that guide the way we think and act.

ethics audit A process through which an organization evaluates its own ethical conduct and makes recommendations to improve it.

ethos   An Aristotelian term denoting persuasive appeal based on a speaker's character and reputation.

evaluation   The fourth step of the public relations process. However, because public relations involves a dynamic process, evaluation can occur at any time.

evaluation research   Fact-gathering designed to help a practitioner determine whether a public relations plan met its goal(s) and objectives.

exchange relationship   A relationship characterized by the giving of benefits to one party in the relationship in return for past benefits received or for the expectation of future benefits.

executive summary   A description, usually one page in length, covering the essentials of a public relations proposal.

external publics   Groups that are united by a common interest, value, or values in a particular situation and that are not part of a public relations practitioner's organization.

extranets   Controlled-access extensions of organizations' intranets to selected external publics such as suppliers.

fact sheet   A who–what–when–where–why–how breakdown of a news release. Unlike a news release, a fact sheet is not meant for publication; instead, it gives just the facts of the story contained in the news release. Fact sheets are often included in media kits.

fair use   A legal principle stating that portions of copyrighted works can be used without the owner's permission under certain conditions. Commonly, fair use includes noncommercial news reporting and certain educational purposes.

false light   A tort in privacy law. A person can be sued for invasion of privacy if he or she presents someone in a false and offensive light, even if the communication in question isn't defamatory.

fault   A burden of proof in libel cases involving private individuals. In that context, to prove fault (falseness) is to show that a defamatory statement is untrue.

Federal Communications Commission (FCC)   A federal agency established to ensure the orderly use of the nation's broadcast airwaves in the public interest.

Federalist Papers   Essays written to New York newspapers by John Hamilton, James Madison, and John Jay under the nom de plume "Publius" in support of ratification of the U.S. Constitution. The essays have been called "the finest public relations effort in history."

Federal Trade Commission (FTC)   A federal agency established to ensure a competitive marketplace. The FTC is the source of most federal regulation governing advertising.

feedback   The receiver's reaction to a message.

feedback research   The examination of evidence—often unsolicited—of various publics' responses to an organization's actions. This evidence can take many forms, such as letters and telephone calls.

feminization   The process through which the increasing influence of women is felt upon social, political, and economic issues.

First Amendment   The constitutional guarantee of freedom of expression, freedom of the press, and freedom of religion. Its ratification in 1789 is considered the most significant event in the development of public relations in the United States.

focus groups   An informal research method in which interviewers meet with groups of selected individuals to determine their opinions, predispositions, concerns, and attitudes.

Food and Drug Administration (FDA)   A federal agency established to protect, promote, and enhance the health of the people of the United States. The FDA regulates the promotion of food, drug, and cosmetic products and services.

food disparagement laws   Laws adopted in several states to protect products and services from defamatory statements that damage their market value; also known as veggie libel laws.

formal research   Research that uses scientific methods to create an accurate representation of reality.

Form 10-K   A comprehensive financial disclosure form that publicly held companies are required to file annually with the SEC.

Four-Minute Men   A speakers' bureau utilized by the Committee for Public Information (Creel Committee) during World War I. Its members would make short presentations in support of the U.S. war effort during the four-minute intermissions between reels at movie theaters.

framing   Communicating an idea in such a manner that an audience, either intentionally or unintentionally, is influenced by the way it is imparted.

Freedom of Information Act (FOIA)   A federal law requiring all government documents, except those covered by specific exemptions, to be open for public inspection.

fully functioning society theory   In public relations, the premise that organizations should help address important social needs, using two-way communication to build consensus, discover shared goals, and help societies reach their humane potentials.

gatekeepers   Members of the news media, such as editors, who determine which stories a given medium will include.

geodemographics   A marketing term for the examination of behavioral patterns based on where people live.

globalization   The growing economic interdependence of the world's people as a result of technological advances and increasing world trade.

global village   Concept first articulated by Canadian communications theorist Marshall McLuhan, suggesting that because of advances in telecommunications technology, we live in a world in which everyone can share simultaneous experiences.

goal   The outcome a public relations plan is designed to achieve.

golden mean   A concept created by Aristotle and Confucius. In Aristotelian ethics, the golden mean is the point of ideal ethical balance between deficiency and excess of a quality—for example, between deficient honesty and excessive honesty.

government relations   The maintenance of mutually beneficial relations between an organization and the local, state, and federal government agencies important to its success.

grassroots lobbying   Organized efforts by ordinary citizens to influence legislative and regulatory governmental processes.

green public relations   Public relations activities geared toward demonstrating an organization's commitment to the environment. Increased environmental commitment is sometimes referred to as "going green."

greenwashing   A term environmentalists use to describe disinformation disseminated by an organization in an effort to present an environmentally responsible image.

gripe sites   Web sites dedicated to airing complaints, either real or imagined, against individuals or organizations.

hackers   Individuals who seek unauthorized access to web sites and computer networks. Sometimes the motivation is personal amusement. However, a hacker's purpose may be to steal, alter, or damage data.

Hofstede's cultural dimensions   Devised by Dutch sociologist Geert Hofstede, five variable elements that help distinguish one culture from another: power distance; individualism versus collectivism; masculinity versus femininity; uncertainty avoidance; and long-term orientation.

hypermedia   Integrated multimedia incorporating audio, visual, and text information in a single delivery system.

identification   A burden of proof in libel. To prove identification is to show that a reasonable person would infer that a defamatory statement applies to the plaintiff.

Image Restoration Discourse   One of the dominant theories of apologia, developed by William Benoit. Benoit identifies five apologia strategies: denial, evasion of responsibility, reduction of offensiveness, corrective action, and mortification.

IMC audit   An organization's examination and analysis of its own marketing communications: procedures, databases, personnel, messages, and so on.

independent endorsement   Verification by a disinterested outside party, which can lend credibility to a message, as when the media decide to air or publish a news story based on an organization's news release.

independent public relations consultant   An individual practitioner who is, in essence, a one-person public relations agency providing services for others on a per-job basis, contract, or retainer.

Industrial Revolution   The period in the 19th and early 20th centuries during which the United States and other Western nations moved from an agricultural to a manufacturing economy.

informal research   Research that describes some aspect of reality but does not necessarily create an accurate representation of the larger reality.

injunctions   Court orders that prohibit the enjoined person from taking a specified action.

insider trading   The purchase or sale of stocks or bonds on the basis of inside information that is not available to other investors. It is a violation of federal law and professional codes of ethics.

instant messaging   An electronic process that allows two or more people to conduct a real-time, written conversation via computer.

institutional investors   Large companies or organizations that purchase stocks and other securities on behalf of their members, usually in enormous quantities.

integrated brand communication   The coordination of an organization's marketing communications to clarify and strengthen individual consumers' beliefs about a particular brand.

integrated marketing communications (IMC)   The coordinated use of public relations, advertising, and marketing strategies and tactics to send well-defined, interactive messages to individual consumers.

intellectual property   Original works of authorship that are fixed in a tangible form of expression.

interconnectedness   The effect of a variety of forces that tend to draw the people of the world closer together. These forces include technological advances, world population growth, and multiculturalism.

internal publics   Groups that are united by a common interest, value, or values in a particular situation and that are part of a public relations practitioner's organization.

International Association of Business Communicators (IABC)   The world's second-largest public relations professional association, with approximately 12,500 members. It was founded in 1970 and is headquartered in San Francisco.

international publics   Groups that are united by a common interest, value, or values in a particular situation and that exist primarily beyond the boundaries of an organization's home country.

Internet   A global network, originally created for military and scientific research, that links computer networks to allow the sharing of information in a digital format.

internships   Temporary, supervised workplace experiences that employers offer students. Some interns work for academic credit. Others receive a nominal wage for their services. Internships are considered a valuable precursor to a public relations career.

intervening public   Any group that helps send a public relations message to another group. The news media are often considered to be an intervening public.

intranet   A controlled-access internal computer network available only to the employees of an organization.

intrusion   A tort in privacy law. In that context intrusion is defined as an improper and intentional invasion of a person's physical seclusion or private affairs.

inverted pyramid   A symbol that represents the traditional organization of a news story. In a traditional news story, the most important information occurs within the first few sentences; as the story progresses, the information becomes less important.

investor relations   The maintenance of mutually beneficial relations between publicly owned companies and shareholders, potential shareholders, and those who influence investment decisions.

issues management   A form of problem–opportunity research in which an organization identifies and analyzes emerging trends and issues for the purpose of preparing a timely and appropriate response.

latent public   A group whose members do not yet realize that they share a common interest, value, or values in a particular situation.

latent public opinion   A behavioral inclination that exists when people have interest in a topic or issue but are unaware of the similar interests of others.

Lee, Ivy Ledbetter   Author of the "Declaration of Principles" in 1906. Lee became the first practitioner to articulate a vision of open, honest, and ethical communication for the profession—but became known by his critics as "Poison Ivy" for not living up to those standards.

libel   A false communication that wrongfully injures the reputation of another. To make a successful claim of libel, a plaintiff must meet the requirements of a five-point burden of proof.

litigation public relations (LPR)   The use of public relations research, strategies, and tactics to influence events surrounding legal cases.

lobby   In a public relations context, an organization that exists solely to influence governmental legislative and regulatory processes on behalf of a client. The word *lobby* may also be used as a verb to denote the act of lobbying.

logos   An Aristotelian term denoting persuasive appeal to the intellect.

lookism   A covert form of sexual harassment: attention that focuses more on a woman's appearance than on her job performance.

macroediting   A stage in the writing process in which the writer examines the "big picture" of a document, including format, organization, and completeness of information.

magic bullet theory   The belief that the mass media wield such great power that by delivering just the right message, the so-called magic bullet, the media can persuade people to do anything.

manipulation   In a public relations context, an attempt to influence a person's actions without regard to his or her self-interests.

marketing   The process of researching, creating, refining, and promoting a product or service and distributing that product or service to targeted consumers.

marketing mix   The four traditional aspects of marketing: product, price, place (distribution), and promotion.

marketing public relations   The use of the public relations process to promote an organization's goods or services.

Maslow's Hierarchy of Needs   Developed by psychologist Abraham Maslow, a multitiered list of ranked factors that determine a person's self-interests and motivations. Under Maslow's theory, people must meet their most basic needs before acting on less pressing needs.

media advisory   A fact sheet that is faxed or e-mailed to news media to alert them of a breaking news story or an event they may wish to cover.

media information center (MIC)   A place where a large number of reporters can gather to collect information on a crisis. It should be close to, but separate from, the emergency operations center established for the crisis.

media kit   A package of documents and other items offering extensive coverage of a news story to the news media. A media kit contains at least one news release as well as other materials, such as backgrounders, fact sheets, photo opportunity sheets, and product samples.

media relations   The maintenance of mutually beneficial relations between an organization and the journalists and other media people who report on its activities.

message The content of a communication that a sender attempts to deliver to a targeted receiver.

microediting A stage in the writing process in which the writer examines each sentence of a document for factual accuracy as well as correct grammar, spelling, punctuation, and style.

mission statement A concise written account of why an organization exists; an explanation of the purpose of an organization's many actions.

modifiers Words or phrases that develop the meaning of another word, such as an adjective that modifies a noun or an adverb that modifies a verb.

monitoring In the context of issues management, the sustained scrutiny and evaluation of an issue that could affect an organization.

Monroe's Motivated Sequence Created in the mid-1920s by Purdue University Professor Alan H. Monroe, a five-step process (attention, need, satisfaction, visualization, and action) that organizes persuasive messages.

multivariate analysis Analysis of research data that examines three or more variables.

mutual fund managers Individuals responsible for purchasing stocks and other securities on behalf of a mutual fund's investors; the investors participate by purchasing shares in the fund.

news conference A structured meeting between an organization's representative(s) and the news media for the purpose of providing information for news stories.

news release A client-related news story that a public relations practitioner writes and distributes to the news media.

The New York Times v. Sullivan Landmark 1964 U.S. Supreme Court ruling that established a higher burden of proof in libel cases brought by public officials.

noise In the context of the communication model, distractions that envelop communication and often inhibit it. Noise can be both physical and intangible. It is sometimes referred to as static.

nonprobability sampling The process of selecting a research sample without regard to whether everyone in the public has an equal chance of being selected.

nontraditional publics Groups that are united by a common interest, value, or values in a particular situation but that are unfamiliar to an organization, but with which the organization now has a relationship.

n-step theory A theory of mass communications suggesting that the mass media influence opinion leaders, who change from issue to issue, and that these opinion leaders, in turn, wield influence over the public.

objectives Specific milestones that measure progress toward achievement of a goal. Written objectives begin with an infinitive, are measurable, and state a specific deadline.

Office of War Information (OWI) An agency created by President Franklin Roosevelt to disseminate government information during World War II. Headed by former journalist Elmer Davis, it was a training ground for future public relations practitioners. It evolved after the war into the United States Information Agency.

open-ended questions Questionnaire items for which the number of possible answers is undefined and unrestricted.

opinion An expressed behavior inclination.

opinion leaders Individuals to whom members of a public turn for advice.

outcomes The actions of a targeted public generated as a result of a tactic or program.

outputs Measures of activity associated with implementation of a particular tactic or program.

partner relationship management The database-driven management of the relationships an organization has with its business partners, including vendors, distributors, and business customers.

passive voice A grammatical term designating that, within a sentence, the subject does not do the action denoted by the verb (see *active voice*).

Instead, the subject is affected by the action denoted by the verb, as in *She was hired*. In most grammatical situations, writers prefer active voice to passive voice.

pathos   An Aristotelian term denoting persuasive appeal to the emotions.

personal attack rule   An FCC requirement that broadcast stations provide free air time to persons subjected to a character attack during a presentation on a public issue.

persuasion   In a public relations context, an attempt to influence a person's actions through an appeal to his or her self-interest.

photo opportunity sheet   A document that promotes the visual interest of an upcoming event. Photo opportunity sheets are sent to photojournalists and television stations. When appropriate, photo opportunity sheets are included in media kits.

pitch   A persuasive message sent by a public relations practitioner to a journalist (via letter, e-mail, or telephone), often on an exclusive basis, describing a newsworthy human-interest story whose publication would generate helpful publicity for an organization.

planning   The second step in the four-step public relations process. Because the process is dynamic, however, planning can actually occur at any time.

podcasts   Downloadable audio essays or programs. Video versions are sometimes called *vodcasts*, though increasingly *podcast* now covers both audio and video.

point of no return   The second stage of a crisis. Once this moment is reached, a crisis becomes unavoidable.

political action committees (PACs)   Organizations representing particular special interests that collect money and contribute it to political candidates.

political speech   Expression associated with the normal conduct of a democratic society. The U.S. Supreme Court historically has been reluctant to regulate it.

Potter Box   A tool designed by Harvard Professor Ralph Potter for ethical decision making. Using the Potter Box involves defining an ethical issue and then identifying competing values, principles, and loyalties.

premarket conditioning   Prior to a marketing campaign, the use of public relations tactics to build a sense of awareness, need, or desire within a targeted public.

press agentry/publicity model   A form of public relations that focuses on getting favorable coverage from the media. In this model, accuracy and truth are not seen as essential.

press secretary   The individual given the responsibility to speak for and handle media inquiries on behalf of a political or government official.

primary public   Any group that is united by a common interest, value, or values in a particular situation and that can directly affect an organization's pursuit of its goals.

primary research   Original research not derived from the results of any earlier researcher's efforts.

priming   Conditioning the memories of people by framing complex issues in the simplest of terms, done in the belief that people will automatically draw on their memories to make judgments.

privacy   A person's right to be left alone and be free from unwarranted publicity.

privilege   Exemption of certain communications from court-ordered disclosure. For example, communication between a client and his or her attorney is considered privileged. However, communication between that same client and a public relations practitioner may not be privileged, and the practitioner could be required to testify.

PRM   See *partner relationship management*.

probability sampling   The process of selecting a research sample that is representative of the population or public from which it is selected.

problem   A commonplace occurrence of limited scope. People often confuse problems with crises.

problem–opportunity research   The gathering of information to answer two critical questions at the outset of any public relations effort: What is at issue, and what stake, if any, does our organization have in this issue?

Progressive Era   Running from the early 1890s until the start of World War I, a period in which a series of political and social reforms, primarily in the United States, occurred in reaction to the growth of business and industry during the Industrial Revolution.

propaganda   A systematic effort to disseminate information, some of which may be inaccurate or incomplete, in an attempt to influence public opinion. A propagandist advocates a particular idea or perspective to the exclusion of all others.

proposal   A formal document that details specific, goal-oriented public relations tactics recommended for a client.

pseudoevent   A special event, often of questionable news value, created for the purpose of attracting the attention of the news media.

psychographic information   Data on attitudinal characteristics of a person or group, such as political philosophy and religious beliefs.

public   In a public relations context, any group of people who share a common interest, value, or values in a particular situation.

public affairs officer   The person responsible for maintaining mutually beneficial relations between a government agency or official and important publics. The term *public affairs* is also used by some nongovernment organizations as a synonym for government relations or community relations.

publication   A burden of proof in libel. In that context, publication is the communication of a defamatory statement to a third party.

publication of private facts   A tort in libel law. In that context, publication of private facts involves the public disclosure of personal information that is embarrassing and potentially offensive.

public figures   For the purposes of libel law, individuals who have widespread notoriety or who inject themselves into a public controversy for the purpose of influencing its outcome.

public information model   A form of public relations that focuses on the dissemination of objective and accurate information.

public information officer   The individual given the responsibility to speak for and handle media inquiries on behalf of a government agency.

Publicity Bureau   The first public relations agency, founded by George V. S. Michaelis and two partners in Boston in 1900.

public official   For the purposes of libel law, any individual elected to public office and/or with substantial public decision-making or policy-making authority.

public opinion   The average expressed behavioral inclination.

public relations   The management of relationships between an organization and the publics that can affect its success. The term to describe the emerging profession was first used in 1923 by Edward L. Bernays in *Crystallizing Public Opinion.*

public relations agency   A company that provides public relations services for other organizations on a per-job basis, by contract, or on retainer.

public relations managers   Practitioners whose job responsibilities are more strategic than tactical in nature. These practitioners solve problems, advise others, make policy decisions, and take responsibility for the outcome of a public relations program.

Public Relations Society of America (PRSA)   The world's largest public relations professional association, with approximately 20,000 members. Founded in 1947, it is headquartered in New York.

Public Relations Student Society of America (PRSSA)   An organization for public relations students. It is affiliated with the Public Relations Society of America.

public relations technicians   Practitioners whose job responsibilities are more tactical than strategic in nature. Their primary role is to prepare communications that help execute the public relations policies of others.

public service announcements (PSAs) Broadcast announcements made on behalf of nonprofit organizations or social causes. Because of legal requirements to serve the public interest, the broadcast media do not charge for PSAs, as they do for commercial announcements. This term is also used to describe free advertising space granted by print media; however, the print media are under no legal requirement to provide the space.

push technology Computer software that permits users to customize information received automatically from the Internet.

rating scale questions Questionnaire items designed to measure the range, degree, or intensity of respondents' attitudes on the topic being studied.

receiver The person or persons for whom a message is intended.

recovery The fourth and final step in effective crisis communications. In this step practitioners evaluate the quality of the organization's response to a crisis and take appropriate actions as a result of the lessons learned.

Regulation FD A regulation issued by the U.S. Securities and Exchange Commission in 2000 designed to tighten corporate disclosure requirements.

relationship management The use of public relations strategies and tactics to foster and enhance the shared interests and values of an organization and the publics important to its success.

relationship marketing Placing relationships with individual consumers above profits, in the belief that good relationships lead to increased profits.

representative sample Population sample selected by procedures that ensure that all members of the population or public being studied have an equal chance of being chosen for the sample. A representative sample must also be sufficiently large to allow researchers to draw conclusions about the population as a whole.

research The first step of the public relations process. However, because the public relations process is dynamic, research can occur at any time.

research strategy A plan that defines what the researcher wants to know and how he or she will gather that information.

resource dependency theory The premise that organizations form relationships with publics to acquire the resources they need to fulfill their values.

response The third step in effective crisis communications. In this step practitioners utilize their crisis communications plan.

return on investment (ROI) A business concept for getting more out of something than the original cost.

rhetoric The use of communication for the purpose of persuasion. In some of its applications, the practice of public relations is a rhetorical activity.

risk assessment The first step in effective crisis communications. In this step practitioners identify potential hazards their organization may face.

salary equity Equal pay for equal work.

sample In a research context, the segment of a population or public being studied to enable researchers to draw conclusions about the public as a whole.

sampling frame The actual list from which a research sample, or some stage of the sample, is drawn.

Sarbanes-Oxley Act Legislation passed by Congress in 2002 that holds corporate officials personally accountable for the truthfulness of corporate financial statements.

satellite media tour (SMT) A series of interviews with reporters in different cities, conducted by means of satellite technology; the newsmaker stays in one location, eliminating expensive and time-consuming travel.

satisfaction When used in the context of Monroe's Motivated Sequence, the process of presenting an audience with a solution to a problem that has already been identified. When used in the context of measuring the strength of relationships, a reference to the degree to which the benefits of the relationship outweigh its costs. When used in the context of Mick Jagger, something of which he "can't get no."

scanning   In the context of issues management, the process of identifying future issues that could affect an organization.

secondary publics   Groups that are united by a common interest, value, or values in a particular situation and that have a relationship with a public relations practitioner's organization, but which have little power to affect that organization's pursuit of its goals.

secondary research   Research utilizing information generated by someone else, sometimes for purposes entirely different from your own; also known as *library research*.

Securities and Exchange Commission (SEC)   A federal agency that administers federal securities laws to ensure that the nation's securities markets are fair and honest.

Seedbed Years   A term coined by public relations historian Scott Cutlip that refers to the period during the late 19th and early 20th centuries in which the modern practice of public relations emerged.

service mark   A legal designation indicated by the symbol ^{SM} to protect names, designs, slogans, and symbols associated with a particular service.

sexual harassment   Unwelcome sexual advances. Workplace sexual harassment is harassment that may affect an individual's employment, unreasonably interfere with an individual's work performance, or create an intimidating, hostile, or offensive work environment.

simple random sampling   A basic and often impractical form of probability sampling that involves assigning a number to every person within the sampling frame, followed by random selection of numbers.

situation analysis   In a written public relations proposal, a statement that accurately and objectively describes an opportunity or threat for which public relations actions are recommended.

social exchange theory   The premise that relationships are built on the exchange of desired resources. Successful relationships are those in which the benefits of the relationship outweigh the costs.

social media   Online technologies and practices that allow people to share information and opinions. They can take many different forms, including text, images, audio, and video. Social media include blogs, wikis, online social networks, and more.

social media news releases   News releases formatted for social media practitioners, particularly bloggers. Rather than standard news narratives, social media news releases feature snippets of information, such as facts and quotes, and links to other information.

social networks   The often-informal structures through which individuals and/or organizations maintain relationships. In social media, social networks link small, personal web sites, often called "profiles," within a larger web site.

soft money   Money donated to national political parties for general expenses. Legislation passed in 2002 restricted such donations but allowed contributions to local political parties and national political conventions.

source   The originator of a message.

spamming   The mass distribution of an advertising-oriented e-mail message.

spim   The unwelcome commercial use of instant messaging.

spin   A popular term used to describe the framing of a message in what the source considers the most desirable context.

spin doctor   A popular term coined by *New York Times* editorial writer Jack Rosenthal in 1984 to describe the activities of political public relations practitioners.

special event   A planned happening that serves as a public relations tactic.

stakeholder   A public that has an interest in an organization or in an issue potentially involving that organization.

stakeholder research   Research that focuses on identifying and describing specific publics important to the success of an organization.

standing plan   A plan that remains in effect over an extended period of time. Its tactics are routinely reenacted to sustain fulfillment of the plan's goal(s) and objectives.

statement of purpose   In a written public relations proposal, a declaration that the proposal presents a plan to address a given situation.

stereotyping   The assumption that all members of a particular group or culture are the same and act in the same manner.

strategies   General descriptions of how practitioners propose to achieve a plan's objectives.

survey research   Formal research conducted through the use of carefully selected population samples and specifically worded questionnaires.

SWOT analysis   An assessment of the strengths, weaknesses, opportunities, and threats that an organization has or could confront.

systematic sampling   A probability sampling technique that uses a standardized selection process to create a sample that is both representative and easy to develop. At its most basic level, systematic sampling involves the selection of every Kth member of a sampling frame.

tactics   Specific recommended actions designed to help an organization achieve the objectives stated in a public relations plan.

text messaging   The process of sending a written message from one cell phone to another.

things return to normal   The fourth and final stage of a crisis. During this stage the immediate threat created by the crisis is over, but its lingering effects are still felt. Although things may have returned to "normal," normality now may be much different from what it was before the crisis.

third-party endorsement   Verification of a story's newsworthiness that the news media provide when they publish or broadcast the story. Appearance in an uncontrolled news medium lends credibility to a story, because the media are neither the sender nor the receiver but an independent third party.

trade magazines   Magazines for members of particular trades or professions, such as carpenters or lawyers.

trademarks   A legal designation indicated by the symbol ® that protects names, designs, slogans, and symbols associated with specific products.

traditional publics   Groups that are united by a common interest, value, or values in a particular situation and with which an organization has an ongoing, long-term relationship.

transition   A device that clarifies the introduction of a new topic within a document. One traditional transition device is a sentence that shows the relationship of the previous topic to the new topic. Such a sentence follows the previous topic and precedes the new topic.

transparency   A quality achieved when organizations and individuals conduct business openly and honestly without hidden agendas.

trust   The willingness of one party in a relationship to open itself to the other.

two-step theory   A theory of mass communication suggesting that the mass media influence society's opinion leaders, who, in turn, influence society.

two-way asymmetrical model   A form of public relations in which research is used in an effort to persuade important publics to adopt a particular point of view.

two-way symmetrical model   A form of public relations that focuses on two-way communication as a means of conflict resolution and for the promotion of mutual understanding between an organization and its important publics.

uncontrolled media   Communication channels, such as newspaper stories, in which a public relations practitioner cannot control the message, its timing, or its frequency.

units of analysis   What or whom a researcher is studying in order to create a summary description of all such units.

univariate analysis   Analysis of research data that examines just one variable.

Universal Accreditation Program   The availability of PRSA accreditation to members of eight additional public relations organizations; established in 1998.

uses and gratifications theory The belief that people have the power to pick and choose the mass media channels that, in turn, influence their actions.

utilitarianism A philosophy developed by Jeremy Bentham and John Stuart Mill that holds that all actions should be directed at producing the greatest good for the greatest number of people.

values The fundamental beliefs and standards that drive behavior and decision making. They are also the filters through which we see the world and the world sees us.

values-driven public relations The values-driven management of relationships between an organization and the publics that can affect its success.

values statement A written declaration of the principles that an organization will strive to follow in all its actions.

variables The logical grouping of qualities that describe a particular attribute. Variables must be exhaustive (incorporating all possible qualities) and mutually exclusive.

veil of ignorance A term and concept created by philosopher John Rawls. The veil of ignorance strategy asks decision makers to examine a situation objectively from all points of view, especially from those of the affected publics.

velvet ghetto Situation that exists when women predominate in lower-paying technical or middle-management jobs, with men dominating upper-level managerial positions.

video news releases (VNRs) Videotaped news stories that an organization produces and distributes to the news media. VNRs often include b-roll footage.

viral marketing Public relations or marketing information that is spread from person to person via e-mail.

virtual organizations Temporary organizations formed by smaller units or individuals to complete a specific job.

virtual public relations A term used to describe the work of many small public relations consultancies; as a result of advances in communications technology, these consultancies can have the look, feel, and service capabilities of much larger public relations agencies.

visual aids Displays presented to an audience to enhance the meaning of a speaker's words. Visual aids can include computer projections, slides, flip charts, handouts, and overhead-projector transparencies.

vox populi Latin for "voice of the people." The phrase refers to the importance of public opinion.

warning stage The first stage of a crisis. If warning signs are recognized and appropriate action is taken quickly, the negative effects of a crisis can be averted or minimized.

Web 2.0 A term coined by Silicon Valley consultants in 2004 to describe a new generation of Internet services that emphasize online collaboration and sharing.

webcast Audiovisual telecasts, usually live, delivered through a web site.

web site A series of computer files maintained by an organization or individual that can be accessed via the Internet. Web sites are created to project an organization's image and to share information with various publics. They are also useful for marketing goods, services, or ideas and for generating feedback.

wikis Web sites or multimedia documents that allow different individuals to contribute and edit content. Also, software packages that make it easy for multiple individuals to author, edit, and remove online content.

work for hire Anything prepared by someone within the scope of employment and, therefore, considered the property of the employer.

World Wide Web A graphics-oriented computer network developed in 1991 that made the Internet more accessible and attractive and helped spur its rapid development.

writing process An organized system for producing effective public relations documents. The writing process begins with the credibility of the writer and moves through 10 separate steps: credibility, research, organization, writing, revision, macroediting, microediting, approval, distribution, and evaluation.

Index

Text Credits

p. 19, courtesy of Hallmark Cards, Inc.; pp. 23–25, courtesy of Judith T. Phair; p. 39, reprinted with permission from the Public Relations Society of America (www.prsa.org); pp. 50–51, courtesy of John Echeveste; pp. 80–82, courtesy of Edward M. Block; p. 108, courtesy, PepsiCo, Inc., Worldwide Code of Conduct; pp. 122–123, courtesy of David A. Narsavage; p. 153, courtesy of APCO Worldwide; pp. 155–157, courtesy of Jane Hazel; p. 181, courtesy of Goodwill Industries; pp. 186–188, courtesy of Cone, Inc.; p. 203, courtesy of the Institute for Public Relations; pp. 224–226, courtesy of David Rockland; p. 241, courtesy of The Boeing Company; pp. 253–255, courtesy of Timothy S. Brown; p. 281, courtesy of Johnson & Johnson; pp. 292–293, courtesy of Deborah Charnes Vallejo; p. 323, courtesy of Kellogg Company; pp. 329–331, courtesy of Regina Lynch-Hudson; p. 350, courtesy of INK, Inc.; pp. 360–361, courtesy of Craig Settles; pp. 398–399, courtesy of Wayne Shelor; p. 413, Copyright © J.M. Smucker Company; pp. 427–428, courtesy of Vin Cipolla; p. 442, courtesy of Special Olympics, Inc. "Special Olympics" is a trademark and tradename owned by Special Olympics, Inc.; pp. 455–456, courtesy of Bill Imada; pp. 496–497, courtesy of James F. Haggerty, photo by Matt Flynn; p. 518, courtesy of the League of Women Voters of the United States; pp. 529–530, courtesy of Kevin J. Saghy; pp. 539–545, reprinted with permission from the Public Relations Society of America (www.prsa.org).